Counseling for Career Development

Second Edition

Counseling for Career Development

E. L. TOLBERT

UNIVERSITY OF FLORIDA

Houghton Mifflin Company   Boston
Dallas   Geneva, Illinois   Hopewell, New Jersey   Palo Alto   London

This book is dedicated, with gratitude and affection,
to Frances, Margaret, Jane, and Yves,
whose diverse careers prove again that each person
is uniquely indispensable.

Printed in the U.S.A.

Library of Congress Catalog Card Number: 79–89452

ISBN: 0–395–28251–9

Contents

Preface

This book is designed for the one-quarter or one-semester course in counselor preparation programs entitled "Career Development," "Career Guidance," or "Occupational Information and Guidance." Some prior study in counselor education is assumed, but it is not essential. The contents apply to the work of the counselor in school, college, and community settings, and the book should also be useful for career guidance workshops, institutes, and in-service education programs. Additionally, it should be useful for those in other specialities—administration, teaching, personnel work—as a source of information on career development and guidance.

The emphasis of the book is on practical applications supported by relevant theory and research. The framework of principles and practices provides a foundation on which the counselor can build as he or she tries out personal ideas, gathers new insights from research reports, and reviews the results of field testing of new programs. This basic framework is essential if practice is to be kept current. In this rapidly evolving field, basic understanding is needed for a start, but keeping up to date is critical.

Since the first edition of this book was published, many changes have taken place in the field of career counseling. The range of settings in which counselors work is increasing. Elementary and middle or junior high schools now offer job opportunities. There are post-high school educational settings—vocational-technical centers, community colleges, colleges, and universities. Community agencies and government programs employ counselors, and there are even some private practice opportunities. Counseling majors, some of whom have entered counselor education as a result of a career change, are headed in many different directions.

New groups are being served—mid-life and older persons, the handicapped, women, minority group members, and other groups with special needs. Legislation focused on the needs of special groups is being enacted and new programs are emerging.

An incredible array of technological devices and material are now available to serve counselor and counselee—computers, microfiche viewers, slide-tape programs, packaged courses, and programmed material for every career guidance purpose. There are even systematic training programs on how to build programs.

New attitudes about work and its meaning to the individual have appeared. A harmonious blending of work and lifestyle is a current goal. Counselors are keenly aware of a growing concern about the economy and energy and the impact of these factors on individuals with whom they will work as well as on the profession itself. Simultaneously, career guidance is being viewed more and more as a collaborative enterprise, one that involves education, community, business, and industry. The fact that all these segments of society need to work together to help individuals with life-long effective career development is increasingly recognized.

All these new developments and changes are covered in this book. Its aim, however, is to enable counselors to expand their roles by taking advantage of new approaches and resources rather than to suggest a different role. The focus is on assisting individuals headed for education, training, or work to make the best possible plans and to carry them out in the most effective ways; no attempt is made to cover the total counselor role.

This expanded role for the counselor does not mean heaping new tasks on already overloaded schedules. It means that effective use of new personnel, new strategies, new technology, new community resources, and collaborative strategies will be essential. The counselor will then be freed to utilize his or her unique talents to provide face-to-face help, to consult with others, to serve as a change agent, to develop new programs and practices, and to evaluate results. This expanded role should clearly demonstrate that career guidance is an essential aspect of the life-long educational and community service enterprise.

The organization of the book illustrates the helping process from identification of needs to final assessment of results. The first three chapters focus on social, economic, and psychological foundations that highlight current deficiencies and suggest models for career guidance. Chapter 1 examines current social and economic conditions and summarizes criticisms of guidance and education. Chapter 2 outlines theoretical concepts of career development; Chapter 3 elaborates on significant factors in these theories. Chapter 4 reviews career-development needs of special groups. Chapters 5 and 6 describe national and local information systems that are essential for effective career development and guidance.

Helping approaches, from one-to-one career counseling to total programs of career development and guidance, are described and illustrated in Chapters 7 through 9. Chapter 7 presents a rationale and strategy for decision-making counseling. Chapter 8 explains how group counseling may facilitate career planning, decision making, and self-understanding. Counselor roles—consultant, change agent, curriculum innovator, program builder—are reviewed in Chapter 9.

Chapter 10 discusses career education in all types of settings. Chapter 11 covers use of support personnel as a way to increase the scope of services. The pros and cons of job placement are examined in Chapter 12 and suggestions are made for developing this service. Finally, in Chapter 13, evaluation and accountability are discussed.

Two appendixes contain major position papers of the guidance profession on the importance of career development services.

This book has been made possible by the generous assistance of a number of persons. Counselor education students and counselors have reacted to much of the material and provided insights and help. Leaders in the field have contributed most generously by providing materials, suggestions, and program descriptions, and by permitting extensive use of their concepts and research. I express my deepest gratitude to these persons.

The author and the publisher are grateful for the assistance of those who made professional reviews of the manuscript. These reviewers, to whom we give thanks, were William Richardson (Western Michigan University), Avraham Sherman (University of Oklahoma), and Donald Zytowski (Iowa State University).

E. L. T.

Counseling for Career Development

1

A Critical Need

GOALS

1
To explain why career guidance is needed.

2
To describe typical career problems faced by individuals over their life span.

3
To identify types of career guidance services needed at various life stages.

4
To present some models for promoting career development.

5
To describe the career-guidance competencies needed by counselors in any setting.

THE CHOICE OF WORK is one of the most important decisions one makes. It determines, to a large extent, how time will be spent, who will be chosen as friends, what attitudes and values will be adopted, where one will reside, and what pattern of family living will be adopted. The job provides an identity for the individual. Loss of work has disastrous effects. The unemployed begins to question his or her identity and purposes in life.

As important as this decision is, it is often made with little thought or assistance. The high school pupil sometimes selects an area of work in imitation of an admired teacher or a popular hero, to resist parental demands, or because it is the first one he or she learns about. The actual amount of consideration given to career planning may be less than that given to buying a pair of shoes. Counselors who have career guidance as one of their major responsibilities may not be asked for help, and the wealth of material they have about occupations and training and educational opportunities may never be used.

Now more than at any time in the past, career planning needs to be done carefully, thoughtfully, and with the help of all of the resources available to the individual. It is important that the school counselor be able to provide effective help at the critical high school stage—no other person is in as strategic a position to do it. But it is equally important that counselors be available to help at critical points throughout the life span. Career-planning needs do not disappear when school attendance ends.

THE NATURE OF THE NEED

A catalogue of the conditions that highlight the need for career guidance includes a wide variety of contemporary problems and issues that affect practically everyone. Furthermore, each year sees the emergence of new pressures and demands that further emphasize the importance of timely and effective assistance. Some of the major conditions are reviewed in the paragraphs that follow.

The Problem of Meaningful Employment

To an increasing degree, individuals are demanding that work provide a sense of accomplishment and identity and are voicing bitter resentment that it does not. Some people seek other avenues to this end through lifestyles that relegate income-producing activities to a position of relative insignificance. Still others turn to leisure and hobby interests for the fulfillment lacking in their jobs.

Suitable work could be one of the most positive of all of the individual's experiences. Among other contributions, meaningful jobs for all could pave the way for racial harmony (Samler, 1970b, p. 8). The potential benefits of suitable work are clarified by the disastrous effects of lack of work. Ginzberg (1952) observed the effects of unemployment in the 1930s, and Gleason (1968) vividly describes them for the 1960s. But though lack of work has the most negative effect, meaningless and monotonous activities on the job also rob the individual of a sense of accomplishment (O'Toole, 1973, pp. 4–5; 1977, pp. 17–18). All jobs may not have the potential to be challenging and stimulating, and in many situations a restructuring of the work setting is badly needed. But better choice and planning could conceivably help many persons find the sort of work that enables them to play their preferred roles in life.

Changes in the World of Work

Not only do employment trends vary in ways that are difficult to predict but new occupations appear and old ones vanish. Service jobs are increasing more rapidly than are production jobs. Laboring jobs of various types, particularly on farms, are decreasing. New occupations have appeared in such areas as computer science and ecology. Some types of machine tending and office work are no longer needed because of sophisticated new equipment that virtually runs itself. The increasing complexity of the work world and the proliferation of choices make the task of career planning more difficult. As Toffler (1970, p. 264) so vividly describes it, the problem is "overchoice" rather than a poverty of choices.

Predicting the nature of occupations and the number of workers needed is particularly hazardous. Yet such prognoses are essential for planning educational and training programs, even though examples of miscalculations abound. After World War II, a surplus of engineers was predicted, and these estimates affected college programs and students' plans. Only a few years later, however, a critical shortage of engineers developed during the Korean War. Following the launching of *Sputnik I* in 1957, a crash program was underwritten by the federal government to identify and develop scientific talent. But in the ensuing dozen or so years, cutbacks in the space program left many highly specialized scientists unemployed. The teaching profession has experienced an oversupply of new workers, partially in response to extensive recruiting. The pessimistic job outlook has turned many would-be teachers toward other fields, and a teacher shortage may be expected at some time in the not-too-distant future. Unexpected changes take place because of energy shortages and the development of new energy sources. Despite the difficulty of predicting future employment patterns, the best available estimates should be used, since the only alternative is complete guesswork. When predictions like those of the Bureau of Labor Statistics are used, however, the individual should be aware that they assume relatively stable social, economic, and international conditions (U.S. Department of Labor, 1978, 1979).

The Problem of Discrimination

There is an increasingly insistent need for help for those who face discrimination in career planning and placement. Though some barriers are falling, accelerated by new legislation, women, blacks, other minority groups, the handicapped, and people over forty still face obstacles of various sorts, including employer and community prejudices. The talented woman who would like to enter a field of work traditionally dominated by men is likely to encounter negative reactions in prepration as well as in seeking employment. The capable black who wishes to earn a position on the strength of his or her accomplishments may be denied employment solely because of race or be hired to serve as a "token black." Career guidance is no routine, easy task under the best of circumstances, but when it is complicated by deeply ingrained and baseless stereotypes, it becomes immeasurably more difficult. Passage of laws such as those promoting education of the handicapped (PL 94-142), training and jobs for the disadvantaged (PL 93-203), elimination of discrimination in education and work (amendments to the Civil Rights Act of 1964), and the removal of compulsory retirement in many occupations has contributed to the substantial progress in the battle against discrimination. Even so, legal actions are only the first steps.

The Problems of Career Changing

Although career changes at ages thirty, forty, or fifty are not a new phenomenon, their frequency is increasing. Some originate in acute job dissatisfaction. Others result mainly from increased self-understanding and awareness of options. Still others are related to the development of a lifestyle that takes the individual in a different direction from that originally chosen. More often than not, these factors interact, with one or the other playing the leading role.

There are also those who take on second careers. Retirees from the armed forces, former housewives returning to the labor force, and new female entrants who must find employment because of the loss of their husbands all represent career changers. None of these is among the typical clientele of the school counselor, but their situations point up the need to learn planning and decision-making skills during the educational process. The high school is the logical setting for at least beginning to develop these competencies.

A new perspective on the total life span as an optimum blending of work, education, and leisure has developed. Retirement increasingly tends to be more a matter of individual choice than an occurrence at a fixed point. Recognition of the need for lifelong education and paid time off from work to engage in training or educational pursuits is also increasing (Kurland, 1978). The pre- and postretirement period more often involves career concerns as age limits to full-time work are erased. These emerging life patterns underline the need for new types of career counseling and guidance.

The Problem of the Dropout

Whether the dropout leaves public school or college, he or she is poorly equipped to find rewarding work in this highly technological society. The magnitude of the problem is staggering. In 1970, approximately 32 percent of the sixteen- to twenty-one-year-olds, or 3 million people, were school dropouts (U.S. Department of Labor, 1972a, p. 42). In addition, about half of those who enter college do not earn degrees. Although the unemployment rate among college dropouts is difficult to estimate, the rate for school dropouts is about twice that of graduates, and the ratio appears to be consistent over the years (U.S. Department of Labor, 1976, p. 43). Further, many jobs appropriate for the unskilled and unprepared dropout are disappearing. The future looks even more grim for those who lack some vocational competency.

The cost of school and post–high school dropouts in terms of incomplete preparation for work is estimated to be over $20 billion a year (Marland, 1974, p. 21). But financial statements do not reveal the personal frustrations and failures of individuals who for one reason or another do not complete an educational program.

The Public School Factor

Work that should be fulfilling and self-enhancing is often described as degrading, monotonous, and dehumanizing. As observed previously, some young people reject occupations requiring long-term preparation, turning instead to a lifestyle that relegates work to an insignificant role. Increasingly, efforts have been made to identify the bases of these and similar negative reactions. A variety of contributing factors appear to be responsible; foremost is the public educational institution itself.

Major new objectives are currently being suggested for public education. "Career education" is among the more recent proposals. Sidney P. Marland, former assistant secretary of education, advocated a major restructuring: "Complete reform of the high school, viewed as a major element of overall preparation of life, cannot be achieved until general education is completely done away with in favor of contemporary career development in a comprehensive secondary education environment" (1972). The adoption of this career-education orientation would require major changes in school organization, with a resulting emphasis on career planning and preparation. Nor is Marland's proposal limited to the high school. Career education would begin in the elementary school and be available throughout one's working life. Criticism of the current educational establishment is clearly evident in this proposal: the schools are not preparing pupils for full participation in the world of work.

Pucinski and Hirach express the same sentiments about the relevance of contemporary education: "Deeper consideration of the issues seems to indicate a need to turn around the entire educational system—with its insensitivities, bureaucracies, professional inbreeding, outdated standards, hesitant leadership, and lack of meaning for life and work in a complex adult world—and to refocus education on the problem of preparing young people for the world of work" (1971, p. x). Venn pinpoints a specific omission in the usual school program: "The schools should assume responsibility for placing students in jobs . . . schools should establish their own extensive placement services which can help all students identify and locate suitable employment and which can continue to offer them counseling on the job and follow them throughout their careers" (1971, p. 41).

The total education program is the target of these criticisms, but much of the onus is placed directly on guidance. The points are well taken, for career guidance is inextricably tied to the work of the schools in preparing young people for adult life.

Criticisms of education are the bases of recommended new practices and alternative educational plans. Accountability, voucher plans, and performance contracting are new terms in the vocabulary of educators, and each concept implies that something new should be done, or that education should be provided in a different way. The most extreme suggestions would eliminate education in its present form (Illich, 1970, p. xix). Most recommendations are more conservative, and underlying many is the increasing cost of public education. The common objective is to relate input to output in terms of demonstrable and significant goals. The most popular and widespread of the new concepts is accountability, which has gained acceptance in many educational, lay, and legislative circles. The latest manifestation of this trend is the rapid spread of minimum competency testing: thirty-three states have instituted specific tests that students must pass before advancing in or graduating from public schools (Pipho, 1978, p. 585).

CAREER-GUIDANCE NEEDS IN SCHOOLS

Over the years, both professional guidance counselors and lay persons have emphasized the need to improve school guidance programs, an issue related to, but somewhat different from, that of career education. One of the more articulate critics of guidance, James A. Rhodes, former governor of Ohio, was unequivocal in his indictment: "The vocational guidance in the public schools has been a failure. It has not provided youth with the understanding of the economic society in which they find themselves, nor encouraged them to follow an educational program which would enable them to compete in such a society" (1970, p. 11). Richard Byrne, a counselor educator, underlines the significance of this criticism: "Increasingly there have been murmurs about the movement's [guidance's] loss of direction, accompanied by increasing statements of dissatisfaction with school counselors and counseling. Now, instead of a murmur there is a loud statement from a governor of a state which consistently has had the best leadership in guidance. You and I had better listen" (1971, p. 875).

The reactions of pupils who should be receiving career assistance and counselors who are either providing it or preparing others to do so emphasize the need for improving career guidance. The National Assessment of Educational Progress (1976, pp. xv–xvi; 1978, pp. 1, 3, 4) reveals that pupils, particularly dropouts, lack knowledge about occupations, how to apply for jobs, and how to cope successfully in the work world. Moreover, although they want help with career planning, they do not feel they receive it (Prediger, Noeth, and Roth, 1973, pp. 8–12; 1974). At the same time, guidance professionals question the concepts and procedures, assumptions, and goals currently used in career guidance (Warnath, 1975; Baumgardner, 1977). Counselors are also aware of the need to improve their skills in providing career assistance (*Guidepost*, 19, No. 15 [1977], 12). The professional associations have clearly recognized this need in two major position papers (National Vocational Guidance Association and American Vocational Association, 1973; Hansen, 1978; see Appendix in this book).

There are conflicting views about where and how guidance services should be concentrated, and these further complicate efforts to improve school guidance. Guidance for the elementary school is an example; the consensus favors it. Marland's proposal for career education at this level implies that career guidance would also be provided (U.S. Department of HEW, 1971, p. 2). Herr and Cramer point out the importance of emphasizing guidance in these grades: "As elementary school children move through the elements of fantasy so characteristic of growth and learning at this life period, work is an important concern to them. By the time they have completed the first six grades of school, many of them have made tentative commitments to fields of work and to self-perceptions" (1972, p. 143). Roberts (1972) describes the help the elementary school counselor can provide in career development and guidance, both directly and indirectly. Hansen also supports extension of guidance into the elementary school: "An integrated, cross-disciplinary program of career guidance as part of the regular school curriculum (K–12) is more consonant with new knowledge about vocational development than some of the isolated, one-shot approaches such as career days, college days, and once-a-year units" (1970, p. 19). In support of this position, a new feature, "Career Guidance in the Elementary School," was introduced in the *Elementary School Guidance and Counseling Journal* to provide for the dissemination of principles and practices for counselors (Leonard, 1972).

In addition, passage of the Career Education Incentive Act (PL 95-207) by Congress in 1967 reflects support for a broad approach, from elementary school through adult life. Hoyt's (1976) definitive statement on implementing career education further indicates the need for comprehensive guidance services by home, school, and employer over the entire K–12 period.

Some people propose a different approach to meeting career-guidance needs. Ginzberg (1971, pp. 278–281), one of the more knowledgeable contemporary experts on conservation of human resources, questions the value of career guidance in the elementary schools. He recommends improvement of high school career-guidance facilities and suggests that major emphasis be put on nonschool agencies for the bulk of career guidance. Along the same lines, Wirtz (1975, Chaps. 3 and 10) recommends an extensive two-stage program for the improvement of career guidance and placement. The first stage emphasizes a required amount of career guidance for all high school pupils, the provision of local and national occupational information, community opportunities for pupils to participate in exploratory work and service, and opportunities for intern- or apprenticeship-type work experiences for those between sixteen and twenty who need them. Community education-work councils would help pupils bridge the transition from school to work. Building on this first stage, the second stage would, among other things, expand opportunities for lifelong education. Wirtz's significant and timely proposal supporting career education is closely allied with Marland's career-education concept, which gives added force to the call for improvement in this area.

The concensus is clearly moving toward widespread support for career guidance that begins in the earliest years and extends throughout the life span. Differences appear to be mainly a matter of where to use the major resources, but the importance of the K–12 period in career development is firmly established.

CASE STUDIES

Facts, figures, and generalizations clarify the need for improved career guidance, but the most vivid evidence is the lives of those who have encountered problems or obstacles. Examples are not difficult to find. The reader can reflect on his or her own life for instances of accomplishments and disappointments. Practically everyone in any community is an example of a career-in-process, demonstrating a pattern of successes and failures. The cases that follow are only a few of many that could be described, but they give human form to the points just made about the need for career guidance.

These cases are based on real persons, although some details irrelevant to the nature of the problems have been changed. Cases from the elementary- and secondary-school level are presented, in addition to post–high school cases and those involving mid-career changers and older persons. This variety of cases is intended to illustrate problems that occur throughout life.

An Elementary School Pupil

Some of the influences with which the elementary school counselor must deal are illustrated in the case of Barry Brown. Note particularly the sources of Barry's attitudes about occupations and the stereotypes beginning to crystallize during the elementary grades. Visualize the problems these attitudes and stereotypes will cause as career planning and decision making are undertaken during the high school years.

Barry Brown's parents insist that his schoolwork be of the highest quality. He is warned repeatedly that if he doesn't complete high school with excellent grades he will not be able to enter a university. His older brother ranked second in his high school graduating class and plans to be an accountant. The books used in Barry's classes are loaded with such professionals as doctors, lawyers, and engineers; firemen and policemen are briefly mentioned. Few skilled workers appear in texts, and those who do are usually in work clothes carrying lunch pails.

Barry's teacher emphasizes the importance of college and the professions for the *best* pupils. Barry spends a great deal of time on his homework. Although his parents do not offer much help, they check carefully to see that it has been done neatly. His father manages a service station, and most of his conversation at home is about the difficulty of finding dependable help and about how competition is making it nearly impossible to make a profit. His mother completed a year of business school and works as a bookkeeper at an automobile dealer's. She talks at length about the lack of opportunity for advancement for those in sales and service jobs.

Barry himself knows very little about work. What he does understand is based on what he hears in school and at home. He chooses one career one day and another the next. Last week he wanted to be an astronaut. This week his choices are professional basketball player, science teacher, and basketball coach. Building model racing cars is his favorite hobby. In Cub Scouts, he and several others with similar interests spend many hours at work on their models. His parents discount these interests, describing them as "toys you will outgrow."

Question: What two or three actions by home and school would you recommend to help Barry gain a more realistic understanding of the world of work?

Some Secondary-School Pupils

At the secondary-school level, educational and occupational problems become acute as decisions must be made and plans implemented. Several typical difficulties are illustrated by the following cases: the confused ninth-grader, the low-achieving pupil with behavior problems, the class-conscious junior, the unmotivated junior, the ambitious senior, and two varieties of dropouts. For each of these cases, identify the critical career problem and suggest at least one action that you feel would help the individual.

Willie Stephens is confused. He is entering the ninth grade next fall and has talked with his junior high counselor and his parents about what academic program he should take. He seems to be headed in the college preparatory direction. His parents are very much in favor of this option and have promoted such careers as law and medicine. (Willie wrote a report on these two occupations as part of a seventh-grade unit on "Choosing Your Occupation.") He has a strong interest in mechanical work and can dismantle and rebuild lawn mower motors with skill and efficiency. He has not investigated any of the vocational programs in the high school, however, because as he says, "People in these programs don't count much. Besides, my parents wouldn't even consider it." Willie doesn't know anything about the vocational programs other than that "you work in shops or in stores." Some orientation was provided for the eighth-graders prior to high school, but Willie says he does not remember much about it.

Both of his parents finished college. His father is a well-known builder and real estate broker. His mother is active in community social and service affairs. It is clear that they have high expectations of Willie, one of which is that he attend a highly competitive college. His records show satisfactory achievement, better than average overall attitude, and strong interests and aptitude in mechanical areas.

In discussing plans, Willie has expressed interest in "making things and fixing things. You bet I like that! I don't even know what time it is when I'm working in my shop." Willie seems relatively happy with his plans but is certainly not enthusiastic. "No, my parents don't tell me what to do. They leave it up to me." He is slightly indignant at the suggestion that he may not be making up his own mind about college. "Oh, I don't think I'll have any problem. I've always managed to get along. As my parents say, 'If you want something enough, you'll get it.'"

Questions: What changes in Willie's parents' attitudes would you suggest? Are there specific actions you feel they could take to help Willie with career planning?

Jack Buell, in addition to being a disciplinary problem, is a sophomore who ought to be a senior. He has had difficulty with the administration, teachers, and the police. He has been picked up twice for speeding, once for "borrowing" a motorcycle without the owner's knowledge, and was suspended from school after being caught with pep pills. In addition, he has been repeatedly disciplined for hostility toward teachers. Jack works hard at baseball and is the team's leading hitter. He recently told the counselor that school "is just a lot of junk. I don't get those subjects. I'm failing most courses. The teachers jump on me all the time." His records show his mental ability to be a little below average, but test results are erratic. His parents are separated, and Jack lives with his grandparents. His ambition is to get a job, be on his own, and buy a car or motorcycle. "I ought to help my parents [grandparents]. They've been good to me and I don't want to keep on being a drain." Jack avoids mentioning his real parents, who left him in a boys' ranch for orphans before his grandparents moved to town and took him in. He has expressed some interest in the school's vocational and work-study programs, but his intense desire to be self-sufficient has eliminated this option. While teachers tend to rate him as low in ability, they agree that he seems to show more intelligence than course grades and test scores indicate. He is a very poor reader, and it has been suggested that he has a reading disability, but no follow-up has ever been done. His attendance has been erratic, and it is obvious that he plans to drop out at the end of the baseball season.

Questions: What do you think are the major obstacles to Jack's career planning? Do you think the school has anything to offer that might be of interest to him?

Mary Jones is a very popular and very class-conscious high school junior. School for Mary is a full-time job. She is bright enough to get A's and B's without much difficulty, but social activities are her "thing." She is president of the school club known as "The Big Wheels," editor of the newspaper, and head cheerleader. She is in the academic program but asserts she couldn't care less about college or "any more of this academic stuff. Sure, I may work a year or so. I'd like to travel, too. Then I'm going to get married. That's my ambition." Though she doesn't say so, she plans to "marry money" and get into the social scene in a big way. In talking to her English teacher, Mary referred to the counselor as "the shrink" and declined to be referred for career planning. "I already know what I want, and only the spacey ones go into this 'counseling' thing."

Even so, she has said that she would like to go into city politics or law. But in her family, social life is the thing, and since it is one of the leading families, she does not need to work. "A girl has a definite role and that's how I'm programmed," she says. In talking about the kind of work she might do in the interim, she says her father can "fix it up" with one of the city offices for her to be a receptionist or do public relations work. But Mary has also said, "I'm really turned on by stuff like this Community Improvement Project and VISTA and things like that. Those don't go over at all in my family. My father thinks they're some kind of socialism and my mother says that they're nice for *others* to do. Maybe I ought to take typing, so I could as least do *something*."

Questions: What conflict in occupational goals does Mary seem to be experiencing? What do you think she could do to resolve the conflict?

Joe Prince is one of those unmotivated and apathetic boys you would seldom notice in class. He is large, amiable, and usually on the fringe of the group when there is some kind of protest or demonstration. Joe says he has no interest in school. He is in the general program and declares that he just wants to "get out of this place and get to work." He thinks he will find some kind of job and talks about engineering, science, electronics, and owning his own flying school. A younger brother in the fifth grade is very much like him. An older sister married and dropped out of high school during her senior year.

In talking with the counselor, Joe expressed little interest in any of the high school programs. He stated that his parents said he should take the college preparatory academic course. Joe's father has a clerical job with the city administration. His mother is a homemaker. Both have high ambitions for Joe, though his test scores indicate average ability.

Joe is generally well liked and goes out of his way to help teachers. He has been assistant manager of the basketball team for two years but has not been outstandingly successful in academic work. A paper route has been his main part-time work experience. Joe is not aware of job openings other than the paper route and has very little realistic information about occupations. He says that cafeteria is his favorite period, and he usually has a couple of candy bars in his pocket.

When asked, "What will you do after high school?" Joe laughs and says, "I wish you'd tell me. *I* don't know."

Questions: How much influence do Joe's parents seem to be exerting on his career plans? If you could make one suggestion to them, what would you say?

Ralph Hart, an ambitious senior, is going to college to prepare for a career—that is the only decision he has made. Now he must make two more decisions, which worry him constantly: (1) "Should I spend the first two years in the community college, live at home, and then transfer to the university, or should I enter the university as a freshman?" and (2) "What should my major be?"

Ralph has heard a great deal about how difficult it is to adjust to the "big university" as a freshman. "You're lost. Just a number. I doubt if I would like that. My parents think it would be good for me to be on my own, but I've heard it's hard to study in the dorms. A lot of people live in apartments, and that makes it even harder to keep up. Then you hear all about drugs and stuff. There's always some of that around, even in high school. But I've heard that the community college courses are so easy that you're not ready for the university once you transfer. I don't know what to do."

Choosing a major also bothers him, but he hasn't done anything about it except look through university and community college catalogues. He has heard that, though a major is not required in the general college program until the junior year, some colleges and departments require specific choices the first year—engineering, architecture, and business administration, for example. "I could waste a lot of time by getting into the wrong program and not having the courses I need," he says. There is no doubt in Ralph's mind that he will attend college, but he has no idea what he expects to get out of it except preparation for a professional job. He more than meets the college entrance requirements and scored high on the National Merit Examination. His interests are widely diversified. He has an uneasy feeling that he may make the wrong choice and not be able to change. Ralph has made only a few important decisions on his own and is reluctant to take even partial responsibility for those he is now facing.

Question: What could you say to Ralph that might lessen his concern about the danger of making a wrong choice in his first year in college?

Henry Fuller dropped out of high school to work when he heard that the new Acme muffler plant was paying good wages to workers with no experience. After six months on the assembly line doing a succession of unskilled operative jobs, there was a cutback. Henry and other high school dropouts were the first to be laid off. Told that the layoff was only for a few weeks, Henry waited, hoping to get his job back. Now he is discouraged by the realization that there are no immediate prospects for re-employment. Henry doesn't know what to do and has no idea where to turn for help. He has no occupational skills. He is sure he couldn't return to high school, even if he wanted to, because he was failing when he left and had announced that he was "through with the dump."

The employment service has been suggested, but Henry says he wants to find his own job; besides, "They give you all those tests and I don't do anything on tests." He is discouraged and pessimistic and blames his troubles on people who have pull, show favoritism, and don't give a new worker a chance. His parents tell him he should go to a vocational school and "learn a good trade." This repeated advice has resulted in Henry's elimination of this possibility. Along with some other unemployed dropouts, he spends most of his time hanging around the shop where motors are rebuilt for drag racing. He is not particularly interested in this but likes to feel accepted by adults with a highly skilled specialty.

Question: What type(s) of assistance might be of value to Henry?

Sam Baker dropped out of school for an entirely different reason than Henry's. He is a bright, ambitious black caught in a job with no future or challenge and is developing deep feelings of frustration. He is working as a "maintenance engineer" in the community college but, as he says, "It's the janitor's job and the same old push broom." Sam did very well in high school but had to drop out during his senior year to go to work. He had hoped to obtain financial assistance to attend the community college or the university and had been accepted at the latter. Recently, he has become interested in the two-year educational aid program at the community college. He has also heard about the occupational specialist program in the school system, which requires no specialized preparation or qualifications other than actual work experience and the ability to get along with others. But Sam must support himself and help meet family expenses. The stipends or scholarships he might receive are not equal to his financial obligations. He is thinking about trying to obtain his high school diploma in the evening adult-education program at the community college, then enrolling for part-time evening studies. Though the two-year program offers an interesting chance for advancement, his real ambition is to study advertising and attend graduate school for advanced work. He feels he will have only one educational chance and that if he selects a two-year program he will have to stay with it. Frustrated with his present work and reluctant to undertake something that is not of major interest to him, he is unable to decide on any positive course of action.

Question: If Sam asked you for your opinion about the two-year program, what cautions should you observe in replying?

A College Student

College brings the individual face-to-face with major career decisions, which involve searching questions of "Who am I?" and "What do I want to be?" For many, it is the first time they are on their own, and peer pressures, independency needs, new lifestyles, and differing values compound the career planning process.

Mary Bell is experiencing a real personal conflict during her first year in college. For the first time in her life, she has realized that women have more than one or two options. She had always assumed that she would attend college mainly for its cultural value, meet a "college man," and get married. She might, if necessary, work a few years at some job, perhaps a clerical one. She might even teach, if nothing else were available. Now Mary is undergoing considerable conflict about women's roles. Some of her friends have been talking about a woman's right to have a career and be a real person, even when married. They even suggest that it would be all right not to marry. She is also torn between a campus "social life" role and a "service" role. These conflicts are so new and personal that she has not been able to discuss them with her parents. To add to her confusion, the same questions come up in classes, where discussions focus on women's exploitation as sex objects and exclusion from many careers. Recently, Mary encountered the first blacks she has ever met on an equal footing, and some of her racial stereotypes have been shaken.

She has always liked mathematics and done well in math courses. Her scores on the college board math test were quite high. She has not revealed her scores to others and has deliberately held down her grades so she would not surpass boys in her class, particularly those she dated or hoped to date. "No boy wants to go with a brain. I'd be some kind of freak. A girl mathematician!"

The prospect of completing college and competing for a job is frightening. Mary has thought about some of her unmarried relatives, who work as clerks and teachers and were always considered "old maids." But recently she has begun to compare her "old maid" stereotype with some of the career women she has read and heard about. Although she has other conflicts about ecology, religion, drugs, and sex, the issue of a career conflict is central. The people she has talked with, including some faculty members, usually strongly support one or the other side of the issue; thoughtful discussion is next to impossible. A visit to the Career Guidance and Placement Center revealed, to Mary's surprise, that many employers are looking for qualified women, even if only as "token females."

Mary almost married when she finished high school, but her parents persuaded her to "at least *try* college." The boy, now a junior, still thinks they ought to get married. As he sees it, she could help him with his work, and his parents would pay most of the expenses. But Mary feels she has to think of her own future; it is important for her to complete college. It makes her furious to feel defensive when he ridicules her thoughts about her future. Besides, he is an average student, and she can easily surpass him in grades.

Mary knows practically nothing about occupations, the preparation they require, or opportunities related to college programs. Her confusion and concern are so severe that she is seriously thinking about dropping out of school and working until she earns enough to pay her own way. Then she will feel free to select the program she prefers.

Question: Do you think Mary is having more difficulty with personal or with social attitudes about appropriate female work roles?

A Mid-Career Changer

Bill Powers struggled hard to get through college, working part-time to help pay his way. Married, with three children and a nice home in the suburbs, he appears to be an up-and-coming young industrial engineer. But recently he began to take stock of where he is going and what he is doing. "It's strange," he told his wife, "the more successful I am the more dissatisfied I feel. I'm away most of the time, and it looks like the future will be more of the same. We don't have any family life. I have to fight commuter traffic every day." Both agree that a major change might be desirable. "But people don't make changes like this, except for the few you read about in the newspapers. It's giving up our social life, two cars, clubs, and all that. We'd like to start some kind of small business or craft shop. But we could lose everything we have. Anyway, it's more or less settled. We're going to make some kind of major change."

Questions: What do you think of Bill's plan? Was any essential information omitted from the description of his original career choice?

The Pre- and Postretirement Years

Orville Harmon has worked for the Empire Office Supply Store for twenty years and is nearing sixty-five, the typical retirement age in his organization. He is still active and alert but has few interests outside of his job and no hobbies. Two grown sons have married and live in distant cities. His wife, Gertrude, sees how aimless some of their own friends have become after retirement and worries about what Orville will do with all the free time. Orville vaguely predicts that he will do all those things he's always wanted to do but never had the time for. He thinks, too, that he might try some part-time work, but he can't name anything that interests him.

Actually, Orville is anxious about the future and prefers to put it out of his mind. As he says, "I'll cross that bridge when I get to it."

Questions: What preparation for retirement would you recommend? Do you think Orville should continue on his job after age sixty-five?

George Fuller has recently retired from the city administrative offices. After the banquet at which he and several fellow retirees received the usual testimonials and gifts, he started to look around for interesting activities to occupy his time. His wife has been active in clubs and other organizations for many years and keeps busy with meetings and appointments. Their retirement income is adequate, so in spite of inflation, the Fullers can maintain their usual lifestyle.

George would like to be of service to the community, to do something that would give him a feeling of importance and usefulness. He has some knowledge of community agencies and institutions but has no idea how to get involved. He notices that he is tending to sit around home and worry rather than taking steps to get out and find some interesting service opportunities.

Questions: What steps would you suggest George take? Why?

Re-entry into the World of Work

Mabel Hillman worked as a secretary for a few years after she married, then stopped because of the frequent moves required by the company for which her husband worked. At the time she left her job, she had risen to an administrative position with considerable responsibility and a substantial salary.

After twenty years of married life, with three children in high school, her husband suddenly announced that he was leaving her and wanted a divorce. Although she receives some financial support from her husband, Mabel finds it necessary to return to work. The prospect is threatening. After having been away from business for so many years, she feels that her skills and social competencies have faded. She wonders if she can learn as rapidly as she once did and imagines that younger workers will be much more efficient than she is. She has contacted several of her former colleagues but has found them rather noncommittal and vague about help. Time has about run out, and she realizes that she has to get started, even though she has no idea of how to begin.

Question: Can you think of anything helpful Mabel might do to build up her confidence about entering the world of work?

Some Handicapped Individuals

Harry Sparks is one of a number of pupils who, by legislative mandate, must be put inthe least restrictive educational environment. Harry has cerebral palsy and is limited in his ability to communicate and needs help in getting about. He is, however, above average in intelligence and has the potential to be very competent in a work setting that takes his limitations into account. The immediate problem is selection of courses to make up a school program in line with his interests and abilities. (Later, vocational rehabilitation will assist with job training.) Harry, however, has no knowledge of occupational opportunities, lacks an understanding of his own interests and aptitudes, and doubts that he will ever be self-supporting.

Question: What do you think a counselor could do to help Harry select a school program?

George Gaines has held a succession of jobs, mostly semiskilled or unskilled. Now in his forties, he left his most recent job because of a heart condition. None of the previous jobs appealed to him, and with the physical limitations now imposed by his condition, he feels that he is through. To complicate his situation further, his wife is a semi-invalid who needs his care as well as financial support. He is not aware of social services that could help him, and after a few visits to the employment service office, George has just about given up looking for anything.

Questions: How might a counselor go about helping George develop a more positive attitude about the future? What is the most difficult block that might be encountered in the process?

In deciding what might be done to help each of these individuals, you may have suggested "talking to someone who knows about jobs" or "helping the individual learn about what he or she can do best." These and similar types of assistance in planning, decision making, and placement compose the career-counseling and guidance service. It is essential that these services be organized to provide the needed assistance at the right time and at a level appropriate to the maturity of those who receive it.

GUIDANCE AND COUNSELING HELP

One strategy to provide career-development assistance in educational institutions is career education. This is not the only way, but the career-education models that have developed vividly illustrate how a school or collegewide program can be built on career-development principles. One such model, developed for the Ohio schools, is shown in Figure 1.1. Note particularly that certain emphases are assigned to the elementary school, to junior and senior high schools, and to post–high school levels.

Career education is defined in this model as a program that endeavors, through the regular curriculum, to provide all young people in school with motivation toward the world of work, orientation to the many job opportunities

> available and exploration of occupations consistent with individual interests and abilities which help youth benefit from and plan for pre-professional instruction or vocational education. The career education program also provides pre-professional instruction leading to further education, vocational educational leading to successful entry and advancement in an occupation of personal choice, and training, retraining and upgrading instruction through-out an individual's work life which is consistent with the technology of the world of work and the individual interests and the needs of out-of-school youth and adults. The successful career education program combines the efforts of the home and the school to prepare youth for successful entry into the world of work. The school integrates the career motivation, orientation, and exploration program with the regular curriculum and includes a strong family life program to develop the positive influence of the home to its fullest potential.
>
> A total career education program consists of the following phases:
> 1. A total *Family Life Program* within the school curriculum with special emphasis for disadvantaged people to help improve the care and motivation of pre-school children and assure a more positive impact of the home on the needs of school age youth.
> 2. A *Career Motivation Program* for all youth in kindergarten through Grade six which develops a positive attitude toward the world of work, inspires

Figure 1.1   Ohio's career-development continuum

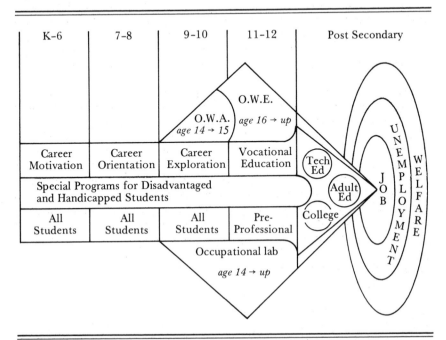

SOURCE: Division of Vocational Education and Division of Guidance and Testing, Ohio Department of Education. Reprinted by permission.

respect for all work and creates a desire to be a part of the world of work.

3. A *Career Orientation Program* in Grades seven and eight which provides all youth the opportunity to become aware of the many occupations open to those who prepare for them.

4. A *Career Exploration Program* in Grades nine and ten, or ages fourteen and fifteen, which provides all youth with the opportunity to examine and gain first hand experiences with several career opportunities consistent with individual interests and ability.

5. A *Career Preparation Program* for youth age sixteen and above which includes:

  a. A comprehensive vocational education program which provides job skills and technical knowledge and develops work habits and attitudes in preparation for employment.

  b. A comprehensive pre-professional education program which provides knowledge and foundations in preparation for professional education beyond high school.

6. A *Career Training, Retraining and Upgrading Program* for out-of-school youth and adults which provides the opportunity throughout adulthood to train, retrain and upgrade skills as technology changes and societal and individual needs and desires dictate.[1]

A summary of the key counseling and guidance emphases in this model is as follows:

1. K–6: Career motivation
2. 7–8: Career orientation and development of awareness of opportunities
3. 9–10: Career exploration to identify occupations appropriate to abilities and interests
4. 11–12: Career preparation for those who will work or enter specialized vocational or technical training. For those planning to attend college, the emphasis is on preprofessional preparation.

The major thrust of the total program is to help young people obtain suitable jobs. Figure 1.1 is a graphic illustration of the model just described. Several terms used in the figure require definition. O.W.A. is an *occupational work-adjustment* program for dropout-prone fourteen- and fifteen-year-olds. O.W.E. is *occupational work experience* for those sixteen years of age and older who are not able to succeed in regular vocational-education programs. The *occupational laboratory* is an in-school experience to help disadvantaged youth become work adjusted.

This program and the one that follows clearly indicate that career education is a concept much broader than career guidance and counseling. Career education involves a reorganization of the educational system, including lifelong education, to help individuals develop effective lifestyles for a technological society. Career development theory provides the basic guidelines for emphases, and career guidance and counseling furnish many of the techniques used both in and out of the classroom. The total concept leads to organized, systematic, community-wide services that facilitate career development.

Another career-education model that illustrates how career development is facilitated through career education is shown in Figure 1.2. This model, developed by the U.S. Office of Education, is based on career-development research and theory. Emphases appropriate for the individual's level of maturity are provided throughout the formal educational program. For example, at the elementary-school level, the focus is on career awareness; at the secondary level, the focus is on career decision making, exploration, and preparation for work or further education. Community agencies and institutions collaborate with the schools, and home and family provide the backdrop for a process that extends from early childhood through the retirement years. Education is lifelong, with entry into and exit from formal programs at appropriate times throughout the life span. Counseling and guidance services are a vital part of this lifelong program.

These representative models, based on the way individuals develop vocationally,

[1]Reprinted by permission of the Division of Vocational Education and the Division of Guidance and Testing, Ohio Department of Education.

Figure 1.2   Career development through career education

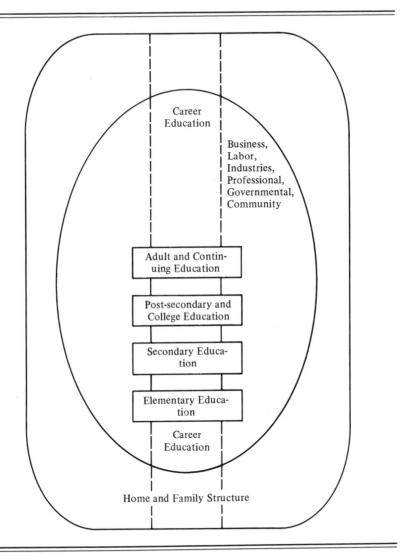

SOURCE: Kenneth B. Hoyt, Office of Career Education, U.S. Office of Education, Department of Health, Education, and Welfare, 1978.

clarify pupil needs and guidance functions for the high school level and later life. Career exploration, decision making, planning, and implementation of plans are the major pupil activities at the high school stage. The career-guidance functions that facilitate these pupil activities are individual counseling, group counseling, provision of information, group guidance, schoolwide course-based career-development procedures, and placement.

Individual and group counseling are the major aspects of the career-guidance program. Augmented by the other services, counseling helps individuals understand themselves, become aware of available options and their personal relevance, make and evaluate decisions, implement the decisions, and assess their suitability. Group counseling introduces the added dimension of feedback from peers for the development of an occupational identity. The information system makes information about occupational and educational opportunities at local and national levels readily available. Guidance activities, such as orientation, help develop readiness for the next step and facilitate successful transition. Support personnel provide routine services that would consume an inordinate amount of a counselor's time and reach individuals who would otherwise easily be missed. Placement in occupations or post–high school preparation programs provides the critical assistance pupils need to make maximum use of the array of services available. Each of these services is considered in depth in the chapters that follow. Each is designed to help individuals work through problems like the ones presented in the case studies.

Career status at any given time involves current development and its relationship to *values, avenues,* and *capabilities.* Figure 1.3 illustrates this concept. *Values* are an individual's sources of satisfaction. *Avenues* are the paths the individual has taken or the institutions he or she has used to arrive at his or her present position. *Capabilities* are the personal attributes, resources, and assets employed in the developmental process. Using this model, the career-education proposals and career-development theories taken up in Chapter 2 may be compared and contrasted. Specifically, values have contributed to current career status; their influence must be taken into account in any program that aims to help the individual develop further in a personally rewarding direction. Avenues, such as the school, provide the individual with the means to implement values and capabilities. If programs or learning experiences are not available, development will be hampered.

ROLES AND RESPONSIBILITIES OF COUNSELORS

Three recent statements make clear the extent and nature of the assistance that counselors in any setting should be prepared to provide. The first, the Career Education Incentive Act of 1977 (PL 95-207), lists the following principles:

1. A major purpose of education is to prepare every individual for a career suitable to that individual's preference.
2. Career education should be an integral part of the Nation's educational process which serves as preparation for work.

Figure 1.3   Influences on current developmental status

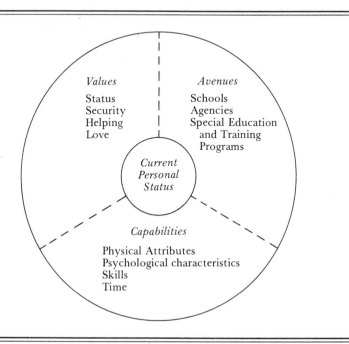

3. Career education holds promise of improving the quality of education and opening career opportunities for all students by relating education to their life aspirations.

4. Educational agencies and institutions (including agencies and institutions of elementary and secondary education, higher education, adult education, employment training and retraining, and vocational education) should make every effort to fulfill that purpose.

The second statement, adopted by the Association for Counselor Education and Supervision (ACES), enumerates fifteen career-guidance competencies that all counselors should have regardless of setting. The statement reflects the professional organization's concern about and responsiveness to social change. The areas of competency are as follows:

1. Career- and human-development theory and research and the skills necessary to translate this knowledge into developmental career-guidance and career-education programs

2. Career-information resources and the necessary skills to assist teachers, administrators, community-agency personnel, paraprofessionals, and peers

to integrate this kind of information into the teaching-counseling process

3. Career-assessment strategies and the skills necessary to assist individuals to use these data in the decision-making process

4. Individual- and group-counseling practices and the skills necessary to assist individuals in career planning using both approaches

5. Career decision-making processes and the skills necessary to implement programs designed to facilitate career decision making for clients in educational and community-agency settings

6. Job-placement services and the skills necessary to assist clients to seek, acquire, and maintain employment

7. The unique career-development needs of special client groups (women, minorities, handicapped, disadvantaged, and adults) and the skills necessary to assist them in their development

8. Sexism and racism and the necessary skills to reduce institutional discrimination in order to broaden the career opportunities available for all persons

9. The roles that lifestyle and leisure play in career development and the skills necessary to assist clients in selecting and preparing for occupations that coincide with various preferences

10. Consultation strategies and the skills necessary to assist others (teachers, parents, and peers) to deliver indirect career-guidance services

11. Synthesizing strategies and the skills necessary to assist individuals to understand the interrelatedness of their career decisions and life roles

12. Program development and curricular-infusion strategies and the skills necessary to design and implement career awareness, self-development, career exploration, and job-placement programs within educational and community-agency settings

13. Organizational development and change processes and the skills necessary to facilitate change in educators' attitudes toward career education

14. Program-evaluation techniques and the skills necessary to acquire evidence of the effectiveness of career-guidance and career-education programming

15. Educational trends and state and federal legislation that may influence the development and implementation of career-guidance programs[2]

These competencies have been utilized in preparing the sequence, content, and approach of chapters of this book. The early chapters deal with theory, need, technology, and materials; later chapters describe and illustrate applications, such as individual counseling, group counseling, and program planning. Note that these career-development competencies build on those gained from other courses and practical work experiences. For example, individual career-counseling strategies are

[2]L. Sunny Hansen, "ACES Position Paper: Counselor Preparation for Career Development/Career Education," *Counselor Education and Supervision*, Vol 17, No. 3, 1978, pp. 168–179. Copyright 1978 American Personnel and Guidance Association. Used by permission.

synthesized with other helping relationships that are used in promoting growth and development.

The third statement, "Career Development and Career Guidance," is a joint position paper of the National Guidance Association and the American Vocational Guidance Association issued in 1973 (see Appendix A in this book). It emphasizes the lifelong need for career guidance, the role of the counselor, and the part that others—teachers, administrators, parents, employers, and peers—play in facilitating career development.

Although the secondary-school setting is the critical place for helping individuals plan, make decisions, and begin to acquire the skills needed for career success and satisfaction, support for services for the total age range and for diverse groups with unique problems is widespread and growing as these three statements illustrate. When one considers the programs, laws, position papers, and other actions being taken that recognize career-development needs, it is clear that the future will see a dramatic surge in support for career guidance and counseling.

This book shows the need for career guidance and facilitation of career development, describes theories of how individuals make plans and decisions, and discusses the importance of factors that affect the developmental process. Unique career needs of special groups are identified. The emphasis then shifts from bases to applications—providing information, counseling, building programs, staffing, and evaluation.

SUMMARY

One of the counselor's most important responsibilities is to assist individuals with career planning and career development. This responsibility, however, has been neglected by counselors in practically all settings, particularly in schools. Considerable reorientation of services is needed, for humanitarian and practical reasons. In this chapter, needs for assistance have been reviewed in terms of finding personal meaning in work, the changes taking place in the world of work, job discrimination, job changing, school dropouts, and educational programs. Case studies have been presented to give further evidence of the need for career guidance throughout the entire life span. Career education as one major strategy to provide guidance throughout the institution has been illustrated by the Ohio and U.S. Office of Education models. Recent legislation illustrates the current wide support for career education and guidance throughout the life span, and the counseling profession has responded to this and other needs by specifying competencies needed by all counselors.

PROJECTS AND EXPERIENTIAL ACTIVITIES

1. Interview an elementary, middle/junior high, secondary school pupil, or older person (selected on the basis of your preferred work setting) to determine

attitudes about occupations, ranking of relative importance to society of several occupations, (for example, physician, engineer, auto mechanic, janitor), and career plans and reasons for them.

2. Check newspapers, television programs, and magazines for items related to career problems and needs. At first you may not locate any, but as you become alert to the vocational implications of news, features, and editorials you should see more and more.

3. Interview a counselor to determine his or her attitudes toward career counseling.

4. Listen to the tape recordings of Kenneth B. Hoyt, "Career Counseling: Beyond Career Development," and Eli Ginzberg, "On Career Guidance," Vol. 1, No. 1 (1972) of the APGA Series, *Counseling: Today and Tomorrow*.

5. List the part-time or full-time jobs you have had and note the factors that influenced you to take each. At what points in your career did you feel the need for guidance assistance?

6. Look over some of the brief autobiographies of leaders in counseling and guidance in William H. Van Hoose and John J. Pietrofesa, eds., *Counseling and Guidance in the Twentieth Century* (Boston: Houghton Mifflin, 1970). Each writer reflects on the persons, preferences, and circumstances that resulted in his or her position of eminence in the field, thus providing examples of the career-development process.

7. Write a brief autobiography (two or three pages) covering your career development to the present time. Include early fantasies, models that influenced you, and occupational goals. Give reasons for selection of goals and for changes made.

8. Form small groups and have each group member in turn briefly summarize his or her career development. At the end, each group should report on the three most inhibiting and three most facilitating factors in career development as illustrated by the individual accounts.

9. Form small groups and discuss the importance of the following factors in the life of each group member: health, marriage, money, travel, career, friends, children, talent, spiritual life, and leisure. Then see whether the groups can arrive at a consensus on the relative importance of each factor and give reasons for the rank assigned to "career."

10. Use a fantasy trip as a small group experience to look into the future. Begin by dimming the room lights, assuming a comfortable position, and using relaxation techniques (deliberately tensing muscles in your face, shoulders, arms, and legs, then relaxing them completely. More extensive getting into the mood would be better, but a brief period should serve for this experience.) Then imagine that it is a day ten years in the future. What time do you get up? How do you dress for work? How do you get to work? What do you do on the job? What are colleagues like? How do you feel when the workday is done? How do you feel about your job? Does your career fit into the lifestyle you prefer? Share what experience reveals to you about the importance of your work, your feelings about it, and how the fantasy trip affects your present plans.

ADDITIONAL REFERENCES

Borow, Henry, ed. *Man in a World at Work.* Boston: Houghton Mifflin, 1964. Chap. 1, "Vocational Guidance in the Perspective of Cultural Change," is an excellent, vivid account of the conditions that have shaped guidance since the beginning of this century. Chap. 3, "Milestones: A Chronology of Notable Events in the History of Vocational Guidance," details the major persons, conditions, and occurrences that have influenced the development of the profession.

————, ed. *Career Guidance for a New Age.* Boston: Houghton Mifflin, 1973. An excellent review of the major aspects of career guidance and a companion volume to *Man in a World at Work,* (1964). Chap. 1, "Historical and Recent Perspectives on Work and Vocational Guidance," covers the history and development of career guidance. Chap. 2, "Social Change and the Future of Vocational Guidance," examines the effects of social change on career planning and choice and helping strategies.

Ginzberg, Eli. *Career Guidance.* New York: McGraw-Hill, 1971. For applications to this chapter, it would be best to read Chap. 3, "Transformations," followed by Chap. 2, "Challenge and Response." The early history of the guidance movement is outlined in the first, and an analysis of developments through the early 1960s, as well as the current situation, is given in the latter.

Herr, Edwin L., and Stanley H. Cramer. *Vocational Guidance and Career Development in the Schools: Toward a Systems Approach.* Boston: Houghton Mifflin, 1972, pp. 4–7. A brief but informative survey of the impact of social needs on the development of career guidance is given on pp. 4–7.

Herr, Edwin L., ed. *Vocational Guidance and Human Development.* Boston: Houghton Mifflin, 1974. The second in the NVGA series on career development and guidance, emphasizing trends since the 1964 book. A comprehensive review and analysis, particularly relevant for this chapter, as it examines the place of work in contemporary society—in the United States as well as other countries. Chapters in Parts 1 and 2 expand on issues and needs introduced in this chapter.

Hoyt, Kenneth. *Refining the Career Education Concept.* Washington, D.C.: U.S. Government Printing Office, 1976. A series of reports describing the development of the concept of career education. Chap. 1, "Counselor Education: A Crusade for Change," describes the concept and identifies strategies for implementation.

Hoyt, Kenneth, Rupert Evans, Garth Mangum, Ella Bowen, and Donald Gale. *Career Education in the High School.* Salt Lake City: Olympus Publishing Company, 1977. One of a series of books by these authors on career education for various educational levels and special groups. Emphasizing the career development stages of decision making and preparation, particularly appropriate for high school years, the book covers all aspects, for instance, bases, program planning, and implementation. Chap. I, "Career Education" is an excellent overview of what career education means for the secondary school.

Marland, Sidney P., Jr. *Career Education.* New York: McGraw-Hill, 1974. Written by the originator of the term *career education,* this book gives a comprehensive and lucid account of the need for and potential benefits of this new approach to education.

O'Toole, James. *Work in America.* Cambridge, Mass.: MIT Press, 1973. A comprehensive and perceptive survey of work in this country, with far-reaching suggestions for improving the quality of life in the workplace. While any chapter offers relevant background material for career guidance, Chap. 1, "Introduction," gives a vivid overview of the work scene today.

————. *Work, Learning, and the American Future.* San Francisco: Jossey-Bass, 1977. The theme of this book, the development of human resources, makes it relevant as background material for career counselors. Chap. 1, "The Case for Change," provides an examination of ways of improving the quality of work and life in America. Chap. 2, "Misuses of Human Resources," brings the reader face to face with the critical problems often confronted by those with whom the counselor works.

Peters, Herman J., and James C. Hansen, eds. *Vocational Guidance and Career Development.* 3rd ed. New York: Macmillan, 1977. An excellent collection of reprinted articles on all aspects of career guidance. Parts 1 and 2 contain a number of selections relevant to the questions and issues raised in this chapter.

Samler, Joseph. *Vocational Counselor and Social Action.* Washington, D.C.: National Vocational Guidance Association, 1970. This brief monograph spells out the responsibilities of the vocational counselor and his or her potential to effect social change.

Slocum, Walter L. *Occupational Careers.* 3rd ed. Chicago: Aldine, 1974. A sociological perspective on such topics as the purposes, settings, requirements, and avenues of advancement in work. Chap. 2, "The Meaning of Work," is particularly useful in learning how attitudes toward work developed and which ones are currently widespread.

Stephens, W. Richard. *Social Reform and the Origins of Vocational Guidance.* Washington, D.C.: American Personnel and Guidance Association, 1970. A very important study that should be read in its entirety.

Williamson, E. G. *Vocational Counseling: Some Historical, Philosophical, and Theoretical Perspectives.* New York: McGraw-Hill, 1965. Much of this book will fascinate the student who wishes to delve into the many facets of the vocational-guidance concept. Chap. 5, "Originators of Systems in Counseling: Parsons, Harper, and Witmer," contains especially interesting excerpts that recapture the flavor of the past. Chap. 6, "Vocational Counseling and Industrial Psychology," is somewhat more technical but valuable as an exposition of how measurement techniques, vocational psychology, and psychological appraisal methods contribute to vocational counseling. In Chap. 7, "After Parsons: The Return to Over-simplification," the author traces the development of helping strategies, the conflicts among them, and the still unresolved issues.

Wirtz, Willard. *The Boundless Resource.* Washington, D.C.: New Republic Book Company, 1975. Any part of this book is valuable reading for the counselor. In fact, a reading of the complete text is highly recommended. As Marland says, the book "should be in the hands of every congressman and his staff; it should be searched by the President's speech writers and by many other parts of the

Executive Branch including the Office of Management and Budget. It should be well comprehended and harkened to by educators at all levels of the enterprise. It should be in the hands of businessmen and labor leaders. It cries out for a renewal of the American spirit, and it offers the apparatus for that renewal in purposeful and logical designs" (1976, p. 626).

Yankelovich, Daniel. "The New Psychological Contracts at Work." *Psychology Today*, 11, No. 12 (1978), 46–47, 49–50. This and additional articles in this issue are significant not only for what they say about changing work attitudes but also because they illustrate wide concern about issues related to work. Other valuable articles are: "What You Really Want from Your Job," "Thinking Clearly about Career Choices," and "The Abrasive Personality at the Office."

2

Theories of

Career Development

GOALS

1

To explain that career-behavior theory has personal meaning
for the individual.

2

To present a vocabulary of common terms used in career
development.

3

To show how career-development theories may be grouped by
similar characteristics.

4

To describe the major theories of career development.

5

To emphasize that theories provide guidelines for practice.

6

To help the student begin to formulate a personally useful
approach to facilitating career development in others.

JOE PRINCE, Mary Jones, and Ralph Hart appear briefly in Chapter 1. Each represents a problem of career development. Joe is the directionless and unmotivated senior. Mary is the socialite who views work as a brief interlude to pass the time until marriage. Ralph is the college-bound senior who is extremely concerned about the selection of a college and a major. A more detailed account of the career development of each will illustrate factors that can lead to difficulties in career planning and development and will also be useful for application to the theories presented in this chapter.

When *Joe Prince* was five years old his family, including an older sister in the third grade, moved from the rural area where his father ran a small service station and did part-time farming. The family had been very close, and was well known and well liked in the community. The move was made for economic reasons and was regarded as a definite advancement for Mr. Prince. The new job with the city utilities department required regular hours away from home, as well as a considerable amount of overtime. Joe had always wanted to be just like his father, but now he seldom saw him; he did not understand why his father was away so much or what he did on the new job.

The parents felt that their children were at a disadvantage in the city schools and pushed them hard to do good work. Joe's sister made average to good grades, but Joe was neither as capable nor as determined. He could not equal her progress. During elementary school he often claimed to be sick to avoid attending school. When his little brother arrived, Joe's mother and father had less time for him; often, his school progress was not noticed until report card time. He was told repeatedly that he should plan to attend college so that he could be a professional. When he entered high school his parents were determined for him to take the academic program, but past achievement indicated that he would probably not be able to succeed in it. Under some pressure from the school, the parents agreed to the general program, with the assurance that it would not preclude college admission.

When Joe's sister dropped out of school during her senior year to be married, the academic pressures on Joe increased. Feeling that he ought to earn some spending money and get some work experience, Joe took over a paper route. He enjoyed working in a routine situation in which he had to make no decisions and could deal with people. At school he found that he could get by best by being friendly to teachers and helping them out. It seemed to help his grades, and he began to feel that he was somebody. He took over as assistant manager of the basketball team because no one else wanted the job. He is relatively happy in his present situation and is really comfortable only in a position in which he need not compete. Tests, such as those required for college admission, cause him considerable anxiety. Any kind of responsibility upsets him a great deal. As a senior, he is beginning to recognize that decisions must be made and tries to hide his concern under an "I don't care" attitude.

Mary Jones has always admired her socially active parents but has never felt close to them—they are like famous and successful persons who notice her now and then. Nevertheless, they have been her models; her primary ambition is to be just like her mother. One of her happiest memories is of being allowed to help with a party given by her parents at the country club. She has been successful at whatever she has attempted. At twelve she was given a horse, and within two years she had won a number of ribbons at shows. At sixteen she won the girls' tennis championship at the club. Bright, sophisticated, and apparently older than her years, she is deferred to in school and in the community because of her parents' social and economic status. In her social group girls neither work at jobs seriously nor become very concerned about education. Many marry after private high school or a year or so of a post–high school finishing school. Furthermore, she sees talking with a counselor as something done only by those who can't make their own decisions.

School and community activities, more than classes, have brought Mary into close contact with a cross-section of people. Near the end of her second year in high school, she has reached a turning point in her values. A conflict about lifestyles has begun to emerge as Mary looks at herself and her subculture from the perspectives of others. It has been a threatening experience to attempt to justify what she believes and how her family and friends live. The matter of a career is one of the sensitive issues. She has begun to question what she wants from life but is reluctant to abandon what she knows and can succeed in for the unknown and threatening.

Ralph Hart says that he decided to attend college when he was in the first grade. At that time his father, a well-known scientist, put aside funds for the boy's education. Ralph says that he has always understood that his father wants to have a famous son. He also says that he sometimes thinks he is competing with his father, and even trying to outdo him. In the fifth grade Ralph won a prize for a science project; since then he has devoted considerable time to competitions, in which he has progressively improved. His nickname, "Einstein," pleases him and he is the authority on all things scientific in the school. He likes to be exact and precise, to foresee eventualities, and to test possibilities carefully rather than jump to conclusions. It bothers him to make a mistake. Uncertainty that cannot be resolved by scientific procedures causes him considerable anxiety. Decisions must be carefully thought out and their consequences foreseen. Though he had thought he was sure of his directions, at times he wonders whether he should consider other possibilities. Is he obeying his father's wishes or his own? He thought that the selection of physics as a major would be easy. He also thought that the state university would be the natural place to go. Now when he reviews his situation he asks himself how he decided on science in the first place. He is baffled that he cannot make quick and positive decisions about the next steps.

These brief cases illustrate blocks to effective career development. The significance of these blocks will become more apparent as this chapter continues.

DEFINITIONS

Career guidance and counseling utilize terms that need to be defined. Some, like *decision making,* are generally understood, but others, such as *vocational development,* are new. Still others have definitions or meanings that are different from everyday usage.

Career   A career is the sequence of occupations in which one engages. Some persons may remain in the same occupation throughout their life spans, while others may have a series of quite different occupations.

Career pattern   A career pattern is the sequence and duration of occupations in the life span of the individual. Career patterns indicate long-term trends, such as upward movement, erratic changes, or dead-end sequences. For example, the career pattern of those at a professional level may show steady upward progression, while for those at an unskilled level it may reveal a succession of occupations at about the same level of pay and responsibility.

Career development   Career development, vocational development, and occupational development are used synonymously in this book. Each refers to the lifelong process of developing work values, crystallizing a vocational identity, learning about opportunities, and trying out plans in part-time, recreational, and full-time work situations. Development involves increasingly effective investigation, choice, and evaluation of occupational possibilities. Career development may be thought of as an aspect of general development. While the term *career* usually refers to the succession of occupations in which one engages during a lifetime, and *occupation* or *vocation* indicate a specific work role, such as physician or machinist, this distinction is not utilized in this book.

Decision making   The everyday usage of this term is not very different from the definition employed in this book, except that occupational decision making is a systematic process in which various data are utilized and analyzed according to explicit procedures, and outcomes are evaluated in terms of desirability. Decision making combines the affective and cognitive domains so that there will be a balance of objective and subjective rewards. For example, "I am studying because previous appraisals have indicated that I have talent, and I feel a deep satisfaction because I can create something unique and personal." It is difficult to imagine a decision-making process without some mix of both elements, although one or the other may carry more weight.

Information   There are three general categories of information—occupational, educational, and personal-social. They overlap considerably. For example, information about occupations usually includes references to educational requirements and important personal attributes. Information is usually in printed form, but filmstrips, slides, audio and video tapes, films, and computer print-outs are also used. "Firsthand" information is that which is obtained directly from the original source, such as an interview with a worker. "Secondhand" information, or information from secondary sources, is that which is derived from data collected by others, such as *The Occupational Outlook Handbook*. Most of the information used in guidance and counseling is from secondary sources.

Job   This term refers to a group of similar positions in a business, industry, or other place of employment. For example, there may be three school counselors at Midtown High School. These three positions make up the job of school counselor in this institution.

Occupation   The occupation of counselor is found in most schools. Thus, an *occupation* is a definable work activity that occurs in many different settings.

Position   A group of activities, tasks, or duties performed by one person is a position. For example, if you are a school counselor at Midtown High School, you are occupying a position.

Work   The term *work* is often used for an activity that is difficult, unpleasant, and done only out of necessity. It is used here for purposeful mental, physical, or combined mental-physical activity that produces something of economic value. Thus, work may produce a service for others as well as a material product.

Placement   In elementary and high school, the term *placement* is often used to mean placement in a course, a curriculum, or a school activity. The meaning of the term as used here is primarily job placement for part-time or full-time work. Placement includes helping the individual locate a job, apply for it, obtain it, and make satisfactory initial adjustment to it. Follow-up to determine the suitability of the job is included.

Leisure   The term *leisure* describes periods of time in which the individual engages in activities or pursuits chosen freely without constraints of any kind. The individual derives a feeling of well-being from these activities. Leisure activities may be different from work, or they may be similar to it (Winters and Hansen, 1976).

Career counseling and career guidance   Career counseling, defined generally in Chapter 1, is really much the same as other kinds of counseling except that it focuses on planning and making decisions about occupations and education. As in all counseling, the personal relationship is critical. It includes exploration of values and attitudes, but information and factual data about the counselee's resources, such as finances for training, are more significant than in personal counseling. Even so, it usually is not possible to help someone with a vocational problem without recognizing such other aspects of his or her life as needs, conflicts, and relations with others.

Career guidance, which includes counseling as a specialized service, encompasses all of the services that aim at helping pupils make occupational and educational plans and decisions.

Career guidance is an organized program to help young people develop self-understanding, learn about the world of work, gain experiences that will help in decision making, and find jobs. For example, using the information system to learn about the work of a secretary is primarily a guidance activity, but discussing the personal meaning of this occupation with the counselor is career counseling. Learning secretarial skills in the business department is a content-oriented course activity that follows guidance and counseling on occupational choice. Career guidance may be provided in many school settings and by a variety of school staff members, such as teachers, support personnel, and pupils as well as counselors. Many of the activities currently used in career education resemble career guidance, for example, role playing, simulated work experience, viewing occupational films, taking field trips, and participating in career conferences and career fairs.

CAREER-DEVELOPMENT THEORY

Theoretical bases for understanding how individuals develop vocationally give the counselor guidelines for helping them to solve problems, avoid blocks, and progress with efficiency and satisfaction. Each counselor, guidance worker, and counselor aide has a set of assumptions that guide his or her actions and constitute his or her theory. A carefully formulated, tested, and consistent theory gives the counselor a rationale for helping that transcends his or her own intuitive guesses.

Career-development theories are relatively new in a profession that is itself not much more than a half-century old. Even so, productive and innovative research and theorizing are increasing rapidly. The sequence of stages postulated for the developmental process underlie the concept of career education. Career development is a high-priority item on an international as well as national scale. The International Association for Educational and Vocational Guidance (IAEVG) is establishing lines of communication between counseling and guidance personnel in different countries. Some developments in England are illustrative of what other countries are doing. There, counseling and guidance programs or courses are offered in approximately a dozen universities. Books that specifically focus on this area—for example, *Career Guidance—The Role of the School in Vocational Development* (Hopson and Hayes, 1972)—are being published, and research programs are being developed. Much of the focus is, in keeping with the theme of this book, on utilizing vocational-development theory and research to improve counseling, guidance, and placement programs. Modules on teaching, decision making, and promoting career self-awareness in the school are available (Hopson and Hough, 1971), and new concepts are being utilized to modernize career-guidance and placement services for young people (Department of Employment, 1971).

Although they are still somewhat tentative, career-development theories are accumulating a broad research base. However, overly enthusiastic use of the data is as inappropriate as complete rejection. Data limitations involve their generalizability and the assumptions on which they are based. For instance, much of the existing research and theory about how people develop vocationally, choose careers, and find and adjust to work are based on data from middle-class white males, who have substantial resources and freedom to pursue career preferences (Herr and Cramer, 1972, pp. 54–55). Their vocational development and career patterns may differ markedly from those in other subcultures. Counselors need to understand the vocational development of a wide variety of groups. The disadvantaged, for example, may not fit typical patterns. The applicability of existing data and theory to women has not been demonstrated; separate career models may be needed for males and females as well as for other subcultures. Further, much of the research and theorizing was done during a period when jobs were more plentiful, and concepts need to be re-evaluated in light of current conditions.

Questions have been raised about the current applicability of systematic models of career development and whether the whole process is so subject to the uncertainties of the world of work that intuition is the most appropriate guide for the individual planning a career (Baumgardner, 1977). In addition, work may not be central to the value systems of all individuals, though all theories assume it to be. Increasingly, it is assumed that work cannot provide a feeling of accomplishment or a sense of identity for everyone and that leisure may play a significant role. Both the position papers of the National Vocational Guidance Association and the American Vocational Association and the policy statement of ACES on career development acknowledge these points. There is considerable agreement that when work opportunities are more extensive than necessary for physical survival in a society in which finding meaning and challenge in work is important, the significance of leisure becomes a major issue. This attitude needs to be taken into account in estimating the utility of career-development theories, but it does not eliminate the need for theories—instead, it emphasizes the importance of the counselor being aware of the relation of leisure to work (Winters and Hansen, 1976). Work is still a central force in the lives of individuals, and knowledge of theories of how careers are developed is essential for counselors.

There is no lack of awareness of the importance of expanding the frontiers of theory and research. Data are accumulating, including a considerable amount on special groups (Betz, 1977; Osipow, 1977). In addition, the position papers of professional associations and individual experts clearly recognize the significance and utility of theories of career development (National Vocational Guidance Association and American Vocational Association, 1973; Hansen, 1978). Hansen, for example, specifies that one critical area for counselors in all settings is to have knowledge of and competency in "career and human development theory and research and the skills necessary to translate this knowledge into developmental career-guidance and career-education programs" (1978, p. 177).

Vocational-development theory is not a general theory of development that can serve as a basis for all counseling and guidance. This may be one reason why some counselors assert either that it offers them little or nothing or that *vocational* counseling is distinct from *real* counseling. Useful vocational-development concepts should be incorporated, along with others, into a comprehensive helping rationale. When the focus is on helping with career planning and development, use is made of principles from vocational-development theory; but when the focus is on, say, family relations or personal conflicts, career-development concepts may not be relevant. Even so, a surprising number of the problems and needs of school and college students, as well as out-of-school youth and adults, revolve around career plans, frustrations, and conflicts.

CLASSIFICATION OF CAREER-DEVELOPMENT THEORIES

Table 2.1 illustrates one way career-development theories may be grouped. Major research projects that are closely related to a particular theoretical position are also listed. In addition, several theorists in related fields whose work contributes to an understanding of career development are identified.

Not all theorists are included, and the contributions of those named in the first column are not of equal weight. Moreover, the brief statements given in the table do not characterize all the theories in the group. The descriptive comments do, however, portray aspects of the approach.

Other classification systems use somewhat the same groupings as the one just given. Herr and Cramer (1972, pp. 30–53) use the following classification and remind the reader that types may be combined to explain career behavior.

1. TRAIT-FACTOR OR ACTUARIAL   The focus is on personal traits such as aptitudes and interests and their relation to traits required by the job.
2. DECISION THEORY   The individual chooses, along the lines of concepts derived from decision theory, the vocational alternative that offers the best return or payoff.
3. SOCIOLOGICAL EMPHASES   Sociological factors, such as one's social group and the social structure, exert an influence on vocational development and choice.
4. PSYCHOLOGICAL EMPHASES   Development and choice depend, to a large extent, on the individual's psychological make-up, for example, motivation, personality structure, and needs.
5. DEVELOPMENTAL EMPHASES   Theories in this group go beyond the previous ones in focusing on the development of the individual over a relatively long period of time.

Crites (1969, pp. 79–116) uses a similar classification system but includes *accidental* and *economic* theories. The latter is related to economic theories of supply and demand, while the former includes chance and contingency factors. Chance factors are those that are unplanned and unexpected, while contingency factors are those whose effects are predictable, "intelligence and socio-economic status" (Crites, 1969, p. 80). More recently, Crites (1978, p. 20) uses trait-factor, client-centered, psychodynamic, developmental, and behavioral theories, although his focus is on the counseling strategy rather than the underlying theory of career development.

There are other theorists who belong in one or another of these classifications or cut across several. Not every theory is covered in this chapter. Those presented, however, should give an adequate overview of the field. In each of the classifications, the work of one or more major theorists is summarized and other contributors are discussed. Some relevant research programs that do not represent independent theories are described. Major theories are outlined in enough detail to provide an understanding of their development and content. With this background it is possible to build a framework for additional reading, make some applications to daily work, compare theories, and relate them to practices. Additional reading is essential. References at the end of this chapter list relevant publications.

Theories may be described from the standpoint of how they deal with specific developmental stages or processes, as is done by Crites (1969, Chaps. 3–7) and Pietrofesa and Splete (1975). Regardless of how they are covered, however, it is unlikely that any one will serve for the many diverse populations in need of assistance (Crites, 1978). The importance of reviewing each theory separately is emphasized by Whiteley (1978, p. 3) when he points out that there are basic differences in the theories on which career counseling is based. An understanding of each makes it possible for the counselor to start to formulate a personally useful approach, somewhat along the lines that Crites (1978a) employs in building his comprehensive model. The counselor will have to decide whether or not one approach will be adequate or a synthesis is needed. Although there is a difference of opinion about this matter (Holland and Gottfredson, 1978; Whiteley, 1978), my position is that one approach can provide the general framework, and useful concepts can be adapted from others.

Table 2.1   Theories of career development and related studies

	Theorists	Major Concepts	Ages Covered	Applications to Guidance and Counseling	Research Support
Trait-Factor or Actuarial	E. G. Williamson Studies: Flanagan	Assessment of traits Matching traits with job factors	High school and adult	At choice points for decision making	Variable results of validity
Developmental	Super Ginzberg Tiedeman and O'Hara Tuckman Studies: Crites, Gribbons and Lohnes Related theorists: Havighurst, Gould, Levinson, Lowenthal, and others	Developmental stages Career patterns Vocational self-concept Vocational maturity	Life span	Counseling and program planning at various ages	Substantial support for major concepts, such as sequence of stages
Needs	Roe, Holland, Hoppock	(Needs arise from attributes and experiences Choices are based on needs	Life span, but emphasis is on child-hood through early choices	Wide applicability of needs concepts in guidance	Varies with theories: Roe, parts supported; Holland, generally valid

Psychoanalytical	Bordin Nachmann Segal Galinsky	Needs are based on a psychoanalytical theory of personality development	Emphasis on personality development in early years, but needs exist throughout life	Primarily in counseling involving needs exploration	Some support for concepts
Sociological	Blau, Gustad, Jessor, and Wilcock Miller and Form Hollingshead	Social influences on development and choice Occupational opportunities play a major role	Life span	Wide applicability	Support for many aspects, such as effect of opportunities on choice
Decision Making	Gelatt Hershenson and Roth Knefelkamp and Slepitza Katz Jepson	Decision making an identifiable process Decisions have a cumulative effect	Life span, but emphasis is on first two or three decades	Wide applicability	Some support
Social Learning	Mitchell, Jones, and Krumboltz Thoresen and Ewart	Utilizes types of learning Coping skills Effects of experience	Life span, but emphasis is on first two or three decades	Wide applicability	Some support, for example, through synthesis of related research

TRAIT-FACTOR OR ACTUARIAL

While this approach may be thought of as primarily a strategy for decision making at a specific time, it may also be viewed as the basis of lifelong career development. The individual becomes increasingly aware of his or her aptitudes, interests, values, and needs and at the same time learns about the demands of occupations. Career development involves matching these two sets of factors—self and occupational. With increasing experience, the matching process becomes more efficient. Williamson (1950, pp. 101–126; 1972, Chap. 4) has been the principal spokesman for this approach and has drawn on it for formulating a counseling strategy employing six developmental steps:

Step 1: Analysis—the collection of data about the individual. Psychological tests are used extensively, but the interview is also frequently employed.

Step 2: Synthesis—the organization of information to identify strengths, weaknesses, needs, and problems. The effectiveness of this step depends on the adequacy of the data collected in Step 1.

Step 3: Diagnosis—the problem and its causes are brought out.

Step 4: Prognosis—the probable success of each option is examined.

Step 5: Counseling—the counselor helps the counselee to understand, accept, and put to use information about self and occupations. Emphasis is on finding a way to deal with the present problem, for example, choosing a course of study or an occupation, but attention is also given to learning how to cope with future problems.

Step 6: Follow-up—a check is made of the suitability of decisions and the need for additional help.

Although affective aspects are considered, the major emphasis in this approach is on relatively objective data about the individual's traits and how well they match factors that are critical to success in work. To varying degrees, the trait-factor approach is present in much occupational planning and counseling today—for example, does one have adequate test scores for admission to graduate schools? Which aptitudes of the handicapped individual appear useful for vocational training?

A large number of research studies provide support for the trait-factor approach. Project Talent is the best known and most extensive.

John Flanagan's Project Talent

This large-scale study, involving pupil attitudes and abilities, career plans, school characteristics, and guidance services, was started in 1960. Over 400,000 pupils in 1,353 high schools took a two-day battery of tests and completed several questionnaires. A 5 percent stratified sample of high schools to insure representation by size was used. Pupils tested were in grades nine through twelve. Instruments used were: forty tests (providing data on eighteen abilities), a student information blank, an interest inventory, an activities inventory, two open-ended essay questions on "My view about the ideal occupation," and two instruments designed to obtain data on schools (for example, faculty qualifications, curriculum) and the guidance service (for example, counselor education preparation, types of counseling help provided).

Follow-ups were scheduled at intervals of one, five, ten, and twenty years after graduation from high school. So far, *Design for a Study of American Youth* (Flanagan et al., 1962), the first book in a series entitled "The Talents of American Youth," has been published. Numerous other publications have been prepared, including one that provides descriptive data about high school pupils and results of the follow-up of those tested as twelfth-graders (Flanagan et al., 1964).

While the project is not based on a vocational-development theory, it is providing a vast amount of data (much of which is stored in data banks) that could conceivably contribute to research on aspects of theories discussed in this chapter.

The purposes of Project Talent are to provide

1. an inventory of the talents and capacities of youth.
2. standards for educational and psychological tests and measurements.
3. guides to estimating occupational success for various patterns of aptitudes, abilities, and other characteristics.
4. information about how occcupations are selected.
5. information about the effect of education on occupational preparation (U.S. Office of Education, 1965).

The next steps in Project Talent are to investigate career patterns to determine the most satisfactory ones, to assess the validity of occupational choice in high school, to analyze the meaning of career changes, and to devise more effective ways to use information. In addition, the twenty-year follow-up will be carried out in 1980.

Findings

Among the findings that focus directly on decision making and career development are the following:

1. A great majority of pupils do not make an appropriate choice of career in high school.
2. In the ninth grade, plans are very unrealistic but there is some improvement by the twelfth grade.
3. About half the pupils make radical changes in occupational choice in the first year out of high school.
4. The original Project Talent pupils tested in 1960 were more definite about occupational plans than were a 1970 group of in-school high school pupils tested for comparison purposes. The percentage of boys who were definite about occupational choices dropped about 8 percent, and girls about 16 percent (Flanagan, 1970).

Project Talent research also shows a growing realism in pupils' career planning between 1960 and 1970 (Flanagan, 1973a). Further, girls have shifted career choices to more nontraditional occupations (Flanagan, 1973b). There are also indications of a seeking for a sense of achievement in work, and the great majority of respondents give their jobs an overall positive rating (Wilson and Wise, 1975, pp. 20, 22).

Project Releases

An outcome of Project Talent data is the development of the Program of Learning in Accordance with Needs, or PLAN. A computer-supported individualized education program in science, mathematics, language arts, social studies, and guidance for grades one through twelve, it is now available for use (Dunn, 1971; Project Talent, 1972).

A career-guidance program, *Planning Career Goals* (Flanagan, 1977), has been prepared, based on data from the ten-year follow-up. This program is designed to help pupils clarify interests in occupational areas and assess information on, and abilities in, these fields.

Another procedure derived from the project assesses the potential of social programs for improving the quality of life (Flanagan, 1978). Fifteen dimensions relating to the quality of life were identified and samples of individuals, including some from Project Talent, were interviewed to determine how well the quality-of-life criteria were being met. In addition to building a model for simulating program impacts, the results provided some valuable data about occupational satisfaction as well as useful case studies. For instance, work is important to over 80 percent of men and women at ages thirty and fifty, and more than half at age seventy. At all ages, over 75 percent reported that their needs in this area are well met (p. 142).

Two publications resulting from the project are of special interest to career counselors. These two books should be used together: the latter does not replace the former. The *Career Data Book* (Flanagan, Tiedeman, Willis, and McLaughlin, 1973) is based on the results of the five-year follow-up after high school. Approximately 100,000 subjects responded in the follow-up. At the time of the follow-up, subjects were twenty-two years old, so they were not necessarily involved in stable plans. Further, the time period was not long enough to judge who was happy and successful; in fact, occupational profiles are based on individuals' plans rather than actual experiences. Each chapter in the book focuses on one of the fifteen occupational groups established for the study. A total of 138 occupations are described by profiles that list thirty-eight scales each. An example of an occupational group is "general teaching and social science" (a group that includes counseling).

A pupil's booklet that provides for self-ratings and gives combined profiles for each major group accompanies *The Career Data Book*. Users can prepare their own ability, interest, and personality profiles, based on similar tests and on estimates, to help in occupational planning. The predictive validity of the profiles is somewhat tentative, but the second book, described next, covers a longer period of time and has more on-the-job data.

Using the Talent Profiles in Counseling (Rossi, Bartlett, Campbell, Wise, and McLaughlin, 1975) includes half the eleven-year follow-up of Project Talent participants, involving approximately 50,000 individuals. This set of profiles, aimed at the career-guidance practitioner, includes the percentage of participants in each occupation covered, information about those most satisfied with their work, and data about positive and negative features as perceived by respondents. Profiles are based on both sexes. The book also includes a very helpful section, with illustrative cases, on how to use the profiles in counseling.

DEVELOPMENTAL THEORIES

In this section, the work of Donald E. Super, Eli Ginzberg, and David V. Tiedeman is discussed first. Following these theorists, the school adaptations of Bruce W. Tuckman are briefly summarized, and the work of existentialists is noted. The major research studies of John C. Crites and Warren D. Gribbons and Paul R. Lohnes are reviewed next to show how they contribute to the developmental approach. Finally, the career-development implications of the works of Robert J. Havighurst, Roger Gould, Daniel J. Levinson, and Marjorie F. Lowenthal and associates are briefly reviewed.

Super's Theory

Super uses the term *approach* rather than *theory* and suggests that his own approach could be labeled "differential-development-social-phenomenological psychology" (1969, p. 9). It focuses on four major elements: vocational life stages, vocational maturity, translating the self-concept into a vocational self-concept, and career patterns. According to this approach, the individual develops vocationally as one aspect of his or her total development at a rate determined in part by his or her psychological and physiological attributes and in part by environmental conditions, including significant others. Specific vocational-development tasks are mastered to attain successive levels of vocational maturity. The progression through vocational life is more or less orderly. Career patterns may in time be predicted when sufficient data are available and the meaning of these data to the individual is known.

Drawing on a wide range of research and theory on development, measurement, occupational adjustment, and related areas, Super formulated a "theory of vocational development" in 1953. The ten propositions he stated at that time still serve as the basic rationale for his research and theory construction.

1. People differ in their abilities, interests and personalities.
2. They are qualified, by virtue of these circumstances, each for a number of occupations.
3. Each of these occupations requires a characteristic pattern of abilities, interests and personality traits, with tolerances wide enough, however, to allow both some variety of occupations for each individual and some variety of individuals in each occupation.
4. Vocational preferences and competencies, and situations in which people live and work, and hence their self-concepts, change with time and

experience (although self-concepts are generally fairly stable from late adolescence until later maturity), making choice and adjustment a continuous process.

5. This process may be summed up in a series of life stages, characterized as those of growth, exploration, establishment, maintenance, and decline, and these stages may in turn be subdivided into (a) fantasy, tentative, and realistic phases of the exploratory stage, and (b) the trial and stable phases of the establishment stage.

6. The nature of the career pattern (that is, the occupational level attained and the sequence, frequency, and duration of trial and stable jobs) is determined by the individual's parental socioeconomic level, mental ability, and personality characteristics, and by the opportunities to which he is exposed.

7. Development through the life stages can be guided partly by facilitating the process of maturation of abilities and interests and partly by aiding in reality testing and in the development of the self-concept.

8. The process of vocational development is essentially that of developing and implementing a self-concept; it is a compromise process in which the self-concept is a product of the interaction of inherited aptitudes, neural and endocrine make-up, opportunity to play various roles, and evaluation of the extent to which the results of role playing meet with the approval of superiors and fellows.

9. The process of compromise between individual and social factors, between self-concept and reality, is one of role playing, whether the role is played in fantasy, in the counseling interview, or in real life activities such as school classes, clubs, part-time work, and entry jobs.

10. Work satisfaction and life satisfaction depend upon the extent to which the individual finds adequate outlets for his abilities, interests, personality traits, and values; they depend upon his establishment in a type of work, a work situation, and a way of life in which he can play the kind of role which his growth and exploratory experiences have led him to consider congenial and appropriate.[1]

The 1957 Career Pattern Study Monograph, *Vocational Development: A Framework for Research* (Super et al, 1957) stated essentially the same propositions and outlined the twenty-year longitudinal Career Pattern Study. This study began in 1951 and involved 138 eighth-grade and 142 ninth-grade boys plus a control group of 173 ninth-grade boys. The sequence of vocational life stages, one of the major concepts in the theory of Career Pattern Study, is as follows:

1. GROWTH STAGE, birth to age fourteen:
General characteristics: "Self-concept develops through identification with key figures in family and school. . . . Needs and fantasy are dominant early in this

---

[1]Donald E. Super, "A Theory of Vocational Development," *American Psychologist,* 8, No. 4 (1953), pp. 189–190. Copyright 1953 by the American Psychological Association, and reproduced by permission.

stage. . . . Interests and capacities become more important with increasing social participation and reality-testing."

Substages of the growth stage are:

Fantasy substage, ages four to ten. Needs are dominant. "Role playing in fantasy is important."

Interest substage, ages eleven and twelve. "Likes are the major determinants of goals and activities."

Capacity substage, ages thirteen and fourteen. "Abilities are given more weight." Job training requirements are considered.

2. EXPLORATION STAGE, ages fifteen to twenty-four.

General characteristics: "Self-examination, role try-out, and occupational exploration in school, leisure activities, and part-time work."

Substages of the exploration stage are:

Tentative substage, ages fifteen to seventeen. "Needs, interests, capacities, values, and opportunities are considered. Tentative choices are made and tried out in fantasy, discussion, courses, work, and other experiences."

Transition substage, ages eighteen to twenty-one. "Reality factors are given more importance as the individual enters the world of work, training, or education, and attempts to implement a self-concept."

Trial substage, ages twenty-two to twenty-four: "A seemingly appropriate choice having been made," a beginning job is obtained and tried out.

3. ESTABLISHMENT STAGE, ages twenty-four to forty-four:

General characteristics: An appropriate or suitable work field is found. Effort is made to "earn a permanent place in it." "There may be some trial early in this period, accompanied by some shifting. . . . Establishment, however, particularly in the professions, may begin without trial."

Substages of the establishment stage are:

Trial substage, ages twenty-five to thirty: The chosen field of work may not be suitable. One or two changes may be made before a suitable occupation is found or the pattern of a series of unrelated jobs is evident.

Stabilization substage, ages thirty-one to forty-four: "As the career pattern becomes clear, efforts are made to stabilize it and develop a secure place in the world of work."

4. MAINTENANCE STAGE, ages forty-five to sixty-four: A place has been made "in the world of work. Now efforts are directed to building it. Little new ground is broken. There is continuation along established lines."

5. DECLINE STAGE, age sixty-five on:

General characteristics: "As physical or mental powers decline, work activity changes, and eventually ceases. New roles must be developed. First, there may be selective participation, next that of observer."

Substages of the decline stage are:

Deceleration substage, ages sixty-five to seventy: Either at the time of retirement or "later in the maintenance stage, demands of work lessen, duties may be changed, or the work itself may be changed to match declining capacities."

Part-time jobs may be found to replace full-time work. Retirement may come after seventy, but there is considerable variation from individual to individual.[2]

Of the additional monographs planned from the Career Pattern Study, *The Vocational Maturity of Ninth-Grade Boys* (Super and Overstreet, 1960) *Floundering* and *Trial after High School* (Super, Kowalski, and Gotkin, 1967) and *Vocational Maturity During the High School Years* (Jordaan and Heyde, 1979) have been published. The final monograph will be a study of determining factors in the careers of the sample of Middletown, New York, men who participated in the project from ages fourteen to thirty-five.

The Career Pattern Study was designed to gain an understanding of career behavior and to develop techniques to assess and predict it. The validity of "propositions," the "vocational life stages," and other elements is being assessed, and identification and validation of dimensions for vocational maturity are major research topics.

Results to date have major implications for counseling, guidance, and education. Indices of vocational maturity have been conceptualized, instruments for measuring them have been developed, and the status of subjects at the ninth-grade level and at various periods of time through age thirty-six has been studied. Ninth- and twelfth-grade indices have been linked to career progress. Some highlights from almost thirty years of research are given next (Super and Overstreet, 1960; Super, 1960; Super et al, 1963; Super, 1964; Super, 1969; Super and Bohn, 1970; Super, Kowalski, and Gotkin, 1967; Jordaan, 1977; Jordaan and Heyde, 1979).

The vocational maturity of ninth-grade boys is characterized by

1. an awareness of the need to make vocational and educational choices.
2. an acceptance of the responsibility for making plans and decisions.
3. some planning and participation in information-getting activities.
4. a lack of readiness to decide on a specific direction or occupation.
5. lack of knowledge about work and training opportunities, failure to utilize resources to obtain information, and little self-understanding.

In the period between the ninth and twelfth grades, modest increases in career development reveal

1. fewer occupations being considered.
2. more adult interests.
3. more confidence about interests.
4. more awareness of important characteristics of occupations of interest and more information about them.
5. more specific plans for obtaining occupational preparation.
6. greater acceptance of personal responsibilities for getting a job or obtaining needed preparation for work.

[2]Adapted by permission of the publisher from Donald Super, John Crites, Raymond Hummel, Helen Moser, Phoebe Overstreet, and Charles Warnath, *Vocational Development: A Framework for Research* (New York: Teachers College Press, 1957), pp. 40, 41. Copyright 1957 by Teachers College, Columbia University.

7. about the same degree of realism in occupational preferences in terms of abilities, interests, and socioeconomic level.[3]

These increases are not substantial, so it is apparent that high school seniors have not progressed as far in vocational development as might be expected. Moreover, since realism of choice and appropriateness of choice do not improve, they cannot be used as measures of vocational maturity (Jordaan, 1977). Throughout the high school years, some pupils mature vocationally, some decline, and others remain the same. Those who are consistent in development tend to be more intelligent, higher in socioeconomic standing, better pupils, and have a better-developed self-concept (Jordaan, 1977).

A high school senior who is most likely to be successful and satisfied at age twenty-five does well in school, is in an academic curriculum, works after school and in the summer, explores school and other activities related to occupational preferences, and exceeds peers in knowledge of the preferred occupation. Moreover, this individual is more likely to have paid work experience that he or she has found by his or her own initiative. Goals are realistic; in other words, socioeconomic level is a significant factor, and the senior is more likely to come from a middle- than a working-class home.

By the age of twenty-five, it was found that career status could be defined by the following five dimensions:

1. career satisfaction—present direction of the career is suitable
2. job satisfaction—likes the present job
3. attained status—higher level of education and occupation than peers
4. career progress—productive occupational moves since high school
5. socioeconomic advancement—upwardly mobile and has surpassed father's occupation level[4]

The self-concept is an important factor in career development; its stability over the high school years is one characteristic of those who are successful at age twenty-five (Jordaan, 1977; Jordaan and Heyde, 1979, pp. 166–170). Researchers are now analyzing how the self-concept is translated into the vocational self-concept, a key process in vocational development (Super et al, 1963). Evidence from several studies suggests that when self-concept and vocational self-concept are congruent, individuals tend to be better satisfied with their work. Changes in self-concepts for those entering new occupations tend to be in the direction of expected roles in the desired work (Super, 1969). Individuals with poorly crystallized views of themselves or poorly organized self-concepts have more difficulty selecting vocational areas than those with better-organized and more positive self-concepts, thus adding emphasis to the key role of the self-concept in career planning (Barrett and Tinsely, 1977).

Other evidence is accumulating to support the theoretical assumptions that occupational maturity increases with age. Strategies for occupational information

[3]In Miller, G. D. (ed.) *Developmental Theory and Its Application in Guidance Programs*. Special Issue of Pupil *Personnel Services Journal*, Vol. 6, No. 1, pp. 41–59, 1977. Minnesota Department of Education, St. Paul.
[4]In Miller, G. D. (ed.) *Developmental Theory and Its Application in Guidance Programs*. Special Issue of Pupil *Personnel Services Journal*, Vol. 6, No. 1, pp. 41–59, 1977. Minnesota Department of Education, St. Paul.

search and elaborateness of reasons for choice increase over the high school years, suggesting more involvement in finding and using information and relating it to occupational choices (Jepsen, 1975), and career development increases systematically over the same period. Pupils learn more about work, how to plan, and how to obtain and use information (Noeth and Prediger, 1978). The more vocationally mature ones make more appropriate choices (Westbrook, 1976).

Two further useful concepts have been derived from the Career Pattern Study. First are the coping behaviors of those entering the world of work. The three positive ones—trial, instrumental, and establishing—have already been mentioned. The two negative behaviors are *floundering* and *stagnating*. These five behaviors provide a meaningful classification system for describing the transition to work and give direction and purpose to guidance and counseling activities.

A second concept is the sequence of developmental tasks that has been postulated for adolescence and early adulthood (Super and Bohn, 1970, p. 141). This sequence entails crystallizing a vocational preference, specifying it, implementing it, stabilizing in the chosen vocation, consolidating one's status, and advancing in the occupation.

Several new developments have enhanced the utility of the theory for practitioners. One is the extension of the rationale and techniques for measuring vocational maturity to cover the life span (Forrest and Thompson, 1974; Super, 1977). A second is Super, Kidd, and Watts's (1977) conceptualization of the career rainbow, later modified to relate the decision-making process to decision points, the multiplicity and intensity of roles one plays (such as child, student, worker), and the theaters in which these roles are played. The resulting model brings together five major elements essential for a complete theory of career development—that is, a lifelong developmental process, decision-making strategies, the impact of social and personal factors, roles in the lifestyle, and career patterns. The conceptualization paves the way for research and demonstration projects to develop ways to improve counseling and guidance practice. With additional refinement and testing, the model could serve as a set of guidelines for providing career-guidance services and as a basis for organizing and implementing career-education programs. It could also provide strategies for career counseling.

Several inventories based on this theory are now available. The Work Values Inventory (Super, 1970b) assesses both intrinsic and extrinsic work values, such as creativity and management, and provides information about some aspects of the work self-concept. The Career Development Inventory, Form I (Super and Forrest, 1972) measures "Planning Orientation," "Resources for Exploration," and "Information and Decision-Making" and gives a total score. This inventory is designed to measure vocational maturity from the sixth grade through high school and is an outgrowth of research on vocational maturity. Form III, based on the results of Form I and an experimental Form II, gives six scores, including separate ones for career-development information, information about the world of work, and information about the preferred occupational group. Work is being done on Form IV for use as a survey instrument for career-education and guidance programs. Forms I and III of the college-level edition, available for experimental use only, are similar in content and purpose to the high school forms, with some items reworded to be suitable for those at the college level. The adult form (Super, 1977) differs from the high school one in both rationale and content and gives a profile of current involvement in career-development stages from exploration on. The adult form of the inventory has considerable potential for use with older persons, a high-priority area today, and it also represents a new approach to understanding stages of career development after the adolescent years, an area that has received relatively little attention prior to this time.

The rationale of the Career Pattern Study has also been used as the basis for a computerized information system, the Educational and Career Exploration System, or ECES. This system, described in Chapter 5, provides information for either a broad survey or an in-depth study of occupations and enables the counselee to compare his or her personal interests and abilities with those required for training and work in his or her areas of interest.

Ginzberg's Theory

Ginzberg's theory of occupational choice is actually a theory of occupational development, representing the combined efforts of an economist, a psychiatrist, a sociologist, and a psychologist (Ginzberg et al., 1951).[5] When the theory was first presented to the guidance profession, it had a pronounced shock effect and generated widespread reaction, both positive and negative. Prior to that time, Ginzberg's work at Columbia University had been primarily in research on human resources. Interest in developing bridges between social and psychological disciplines and studying the role of work in society led to his research and theorizing in the vocational-choice area. Formulation of the theory was one step in the general research program (Ginzberg, 1952, 1970).

According to this developmental theory, the individual moves through a series of related stages. The *process* of occupational choice, rather than a one-time decision, is central to the theory. Values, environmental realities, psychological attributes, and educational opportunities and achievement affect the process. Movement is largely *irreversible*—one cannot go back and take a different option. *Compromise* between desires and reality enters into the choice, and one has to give up options in order to attain a desired goal. It may not be possible to utilize one's abilities or realize one's goals to the fullest extent. Finally, it is assumed that vocational decision making can be portrayed in the following stages (because age eleven is identified as the point in the individual's life when he or she first realizes that he or she will eventually have to work, little attention is given to earlier periods):

1. FANTASY PERIOD, before age eleven: Needs and impulses are translated into occupational choices. Children feel that they can do whatever they want to do.

2. TENTATIVE PERIOD, ages eleven to seventeen: Interests, abilities, and values are used in making choices. Choices are tentative because reality factors are not adequately considered.

[5]Material in this section is based on Eli Ginzberg, "Toward A Theory of Occupational Choice: A Restatement," *Vocational Guidance Quarterly*, 20, No. 3 (1972b), pp. 169–172. Copyright 1972 American Personnel and Guidance Association. Used by permission.

Substages of the tentative period are:

Interest substage, about ages eleven to twelve: Interests are the primary basis for choice, but abilities are seen as necessary.

Capacity substage, about ages thirteen to fourteen: Capacities are considered in planning, but knowledge of them is incomplete, so choices are tentative.

Values substage, about ages fifteen to sixteen: Values enter the choice process, dominating interests and capacities.

Transition substage, about age seventeen: Factors listed previously are joined and used in choosing. Reality factors are not yet appreciably involved; plans are still somewhat tentative. The individual realizes that current decisions will affect his or her future.

3. REALISTIC PERIOD, age seventeen to young adulthood: Choices are made during this period. There are compromises between reality factors—job requirements or educational opportunities—and personal factors.

Substages of the realistic period are:

Exploration: The realistic stage begins with exploration; opportunities are investigated for virtually the last time, and options are checked out.

Crystallization: The individual actually makes a choice. Compromise is an important factor.

Specification: The choice is delimited; the individual becomes quite specific and takes steps to implement the decision.

From the original research on which this developmental process is based, described later in this chapter, several other aspects of career choice were identified. Definite patterns were observed in the development of the individuals in the sample: some exhibited early choices and commitment to a specific goal; others began with broad but poorly defined interests and progressively narrowed them. There was also considerable variation in the timing of crystallization of choice. Although this stage usually took place between ages nineteen and twenty, for some it occurred much earlier and for others much later. Occasionally, an individual seemed unable to arrive at a decision at all, either because of extreme passivity or, as Ginzberg expresses it. "because he is so pleasure-oriented that he cannot make the necessary compromises" (1952, p. 493).

Ginzberg's career-development theory is based on interview data from male students at the Horace Mann University School and Columbia University. A check on the relevance of the theory for other socioeconomic levels and for women was made by interviewing an additional seventeen boys, thirteen to eighteen years of age, from lower-income families and women college students aged eighteeen to twenty-one. Patterns revealed in the two additional samples tended to support the theory. These samples were limited, however, and Ginzberg has urged that replication as well as additional research be carried out with such other groups as southern blacks.

Others' research has tended to support the theory, particularly the concepts of vocational development as a process, increased realism with age, compromise, and the effects of values and personality factors in the selection of the preferred work role. Small (1952, 1953) investigated the interaction of reality and fantasy. His results indicated that the concept of compromise was supported but not the progression toward greater reality of choice. Small concluded that reality in choice is a function of ego strength. Davis, Hagan, and Strouf (1962), using sixth-graders of differing socioeconomic levels, found, as the theory predicts, that tentative choices exceeded fantasy choices. Hollander's (1967) study also provides support for the increasing-realism-with-age aspect of Ginzberg's theory. Using pupils in grades six through twelve as subjects, he found that increased realism was related to both age and grade. Jepsen's (1975) study tended to confirm the increase in realism, but Howell, Frese, and Sollie (1977) failed to obtain confirmation for the theory-derived assumption that goal blockages would lower expectations, that is, increase realism of choices.

Ginzberg has made some major modifications in his theory. One of the most significant is that, instead of a more or less final choice in the early or middle twenties, "the choice process is coextensive with a person's working life; he may reopen the issue at any time" (1970, pp. 63–64; 1972b, p. 169). Additional major revisions are as follows:

1. The *process* of vocational choice and development is lifelong and open-ended. Major causes of later occupational change seem to be feedback of satisfactions related to the original choice, the amount of freedom associated with changing responsibilities, and pressures or options in the individual's current work.

2. *Irreversibility* is no longer considered valid. As Ginzberg states, "The principal challenge that young people face during their teens is to develop a strategy that will keep their options open, at least to the extent of assuring their admission to college or getting a job with a preferred employer" (1972b, p. 171; 1975, p. 41).

3. *Optimization* replaces *compromise*. Finding the most suitable job is a continuing process. There is an ongoing effort to satisfy the most important needs via the opportunities available, with recognition of the operative restraints.

4. *Constraints* need to be given considerable weight. Ginzberg identifies these as low-income family situation; parental attitudes and values; inadequacies of the educational institution, including its failure to keep up with changing opportunities for women; minority group membership; and ineffective linkages among school levels and between schools and jobs, community institutions, the armed forces, and other institutions.

5. The *opportunity structure* of the world of work is given more weight, as is the importance of the individual's perception of opportunities that have in the past been closed to him or her.

6. *Value orientation* is now given more weight and is considered to play a major role in the individual's search for satisfaction. One's lifestyle also has an impact on vocational decisions as an effort is made to achieve a balance between work and other activities.

Ginzberg's recommendations for the provision of services that take into account these revised principles include increased emphasis on vocational counseling after the high school period; recognition that although the individual is the center of the process, reality factors play a major role; and an emphasis on a lifelong process of helping individuals learn about options and how to take advantage of them (1971, pp. 288–289; 1972b, pp. 174–175; 1975, pp. 38–44).

Tiedeman and O'Hara's Career-Development System

In this approach, career development is defined as the process of building a vocational identity through *differentiation* and *integration* as one confronts work. The newness of the experience demands that a new identity be formed (Tiedeman and O'Hara, 1963, pp. iv–vi). The goal is the formulation of an ego identity for work. As Tiedeman and O'Hara define it:

> Ego identity is the accumulating meaning one forges about himself as he wrestles with his meeting with society. Ego identity is a psycho-social phenomenon. It is the crystallizing premises of existence which one forges both where one can and where one may in order to establish one's self in the world. Career development includes the development of an orientation toward work which evolves within the psycho-social process of forming an ego-identity (1963, p. 4).

Career development is a continuing process of defining one's identity in vocational terms.

The developmental–decision-making process of differentiation and integration consists of a series of steps, which may be repeated throughout one's lifetime. An individual may be at different stages in dealing with different problems. The decision-making process begins when one encounters a problem or experiences a need and realizes that a decision must be made. First, there is a phase of *anticipation* or *preoccupation,* consisting of four steps:

EXPLORATION   Various goals are considered. The individual may review past experiences, consider abilities, weigh the desirability of goals, predict the results of his or her actions, and try out roles in his or her imagination.

CRYSTALLIZATION   Considering values, goals, and possible rewards, the individual prepares to move in a specific direction. There is a stabilization of thought. The individual gets ready to make an investment along the lines that seem most desirable.

CHOICE   A choice of decision follows crystallization. The individual can state what he or she wants to do or be.

CLARIFICATION   This step concludes the differentiation phase of decision making. Clarification involves further analysis of the choice and provides an opportunity for the review and resolution of doubts and uncertainties.

The individual is now ready to implement his or her choice in the phase of *implementation* and *adjustment.* Plans are put into effect. There is a tryout of the tentative decision. The three steps in this phase are:

INDUCTION   The individual enters the situation—for example, the job or school. He or she seeks approval and recognition. To some extent, he or she surrenders aspects of self to the new group or organization.

REFORMATION   Now that the individual is accepted, he or she may become more assertive, by, for example, convincing others to share his or her views and expressing a sense of self.

INTEGRATION   A balance is achieved between the demands of the group and the individual's needs. This is not a static condition but one of "dynamic equilibrium." It may change and therefore initiate the process of differentiation and integration all over again (1963, pp. 38–45).

The process just described is most effective when it is carried forward rationally and thoroughly. It may take place in a number of problem areas in an individual's life simultaneously. A decision in one area affects the process in another. For example, a decision to move to another part of the country may affect those involving job and family life. Each decision leads to a new sequence of differentiation and integration, although it may not follow immediately; for example, selection of a job may result in a slowdown in decision making as long as the job is suitable.

Time and discontinuity are elements in career development. The way the individual utilizes each day as well as the time he or she devotes to such major life periods as preparation for work are affected by biological demands and cultural factors. For example, the individual should complete training and be ready to begin work at a culturally determined period or age. Discontinuities—that is, moves from one activity to another—require decision. Awareness of these discontinuities affects the way the individual handles the tasks of differentiation and integration as he or she plans for the future. A decision is not usually required when the child moves from elementary school to junior high school, but one is necessary when the student completes high school and is considering a job, vocational training, or the university.

Tiedeman and his colleagues have drawn on the work of others, primarily Super and Ginzberg, in formulating and testing their theory. They do not claim that it is comprehensive, stating rather that it is "a concatenation of concepts that seem to be needed as primitive terms in a science of career development relating personality and career through the mechanisms of differentiation and integration as a chooser chooses and experiences in the evolution of his life problems" (1963, pp. v–vi). A large amount of research has been conducted to test its various aspects. Studies such as those of O'Hara and Tiedeman (1959) and Harren (1966) support hypotheses that there are changes in the vocational self-concept with increasing age, that clarification of the self-concept and increased self-knowledge occur, that steps in the differentiation and integration process are identifiable, and that the individual may be at different steps on different problems. Research on Erikson's stages of psychosocial development and vocational choice have tended to validate Tiedeman's use of this model of personality development; in other words, those individuals who have resolved developmental crises also show more suitable vocational choices (Munley, 1975, 1977).

Tiedeman and his associates (Tiedeman and Miller-Tiedeman, 1975; Dudley and Tiedeman, 1977; Peatling and Tiedeman, 1977) are continuing work on the teaching and improvement of decision-making processes, using new conceptualizations of the process and advanced computer technology. Emphases involve stress on futurism, on individuals becoming self-constructionists, and on developing "I-power," or the ability to comprehend the process of development. As Tiedeman says, "What is needed is not the attainment of a particular career status. Instead, what is needed is knowing how we know and how we apply knowledge of our actions so that we guide our actions by knowledge" (1977, p. 14). It is suggested that counselors are the ideal persons to introduce the study of futurism into schools and colleges as a strategy to enable individuals to control their futures (Tiedeman, 1978). Materials and procedures have been developed to help pupils develop "I-power"—for example, through making deliberate decisions about better use of study time (Tiedeman, 1978).

The decision-making process has been used as the basis for a career-guidance computer system, the Information System for Vocational Decisions, or ISVD, described in Chapter 5. The computer career-guidance system is not now operating, although a series of annual reports on it will be published by the Character Research Press.

Tuckman's Career-Development Education Theory

Tuckman (1974) has formulated an eight-stage career-development theory whose major components are self-awareness, career awareness, and career decision making. The theory serves as the basis for what he calls career development education; that is, it includes all aspects of career education except skill training. Starting with a child-development model based on the work of a number of theorists, he describes the stages as follows[6]:

Stage 1, grades kindergarten—one: *unilateral dependence.* There is a reliance on external controls. The emphasis is on career awareness, including information about work in the culture and the nature of tools found in the home.

Stage 2, grades one—two: *some assertion of self.* The emphasis is on automomy, more varied knowledge of work, work climates, and the fact that careers are actually chosen.

Stage 3, grades two—three: *conditional dependence.* The child realizes some independence and makes some choices, for example, friends. The focus of the self-awareness of this stage is on motives, needs, and orientations toward relations with others. The process of decision making is given attention.

Stage 4, grade four: *interdependence.* The child explores the world and theorizes about how it works. The focus is on awareness of skills and jobs and their place in society and on practice in making decisions.

[6]Material in this section based on Bruce W. Tuckman, "An Age-Graded Model for Career Development Education," *Journal of Vocational Behavior,* 4 (1974), pp. 193–212. Used by permission of the author and Academic Press, Inc.

Stage 5, grades five–six: *external support*. The child seeks external support and approval as an indication of success. The emphasis is on interests and goals, the requirements of work settings and jobs, and further clarification of decision-making processes.

Stage 6, grades seven–eight: *self-determination*. The sense of self becomes more pronounced, and there is an effort to assert self and establish one's own rules and norms. The focus is on self-awareness factors involving abilities as well as previously explored self-aspects. Career values and occupational clusters are explored. Essential factors in decision making are explored.

Stage 7, grades nine–ten: *mutuality*. Peer culture factors and the establishment of close relationships become more important, and group values enter into career choice. The focus is on self-awareness of motivations, attitudes, and values in occupational choice; work expectations, work climates, and need-meeting potential of occupations; and increased proficiency in decision making, including the effects of stereotypes.

Stage 8, grades eleven–twelve: *autonomy*. The individual now knows who he or she is, and is ready to try out new experiences, including exploratory vocational activities. The focus is on engaging in these new experiences for appropriateness, learning about specific work or educational requirements, and narrowing the range of choice possibilities.

The model, of which only a few major points are given, also includes suggested media and experiential activities. Tuckman points out that it is designed to suggest testable hypotheses rather than provide a complete and definitive theory and application. Even so, it is well designed and synthesizes a large amount of existing research and theory; thus, it has considerable utility for the practitioner.

Career Awareness in Developmental Theories

The element of career awareness is an important factor in developmental theories, and the concepts of Wise, Charner, and Randour (1978) are helpful in understanding its utility in guidance and counseling. Four major elements make up their model: influences, such as family, school, mass media, and community groups; skills, such as self-assessment; awareness, such as values and preferences; and decision making. When making a choice, the individual draws on awareness factors—knowledge of work, values, and preferences and self-concepts about abilities and chances for success. These factors allow the individual to evaluate the conditions of work and what is done on the job, the rewards, and the requirements, such as education. The individual needs to be able to assess personal attributes, to decide what is important to him or her. Decision-making skills involve the clarification of goals, collection of information, anticipation of the future, identification of options, and estimation of chances of success and the potential rewards.

Viewing career awareness as consisting of these four interacting dimensions assists the counselor in understanding what is involved and in planning ways to implement helping strategies as part of a developmental framework.

Existential Concepts in a Developmental Approach

Although a relatively small amount of career-development theorizing has been done from the existential point of view, several concepts have particular relevance for the lifelong process of choosing and finding meaning in work. Simon (1966) points out that existential philosophers would find much to agree with in the writings of current career-development theorists and presents not a theory but "a discussion of an existentialist's view of vocational development." Drawing on Sartre, he takes a developmental view of vocational life. There is a drive within the individual that moves him or her from the "I-It" stage (treating people as objects) through the "Thou" stage (discovering the true nature of others) to the "I-Thou" stage (self-understanding, objectifying, or discovering one's own objective or real self). Each step in the process involves an unsettling experience that must be accepted if the person is to move toward fulfillment and maturity.

Standley (1971) relates existential philosophy to career development in summarizing Kierkegaard's views that the choice of a vocation is a critical event in the process of "objectifying oneself." The person moves through aesthetic (love of pleasure and lack of commitment), ethical (a new level of commitment), and religious (commitment and meaning in life) developmental stages. She sees Kierkegaard's concerns as similar to those expressed by vocational-development theorists: "the importance of vocation to man's total development, vocational choice as an objectification of the self-concept, vocational development as occurring in a sequence of life stages, vocation as a pivotal source of life's meaning" (p. 122). The reality of the environment must be faced. Accepting the realities in the process of discovering one's true self enables one to find meaning and purpose in an occupation.

Crites's Vocational-Development Project

The construct of vocational maturity was developed by the staff of the Career Pattern Study, of which Crites was a member. Work on a practical-inventory type of instrument was started at the same time, and concepts currently used are related to those Super and his associates developed. The Vocational-Development Project is thus related to that theory of career development and does not constitute a new approach. Crites's project merits specific attention here because of the longitudinal nature of the design (although data so far are cross-sectional), the instruments that have been developed, the specific variables covered, and the systematic research program (Crites, 1961; 1968; 1971, Chaps. 1, 2).

Of the two major scales planned, the *attitude scale* has been completed and tested, and the *competence scale,* although not as adequately validated, is in use. The latter scale measures competence in five areas: goal selection, occupational information, planning, problems, and self-knowledge (Crites, 1971, p. 17). Westbrook (Norton,

1970; Westbrook and Cunningham, 1970) has developed a comprehensive scale to measure the cognitive aspects of vocational maturity Crites hypothesized (see Chapter 3).

The attitude scale includes items from both counselees and vocational-development theorists. The following areas are covered:

1. Involvement in the process of vocational choice
2. Orientation toward the problem of vocational choice
3. Independence in decision making
4. Preference for factors in vocational choice
5. Conceptions of vocational choice (Crites, 1971, p. 17)

The project has provided an easy-to-use inventory for measuring attitudinal and cognitive factors in vocational development suitable for grades five through twelve and also usable with college first-year students. The inventory items are monotonically (rising continuously) related to age and grade. Results show that students in vocationally oriented school courses tend to be less mature, as do those from the lower socioeconomic and minority ethnic and racial groups (Crites, 1971, pp. 72–73). Research on the competence part of the inventory is progressing (Crites, 1974, 1978c); eventually, results will be related to those of the attitude scale, and both will constitute a technique to measure career-choice competencies and career-choice attitudes, two of the four dimensions Crites has postulated as indicators of career maturity.

Four major research approaches are now in process or planned: survey, technique, theoretical, and applied. Much of the work on the first two types has been completed. The focus is now on the last two, involving the testing of hypotheses from vocational-development theory and the investigation of the effects of procedures to increase vocational maturity. Results of the latter activities have been mixed. However, indications are that both individual and group counseling can help in increasing the maturity of vocational attitudes (Crites, 1971, p. 74). A substantial amount of research has been done by Crites and others on the Career Maturity Inventory (for example, Westbrook, 1976).

In addition to developing a synthesis of career-counseling approaches (Crites, 1978a, 1978b), Crites has developed a model for career development in early adulthood (1976) that combines the elements of career adjustment, career life stages, organizational climate, and environmental influences. Work is in progress to construct a career-adjustment inventory to measure the variables considered necessary for the transition to work that are not assessed by other techniques, such as coping with thwarting elements in obtaining and progressing in a job.

Gribbons and Lohnes's Study

Primarily focusing on readiness for vocational planning, Warren D. Gribbons and Paul R. Lohnes used interviews to study the progress of 110 boys and girls first contacted in the eighth grade in schools near Boston. The study (Gribbons, 1960) was an outgrowth of Gribbon's research on the effectiveness of the Educational Testing Service Group Guidance Unit, *You: Today and Tomorrow* (Katz, 1958). (The workbook-type unit was found effective in promoting educational and vocational planning.) The wealth of interview information suggested to Gribbons that a longitudinal study of career development would be of value. Plans were then made for a study involving biannual contacts until two years after high school, with an additional five years of data gathering tentatively envisioned (Gribbons and Lohnes, 1968, p. 7).

Scales to measure readiness for vocational planning were prepared for scoring semistructured interviews (Gribbons and Lohnes, 1964a; 1964b; 1968, pp. 15–16). Scales included the following:

1. the factors in curriculum choice, including the pupil's knowledge of abilities, interests, and values, and their relation to curricula; courses in various curricula; and how the curriculum choice relates to occupational choice

2. the factors in occupational choice, including abilities and information about occupations

3. ability to describe strengths and weaknesses and to relate them to educational and vocational choices

4. accuracy in estimating abilities and achievements, for example, academic ability test scores

5. adequacy of the evidence the individual uses in self-ratings, for example, data used to estimate academic ability

6. awareness of interests and how they relate to occupational choice

7. awareness of values and how they relate to occupational choice

Similar interviews were used in the eighth, tenth, and twelfth grades, and two years after high school (Gribbons and Lohnes, 1968, pp. 117–133). The major report covers this period. A later report covers an additional two years but deals mostly with the development of a single score for the readiness for vocational planning scales and the use of three variables—sex, socioeconomic status, and IQ—in predicting curricula. The single score for vocational maturity was found to contribute to predictions utilizing the Project Talent "career tree" concept of occupational paths (Gribbons and Lohnes, 1969).

Analysis of the eighth-grade to post–high school data showed that readiness for vocational planning scores, indicating greater maturity on the eight scales listed previously, increased from the eighth to the tenth grades. But eighth-grade scores were better predictors of the extent of educational and vocational planning, educational aspirations, post–high school career adjustment, and other criteria and were as effective as the tenth-grade scores in predicting curriculum choice and level of occupational preference. It would be expected, however, that readiness for vocational planning would increase with age. In spite of the questions raised by the relative superiority of the eighth-grade scores, Gribbons and Lohnes concluded that, for guidance purposes, readiness for vocational planning may be validly assessed as early as the eighth grade (1968, pp. 98–99). The lack of agreement with other types of measurements and lack of increase with chronological age, however, raise questions about the validity of the scales, concepts, or methodology (Super 1969b, p. 6).

Gribbons and Lohnes define four career processes, somewhat similar to Super's coping behaviors:

1. constant maturity, indicating persistent efforts to attain the first-chosen goal
2. emerging maturity, involving movement through the stages defined by Super, such as crystallizing and specifying a vocational preference
3. degeneration, involving progressive deterioration in plans and efforts, increasing frustration, and decline in status
4. constant immaturity, defined as the adoption of unrealistic goals with no improvement or advance in achievement (1968, pp. 68–69, 100)

Gribbons and Lohnes's data support the concept of different career processes. All the subjects in the study could be assigned to a specific process group, with the largest number belonging in Emerging Maturity and the next largest in Degeneration. Boys and girls were about equally represented in each category, with more girls in Constant Maturity and a few more boys in Constant Immaturity (1968, pp. 71–100). Membership in a process group, however, could not be predicted with eighth- or tenth-grade readiness for vocational planning scores.

A statistical procedure called Markov chain analysis was used for predicting successive positions in vocational behavior. The technique was shown to be a useful tool, and it provided additional data about the vocational development of the group. For example, individuals tend to be consistent from year to year. If the individual is coping inefficiently (floundering or stagnating) in the eighth grade, the chances are about 2 to 1 that he or she will be in this pattern two years after high school (Gribbons and Lohnes, 1968, pp. 188–189).

The interview questions are useful material for counseling and guidance (Gribbons and Lohnes, 1968, pp. 119–154). Perrone (1972) utilized the interview guides and manuals to stimulate the interest of eighth-grade teachers in career development. Results of a pretest were used to identify pupil needs and to serve as clues for selection of teaching materials and procedures. Posttests with the interview guides showed significant improvement among suburban school low- and average-achieving students, but not with inner-city school pupils (Perrone, 1972). The study employed readiness for vocational planning scales for motivational purposes, curriculum planning, and pupil development, and it suggests innovative uses of the materials developed by Gribbons and Lohnes.

Some Related Theories of Development

Although they do not specifically deal with career development, several theories about life stages include work as one of the major elements. Havighurst's (1972, pp. 1–98) developmental tasks covering physical, psychological, and cultural factors encompass stages from early childhood through later maturity. In the early stages of infancy and early childhood, little is said about career development, but beginning in middle childhood comes awareness of role and development of values, and occupational factors begin to be visible. One major task of the adolescent period is increasing readiness for occupational choice and preparation. Following this stage, one major task of the next, early adulthood, is choosing an occupation. Clearly, this selection is a result of the completion of many earlier tasks, rather than an isolated event, and is thus part of a developmental process. Later tasks also include those that involve progress and establishment in work. Havighurst (1964, p. 216) has also formulated seven stages of vocational development, drawing on his own concept of tasks, Erikson's psychological crises, Super's vocational stages, and others. Havighurst's stages resemble those of other developmental theorists; for example, the early years involve an awareness of the role of work in one's life, and the middle years are the time for establishing a place in the work world.

Gould's (1975) studies of adult development identify seven stages with the following age periods: sixteen to seventeen, eighteen to twenty-one, twenty-two to twenty-eight, twenty-nine to thirty-six, thirty-seven to forty-three, forty-four to fifty, and fifty-one to sixty. Data about the stages cover a wide range of factors; some relate specifically to career development. Feelings that it is too late to change careers increase sharply in about the middle thirties and remain relatively high from the middle forties on. Concern about not making enough money is relatively high up into the middle thirties, and peaks in that decade; from then on it drops about to an average level. The twenty-two to twenty-eight age period is viewed as the time to build professionally for the future, but in the twenty-nine to thirty-four period, questions often arise about what one is doing and why.

Further clarification of developmental stages is provided by Levinson (1977), who emphasizes that development means building a life structure that is made up of one's sociocultural world (of which occupation is a part), one's participation in this world (for example, role as worker), and both inhibited and self-expressed aspects. Occupation and family life are considered to be the most significant components of the life structure.

In the developmental process, the structure changes, going through alternating periods of stability and transition. In the first, the stable period, the primary developmental task is to build a life structure around choices and goals. During the transitional period, the primary task is to terminate the existing structure and get ready for the new one. For example, the early adult transition stage lasts from age seventeen to age twenty-two. During this time, the individual has to sever connections with the preadulthood period and move into the adult world.. One aspect of this period is development of an occupation that enables the individual to implement his or her dreams of accomplishment, and conflicts may arise about keeping options open versus searching for stability. Considerable attention has been given to the mid-life transition period, when there is a need to seek new sources of vitality and to avoid stagnation. Both the concepts of transition and stable periods and the characteristics of each phase have important implications for the process of career development and suggest strategies for counseling interventions (Fozard and Popkin, 1978).

Other studies and publications throw light on the developmental process in ways that help in understanding career development. In analyzing men and women at four stages of life—high school seniors, young newlyweds, middle-aged parents, and those about to retire—Lowenthal, Thurnher, Chiriboga, and associates (1976, p. 3) classified individuals at each stage by the way roles and activities combine to produce various lifestyles: *simplistic* (few roles and limited range of activities), *diffuse* (few roles and varied activities), *focused* (wide role scope and a narrow range of activities), and *complex* (many roles and a varied pattern of activities). High school boys seem to have little awareness of what their occupational careers will be like; they tend to fantasize being a great success. They recognize that work will be a part of their life but do not look forward to it. There is little focus in lifestyles. High school girls tend to view work as an interim activity between school and marriage and tend to be even less focused. At the next stage there is a greater degree of realism, the importance of the occupation to the individual increases, and the individuals question the suitability of what they are doing. During the middle years, men are very committed to work but wonder if success through their own efforts is possible. Focus for men is quite high, but it is less significant for women. This concept of lifestyles, which includes work career as one factor and utilizes roles and activities as dimensions of lifestyle, provides an interesting view of how major aspects of life are related over the span from high school to preretirement. The concepts give needed emphasis to the place of the career as a major element in lifestyle.

Passages (Sheehy, 1976) used the research of those mentioned as well as others to describe life patterns of men and women, emphasizing passages from one stage of development to the next. Although the book helps to explain the developmental process, its suggestions for surmounting obstacles should be carefully considered, for they may not be applicable or useful in all cases.

Any research and theorizing on the developmental process almost inevitably has implications for career development regardless of the discipline involved or the focus of the study; the work life of the individual is necessarily one of the major aspects considered. It is, therefore, important that career-guidance workers be aware of progress in related areas.

NEEDS THEORIES

Although psychological needs are acknowledged in the theories already considered, as well as in those that follow, some theories make them central concepts. Needs theories derived from psychoanalytic personality theory are considered separately; they represent a special case.

Roe's Theory

From research on the effects of childhood experiences on adjustment, creativity, and intelligence, Anne Roe concludes that the early home climate has significance for career choice. Based on this general position, she developed a theory whose major propositions are as follows:

PROPOSITION 1   Genetic inheritance sets limits to the potential development of all characteristics, but the specificity of the genetic control and the extent and nature of the limitations are different for different characteristics.

PROPOSITION 2   The degrees and avenues of development of inherited characteristics are affected not only by experiences unique to the individual but also by all aspects of the general cultural background and the socioeconomic position of the family.

PROPOSITION 3   The pattern of development of interests, attitudes, and other personality variables with relatively little or nonspecific genetic control is primarily determined by individual experiences through which involuntary attention becomes channeled in particular directions.

  a. These directions are determined in the first place by the patterning of early satisfactions and frustrations. This patterning is affected by the relative strengths of various needs, and the forms and relative degrees of satisfactions they receive. The two latter aspects are environmental variables.
  b. The modes and degrees of need satisfaction determine which needs will become the strongest motivators. The nature of the motivation may be quite unconscious.

Possible variables are:

1. Needs satisfied routinely as they appear do not become unconscious motivators.
2. Needs for which even minimum satisfaction is rarely achieved, will if higher order (as used by Maslow, 1954), become expunged or will, if lower order, prevent the appearance of higher-order needs and become dominant and restricting motivators.
3. Needs, the satisfaction of which is delayed but eventually accomplished, will become (unconscious) motivators, depending largely on the degree of satisfaction felt. Behavior that has received irregular reinforcement is notably difficult to extinguish. The degree of satisfaction felt will depend, among other things, on the strength of the basic need in the given individual, the length of time elapsing between arousal and satisfaction, and the value ascribed to the satisfaction of this need in the immediate environment.

PROPOSITION 4   The eventual pattern of psychic energies, in terms of attention directedness, is the major determinant of interests.

PROPOSITION 5   The intensity of these needs and of their satisfaction (perhaps particularly as they have remained unconscious) and their organization are the major determinants of the degree of motivation that reaches expression in accomplishment.[7]

[7]Adapted with permission from Anne Roe and Marvin Siegelman, *The Origin of Interests* (Washington D.C.: American Personnel and Guidance Association, 1964), p. 5. Copyright 1964 by the American Personnel and Guidance Association.

Roe adopted Maslow's personality theory to clarify the meaning of work and developed a "fields by levels" classification of occupations to systematize the world of work. Figure 2.1 illustrates the hypothesized relationships of early home climate and occupational preference.

Figure 2.1 shows the relationships to parental types, preferred modes of interacting with others, and predicted occupational choices. Warm and cold home climates are defined by the following parental characteristics:

Cold
1. AVOIDANCE OF THE CHILD
   a. Rejecting: cold, hostile; points out inadequacies and disregards the child's preferences and opinions
   b. Neglecting: provides a minimum of physical care; gives no affection, cold but not derogatory

Warm or Cold
2. EMOTIONAL CONCENTRATION ON THE CHILD
   a. Overprotecting (tends to be warm): indulgent, affectionate, allows little privacy, guards from injury
   b. Overdemanding (tends to be cold): sets high standards, pushes to high academic performance, in extreme form tends to be rejecting

Warm
3. ACCEPTANCE OF THE CHILD
   a. Casual: mildly affectionate, responsive if not otherwise distracted, unconcerned about the child, makes few rules and does not enforce them
   b. Loving: gives warm and loving attention, helps with projects, uses reason rather than punishment, encourages independence (Roe, 1957; Roe and Siegelman, 1964, p. 7)

The related hypotheses are

1. Loving, protecting, and demanding homes would lead to person orientation in the child and later person orientation in occupations.
2. Rejecting, neglecting, and casual homes would lead to non-person orientation in occupations.
3. If extreme protecting and extreme demanding conditions were felt by the child to be restricting, he might, in defense, become non-person oriented.
4. Some individuals from rejecting homes might become person oriented in a search for satisfaction.
5. Loving and casual homes might provide a sufficient amount of relatedness that other factors such as abilities would determine interpersonal directions more than personal needs.[8]

[8]Adapted with permission from Anne Roe and Marvin Siegelman, *The Origin of Interests* (Washington, D.C.: American Personnel and Guidance Association, 1964, pp. 7–8. Copyright 1964 American Personnel and Guidance Association.

Figure 2.1   Early home climate and its relation to occupational classification

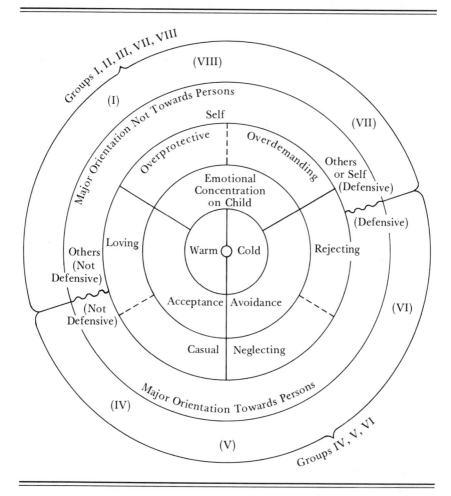

SOURCE: Anne Roe and Marvin Seigelman, *The Origin of Interests* (Washington, D.C.: American Personnel and Guidance Association, 1964), p. 6. 1964 copyright. American Personnel and Guidance Association. Reprinted with permission.

The two-way occupational classification plan in Table 2.2 is related to the home environments as identified by the Roman numerals around the outside part of the circle in Figure 2.1. An earlier classification using the level and function organization (Roe, 1954) was revised by Moser (1956). The revision was accepted and used by Roe and is the one illustrated here (1956, p. 151; 1957).

The *fields of work* listed across the top are classified by interest and by the primary focus of the occupations. The *levels* on the left side represent degrees of responsibility, capacity, and skill. Research has dealt mainly with fields of work, and only a relatively small amount has been done on levels. Proposition 5 is related to levels; the intensity of needs has a pronounced effect on the level an individual will reach in the chosen field.

Roe's studies (Roe and Siegelman, 1964) give modest support to the hypothesis that early home experiences are related to later orientation toward or not toward persons (about 10 percent of the variance in later orientations) but very little to hypotheses involving occupational choice. It was not possible to differentiate between the occupational groups, although the male engineers had the least stressful home backgrounds, and women in the same occupation tended to have had good home relations and to identify with their fathers. For both men and women social workers, there was more stress and less affection from parents (Roe and Siegelman, 1964, pp. 61–67). Other studies focusing on the same hypotheses have not supported the theory (Grigg, 1959; Hagen, 1960; Switzer, Grigg, Miller, and Young, 1962; Utton, 1962; Brunkan, 1965; Green and Parker, 1965).

Although evidence has not supported aspects of the theory relating early home climate to occupational choice, lack of adequate instruments, subjects' difficulties in recollecting the early atmosphere, and deficiencies in research designs may have prevented a fair test. Furthermore, the *difference* between parental attitudes may be the important factor (Switzer, Grigg, Miller, and Young, 1962). *Perceived* parental attitudes have been studied, but vocational behavior may be more closely related to *actual* parental behavior (Berdie, 1964).

The occupational-classification aspect of the theory has proved valuable in a number of ways, even though it has not been shown to be related to early home climate. It groups together occupations with similar psychological climates, and adjacent groups are more alike than widely separated ones (Osipow, 1966; Roe, Hubbard, Hutchinson, and Bateman, 1966; Hutchinson and Roe, 1968). It is easy to use for classifying occupations (Lunneborg and Lunneborg, 1968; Roe, 1972a, p. 74). Students' classifications of their own and their fathers' occupations effectively predict academic achievement. The classification plan has also been shown to be useful in testing the reliability of interest measurement and for predicting the extent of occupational changes by individuals (Knapp, Knapp, and Buttafuoco, 1978).

The classification plan has been refined, and further verification of the fields-and-levels concept has justified confidence in it (Roe and Klos, 1972, pp. 209–211). The classification system may be meaningfully arranged as a cone, with the greatest diameter at the highest level. At low levels, such as Level IV, the differentiations of groups may not be as meaningful (Roe and Klos, 1972, pp. 212–214). Two structures have been extracted by an analysis of the total group-by-level organization; the resulting patterns—excluding arts and entertainment, which fit neither one—provide useful guides for occupational counseling (Meir, 1970).

Super has suggested a third dimension of "enterprise" (Super, 1957, pp. 47–50). Roe agrees with this addition but not with Super's categories. Her addition is a classification somewhat like that for occupational groups, for example, "service—these employers are non-profit organizations concerned with health, welfare, recreation, the military, or government" (Roe and Klos, 1972, p. 214). *Level* in this

Table 2.2 A modification of Roe's field by levels occupational classification

Level	I Service	II Business Contact	III Business Organization
1. Professional and managerial (Higher)	Research scientist (Social)	Sales manager (large corporation)	Cabinet member President (large corporation)
2. Professional and managerial (regular)	Administrator (social welfare) Manager (penal institution) Probation oficer Social worker	Personnel manager Sales engineer	Banker Broker CPA Hotel manager
3. Semi-professional and managerial	Employment interviewer Nurse (registered) Physical director (YMCA) Recreational therapist	Confidenceman Freight traffic agent Salesman, auto, in-surance, bond, real estate Wholesaler	Accountant Owner (small grocery) Postmaster Private secretary
4. Skilled	Army sergeant Barber Chef Headwaiter Policeman Practical nurse	Auctioneer Canvasser Survey worker Salesman (house to house)	Compiler Morse operator Statistical clerk Stenographer
5. Semi-skilled	Chauffer Cook Elevator operator Fireman (city) Fortune teller Navy, seaman	Peddler Salesclerk Ticket agent	Cashier Clerk (file) Mail carrier Telephone operator Typist
6. Unskilled	Bellhop Janitor Streetsweeper Watchman	Newspaper boy	Messenger boy

SOURCE: Helen P. Moser, William Dubin, and Irving M. Shelsky, "A Proposed Modification of the Roe Occupational Classification," *Journal of Counseling Psychology,* vol. 3, 1956, p. 30, Copyright 1956 by the American Psychological Association. Reprinted by permission.

IV Technology	V Outdoor	VI Science	VII General Cultural	VIII Arts and Entertainment
Inventor (industrial research) Research scientist (engineering)	Research engineer, mining	Dentist Doctor Research scientist (physics, chemistry)	Judge Professor (history, math, etc.)	Orchestra conductor T.V. director
Air Force (pilot) Engineer Flight analyst Superintendent (factory)	Conservation officer Fish and wild-life specialist Geologist Petroleum engineer	Chemist Geneticist Pharmacist Veterinarian Physicist	Clergyman Editor News commentator Teacher (high school, primary)	Architect Baseball player (major league) Critic Sculptor
Aviator Brine foreman (DOT foreman II) Contractor (general, carpentry, etc.) Engineer (locomotive)	Apiarist County agent Farmer (small independent owner) Forest ranger	Chiropodist Embalmer Physical therapist	Justice of the peace Law clerk Librarian Reporter	Ad artist Athletic coach Interior decorator Photographer
Blacksmith Carpenter Dressmaker Paperhanger Plasterer foreman (DOT foreman I) Shiprigger	Landscape gardener Miner Rotary driller (oil well)	Medical technician		Chorine Illustrator (greeting cards) Window decorator
Carpenter (apprentice) Crane operator (portable) Meat curer Railroad switchman Truck driver	Farm tenant Fisherman Gardener Hostler Nursery worker Trapper		Library attendant	Clothes model Lead pony boy
Carpenter's helper Deckhand Laborer, foundry	Animal tender Ditcher Farm laborer Nursery laborer		Copy boy	Stagehand

plan is correlated with prominence, for example, the size or scope of the employing establishment. The system is described in detail by Roe and Klos (1972, pp. 214–220).

Several instruments have been developed by Roe and her associates and by others, and there have been computer applications for some aspects of the theory. The Family Relations Inventory, or FRI, developed by Brunkan and Crites (1964) to measure perceived parental attitudes, and the Roe-Siegelman Parent-Child Relations Questionnaire (Roe and Siegelmen, 1964, pp. 94–98) are examples. Roe's occupational-classification system is used as the basis for the Computer Assisted Vocational Information System (CVIS) now in operation in Willowbrook High School, Villa Park, Illinois. The system is described in Chapter 5.

Holland's Theory

John L. Holland's work is often identified with the National Merit Scholarship Program and the American College Testing Program, but it actually has a much broader base. In his original theory, six occupational environments and six personal types were postulated (1966, pp. 54–59, Chaps. 2, 4). The environments were realistic, intellectual, social, conventional, enterprising, and artistic. The similarly named personality types represented personal orientations or lifestyles. Each environment included levels somewhat similar to Roe's. The individual's personal-orientation hierarchy determined the environment he or she chose. The more clear-cut his or her hierarchy, the more effective the search for a suitable environment. Knowledge about both self and environments are needed for suitable choices. The revised theory (Holland, 1973) uses quite similar terms for personality types and environments. The types are realistic, investigative, artistic, social, enterprising, and conventional. Thus, the only type-name change is that intellectual is now investigative. The same is true for the environments.

The development of personality types is the result of interactions of heredity and environmental factors. These interactions lead to preferences for special kinds of activities, which in turn direct the individual toward certain types of behaviors. Summaries of the type descriptions follow[9]

Realistic Type (REAL)

Prefers systematic manipulation of objects, tools, machines, and animals. Dislikes helping or educational activities. Preferences lead to development of competencies in working with things, animals, tools and technical equipment, and neglect of social and educational competencies. Thinks of self as good in mechanical and athletic ability and not proficient in social and human-relations skills. Values tangible things, such as money and power. Typical characteristics are materialism, practicality, stability, conformity. May prefer skilled trades and technical occupations.

[9]Based on John L. Holland, MAKING VOCATIONAL CHOICES, © 1973, pp. 14–18, 29–33. Adapted by permission of Prentice-Hall, Inc., Englewood Cliffs, New Jersey.

Investigative Type (INT)

Identifies the type of individual who prefers activities in the physical, biological, or social sciences. Social, persuasive, and routine types of activities are disliked. Scientific and mathematical competencies are developed, and persuasive and social ones are neglected. Values science. Perceives self as scholarly and scientifically competent. Typical characteristics are analyticalness, curiosity, methodicalness, and reservation. Occupations are mainly in the scientific area.

Artistic Type (ART)

Prefers ambiguous, free, and unsystematized activities to create artistic products, such as painting, drama, writing. Dislikes systematic, orderly, and routine activities. Competencies in artistic endeavors are developed, and routine, systematic, clerical skills are neglected. Perceives self as expressive, original, independent, and having artistic abilities. Some typical characteristics are emotionalism, imagination, impulsiveness, and originality. Artistic occupations are usually in painting, writing, acting, and sculpture.

Social Type (SOC)

Prefers activities involving others in which the emphasis is on helping, teaching, or otherwise providing assistance. Dislikes routine and systematic activities involving objects and materials. Social competencies tend to be developed, and manual and technical ones deprecated. Perceives self as competent in helping and teaching others and values social relations activities. Some typical characteristics are cooperation, friendliness, persuasiveness, and tact. Social occupations include those in teaching, counseling, and social welfare work.

Enterprising Type (ENT)

Prefers activities that involve manipulation of others for economic gain or organizational goals. Dislikes systematic, abstract, and scientific activities. Leadership and persuasive and supervisory competencies are developed, and scientific ones rejected. Perceives self as aggressive, popular, self-confident, and having leadership ability. Political and economic achievement is valued. Typical characteristics are ambition, domination, optimism, and sociability.

Conventional Type (CONV)

Prefers activities that involve orderly, systematic, precise, and prescribed use of data for contributing to the organization's goals. Dislikes ambiguous, free, and unsystematic activities. Competencies are developed in clerical, computational, and business-system areas. Artistic and similar activities are neglected. Perceives self as orderly, conforming, and possessing clerical and numerical skills. Some typical characteristics are efficiency, orderliness, practicality, and self-control. Representative occupations are banker, cost estimator, tax expert, and bookkeeper.

The worker environments have the same names as the personality types and require certain personal characteristics. They also offer opportunities to put to use specific interests and competencies. The majority of people in a particular work environment are individuals with the parallel personality type. In a sense, the individuals create the environment; the environments in turn attract similar personality types. The brief descriptions of environments that follow show how each provides a favorable, stimulating workplace for the associated personality type.

Realistic Environment (REAL)

Individuals have the opportunity and are stimulated to work in an orderly, systematic manner with tools, machines, or animals along with other persons of the realistic type. The environment provides rewards for competence in those types of activities and tends to reject the importance of inappropriate competencies, such as those in social relations. Traits that are reinforced in this type of environment include conformity, normality, practicality, thrift, and the ability to remain uninvolved.

Investigative Environment (INT)

This environment demands and rewards systematic, creative study in the physical, biological, or social sciences. Individuals tend to see themselves as competent in mathematical and scientific ability and capable of dealing with abstract concepts. Traits such as analyticalness, curiosity, independence, precision, and rationality are reinforced.

Artistic Environment (ART)

This environment requires and rewards free, ambiguous, and unsystematized activities and encourages members to see themselves as original, intuitive, nonconforming, and having artistic abilities of some sort. Those who display artistic values are rewarded; traits such as complexity, disorderliness, emotionalism, imagination, and intuition are reinforced.

Social Environment (SOC)

There are opportunities and demands for individuals to help, cure, or teach others. In this climate, social skills are fostered and reinforced; individuals tend to perceive themselves as interested in helping others, as sociable, and as understanding others.

Social values are rewarded, and traits such as cooperation, generosity, helpfulness, idealism, and sociability are reinforced.

Enterprising Environment (ENT)

This environment has demands and rewards for individuals to manipulate others for profit or to attain organizational goals, to act in leadership roles, and to value power, status, and responsibility. Individuals are encouraged to see the world in relatively stereotyped and simple terms. Among the traits that are reinforced are ambition, energy, impulsiveness, pleasure seeking, and sociableness.

Conventional Environment (CONV)

In this environment, individuals are encouraged to engage in and find reward in activities involving the orderly and systematic manipulation of data. They see themselves as conforming, orderly, and competent in clerical activities. Traits such as conscientiousness, efficiency, persistence, practicality, and self-control are reinforced.

The classifications of personality types and work environments are central concepts in Holland's theory. Individuals think, perceive, and act in ways in which one of the six types is dominant. In actuality, no individual is one pure type but exhibits some amount of each—in other words, has a profile that constitutes his or her personality pattern. The work environments are shaped by individuals with similar profiles and by characteristics of the particular work setting.

Occupational Choice

The process of occupational choice involves a search for environments that enable the individual to utilize his or her competencies and express his or her interests and values. And to some extent, environments search for suitable individuals, through recruiting and other methods. Behavior is determined by the interaction of personality and environment. Some personality types are more closely related than others, and the possession of related ones tends to lead to a more clear-cut occupational preference. Figure 2.2 shows the relationship of types. Thus, the individual who prefers types that are next to each other has more consistent preferences. For instance, investigative and realistic are adjoining types and correlate .46. Investigative and enterprising, however, are quite far apart and correlate only .16. The hierarchy of the top three types is typically used to determine the most suitable occupational environment.

A number of predictions have been made about an individual's behavior on the basis of these personality type combinations. For example, other things being equal, achievement in the occupation will be positively related to the following order of types: enterprising, social, artistic, investigative, conventional, and realistic (Holland, 1973, pp. 24–25). The top three types are used for career-guidance

Figure 2.2 A hexagonal model for defining the psychological resemblances among types and environments and their interactions

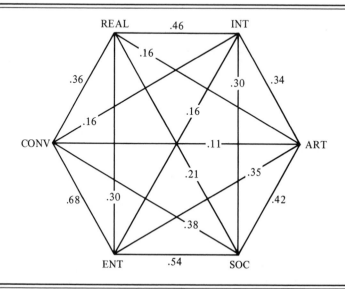

SOURCE: John L. Holland, MAKING VOCATIONAL CHOICES, © 1973, p. 23. Used by permission of Prentice-Hall, Inc., Englewood Cliffs, New Jersey.

purposes, as, for instance, in the Self-Directed Search, discussed later, but any number from two to six could be considered. For example, for the individual who has social, enterprising, and conventional traits in that order, occupations such as director of social services, employment interviewer, or dormitory director are among those suggested for consideration.

Research and Results

The concept of levels has not been as thoroughly investigated as have the personal-orientation and vocational-environment classifications. A study designed to determine whether or not level reflects self-evaluation, however, does give support to the concept. Schutz and Blocher (1961), using several measures of occupational-level preference with twelfth-grade students, found a significant relationship. Holland reports additional confirming evidence from a comparison of the level of probable college major for National Merit finalists with status as measured by the Vocational Preference Inventory and scores on the Scholastic Aptitude Test (1961). In general, self-evaluation plus intelligence is considered to be an indication of the level of potential achievement (Holland, 1973, p. 58), although some research has used combinations of personality types and degree of consistency to suggest educational level. There is some support for the position that the more clear-cut the differences in the scores and the more consistent the pattern, the higher the level of academic achievement (O'Neil, 1977).

More attention has been devoted to validation of the hypotheses about occupational environments and personality patterns and their relationship. Holland's interest inventory has been used successfully to differentiate educational groups (Holland, 1961). There is evidence that students tend to report changes in their dominant personality orientation as expressed in the college major (Walsh and Lacey, 1970). Additional support was derived from a study by Elton and Rose (1970), who predicted the occupational orientations of graduating college males from data from their first college years. While personality and aptitude measures did not predict senior occupational group any better than did expressed interest, results revealed that retention or transfer of major was related to predictions made from the theory. In general, the constructs of personality type on occupational environment have been supported (Osipow, 1976; Betz, 1977).

Holland's theory appears to be appropriate for potential high school dropouts as well as for college students (Cunningham et al., 1977). Although much of the developmental work on the theory has been done with college students (Thoresen and Ewart, 1978, p. 179), there are indications that it is useful with others, such as nonprofessional workers (Salomone and Slaney, 1978).

Older men between the ages of forty-five and fifty-nine tend to give more weight to personality types when job changes are made than on initial entry into a job; the latter is more a function of job availability than personality factors (Parsons and Wigtil, 1974). Personality patterns are also useful in identifying desirable counselor characteristics—in other words, the social type was selected, rather than a type similar to the individuals seeking help (Cox and Thoresen, 1977). Stability of patterns appears to be about the same as for those derived from other major occupational classifications (McLaughlin and Tiedeman, 1974).

In putting theory into practice, Holland (1978a, pp. 60–61; 1978b, pp. 134–135) urges career counselors to use a variety of methods and techniques and suggests that one-to-one counseling is neither the most practical nor the most efficient approach. In addition, he believes that his approach, using types and environments, offers more productive answers to the critical questions about career guidance than do those based on developmental stages (Holland, 1978, p. 156).

Holland has developed two instruments related to his theory. The first, the Vocational Preference Inventory, or VPI (1965, 1975), has been used in the research previously reported. It consists of 160 occupational titles, to which the individual responds with "yes" or "no" to express preference or rejection. In addition to the six occupational-environment scales, there are scales to help facilitate interpretation that measure such characteristics as self-control, masculinity, status, infrequency, and acquiescence. The inventory is suitable for ages fourteen and above and is most appropriately used as a "brief screening inventory for high school and college students, and employed adults" (Holland, 1965, p. 1). The results should not be used alone; interpretation should be related to other data about the individual. Technical aspects appear to be satisfactory (Holland, 1965, p. 9), and the inventory should be helpful in guidance and counseling (Stahmann, 1972).

The second instrument, the Self-Directed Search, or SDS (Holland, 1977), is relatively new and is unique in two ways. It is self-administered, scored, and interpreted, and it is based directly on a specific vocational-development theory. The new edition (Holland, Gottfredson, and Holland, 1977) has been improved by reducing sexual bias, simplifying scoring, and making other changes to increase the occupational options considered by the user and to facilitate the development of self-understanding. In addition, the number of occupations in the *Occupations Finder* (the interpretative booklet used with the SDS) has been increased from 456 to 500. A new, simplified form (Form E, Easy) has been prepared for use with adolescents and adults with reading levels between the fourth and sixth grades. Reviews of the SDS (Brown, 1972; Cutts, 1977; Dolliver and Hansen, 1977) give generally positive evaluations.

A new career-guidance system called the Vocational Exploration and Insight Kit, or VEIK (Takai and Holland, n.d.), which includes the Self-Directed Search, a revised Vocational Card Sort, and an Action Plan, does not lead to an increase in the number and variety of occupational options considered and in the degree of satisfaction with plans when compared with SDS alone. The results suggest that various individuals may need help tailored to their specific needs and that there may be a ceiling effect in the use of several techniques in combination.

The rationale of the SDS appears to be sound (Edwards and Whitney, 1972), and research on it has given positive results. Both the published version and another that did not include the "self-directed" aspects increased the number of occupations that high school pupils considered. Those who took the published version considered occupations that were more realistic and appropriate in terms of abilities, interests, and self-descriptions. Pupils who took either version expressed increased satisfaction with their plans, and those who used the published version appeared to feel less need for immediate counseling (Zener and Schnuelle, 1972). Previously criticized sex bias has been reduced, and the theory has been found to apply to minority group members. Holland's classification has been shown to be capable of reflecting patterns of job changes for both young men and young women (Nafziger, Holland, Helms, and McPartland, 1974). Levels of consistency of patterns have been shown to be related to future plans (O'Neil and Magoon, 1977) and also to academic potential as measured by tests of academic ability (O'Neil, 1977). Further, the classification system as assessed by the VPI has been shown to be appropriate for high school pupils, including potential dropouts (Cunningham, Alston, Doughtie, and Wakefield, 1977). Some aspects of Holland's theory also serve as the basis for the major career clusters and vocational-interest inventory in the American College Testing Program's Career Planning Profile (American College Testing Program, 1972, pp. 9–10). Without question, the instrument, as well as the theory on which it is based, has considerable utility for career guidance and counseling.

Hoppock's Composite Theory

Robert Hoppock describes his contribution to vocational-development theory as minute (1970, p. 93), but his composite theory has probably had a substantial impact on counselors and guidance workers. His publications have been among the most widely used by practitioners, and he has been the most articulate member of the profession on the importance of occupational information. His theory was developed in response to a request for a rationale for his proposals on the use of occupational information (1970, p. 93). Hoppock questions whether research will serve as a basis for accepting or rejecting any of the available theories and emphasizes the importance of the counselor's familiarity with the best that is available in order to provide the most effective help in day-to-day work.

According to Hoppock, the effects of a variety of personal and environmental factors should be recognized; personal need is central to his theory, but environmental information is a critical factor in effective vocational development and decision making. The ten postulates of his theory are given in his book (1976, pp. 91–92) and should be read to appreciate the utility of the theory.

PSYCHOANALYTICAL THEORIES

Work has not been an issue of paramount concern to psychoanalysts. Freud was ambivalent about its importance, seeing it as both essential for organized society and an unpleasant duty to be performed, but some neo-Freudians have been more explicit about the meaning of work for the gratification of needs and for psychological development (Neff, 1965). Some recent theorists have used the psychoanalytic theory of personality as a basis for research on the role of work in the individual's life and the factors involved in choice.

The major comprehensive statement of a psychoanalytic vocational-development theory grew out of four studies of occupational groups (Nachmann, 1960; Segal, 1961; Galinsky, 1962; and Bordin, Nachmann, and Segal, 1963). With encouraging results from these studies, Bordin, Nachmann, and Segal constructed a "framework for vocational development." The major elements of this framework or theory are as follows:

1. There is a continuity in human development. The simplest and earliest psychological and physiological processes in infancy are connected with the most complex intellectual and physical activities of adult years.
2. Instinctual sources of gratification are the same for complex adult behavior as for the simpler behavior of infancy.
3. The individual's pattern of needs is determined in the first six years although it may be modified somewhat during his lifetime.
4. The occupation which one seeks is determined by the needs developed in the first six years.
5. The theory applies to all ages and all levels and types of work with the following limitation:
   a. It does not apply to those who are either restricted or motivated by external factors, e.g., cultural or financial. There must be enough freedom of choice for needs to determine behavior.
   b. It does not apply to those who can find little or no gratification in work.

6. Work represents sublimation of infantile impulses in the broadest sense of the term into socially acceptable behaviors.

7. A lack of knowledge of occupations can result in the selection of one which does not fulfill expectations. But emotional (neurotic) blocking of information about opportunities is a psychological mechanism and thus is an aspect of the theory.

8. All jobs can be described in terms of clusters of dimensions which represent psychoanalytic needs.[10]

Other studies have tended to provide some support for the theory. Beall and Bordin's (1965) analysis of the experiences of engineers, drawn from speeches, diaries, and other documents, revealed some developmental patterns and impulse gratification related to the theory. Identity formation, an aspect of infant and early childhood development, was found to be related to problems in vocational choice (Galinksy and Fast, 1966). Barry and Bordin (1967) used a variety of data, including the same type employed by Beall and Bordin, in research on ministers, priests, and rabbis. They found some support for predictions based on psychoanalytic theory.

Research methodology and theoretical restrictions present problems for the theory, however. Measurement problems are difficult to solve (Bordin, Nachmann, and Segal, 1963, p. 116). Eliminating environmental factors limits the theory's applicability and potential utility (Roe, 1963, p. 117). The assumption that adult behavior, including occupational behavior, has the same instinctual sources of gratification as does infantile behavior has been questioned (Roe, 1963, p. 117; Ashbrook, 1967, p. 404). Nonetheless, although it is difficult to draw specific guidance procedures from the theory, it has a value in emphasizing the importance of the psychodynamics of each individual when helping with career planning and choice (Crites, 1978, p. 36).

SOCIOLOGICAL THEORIES

The effects of social institutions, such as the family, home, and occupational structure, are taken into account by practically all theories, but emphasis varies considerably. Some approaches to explaining behavior give heavy weight to sociological factors. August B. Hollingshead, a sociologist (1949, pp. 281–287), found that social class has a marked effect on job plans, job availability, and feelings of certainty about plans; the lower the class, the lower the adolescent ranked on each of these factors. "Job channels" with associated levels represented sociological influences on the occupational paths available and those levels that could be reached (1949, pp. 360–370). Occupational choice and development have also been major concerns of industrial sociologists.

Sociological theories have included descriptions of work-life stages in which economic and sociological factors typically play a major part:

[10]Adapted from Edward S. Bordin, Barbara Nachmann, and Stanley J. Segal, "An Articulated Framework for Vocational Development," *Journal of Counseling Psychology*, 10 (1963), 110. Copyright 1963 by the American Psychological Association, and used by permission.

1. PREPARATORY   Orientation to work is developed
2. INITIAL   The initial work period, which includes part-time work experience and formal education
3. TRIAL   The trial-work period, consisting of the time from entry into the world of work until a satisfying job has been found
4. STABLE   The stable work period, with establishment in work and community
5. RETIREMENT   The period when there is a decline in work interests (Miller and Form, 1951, pp. 519–786).

The theoretical formulation of Blau, Gustad, Jessor, and Wilcock (1956), which they describe as a conceptual framework rather than a theory, specifies variables and interactions that should be taken into account. Research is needed, however, to develop a theory from this conceptualization. The statement has a cross-disciplinary origin. In order to insure that psychological, economic, and sociological perspectives on occupational choice and development would be included, the framework was developed by representatives of each of these fields. The conceptualization is graphically portrayed in Figure 2.3, which shows the impact of sociological factors on choice in two major ways: (1) by the influences on personality development, and (2) by the number and types of jobs available. The case example at the top left of the figure shows an individual, Y, who is looking for a job. His first preference is job A; but he is not qualified for it and so does not apply. He instead applies for the next job, B. He gets it and therefore does not bother to decide what the third choice would be.

At the top right of the figure, the *occupational* side of the process is illustrated. Two hundred employees are needed. Fifty with Y's training and experience are available and are employed. Since 200 are needed, 150 with fewer but adequate qualifications are also employed. It is not necessary to further lower requirements to obtain an adequate number of employees.

The point of "occupational entry" is shown at the top, and below are the circumstances and conditions that precede it. The four personal factors in box 1 and the four occupational factors in box I interact to lead to occupational entry and are related to the factors in the boxes immediately above them—for example, preferences are tempered by *expectancies*. This top left box involves the individual's decision processes.

Boxes 2 and II involve possible influential factors. Unless they affect factors in 1 and I, they do not play a part in occupational entry.

Boxes below the dotted line represent historical, personal, and occupational factors that led to the current entry situation. Choice is a point in the developmental process, which extends back into early family life. Changes in the world of work have also affected the present entry opportunities.

The same conceptualization could be applied to other choice points in the individual's development, for example, selecting school courses, evaluating the suitability of a job after a period of work, or formulating goals after being rejected for a job.

An extensive review of research and theory was used in the initial formulation. Adaptations of the model have been used by Super and others as one element in a

Figure 2.3   A sociological view of career choice and development

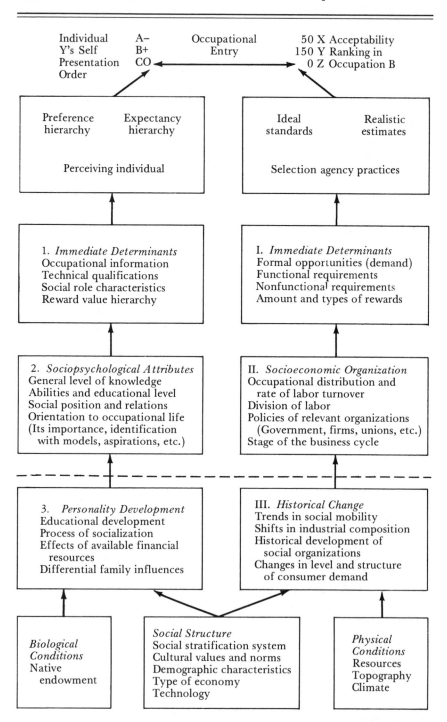

SOURCE: *The Industrial and Labor Relations Review,* 9, No. 4 (July 1956). Copyright © 1956 by Cornell University. All rights reserved. Reprinted with permission.

developmental framework (Super, Kidd, and Watts, 1977). As the authors point out, however, its value will be realized only if empirical research determines how and why the variables explain occupational choice and development. There is already a considerable amount of research on various aspects, such as personality development, the effects of occupational information, and the impact of the job market and industrial development on employment, but the postulated relationships have not been tested.

DECISION-MAKING THEORIES

Several well-known occupational-choice and development theories demonstrate how decision-making processes previously utilized in economics and to some extent in psychology can be used to explain career behavior. Decision making is an element in all theories, but the uniqueness of this classification lies in its extensive incorporation of decision-theory concepts and decision processes.

Gelatt's theory, discussed first, puts major emphasis on decision-making concepts. Hershenson and Roth give relatively more attention to the developmental aspects; thus, their theory shares characteristics with the developmental group, even though I consider it appropriate for the decision-making category. The model advanced by Knefelkamp and Slepitza also has developmental emphases but focuses on changes in decision processes. Jepsen's work deals specifically with how decisions are made and is described more fully in Chapter 7. Other studies and applications are discussed at the end of this section.

Gelatt's Theory

H. B. Gelatt's theory has been selected for detailed analysis because it illustrates the nature of the general approach and applies to the work of the school counselor. The theory is actually designed as the basis for an approach to counseling but serves very well to illustrate the cyclical process of decision making in vocational choice and development, the effects of past experiences, and the relationship of immediate, intermediate, and distant decisions. Other decision-theory concepts, such as weighing the value of alternative goals, using data to estimate the possibility of achieving each, and assessing the value and utility of the goal, are included. The process is illustrated in Figure 2.4.

Decision making begins, as shown at the top of Figure 2.4, with a *purpose* or *objective*. The individual is aware that a decision needs to be made, that information is needed, and that there are at least two possible courses of action. Next, data are collected. The purpose of the decision indicates what is needed; for example, if the individual is trying to decide whether to enroll in a training program in mechanical work, he or she needs information about his or her mechanical aptitudes, interests, and abilities and descriptions of the programs at the vocational-technical center.

Utilization of data is central to the process. The strategy shown in the right-hand area is the sequence of activities. Relating this to the case of Ralph Hart, the strategy

Figure 2.4 Gelatt's decision-making frame of reference

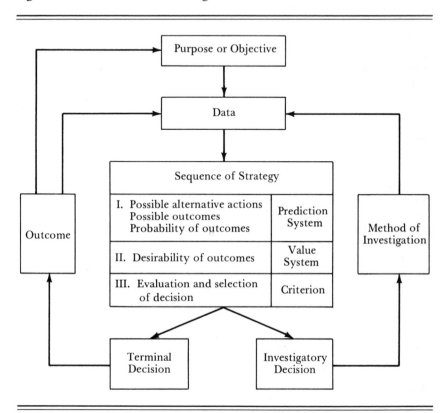

SOURCE: H. B. Gelatt, "Decision-Making: A Conceptual Frame of Reference for Counseling," *Journal of Counseling Psychology*, 9, (1962), 242. Copyright 1962 by the American Psychological Association and reproduced by permission.

would involve identifying *possible* majors, predicting the *possible* outcomes of selecting each one, and estimating the *probable* results. Next, the strategy would involve an evaluation of the *desirability* of each outcome. Which does he value most? Which one enables him to be what he wants to be? In the final step, he selects a specific major.

The individual's prediction system determines the way he or she looks at possible and probable outcomes, as well as the alternatives considered. The individual must have some idea of how well the available data apply to the possible choices. For example, if Ralph is considering a major in science or engineering, he needs to know the requirements of the programs and how he compares with others. He may use information in college catalogues and school marks and test scores. Other factors, such as finances and college admission criteria, must also be considered. Difficulties often arise at this point because the individual has very limited occupational or educational horizons and knows little about opportunities.

Estimating *possible* outcomes and probabilities makes heavier demands on the individual's prediction system. Past experiences of success, the self-concept, and the level of aspiration enter the process. The individual may predict too optimistically, too pessimistically, or quite accurately. Available data typically permit only very rough estimations. The individual's prediction system may be ineffective or efficient, in relation both to the data selected and to the weights used.

The next step in the strategy is the individual's estimates of the *desirability of outcomes.* He or she compares goals with his or her hierarchy of values. If, for example, making money is the individual's highest value, he or she would be very likely to choose the course of action that provides the largest income. Comparison of outcomes with values is not a discrete step, it is emphasized as success in various options begins to appear possible. For example, Ralph may conclude that he could obtain a degree in physics and then do advanced study. The questions he asks are, "Is this what is most important to me?" and "Is this what I really want to be?" While some critics of decision-making approaches charge that values do not play a part in the process, they constitute a major element in Gelatt's strategy.

Finally, a decision is made. It may be either "terminal" or "investigatory." From either type feedback into the decision-making loop occurs; the suitability of the decision is assessed by tryout, or further investigation is planned. Both these courses of action provide new data for decision making. The cyclical process is more or less continuous. The individual may be at different stages on different problems at any given time. Each decision changes or adds to the available data for the next one.

The implications of this model for guidance and counseling will be taken up in Chapter 7. Our purpose here is to illustrate how a decision-making approach may explain vocational choice and development. The model deals more specifically with choice, but it shows how development is a series of choices, each drawing on antecedent conditions and changing the future (Gelatt, 1962; Clarke, Gelatt, and Levine, 1965; Gelatt, 1967).

Gelatt has not developed all aspects of the model and mentions specifically that *value* and *utility* need further clarification. Some other concepts, such as *risk,* need to be incorporated. However, many relevant concepts are included, such as assessing the value of *alternative choices* and the *subjective probability* or likelihood that each can be attained; *maximizing* expected value in decision making; and *sequential decision making* (Brayfield and Crites, 1964, p. 311).

Research on the types of information pupils use, the types needed, and the types that improve decision making has revealed that adequate information is often unavailable. If local and relevant information were used, pupils could carry out more effective decision making (Clarke, Gelatt, and Levine, 1965; Gelatt and Clarke, 1967; Kroll, Dinklage, Lee, Morley, and Wilson, 1970, p. 170).

Hershenson and Roth's Theory

David Hershenson and Robert Roth (1966) conceptualize vocational development as a decision-making process in which two trends pervade repeated choices. The range

Table 2.3 Life stages of vocational development

Freud Stage	Erikson Issue	Vocational Development Stage	Energy Utilization	Vocational Mode
Receptive ORAL Sadistic	Basic trust	Social-amniotic	Awareness	Being
Expulsive ANAL Retentive	Autonomy			
GENITAL Oedipal resolution	Initiative	Self-differentiation	Control	Play
LATENCY Puberty	Industry	Competence	Directed	Work
ADOLESCENCE	Identity	Independence	Goal-directed	Occupation
MATURITY	Intimacy Generativity Ego integrity	Commitment	Invested	Vocation

SOURCE: David B. Hershenson, "Life-Stage Vocational Development System," *Journal of Counseling Psychology*, 15, No. 1 (1968), 26. Copyright 1968 by the American Psychological Association. Reprinted by permission.

of possibilities is narrowed, and the strength of those that remain is increased; in other words, the individual becomes more positive about them and adapts to the conditions of the remaining choices. As the series of decisions made by or for the individual leads him or her in a specific direction, the end result or goal becomes more inevitable. For a disconfirming experience to affect a trend materially, it must be increasingly powerful the further the individual is along in the certainty-of-choice path. The shapes of the curves representing these two factors are unique for each individual. One person may rapidly narrow choices while another does so quite slowly.

In a later formulation, Hershenson (1968) views career development as a five-stage sequential process, with the emphasis on the order of stages rather than on

Vocational Question	Measurement Construct	Typical Measures	Relevant Vocational Theorists
Am I?	Socialization to: (1) culture (2) family	Family SES, trust scale, anomie scale, cultural conformity measures	Social psychological: Lipsett, 1962; Roe, 1957; Bordin, Nachmann and Segal, 1963
Who am I?	Affective self-concept, attitudes, values	Who are you? Adjective checklist, Q sort, Allport-Vernon, Stern Activities Index, Values Inventory	Bordin, 1943; Super, 1957; Tyler, 1955, 1961
What can I do?	Abilities	DAT, GATB, miniature tasks, TOWER	Adler, 1938; Holland, 1959; White, 1960; Flanagan, 1962
What will I do?	Interests	Verbalized, Kuder; SVIB, OII (Lee-Thorpe), MVII	Decision theories: Ziller, 1957; Tiedeman, 1961; Hilton, 1962
What meaning does what I do have for me?	Satisfaction	Verbalized, questionnaire, critical incident	Existential: Simons, 1966; Herzberg, 1959

the individual's chronological age. That is, the counselor needs to look at the stage in which the individual is actually functioning, rather than comparing him or her with others of the same age. Also, it is assumed that development in each stage sets limits on what can be accomplished in those that follow.

Table 2.3 shows the five vocational stages, along with related ones from Freud and Erikson. The typical modes of the stages, rationales, instruments for measurement of progress, and related theorists also are shown.

The stages, based partly on those of other vocational theorists, are differentiated by the way the individual uses energy. For example, in the first stage, social-amniotic, energy is used mainly to receive input from the environment and to become aware of one's own existence. The family and immediate environment have the most pronounced effect at this stage; severe deprivation will limit development at this and later stages.

In the second stage, the individual goes on to differentiate the self as an individual, to assert the self, and to exert some control, arriving at an answer to the question "Who am I?" mainly through play experience with objects and persons and by taking roles. The competence stage follows, in which the individual attempts to find out what he or she can and cannot do; often this search is in the area of schoolwork. Next, the individual must decide which activity—which occupation— to concentrate on. This is called the independence stage, since it is the first time the individual must deal with real choice.

Hershenson states that real occupational interest must follow the development of competence and that the capacity for directedness must precede goal directedness. This is a reversal of the usual order, based on unique use of the concept of occupation. The final stage of vocational development is a commitment to an occupation.

Stages are sequential. An individual cannot perform the tasks at one stage until those at earlier stages are mastered. For example, an individual cannot work toward a goal until the capacity for goal directedness is achieved. The author suggests that the formulation may offer ways for further analyzing other theories, for instance, Roe's theory and its failure to reveal a substantial relationship between early home climate and occupational choice.

Studies by Hershenson and Langbauer (1973) and Hershenson and Lavery (1978) have tended to support the sequence of stages. Three different populations were used (deaf, socially disadvantaged, and mid-career occupation changers). However, only cross-sectional data were used, and longitudinal research is needed for a more definative evaluation of the theory.

A Cognitive-Developmental Model

The concept of L. L. Knefelkamp and R. Slepitza (1978) could be placed in the developmental classification as well as in the decision-making group; it includes a great deal of both approaches and synthesizes them uniquely. The model, which is primarily focused on college students at this point in its development, deals with stages of cognitive development in occupational choice, from a simple view of career planning and decision making to a qualitatively different and much more complex and integrative perception that takes into account personal characteristics, social factors, and the process of career choice and involvement.

The nine variables that represent areas of qualitative change in development and growth are grouped into four major categories:[11]

[11]Material in this section adapted from "A Cognitive-Developmental Model of Career Development—An Adaptation of the Perry Scheme," by L. L. Knefelkamp and R. Sleptiza. In J. M. Whiteley and A. Resnikoff (Eds.), *Career Counseling.* Copyright © 1978 by Wadsworth, Inc. Reprinted by permission of the publisher, Brooks/Cole Publishing Company, Monterey, California.

DUALISM   There is no one right occupation. Some authority will provide the answer. Locus of control is outside the person.

MULTIPLICITY   There is a shift to consideration of more factors and a belief that a good decision-making process is all that is needed to find the right answer. Reliance on outside factors continues; the locus of control is still outside the individual.

RELATIVISM   The locus of control is now within the individual. Personally developed decision processes are used, and responsibility for decisions is accepted.

COMMITMENT WITH RELATIVISM   Increased responsibility for career choice is assumed. Career and self-identity become confused. After initial narrowing, the individual's career world expands.

A brief summary of the nine stages that are subdivided to fall within these categories is as follows:

Dualism	*Stage 1*	Reliance on authority for pointing out the right occupation.
	Stage 2	The possibility of a right or wrong decision is recognized.
Multiplicity	*Stage 3*	The authority is the decision-making process. More factors that need to be considered are recognized.
	Stage 4	The self is not yet fully involved in the choice, and the individual does not yet accept full responsibility for choices.
Relativism	*Stage 5*	Self now the major motivational force in decision making, and the counselor is seen as a helper rather than the authority.
	Stage 6	A reflective stage, in which the individual is not yet ready to commit self.
Commitment with relativism	*Stage 7*	Integration of self and career role is experienced. A realization that the individual defines the work role, following a preliminary fear of being confined and constricted by it.
	Stage 8	The meaning of the occupational commitment is experienced. There is a high degree of integration of all aspects of life.
	Stage 9	The individual knows who he or she is, what he or she wants, how one affects others, and seeks to reach potential. More searching and risk taking is done.

Data collected in studies of college students tend to support the concept of qualitative changes in relation to educational level and status in occupational planning. One particularly interesting finding is that students sometimes parrot career-development maxims without understanding or accepting their personal meaning. Knefelkamp and Slepitza acknowledge that, for practical applications, more work must be done on longitudinal studies to validate stages, assessment methods should be developed, and programs must be set up to try out the models with individuals. Even so, the concepts appear to hold considerable promise for understanding and facilitating the career-development process and represent a much-needed concern with cognitive processes in the career-planning process.

Jepsen's Work

The studies of David Jepsen (1974a, 1974b, 1975) on the decision-making process are significant for their contribution to an understanding of an element that is vital to any theory of career development. Jepsen has identified patterns of decision making, described strategy-types of pupils, and shown that as high school pupils progress through school, they tend to engage in more complex information-search strategies and to develop more elaborate rationales to support occupational choices; these increases contribute to the degree of confidence about choices. However, pupils fail to reduce the number of discrepant choices, that is, different types or levels of occupations chosen. Jepsen's studies add to the understanding of how pupils make decisions and provide valuable guidelines for designing career-guidance services.

Other Decision-Making Theories

Martin Katz (1963, 1966) has specified the choice points in school that require decisions; emphasized the importance of the value systems as the synthesizer of perceptions, needs, and goals in vocational choices; and described a model combining the three systems used by the individual—an information system, a value system, and a prediction system. The exploration of choices begins with values (see SIGI in Chapter 5). Katz's description of how values are investigated could be a useful procedure for Gelatt's model, which was described previously. The incorporation of risk-taking tendencies in career decision-making theory has been investigated by Ziller (1957). Willingness to take risks varies with the occupations selected. Other research by Slakter and Cramer (1969) found only a weak relationship between risk taking and choice of an educational program or occupation. The use of the concept is questionable until there is more definite research to clarify its role in career decision making. Dilley (1965) found evidence that decision-making ability is related to intelligence, achievement, and participation in extracurricular activities. Since these three variables are related to vocational maturity, he concluded that vocational maturity and decision-making ability are related.

A number of guidance programs utilize decision-making concepts to facilitate vocational development and improve decision making (Chick, 1970; Hansen, 1970; Martin, 1970). Several will be described in Chapter 5, but two are particularly relevant here. DECIDING, a programmed workbook for the high school level (Gelatt, Varenhorst, and Carey, 1972) is designed to help pupils make rational decisions, acquire and use information, and keep options open as long as possible. Gelatt's decision-making plan interweaves values throughout the process. The workbook includes simulation career games and incorporates other aspects of decision theory, including the concepts of *risk* and *alternative strategies*. The Career Planning Program (ACT, 1972) utilizes decision-making concepts to help pupils make post–high school plans. A profile covering values, goals, interests, abilities, and other personal data is a basic source of information for planning. An exceptionally well-designed student booklet based on decision-making processes explains data and their relationships to post–high school preparation and occupations. This booklet is a model of a lucid, interesting, and complete presentation; it includes well-organized information about career clusters and identifies related training and educational programs. Appropriate emphasis is given to the often-neglected vocational- and technical-education training programs and to related careers. The counselor's manual suggests individual and group counseling approaches and includes a summary of the major vocational-development theories, particularly useful with this chapter (ACT, 1972).

SOCIAL-LEARNING THEORY

Although a number of theories already covered make use of social learning, some extensively, the work of Anita Mitchell, G. Brian Jones, and John Krumboltz (1975) on career development and C. E. Thoresen and C. K. Ewart (1978) on learnable cognitive processes merits special attention. The Mitchell, Jones, and Krumboltz social-learning theory, which draws on concepts from psychology, economics, sociology, guidance, and education and synthesizes a large number of research studies (1975, pp. 40–53), gains credibility through the way it was developed and its adequacy in terms of testability, consistency with known facts, potential for generating hypotheses, and parsimoniousness. The authors characterize their approach as one that

> attempts to encompass a total process, not just some phase of it. It explains the development of career aspirations and achievements which are so important in the trait-factor approach; reinforces the notion that career selection is a developmental process at the same time (although contesting the validity of lock-step developmental stages and phases); clarifies the role of decision-making and the evolution of decision-making skills; allows for the influence of economic and sociological variables; and is compatible with critical aspects of personality theories (Mitchell, Jones, and Krumboltz, 1975, p. 12; Krumboltz, 1979, pp. 19–49).

The social-learning theory is composed of the following four categories of factors that influence career decision making:

1. Genetic endowment and special abilities, such as race, sex, intelligence.
2. Environmental conditions and events, such as job and training opportunities and family experiences.
3. Learning experiences, such as instrumental and associative learning
4. Task-approach skills, such as learning skills like good work habits.

These four types of influences interact to produce three kinds of consequences.

1. Self-observation generalizations, such as "I am good at mathematics"
2. Task-approach skills, such as setting an occupational goal and using information to choose a college
3. Actions, for example, based on interactions of self-observations and task-approach skills; the individual takes an action such as enrolling in a drafting course.[12]

The process of career planning and development involves the effects of genetic and environmental factors on the cumulative learning experience. The individual arrives at a choice, but at a point in the developmental sequence rather than at the end. Learning experiences are both affective and cognitive. Decisions and actions affect future behavior, as when being successful in a drafting course causes the individual to consider the possibility of being an architect. Negative experiences reduce the likelihood of further participation in similar learning experiences in the future.

A number of propositions and hypotheses have been developed from social-learning theory, for example:

> Proposition IA1. An individual is more likely to express a preference for a course of study, an occupation, or the tasks and consequences of a field of work if the individual has been positively reinforced for engaging in activities she/he has learned are associated with successful performance of that course, occupation, or field of work. Illustrative hypothesis: Boys who are reinforced for their basketball performance are more likely to indicate an interest in a basketball career than those who are not so reinforced.
>
> Why are some boys reinforced for basketball playing and others not? A boy whose heredity and nutritional environment enable him to grow six feet ten inches tall is more likely to be reinforced by his basketball coach than a boy who grows to be only five feet two inches tall. Genetic and environmental factors play a major role in which learning experiences get reinforced.[13]

[12]From "A Social Learning Theory of Career Selection," by J. D. Krumboltz with A. M. Mitchell and G. B. Jones. In J. M. Whiteley and A. Resnikoff (Eds.), *Career Counseling.* Copyright © 1978 by Wadsworth, Inc. Reprinted by permission of the publisher, Brooks/Cole Publishing Company, Monterey, California.

[13]John D. Krumboltz, "A Social Learning Theory of CDM," in Anita M. Mitchell, G. Brian Jones, and John D. Krumboltz (eds.), *A Social Learning Theory of Career Decision Making.* (Palo Alto, Calif.: American Institutes for Research, 1975), pp. 13–39.

An illustrative case involving a hypothetical person, "Barbara," is shown in Figure 2.5. The factors that affect her occupational selection are displayed and the circles represent associative learning experiences. Triangles contain self-observation generalizations. Parallelograms show task-approach skills. Only a few of the learning experiences having an effect on "Barbara's" educational and occupational selections are shown.

The social-learning model has received considerable evaluation through use of previously completed research. But, as is true for other theories of career development, additional testing and validation are needed. Social-learning theory does, however, provide hypotheses that readily fit into research studies and that provide guides for program-building evaluation.

A model by Thoresen and Ewart in the same general area utilizes concepts of behaviorial self-control drawn from self-management psychology to serve as a basis for career development and guidance.[14] Behavioral self-control, as defined by Thoresen and Ewart, means *"learnable cognitive processes that a person uses to develop controlling actions which, in turn, function to alter factors influencing behavior"* (1978, p. 191). This definition recognizes that the individual not only learns self-control skills but also uses them to change personal behavior. Behavior includes both internal (for example, self-statements) and external (for example, overt actions) types.

There are four major areas in which self-control skills are involved:

1. COMMITMENT   The individual develops and sustains motivation. For example, reasons for present behavior are assessed and possibilities for change are reviewed. Motivation is used to build commitment.

2. AWARENESS   The individual observes his or her own behavior and notes what is done in specific situations. The activity serves as a guide in determining what to change in one's personal situation.

3. RESTRUCTURING THE ENVIRONMENT   The individual modifies particular aspects of the environment that are inhibiting so that they serve to facilitate change. For example, the individual may get other persons to help him or her to learn about occupations.

4. EVALUATING CONSEQUENCES AND STANDARDS FOR SELF-EVALUATION   The individual arranges events so that they will be supportive. Short-term goals are set up. For example, the individual gives himself or herself an immediate reward for obtaining information about an occupation.

Thoresen and Ewart point out that self-control procedures have not yet been used in career development, but they suggest questions that are relevant for this area, such as: can unrealistic plans be changed by using explicit criteria for short-term goals? Self-control skills could be taught in schools to help individuals become more in charge of their own lives. Single-case research procedures could be used to evaluate effects. Other designs could be employed to assess the impact of particular features of the program.

[14]Adapted from "Behaviorial Self-Control and Career Development," by C. E. Thoresen and C. K. Ewart. In J. M. Whitely and A. Resnikoff (Eds.), *Career Counseling.* Copyright © 1978 by Wadsworth, Inc. Reprinted by permission of the publisher, Brooks/Cole Publishing Company, Monterey, California.

Figure 2.5 Illustrative excerpt of factors affecting "Barbara's" occupation selection

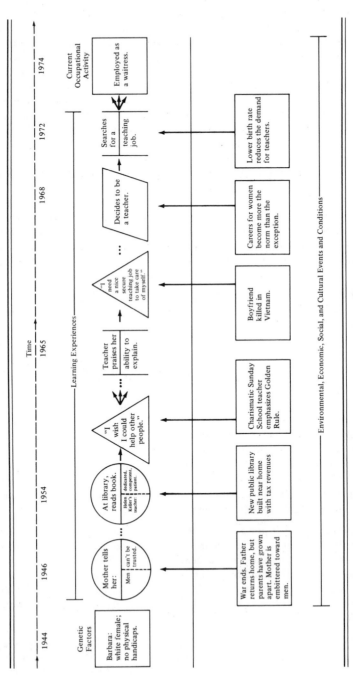

SOURCE: From "A Social Learning Theory of Career Selection," by J. D. Krumboltz with A. M. Mitchell and G. B. Jones. In J. M. Whiteley and A. Resnikoff (Eds.), *Career Counseling*. Copyright © 1978 by Wadsworth, Inc. Reprinted by permission of the publisher, Brooks/Cole Publishing Company, Monterey, California.

MY POINT OF VIEW

My point of view about career development and its relationship to guidance and education is a compendium of concepts from previously discussed theories[15] that appear to have the most validity and utility for practice. These concepts can be stated as follows:

1. Career development reflects cultural and political attitudes and values. Moreover, in a society that has a linear type of progress, the process of career development does not change, but the nature and content of stages do.

2. Each individual is unique in potential, tendency to commit, level of activity, and preference for type of activity.

3. Career development is a major part of the total developmental process, extends throughout life, and is one of the principal organizing themes of life. Partly biologically and partly socially determined, it reflects the culture and subculture in which it exists.

4. Career development is largely determined by social learning, with models exerting a major influence on its progress; other types of learning, however, are also involved. The family, community, and media are particularly influential, but institutions such as the school also play a part. These influences are usually too subtle to be easily identified by the individual.

5. The self-concept, the result of genetic and social learning factors, is the major motivating force in career development. It guides the individual in determining what he or she wants to be vocationally.

6. Career maturity is similar to other types of maturity and indicates how well the individual is mastering the career-developmental tasks appropriate for his or her age. The more successful one is in coping with current tasks, the greater the chance of success in mastering future ones.

7. Career development involves a lifelong series of choices, some minor and some major. The latter come at times of significant changes in roles, such as from student to worker.

   a. Major choice points are primarily culturally determined (work, marriage, retirement), but personal factors play a part. The time involved may be brief or extensive; a decision, for example, may involve a period of several years. Each choice point involves, to some extent, the sequence of career development—awareness, exploration, choice, tryout.

   b. Subcultural norms and mores affect major choice points.

   c. Disabilities may affect the time involved but do not eliminate stages.

   d. Decisions involve both logical and intuitive processes, and the style varies with individuals. Either extreme is usually ineffective.

[15]While concepts were borrowed from a number of theories, special mention should be made of the following sources: John D. Krumboltz, Anita M. Mitchell, and G. Brian Jones, "A Social Learning Theory of Career Selection," *Counseling Psychologist,* 6, No. 1 (1976), 71–81; Donald E. Super, Jennifer Kidd, and A. G. Watts, "A Life-Span and Life-Space Approach to and Descriptive Framework of Career Development," mimeograph (Cambridge, Eng., 1977); and David V. Tiedeman, "Guidance for the Knowing, Not just the Status, Career," mimeograph (Northern Illinois University, 1977).

    e. Although the decision process is unique for each person, each decision involves the following elements:
      1. a decider
      2. choices, even if one option is not to decide
      3. estimation of chances for success in options considered—in other words, a projection into the future
      4. consideration of the risk involved
      5. consideration of the value and personal importance of success
      6. awareness of what one must give up in selecting an option
      7. expectations of self and others
      8. tryout for verification of suitability

8. Career development involves stages in which one process dominates, but all processes are present throughout one's working life. The major stages are awareness, exploration, choice and preparation, establishment, and reassessment. Stages differ for special groups, largely due to cultural and economic influences. Career patterns reflect the style in which individuals progress through career development; similarities in patterns permit groupings.

9. The career role is a major aspect of the lifestyle but is only one of a number of aspects. All roles the individual plays interact, but the career role exerts a major influence on others.
    a. The lifestyle is the major source of satisfaction and personal meaning for the individual, and occupation is the major factor in determining the lifestyle. Occupational satisfaction is based on the degree of congruence between lifestyle and occupation as well as suitability of occupation.
    b. Leisure is one of the lifestyle roles, is largely culturally and occupationally determined, and is signifcant in relation to the time and resources available. It follows a developmental sequence somewhat similar to the career and in some cases can dominate the lifestyle (for example, fantasy play, business-contact golf, postretirement community service).

10. Accuracy of perceptions of the environment is a major factor in career development. The better understood the environment, the greater the individual's feeling of "I-power," and the less likely there will be negative impact from encountering the actual opportunities and barriers in the world of work (for example, one is less likely to prepare for an occupation that is overcrowded; institutional constraints are more likely to be perceived as conditions to overcome rather than blocks to aspirations). Moreover, the individual can more effectively project the self into the work setting, test out the opportunity to be what he or she wants to be, and relate possible and preferred lifestyles.

11. Work satisfaction is a function of how the individual perceives
    a. himself or herself as regarded by others in the work setting.
    b. the attractiveness of the actual tasks carried out.
    c. attitudes of family and acquaintances about the occupation.
    d. the time demands of work.
    e. the adequacy of remunerations to enable the preferred lifestyle to be maintained.

f. the availability of attractive alternatives.

The rewards of an occupation are unique for each individual; thus, any occupation can be satisfying to some individuals. Changes in perception of adequacy of those elements lead to efforts to change jobs.

12. Retirement introduces a particularly difficult task in career development. Since occupation is the major role in lifestyle, or at least one of the two or three major ones, all roles suffer. The more highly structured the previous work, or the more central to the lifestyle, the more difficult it is to perceive oneself in another what-I-want-to-be role.

IMPLICATIONS OF THEORIES

This chapter on theories of career development, together with related studies, brings together material that serves as guidelines for practice. The applications are described and illustrated in the chapters that follow; each of the techniques or procedures covered derives its rationale from the theoretical principles described on the preceding pages. To help provide a link between this, the theory chapter, and later applied chapters, the implications of the theories are summarized in Table 2.4. In addition, the cases presented at the beginning of the chapter are discussed.

Table 2.4 identifies some of the major implications of the theories, although space limitations do not permit a detailed listing of them or an explanation of what should be done and how. For example, for developmental theories, a complete statement of "identification of factors" would include preferences, values, home influences, abilities, goals, status of career development, hobbies, models, leisure activities, and work or part-time work experiences. The developmental theory also suggests which factors should be given the most weight at each life period, for example, the exploratory stage. A detailed study of each group of theories is necessary to understand the implications for practice. In the chapters that follow, many of the applications are described and illustrated. A good grasp of theories, however, enables the counselor to develop and try out new and original applications. Thus, theory frees one to move beyond techniques and procedures developed by others and use creativity in day-to-day work.

The cases presented at the beginning of this chapter provide another way to show theory implications. For example, how could one or more theories explain Joe Prince's behavior and suggest helping strategies? A trait-factor approach would give some valid indications of his abilities and allow the counselor to relate them to expected success in school and level of education. This approach would also point out that parental expectations might be more realistic. From developmental as well as several other theories, the concepts of models could be used to help explain Joe's indecision and confusion. His father, whom he admires, not only is away a great deal of the time but for other reasons is no longer an example for Joe to emulate. It is apparent that career-development tasks have not been mastered, that work values have not crystallized, and that Joe has not, from a needs theory point of view,

Table 2.4 Implications for practice, practical applications

Theory	Identification of Factors	Providing Occupational Information	Individual Counseling	Group Counseling	Program Development	Placement	Evaluation
Trait-Factor or Actuarial	Assess personal traits Analyze occupational requirements	Need to match personal factors with occupational requirements	Help relate personal and occupational factors	Same, and feedback from members	Need systematic assessment and occupational information resources	Indicates realism of plans	Assess suitability of choices
Developmental	Theory indicates critical ones by stage	Stage indicates what is needed	Relate to level of career maturity Provide help to reach appropriate level of maturity	Same, and test roles Get feedback from members	Indicate the major emphasis, for example, exploration is a lifelong process	Part of the developmental process	Mastery of tasks at each developmental stage
Needs	Identify needs	Provide information about needs and characteristics of work settings	Explore needs and values Relate to occupational settings	Same, and get feedback on needs	Help individuals identify needs Explore occupations	Identify needs met in settings	How well choices meet needs

Psycho-analytical	Identify needs and conflicts based on psychoanalytical theory	Provide information about work settings	Explore drives and needs Resolve conflicts	Same	Help individuals define needs Identify critical factors in occupations	Help to satisfy identified needs	How well choices meet needs
Sociological	Theory indicates critical ones, such as aptitudes, education, goals	Provide extensive information about economic and other conditions of work settings	Explore personal attributes and occupational factors Relate the two sets of factors	Same, and interact to clarify goals	Help individuals to understand themselves Provide information, particularly at choice points	Help to identify opportunities	Assess adequacy of information, success in finding an occupation
Decision Making	Extensive and accurate self- and occupational information needed	Stages in decision making show what information is needed	Describe skills that should be learned to aid in decision making	Same, and get feedback from others	Services and personnel needed and times to provide services	A process to use in selecting and changing jobs	Efficiency of each step and suitability of decision
Social Learning	Identify influences, models, and learning skills	Need models and other learning experiences of successful behavior	Explore social learning Use models to improve skills	Same, and use small-group learning experiences	Schedule development of coping skills Provide effective models	Develop skills in finding and holding a job	Suitability of decisions Effectiveness of coping skills

93

identified a field of work that is in line with personal interests, values, abilities, and goals. A social-learning approach suggests, among other things, that such coping methods as task-approach skills are deficient and that he does not have a clear concept of who he is.

The behavior of Mary Jones can be explained quite readily by several theories. She has not developed occupationally in a productive direction as might be expected of someone with limited exploratory experiences and relatively powerful models close at hand. Not having had the opportunity to explore, investigate, and try out a variety of experiences, she is confused by the challenges to subcultural values that she is encountering. In her case, too, career-development theories provide guidelines for counseling and guidance to assist her in formulating career goals and planning ways to reach them.

Theories, particularly developmental and social learning, explain how Ralph Hart became locked into a career field that does not necessarily appeal to him. He did not go through growth and exploration stages, he has not learned how to make decisions, and he is not aware of his own needs. The scientific area may be suitable for him, but he should have his own reasons for entering it.

The difficulties faced by other individuals described in Chapter 1 also may be explained by career-development theories. Barry Brown is developing some potentially limiting occupational stereotypes; he should be building an awareness of the place of work in one's life and playing out fantasy roles. Henry Fuller is quite retarded in career development; he is particularly lacking in exploratory and coping skills and a concept of self at work. The mid-career and pre- and postretirement cases also present problems that can be addressed by career-development theory.

In all these illustrations, some theories appear to fit better than others. But all usually contribute to both understanding the cause of difficulty and planning strategies for helping. Each counselor and guidance worker should build a personal synthesis for applications to day-to-day work.

SUMMARY

In this chapter, a number of individuals have been described to illustrate problems in career development. Some of the terms used in career counseling and guidance have been defined. Classification systems for career-development theories have been reviewed. The major categories used in this chapter are trait-factor, developmental, needs, psychoanalytical, sociological, decision-making, social learning, and existential. In each of these categories, the work of one or more well-known theorists has been summarized in sufficient detail to provide the reader with a framework on which to build. The explanations were brief, so additional reading is essential for a comprehensive understanding of theories.

The assumptions made by these theories should be considered by the user. First, they were developed primarily through research on middle-class, relatively affluent individuals. (More attention, however, is now being given to special groups.) Second, they assume that work is important to the individual. Third, they reflect relatively less concern for environmental variables than for psychological ones, and there is the implication that the individual is relatively free to make full use of his or her abilities and interests. Each theory attempts to explain the vocational behavior of individuals and provides some insight into the career-development problems illustrated in the three cases. My point of view on career development, which consists of points adapted from various theories and research studies, emphasizes career-development stages, subculture influences, the major role of decision making, and the critical importance of information about the world of work and education. The implications of theory for education and guidance point to the need to synthesize career-development concepts with the school program at all levels, work jointly with the home and community for maximum effectiveness, provide opportunities to practice decision-making skills, and give special attention to choice points in the educational process and throughout the life span.

PROJECTS AND EXPERIENTIAL ACTIVITIES

1. Interview a person who has had substantial work experience, preferably someone near retirement, and relate your findings to one of the theories. A list of questions based on the stages and significant factors identified by a particular theory may be prepared to serve as an interview guide.

2. Prepare a career pattern report on your own experiences to date. Include your early plans, choices, and the reasons for your choices.

3. View the films *A Dialogue on Vocational Development Theory, Parts I and II* (Film Department, American Personnel and Guidance Association, 1607 New Hampshire Avenue, N.W., Washington, D.C. 20009).

4. Formulate a brief statement of your "theory" of career development. Interpret your own career behavior in terms of your formulation. For example, does it explain the factors or influences in your choice of a college or major?

5. Form small groups and ask each person to give a brief summary of his or her career development up to the present. Then ask group members to select one of the individual's accounts and relate major features to one of the theories. Estimate how well the theory explains the career. Ask each group to report results to the class.

6. Form small groups and have each group use one of the instruments described in this chapter, such as SDS, VMI, or VPI. Before completing the instrument, describe for the class the major factors measured and ask each member of the small groups to rate each other group member on the factors. Then ask members to complete the instrument, score, and react to similarities and differences in others' rankings. Compare with inventory results.

7. Designate four or five places in the room as home base for a theory or a type of theory. For example, you could use developmental and needs, or Holland and Super, as areas. Then ask each member of the class to move to the area that represents his or her theory preference. Announce that they will have ten to

fifteen minutes to decide on five reasons why the selected area is the most useful one. Ask each group to discuss its reasons briefly for the class.

8. Use small groups and ask members to think back to a point when they were relatively uncertain about occupational plans. (It may be at that time when they were considering counselor education as a major.) Then ask each group to agree on the top two theories they would have liked a counselor to have used in helping them make a decision. Have each group report on and explain its selections to the class.

9. Ask each small group to construct a theory by agreeing on five concepts selected from the theories discussed in this chapter (using one concept from each of five theories). Ask each group to report its results to the class.

10. Use a fantasy exercise (see item 10 in "Projects and Experimental Activities," Chapter 1) to have class members look twenty years into the future. Ask that they imagine they are telling a beginning counselor about the most meaningful event that has taken place in their lives in the past twenty years. Ask for volunteers to describe these events. Then discuss how career-development theories might explain these events.

ADDITIONAL REFERENCES

Most of the major references for the career theorists are noted in the text and are the primary sources for in-depth study of their positions. The following either are complete statements of the theories presented or summaries and evaluations of them.

Borow, Henry, ed. *Man in a World at Work.* Boston: Houghton Mifflin, 1964, Chap. 12, "Major Programs of Research on Vocational Behavior," is the most useful. Although this book is somewhat older than most listed, it gives an excellent account of the status of career-development theory in the early 1960s. Many of the questions raised are still relevant.

Crites, John O. *Vocational Psychology.* New York: McGraw-Hill, 1969. The author has organized his material around such topics as "theories of choice" and "development of choice," making it necessary to refer to the index for appropriate passages. Research is described and evaluated, and critical analyses are provided. This book is one of the most valuable references for this chapter, although more recent studies should also be read to update the theories.

Herr, Edwin L. *Vocational Guidance and Career Development in the Schools: Toward a Systems Approach.* Boston: Houghton Mifflin, 1972. Chap. 2, "The Ingredients of Career Vocational Development," is a helpful summary of approaches. It develops the concept of *vocalization,* a term analogous to *socialization.*

Holland, John L. *Making Vocational Choices.* Englewood Cliffs, N.J.: Prentice-Hall, 1973. The most detailed statement available of Holland's theory, this book is essential for an understanding of the theory, its research support, and ways of applying it in guidance and counseling programs.

Jordaan, Jean Pierre, and Martha Bennett Heyde. *Vocational Maturity During the High School Years.* New York: Teachers College Press, Columbia University,

1979. This is the third monograph in the Career Pattern Study series. It analyzes changes in the career behaviors of pupils from the ninth through the twelfth grades. Practical applications are explored. An extremely valuable reference for both researcher and practitioner.

Mitchell, Anita M., G. Brian Jones, and John D. Krumboltz, eds. *Social Learning and Career Decision Making*. Cranston, Rhode Island: Carroll Press, 1979. A comprehensive collection of articles on social learning theory of career development by the major authorities in the field. The Krumboltz theory summarized in this chapter is included. The processes of career development and career decision making are thoroughly analyzed and applications are discussed. A valuable reference on this relatively new approach to career development.

Osipow, Samuel H. *Theories of Career Development*. New York: Appleton-Century-Crofts, 1968. This is the only available book devoted exclusively to a thorough and critical evaluation of vocational-development theories. Although a considerable amount of research has been done since its publication, it is a must for students of career development.

Rossi, Robert J., Wendy B. Bartlett, Emily A. Campbell, Lauress L. Wise, and Donald H. McLaughlin. *Using the Talent Profiles in Counseling: A Supplement to the Career Data Book*. Palo Alto, Calif.: American Institutes for Research, 1975. In addition to the actual occupational profiles that comprise the major section of the book, strategies for counselors to use in career counseling are described and illustrated on pp. 3–23.

Super, Donald E., ed. *Measuring Vocational Maturity for Counseling and Evaluation*. Washington, D.C.; National Vocational Guidance Association, 1974. This is the first and still the most complete review of the measurement of vocational maturity. Although some new developments have taken place, this monograph is essential reading for researchers and practitioners interested in career maturity. The final chapter ("Retrospect, Circumspect, and Prospect") is a good overview of the book.

Tiedeman, David V., and Anna Miller-Tiedeman. *Choice and Decision Process and Careers*. DeKalb, Ill.: ERIC Clearinghouse in Career Education, n.d. A complex review of the Tiedeman concept of the decision-making process, with an extensive list of annotated references from the ERIC system.

Whiteley, John M., and Arthur Resnikoff, eds. *Perspectives on Vocational Development*. Washington, D.C.: American Personnel and Guidance Association, 1972. Developments in the theories of Super, Holland, Tiedeman, and Roe are considered in detail. This is a very useful reference for use in conjunction with the more recent statements of some of the theorists.

————, eds. *Career Counseling*. Monterey, Calif.: Brooks/Cole, 1978. The reports in this book, drawn on extensively in this chapter, are reprints from two issues of the *Counseling Psychologist* devoted to career development and guidance (Vol. 4, No. 3, 1974, and Vol. 6, No. 3, 1976). The following paragraph indicates which readings are most relevant for specific parts of this chapter. If the journals are used, articles may be located by titles, with the exception of Chap. 1, which was prepared specifically for the book.

Chap. 2, "Career Counseling: A Review of Major Approaches," and Chap. 4, "Career Counseling: A Comprehensive Approach," review major theories and suggest a synthesis for helping interventions. Articles in Chap. 3 by Holland, Vetter, Harmon, and others relate to Crites's Chap. 2 and will be helpful in connection with it. Chap. 5, "A Social Learning Theory of Career Selection," by Krumboltz, Mitchell, and Jones is a complete presentation of the theory discussed in this chapter. Chap. 6 contains commentaries by Holland and Roe of theories presented in Chap. 4 and 5 and a response by Krumboltz. Chap. 7, "Using a Typology of Persons and Environments to Explain Careers: Some Extensions and Clairifications," by Holland and Gottfredson, is an advanced discussion of the use of Holland's typologies. Chap. 8, "Behavioral Self-Control and Career Development," by Thoresen and Ewart is the complete statement from which the brief summary in this chapter was drawn. Chap. 9, "Research Priorities and Resources in Career Decision Making," has not been mentioned in this chapter but is useful here, particularly in connection with Chap. 5 on the social-learning theory; it identifies research questions related to the theory. Chap. 10, "A Conceptual Framework for Career Awareness," by Wise, Charmer, and Randour is the source for material in this chapter. Chap. 11, "A Cognitive-Developmental Model of Career Development—An Adaptation of the Perry Scheme," by Knefelkamp and Slepitza is the source from which the summary in this chapter was drawn.

Zaccaria, Joseph S. *Theories of Occupational Choice and Vocational Development.* Boston: Houghton Mifflin, 1970. Zaccaria makes a distinction between choice and development and provides a concise, helpful review of major theories. Although there is some duplication, a reading of Chaps. 1–3 will be helpful in conjunction with this chapter.

3

Understanding

Career-Development Factors

GOALS

1

To identify the major factors involved in career development.

2

To explain how these factors may be assessed.

3

To emphasize the importance of these factors for the
individual's career development and to describe how they
facilitate or impede the process of career development.

4

To help the student begin to appreciate the importance of
these factors in services designed to help others with
career development.

SUCH FACTORS AS APTITUDE, interests, and economic conditions are important in the process of career development. Their meaning and assessment should be understood both for better comprehension of theories and to permit applications that facilitate growth and remove blocks. Both the ACES position paper (Hansen, 1978) and the NVGA/AVA statement (1973) emphasize the importance of helping individuals become aware of the personal significance of these factors. This chapter is devoted to a discussion of the significance of these several aspects of career development.

Specific theories may emphasize a particular factor, but most of the factors described here play a part in each theory. Furthermore, their interactions are more significant than the individual effects of each. The factors affecting career development may be categorized as follows:

1. OCCUPATIONAL APTITUDES   Academic aptitude or intelligence, as well as specific occupational aptitudes such as mechanical or clerical

2. OCCUPATIONAL INTERESTS   Interest in specific occupations or broad areas of work

3. PERSONALITY   Characteristics such as the self-concept, values, needs, and ways of relating to others

4. CAREER MATURITY OR DEVELOPMENT   Additudinal and cognitive factors showing one's status in the process

5. ACHIEVEMENT   Proficiency in school subjects, vocational skills, or other areas.

6. HOME, FAMILY, SEX, AND RACE   Family composition, race, sex, national origin, socioeconomic level, parental occupations, and subcultural characteristics

7. HANDICAPS   Social, physical, and psychological handicaps. Some conditions are clearly handicapping, while others are limiting only because of public attitudes.

8. EDUCATION   The limiting and facilitating effects of schools, colleges, and other types of training or educational programs.

9. ECONOMIC CONDITIONS   The conditions of the economy, employment trends, the effect of technology, and the job market.

Both personal and environmental factors are included in this list, and the classifications are quite broad. Many subcategories could also be identified; for example, the effects of a war economy on employment opportunities, or the effects of changes in the types of energy used.

Specific theories may emphasize these factors to varying degrees. Super's theory, for example, makes use of most of them, while the psychoanalytic rationale gives most emphasis to personality needs and little to economic and educational factors. A review of Table 2.4 and the theories discussed in Chapter 2 clearly indicates which factors are the most relevant for each specific theory.

Factors may be assessed by a variety of approaches. Those that are psychological in nature are usually measured, at least in part, by a test or inventory. Others, such as economic conditions, are determined from reports. Direct observation may also be employed. The use of psychological measurements for assessment presents some special problems involving selection of instruments and interpretation of results.

Although measurement principles are covered in specific courses, several particularly important concepts are reviewed briefly here to indicate their importance for assessing career-development factors.

ELEMENTS OF FACTOR ASSESSMENT

A complete review of measurement principles is beyond the scope of this chapter, but a brief review of types of tests and inventories, reliability, validity, norms, scores, test administration, and interpretation of results should be helpful at this point.

Types of Tests and Inventories

The major types are aptitude (including academic aptitude), achievement, occupational interest, career development, and personality. These types of tests are similar in name to factors in vocational development, and tests are frequently used to provide information about the factors. For example, when intellectual ability is identified as an important variable in Roe's and Super's theories, the source of evidence about it is usually a test score. Later in this chapter, more is said about instruments, and examples are given in the section on factors.

Reliability

In using tests, inventories, and ratings, it is necessary to be able to estimate factors affecting the scores. Reliability is often thought of as involving only the stability of the test over time, but other types of stability are also important. This is not to say that stability over time is of little concern. If an interest inventory has this type of reliability, we can give Maria Sanchez the inventory today and be certain that if we give her another one like it next year, the results will be very similar. But conditions other than time also cause variations. For example, her interests may change, the particular items in the inventory may affect the results, or she might feel bad. Some of these influences are long-term and some are transitory. If we are using the results to help Maria plan her program for the next term, we are interested in conditions that affect the short-term stability of the inventory. The counselor might wonder, "Do these scores give an accurate picture of the things Maria likes at this time?" If, however, the counselor is using the results to help Maria plan post–high school education, he or she is more interested in long-term stability. He or she might thus ask, "Can we expect that Maria's future interests will be similar to her current ones?" Different uses of tests and inventories call for different kinds of reliability. The test manual may or may not provide what is needed, but the user should at least know how well a given reliability fits the purposes for which the test is being used.

Validity

The test or inventory should provide information, with some degree of accuracy, about what the individual will do, likes to do, has learned, or can say, for example, that nine out of ten people with similar scores were successful as science majors at a particular college. Tests will help the individual, *provided* that the relationship of test scores to success in science courses has been determined or, even better, that scores on the *specific* tests taken have been related to success in the *particular* science program under consideration.

Test and inventory scores, however, indicate how a *group* of individuals may be expected to perform, not what Louis in particular will do. We can never be absolutely sure what Louis's marks will be, but we can say, for example, that nine out of ten people with similar scores received a B average for the first quarter.

Validity is related to the type of instrument and to the way it is used. For example, Louis's academic aptitude test is valid if it predicts marks in college. An achievement test in physics is valid if it covers the important concepts in physics.

Validity is essential for instruments used in career development. In all theories, prework data are related to vocational choice; successful translation of theory into practice depends on valid measurement of personal factors.

Norms, Scores, and Test Administration

In using measurements to understand and facilitate career development, application of the correct norm group is of critical importance. For example, if a pupil is planning to enter vocational-technical training, he or she should be compared with students in vocational-technical programs on general ability, specific aptitudes, and interests. In making these comparisons, however, caution should be exercised in estimating the potential of those who have been severely deprived educationally, socially, or occupationally. Such comparisons are better interpreted as indicative of needed remedial work than as predictive indices. Predictions are as accurate for the disadvantaged as for typical groups, since test results reveal only the deficiencies that will cause difficulty in training and work. But if the use of results stops with prediction, the counselor will only perpetuate the cycle of deprivation. A diagnostic and remedial approach will help to promote positive career development.

The use of *criterion-referenced* scores may enhance the utility of measurements in assessing career development. In this type of score, the individual is not compared with a group (as with *norm-referenced* scores) but with a standard of what is adequate, for example, the ability to use decimal fractions.

The test-taking situation can itself contribute to poor performance by those who have had little or no experience with tests and for whom they represent a threat. Unfamiliarity with procedures, lack of confidence, and apprehension can negatively affect results. Using measurements with the disadvantaged requires special skill in administration, interpretation, and application of results (APA, 1969; Mathis, 1969; Reed, Seiler, and Lesher, 1969; Seiler, 1971).

Interpretation of Results

Test data can help facilitate career development. They can help with planning, decision making, and overcoming obstacles that might otherwise disrupt the process. For example, a boy who thinks he has low ability might elevate his goals if he finds that he should be able to do the course work in the community college. A girl who assumes that she should aim for a typical female occupation might change her career directions if she finds that her interests point toward occupations she had not previously considered.

The value of tests in career counseling is a subject of considerable controversy. Goldman has described efforts to combine the two as a marriage failed (1972). His pessimistic conclusions stem from several factors. First, tests were developed primarily for use in selection and placement, and they are not relevant for counseling. Second, predictions are not precise enough for practical use. Third, they evoke negative reactions from the disadvantaged. Finally, counselors don't know how to use them. Wesman (1972), taking the opposing point of view, describes Goldman's conclusions as a case of murder and suicide—murder for tests and suicide for the counselor who must proceed without their help. Wesman goes on to say that, although tests can be improved, they provide accurate, dependable information that cannot be obtained in other ways and thus are useful without having the level of predictive accuracy some critics assert is necessary. Use with the disadvantaged is defended because test results give an estimate of their standing and thus provide bases for remedial work. As Wesman says, you don't kill the messenger who brings the bad news.

Most of these issues would be resolved if test data could be put in a form that would facilitate career development. This would require that results and their practical use be clearly understood. Much progress is being made in this direction. One example is the American College Testing Program's Career Planning Program, or CPP (Hansen and Cole, 1972; Prediger, 1976), which provides information relevant for career development by using abilities, interests, career-related experiences, and data/ideas, people/things work-task dimensions to suggest occupational clusters or postsecondary education/training areas for exploration. Vocational Interest, Experience, and Skill Assessment, or VIESA, is a short form (forty-five minutes) of the CPP designed to assess interests, experiences, and skills using the same data, ideas, people, and things dimensions and exploratory strategies (Vocational Interest, Experience, and Skill Assessment, 1976). Predictive data are given in terms that are helpful for planning without attempting to be unrealistically precise. The revised Differential Aptitude Test, or DAT, is another example (Bennett, Seashore, and Wesman, n.d.; Mastie, 1976). Nine scores are shown on a profile, and a computer-printed career-planning report analyzes the relationship of scores to career plans.

The necessary relation between test data and career development is made clear in Prediger's (1972) statements of facilitative uses. He emphasizes the need for a new approach based on career development and decision making to promote occupational exploration, self-understanding, and estimates of probable success in occupational options. Data should be in a form that will have an impact on career development. In response to his own mandate, Prediger (1971a, 1971b) describes a technique that plots various training or occupational groups in a similarity score profile and enables the pupil to determine the group he or she resembles. A number of measurement factors can be used to locate the occupational or educational plots, and it is thus possible for the pupil to understand *why* he or she is more like, for example, drafting students than like those in auto mechanics. This type of information encourages the pupil to look at himself or herself in various options and to plan ways to become more like a particular group, for example, taking courses, talking with workers, and doing part-time work so as to more closely resemble draftsmen. Although the approach is designed for counseling, it could be more widely applied to make such information available to all pupils at strategic points in their career development. Finally, a person-referenced approach to test interpretation (Bradley, 1978) is suggested as a way to go beyond both norm- and criterion-referenced methods and make the test interpretation a personally relevant learning experience.

For effective use of measurement information in career development, data-processing facilities are necessary. The amount of computation required, including the extensive use of information on local trends and opportunities, is beyond the capabilities of counselors. Further, support personnel are needed for clerical assistance and collection of local information. Any steps to make measurement data more useful in career development will be expensive, but the gain should far outweigh the cost.

DETAILS OF FACTORS AND ASSESSMENT

The factors enumerated at the beginning of this chapter are discussed briefly in the following paragraphs, and some of the widely used methods and instruments for assessment are described. Factors in career development cut across such areas as psychology, economics, and sociology, and career development encompasses the total life of the individual.

Occupational Aptitudes

Intelligence or academic aptitude, vocational aptitudes, and special talents play significant roles in career development. Intelligence, or academic aptitude, probably has the most pronounced effect on the level of education or occupation reached. Specific vocational aptitudes, such as mechanical or clerical, have less predictive efficiency for training or occupations but are useful in guidance and planning. There are minimum levels of intelligence necessary for success in work or training beyond which other factors begin to make substantial differences in achievement. Aptitude levels have been established for a variety of occupations (U.S. Department of Labor, 1965a, Vol. II). Figure 3.1 illustrates these levels based on the *Dictionary of Occupational Titles* (DOT). Long-term research has shown that aptitudes may be used

Figure 3.1 The occupational group for guidance and counseling, *Dictionary of Occupational Titles,* 3rd ed.

GUIDANCE AND COUNSELING
.108; .208

Work Performed

Work activities in this group primarily involve guiding and/or counseling individuals or groups in the solution of occupational, educational, personal, or social problems. Typical situations would be assisting prison parolees in gaining employment and adjusting to society; counseling high school students about college admission requirements and curricula; counseling unhappy or frustrated workers or jobseekers into more fulfilling work; and assisting troubled individuals or families toward normal social adjustment and development.

Worker Requirements

An occupationally significant combination of: Sympathetic attitude toward the welfare of others; capacity to absorb training and apply knowledge to the solution of diverse problems; verbal facility to relate to people at all levels; organizational ability in order to plan and direct guidance programs; tact, poise, and general demeanor that tend to inspire confidence and esteem.

Clues for Relating Applicants and Requirements,

Volunteer welfare work for local church group.
Expressed preference for public contact work.
Membership in school debating club.
Successful academic record in pertinent courses, such as psychology or education.
Poise and self-confidence exhibited in an interview.
Elective office in school.

Training and Methods of Entry

A college degree is the minimum requirement for entry into this field. In most cases, education beyond the 4-year college level is required, varying according to the individual situation.

Most municipal and State governments and private organizations require 2 years of graduate study from applicants who are interested in pursuing social work as a career.

Openings in school-counseling work are usually available to individuals who have State teaching certificates and special certificates for school counseling. Most States issue counselor certificates only to people with a master's degree or the equivalent in counselor education, as well as actual teaching experience.

A graduate degree in psychology serves as an excellent qualification for entry into numerous positions, particularly those in industry.

RELATED CLASSIFICATIONS

Administration (.118 .168) p. 237
Interviewing, Information-Giving, and Related Work (Vocational, Educational, and Related Activities) (.168; .268) p. 250
High School, College, University, and Related Education (.228) p. 341
Social Science, Psychological, and Related Research (.088) p. 294

QUALIFICATIONS PROFILE

GED: 5 6
SVP: 7 8
Apt: **GVN** SPQ KFM EC
     1 1 3   4 4 4   4 4 4   5 5
     2 2

Int: 4 6 5 8
Temp: 5 9 4
Phys. Dem: S L 4 5 6

SOURCE: U.S. Department of Labor, *Dictionary of Occupational Titles,* 3rd ed., Vol. 2 (Washington, D.C.: U.S. Government Printing Office, 1965), p. 296.

to predict occupational membership (Thorndike and Hagen, 1959, pp. 316–317). The follow-ups of Project Talent (see Chapter 2) also illustrate the use of interest, aptitude, and personality data in occupational prediction.

Intelligence is usually expressed in terms of scores on tests that measure ability to use abstract symbols. Test content resembles school tasks, and the scores typically correlate more highly with school marks than with such other criteria as occupational success. The correlations between school marks and test scores are usually in the 40–60 range, so a great deal of variability in marks is not accounted for by scores. Even so, academic-ability tests and previous school achievement are the best predictors of future success in academic work.

There are sharp differences of opinion about the suitability of these tests for the disadvantaged (Brazziel, 1970; Cameron, 1970). Tests validly measure important variables in career development and choice. Misuses, rather than technical flaws, appear to account for the major criticisms. One possible approach is to modify the testing procedures to eliminate, as much as possible, biases that may favor those with better academic preparation and middle-class socioeconomic backgrounds. Nonverbal tests and work-evaluation procedures, discussed later, provide two promising approaches.

Occupational aptitudes are increasingly measured by batteries of tests. Their purpose is to provide profiles that indicate occupational directions the individual might profitably take, but the goal of differential occupational prediction has not been realized. Even so, well-developed batteries, such as the General Aptitude Test Battery, or GATB, and the Differential Aptitude Test, or DAT, give valuable information for planning programs or choosing occupations. A particularly useful feature of the GATB is its correlation to occupational groups in the *Dictionary of Occupational Titles,* Vol. II. Figure 3.1 shows how these test scores provide an aptitude profile for an occupational group and indicates the significance of a number of other factors, such as previous part-time work experience, physical abilities, temperament, and interests.

The Qualifications Profile includes aptitudes tested by the GATB, measured on a scale ranging from a high of 1 to a low of 8. Boldface letters indicate the most important aptitudes. G (Intelligence), V (Verbal), and N (Numerical) aptitudes are required at high levels and are quite important. Others, such as F (Finger dexterity), are less important.

One of the most promising approaches to evaluation of the occupational potential of those for whom the usual tests are not suitable and who need to see a relationship between the evaluation procedures and the actual job is *work evaluation* (Neff, 1966). The term is used to indicate "any process which assesses the physical, mental, or emotional abilities, limitations, and tolerances of a person, so that his current and future vocational potential and adjustment may be reasonably predicted" (Daughtrey, 1972, p. 13). The process involves assessing performance in various situations that closely resemble work, helping the individual to assess himself or herself, evaluating the meaning of his or her performance, and assisting him or her to make vocational plans. Thus, it facilitates career development (Hoffman, 1972). The Singer/Graflex Vocational Evaluation System is an example of a commercial package that provides for the evaluation of vocational aptitudes, interests, and work tolerances. Ten work sampling stations, such as drafting, plumbing, and pipe-fitting, are used to evaluate one thousand job areas.

Vocational evaluation is used in vocational schools, penal institutions, and rehabilitation agencies. It appears to be a successful way to assess the occupational potential of those who, because of lack of motivation, educational deficiencies, cultural deprivation, or negative attitudes toward tests, do not demonstrate their potential on typical paper-and-pencil aptitude tests.

Aptitude testing is a complex and rapidly growing specialty. More sophisticated instruments are being developed, and computers are making it possible to predict performance in educational programs and jobs quickly, to an extent that was heretofore impossible. Tremendous quantities of data can be easily handled. Pupils can obtain predictions for themselves using computer terminals. Programs such as PLAN provide achievement and career-development feedback and will no doubt have a significant impact on pupil growth and planning. Career education will certainly involve aptitude measurement, but the means has not been determined yet. Counselors and guidance workers will play key roles in helping pupils make effective use of aptitude data, and they should be experts on the contributions and limitations of these measurements as well as the technology that will make them available in usable form.

Occupational Interests

Interests in activities, relationships, and tasks associated with occupations are also critical variables in vocational development. They are only slightly related to abilities. The existing systems of classification tend to be similar. Interests are related to occupational choice, job satisfaction, and job tenure. Needs and interests are related, and inventoried interests tend to be more stable than expressed or manifest interests. Regardless of the way interests are identified, they tend to be quite variable in childhood and to become more stable with increasing maturity. Vocational interests play a part in every theory of vocational development.

Interest measurement may open up new career avenues for those whose opportunities have previously been limited. Research on the patterns of men's and women's interests suggests that they are similar and that women's career options may be expanded by relating their interests to occupations traditionally identified as exclusively male (Cole, 1972).

The measurement of interests has been one of the most thoroughly researched areas in psychometrics. But like other types of measurement, it evokes heated controversy. Those who use tests and inventories should be familiar with the pros and cons argued by knowledgeable persons and should develop a reasonable but not overenthusiastic approach to application of results.

Critics of interest inventories challenge their fakability, forced-choice format, validity, and the appropriateness of questions. Rothney (1972, pp. 78–85), one of the most articulate critics of tests, is particularly concerned about the lack of sophistication demonstrated by counselors in the use of interest measurements but concludes that tests can help in career planning. Bauernfeind (1968, pp. 43–46) points out that the *ipsative* scores obtained from forced-choice interest inventories can be interpreted in any of a number of ways. One has only to read the reviews in Buros's *Mental Measurement Yearbooks,* particularly the eighth edition, to become aware of limitations that should be observed.

The Strong Campbell Interest Inventory or SCII, formerly called the Strong Vocational Interest Blank, is probably the most widely used interest inventory for the college bound (Hansen, 1977). It represents the greatest amount of longitudinal research and has proved effective for predicting occupational membership over long periods of time. The male and female forms have been merged into a new unisex form that contains three major sets of scales: occupational themes, basic interest, and occupational scales. Separate ratings are provided for men and women on the last scale. Scores indicate whether the individual's pattern of preferences more closely resemble that of a general sample of men or women or members of an occupational group. Basic interest scales are included to facilitate the interpretation of the occupational scales. The theme scales are based on Holland's six personality types. Two nonoccupational scales are also provided.

Another interest inventory that includes nonprofessional as well as professional occupations is the Occupational Interest Survey, or KOIS (Kuder, 1970). College major preference scores are also given. Results represent the degrees of similarity between the individual's responses and those of persons in specific occupations and academic majors.

Interest inventories designed for those planning to work after high school should be particularly useful to career development. The Minnesota Vocational Interest Inventory, or MVII (Clark, 1961; Clark and Campbell, 1965) includes occupations such as baker and truck driver and work areas such as mechanical and health service. Occupational scores represent the degree of similarity to members of occupational groups compared with tradespeople in general. Area scores reflect levels of interest in types of activities and help in the interpretation of the occupational profile.

The second vocationally oriented inventory is a relative newcomer that shows considerable promise. The Ohio Vocational Interest Survey, or OVIS (D'Costa, Wineforder, Odgers, and Koons, 1970), is related to the DOT classification of data-people-things (see Chapter 5) and includes work areas and specific occupations, such as manual work and nursing. It is for grades eight through twelve, both boys and girls. Norms for grade thirteen in community colleges are also available. Reliability appears to be satisfactory, and stability over a two-year period is substantial. More validity data, for example, predictions of occupational choice and satisfaction, are needed however (Sorenson, 1974). Pupil information, such as occupational plans, is also obtained, and provisions are made for the inclusion of local survey questions. An interesting feature is the index of clarity, which measures consistency of preference. Occupational interests may also be measured in terms of local norms. Materials include a *Guide to Career Exploration,* a looseleaf book containing detailed information about the twenty-four OVIS job clusters, and a Career Exploration leaflet, which helps pupils with career planning and decision making.

One promising trend in interest inventory design is the identification of occupational *satisfiers* and worker needs (Gay et al, 1971). Needs assessed by an inventory are matched with satisfiers provided by occupations, and potentially suitable occupations are identified. An example of a need is "ability utilization." The inventory is based on a theory of work adjustment that involves "interaction between *work personality* and *work environments* as a way of conceptualizing the process by which an individual adjusts to work" (Lofquist and Dawis, 1972, p. 1). The significant aspects of the work personality are abilities and vocational needs; those of the work setting are ability requirements and reinforcer systems. The results of the interaction of the individual with the work setting can be expressed in terms of satisfactoriness, satisfaction, and tenure. Reinforcer patterns have been developed for a number of occupations (Rosen, Weiss, Hendel, Dawis, and Lofquist, 1972). More recently, the theory of work adjustment has been extended to include a description of the work-adjustment process, for instance, relating personality style to the counseling approach and work setting (Dawis and Lofquist, 1976).

One of the more controversial aspects of interest inventories has to do with sex bias (Diamond, 1976; Betz, 1977). A certain amount is present in most instruments, but steps are being taken to reduce bias by analyzing instruments and setting up guidelines for their construction (Diamond, 1978).

Personality

Under the general rubric of *personality* could be listed values, needs, prestige rankings, self-concept, and level of aspiration. Values appear to be related to interests and needs, and all three are involved in occupational choice. Occupational prestige exerts an influence. The self-concept, which plays a major role in some theories, is related to occupational choice, educational achievement, and broader aspects of life, although it is not clear just how it is translated into an occupational self-concept. Perceptions may lead to unrealistic choices for a number of reasons, including achievement needs, social pressures, and prestige ranking of occupations. Willingness to take risks may be a general personality characteristic that enters into choice (Witwer and Stewart, 1972). Personality factors appear to be particularly important in the career development of women, the disadvantaged, and minority groups. The individual's attitudes about the self, occupational roles, locus of control, career salience, and the expectations of others have an effect on career development and occupational choice (Putnam and Hansen, 1972; Greenhaus, 1976; Osipow, 1976). Holland's theory of career choice and development involves measuring occupational preferences to identify personality types; occupational-interest inventories are classified as personality inventories (1973, p. 7).

Two aspects of personality, career salience and locus of control, have recently captured attention in investigations of career development. *Career salience* is the importance of work to an individual in comparison to other aspects of life—in other words, how much career stands out. The more pronounced the salience, the more likely it is that individuals view their chosen occupation as ideal. In addition, there is evidence that those who are vocationally undecided may be low in career salience—work is just not very important to them (Greenhaus and Simon, 1976, 1977). Much more needs to be done to substantiate the usefulness of this concept for career counseling and guidance for various age levels. It does, however, appear to be a very promising factor in understanding the process of career development.

Locus of control refers to the location of the individual's feeling of control or power—internal or external. The more one feels in control of his or her life, decisions, and environmental conditions (has an internal locus of control), the more one is pleased with work activities and the more one progresses in an occupation (Osipow, 1976; Betz, 1977). Again, research has emphasized specific groups, and application to the wide range of personalities has not yet been established.

Neither of these concepts has a demonstrated direct relationship to the theories of career development discussed in Chapter 2. Even so, career salience has implications for the developmental process because of the importance of occupation in an individual's lifestyle. Locus of control almost certainly enters into the way one goes about making career decisions, but research is needed to shed light on the process.

A number of other personality factors play a part in career development. The prestige or social status of occupations, which is remarkably stable over time, is assumed to serve as a powerful attraction for those types of work that rank high, such as physician and lawyer (Kanzaki, 1976). Characteristics of the work personality have been hypothesized to be influential in work adjustment. Examples of these characteristics are flexibility, activeness, reactiveness, and celerity, or the speed at which the individual achieves work personality–work correspondence (Dawis and Lofquist, 1976).

A rather surprising personality characteristic that has recently been identified is the motive to avoid success (Esposito, 1977). White females seem to have a tendency to expect high achievement and success to result in negative consequences and thus to reject them. This type of behavior obviously has a great deal of significance for women's career development.

Methods of assessing personality include paper-and-pencil inventories, projective tests, interviews, situational tests, and unstructured self-reports. Some instruments or techniques for measuring occupational interest and personality are quite similar and are used for both purposes. Holland's VPI and the Myers-Briggs Type Indicator (Myers, 1970) are examples. Personality data are also obtained from behavior on other types of tests, such as the pupil's approach to a difficult task in an aptitude test.

Career Maturity or Development

In recent years, substantial progress has been made in the area of identification and measurement of specific factors that indicate one's status in the process of achieving career maturity. These factors or dimensions for school-age youth have been identified by Super (1974, p. 18) as planfulness (attitudes of concern and planning for the immediate and distant future), exploration (attitudes about the use of resources for learning about work), cognitive information (about job requirements, working conditions, and others), decision making (how you do it), and reality orientation (self-knowledge, suitability of choice). Crites (1974, p. 25) has specified four dimensions: career-choice competencies (how to decide, amount of information obtained); career-choice attitudes (importance of the task of deciding); realism of career choice (how much it is in line with abilities); and consistency of career choices (in related families and at a consistent level).

Specific factors are related to specific age levels. The preceding examples are suitable for high school and college individuals, but others are needed for adults. Sheppard (1971) and Walls and Gulkus (1974) inventoried past vocational decisions to specify four dimensions that represent male adult vocational maturity: involvement in the vocational-choice process, orientation toward work, independence in decision making, and preference for vocational-choice factors.

For his measurement of adult vocational maturity, Super (1977) modified the five factors he had identified as measuring the vocational maturity of school-age youth. Although the basic factors are the same, the tasks, the areas to be explored, and the information needed are different for adults. In the measurement process, part scores are derived for the stages of exploration (about ages fourteen to twenty-five), establishment (about ages twenty-five to forty-five), maintenance (about ages forty-five to sixty), and decline (about age sixty on). Each of these stages has three areas of concern relating to completed, currently faced, and anticipated tasks, that is, indicating the individual's current involvement with tasks of these stages (Super, Zelkowitz, and Thompson, 1975).

Westbrook (1976), emphasizing cognitive aspects, specified the following factors for measuring career-choice competencies, one dimension in Crites's four-dimensional model:

1. Fields of work (the individual knows occupations in various fields)
2. Job selection (the individual can select occupations for a hypothetical pupil)
3. Working conditions (the individual is aware of the working conditions of various occupations)
4. Education required (the individual knows the extent required for a wide range of occupations)
5. Attributes required (the individual knows the abilities, interests, and values required for various occupations)
6. Duties (the individual can identify what various jobs entail)

A total score combines these separate factors into a rating for the dimension.

One other approach involving cognitive factors identifies the dimensions of knowledge of work habits and work application procedures (Yen and Healy, 1977). Results of research suggest that these two factors increase with work experience.

Research has supported the utility of the factors Super proposed for those at the high school and college levels as well as for adults. Although instruments designed to assess these factors are considered to be at the experimental stage of development, research data have shown their practical utility for counseling and guidance.

Crites's (1974, 1978c) inventories have been published and are widely used. Scales have been designed to measure two dimensions of the four he postulated. A substantial amount of research on the attitude scale has been carried out; results suggest that it is useful for assessing career-maturity attitudes for people of high school age. There is a question, however, of its adequacy for college students. A number of research studies have been done on the competency test, and it holds promise of serving as a useful measure of one of the four major factors of career maturity.

Research on Sheppard's adult scale has been limited, but it has been shown to differentiate groups that are assumed to be unlike in career development and to be related to occupational values of various levels of maturity. Westbrook's Cognitive Vocational Maturity Test (Westbrook and Mastie, 1974) also has been the subject of considerable research and has been shown to be useful for screening, diagnosis, and evaluation in connection with career-development and career-education programs. The test has been incorporated into the American College Testing Career Guidance Program and the Assessment of Career Development published by Houghton Mifflin (American College Testing Program, 1974; Noeth and Prediger, 1978).

Substantial progress is being made in specification and measurement of career-development factors. Most of the instruments described here are now being tested in a variety of situations, and their usefulness is being verified. Specific studies are also being carried out to determine their applicability to minority groups, women, and those with varying degrees of commitment to work (Super, 1974). These measurements should become some of the most valuable techniques in career guidance.

Achievement

Progress in school courses, social skills, and vocational proficiencies are types of achievement. Tests, as well as school marks, may be used to assess academic achievement. Work samples and trade tests represent two ways to assess vocational proficiency. Past achievement is one of the best indications of future performance, particularly in the academic area, and is an important factor in career development. The pupil who has a serious deficiency in achievement will find many career avenues closed.

An example of the relevance of this factor to an occupational group is shown in Figure 3.1. General Education Department, or GED, and Specialized Vocational Preparation, or SVP, indicate the achievement levels necessary. The three factors in GED are *reasoning development, mathematical development,* and *language development,* and the scale ranges from a high of 6 to a low of 1; high levels of achievement in these three areas are needed for the occupation in the illustration. SVP indicates that between two and ten years of specialized preparation is needed.

The trend toward basic skills and literacy testing in the schools will have an impact on career development in that it may impede some individuals' progress through school, but it will no doubt give others a higher level of competence for coping with work demands.

Home, Family, Sex, and Race

The factors included in this general area exert a powerful influence on career development. The father's occupation, for example, has considerable influence on the son's choice and is, in addition, a major determinant of the socioeconomic level of the family (Krippner, 1963). Occupational and educational values and roles are substantially influenced by home and family. Barnett (1971) found that home and family factors were related to the career commitment and career implementation of college women. Theories typically recognize the role of the early home life in the formulation of needs, values, and occupational stereotypes, and some give it considerable weight. Subcultural pressures and rewards are transmitted to the child through the home, and the resulting patterns of behavior may enhance or retard career development. Patterns may cause severe problems for the disadvantaged, who have few if any opportunities to learn to cope effectively with career-development tasks (Gordon, 1968, pp. 140–141).

The impact of sex on career development has only recently become a source of widespread concern. Problems in this area have existed for many years, of course, but social awareness, research, and writing have increased so much in the past decade or so that the issue merits special treatment. Race presents a somewhat similar situation. Concern about the unique career-development problems related to race has grown considerably in recent years; the needs and problems of this issue also merit special attention (see Chapter 4).

Handicaps

Physical, mental, and social handicaps may sometimes influence career development more as a result of public attitudes than because of actual occupational limitations. Although attitudes cause problems in the occupational placement and adjustment of the physically and mentally handicapped, they may provide an even greater barrier to career development for the socially handicapped. Sex, race, age, and national origin may not be viewed as *handicaps,* yet they may limit the individual's educational opportunities and success in job seeking. The social handicaps of the disadvantaged tend to lock them into a cycle of low-level jobs. The former prison inmate, for instance, may find suitable employment difficult or impossible to obtain. Although recent legislation is aimed at reducing discriminatory practices, physical and mental handicaps have effects on career development that range from mild to drastic. (Chapter 4 includes a more extensive discussion of the career-development problems and needs of those with handicaps.)

Education

Ginzberg (1972) is among those who have urged that more attention be given to the effects of social institutions on career development. The school, as one of the major social institutions for youth, may facilitate or retard the individual's progress toward career success. Career roles are influenced by the school, and stereotypes, particularly of sex-linked careers, are reinforced (Berstein, 1972). The relationship of social class and school progress has been documented repeatedly since Hollingshead's Elmtown study (1949). Job-bound pupils do not see the school as concerned about them or as offering relevant career-planning assistance (Betz, Engle, and Mallinson, 1969). The educational establishment, K–college, is the avenue through which some individuals make effective strides in career development and in which others encounter obstacle after obstacle.

Economic Conditions

Economic conditions may be among the most pervasive factors in career development. Opportunities, the structure of the work world, the effects of technology, the impact of international actions such as an oil embargo, the effects of taxpayer revolts, and income levels are major influences on the choice of education and work. The phasing out of such projects as the space program and changes in federal financing of social service activities have reduced job openings and caused individuals to change career plans. If career education provides for more efficient dissemination of occupational-opportunity information, economic conditions should have an even greater impact.

THE ROLE OF JOB SATISFACTION

The individual's success and satisfaction with the jobs he or she obtains are major elements in career development, for example, in accomplishing developmental tasks, meeting needs, and making good decisions. Each theory either explicitly or implicitly considers dimensions of job satisfaction. Super (Super, Kowalski, and Gotkin, 1967, pp. IX 7–IX 8) has specified occupational and career success as criteria for validating measurements of vocational maturity. These dimensions provide a helpful way to think about job satisfaction. The major elements are as follows:

1. Satisfaction with career plans
2. Continued self-improvement through education and work
3. Success in obtaining and holding jobs
4. Economic self-sufficiency
5. Becoming established in a satisfactory occupation

Specific criteria, such as the opportunity to utilize strengths, attainment of the occupational level desired, stability of employment, and achievement of career goals, are subcategories. The Career Pattern Study research (see Chapter 2) has been quite specific in defining the nature of occupational success; the dimensions it specifies are correlated with data from other job-satisfaction research.

Summaries by Pallone, Rickard, and Hurley (1970, 1971) report trends and major findings of studies of job satisfaction and indicate that such familiar factors as salaries and wages, types of supervision, and fringe benefits still relate to satisfaction. Little evidence, however, was found to support the two-factor concept of job satisfaction, which sees one set of factors as satisfiers and a second set as dissatisfiers.

Since this theory hypothesizes that intrinsic factors involving self-actualization are primarily satisfiers and that job context factors tend to be dissatisfiers, verification would be quite significant for career development. Research, however, tends to support the position that the *same* factors may operate as satisfiers or dissatisfiers (Crites, 1969, p. 520). Although later research has not found such factors as interest, aptitude, and tenure to be highly relevant to job satisfaction, the bulk of previous research does in fact tend to identify these as important (Crites, 1969, pp. 515, 525; Super and Bohn, 1970, p. 79). Less support has been found over the years for personality characteristics. Pallone and others (1970, 1971) suggest that sources of satisfaction may derive more from the work situation than from the personality of the worker. Kaplan suggests that just having a job is a potent source of satisfaction for many workers; not everyone wants to be creative or have responsibility. Sears (1977) found that as early as age thirty, indications of lifelong work satisfaction are evident.

Self-esteem appears to be one of the major factors in work satisfaction. Feelings of accomplishment and opportunities to be one's own boss serve as a basis for the building of self-esteem on the job. In a large-scale study, workers rated personal-satisfaction types of factors, such as interesting work and adequate help and equipment to get the job done, highest in importance (O'Toole, 1973, pp. 12–13, 17). The importance of the relationship between satisfiers provided by the work situation and the needs of the worker is being investigated. Evidence is accumulating that matching worker needs to occupational satisfiers does result in job satisfaction (Gay, Weiss, Hendel, Dawis, and Lofquist, 1971, pp. 54–55). This approach supports the hypothesis that personality needs are important in job satisfaction.

One particularly important career-development question is whether or not there is a relation between school preparation and job satisfaction. Johnson and Johnson (1972) found that being in an occupation related to high school preparation contributed to job satisfaction.

A summary of the major factors in job satisfaction illustrates its relationship to career development. The following are most significant:

1. Supervision and relations with the supervisor
2. Salary and wages
3. Fringe benefits
4. Occupational aptitudes and general ability
5. Relationship of job to preparation
6. Occupational interests
7. Tenure

Two new aspects of job satisfaction merit special attention. One is the effort to humanize work by emphasizing such conditions as security, individuation, and democracy (Herrick, 1975). The other is the way leisure is used to meet needs not realized in work (Adams and Stone, 1977). These two aspects are certain to become more visible in career-guidance practices.

The relation of job satisfaction to career development provides a way to approach accountability. School programs that lead to job success and job satisfaction would certainly fulfill long-range accountability criteria.

SUMMARY

Factors such as aptitudes, interests, and socioeconomic level have been given various weights by different career-development theories. To understand and apply such theories, it is necessary to become familiar with the nature and assessment of these factors. Improvement is needed in the utilization of measurement data if they are to be useful in facilitating career development and planning. The influential factors in career development are aptitudes (including academic aptitude or intelligence), occupational interests, personality characteristics, career-development achievement, home and family, sex, race, economic factors, and handicaps. Job satisfaction is an aspect of career development and provides a way to assess the effectiveness of school programs and to establish accountability measures. Theories of career development should incorporate concepts of job satisfaction, leisure, and the effects of sex and race.

PROJECTS AND EXPERIENTIAL ACTIVITIES

1. Review the theories outlined in Chapter 2 to estimate the importance each gives to the factors discussed in this chapter.
2. Estimate your status in regard to each of the factors that applies to the individual and the influence each has had on your plans.
3. Take a battery of aptitude, interest, and other tests and relate the results to your own career development. For example, compare your career interests with your present goals.
4. Interview workers at several different occupational levels—professional, trade, service, and unskilled—to determine the main work satisfiers for each. See if you can determine a relationship between satisfactory performance on the job and job satisfaction.
5. Interview a worker about feelings about his or her job. First, find out how well the individual likes the specific job. See if there is a difference in satisfaction between using skills or competencies and the total job setting.
6. Interview an employer to learn what his or her establishment does to enhance the employees' job satisfaction.
7. Take one or more of the career maturity/development inventories mentioned in this chapter. Note the questions raised and judge how well they apply to you at your present stage of development. (For example, note that questions may be designed for the high school individual.)

8. Form small groups in which each person identifies the first, second, and third factor in job satisfaction. Each group should report its results to the class, noting similarities and differences in groups.

9. Form small groups in which each person ranks (and gives the reason for a ranking) one other individual high, average, or low on the career-development factors of one of the theorists—Super, Crites, Westbrook, or Sheppard—without identifying the person ranked. Put the unsigned rankings in a stack and then have a member select and read one ranking. See if group members can guess who the rankings apply to. After a few minutes' discussion, the teacher will reveal which person the ranking is supposed to fit.

10. Discuss and illustrate measures of career development for the class. Then, using small groups, ask each group to prepare a ten-item test of vocational maturity for the counselor-preparation program. (Suggestion: What would be the appropriate stage of development for the first-quarter student? The last-quarter student?) Ask each group to report its results. Also, give its group rating on the scale. In addition, as each group reads its scale, have other class members score themselves on each item.

11. Read one or more of the cases in Studs Terkel's book *Working* and discuss in small groups the positive and negative factors brought out by the interviewee. Which ones appear to be the most influential in the individual's job choice and satisfaction?

ADDITIONAL REFERENCES

Brown, Duane. *Students' Vocational Choices: A Review and Critique.* Boston: Houghton Mifflin, 1960. This book is particularly helpful in conjunction with this chapter, as it summarizes a tremendous amount of research on factors that influence career development from preadolescence through the adult years.

Crites, John O. *Vocational Psychology.* New York: McGraw-Hill, 1969. A discussion of factors related to career development is provided in Chap. 6, and occupational satisfaction is covered in Chap. 11.

Herr, Edwin L. *Decision-Making and Vocational Development.* Boston: Houghton Mifflin, 1970. Chaps. 3 and 4 give concise and relevant summaries of the factors affecting career development.

Isaacson, Lee E. *Career Information in Counseling and Teaching.* 3rd ed. Boston: Allyn & Bacon, 1977. The author provides a comprehensive review of factors influencing career choice and development in Part 2. Chap. 3, "Psychological and Physical Factors," is useful reading for this chapter. Chap. 4, "Sociological and Economic Factors," is an interesting review of a very important area and includes some aspects of the sociology of work.

Super, Donald E. *The Psychology of Careers.* New York: Harper & Brothers, 1957. Part 3, on factors in career development, is one of the most complete references on the subject. More recent material should also be consulted, however.

————, ed. *Measuring Vocational Maturity for Counseling and Evaluation.* Washington, D.C.: National Vocational Guidance Association, 1974. The best single source of information on the measurement and use of dimensions of vocational maturity. Chap. 13, "Retrospect, Circumspect, and Prospect," provides a quick overview. Most of the instruments discussed in this chapter are covered in detail, although recent developments are not included.

Zytowski, Donald G. *The Influence of Psychological Factors Upon Vocational Development.* Boston: Houghton Mifflin, 1970. Chaps. 3 through 7 cover the factors affecting vocational choice and development and provide one of the most useful references available on the topic. This book is highly recommended.

4

Career-Development
Needs of Special Groups

GOALS

1
To describe the special groups with whom the counselor
may work.

2
To explain the unique career-development and guidance needs
of these groups.

3
To emphasize the importance of being sensitive to the
characteristics and needs of special groups without
stereotyping them.

4
To explain why specific career-guidance and counseling
strategies should be used with members of special groups.

THE CLIENTELE OF CAREER COUNSELORS has expanded to the extent that many who formerly were neglected or overlooked are now being assisted. The NVGA/AVA position paper emphasizes this trend by pointing out that there is "increasing national concern with the need to develop all human talent, including the talents of women and minorities" (1973, p. 6). The ACES statement expresses its concern in even more clear-cut terms. All counselors should have knowledge of and competencies in "the unique career development needs of special client groups (women, minorities, handicapped, disadvantaged, and adults) and the skills necessary to assist them in their development"[1] The importance of this area of competency and concern for the counselor cannot be overemphasized. It has emerged only in recent years and is certain to expand considerably in the future. This chapter presents an overview of these special groups.

THE SPECIAL GROUPS

Any group can be defined as special—adolescents, dropouts, rural dwellers, high achievers. The term can easily be expanded to the point where it loses all meaning. In this chapter, those groups with unique career-development needs are singled out for discussion. For the most part, the groups are based on social-psychological-racial-sexual conditions. These groups are primarily ones that need better understanding and are often neglected. Their career-development needs often require special emphases in provision of services. These groups include women, minorities, disadvantaged individuals, mid-life and older persons, handicapped individuals, and the gifted and talented.

Sue (1977, p. 5) supports the need to understand the behavior, needs, and goals of specific groups but warns against the danger of building stereotypes in which group members are regarded as all alike. Broad generalizations are needed as the backdrop against which to identify and accept the individuality and uniqueness of each person. But reading about group characteristics tends to accentuate the danger of stereotyping, and if the potentially negative results of reading are to be balanced, personal contact with individuals of each group is needed.

Women

As a group, women can be further divided into subgroups with special other needs—such as returnees to the job market, blacks, and widows. Farmer and Backer (1975, p. 138) point out the need for personal contact with members of these subpopulations so the counselor can become aware of special needs. For example,

---

[1]L. Sunny Hansen, "ACES Position Paper: Counselor Preparation for Career Development/Career Education," *Counselor Education and Supervision,* 17, No. 3 (1978), pp. 168–179. Copyright 1978 American Personnel and Guidance Association. Used by permission.

women re-entering the labor force often lack self-confidence, up-to-date skills, and know-how for job searches. Black women differ in occupational attitudes from white women and from each other according to social class. Those who are better educated have less fear of success than white women and are much more self-confident and career motivated than black women at lower socioeconomic levels. Recently divorced or widowed women suffer from a sense of helplessness and lack of confidence in handling their own affairs (Farmer and Backer, 1975, pp. 118–147).

Participation of women in the labor force has far outdistanced the development of appropriate guidance services and equitable treatment insofar as pay and advancement opportunities are concerned. In mid-1977, approximately 40 million women were in the labor force, amounting to over 40 percent of the entire work force in this country. Almost half the women over sixteen years of age were employed. More than one-third of the mothers of children under three years were involved in paid work outside the home. But women's median earnings were only about half that of men. Males with high school diplomas earn about the same as women with college degrees. Young women starting out get jobs of the same type as those held by women who have been working for some time, a result of a narrow range of opportunities and limitations on advancement (Wirtz, 1975, pp. 29, 128–129).

Social Attitudes

Despite women's extensive involvement in the work world, misconceptions about their efficiency and productivity abound. Some typical ones are shown in the following list:

The Myth and The Reality[2]

THE MYTH	THE REALITY
1. A woman's place is in the home.	Homemaking itself is no longer a full-time job for most people. Goods and services formerly produced in the home are now commercially available; laborsaving devices have lightened or eliminated much work around the home.
2. Women aren't seriously attached to the labor force; they work only for extra pocket money.	Today, more than half of all women between eighteen and sixty-four years of age are in the labor force, where they're making a substantial contribution to the nation's economy. Studies show that nine out ten women will work outside the home at some time in their lives.

[2]Women's Bureau, Employment Standards Administration, U.S. Department of Labor. *The Myth and the Reality*. Washington, D.C.: Superintendent of Documents, U.S. Goverment Printing Office, 1974 (revised).

Of the nearly 34 million women in the labor force in March 1973, nearly half were working because of pressing economic need. They were either single, widowed, divorced, or separated or had husbands whose incomes were less than $3,000 a year. Another 4.7 million had husbands with incomes between $3,000 and $7,000.

(The Bureau of Labor Statistics estimate for low standards of living for an urban family of four was $7,386 in the autumn of 1972. This estimate is for a family consisting of an employed husband age thirty-eight, a wife not employed outside the home, an eight-year-old girl, and a thirteen-year-old boy.)

3. Women are out ill more than male workers; they cost the company more.

A recent Public Health Service study shows little difference in the absentee rate due to illness or injury: 5.6 days a year for women compared with 5.2 for men.

4. Women don't work as long or as regularly as their male coworkers; their training is costly—and largely wasted.

A declining number of women leave work for marriage and children. But even among those who do leave, a majority return when their children are in school. Even with a break in employment, the average woman worker has a work-life expectancy of twenty-five years as compared with forty-three years for the average male worker. The single woman averages forty-five years in the labor force.

Studies on labor turnover indicate that net differences for men and women are generally small. In manufacturing industries, the 1968 rates of accessions per 100 employees were 4.4 for men and 5.3 for women; the respective separation rates were 4.4 and 5.2.

5. Married women take jobs away from men; in fact, they ought to quit those jobs they now hold.

There were 19.8 million married women (husbands present) in the labor force in March 1973; the number of unemployed men was 2.5 million. If all the married women stayed home and unemployed men were placed in their jobs, there would be 17.3 million unfilled jobs.

Moreover, most unemployed men do not have the education or the skill to qualify for many of the jobs held by women, such as secretaries, teachers, and nurses.

Such attitudes clearly indicate the problems women face, problems that must be overcome if productive, effective career development is to take place.

Social attitudes exert a persuasive effect on women's roles, ambitions, and achievements. As Wirtz points out, *"The problems women encounter in the world of work warrant basic revision in the early socializing processes that shape boys and girls alike in their senses of identity and their ranges of life expectations"* (1975, p. 131). The socializing process tends to direct girls toward traditional "female" occupations—nurse, secretary, elementary school teacher. Newspapers, magazines, radio, television, school textbooks, and a host of other materials and activities tell girls that certain occupations are not suitable, that less achievement is expected of them than of boys, and that if their achievement is high, particularly in math, science, and technical areas, they will be less feminine. Counselors themselves are not without attitudes that limit women's career development (Bingham and House, 1973). Changing the perceptions and customs of society is a difficult but needed step, and one that would certainly eliminate many barriers that now exist.

Removal of barriers is proceeding along several fronts—legislation, women's organizations, and educational programs. Title IX of the Education Amendments of 1972, a landmark legislative step, is one of a series of congressional actions aimed at ending sex discrimination. It prohibits sex discrimination in educational institutions receiving federal financial aid (Sandler, 1977). The effects of Title IX are already being demonstrated in women's increased admission to and participation in higher-education programs. But the transition from school to work, in terms of equal pay and opportunities for advancement, is still filled with obstacles.

Research Information

Much of the currently available research and theorizing has not considered the wife and mother facets of the female role (Richardson, 1974, pp. 137–138). However, patterns have been described in ways that help in planning, and there are some useful data on women's career maturity. Richardson (1974, pp. 138–139) suggests three patterns: a continuous, uninterrupted work pattern that may also include homemaking; a work-oriented pattern that involves a compromise between home and work; and the homemaking pattern, in which work, if done at all, is more or less incidental. Little is know about vocational maturity in terms of these types of role development.

In his postulates about the career development of women, Zytowski (1969) takes the position that there are fundamental differences between the career developments of men and women, and he includes, among other things, differences in roles, developmental stages, and other factors affecting participation. The postulates highlight these differences, although Zytowski states that he hopes social and technological developments will make the postulates obsolete. There is some evidence that women's career patterns are not predictable by data available at the time of college entrance but can be predicted from data available five years later. Education and marriage are the most effective predictors; that is, more education and an unmarried status are most typical of those who are work oriented (Wolfson, 1976).

Super's (1957, pp. 76–78) formulation of women's career patterns, which consists of four patterns shared with men and three patterns unique for women, are still among the more useful. The four shared patterns are stable, conventional, unstable, and multiple trial. Those unique to women are interrupted (for marriage and child-rearing), stable homemaking (with homemaking viewed as a career), and double track (work while raising a family).

Several attempts have been made to apply career-development theories to women's career development (Vetter, 1973; Farmer and Backer, 1975, pp. 122–138). Although many of the aspects are relevant, such as developmental stages, demands of the work world, and importance of needs in career choice, none has been shown to be well suited as an explanation of women's career development or as a basis for assessing career maturity.

One recently identified factor that merits attention in a review of needs of women is the motive to avoid success, also called *fear of success* (Farmer, 1976; Esposito, 1977). This learned attitude tends to lower occupational aspirations and direct the individual toward the traditional female occupations. Career development could be hampered unless this attitude is altered through education and guidance, particularly through provision of situations in which individuals can come into contact with high-achieving female role models.

More should be done to reduce or eliminate sex bias in career information and psychological measurements, particularly those that assess occupational interests (Betz, 1977), although mere recognition of the problem represents a major step forward. Some progress has been made in identifying biased test items, developing scoring methods to reduce bias, and constructing bias-free instruments. The new DOT has been edited to reduce sex bias as much as possible. Still, bias in occupational information has been found in both governmental and privately produced publications, including computer-guidance programs (Farmer and Backer, 1975, pp. 151–154).

Personal Needs

Another group of career-development needs centers around the internal attitudes and knowledge of women themselves. Girls and women need to know that societal pressures exist, that they affect others' perceptions, but that they can be handled. Obviously, attitudes such as self-limiting of choices and viewing traditional occupations as appropriate or "right" are the product of the socializing that Wirtz would change. But these attitudes have been adopted by many girls and women, and they are used as guides for planning. For example, a girl who has the ability and interest to become an engineer may reject this option because her family and friends do not think women can or should be engineers. Male attitudes are often significant in the occupational plans of women. A boy friend or husband may not believe that a girl should work at all, work in a male-dominated occupation, or equal or exceed his occupational level.

Data from the National Assessment (Aubrey, 1978; Miller, 1978; Mitchell, 1978b; Westbrook, 1978) show some sex differences in career attitudes and competencies at ages nine, thirteen, and seventeen, and in adulthood. For example, at age thirteen, girls tend to reflect sex stereotyping in their knowledge of occupations (Aubrey, 1978, p. 16). In addition to personal attitudes about what is appropriate, many girls know about only a narrow range of occupations. Thus, there are lessened opportunities because of a lack of knowledge about options.

Minorities

There is a tendency to use the terms *minority* and *disadvantaged* as if they are synonymous, or at least approximately the same. The position taken here, however, is that although there may be some overlap of groups classified by each term, the meanings are different. Minority groups in the United States may include some disadvantaged members, and membership in a minority group often results in some sort of discrimination, but disadvantaged status, involving social, economic, and educational deprivation, is another matter. The career needs of these two groups are therefore considered separately in this chapter.

The large minority groups in this country are blacks, Hispanic Americans, American Indians, Puerto Ricans, and Asian Americans. Others exist, but these are the major ones and also the ones with the most pressing career needs.

The two major problems that each of these groups experience are discrimination and stereotyping. These problems are related because a stereotyped view of a group is often the basis of discrimination. Even with little or no stereotyping, language, customs, and values may make communication and mutual understanding more difficult than they should be. For example, the Hispanic American who has difficulty understanding English will experience career-development problems regardless of attitudes about his or her ethnic group.

Blacks

This minority group is by far the largest. For a number of reasons, including early status in this country, blacks have encountered the most pervasive barriers to career development. Their unemployment rate is high, particularly for young males. Discrimination in regard to college admission has been pronounced in past years and still operates in more or less subtle ways. Affirmative-action policies provide some assistance for those who have had inferior preparation and limited social-cultural advantages, but this approach is itself embroiled in controversy.

Unemployment and underemployment are conditions faced by all groups, but particularly by blacks; the unemployment rate for young black males is approximately 40 percent. Underemployment is more difficult to determine, but it appears to be quite widespread. Moreover, in an economic slowdown, blacks (as well as other minority group members and also women) are the first to be laid off. These conditions make progress on the job difficult or impossible, and they also limit opportunity for the type of exploratory activities that are needed in career development.

Social Attitudes   Stereotypes and the attitudes they evoke in connection with blacks have great impact. One stereotype, for example, is that blacks are lower in intelligence than whites. Another is that they are not dependable. A third is that blacks do not like hard, exacting work. There is no valid support for any of these beliefs, but they show the potential effect that a rigid way of thinking has on the career development of those about whom the attitudes are held.

Research Information   Lack of accurate, comprehensive, up-to-date career information is another problem, but it is not unique for blacks or any other minority group. The minority culture does not provide models and exploratory experiences, media information tends to emphasize the white, middle-class majority, and educational materials fail to show minority group members in a variety of types and levels of occupations; the information base for planning, therefore, is biased. There are also questions about how well measures may assess the vocational maturity of minority groups because of educational and social differences (Locascio, 1974; Osipow, 1976). Thus, it may be inappropriate to use these instruments in guidance. An opposing point of view states that it is essential to use norms reflecting the cultural expectations of the middle class; they show what must be accomplished. Either course of action has advantages and disadvantages.

Results of the National Assessment Career Development Survey of attitudes and information (Aubrey, 1978; Miller, 1978; Mitchell, 1978b; Westbrook, 1978) reveal areas that appear to need remediation. For example, at ages nine and thirteen, blacks appear to be lower than whites in occupational knowledge (Aubrey, 1978, p. 16; Miller, 1978, p. 15); at age seventeen, they are lower than whites on matching occupations with physicial characteristics and skills (Mitchell, 1978b, p. 14); and as adults, they have less information than whites about occupations (Westbrook, 1978, p. 16). Although race does not differentiate results in all cetegories, there are suggestions that some aspects of career development, including the informational one mentioned, need considerably more emphasis.

Personal Needs   Models that represent successful black individuals in a variety of occupations are lacking. Seriously considering an occupation in which one sees no successful workers of similar ethnic group makes excessive demands on one's self-confidence. Models are needed to make the possible seem probable.

Helping services provide one avenue for meeting career-development needs, but quite often they are not utilized, or counselors may not be attuned to the unique requirements or may not understand the cultural characteristics of minority groups.

Many counselors reflect an educationally oriented, middle-class background and lack of associations and experiences may not provide the conditions they need for growth. Thus, a clear-cut career-development need is for readily available teachers and counselors who understand the barriers blacks meet and can appreciate their need to achieve an identity.

Hispanic Americans

This minority group, the second largest in the United States, is composed of several subgroups, including Mexican Americans and Cubans. These subgroups tend to be concentrated in urban areas near the countries from which they originally came—Cubans in Florida and Mexican Americans in Texas and California (Ruiz and Padilla, 1977).

Social Attitudes   Most Hispanic Americans are members of a specific religious group, have strong family ties, demonstrate clearly defined sex roles, exhibit a tendency to hold onto their language, and prefer personal and informal contacts, but these tendencies do not necessarily cause career-development problems. But they may tend to foster stereotypes and cause difficulties in obtaining jobs and progressing in occupations and in making use of counseling and guidance services (Brammer, 1978). The employment and educational levels of this population are lower than those of the general population; Hispanic Americans do more menial work and receive lower pay than the general population (Kuvelsky and Juarez, 1975, p. 280; Ruiz and Padilla, 1977). They have few role models, and outside pressures, such as those resulting from stereotypes, generate stress (Ruiz and Padilla, 1977). Occupational horizons are restricted (Greco and McDavis, 1978), and in a sense, individuals are caught between two cultures that differ significantly in the way they view work. However, Hispanic Americans want to share in the "American dream" (Kuvelsky and Juarez, 1975, pp. 280–283) as much as anyone else. School dropouts as well as graduates have educational and social aspirations; leaving school before graduation is typically due to home and other problems rather than lack of interest in education (Kuvelsky and Juarez, 1975, pp. 277–281).

Personal Needs   Relatively low utilization of counseling and guidance services is partly due to cultural factors (help is often provided by the extended family), communication problems, attitudes toward these types of help, and the fact that no one counseling program is suitable for all subgroups included within the Hispanic American population (Ruiz and Padilla, 1977; Brammer, 1978; Greco and McDavis, 1978).

Counselors, except for those from the same ethnic group or those who have extensive contact with the culture, no doubt frequently do not understand the difficulties faced by Hispanic Americans in coping with relatively commonplace facts about the world of work and dealing with the stereotypes and discrimination they encounter in education and occupations.

American Indians

There are about 800,000 American Indians in this country and about 50 percent of them are concentrated in five states (Youngman and Sadongei, 1974). Their career-development needs are acute, because the gulf between the reservation and the major culture seriously retards their knowledge of the world of work. The major career opportunities are outside the reservation, a situation that accentuates differences between cultural values, customs, and preferred lifestyles. For example, Indians believe that it is bad manners to speak of one's accomplishments (Youngman and Sadongei, 1974). Thus, not only is there a need to understand job-getting skills and to broaden occupational horizons but also to understand how personal preferences and attitudes relate to the world of work and work-getting customs and expectations.

Changes in national policy from paternalism to self-determination tend to highlight existing career-development problems and to generate new ones. Spencer, Windham, and Peterson's (1975) study of the Choctaws illustrates the existing and potential difficulties, although their results do not necessarily apply to other tribes. (Little research has actually been done on career-development needs of Indians.) There is a tendency to select occupations that are highly visible on the reservation, such as teacher, and to assign prestige to technical, skilled, and semiskilled occupations, with accessibility being the basis for the preference. What is needed is a variety of models in various occupations, a bicultural education that will facilitate coping with life both on and off the reservation as well as dealing with those in other walks of life, and realistic information about occupational opportunities (Spencer, Windham, and Peterson, 1975, pp. 216–218). More information is needed about other Indian groups, since there is considerable diversity among them. Even so, it is likely that most face the problems of whether to leave the reservation and of deciding which occupations offer realistic and rewarding options.

Puerto Ricans

Puerto Ricans share problems of unemployment, menial jobs, insufficient education, and few successful career models with other minority groups (Christensen, 1977). They face the typical prejudices directed at the foreign, and their culture is "either ignored or lumped together with others under the rubric of 'Spanish-speaking'" (Christensen, 1977, p. 413). Moreover, they prefer to use family members for assistance rather than utilize counselors, especially in Puerto Rico.

The family influence, however, particularly the mother's influence, may be eroding for those who have come to the United States. In fact, Puerto Ricans, like some other minorities, may be caught between two cultures, and the strong, extended family influence that existed in their country may not have the motivating effect it once had. As Christensen (1977) says, however, many with whom the counselor will work will be recent arrivals, and so it will be important to work with and through the family to facilitate career development to meet the needs identified earlier.

Asian Americans

The career-development needs of Asian Americans have received little attention until recently. As Sue (1975, p. 97) points out, however, current work has done little to dispel stereotypes and to provide the basis for helping with career development. However, it is apparent that some career-development problems are shared with other minority groups, but some major ones are unique for this subgroup. Moreover, although historical conditions affect the present status of all minority groups, these conditions are of critical significance for Asian Americans (Sue, 1975, pp. 99–104). Antecedent factors and present characteristics have helped to build a stereotype of successful coping and have obscured the cultural conflicts, inequities in opportunity, discrimination, and isolation that exist. Contrary to a number of other minority groups, Asian Americans have attained a high level of education. But because of cultural characteristics and the reactions of others to personal traits (restraint of strong feelings, language facility), the occupational options have been narrowed, in that math and science are emphasized (Sue, 1975, pp. 98, 105–106).

Although relatively little information is available about career interests, Asian Americans appear to show a preference for concrete, impersonal, and practical occupations. A concentration on these areas and perceived barriers to other areas do much to limit opportunities (Sue, 1975, pp. 108–109). In some unknown way, these conditions affect the critical exploratory process in career development and limit decision processes. It is logical to assume that both stereotypes and perceived opportunities have a decided effect on mid-career changes. Moreover, the three coping styles that Sue (1975, pp. 103–104) identifies—traditionalist, rejectionist, and "Yellow Power"—have implications for career development. As data are accumulated and related to career-development theory, bases for facilitative intervention should become available.

Disadvantaged Individuals

This group is discussed separately because these individuals can come from any racial or subcultural group. Any individual may be so deprived economically, socially, or culturally that the classification applies. At times the term *disadvantaged* is applied loosely to a very large number of persons; for example, Joe is called disadvantaged because his parents do not have the funds to send him to college. Beverly is disadvantaged because she is failing Spanish. Mark is disadvantaged because his accent is different from others in the part of the country in which he lives. These are relatively mild levels of handicap; the term is used here to indicate those persons who are so adversely affected by the cumulative effects of deprivation that they are not able to cope with the social and economic demands of the society.

Racial and subcultural factors can be involved if language, work attitudes, and occupational values prevent school progress or occupational success. Thus, minority group members may end up in this category in disproportionate numbers. But minority and disadvantaged status are not synonymous.

The career-development needs of the disadvantaged run the gamut from an awareness of the place of work in one's life in a technological society to adapting to and being successful on the job. Problems often arise because of basic skill deficiencies in school. Poor achievement and a tendency to drop out are typical during the middle-school and early high school years. Finding a job presents severe problems, but keeping and making progress in it are even more difficult. The older disadvantaged person faces even more difficult problems in terms of career development—in addition to the failure to accomplish the earlier career-development tasks, age is a further limiting factor.

Research Information

Not a great deal is known about the career-development process of the disadvantaged. In particular, the crucial phase of transition from school to work is not understood; this process is currently one of the high-priority research areas. Measurement instruments may not be effective in assessing interest, abilities, and personality characteristics because of background attitudes about testing and test-taking skills. Assessment of the vocational development of dropouts or those bordering on this classification can not be done effectively with currently available instruments (LoCascio, 1974; LoCascio, Nesselroth, and Thomas, 1976). But it has been found that low-socioeconomic-level teenagers (not the severely disadvantaged, however) tend to be more realistic in terms of job expectations than in plans (Thomas, 1976). Dropouts also are consistently lower than in-school pupils on knowledge, attitudes, and skills that will help them in getting and keeping a job (National Assessment of Educational Progress, 1978, pp. 1, 3–4). Dropouts and potential dropouts, however, are not necessarily severely disadvantaged, although the latter group would be expected to be far more deficient than pupils in general in occupational knowledge and other career-development skills and attitudes.

The disadvantaged also exhibit poor work skills and poor work attitudes acquired from associates who cannot adjust to work, emotional problems that interfere with work adjustments, and lack of necessities such as transportation (Miller and Oetting, 1977). The work-adjustment hierarchy of Miller and Oetting (1977) clearly illustrates problems of career development of the severely disadvantaged. The eleven levels shown in Table 4.1 are similar to developmental tasks; earlier ones must be successfully achieved before later ones can be undertaken.

Three major groups make up the levels shown in this table:

1. The acquisition group, which includes the steps to be accomplished prior to going to work
2. The maintenance group, which includes the four levels to be mastered to meet conformance requirements of the new job
3. The upgrading group, which includes the cycle of competence development that leads to advancement

This developmental hierarchy indicates that work adjustment is a series of steps, and it specifies career-development needs.

Table 4.1 The hierarchy of work adjustment

		Level	Successful Outcome
(C) Upgrading Group	Level XI	High-level job maintenance	Satisfactory and satisfied in new position
	Level X	Job or promotion getting	Gets promotion or better job
	Level IX	Advancement readiness	Applies for promotion or job
	Level VIII	Orientation for change	Motivated to seek improvement
(B) Maintenance Group	Level VII	Skilled performance and job satisfaction	Permanent employment except for job changes
	Level VI	Interpersonal relations	Long-term employment
	Level V	Entry-level performance	Still employed beyond usual probation period
	Level IV	Job conformance and adaptation	Not fired and does not quit in first few days
(A) Acquisition Group	Level III	Job getting	Obtains job
	Level II	Job readiness	Applies for job
	Level I	Work orientation	Motivated to seek work

Source: Gene Oetting and C. Dean Miller, "Work and the Disadvantaged: The Work Adjustment Hierarchy," *Personnel and Guidance Journal*, 56, No. 1 (1977), 29–35. Copyright 1977 American Personnel and Guidance Association. Used with permission.

Personal Needs

Personal deficiencies reflect a lack of several major characteristics considered essential for career development. There is typically a lack of models exhibiting positive work attitudes, roles, and goals. Deprivation in occupational exploratory and educational opportunities and work experience is also present. Self-concept related to career and educational achievement is low, and level of vocational maturity is below that of a comparable age group. Poor verbal skills and other characteristics associated with disadvantaged status set up barriers to educational and training programs and help generate feelings of alienation and rejection. Negative forces may be present that inhibit early career development. Thus, the school not only must help the student but also attempt to change the parents, guardians, or institutions, or at least lessen their negative influences.

Mid-Life and Older Persons

Although concern about special groups in general is a relatively recent phenomenon, interest in those at mid-life and older in particular is probably the most recent. *Newsweek* magazine considered this concern of enough popular interest to present a feature article, "The Graying of America." The authors of that article (Clark and Gosnell, 1977) point out the startling increase in the average age of Americans, which in part accounts for the increasing interest in them as their political power grows with their numbers. At the time of the first census in 1790, half of the American population was under sixteen years of age. In 1970, the median age was twenty-eight; by 2030, it is expected to be near forty. It is predicted that one out of every six Americans will be over sixty-five at that time. Hence, drastic social, economic, and political changes are anticipated in the years ahead. Some of these changes are already here: recent legislation in the form of the Age Discrimination in Employment Act Amendments of 1978 (PL 95-256) has removed the compulsory retirement age for many groups of workers, and there appears to be a definite trend to eliminate age as an employment and retention factor for the world of work. And the Career Education Incentive Act has recognized the importance of expanding services beyond the high school to include adults.

Research Information

Research on the career-development needs of mid-life and older persons has increased greatly. The process of career development throughout the life span has come under increased scrutiny, and techniques for measuring career maturity have been developed. Services are being established and related issues such as lifelong education are being debated.

Super's Adult Career Inventory (see Chapter 3) covers this period, with "establishment" including the years from twenty-five to forty-five and "maintenance" covering the forty-five to sixty period. For each period, the career-development tasks are specified (the major mid-career tasks are given in Chapter 2 in the discussion of Super's theory). Ginzberg has recently revised his career-development theory to emphasize the importance of keeping options open throughout the life span as opposed to being in an irreversible occupational path. Crites has recently turned his attention to adult career development, giving weight to dimensions that relate to career adjustment, particularly how the worker copes with frustrating experiences. The needs and problems of the period have also captured the interests of researchers in developmental psychology.

Even though there is considerable research and theorizing about the career-development needs of this period, a great deal still needs to be done to specify them more precisely and to determine what should be done to help individuals at mid-life and at older ages. There is enough data, however, to make a start in specifying the major career-development needs of the mid-career years.

The characteristics of the middle years give a good indication of career-development needs. It is a time of possible mid-life crisis in which there is considerable ambiguity; the individual may have difficulty in making decisions, particularly if elements of moral judgment are involved (Peatling, 1977). Security needs tend to increase, reaching a peak around age fifty, if job stability seems to be shaky (Osipow, 1976). There may be a period of renewal or of career readjustment in which self-concept, values, and goals change (Betz, 1977). At mid-life, people may discover that leisure can help them find a sense of accomplishment and self-fulfillment that other aspects of life, including work, have failed to provide (McDaniels, 1977). Economic independence and increased free time may open up opportunities previously unavailable. But work is a potent factor in the quality of life for men and women at the mid-life period (more important for women than men), and this appears to be a prevailing attitude. At the same time, however, work is a greater source of stress for men than women. Adverse economic conditions appear to have a greater impact on men at the mid-life period than at other times (Heddesheimer, 1976; Sheppard, 1978, pp. 123, 173–174).

The needs of re-entry women are of special concern. Those who return to work after a period of absence often lack self-confidence about academic and work skills and have special needs relating to child care and job-search skills. Exploration of opportunities is a major need. Divorced or widowed women may be much more concerned with economic, security, and emotional needs than with actualizing potential, at least in the early stages of re-entry into educational programs or work (Farmer and Backer, 1975, pp. 139, 146).

Mid-Career Changers

The career-development needs of the mid-life group are thrown into sharp relief by the characteristics of mid-career changers, their reasons for changes, and the gains expected. Not all changes result from desperation; often they arise from shifts in roles, goals, and attitudes toward life. In some cases, men who have been more mastery oriented tend to move to a passive, introspective point of view, while women in passive or nurturing roles shift to ones that are more mastery oriented

(Heddesheimer, 1976). An interesting way to look at career changes is portrayed by Heddesheimer in a description of multiple motivations. Table 4.2 shows four possible career patterns resulting from varying degrees of pressures from self and environment. Other factors stimulating mid-life changes are the impetus of the women's movement on female participation in the work force, the effects of technology on occupations, unemployment, the relationship of life expectancy to retirement, and the effects of the psychological dimensions of the mid-life period (Entine, 1976).

Other attempts to classify job changers by motives have been made. One interesting typology, derived from the study of a small number of those who left highly demanding executive positions to set up their own businesses, showed that men could be grouped by high and low success orientation and tough- and tender-minded dispositions (Thomas, Mela, Robbins, and Harvey, 1976). Using these two dimensions, the changers could be classified as "Counterattackers," "Flankers," "Retreatists," and "Own Drummers." These categories are fairly self-explanatory—for example, "Own Drummers" are low in achievement/success orientation, tender-minded, independent, and show some concern about others. In the small sample used, there were as many of this "Own Drummer" category as the other three combined. Other data suggest that changes may sometimes take place because of life structure changes (Thomas, 1977). For a variety of reasons not well understood, a number of individuals who frequently consider changing jobs actually do not do so. There is some evidence that if the think-about-changing individual does become unemployed, he or she makes a more successful adaptation than those who do not consider changing (Sheppard, 1978, pp. 123, 173–174).

The bases for mid-life career changes are just beginning to be uncovered and clarified. The future is certain to witness more detailed studies of this age range and the establishment of counseling and guidance services (Harrison and Entine, 1976). Moreover, expanded opportunities, such as lifelong educational programs, are being given increasingly serious consideration (Mondale, 1976).

Pre- and Postretirement Individuals

The career-development needs of the pre- and postretirement group are also capturing the attention of theorists and researchers. Need levels change during this period; there appears to be less need satisfaction in regard to security and keeping up with what is happening than at other ages (Osipow, 1976). Sinick (1976) identifies adjustment, use of time, and more mundane matters, such as budgeting and housing, as needs of older persons. Since the retirement age is likely to be lowered in the years ahead, this group's needs are expected to be more visible. It is estimated that by the year 2000, the average age at retirement will be fifty-five. At the same time, it is anticipated that there will be approximately 55 million persons over this age in the population (Entine, 1976). Thus, there will be a large number of active, healthy individuals who are looking for new types of work, interesting leisure activities, productive educational experiences, part-time work, or volunteer

Table 4.2   Career patterns and Mid-life changers

Pressures from the Environment	Pressures from Self	
	Low	*High*
Low	Routine career	Self-determined career
High	Situationally determined career	Self-directed accommodation career

SOURCE: Janet Heddesheimer, "Multiple Motivations for Mid-Career Change," *Personnel and Guidance Journal*, 55, No. 3 (1976), 109–111. Copyright 1976 American Personnel and Guidance Association. Reprinted with permission.

involvements. Job changing will be important for many; it is not exclusively the province of the mid-life group.

Unfortunately, Social Security regulations presently limit the work participation of older persons. This state of affairs contrasts with practices in some other countries that provide for gradual retirement for some workers, special vocational training for older workers to help them retain present jobs or transfer to new ones, and assistance to those who may be laid off if the employer encounters financial difficulties. In some other countries there is, in fact, an active searching for alternatives to laying off older workers. In some cases, specific jobs are set aside for older persons (Sheppard, 1978, pp. 219–225).

Inevitably, changes in the average age of the population, changes in compulsory retirement age, an increase in life expectancy, affirmative action policies, and changing attitudes about older persons will have a profound impact on the career development of this age group. This life period is receiving increasing study, and useful data for social policy, guidance, and counseling services are already available. Much more needs to be done, however.

Handicapped Individuals

There is a difference between a handicap and a disability. An individual may be physically, emotionally, intellectually, or physically impaired or disabled, but the condition in itself is not an occupational handicap unless it interferes with employment or job progress. Although not all impairments and disabilities are handicapping, most are. Thus, both are included in this section.

Legislation and public concern are becoming increasingly focused on the rights to education and work of disabled people. The provisions of the Education for All Handicapped Children (PL 94-142)—a landmark legislative step in the education of the handicapped—reflect sensitivity to the educational development needs (which are part of the career-development process) of the learning disabled and identify two major needs of those with disabilities, regular association with nonhandicapped persons and programs designed to meet unique needs. The number of preschool and inschool handicapped individuals alone is estimated at around 8 million (Brenton, 1977, p. 7). Counselors will have increased responsibilities for evaluating the potential of disabled pupils, planning programs, monitoring programs, working with parents, and consulting with teachers (Humes, 1978). These responsibilities may require role modifications and quite likely will be added to the usual counseling duties with no additional provision of funds or time. But the time has come when the career-development needs of this special group, like the others already mentioned, are a major concern of guidance workers.

Generalized Needs

Remediation, therapy, or other needed types of assistance to help the individual be as effective as possible in training or educational programs are essential. Help could involve assessment of strengths and limitations, assisting the individual to relate abilities to areas of interest, treatment (therapy, prosthetic devices) to reduce limitations as much as possible, and counseling to help the individual accept conditions that cannot be reduced or eliminated. Each of these services calls for a high level of expertise on the part of counselors and medical personnel; many of the usual assessment instruments may not be adequate to tap the potential of the disabled individual.

The task of planning programs based on needs and in tune with occupational goals is complicated. Batelaan's program (Wheeler, 1978) for the vocational education of the handicapped began with a needs survey to identify those to be served. Categories of disablement were then established. They included mental retardation, visual impairments, hearing impairments, emotional disturbances, learning disabilities, physical limitations, and speech problems. In addition to surveying all those responsible for the education, rehabilitation, and job placement of individuals with special needs, information was obtained from the individuals themselves and their parents. Then, for each of the preceding categories, an advisory unit was set up that included an employed adult with the disability, a parent of a student with the disability, and a person who worked with pupils having the disability. The advisory units had as their goals removing barriers to employment, devising effective ways to provide career-related experiences, and assisting with employment and use of resources. Workshops for personnel involved were conducted for preparation, input, and planning. One outcome of the workshop task of specifying staff usage included a statement that the counselor's role should be that of liaison among various personnel and a resource for pupil information from files.

The sequence of goals set up by Batelaan and Wheeler's program illustrates the career-development needs of handicapped pupils and also shows that those needs are similar to those of all pupils:

SCHOOL LEVEL OR TIME	NEED
1. Elementary	Career awareness
2. Middle	Work adjustment
	Prevocational skill training
	Career exploration
3. Secondary or postsecondary	Vocational training
	On-the-job training
4. When ready	Vocational placement
	Follow-up
	Additional training or retraining

This program emphasizes the need for acceptance and understanding as a person and as a productive worker by employers and cooperation by parents in work adjustment. Handicapped persons have demonstrated over and over again that they can perform well in work in which their limitation is not a critical factor. It is important, therefore, that others, particularly employers and family members, do not adopt a condescending attitude.

Experiences that enable the individual with limitations to understand his or her interests and abilities are particularly important. They must be well planned so the individual will be able to explore a range of occupations wider than the usual ones considered satisfactory for the stereotype of the handicapped person. Job development may be needed to tailor work for the individual. In some cases, sheltered workshop exploration and work may be needed for the severely handicapped. But the theme of PL 94-142—that it is desirable to use the least restrictive learning environment—is a useful principle for occupational placement.

Personal Needs

Handicapped individuals need an understanding of the opportunities, problems, and demands of various occupations and occupational goals with a realistic expectation of what will be encountered. This endeavor necessitates a type of information that is not available to the extent needed, although the ability profiles in the *Dictionary of Occupational Titles* are a useful aid. It is particularly important for handicapped persons to plan educational and training programs in line with occupational goals, since they have less flexibility in moving about in the world of work.

Additionally, these individuals may also need related services. Instruction in personal care and grooming, advice on clothing, and transportation may be required to enable them to cope successfully with job demands and human relations in the work setting.

The Gifted and Talented

Quite often there is a general feeling that the gifted and talented do not need any special attention; they can take care of their own career planning. Their exceptional abilities enable them to understand far more about themselves and occupations than the average person can, and they can find suitable education and work with little or no difficulty. In my opinion, these and similar concepts are myths—myths that can do a great deal of harm to the career development of those who are gifted and talented.

Social Attitudes

Having superior intellectual ability or an exceptional amount of talent in an area or field of study does not necessarily mean that an individual has greater than normal self- or occupational knowledge, decision skills, or satisfying career goals. In fact, with so many possible options and the likelihood of scattering energies in all directions, it is reasonable to conclude that such an individual needs *more* career-planning assistance than the average person—at least as much as a person with a handicap. But the allocation of funds and facilities clearly shows that this is not a widely accepted position; special programs for the talented receive a minuscule amount of support compared with that for those with handicaps. Exceptions do occur; in time of national emergency, programs often are established to identify and prepare those with above-average ability. The National Defense Education Act, which set up a program to identify individuals with scientific talent and help them obtain higher education, is an example.

Research Information

Although no single criterion can be used to identify giftedness, those so designated usually have above-average though not necessarily superior general ability, task commitment, and creativity (Renzulli, 1978). Multipotentiality often causes problems in career choice. Moreover, there is a desire to do more than just find an occupation—gifted individuals want one that will provide for self-expression and an opportunity to implement a philosophy of life (Hoyt and Hebeler, 1974, pp. 104, 115).

Personal Needs

Career-development needs of the gifted and talented may be grouped in five broad areas: personal work and study skills; self-understanding and self-direction; understanding of relevant opportunities in the work world; understanding and support by others; and challenge in educational programs and materials. However, relatively little is known about career development and career maturity of members of this group. For example, does the exceptionally talented individual typically go through the phase of exploration at about the same time that others do?

Those with exceptional ability may find that they can accomplish school assignments with relative ease and may be well ahead of classmates in some subjects. One result may be development of some very ineffective work skills; the individual has no need to be efficient. Later, if competition increases or there is a desire to achieve in line with ability, the poor learning habits get in the way. The tasks can become frustrating for someone who has up to that time felt highly capable and competent.

Self-understanding, particularly accurate assessment and acceptance of special abilities, may be lacking. Feedback may be confusing and objective input difficult to obtain. Accounts of the lives of exceptional achievers are full of examples of discouragements and negative opinions from others. This seems to be particularly true in the case of women with talent in nontraditional fields and minority group members in almost every field. At times, the indications of special abilities are so at odds with the individual's self-perceptions that they are not acceptable—the response may be, "I don't believe it. There must be a mistake."

In addition, the problem of overchoice further complicates effective use of information: it may be difficult to give up some options to concentrate on a few. Some talents may be in highly specialized fields and occupational roles, where avenues of progression are not as clear-cut as for more everyday work; a certain amount of risk may be involved in earning an adequate income. Role models of successful individuals are particularly important in helping with career planning, but they may not be available in the school or community.

The possession of exceptional abilities may cause problems with parents, peers, and teachers. If the individual's talents are quite out of line with those of family members, there may be strong support or equally strong negative attitudes. The level of verbal communication, topics of interest, and ways of spending time may be so different from peers and siblings that alienation results. The individual may not fit in the classroom for a number of reasons; for example, he or she may not be interested in the typical assignments. Teachers and others sometimes believe that the gifted individual is teetering on the borderline of emotional breakdown. Counselors may have had little or no experience in working with these individuals and may not provide effective help.

One of the major reasons for difficulties with others, particularly teachers, results from the fact that many learning activities and materials lack appeal and provide no challenge. For example, the individual may be far ahead of others in verbal skills, general knowledge, reading ability, or artistic achievement. At times, the individual may deliberately or unintentionally challenge the teacher; some instructors feel threatened by this and react negatively. Even if the special abilities are recognized and accepted, there may be no programs that will facilitate their development. If there are programs, those who have been severely culturally deprived may be so deficient in basic skills, they will be overlooked in the identification process or will have to spend most of their time on remedial work.

Much more concern should be given to the career-development needs of the gifted and talented. The assumption that they can get along leads to neglect of the individual who is entitled to assistance and may very well result in the loss of a valuable social contribution.

SUMMARY

The recognition of the career-development needs of special groups—women, minority group members (blacks, Hispanic Americans, American Indians, Puerto Ricans, and Asian Americans), disadvantaged individuals, persons at mid-life and retirement stages, the handicapped, and the gifted and talented—is not new, but it has only recently moved into a major position in the concern of theorists, researchers, practitioners, politicians, and the general public. A host of social, ethical, economic, and political conditions has contributed to the emergence of this concern. Research data on needs and effective helping strategies have been accumulating and have made possible the establishment of services; it is obvious, however, that we are only at the threshold of knowledge of the career-development processes of the special groups most in need of career-development assistance.

The counselor needs to have an understanding of the characteristics and career-development needs of these special groups, to enhance this knowledge by use of research studies as well as personal contacts, and to guard against stereotyping. The overriding need is to regard each person, regardless of group membership, as a unique individual.

PROJECTS AND EXPERIENTIAL ACTIVITIES

1. Interview several members of one of the special groups discussed in this chapter. Identify the top three career-development needs.
2. Make up a brief list of the career-development needs of a special group. Use information from this chapter, additional reading, and your own experience for its construction. If possible, ask one or two members of that group to check the list to see if they agree with you.
3. Arrange to participate in a setting (such as volunteer work) in which you will have personal association with members of a special group. Keep a diary to record what you have learned.
4. Class members representing subgroups can identify the career-development needs they have experienced and discuss how representative they consider them to be.
5. Make up a number of signs for a classroom activity, each sign indicating membership in a specific group discussed in this chapter. Put a sign on each person's back, without the student's knowledge of what is on the sign. Then have members circulate and interact in accordance with the identifying signs. After a period of interaction, tell members what groups were included and ask them to deduce the one with which they were identified. Discuss the feelings involved in being a member of a special group.

6. Invite individuals who are members of several of the special groups and who are active in guidance and counseling with these groups to meet with the class. Use committees to prepare lists of career-development barriers for various special groups discussed in this chapter, with the visiting representatives sitting in with appropriate committees to serve as consultants. Each committee should report to the class.

7. Use a fantasy exercise (see item 10 in "Projects and Experiential Activities," Chapter 1) to have the class members imagine they are members of a subgroup not represented in the class, or use role reversals—males take female roles, whites take black roles. Utilize a workday for the fantasy trip. Emphasize reactions of others, rewards and negative features of the work, and opportunities for advancement. At the conclusion, discuss feelings about the experiences and what was learned about the subgroup.

8. Make up a list of groups with special needs (those in this chapter and any others you wish to add). Then ask small class committees to assume that they each constitute a counseling service that can serve only one of the groups. They must eliminate the others in rank order. When the eliminations have been completed, ask each committee to report, giving reasons for each choice and for selecting the one group to help.

ADDITIONAL REFERENCES

Drier, Harry N., and Edwin L. Herr. *Solving the Guidance Legislative Puzzle.* Washington, D.C.: American Personnel and Guidance Association, 1978. A review and analysis of legislation affecting guidance and counseling that indicates growing concern for special groups and specifies the types of programs mandated by Congress. See especially Chap. 5 on "special populations."

Farmer, Helen S., and Thomas E. Backer. *Women at Work: A Counselor's Sourcebook.* Los Angeles: Human Interaction Research Institute, 1975. A very useful source book for understanding career-development needs of women of all ages. Strategies for helping are described, and an excellent list of program resources is given.

Foster, June C., Claire Olsen Szoke, Pelly M. Kapisovsky, and Leslie S. Kriger. *Guidance, Counseling, and Support Services for High School Students with Physical Disabilities.* Cambridge, Mass.: Technical Education Research Center, Inc., 1977. A book designed specifically for the school counselor to provide assistance in the new responsibility of working with pupils with physical disabilities and chronic health problems. It contains an overview of a number of disabling conditions and a comprehensive discussion of helping strategies. Several chapters deal specifically with career development and closely related topics. State and national resources are identified. (A detailed state resource list is available.)

Hoyt, Kenneth. *Career Education Needs of Special Populations.* Washington, D.C.: U.S. Government Printing Office, 1976. An excellent review of the career-guidance needs of minority, low-income, gifted and talented, and handicapped individuals.

Kahl, Anne, Jon Q. Sargent, Philip L. Rones, Chester C. Levine, John Franklin, and Lois Plunkert Terlizzi. "Working with Older People." *Occupational Outlook Quarterly,* 20, No. 3 (1976). Although the major thrust of this special journal issue prepared by the Bureau of Labor Statistics for the Administration on Aging of the U.S. Department of Health, Education and Welfare is on occupations that involve working with the elderly, it is a valuable source of information about the career-development needs of this increasingly important subgroup.

Mangum, Garth L., G. Donald Gale, Mary L. Olsen, Elwood Peterson, and Arden R. Thorum. *Your Child's Career.* Salt Lake City, Utah: Olympus Publishing Co., 1977. Chap. 9, "The Handicapped and Career Education," is an excellent review of career development for the handicapped for anyone working with this special group, not just parents. The point is clearly made that career development is essential for all those with disabilities and that the home and school have major responsibilities for facilitating its growth.

Peters, Herman J., and James C. Hansen, eds. *Vocational Guidance and Career Development.* 3rd ed. New York: Macmillan, 1977. A number of excellent articles on special groups (mid-life and older adults, disadvantaged, and women) are included in this book of readings.

Picou, J. Steven, and Robert E. Campbell, eds. *Career Behavior of Special Groups.* Columbus, Ohio: Charles E. Merrill, 1975. An excellent series of articles and reports on needs of special groups. It covers theoretical questions and issues and has comprehensive reviews of the needs of a number of subgroups plus discussions of policy issues and programs. This book is one of the most useful references available on this topic.

Sinick, Daniel, ed. "Counseling over the Life Span." *Personnel and Guidance Journal,* 55, No. 3, (1976), 100–101. A special issue that is a valuable reference for understanding counseling needs over the life span. Although the focus is not specifically on career development, much of the content inevitably touches on this facet of life.

Super, Donald E. *Career Education and the Meaning of Work.* Washington, D.C.: U.S. Government Printing Office, 1976. An excellent review, in booklet form, of life stages, developmental tasks, and career patterns and how these factors relate to the career development of special groups.

Verheyden-Hilliard, Mary Ellen. *A Handbook for Workshops in Sex Equality in Education.* Washington, D.C.: American Personnel and Guidance Association, n.d. Although this is primarily a manual for workshop leaders in Sex Equality in Guidance Opportunities, a project of the American Personnel and Guidance Association, several sections are valuable for information on career needs of women. See especially pp. 9–18, "Workshop Leader's Backup Information" and appendixes such as Title IX of the Education Amendments of 1972 (pp. 35–54) and the Women's Educational Equality Act (pp. 70–72).

Women's Bureau. *1975 Handbook on Women Workers.* Washington, D.C.: U.S. Department of Labor, 1975. A comprehensive review of a number of factors of concern (educational and work status, legislation, resources for assistance) to those providing career guidance to women. An essential reference for the career counselor working with women.

5

The Information System

GOALS

1
To state the importance of occupational, educational, and training information for career guidance and counseling.

2
To cite major types and sources of information.

3
To explain how to judge the accuracy and appropriateness of informational materials.

4
To describe how technology is used to provide career and educational information.

5
To describe how to set up an information service in schools or other settings.

INFORMATION PLAYS A MAJOR ROLE in career development. Career-development theories emphasize its importance even at the earliest years. Even elementary school pupils begin to develop attitudes about work. Barry Brown in the fourth grade is picking up information from home and school about the high prestige of college and the professions. In high school, a lack of needed information can cause him difficulty. Willie Stephens, in the ninth grade, has a superficial knowledge of two occupations, derived from rather apathetic research in the library. Joe Prince has no information about the personal qualifications and training required for his tentative occupational preferences. This list of potential problems could be extended. You probably remember occasions when you or a friend needed information about occupations, education, or training and it was not available.

Counselors in any setting need competencies in all aspects of information used in guidance. The NVGA/AVA position paper emphasizes this need by pointing out that the world of work is becoming more complex and that information about demands, working conditions, rewards, and resources for assistance are required for good career decisions. (see Appendix). The ACES statement of counselor competencies further highlights the critical importance of skills in this area. Counselors should have knowledge of and competence in "career-information resources and the necessary skills to assist teachers, administrators, community-agency personnel, paraprofessionals, and peers to integrate this kind of information into the teaching-counseling process."[1] A thorough understanding is a prerequisite to helping others utilize materials and technology.

Although this area is extremely important and much has already been done, information resources have not matched counselors' needs. Wirtz's (1975, p. 171) proposal of a system to report national and local occupational opportunities is a step in the right direction; the demand for information is one of the major themes of his timely book. The gaps that currently exist make it even more imperative that the most effective use possible be made of what is available.

This chapter is about various types of information that should be available in the school, college, or other setting where career guidance is provided. It begins with a broad survey of work- and career-preparation opportunities. Types of information are described, and ways of organizing information for use by pupils and other counselees, teachers, parents, and counselors are reviewed. Discussion on how to develop the school information center concludes the chapter. The actual use of information—for example in individual and group counseling, group guidance, and career education—is covered in later chapters.

THE LABOR MARKET

Information about occupational distribution and trends, ranging from the national to the local level, is essential. At the national level, information is readily available

[1]L. Sunny Hansen, "ACES Position Paper: Counselor Preparation for Career Development/Career Education," *Counselor Education and Supervision*, 17, No. 3 (1978), pp. 168-179. Copyright 1978 American Personnel and Guidance Association. Used by permission.

in the form of the *Occupational Outlook Quarterly* (U.S. Department of Labor, 1978). This publication gives detailed information about the present situation and makes predictions for the future. Distribution data and some predictions are quite reliable. For example, the number of eighteen-year-olds entering the labor market in 1985 can be predicted quite accurately from actuarial formulas. The number working in a particular occupation or industry until the middle of the next decade is more difficult to predict accurately, but some information of this type is available (U.S. Department of Labor, 1978, p. 5). Predictions are based on the following five assumptions:

The institutional framework of the U.S. economy will not change radically.

Current social, technological, and scientific trends will continue, including values placed on work, education, income, and leisure.

The economy will gradually recover from the high unemployment levels of the mid-1970's and reach full employment (defined as an unemployment rate of 4 percent) in the mid 1980's.

No major event such as widespread or long-lasting energy shortages or war will significantly alter the industrial structure of the economy or alter the rate of economic growth.

Trends in the occupational structure of industries will not be altered radically by changes in relative wages, technological changes or other factors (U.S. Department of Labor, 1978, p. 17).

Figure 5.1 depicts the growth of the civilian labor force from 1950 to 1985. The 1985 labor force will be approximately 104 million persons, a 19 percent increase over 1976. The marked growth since 1960 results partly from the increased number of women entering the labor market. The rate for women entrants will continue to increase, but there will be a slight decline for men (U.S. Department of Labor, 1978, pp. 19–20).

The labor force occupational distribution is illustrated in Figures 5.2 and 5.3. The first shows the number of workers in major occupational groups in millions in 1976. "Operatives" include those who operate machinery and vehicles; the "clerical" group consists of those who type, keep records, and do similar work. These are the two largest groups,. although "professional and technical workers" is a close third. The *Occupational Outlook Handbook* describes trends and gives detailed information about a number of specific occupations in each of these classifications (1978, pp. 22–25). For example, under "professional" is the subgroup "counseling," and within it four specific occupations: school counselor, employment counselor, rehabilitation counselor, and college career planning and placement counselor.

Figure 5.3 portrays growth in these occupational groups for the 1976–1985 period. The greatest increase is anticipated in clerical workers, followed by service workers, excluding private household workers. This group includes a wide range of workers, from firefighters to janitors to cosmetologists. The third greatest increase is expected in craft workers (skilled workers like carpenters, machinists, and electricians). Growth in the professional and technical area, fifth in size, will be substantial—about 18 percent. Part of this growth reflects a demand for scientists

Figure 5.1   Civilian labor force growth, 1950–1976, and projected to 1980 and 1985

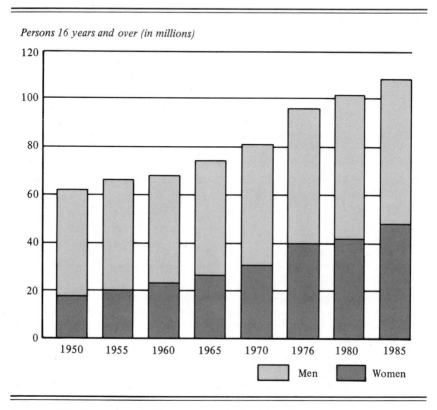

Persons 16 years and over (in millions)

SOURCE: U.S. Department of Labor, *Occupational Outlook Handbook* (Washington, D.C.: U.S. Government Printing Office, 1978), p. 19.

and engineers in energy production, transportation, and environmental protection. Private household workers and farm workers are expected to show a negative change. Even though there is a demand for private household workers, the unattractive nature of the work is a major reason for the decline. Trends toward larger farms and more efficient production methods are largely responsible for the decline in farm workers.

Several other trends of significance for the counselor are as follows:

1. Service-producing industries (trade, government services, transportation) will increasingly offer more jobs than those providing goods (manufacturing, mining).

2. The shift toward white-collar occupations will continue. They now represent almost half the total labor force.

Figure 5.2   Occupational distribution of the labor force

Workers, 1976 (in millions)

SOURCE: U.S. Department of Labor, *Occupational Outlook Handbook* (Washington, D.C.: U.S. Government Printing Office, 1978), p. 22.

3. The need for replacements in occupations due to deaths and retirements is expected to account for most job openings in practically all occupations. Growth will be a less significant factor.

4. Individuals who have a college education will continue to have a lower rate of unemployment than those who do not, and high school graduates will have a lower rate than dropouts. This is true even though the percentage of those in the labor force with four years of college has risen from 7.9 in 1952 to 16.5 in 1976, and many jobs do not require a college degree. Moreover, income will increase with the number of years of education.

5. Many occupations that have experienced the most rapid growth require vocational, apprenticeship, or community college preparation, for example, science and health technicians. In the past decade, enrollments in public vocational schools have tripled, and the number registered in apprenticeship programs has increased 40 percent.

6. Clerical workers are the largest and fastest-growing occupational group. Even though the use of computers and other technology will lessen the need for machine operators and other similar types of workers, occupations that involve personal contact, such as receptionists, will show increases.

Figure 5.3   Growth in occupational groups, 1976–1985

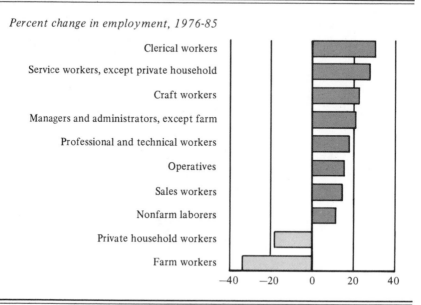

Percent change in employment, 1976-85

Clerical workers	
Service workers, except private household	
Craft workers	
Managers and administrators, except farm	
Professional and technical workers	
Operatives	
Sales workers	
Nonfarm laborers	
Private household workers	
Farm workers	

−40   −20   0   20   40

SOURCE: U.S. Department of Labor, *Occupational Outlook Handbook* (Washington, D.C.: U.S. Government Printing Office, 1978), p. 24.

A more detailed study of the world of work is needed for an understanding of these and other trends. Since the counselor is not expected to have a vast amount of detailed information at his or her fingertips, knowing where such information can be found is essential. Some of the systems described later in this chapter provide considerable assistance in locating needed information. Nevertheless, the counselor needs to know the types of information that can be retrieved and the sources from which they were obtained.

OPPORTUNITIES FOR CAREER PREPARATION

Career preparation is a complex and confusing area. New programs, new types of schools, and new emphases in traditional programs complicate the counselor's job of keeping up to date. The following list illustrates the scope of preparation programs:

1. Vocational education in public schools
2. Private vocational schools

3. Federal apprenticeship programs
4. Employer training
5. Armed forces training
6. Comprehensive Employment and Training Act (CETA)
7. Work Incentive Program (WIN)
8. Home study courses
9. Junior or community colleges
10. Vocational-technical schools and centers
11. College and university training

At the risk of being unfair to many counselors, it may be said that counselors and guidance workers tend to know little about numbers 1 through 10. The reason is obvious; educators have typically followed the academic route. Many have worked only in educational institutions and had little or no contact with other types of career-preparation programs.

The following survey of vocational-education programs focuses on some important features of each of the types just listed. Supplementary reading and experience, preferably including actual visits, will be of great help in understanding what each program does, who can profit from it, and the occupations to which it leads.

Vocational Education in Public Schools

There are usually several vocational-education programs in the high school. The two oldest are vocational agriculture and vocational home economics. These two programs have changed, however. There is more emphasis on the job market. Preparation has expanded to include a number of related occupations, such as agribusiness, child care, and clothing management. There are many home economics opportunities for boys in the latter program. Another innovation is the cooperative program, in which pupils attend school part of the day and work at a job for the remainder. Cooperative programs usually involve office work, sales work in retail establishments, and mechanical and automotive repair work. However, a number of other occupations are also included. In fact, such a program is applicable to practically all occupations for which a high school education is adequate. Names like distributive education (DE), diversified occupations (DO), vocational office training (VOT), and cooperative training (CT) are often given to cooperative programs, but the terms change with the expansion and modification of programs. Many schools are introducing exploratory programs in the junior high school and middle school. Some schools offer the option of a full-time job during the senior year, with credit toward graduation. There are many innovative approaches, such as ABLE, which involves eleven broad areas and over two hundred specific occupations (Morrison, 1970).

Learning about a school's programs is best accomplished through firsthand contact. Counselors and other staff members are often genuinely surprised to learn what is actually done in the shops, cooperative programs, and other vocational programs in their own schools when they participate in tours and orientation activities.

Private Vocational Schools

Private schools prepare pupils for a multitude of career areas, the major ones being business, trade and technical jobs, cosmetology, and barbering (U.S. Department of Labor, 1971c, p. 18). Many students prefer private vocational schools; the skill-oriented nature of the preparation seems to be one of their main appeals (Crawford, 1969). Since many private vocational schools accept students who have not completed high school, they provide good training opportunities for older unemployed persons (Belitsky, 1970).

Lists of schools are often prepared by professional and trade organizations. The *Occupational Outlook Handbook* lists the addresses of these organizations at the end of each occupational description.

Federal Apprenticeship Programs

Apprenticeship programs provide training in such crafts as carpentry, masonry, and machining. In 1971, there were approximately 350 apprenticeable occupations with about a quarter of a million trainees (U.S. Department of Labor, 1971a). Training periods range from two to four years, the entering age is about seventeen, and pay begins at about one-half of the skilled worker's wages (Stevenson, 1971). Information about programs and openings may be obtained from state employment service offices and from the Department of Labor. State apprenticeship agencies and local councils also provide information. Apprenticeship information centers (Stevenson, 1971) have been established in a number of cities. Friend (1972) compares apprenticeship training with college and concludes that much better dissemination of information about craft training, particularly in the schools, is needed. Minority group participation in apprenticeship training has increased, due largely to federal outreach programs (U.S. Department of Labor, 1971a; "Words and Figures," 1972). More opportunities for minority group members should be available in the future (Egan, 1978).

Employer Training

This type of training, excluding apprenticeships, may range from brief contacts to systematic programs that include classroom work. Little information is available about the number of persons trained or about training opportunities (U.S. Department of Labor, 1971c, p. 18; Issacson, 1977, p. 30). Direct contact with local employers is perhaps the best way to obtain information. Some organizations prepare detailed descriptive material about entry training and later programs to prepare employees for advancement. Much of this is on-the-job training, but classroom work may be included. This is an important training resource, but one that calls for local investigation by the counselor.

Armed Forces Training

The extensive training programs in the armed forces constitute a major source of occupational preparation. Furthermore, most military specialties have civilian counterparts, and work skills may be used after discharge from the service. Aids like the *Military-Civilian Occupational Sourcebook* (1978) relate military to civilian occupations.

Comprehensive Employment and Training Act, or CETA

This act, which became law in 1973, has established a new pattern for federal aid and training programs. Funds go directly from the federal government to local prime sponsors to use as they see fit to provide occupational training and placement and to promote the career development of those served. A prime sponsor may be a county, a city, or a state with a population of 100,000 or over. Grants are awarded on the basis of the number of disadvantaged individuals and the rate of unemployment. Thus, there is extensive local control—a procedure that at times provides excellent programs but that also allows waste, mismanagement, and the initiation of programs that are more controversial than helpful.

Some programs taken over by CETA may be continued if the local sponsor chooses to do so; the Manpower Development and Training Act, or MDTA, is an example. Others, such as the Job Corps, are continued under CETA. The various titles in CETA provide for an impressive array of program types designed to benefit practically any individual who is unemployed, underemployed, disadvantaged, or in need of career-development assistance.

Title I calls for establishment of planning councils to guide prime sponsors in allocating funds. Within the limits of the client population, funds are to be used to train and place people in appropriate employment. Informational and counseling services may be included.

Title II supports public-service employment programs designed to enable individuals to make the eventual transition to jobs in non–CETA-supported agencies or in private enterprise. Jobs provide needed public services and also help individuals develop skills and competencies to make the transition. Special provisions are made for Indian tribes.

Title III calls for a wide variety of training opportunities and establishment of a comprehensive system of occupational information and nationwide job-placement facilities. Special programs provide assistance to pupils who must work to remain in school and older persons who lack employment skills, summer work for youth, and assistance for older persons who are laid off from work and others who have difficulty in securing or keeping a job. All types of training are provided, and assistance to special target groups, like those described in Chapter 4, is a priority.

Besides being a major training and educational program designed for those with career-development problems, CETA was intended to put considerable emphasis on career guidance and information. APGA has expressed concern, however, that the guidance and counseling component is not receiving adequate emphasis; it recommends that this component be placed on equal status with training and placement functions. A task force on CETA has been established in APGA to communicate suggestions and recommendations to CETA and to appropriate congressional committees. The major themes of current recommendations are to include counseling assistance along with the total admission, training, placement, and job-adjustment process; to use qualified counselors to provide special services and train paraprofessionals; and to utilize CETA funds for in-school counseling (*Guidepost*, 1978; Hooper, 1978).

Work Incentive Program, or WIN

This program, not included in CETA, is aimed at helping employable individuals in families now receiving Aid to Families with Dependent Children to become economically independent. Under it, state employment services provide vocational testing, counseling, occupational training, or placement—whichever is needed. The program was extensively revised in 1973, and its emphasis is now on preparing welfare recipients for productive work. Training is designed to increase the individual's employability, and employers receive tax-credit benefits.

Home Study Courses

A great variety of courses, ranging from kindergarten through college, are offered for home study. Colleges, trade associations, and private schools are their major sources. The National Home Study Council (1601 18th St., N.W., Washington, D.C. 20009) publishes a semiannual directory of accredited private schools. Additional information may be obtained by contacting colleges and trade associations. (See "Sources of Additional Information" in the *Occupational Outlook Handbook*.)

Junior or Community Colleges

These institutions are more and more frequently identified as community colleges because, in addition to providing the first two years of work leading to the bachelor's degree, they offer two-year-or-less terminal programs in career preparation, provide adult education not related to degree work, and may, in cooperation with local business or government agencies, offer special programs to meet the needs of employees. Career-education offerings are typically quite extensive, and new programs are frequently added. Local needs are emphasized in the curriculum, since graduates more often than not work in the community. General information on public institutions may be obtained from state departments of education or local school board offices. National directories are also available; examples are listed later in this chapter.

Vocational-Technical Schools and Centers

These institutions may offer career preparation somewhat like that of the community college. Often they are tied in with the public schools, and high school pupils sometimes take related training at the vocational-technical center. Although the vocational-technical school primarily offers post–high school education, individuals who have not received diplomas are often admitted. The admission procedure usually emphasizes assessing potential for the job. Program lengths are usually computed in hours and may range from several months to two years. Centers frequently cooperate with local schools to inform dropouts and potential dropouts about career-training opportunities. Typical courses include air conditioning, refrigeration, and heating technology; automotive technology; and carpentry. Further information can be obtained from state departments of education, local school superintendents, and the centers themselves. Representative directories are given later, but information obtained locally is more up to date and comprehensive. A tour is an excellent way to learn about the programs.

College and University Training

Opportunities at this level are probably the most familiar to counselors and guidance personnel. More well-developed directories, information systems, and placement services are available for college training than for any other type of career preparation. "College Days" bring institutional representatives to high schools for face-to-face meetings with pupils. To some extent, the abundance of information causes problems, and pupils need help in understanding admission requirements, the campus atmosphere, majors, required courses, and the like.

This brief survey illustrates the almost overwhelming variety of training and educational resources available to the high school pupil. No counselor could possibly remember all the relevant details, and frequent changes in programs and other factors make an attempt at encyclopedic knowledge pointless. It is essential to know *what* is available and *where* to locate the necessary information. For example, the knowledge that such an institution as a vocational-technical center exists, and familiarity with its admission requirements and offerings is enough to begin helping the pupil to explore this training opportunity. The exploration could move on to more specific data if the pupil showed enough interest. Directories, pamphlets published by the centers, filmstrips about related occupations, and visits could be used. Such information should be organized in a system that enables both counselor and counselee to use it with a minimum of difficulty.

TYPES OF INFORMATION

Information may be printed or recorded on tapes, slides, transparencies, film, or videotapes. It can be obtained directly from persons or organizations and made available in recorded or written form. The counselee may obtain career information by talking with or observing a worker. In this section, informational media are discussed briefly, and suggestions are made on how to obtain and evaluate materials. Each of these topics could easily merit a chapter or an entire book. The purpose here is to describe each type briefly, identify some representative materials, and thus provide a first step toward further intensive investigation.

Printed, Audio, and Visual Materials

The quantity and variety of printed material in leaflets, brochures, monographs, booklets, and books is practically limitless. Industries, businesses, and professional and trade associations provide information about jobs within their areas. Private publishers of booklets (and whole information systems—see "A Survey of Systems" on page 161) produce and distribute materials that are usually of high quality. The U.S. Government Printing Office sells some of the best and most reasonably priced materials available. Luckily for the counselor, several guides make it possible to locate, select, and obtain the kinds of material needed with relative ease. Let us look briefly at the major guides.

The Occupational Outlook Handbook

This publication, often referred to as the OOH, is one of the most valuable books in career guidance and counseling. Originally prepared to provide career information for returning World War II veterans, it has become a standard reference for counselors and placement workers. One must use it to begin to understand and appreciate its tremendous value. Its coverage is more complete for sales and professional and related occupations than for other categories, and occupations included represent over nine-tenths of all workers in these occupational groups. About two-thirds of the skilled, clerical, and service workers are employed in the occupations discussed. Semiskilled, managerial, and laboring occupations are less well represented. The introductory sections to the major occupational divisions include information about additional jobs, trends, and other helpful material.

The introductory section of the handbook, "Tomorrow's Jobs," is an excellent brief overview of the world of work. The two major sections that follow constitute the body of the handbook. The first covers occupations and is subdivided into such sections as "professional and related," "managerial," and "sales." Each section is introduced by a short exploration of general trends. Specific occupations are discussed under the following headings:

Nature of the Work
Places of Employment

Training, Other Qualifications, and Advancement

Employment Outlook

Earnings and Working Conditions

Sources of Additional Information

The last section is useful for obtaining material for one's occupational and educational files.

The DOT six-digit code number (discussed in the next section) is also given. This code enables the counselor to correlate information in the DOT and the OOH.

The second section of the handbook contains discussions of some major industries, such as manufacturing, construction, and government. Representative occupations within these industries are also described—for example, "soil scientist" is discussed under agriculture. This portion of the book allows career planning to be approached from an industry-centered point of view; it answers the question "What kinds of occupations could I consider if I were interested in the aircraft manufacturing industry or in television broadcasting?"

Finally, there is an alphabetical index to occupations and industries, which helps the reader locate topics quickly and easily.

One additional feature enhances the practical utility of the materials: reprints of the sections on specific occupations and industries are available. These are well suited for filing, lending to pupils, display racks, and other similar uses.

The Dictionary of Occupational Titles, Fourth Edition

This fourth edition is the result of the U.S. Employment Service's research on the changing occupational structure in this country, and it contains a number of new features. It is a one-volume book, in contrast to the two-volume 1965 third edition, and several supplements are planned.

A second new feature is the listing of occupations on the basis of job relationships. Nine broad occupational categories are used, and the order of listing is determined primarily by the first digit in the code number assigned to each occupation. The first digit is the *occupational category;* for instance, zero indicates occupations in the professional, technical, and managerial category. An example is "occupations in social science," which is 04; the second digit indicates the professional division. The third digit indicates the specific group, of which 559 are used. Occupations are then listed in order from low numbers to high. The book also has an alphabetical list of titles, so that occupations may be looked up in this way. Descriptions of over 20,000 occupations are given, covering nearly all of those in the United States.

Several other significant changes increase the utility of the book.

1. More than 2,100 new occupations have been added and over 3,500 deleted.
2. Job definitions have been updated and verified, and codes have been changed to reflect actual worker function ratings.
3. A nine-digit code number is used for each occupation. The last three digits indicate the order of occupational titles within the six-digit group. They are

primarily for computer use; only one occupation can have a specific nine-digit code, whereas several may have the same six-digit code. (These codes are explained in more detail later in this section.)

4. Significant military occupations are now included.

5. Occupations are grouped by industry.

6. Master titles (work duties common to a number of jobs, such as "apprenticeship") are listed.

7. Term titles (titles common to a number of jobs that may differ widely in required job knowledge) are given. "Electronics assembler" is an example.

8. The coding permits the DOT classification system to be related to other systems, such as those of the Bureau of Census and the U.S. Office of Education.

Two occupational definitions illustrate the wealth of information provided by the DOT and also clarify the meaning of terms already used. At the top of Figure 5.4 is the three-digit classification for occupations in psychology. This number indicates the specific group into which the two occupations fall. The examples are "counselor" and "psychologist, counselor."

For the occupation of counselor, the first item is the nine-digit code number. The first digit, zero, indicates that the occupation is in the professional, technical, and managerial category. The second digit, 4, indicates that it is in the social science division. The third digit, 5, places the occupation in the psychology group. The next three digits indicate the degree of complexity and responsibility of the occupation in terms of data, people, and things. The lower the number, the more demanding the work. Both occupations have 1 for data, indicating they are next to the highest level. The zero for people is the highest level. The "7" for things is the lowest level of complexity.

The final three digits indicate the number of occupations with the same six-digit classification and the alphabetical position of each one. These three digits are in increments of four, for example, 010, 014, 018, 022, 026. If only 010 is used, there is one occupation with that six-digit code. In the example of counselor, there are several, as counseling psychologist has a higher number.

Following the code is the basic title, the name by which the occupation is usually known, in boldface type. The industry designation is shown in parentheses; in these examples, it is professional and kindred, which shows that the occupation occurs in a number of work settings. Alternate titles are given next; they are synonymous with the basic title but not as commonly used. Alternative titles are included in the alphabetical index to enable the occupational definition to be located.

The major section of the entry is the definition, which includes the following:

1. LEAD STATEMENT　This summarizes the data about the occupation and is followed by a colon. For the occupation of counselor, the lead statement is "Counsels individuals and provides group education and vocational services."

2. TASK ELEMENT STATEMENTS　These explain the specific tasks workers perform to accomplish the job described in the lead statement. Several are given in the two illustrative definitions—for example, "Collects, organizes, and analyzes informa-

Figure 5.4   Entries from the *Dictionary of Occupational Titles*

---

045   OCCUPATIONS IN PSYCHOLOGY

This group includes occupations concerned with the collection, interpretation, and application of scientific data relating to human behavior and mental processes. Activities are in either applied fields of psychology or in basic science fields and research.

045.107-010   COUNSELOR (profess. & kin.) guidance counselor; vocational adviser; vocational counselor.

Counsels individuals and provides group educational and vocational guidance services: Collects, organizes, and analyzes information about individuals through records, tests, interviews, and professional sources, to appraise their interests, aptitudes, abilities, and personality characteristics, for vocational and educational planning. Compiles and studies occupational, educational, and economic information to aid counselees in making and carrying out vocational and educational objectives. Refers students to placement service. Assists individuals to understand and overcome social and emotional problems. May engage in research and follow-up activities to evaluate counseling techniques. May teach classes. May be designated according to area of activity as COUNSELOR, COLLEGE (education); COUNSELOR, EMPLOYMENT DEVELOPMENT DEPARTMENT (education); COUNSELOR, SCHOOL (education); COUNSELOR, VETERANS ADMINISTRATION (gov. ser.).

045.107-026   PSYCHOLOGIST, COUNSELING (profess. & kin.)

Provides individual and group counseling services in universities and colleges, schools, clinics, rehabilitation centers, Veterans Administration hospitals, and industry, to assist individuals in achieving more effective personal, social, educational, and vocational development and adjustment: Collects data about individual through use of interview, case history, and observational techniques. Selects and interprets psychological tests designed to assess individual's intelligence, aptitudes, abilities, and interests, applying knowledge of statistical analysis. Evaluates data to identify causes of problem of individuals and to determine advisability of counseling or referral to other specialists or institutions. Conducts counseling or therapeutic interviews to assist individual to gain insight into personal problems, define goals, and plan action reflecting interests, abilities, and needs. Provides occupational, educational, and other information to enable individual to formulate realistic educational and vocational plans. Follows up results of counseling to determine reliability and validity of treatment used. May engage in research to develop and improve diagnostic and counseling techniques. May administer and score psychological tests.

SOURCE: U.S. Department of Labor, *Dictionary of Occupational Titles,* 4th ed. (Washington, D.C.: U.S. Government Printing Office, 1977), pp. 48–49.

tion about individuals through records, tests, interviews, and professional sources to appraise their interests, aptitudes, abilities and personality characteristics, for vocational and educational planning."

3. "MAY ITEMS"   Many definitions contain sentences beginning with "may." This terminology indicates that in some settings, these duties may be required. For example, in some jobs, counselors "may engage in research and follow-up activities to evaluate counseling techniques."

Italicized words are defined in the glossary; these words usually are those used in a way that is different from the everyday definition or meaning. Finally, one or more undefined related titles may be given; these are preceded by the statement "May be designated according to. . . ."

Practice with the DOT is the best way to become familiar with the information it provides and to make effective use of it in guidance and counseling.

NVGA Publications

Each issue of the *Vocational Guidance Quarterly,* or VGQ, published by the National Vocational Guidance Association, contains an annotated listing of current career information, classified by type of publication and reading level and rated for quality. Materials from private publishers, businesses and industries, professional and trade associations, and the federal government are included. Prices are given, and much free material is listed. Films and filmstrips are also described and evaluated, although not in every issue. At intervals, this information is compiled in book form as the NVGA *Bibliography of Current Career Information* (1978).

The series of pamphlets and books prepared under NVGA direction, some of which have already been mentioned, are of outstanding value to the counselor. The following are particularly relevant here:

Looking at Private Trade and Correspondence Schools (1963), a guide for pupils considering this type of training.

How About College (1968), a guide to help pupils choose and apply to a college.

Career Decisions (1969), a guide for pupils and parents on how to make career decisions.

How to Visit Colleges (1972), a guide for pupils visiting a campus to learn about a college's environment and facilities.

In addition, Inform, the National Career Information Center of APGA, provides several services, including a newsletter, information bibliographies based on career clusters, and special publications on such topics as career opportunities for those in vocational-technical training. The emphasis is on identifying hard-to-find materials, describing effective information-dissemination methods, and providing material and suggestions to meet special needs and problems as they arise in the profession. A listing of all APGA and NVGA publications may be obtained by writing to the American Personnel and Guidance Association, Two Skyline Place, Suite 400, 5203 Leesburg Pike, Falls Church, Virginia 22041.

Department of Labor Women's Bureau Publications

Career information specifically relating to the problems and needs of women is becoming more readily available. There is, however, a continuing shortage. The publications of the Women's Bureau are timely and valuable and include fact sheets, booklets, and career guides. A recent brochure-poster, "Get Credit for What You Know," gives information about obtaining course credits through high school and college proficiency examinations. The *1975 Handbook on Women Workers* (U.S. Department of Labor, 1975) is an invaluable source of information for counselors. The address is Women's Bureau, Employment Standards Administration, U.S. Department of Labor, Washington, D.C. 20210.

Other Materials

Several types of printed information and several outstanding films will be mentioned because they represent innovative attempts to meet current needs. One of these projects, *Vocational Biographies,* aims at providing in brief leaflet form more of the sociology of work than is usually included in career information. No data are available on the effectiveness of this approach, but the materials appear to be stimulating and well prepared. (They are published by Vocational Biographies, Sauk Center, Minnesota 56378.)

The twelve Project WERC films, titled *Why Not Explore Rewarding Careers?*, are available from the American Personnel and Guidance Association. They provide in an exciting way information about occupations that do not require a college degree. Descriptive material and scheduling information may be obtained from the Film Department of APGA.

Two government publications are of special interest. One is a series of articles on relatively little-known occupations carried in the *Occupational Outlook Quarterly* under the title "You're a What?" For example, the spring 1977 issue contains a description of the work of a topiarist (a person who shapes plants by training, cutting, and trimming). Another is a series of publications by the Bureau of Labor Statistics (1978), prepared in collaboration with state employment security agencies, which gives the occupational outlook for a large number of occupations until 1985, estimates of the number employed in 1974, the number being prepared, the number of annual openings to 1985, and a narrative description of trends.

Directories

A number are available for colleges and universities, community colleges, and vocational and technical schools. There are also computerized directories that match students and colleges. Publishers should be contacted for descriptions and prices of the most recent editions. Representative directories are

The College Blue Book, published by Macmillan Information, Macmillan Publishing Company, Inc., 200D Brown Street, Riverside, New Jersey 08370. The new sixteenth edition includes listings of technical, trade, paraprofessional, and business schools; narrative descriptions of colleges; degrees offered by college and subject; and scholarships, fellowships, grants, and loans.

Barron's Profiles of American Colleges, published by Barron's Educational Series, Inc., 113 Crossways Park Drive, Woodbury, New York 11797. Two volumes contain college descriptions and an index to major areas of study. Regional editions providing in-depth descriptions of institutions are also available.

Barron's Guide to the Two-Year Colleges in two volumes is available from the same publisher. The books provide detailed descriptions of colleges and data to help with occupational program selection.

A different approach to the educational directory is the in-depth treatment provided by *Barron's College Profile Series.* These are booklets published by Barron's Educational Series that contain detailed information about the campus, admissions, costs, academic atmosphere, and student activities of various colleges.

Directories are also published by professional and trade associations. For example, the Accrediting Commission for Business Schools, 1730 M Street N.W., Washington, D.C. 20036, distributes a free list of accredited institutions. The National Association of Trade and Technical Schools, 2021 L Street N.W., Washington, D.C. 20036, also makes available a list of accredited private-residence schools offering job-oriented training.

College-placement services utilize computerized directories to locate openings for applicants. (These are discussed in Chapter Twelve). Some additional college information services are reviewed in a later section of this chapter.

Resource Persons and Agencies

These sources are primarily for local information, although one may have recourse to a regionally or nationally based individual or organization. Workers, employers, retired persons, and specialists in a career area who have a comprehensive knowledge of an occupational field are often valuable resources. Resource agencies include governmental offices such as the employment service, apprenticeship councils, chambers of commerce, service clubs, private employment services, and unions. The list could be greatly extended; the examples illustrate the typical sources found in the community.

EVALUATING INFORMATION

Although some help in selection is available in the NVGA publications already mentioned, the counselor will, in the final analysis, have to depend on his or her own evaluation of the "best buy" for his or her situation.

The NVGA publication *Guidelines for the Preparation and Evaluation of Career Information Media* (NVGA, 1971), although designed for publishers and others who prepare information, is a basic source of criteria for the purchaser and user. Films, filmstrips, and literature are covered. For each type, criteria are given for materials on individual occupations, occupational fields (for example, clerical and mechanical), and industry occupations (for example, the electronics industry).

The discussions, organized by such topics as "work performed," "work setting," and "potential personal rewards," contribute to an understanding of the scope of career information, as well as provide criteria for selection. A useful technique for evaluation is to arrange criteria as a scale for which quantitative ratings are given.

Date of publication, sources of information, and the qualifications of the publisher are important criteria. One point that the counselor should keep in mind is the *recruiting* purpose of much material. Businesses and industries are interested in presenting themselves positively.

A recent publication, *Guidelines for the Preparation and Evaluation of Non-print Career Media* (NVGA, 1977) gives criteria for the evaluation of films and similar materials, stressing content, institutional design, bias, and quality of information. A modification specifically designed for the evaluation of simulated material of all types has been prepared by Weinrach (1978).

A SURVEY OF SYSTEMS

The term *system* is used rather loosely here; it is applied to any standardized procedure for obtaining, filing, and making information available. Some systems, particularly those built around computers, qualify as systems in a strict sense of the term. They are highly complex, expensive, and sophisticated; general use is undoubtedly impending, but many are still in the field-trial and experimental stage.

Three types of systems of varying complexity have been developed to provide career information. Computer systems are the most sophisticated. Those that make some use of technical aids, such as the reader-printer, are less complex. The simplest are systems that include guides or indexes requiring the user to locate, read, and synthesize information.

COMPUTER SYSTEMS

The development and use of computers for career guidance has accelerated in the past few years. The help they can provide is in line with needs expressed by both pupils and counselors (Harris-Bowlsbey, 1975, pp. 39–40).

Table 5.1 shows the primary and shared responsibilities for the career-guidance services of computers, counselors, teachers, and the community. The table clearly shows that while computers can do several career-guidance tasks, they share responsibility for some and cannot provide for others. Exploration of educational and career options and implementation of choice are the two tasks that most effectively use computer characteristics. New developments may enable computers to be more effective in some tasks—teaching decision-making skills, for example—and to serve as an aid to others, such as teaching of job-seeking skills. But it is readily apparent

Table 5.1 Components of career education and guidance, with assignment of responsibility

Theme	Teacher/ Curricu- lum	Computer	Counselor/ Group	Counselor/ One-to- One	Community
Activities for the formation and clarification of self-concept		*	⊛	*	
Activities which promote broad exploration of educational and vocational options	⊛	⊛			*
Activities which assist individuals to relate self-information to occupational and educational info		*	⊛	⊛	
Deliberate teaching of career-planning and decision-making skills	*	*	⊛		
Opportunities for reality testing of occupational alternatives	*			*	⊛
Assistance with implementation of choice (job placement, college or tech. school selection, financial aid)		⊛	*	*	
Teaching of vocational skills	⊛		*	*	*
Teaching of job-seeking and holding skills and attitudes	⊛		⊛	⊛	*
Economic awareness and planning	⊛		*	*	*

⊛ = primary responsibility
* = shared responsibility
SOURCE: Jo Ann Harris-Bowlsbey, *Structure and Technology for Facilitating Human Development Through Career Education* (De Kalb, Ill.: ERIC Clearinghouse in Career Education, 1975. Reprinted with permission.)

that computers will not replace counselors. They can save enormous amounts of time for counselors, who can then devote their energies to the duties for which their preparation and experience uniquely qualify them—face-to-face counseling and consulting.

System of Interactive Guidance and Information, or SIGI

Martin Katz, supported by the Carnegie Corporation, is developing a system designed to help junior college students with the process and content of career decision making. Katz places considerable emphasis on values in the choice process, and values play a major role in SIGI.

The system contains six subsystems and an introduction that helps the user understand concepts and estimate current status in career planning. Following the introduction, the student identifies values (values subsystem), locates occupations in line with values (locate subsystem), obtains additional details about occupations of interest (compare subsystem), predicts grades in preparation programs (prediction subsystem), obtains detailed data about preparation programs, occupational requirements, and sources of aid (planning subsystem), and evaluates occupations in terms of rewards and risks involved (strategy subsystem).

Students can usually go through the program in several hours, but the process can be broken down into several shorter periods. Vocabulary is satisfactory for an eighth-grade reading level. About 220 occupations are included, and information is updated regularly.

Field testing of SIGI has been in process for several years at seven colleges, and evaluation data are generally very positive. Users rate the program as helpful and interesting and the number of occupations as adequate. Usage tends to be heavy, and additional terminals have been added at some test sites.

In addition, a number of research studies have been carried out. For example, the use of self-estimates of ability has been shown to be valid for the SIGI prediction system (Norris and Cochran, 1977), confirming the findings of ETS on the same process. Several dissertations have involved evaluation of effect on career maturity and have tended to show positive results (ETS, n.d.), although the effectiveness of the system probably should be measured by more specific criteria than a global estimate of career maturity. There is at least tentative evidence that SIGI can help with development of the decision-making skills involved in the choice of a college major. When SIGI is used as part of an organized career-guidance program, it is well received and rated higher in value (Cochran and Rademacher, 1978). SIGI is one of the systems that Harris-Bowlsbey (1975, pp. 35–36) describes as incorporating a mediating function, but this computer function is still in its infancy.

Career Information System, or CIS

Formerly called the Occupational Information Access System, or OIAS, CIS is a statewide interagency consortium in Oregon that provides current labor-market and educational information to individuals, schools, and agencies (Harris-Bowlsbey, 1975, pp. 26–27; Oregon Career Information System, n. d.). Its purpose is to help agencies and institutions offering career guidance by making information available, developing occupational and educational information systems, and providing training for system users.

CIS delivers several types of assistance, based on the needs revealed by the individual's completion of QUEST, an introductory questionnaire that helps users explore occupations related to self-assessed interests and abilities. The computer draws on a data file of 240 occupations to identify those that meet personal requirements. Moreover, by changing questionnaire responses, the user can explore other occupations. Brief three-hundred-word summaries of occupational duties, pay, outlook, and working conditions, emphasizing both state and national labor-market information, may be obtained. The user may request a listing of books and other material for each occupation in the system, names of local resource people, clubs that provide occupational exploratory experiences, guides to preparation for occupations, descriptions of training and educational programs in Oregon, and data to facilitate comparisons of school costs and services.

Evaluative data about the effects of CIS on users and contribution to staff effectiveness indicate that it appeals to a wide range of students, is easy to use, helps in career decision making, and is effective in a variety of school, higher-education, and community settings (McKinlay, 1974, pp. 134–157).

CIS is currently serving over 200,000 individuals and about 350 schools and agencies in Oregon, including junior and senior high schools, community colleges, colleges and universities, and social agencies such as those for correctional, community action, and vocational rehabilitation.

Guidance Information System, or GIS

This system, formerly called the Interactive Learning System, contains four main information banks the user can question and receive immediate printed information from. The four files are as follows:

1. THE OCCUPATIONAL FILE   This file contains information about more than 1,200 occupations. Both the fifteen job clusters of the U.S. Office of Education and the nine categories of the DOT provide bases for exploration. In addition to information about occupations, details about education and training opportunities may be identified by switching to other files.

2. THE FOUR-YEAR COLLEGE FILE   This file contains information about more than 2,600 colleges, universities, and technical institutes. Information may be obtained about institutions on the basis of student-selected needs.

3. THE TWO-YEAR COLLEGE FILE   This file contains the same kind of information as the four-year college file.

4. THE SCHOLARSHIP AND FINANCIAL-AID FILE   This file contains information on financial-aid opportunities utilizing funds amounting to more than $200 million.

An extensive array of multimedia information is cross-referenced to the occupational file—for example, there are audiovisual filmstrips and cassettes on occupational clusters. A microfiche kit of two- and four-year college catalogues supplements the college files.

The system is an excellent example of how a career-information center can be automated with enormous savings of counselor time. The program is in use in over 1,400 career information centers in twenty-six states.

Experimental Education and Career Exploration System, or ECES[2]

This system will be described in detail both because it has certain unique features and because extensive field testing has been carried out on it. It was initially sponsored by IBM's Advanced Systems Development Division; the principal investigators are Frank J. Minor, representing IBM, and Donald E. Super and Roger A. Myers of Teachers College, Columbia University. In 1971, IBM discontinued development of the program and gave it to the state of Michigan.

The developers specified major counseling and guidance problems as indications of need. The school counselor is responsible for providing vocational orientation and helping pupils explore occupational alternatives, a task that is often neglected. It is difficult to keep information about careers, educational opportunities, and pupil abilities, aptitudes, and interests on hand for immediate use when needed. Presenting data to the counselee is too time-consuming, and the usual printed matter available is of limited value. The computer offers a way to store, retrieve, analyze, and display information rapidly and efficiently.

Vocational development is viewed as a lifelong process consisting of an orderly succession of stages. These stages, listed in the discussion of the Career Pattern Study in Chapter 2, include growth and exploration. The system, characterized as a support facility for the school, was designed to help the counselor as well as to assist pupils in occupational exploration. The benefits to pupils are that the system will enable them to become aware of and explore occupational alternatives, assist them to understand their potential, help them to relate personal attributes and goals to educational and occupational opportunities and to increase their occupational mobility, provide the opportunity to explore post–high school training and educational options, and assist them in identifying a suitable post–high school educational or training institution. The benefits to the counselor are that counselees will be ready for problem solving and planning, information may be obtained from the system to help in understanding the counselee, and extensive and complex information files will not be needed.

[2]Adapted from Frank J. Minor, Roger A. Myers, and Donald E. Super, "An Experimental Computer-Based Educational and Career Exploration System," *Perspectives on Vocational Development,* eds. John M. Whiteley and Arthur Resnikoff (Washington, D.C.: American Personnel and Guidance Association, 1972), pp. 173–181. Copyright 1972 by the American Personnel and Guidance Association. Adapted with permission.

The ECES system was designed for high school pupils with a wide range of socioeconomic backgrounds and post–high school plans. Occupational exploration is followed by in-depth investigation. The system is controlled by the pupil-operator, who can communicate with the computer by keyboard. The newest version, ECES IV, provides six steps through which pupils progress. These are as follows:

1. *Step One: Awareness*
   Pupils are helped to become aware of who they are and what they want from life. They enter interests, planned educational level, work values, personal values, and learning abilities. The computer holds school record data and it presents data via color filmstrips and microfiche. Much of this step is off-line from the computer, and materials can be used in group guidance or classroom settings. The Ohio Vocational Interest Survey (OVIS) is administered. A student manual, in workbook form, explains and illustrates each step. Preferences for this step are entered in the computer and used in future interactions.

2. *Step Two: Search*
   The computer searches for occupations that fulfill the pupil's requirements and provides a list of suitable occupations. Six criteria are used in the search: preferred high school courses, interest-test scores, self-estimates of interest, desired salary level, planned level of education, and favorite work activities. Occupations that meet any or all of these criteria are identified, and the computer provides a list for further exploration.

3. *Step Three: Explore*
   In this step, pupils can use a library containing information about 400 occupations, 300 educational programs, over 4,500 courses, more than 3,000 schools and colleges, labor-market statistics (updated daily), and charts that show the results of exploration. The occupations library provides color pictures of occupational information in cassettes. The user inserts cassettes at appropriate times for exploratory information, and exploration is continued until one preferred occupation is identified.

4. *Step 4: Experience*
   This step is a unique day-on-the job experience. The computer schedules the experience and gives instructions on how to write a letter of application for it and to prepare for the job interview. Pre- and postexperience readiness and suitability ratings are made by pupil, teacher, and employer. The results of the day-on-the-job experience are used in the following steps.

5. *Step 5: Plan*
   The pupil chooses an occupational goal and formulates the strategy to reach it. The computer checks the strategy's suitability and suggests any additional factors to be considered. The decision-making processes may be taught at the computer terminal, in group guidance meetings, or in the classroom. In addition, parents, pupils, teachers, and counselors review career plans.

6. *Step 6: Placement*

Both pupils and employers are involved here. Pupils may locate information about job openings, and employers may learn about those looking for work. The computer teaches users to write résumés and to develop interpersonal work skills. In addition, pupils are assisted in locating schools and other institutions that provide needed preparation.

Field testing on the original version at Montclair High School, Montclair, New Jersey, in 1969 involved data from experimental and control groups and an assessment of reactions of pupils, teachers, parents, and counselors. Experimental group members had the choice of using the system; practically all did so. Reactions to the system were very positive; students not planning to attend college and the disadvantaged were among the most enthusiastic users. The short trial period of three months, however, did not substantially affect vocational maturity. Counselors, parents, and teachers were generally favorable and expressed a desire to have the system available in the school (Bohn, 1970).

After changes and modifications based on the field-trial results, additional field testing was done at the Genesee Intermediate School District, Michigan. Tenth-graders in thirteen high schools served as the experimental group, and control groups were used. The Career Development Inventory (CDI) developed by Super was used in the evaluation. Each pupil spent a minimum of two two-hour sessions with the computer, and results showed that these students exceeded nonusers in awareness of occupational resources and quality of resources used. Enthusiasm was high. Interestingly enough, the most positive attitudes were expressed by nonurban and female pupils. Counselors and parents also reported highly favorable reactions (Myers, 1972).

More recent investigations of the system's effectiveness (prior to ECES IV) have shown that it has a positive impact on some aspects of career development, for example, planfulness and use of resources for exploration. Further, indications are that there may be both lower and upper limits to optimum time spent on the computer (Myers, Lindeman, Thompson, and Patrick, 1975). Current evaluations are being carried out as part of the COMPASS Project, a federally funded study. There are a total of twenty-eight terminals in Michigan, and plans are being made to install a number in another state.

ECES IV is the first complete computer-based career-development system and is the result of ten years of research and development. It was identified as the career guidance system of the 1980s at a recent APGA convention.

Computerized Vocational Information System, or CVIS

This system was developed by Joann Harris, director of guidance, and the guidance staff at Willowbrook High School in Chicago. CVIS began operation in 1967.

Originally, CVIS was developed in one high school, but because of widespread interest, a group of users was organized in 1972 to share information and provide data-file updates to members. Then, in 1975, the CVIS consortium was formed as a nonprofit organization. The CVIS product was released to the consortium by the state of Illinois, and the headquarters is now in Westminister, Maryland. There are about fifty institutional members, with secondary schools making up about three-fourths of the total. The consortium distributes CVIS products, supervises the updating of national data files, promotes new developments, and provides for communication among users. CVIS is now operational in close to four hundred sites across the nation, with from one to eighty terminals at a site.

The guidance staff began by identifying several pressing needs involving career information. Pupils lacked motivation to read material on occupations. They needed assistance in relating career information to interests, abilities, and goals. Furthermore, the job of maintaining an up-to-date supply of career information was extremely burdensome. A decision was made to use computer technology; a proposal was prepared, and financial support was obtained.

Roe's fields-by-levels occupational classification was adopted as the basic format for career information. Data on about four hundred occupations, all colleges and universities, local training programs, and local occupational opportunities are stored in the computer, along with an 1,100-character cumulative record for each pupil. With these data and prepared scripts, a pupil can explore educational and occupational opportunities, guided by the fields-and-levels concept, and obtain an estimate of his or her potential for various options.

The guidance system has been expanded to serve the junior high school and the community college. At the junior high school level, the pupil can explore occupations classified according to the six environments hypothesized by Holland's theory. Exploration is based on pupil personality, abilities, and interests, and may lead to planning a high school program. At the community college level, the student may compare himself or herself with various groups, including those planning to transfer to four-year colleges. The most recent additions are a financial-aid bank, which makes possible a search for sources of financial assistance, and a select-a-course function that allows students to register for courses the following year (in both high school and college).

To use the system, the pupil sits at a console with a typewriter-like keyboard, a screen, and a printer. The pupil types responses to multiple-choice questions and gives "free" responses to questions about such matters as financial resources for training. Orientation to the classification system is accomplished in a preliminary vocational unit. The pupil gives his or her "student number," which enables the computer to locate his or her record. A game of tick-tack-toe develops familiarity with the computer's operation. The system then reviews the pupil's record, asking questions about achievement and self-estimates of ability. The computer responds by verifying, raising questions, or indicating discrepancies.

As exploration continues, the pupil responds to the computer's request for a field of interest and an expected level of attainment. The computer provides a list of occupations in the field-level categories selected and brief definitions of each occupation given. Longer descriptions, of around three hundred words, may be printed if requested. Additional reading references, including page numbers, may also be provided. The exploratory process may be discontinued and resumed later.

The computer will begin at the point where exploration ended at the previous session.

New scripts enable the pupil to explore colleges, specialized schools, apprenticeships, local jobs, and military service.

The system may also be used by counselors to recall student records, schedule pupil use of the computer, retrieve occupational and educational information, and obtain "discrepancy" messages counselees have received. A discrepancy message may be major or minor. A minor discrepancy might be the choice of a lower educational goal than is suggested by ability. A major one might be the selection of a program that appears to be much too difficult. The computer may suggest that a counselor be consulted.

Several additional features of CVIS are significant for the development of computerized guidance systems. The cost is held down by including administrative data and computer-assisted instruction in the system. Currently, thirty-one terminals are in schools in DuPage County, Illinois, which makes CVIS the largest computer-guidance system in operation. Informational and instructional services, including a 16mm color film on CVIS, are available to interested schools and school systems. Because the program is in the public domain, the programs and documentation are available to nonprofit educational institutions at a cost of approximately $1,000. (A number of factors, however, must be considered in estimating the cost of instituting the system.)

Research and evaluation have been built into the system by storing data on use, decisions made, and the like. Evaluation of the vocational exploration aspect of CVIS revealed that pupils are highly enthusiastic about the system. Substantial majorities stated that they learned a great deal about themselves and about occupations of interest. They like the scripts and felt that they knew more about making occupational decisions then did nonusers. CVIS also increased pupils' information about occupations and their levels of vocational maturity. Use with academically disadvantaged vocational pupils resulted in more gain in cognitive aspects of vocational maturity than a counselor-based process (Maola and Kane, 1976).

DISCOVER

The newest computer career-guidance system, a third-generation system, has gone through four years of development and is now in use, marketed by IBM. In addition to the capabilities of the second generation—direct interaction between computer and user, storage of information about the user and about previous interactions, and feedback on effectiveness of choices—DISCOVER includes the following features:

1. A systematic program of guidance materials for use over a relatively long period of career development
2. Computer-assisted instruction and simulation exercises in values clarification, decision making, and classification of occupations
3. Capability for on-line administration and interpretation of tests

4. A light pen for selection of responses

5. The incorporation of a systematic model of career development (Rayman and Harris-Bowlsbey, 1977)

The original DISCOVER system is designed for grades seven through twelve. There is also a model for college-level and adult use that has undergone two years of development and field trials (DISCOVER Foundation, 1977; Rayman, Bryson, and Day, 1978). Both cover self-information, occupational exploration, decision making, self and occupational factors relationships, and choice implementation in twelve interactive modules.

Figure 5.5 shows the eleven major modules (the first entry is not shown in the figure) with Super's and Tiedeman's career-development stages in the lower part of the figure to illustrate the career-development organization of the modules. The submodules of information, for use with Module 8, are shown in the box at the right of the figure.

The purposes of the modules are as follows:

00 ENTRY

Introduces the user to the system and monitors entry and exit. The Survey of Career Development is taken and serves as a guide in selecting appropriate modules.

1a. UNDERSTANDING MY VALUES

Provides experiences to enable the user to identify values and to ask the computer to search for occupations in which these values may be put into play. The list of occupations obtained is stored in the computer for later use.

1b. PLAYING A VALUES GAME

Involves a Monopoly-like game to help user understand values and career goals.

2a. LEARNING TO MAKE DECISIONS

Assists user in learning how to make decisions and in identifying present decision-making strategies.

2b. PRACTICING CAREER DECISIONS

Illustrates the decision tree, provides decision-making practice, and gives the user the opportunity to try out some low-risk decisions.

3a. LEARNING HOW OCCUPATIONS CAN BE GROUPED

Presents the data-people-things and the Holland classification plans and provides practice in classification.

3b. BROWSING OCCUPATIONS

Allows the user to select titles from 320 in the module using Holland's Occupational Classification System and receive a one-display description of settings and duties.

4. REVIEWING MY INTERESTS AND STRENGTHS

Uses Holland's Self-Directed Search and gives the pupil an on-line interpretation. These data are used in world of work exploration.

5. MAKING A LIST OF OCCUPATIONS TO EXPLORE

Gives ways to make a list of occupational options to explore. These are personal work values, the Self-Directed Search, selecting from a list by the terminal,

Figure 5.5 DISCOVER: A MODEL FOR A SYSTEMATIC CAREER-GUIDANCE PROGRAM

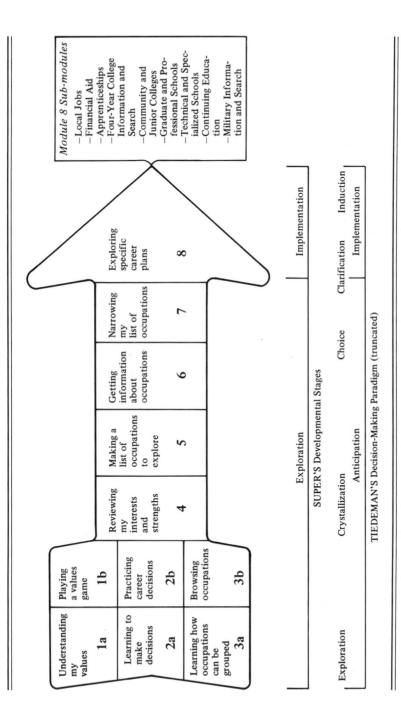

SOURCE: Jack R. Rayman and Joann Harris-Bowlsbey, "DISCOVER: A Model for a Systematic Career Guidance Program," *Vocational Guidance Quarterly*, 26, No: 1 (1977), 3–11. 1977 Copyright. American Personnel and Guidance Association. Reprinted with permission.

combining characteristics (such as place and salary), and favorite school subjects.

6. GETTING INFORMATION ABOUT OCCUPATIONS

Provides extensive information about occupations. Personal information may be compared with occupational requirements and duties. The user ends up with a list of those jobs in which he or she has a serious interest. This list may be the same or different from the one brought to the module.

7. NARROWING MY LIST OF OCCUPATIONS

Helps the user select a first-choice occupation and a few others in rank order of preference. The individual is assisted in the narrowing process by being given more information, by comparing occupations, and by further analysis in terms of such factors as work values.

8. EXPLORING SPECIFIC CAREER PLANS

Explores one occupation at a time. The computer identifies pathways to the occupation; the user may choose any pathway to explore and may go to any of the nine submodules shown on the right of Figure 5.5, such as apprenticeship and technical and specialized schools, for data. The nine submodules contain a wealth of information, including local job data, sources of financial aid, the names of all four-year colleges and universities in the United States, and the names of approximately 11,000 technical and specialized schools. Not only do the submodules contain basic information about work and education, they also have instructional materials, such as "How to Look for a Job."

Some local data files, such as those containing job data, must be developed by the site. Other local information, such as data about community colleges and specialized schools, is part of the regular national data bank.

The college and adult version is substantially the same as the one described, but several modules are designed specifically for adults who have unique career-development problems. For example, there is a submodule for mid-career job entrants and changers.

The system's model of career development may be utilized as the basis of counseling and guidance services, even if a computer is not readily available. The modularized format of DISCOVER makes it relatively easy to phase in the program module by module later if it is adopted.

Field testing and evaluation data give substantial evidence of the system's acceptance and effectiveness. Both junior and senior high school pupils' reactions were quite positive. Parents reported that their sons and daughters had discussed DISCOVER and factors in career planning at home, and parents rated the system as valuable for young people. In addition, DISCOVER helped pupils specify career plans, understand occupations, and increase their self-understanding. Effects on career maturity, as measured by standardized instruments, were inconclusive, due probably to limitations of field-test designs and other similar factors; additional study of this aspect is needed.

Field tests also provided feedback for modification and improvement of the system. For example, the extreme flexibility, which permits users to move quickly to any part, has both positive and negative results. Also, DISCOVER may be viewed as a warm, personal experience, but in some cases users may skip essential sections (Bowlsbey, Rayman, and Bryson, 1976, pp. 16–23).

Other Systems

One computer program (Farmer, 1976) was designed for adults who are changing careers or entering the world of work. The guidance process is very much like those of the interactive programs already described. The DAT Career Planning Report is an example of a program that compares test results with personal data to give the user a printed analysis of the occupational plans and goals (Super, 1974b). These computer interpretations appear to be equal in effectiveness to those provided by counselors (Sharf, 1978). Preparation of counselors may be carried out by having students respond to a computer "counselee" that evaluates the appropriateness of techniques utilized (Hummel, Lichtenberg, and Shaffer, 1975). A placement program, called GRAD II, designed by the College Placement Council, Inc., matches students looking for jobs with employers' needs, thus paving the way for better campus interview scheduling.

Technical Aid Systems

Several other career-guidance systems and programs involve new technology and may use computers at one or more stages. Vital Information for Education and Work, or VIEW, is one such system; the computer may be used in preparing information, but it is not a central feature. A second system, JOB-FLO, makes extensive use of computer-generated data. A third, the Occupational Information Systems Grants Program, supports various kinds of delivery systems development; computers may be components of these programs.

VIEW

The VIEW system was developed by the Department of Education, San Diego County, California, at the request of school administrators and vocational curriculum specialists who wanted local labor-market information in a form convenient for counselors, teachers, and pupils. The first step was establishment of a regional career-information center to serve high schools and junior colleges in the area. Phase I of the project involved identification of both types and sources of information needed by counselors and pupils and methods of collection. Phase II was the development of the vehicle for presenting the information, the microfilm aperture card. One card contains about four pages of general occupational information, including the DOT code number, a brief description of the nature of the work, pictures of local workers, criteria for applicants, training needed, wages or salary, and other pertinent information. The second card gives local information, such as nearby training opportunities, local employment opportunities, and sources

Figure 5.6   VIEW card for an occupation

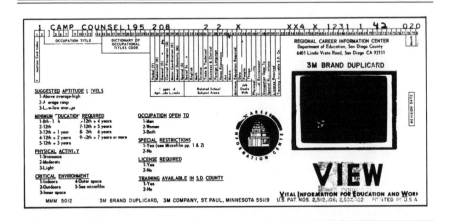

SOURCE: Superintendent of Schools, Department of Education, San Diego County, San Diego, California. Used by permission.

of additional information. A scale by which pupils can rate their suitability for the occupation may be included. Figure 5.6 shows a card, and Figure 5.7 illustrates the first page of the card containing general information.

The system is relatively easy to use. A packet of cards is selected, either by the pupil alone or by the pupil and counselor. Seated at the reader-printer, the pupil goes through the cards, reading the projections on the screen before him or her. When the pupil finds material of interest, he or she may read the general card and, if he or she wishes, the local one. Any of the material may be printed and kept by the pupil.

The California program is an excellent example of an outstanding state-level system. The work of the information center has expanded; in addition to VIEW, there are now components that involve an inventory of career-guidance measurements; an inventory of materials on occupational competency; strategies and materials for staffs implementing career-development activities; and the collection, coordination, and distribution of career information. Work is being done to combine VIEW with a computer career-guidance system (California Pilot Career Guidance Center, 1974, Whitfield, Miller, and Johnson, 1978, pp. 1–2). Information may be obtained from Edwin A. Whitfield, Project Director, California Regional Career Guidance Center, 6401 Linda Vista Road, San Diego, California 92111.

The trend toward expanding VIEW systems is further exemplified by the Florida Center for Career Development Services, formerly called Florida VIEW (Woolley, 1978). In addition to preparing and updating the VIEW system, the center handles Computer Assisted Placement Services, or CAPS, which it has recently taken over.

Figure 5.7   The first page of a VIEW card for the occupation of carpenter

D.O.T.: 860.381
Revision date: October, 1967

VIEW

VITAL INFORMATION FOR EDUCATION AND WORK

CARPENTER
(CARPENTER APPRENTICE)

The Carpenter constructs, erects, installs, and repairs structures and fixtures of wood, plywood, and wallboard, using carpenter's handtools and power tools, and conforming to local building codes.

REQUIREMENTS AND QUALIFICATIONS

You Should Have These:

Personal Traits	Aptitudes	Physical Traits
• Accurate and precise	For an explanation of aptitudes, you are urged to:	• Good physical condition
• Work well with others		• Good sense of balance
• Pride in work	• See your Counselor or Advisor	• Manual dexterity
• Patience		• Stamina
• Reliable	or	• Average coordination
	• Visit an office of the California Department of Employment	• Normal vision and hearing (or corrected)

You Must Be Able To:
- Climb, balance, stoop, kneel, crouch, crawl
- Reach, grasp and hold
- Work outside and indoors in rough surroundings
- Tolerate noise and dust
- Tolerate cuts and other injuries from sharp tools
- Provide own protective clothing such as hard hats and safety shoes

You Should Know That:
- You may have to purchase protective clothing, tools, and textbooks as an apprentice
- Carpenters are subject to seasonal fluctuations in employment
- Bad weather will affect earnings through lost time
- You may have to provide your own transportation to construction sites
- Total material costs to apprentices is about $275
- Hazards are plentiful in the Carpenter's trade

The VIEW system itself has been expanded by addition of a new career deck on apprenticeships. Additional information may be obtained from the Center for Career Development Services, Florida Department of Education, Knott Building, Tallahassee, Florida 32304.

JOB-FLO

A relatively new program provided by the U.S. Department of Labor, JOB-FLO started in 1976 to provide available information about career fields that need workers (Baxter, 1976). It is designed to make information on high-demand occupations available from the two hundred job-bank districts in the United States. From the JOB-FLO reports it is possible to tell whether a large-scale demand exists for specific kinds of workers in a particular city or region. Reports also show pay, industries needing workers, and required experience and education. Job banks, currently operating in practically all states, list available jobs and are revised daily. These lists are made available to local employment service offices through computer generated print-outs or microfiche. A job-bank openings summary prepared by the U.S. Department of Labor, Employment, and Training Administration shows all job-bank openings throughout the country for the previous month. From this listing, those occupations for which there is a high demand (and that meet several other criteria) are listed in JOB-FLO.

Although the jobs may be filled by the time JOB-FLO is available, the listing of a large number of openings suggests that there is an undersupply and that opportunities for employment exist. Even though JOB-FLO is not a placement service, the interested person can find out from the local employment service which jobs are available that day in another city—in other words, the job bank can be consulted for current job openings. Counselors may obtain JOB-FLO information for their local areas from the Department of Labor.

Less Complex Systems

Subscription and related services available from commercial publishers also represent information systems. A publisher may, for example, market a set of materials organized to facilitate exploration and choice and provide regular issues of new materials to update and expand the system. Several representative systems are identified and briefly described in the following list. (Current information about prices and content may be obtained from the publishers.)

1. Science Research Associates, Inc., 254 East Erie Street, Chicago, Illinois 60611, is one of the largest publishers of occupational materials. Kits such as the following are available.
   a. Widening Occupational Roles Kit (WORK), grades 6–10. The set is designed to be used with individuals or groups for career exploration.
   b. Job Experience Kits, grades 8–14. Work simulation is provided for twenty occupations.

c. Occupational Exploration Kit, grades 9–14. This kit contains four hundred occupational briefs, seventeen job-family booklets, and other career material.
2. Chronicle Guidance Publications, Inc., Moravia, New York 13118, markets a number of useful and well-designed sets of materials. An occupational file based on the DOT and a desk-top file are available. Two types of "system" equipment assist the pupil with exploration and decision making. The Occupation View-Deck and the College View-Decks use perforated cards to enable the user to narrow his or her choices of occupations or colleges.
3. Careers, Largo, Florida 33540, distributes a number of desk-top kits and offers subscription services to keep them up to date. Representative kits include Career Desk-Top Kit, Semi-Skilled Careers Kit, and Industrial Careers Kit (skilled and technical). Other subscription services and materials are available.
4. Houghton Mifflin Company, One Beacon Street, Boston, Massachusetts 02107, distributes desk-top career files for use in occupational exploration at the high school level. Specialized kits for industrial careers, business, and other areas are available.
5. The College Selection Program, Houghton Mifflin Company, One Beacon Street, Boston, Massachusetts 02107, is a computer-based college-guidance program that assists pupils and parents from the initial consideration of a college during the junior year until action is taken on the college application by the institutions selected. After use of the planning guides and conferences with the school counselor, there is a computer search to identify colleges that meet the pupil's needs. This list is then used to prepare applications.
6. The National College Catalogue Service is a microfiche file of the latest catalogues of degree-granting American institutions with provisions for regular updating. Available sets include four-year, two-year, and graduate-level institutions. Materials are available from Time Share, 630 Oakwood Avenue, West Hartford, Connecticut 06110. The GIS computer guidance system described earlier is also available from Time Share.

Kits and simulation materials that emphasize an experiential mode have increased tremendously in recent years. Production has been so extensive and use so widespread that guidelines have been included in the *Personnel and Guidance Journal*. Extensive use is made of slides, audio cassettes, films, and games in these kits. Directions for group activities are often included. Production of this type of material has been stimulated by and is often incorporated in career-education programs. Some are best classified as group counseling and group guidance. Thus, additional comments about typical programs are included in later chapters.

An example that illustrates features of this type of new program is the Job Game, which is reviewed in the *Personnel and Guidance Journal* (Feinberg, 1977, p. 60). This program is designed to help individuals with occupational planning and obtaining employment through activities and exercises such as role playing, fantasy trips, science fiction language, and case studies. Audiocassettes and student workbooks are used. Pupils go through a process of identifying skills and interests, choosing appropriate occupations, learning about job characteristics, practicing interviewing for jobs, and trying out other employability skills.

Other systems could be listed, and new ones appear regularly. Perhaps the best sources of information about the wealth of new materials are the "Current Career Films" and "Current Career Literature" sections (particularly the one entitled "Supplementary Information") of the *Vocational Guidance Quarterly* and reviews in the *Personnel and Guidance Journal*. Sample materials may sometimes be obtained free of charge, and some publishers provide personnel and equipment for demonstrations.

DEVELOPING THE SCHOOL OR AGENCY INFORMATION SYSTEM

Establishing an information system begins with a clear statement of needs, goals, and objectives. Next, the criteria for assessment are formulated. Following these steps, a rationale is prepared, local resources and services inventoried, components selected, and a plan of organization developed.

Establish the Need

This process is based on user and community information. The critical questions are: Where do graduates and dropouts go? What happens to them? What are the plans, abilities, interests, and special achievements of those still in school? What are the opportunities and limitations of the school community? This community may be defined as extending far beyond the school's attendance area. Seeking answers to these questions, one school guidance staff realized that its guidance service was heavily stocked with college- and professional-level information, but most graduates attended one of three vocational-technical schools or worked in one of two local industries.

State the Rationale

This procedure may appear to be an unnecessary step. "Everybody knows that an information service is needed!" Even if this kind of agreement exists, a statement of *why* information is needed and *what* help it is supposed to provide is necessary. If counselors, for example, have not articulated how information will facilitate growth and decision making in individual and group counseling and guidance, if they use it sporadically, or if they consider it distinct from counseling and guidance, the system will never attain its potential.

Inventory Local Resources and Current Services

Once those involved agree on what is needed—for example, information about apprenticeships, semiskilled mechanical work, or entry jobs—the sorts of information already available in the school can be identified. For example, a science teacher may be a widely consulted source of information about jobs in photography, or the home economics teacher may have an extensive file on occupations in food services, child care, and clothing production. Often a great deal of information is already available, but unsystematic, isolated, and little known.

This step is primarily an inventory of existing and prospective services within the school. Community resources, discussed later, could also be part of the system.

Identify Components and Plan Organization

Four elements are considered here: the specific materials and equipment needed, the relations of components, methods of utilization, and feedback from evaluation and modification. The survey of materials and equipment provided in this chapter can serve as a framework for identifying components. Career-development theories provide guidelines for determining how components are related and how their use may be planned. The system does not exist in a vacuum; it is a part of the total guidance system.

Feedback is often neglected; it is so important, however, that it should be provided for at the outset of planning. For example, suppose you have a good, up-to-date file of occupational information, but it is very seldom used. Why? Where does the system fail? Who should do what to improve the situation? A modified, informal *systems analysis* procedure is useful here. You have identified the components, both persons and equipment, in the system. You have described how they work together. But some part or person is not functioning properly. Analysis of the system will reveal the source of difficulty and suggest how it may be remedied.

State the Objectives

Objectives are derived from needs and should be stated in terms that specify what the system is supposed to do and how results will be evaluated. Mager (1962, p. 43) identifies the key elements in goal formulation as specifying the desired outcome, the means by which the individual demonstrates mastery, and the criteria for judging success. This approach can be applied to the information system as well as to other aspects of career counseling and guidance. As Mager says, "if you're not sure where you're going, you're liable to end up someplace else" (1962, p. ix).

The California model of career development illustrates this approach (Cunha et al, 1972, pp. 10, 17–18). A general objective or need, for example, is for pupils to learn about themselves and the variety of occupations that might be suitable for them. The specific behavioral objectives are classified as *awareness, accommodation,* and *action.* An *awareness* objective might be preparation of a chart showing how class members' interests differ. An *accommodation* objective might be the pupil's comparison of his or her abilities and interests to those of an occupation in the *OOH.* An *action* objective might be selection of career conference meetings appropriate to abilities and interests. For each of these goals, an acceptable level of performance is specified. The National Assessment (1971, p. 49) suggests such general goals as "Can write position-wanted ads." This goal could be stated in terms that make clear the behavior that is desired, and how and under what circumstances the individual can demonstrate mastery. For example, it could be stated that at the end of the first term of the senior year, the pupil should be able to compose, in fifty words or less, a position-wanted ad that summarizes his or her qualifications and the specific type of job sought, using titles from the DOT.

Jacobson (1975) has described the evaluation of information centers and recommendations for building and staffing them. Recommendations cover all aspects of the organization and operation of career centers; particularly noteworthy is the emphasis on the use of volunteers to free the counselor for work with individuals and groups on decision making and career planning (pp. 111–112).

The procedure used by Reardon and Domkowski (1977) gives helpful guidelines for emphasizing self-help in a career-information center. A set of modules, each with an overview, pretest, learning activities, and a posttest, was constructed. The systems approach was used in designing the program to meet student needs and for evaluation and accountability. Introductory modules explain the service; help in identifying abilities, interests, and occupations to explore; and state what steps to take in planning. One, for example, covers campus and community career-development resources. The development of the service illustrates steps outlined earlier in this section.

SUMMARY

This chapter has surveyed the multitude of information resources and has alerted the counselor to those that may be incorporated into an information system. Major occupational trends and predictions have been reviewed first, to illustrate the complexity of the world of work and to provide some general information. Trends, for example, show an increase in professional, technical, and service jobs and a decrease in opportunities for the unskilled. The opportunities for vocational education in the high school and for post–high school training and education are extensive, and the counselor will need to keep in touch with vocational teachers and community agencies such as the state employment service to keep abreast of new developments. Many new programs are aimed at the disadvantaged and hard-to-employ.

Resources for the information system are extensive and represent varying degrees of sophistication. They include computer systems, files, subscription services, and individual publications like the *Occupational Outlook Handbook*. Many promising computer systems have been developed, but several have been discontinued for lack of funding. Others, however, such as ECES, CVIS, and DISCOVER, are currently in operation and proving quite effective. New guidance systems are being developed, and it seems likely that the career-education approach to public schools will stimulate more efforts in this direction. The counselor has a responsibility to insure that the information provided is accurate, up to date, and unbiased. Much free material is designed specifically for recruiting and should be recognized as potentially biased. Each school should design its own information system by identifying needs, formulating general purposes, surveying resources, and specifying goals. A built-in feedback process is essential to keep the system up to date, efficient, and responsive to changing needs.

PROJECTS AND EXPERIENTIAL ACTIVITIES

1. Interview a worker to determine how much prior information he or she had about the present job and how the information was obtained.
2. Look for items in the newspaper about occupational trends. Compile a scrapbook about local trends and training opportunities.
3. Tape-record a three- or four-minute summary of the information on any occupation in the *Occupational Outlook Handbook*. Play it back to judge its clarity and completeness.
4. Visit a vocational-technical center or community college and obtain information about its programs. Talk with students about their work, the satisfaction it provides, and their occupational goals.
5. Visit a career-guidance computer center and go through the program. (Keep in mind that the program may not be suitable for graduate students.) Talk to students who have used the program to determine their reactions. (If a career-guidance computer system is not available, visit any type of computer center to learn something about procedures and language. One will probably be available on campus.)
6. In the classroom, divide into small groups and discuss the one most helpful and the one least helpful source of educational/career information you have utilized. At the conclusion of these discussions, report to the class. What types of information appear to have been most helpful? The least helpful? Why?
7. Select one or several occupations, preferably those with which you are not familiar and come up with a group consensus about whether both men and women can do the job equally well and how many years of special education or training are necessary. Using ratings of from 1 to 5 (1 being low and 5, high), rate the importance in the selected occupation of working with data, people, and things. Report your results and discuss your agreements and disagreements with the class as a whole.
8. Organize committees to take an inventory of all the career-development material in the library (educational directories, training guides, occupational-information books, scholarship information, and so on) and prepare an annotated listing. Include items in the media center.

ADDITIONAL REFERENCES

Chick, Joyce M. *Innovations in the Use of Career Information.* Boston: Houghton Mifflin, 1970. This entire book is an excellent discussion of new and innovative career-dissemination methods. Chap. 2, on computers, is particularly helpful; the pros and cons of computer use are relevant for this chapter.

Hansen, Lorraine Sundall. *Career Guidance Practices in School and Community.* Washington, D.C.: National Vocational Guidance Association, 1970. This book, prepared under the direction of ERIC Counseling and Personnel Services Center, is a must for anyone working in career development. Chap. 4, "Career Guidance Utilizing Advanced Media and Technology," is appropriate here.

Harris-Bowlsbey, Jo Ann. *Structure and Technology for Facilitating Human Development Through Career Education.* De Kalb, Ill.: ERIC Clearinghouse in Career Education, 1975. One of the ERIC Information Series on career education, this book is especially useful with this chapter for a summary of career-guidance and career-education concepts, brief descriptions of innovative programs, and an annotated list of resources. Chap. 3, "Technology for Career Guidance," and Chap. 4, "Toward an Integrated Approach for Facilitating Human Development Through Career Education," are particularly recommended.

Hoppock, Robert. *Occupational Information.* 4th ed. New York: McGraw-Hill, 1976. Hoppock's book has been a standard reference on the use of occupational information for many years. Chap. 4, "Sources of Occupational Information," Chap. 5, "Appraising Occupational Literature," and Chap. 6, "Classifying and Filing Occupational Information," are very useful with this chapter as guides in building the occupational library.

Isaacson, Lee E. *Career Information in Counseling and Teaching.* 3rd ed. Boston: Allyn & Bacon, 1977. Part 5, "Materials Describing the World of Work," covers all types of information, filing, and technology, including computers, and provides a good overview of resources. Pp. 294–307 contain a comprehensive review of apprenticeship training, on-the-job training, and CETA.

Miller, Anna L., and David V. Tiedeman. "Technology and Guidance: The Challenge to More Elastic Existence Amid Accelerating Obsolescence." In *Vocational Guidance and Human Development.* Ed. Edwin L. Herr. Boston: Houghton Mifflin, 1974, pp. 381–398. A provocative review of what technology can do to facilitate the guidance process.

Norris, Willa, Franklin R. Zeran, Raymond N. Hatch, James R. Engelkes, and Bob B. Winborn. *The Information Service in Guidance,* 4th ed. Chicago: Rand McNally, 1979. This is an excellent, comprehensive text of all facets of the information service. Chap. 2, pp. 65–96, describes classifications systems, including the DOT and the Standard Industrial Classification (SIC).

Sinick, Daniel. *Occupational Information and Guidance.* Boston: Houghton Mifflin, 1970. Occupational "families," an important concept in organizing and using information, are discussed on pp. 16–24. Useful material for the job- or training-oriented pupil is discussed on pp. 27–38.

Super, Donald E. "Computers in Support of Vocational Development and Counseling." In *Career Guidance for a New Age.* Ed. Henry Borow. Boston: Houghton Mifflin, 1973, pp. 285–315. An excellent brief review of computer developments and their use in counseling and guidance.

————, ed. *Computer-Assisted Counseling.* New York: Teachers College Press, Columbia University, 1970. Computer systems are described by development-program directors. The discussions of the use of computers in guidance and counseling (Chaps. 1, 2, 10, and 11) are perceptive statements of their values and limitations.

U.S. Department of Labor. *U.S. Workers and Their Jobs: The Changing Picture.* Washington, D.C.: U.S. Government Printing Office, 1976. A short, easy-to-understand booklet prepared to mark the bicentennial year. Using well-done charts and brief comments, it gives an engrossing picture of the current status of and major trends in work in this country. Highly recommended for a quick orientation.

————. *Dictionary of Occupational Titles,* 4th ed. Washington, D.C.: U.S. Government Printing Office, 1977. See the discussion of this book in the chapter.

————. *Occupational Outlook Handbook.* Washington, D.C.: U.S. Government Printing Office, 1978. See the discussion of this book in the chapter.

6

Finding and Organizing
Local Information

GOALS

1
To identify local sources of career-development information.

2
To explain the types of help these sources can provide.

3
To describe how to obtain career data by surveys and
follow-ups.

4
To explain how to set up and implement plans to collect and
use local career, educational, and training information.

ONE DILEMMA FACING COUNSELORS in all settings is that most individuals need information about *local* occupations, training opportunities, job openings, and educational programs, but this type of data is the least readily available. In contrast to the abundance of well-prepared, up-to-date, national-level information, local information is scattered, fragmentary, and difficult and time-consuming to obtain. Further, the counselor must obtain it while attending to other responsibilities.

The job is not as overwhelming as it might seem, however. Some of the information systems discussed in Chapter 5 include local information. Many organizations are ready and eager to help. In Chapter 11, the role of support personnel in obtaining local information is discussed. But the counselor is the leader and planner, and his or her understanding of what is available and how to get it will determine the quality of this critical service. This chapter is designed to help the counselor build up the quantity of local information in the information system.

The collection and use of local information has strong support from both the NVGA and AVA and ACES position papers. All that was said in Chapter 5 about the importance of information applies at the local level as well as at regional, state, and national levels. Particular importance is given to identification and use of local resources for data about work and training, for exploratory experiences, and for help in finding and maintaining employment. Additionally, Wirtz (1975, pp. 36–37) emphasizes the critical need for local information for development of human resources and suggests ways to collect and make it available. Many of the programs discussed in the previous chapter can provide local as well as national occupational and educational information. The school can and should be a major resource for information about local occupations, trends, training, and educational opportunities, and about community agencies that provide assistance for training and placement (see Chapter 10).

TYPICAL SOURCES

The first step in building the local information service is to identify the vast array of persons, establishments, agencies, and services willing and able to help. Among the typical sources and services are the following:

1. EMPLOYERS   Publications, resource persons, sites for visitations
2. EDUCATIONAL AND TRAINING INSTITUTIONS   Schools, colleges, vocational-technical centers, apprenticeship programs, and special emergency programs
3. LOCAL AGENCIES AND ORGANIZATIONS   State employment services, vocational rehabilitation offices, the Chamber of Commerce, the Junior Chamber of Commerce, information and referral centers, and service clubs
4. SPECIAL CAREER-INFORMATION AND GUIDANCE PROJECTS   Programs established to fulfill this special function—VIEW, computer guidance systems
5. WORKERS AND OCCUPATIONAL GROUPS   Local groups representing professions and trades, as well as individuals willing to give information and interviews about their jobs

6. NEWSPAPERS AND OTHER LOCAL MEDIA   Feature articles, news about new industries or businesses, the telephone directory, television and radio programs

Almost every community has some representative sources in each of these categories. Surveys of local resources in which I have participated have inevitably resulted in lists so extensive that everyone involved was genuinely amazed. A closer look at each of these local resources will reveal their information potential.

Employers

Many employers, particularly those who have a sizable number of employees, distribute printed or mimeographed information about entry jobs, training programs, and advancement opportunities. Large organizations with local branches often publish elaborate and attractive brochures. Kunze (1967) gives an excellent description of the resources available, using "spectrum of occupational information media." Table 6.1 illustrates these types of resources.

"Extent of directness" indicates how closely the type of information approximates actual work experience. Not all industries and businesses provide all these experiences, but the trend, as Kunze points out, is for greater business and industrial participation and interest in providing information. Counselor requests usually receive favorable responses.

The types of experiences listed in Table 6.1 are widely used and considered valuable for occupational exploration and planning. Specialists in various fields are available for interviews, visits to schools, and career conferences. Industries provide personnel and equipment for career fairs and expositions (Musselman, 1969). Some have supported summer institutes in which teachers and counselors study local employment opportunities and prepare information for use in schools (Capehart, 1967; Patterson, 1976). Carr and Young (1967) describe a number of ways industry has made local occupational information available, including career seminars for potential dropouts and summary industrial work experience for counselors. Local leaders in business, industry, labor, and education have established councils to conduct occupational surveys and sponsored workshops to help counselors learn about occupations (Ching, 1967).

One of the oldest and most valuable methods of providing local information is the plant or business tour (Hansen, 1970, pp. 63–68). Hoppock (1976, pp. 176–187) gives one of the best explanations available on planning, carrying out, and critiquing tours.

Educational and Training Institutions

Most institutions provide attractive booklets, leaflets, and catalogues listing and describing their programs. The rapidity with which programs change, particularly in the vocational-technical area, makes it mandatory that new material be obtained each year and that communication between counselor and institution be maintained.

Some community colleges and vocational schools have films, sets of slides, or other visual material describing their programs. Although materials may be

Table 6.1   Spectrum of occupational information data

Extent of Directness	Classifications	
10	On-the-job tryout: part-time, summer jobs, work-study programs	Provides direct contact with actual work situations
9	Directed exploratory experiences: work samples, work-evaluation tasks	
8	Direct observation: visits to work settings	
7	Synthetically created work environments: combination of stimuli and environmental manipulation	Simulation of work settings and occupational roles
6	Simulated situations: career games, role playing	
5	Interviews with experts: questioning representatives of occupations, career days	Information is processed by and adapted to the needs of the individual
4	Computer-based systems: computer systems that store, retrieve, and process occupational data in response to individual requests	
3	Programmed instructional materials: books and workbooks	Information is prestructured, fixed, and designed for general use
2	Audiovisual aids: films, tapes, slides, etc.	
1	Publications: books, monographs, charts, etc.	

SOURCE: Adapted with permission from Karl R. Kunze, "Industry Resources Available to Counselors," *Vocational Guidance Quarterly,* 16, (1967) Copyright 1967 by the American Personnel and Guidance Association. Reprinted with permission.

borrowed, the discussion and explanation is best handled by a member of the college or school staff.

A well-planned visit is the best way for pupils and counselors to obtain information about local training and educational programs. The most effective visits in which I have participated included an orientation session, in which the director described the overall program using films, slides, and handouts. This session was followed by a visit to each department. Staff members described the work, allowing students to demonstrate the major activities of the program. Questions were answered at each stop, and there was a final meeting for questions and discussion. One institution even gave a brief pre- and posttest with prizes!

The local apprenticeship representative may be invited to speak to individuals and groups and to provide material about programs. A visit to sites where apprentices are working is also helpful, but it should follow an orientation to both the occupation and training programs.

Information about new programs, primarily for the disadvantaged, hard to employ, and unemployed (some programs were mentioned in Chapter 4), can be obtained from the state employment office, the local superintendent of schools, the community college, and the vocational-technical center. Since these programs frequently change, expand, or merge, fairly frequent checks are necessary. References such as Gleason (1968) and *Breakthrough for Disadvantaged Youth* (U.S. Department of Labor, 1969) are useful for orientation.

Information about local colleges is perhaps the easiest to collect but the most difficult for both counselor and pupil to understand. College catalogues often do not provide all the information needed. An error in planning caused by obsolete material or counselor misinterpretation may be costly for both high school graduates entering college and community college transfers. I have participated in several conferences in which college first-year students and junior transfers talked with their former counselors about the transition to college. Students cited repeated instances in which incomplete and inaccurate information were major impediments to smooth transition.

Information about local training and educational resources—in addition to counselor familiarity with courses, types of students, and institutional environments—is a valuable part of the information system. Even information about in-school programs, such as cooperative vocational preparation, should be included. It is sometimes erroneously assumed that everyone knows about such programs because they are nearby.

Local Agencies and Organizations

Both governmental and private agencies and organizations are excellent sources of information. Some of the Bureau of Labor Statistics' publications give regional and local information on trends and wages. It is well worth keeping in touch with the regional office of the bureau for news releases.

The state employment service is by far the most fruitful local source. Its services are outlined briefly in the *Occupational Outlook Handbook* (U.S. Department of Labor, 1978). A visit is the most effective way to learn about its programs and services and to establish working relationships. There is some evidence that rapport and understanding between counselors and employment service employees could be improved (Rossman and Prebonich, 1968). Some innovative approaches to building better relationships have been reported as quite successful. For example, school counselors have worked during summers as employment service counselors (Sudweeks, 1972).

Community organizations, in cooperation with local governmental agencies, often produce occupational and educational information. The Chamber of Commerce is a good source of information about business trends, prospective new industries, and major employers. Other services are usually available. In one community, the chamber provided the stimulus and some of the funds for a community occupational survey. Service clubs like the Rotary, Lions, and Kiwanis have committees on local training and employment opportunities. It is worth the effort to contact all of these organizations. Since many local business and industry executives are members, contact with these organizations may help to identify employers who have been overlooked.

The local office of vocational rehabilitation is another valuable community resource. A personal visit is recommended, both for an up-to-date explanation of its services and to establish communication and working relationships. The local civil service office may provide information about occupational opportunities and qualifying examinations. This information is likely to be more regional and national than local in scope but the announcements are of interest to many pupils and will contribute to the comprehensiveness of the school information system.

Many communities support information and referral centers that maintain current lists of all types of educational, training, and placement programs. This type of agency is a good starting point for identifying community career-development resources.

Special Career-Information and Guidance Projects

The Educational Resources Information Center, or ERIC, funded in 1966 and moved to the National Institute of Education in 1972, is the best system for locating information about career guidance and career education. Sixteen clearing-houses, each responsible for a specific area of information or type of service, provide copies or guides to sources of research report and project descriptions. The "fugitive" material (Brandhorst, 1977)—difficult-to-locate or obtain material, such as project descriptions and curriculum material—is listed and annotated in the monthly catalogue, *Research in Education*, published by the U.S. Government Printing Office. Journal articles are covered by *Current Index to Journals in Education*, published by Macmillan Information, 866 Third Avenue, New York 10022.

Of the sixteen clearing-houses, the ones most likely to have career-development information are

ERIC Clearinghouse on Career Information
Ohio State University
Center for Vocational Education
1960 Kenny Road
Columbus, Ohio   43210

ERIC Clearinghouse on Counseling and Personnel Services
University of Michigan
School of Education Building, Room 2108
Ann Arbor, Michigan   48109

ERIC Clearinghouse on Handicapped and Gifted Children
Council for Exceptional Children
1920 Association Drive
Reston, Virginia   22091

More than six hundred microfiche collections are available around the country, and more than a thousand terminals in various locations have on-line access to ERIC. The user can locate material in *Research in Education,* a publication available in nearly all major libraries in the world. Reports can be located in the microfiche files and read on the microfiche reader; many libraries can provide hard copy from the microfiche cards. Noncopyrighted material may also be obtained in either microfiche or hard-copy form from

ERIC Document Reproduction Service
Computer Microfilm International Corporation
P.O. Box 190
Arlington, Virginia   22210

The ERIC system provides access to all sorts of educational studies, reports, program descriptions, and evaluations; everything listed is either available directly or in a relatively easy-to-locate source such as a guidance journal. ERIC is an invaluable source of the types of data so necessary to counselors but so hard to obtain.

The newest and potentially one of the most comprehensive and useful sources of local information are computer guidance systems, such as those described in Chapter 5. National data banks also cover many local training and educational institutions. Information about local occupations, however, must be obtained and processed in the specific area. One example is the INQUIRY project (see Chapter 5) (Farmer, 1976). Subsystems contain local occupational and educational data in addition to a national data bank. ECES IV (Educational Career Exploration System) provides information on local training and educational opportunities, but it is particularly helpful locally through its placement step, in which information about job openings is provided. Employers can also use this file to identify students available to fill jobs. The junior high school CVIS (Computerized Vocational Information System) provides pupils with information about high school programs related to occupational preferences. The high school version contains local data about community colleges, companies offering apprenticeships, technical and specialized schools, and entry information about jobs. The program is designed so that there is practically unlimited opportunity for local programming. DISCOVER also has several local data files. Submodule 8a, local jobs, helps the user develop his or her own job bank. National files on apprenticeships, community colleges, technical and specialized schools, and continuing education also include local information.

The Oregon Occupational Information Access System (OIAS) is designed to provide both statewide and local information. After the user completes occupational exploration, the computer provides labor-market data, a description of the nature of the work and working conditions of occupations, and names of state training and educational institutions. A unique type of local information contained in the computer is the names of local individuals who are willing to discuss their occupations with students. The computer also provides information about the availability of taped interviews with workers in various occupations.

The type of data generated in the JOB-FLO program is also local. Moreover, the individual who wishes to locate a specific job opening may do so with the assistance of the employment service in his or her own community. The major emphasis of the occupational system's grant program is to insure the provision of local information to pupils and adults who need it.

Workers and Occupational Groups

Local groups representing all categories of occupations are potentially fruitful sources of information. They can usually provide lists of accredited preparation programs, general occupational descriptions, and information about local opportunities. They may provide speakers for career conferences and may help the counselor build a list of resource persons who will meet with pupils for informational interviews. Although this resource is time-consuming to establish, its potential benefits are substantial. A face-to-face interview with a worker in the job setting, for example, the dentist's office, the machinist's shop, or the buyer's store, will give the pupil a more vivid and realistic picture than could be obtained from any other source short of actual work experience. True, the information may be biased. The person interviewed may try to promote his or her occupation. But if the counselor helps in planning for the interview and follows it up with a discussion of its content, misinformation and biases may be corrected.

Newspapers and Other Local Media

In addition to the want ads, which give fragmentary information about local occupational needs, features and news articles often provide announcements and descriptions of new businesses or industries, educational and training programs, and agencies to help job hunters. Coverage is variable, however. Some occupational areas fare much better than others, and a considerable amount of material is rated as difficult reading for potential consumers (Gutsch and Logan, 1967).

Radio and television programming devoted specifically to occupational information is usually not extensive, but much data are broadcast in news programs, special features, and spot announcements. News items that give information about summer job placement programs, for example, provide valuable information for the counselor. Announcements about vocational-technical education are widely distributed and appear to be well designed and stimulating. On the negative side, occupational stereotyping, often characteristic of drama and sometimes even of documentaries, can be quite misleading.

THE COMMUNITY OCCUPATIONAL SURVEY

Surveys may be of many types, serve different purposes, and be organized in different ways. Baer and Roeber (1964, pp. 342–344) identify four types: career development (pupils' futures); occupational (the local occupations); educational (the training and educational opportunities); and community services and resources (agencies and organizations that provide placement, financial aid, training, and so on). Data may be collected by mailed questionnaires, pupil interviews, counselors and teachers, or community volunteers. A survey may focus on a specific topic, such as entry jobs in manufacturing, or may cover a representative sample of employers in the community.

In-service education can be combined with data collection. Elder (1969) describes a community occupational survey done by counselors for which college credit was awarded. Clark (1962) conducted a local survey and gained a comprehensive understanding of the climate of industrial jobs while collecting information of value for guidance and curriculum planning.

Pupils can learn about jobs by doing brief personal-interest surveys (Vineyard and Brobst, 1962). This type of activity may be expanded, making coverage systematic and the results available for others to use. Surveys of this type made by counselors (Laramore and Thompson, 1970) have had multiple benefits: counselors learned about the world of work, became involved in producing career information, and developed a tape library for the school. Hoppock describes a procedure in which pupils survey beginning jobs as a way of finding employment and making a larger vocational choice. The survey is cooperatively planned to help pupils identify jobs that might otherwise have been overlooked, obtain a list of prospective employers, gain a realistic picture of the world of work, and gain skill in interviewing employers. The method is described fully, and surveys made by others are summarized (1976, pp. 203–208).

Job analysis is a formal and systematic process not usually associated with the survey. The general approach, however, can be used in visits to observe workers (Sinick 1970, pp. 46–50; Norris, Zeran, Hatch, and Engelkes, 1972). Awareness of the criteria used in job analysis will sharpen the counselor's perceptions when talking with employers and observing workers. Carrying out several job analyses to gain an understanding of job demands and working conditions is valuable.

Let us now briefly review the usual steps in a community occupational survey. More complete directions are available in Norris, Zeran, Hatch, and Engelkes (1972, pp. 300–323), including a checklist of steps to be taken and sample forms to be used. Elder's report[1] of an in-service workshop survey also gives some helpful suggestions.

1. *Identify the Need for the Survey*
   a. Specify the problem, for example, youth unemployment or lack of local information for counselees.
   b. Decide on the general types of information needed.

2. *Build Interest*
   a. Talk with other individuals and groups who may participate and lend support.
   b. Hold a meeting to discuss the purpose of the survey and how it may be achieved.

[1]Lawrence A. Elder, "An Inservice Community Occupational Survey," *Vocational Guidance Quarterly*, 17, No. 3 (1969), pp. 185–188. Copyright 1969 American Personnel and Guidance Association. Used by permission.

3. *Set Up a Survey Committee and Subcommittees*
   a. Have the survey committee appoint a director, establish a budget, and state its specific purposes. Set geographical limits, select methods of data collection, develop a timetable, and appoint subcommittees. Most of these tasks can be turned over to the survey director after the committee has established its policy—that is, after the purposes, types of information to be collected, and geographical area have been agreed on.
   b. Appoint subcommittees for the following functions:
      (1) Preparation of the lists of employers to be contacted
      (2) Publicity, including advance notice to the employers selected
      (3) Preparation of data-collection instruments. Training of interviewers, if this technique is employed. Computer use should be investigated
         (a) Tryout of instruments on subjects similar to those to be surveyed and subsequent modification, if necessary
      (4) Preparation of forms for a data summary. A close tie-in with the work of the instrument-preparation committee is essential; otherwise, needed information may be overlooked, unnecessary data may be collected, or it may prove difficult or impossible to tabulate and summarize the data collected.
      (5) Survey of data already available. Similar surveys may have been done. Some information may already be in usable form. The preliminary contacts with individuals and groups (Chamber of Commerce, apprenticeship council, union, employment service) may have identified relevant information. Asking an employer for detailed information he or she has just provided to another survey or that is contained in readily available reports evokes negative reactions.
      (6) Preparation of the report and utilization of results. An adequate number of copies of the final report should be prepared for counselors, teachers, and key persons in the community. This committee should work closely with the publicity committee to prepare releases for newspapers, television, and radio. Materials for presentation to community groups and classes could be prepared in cooperation with school media departments.
      (7) Updating the survey. Plans should be made for keeping the survey data current and for conducting future surveys.

4. *Carry Out the Survey*
   a. Make the timetable reasonable and flexible. Typically, contingencies arise and delays occur. It is quite easy to underestimate the time needed to obtain returns on mailed questionnaires or to interview employers. The PERT approach (Cook, 1966) is useful in identifying steps and making up a sequential chart of activities.
   b. Use a variety of methods to increase the percentage of mailed returns or completed interviews. Telephone calls, mailed follow-ups, and personal visits may elicit additional replies. It may be necessary to make several trips for a difficult-to-schedule interview. Publicity may give the survey visibility and status and thus increase returns.

5. *Analyze Data and Prepare the Report*
   a. Designate sections of the report to correspond to purposes of the survey. Elder (1969, p. 187) used the following outline for a report on employment opportunities in Santa Cruz County, California:

   (1) A list of employers, job titles in each establishment, and names of persons to contact
   (2) A list of jobs with code numbers
   (3) A summary for each job, including:
       (a) Employment potential
       (b) Remuneration
       (c) Training requirements
       (d) A cross-reference to "1" above, showing establishments in which the job area is found
   (4) A cross-reference by establishment and job title
   b. Design multimedia presentations for classes and community groups. Slides, transparencies, and audio tapes increase the impact.

6. *Make Plans to Update the Survey*
   a. Use data-processing cards so that new information can be added easily.
   b. Appoint a standing committee to keep the updating process current.

Community occupational surveys have tremendous potential for enhancing local information. But multiple benefits are almost inevitable. The business and industrial community and the schools experience increased rapport. Survey participants learn about work. The public is impressed with the school's interest in the community and its practical activity.

THE FOLLOW-UP STUDY

Follow-up of former pupils is a valuable technique for assessing the effectiveness of the total guidance and counseling program, as well as the information system. It may also be used to provide information on local occupational, educational, and training opportunities. Norris, Zeran, Hatch, and Engelkes (1972, pp. 314–323) point out that the follow-up is infrequently used to obtain local occupational and educational information, but that it could be used to provide data about local employment opportunities, requirements, on-the-job training, and advancement possibilities. Data can also be obtained about educational and training opportunities, such as admission requirements, characteristics needed for success, and occupations to which the preparation leads.

Pupils can benefit from conducting the follow-up. Hoppock (1976, pp. 164–175) recommends this procedure as a way to help pupils gain a realistic picture of the world of work.

Career development can be studied. Baer and Roeber (1964, pp. 349–357) describe a follow-up procedure of this type. I have followed up counselors to obtain data on career patterns for use with currently enrolled students. I also used a variation of the follow-up to help college students find summer jobs. A file of summer jobs was built by asking graduating seniors and those who did not plan to return to the same job the following summer to fill out a card listing address, person to contact, remuneration, and reactions. The file was widely used and seemed to be more accurate than many directories listing summer employment opportunities.

The follow-up as an evaluation technique seems to be infrequently used (Kramer, 1970). Although I know of no statistics on the use of the occupational follow-up, it is likely that this specialized approach is used even less frequently. With the increasing emphasis on accountability, however, we may expect to see a resurgence of interest in the "payoff" criterion—what happens to the schools' products?

The mechanics of follow-up studies are explained in several sources (Hansen and Herr, 1967, pp. 100–114; Norris, Zeran, Hatch, and Engelkes, 1972, pp. 314–323; Hoppock, 1976, pp. 164–175). The steps in a follow-up resemble those in the occupational survey.

1. *Determine the Purpose*
   a. Remember that the focus is on occupational and educational information and be sure to cover the following areas:
      (1) Job now held
      (2) Nature of the work
      (3) Training and/or experience required
      (4) How the job was located
      (5) Reactions to the work
      (6) High school courses that are beneficial
      (7) Opportunities for advancement, including employee training

2. *Enlist the Support of Others*
   a. Contact school and community persons and agencies for assistance and financial support.
   b. Check on follow-up activities in the school.
      (1) Some departments, for example, vocational, agriculture, and home economics, routinely follow up pupils.
      (2) Some post–high school educational and training institutions regularly give the school feedback on former pupils.

3. *Form a Follow-up Committee*
   a. Enlist wide representation from school departments.
   b. Use lay persons and community agencies.
   c. Decide on groups to be followed up, data to be collected, and method of data collection. The mailed questionnaire is widely used, but some follow-ups have used pupils to establish contact and deliver and pick up questionnaires.

4. *Assign Staff Responsibilities or Set Up Subcommittees*
   a. Make specific assignments, including the following:
      (1) Preparation of the lists of names and addresses
      (2) Preparation of the data-gathering instrument

(3) Preparation of forms for summary and analysis (Data-processing equipment will greatly facilitate the process, from printing of address labels to analyzing results)

(4) Publicity on the follow-up. Orientation for current pupils and news releases to the community are helpful. Pupils may encourage respondents to return the forms and be motivated to reply themselves when they have left school

5. *Carry Out the Follow-up*
   a. Set up a time table. PERT (Cook, 1966) is a helpful approach.
   b. Use a variety of methods to increase the percentage of returns. Many subjects will not return the first questionnaire. Additional mailings will inevitably be needed. Some will never respond. Telephone calls, visits, and messages carried by pupils may help in some cases. A low level of response may seriously bias the results. Its effects should not be as harmful for the occupational as for the evaluation survey, but the value of the former will be considerably lessened by partial returns.

6. *Summarize Data; Prepare and Distribute the Report*
   a. Make enough copies so that all interested persons may receive one.
   b. Prepare a multimedia presentation of the important findings for the school staff, pupils, and community groups.
   c. Suggest ways in which the results of the survey may be used, for example, counseling, group guidance, and career days.

7. *Prepare Plans for Additional Follow-ups*
   a. Modify procedures and techniques, in response to the results of the completed follow-up.
   b. Prepare a step-by-step plan for the continuation of follow-up procedures.

There are several other methods for collecting and making available local occupational, educational, and training information. Some innovative approaches are described next.

OTHER SOURCES

In each of the following procedures, counselors have shown creativity and ingenuity in devising ways to obtain information and have often involved pupils in an active learning experience. Bradley and Thacker (1978) prepared slide presentations with cassette tapes of local occupations. Establishing contacts with employers is reported as one of the chief benefits of the project. Munger's (1967) "Speaker's Bureau" was composed of students who used local interviews and observation, as well as information from printed material, to prepare brief talks to group guidance classes and home rooms. The pupil-speakers were well received by classes and faculty. After the presentations, the demand for occupational information increased substantially. Demain and DuBato (1970) used pupils to plan and run career conferences. Pupil needs were identified, local speakers obtained, and introductions at meetings given by pupils. Evaluations indicated that the active participation was a valuable learning experience. Other programs with which I am familiar involve pupils in planning and conducting career fairs, making 8mm movies and tape recordings of workers, and collecting printed information for the occupational file.

Students in graduate guidance and counseling courses may be used to collect local information. Laramore (1971) describes the preparation of occupational-information packages, consisting of 8mm films or slides and scripts, by students in an introductory guidance course; the packages were made available to pupils and counselors at a reasonable price. The visual information illustrated the major tasks of the occupation, and the tape-recorded script took the form of a dialogue, tour, or other appropriate activity. The experience was rated by counselors as an effective way to learn about occupations. The packages were described as well done and very helpful.

Smaby and Holton (1975) describe a unique program to prepare resource persons to give information to small groups of students. A model was presented to help those representing occupations communicate with pupils, including a brief review of human-relations skills. Evaluations were highly favorable to the program.

Finally, local information may be available within the school. Johnson and Briggs (1972) found that forty-one school staff members had worked in well over a hundred occupations, attended forty-eight colleges and universities, and traveled widely.

Local information is valuable to the extent that it is used to help pupils, either directly or indirectly. indirect help, through curriculum planning, is discussed in Chapter 9. Direct help is provided by making it a part of the information system.

WORKING WITH SOURCES

The first step in setting up the local information aspect of the information system is to establish priorities. Everything cannot be done at once. The following suggested procedures could be adapted to the local situation. Items 1, 2, and 3 would be carried on concurrently, with emphases in the order given. The suggestions may appear overly detailed and elementary, but my experience suggests that these little details are important and worth the time and effort they require.

1. *Establish a File of Major Employers in the Community*
   a. Contact the employment service and the Chamber of Commerce for the names of those employing the largest number of workers.
   b. Use the telephone and a state directory of business and industry (if available) to help build the list.
   c. Begin calling or writing these establishments to identify a person who can serve as a contact and to request information on job opportunities. Emphasize entry jobs at this stage.
   d. Make up 3 × 5 cards with the names of establishments and the names and telephone numbers of contact persons.

e. Plan to visit each one over a period of six months or a year to establish working relationships, gather additional information, and learn about the business or industry.

f. Use the card file for referral of pupils. File the material obtained in manila folders in a local employers file. Since each establishment will have different types of jobs, the employers file should be cross-referenced to the occupational file.

g. Include occupational-survey material in the employers file. It is suggested that the survey be a lower-priority item and, if made, scheduled for the second year.

2. *Establish a File of the Major Resource Agencies in the Community*

a. Begin with the employment service and the vocational rehabilitation office. Call for an appointment. Visit each, obtain a list of services provided, and discuss the procedures they prefer for referrals. Obtain names and telephone numbers of contact persons.

b. Continue the list by adding the names of other agencies. Call to make an appointment for a personal visit. Follow the procedure just outlined for each one. The result will be a card file giving the agency's name and function, the name and telephone number of the person to contact, and notes about its services.

3. *Begin to Build a List of Resource Persons*

a. Use various methods to obtain names, telephone numbers, addresses, and occupations of individuals who will serve as information resources for pupil interviews, career days, and group guidance sessions. Among the methods of building such a list are the following:

   (1) Prepare a notice for pupils to take home so that parents can indicate interest in participating.

   (2) Survey school staff members for occupational experience.

   (3) Announce the program on local newspaper, radio, and television and ask for volunteers.

b. Prepare guidelines for occupational interviews and discuss them at a meeting of interested persons.

c. Screen the list of volunteers, with the help of school staff members who know the community. (Not everyone who volunteers will be a suitable resource person!)

d. Use the file to refer pupils and follow up for reactions.

4. *Begin to Plan an Occupational Follow-up of Pupils*

a. Begin by discussing the plan with current seniors. Concentrate on building enthusiasm for responding to a follow-up at the end of their first year out of school.

b. Plan to expand the follow-up by including dropouts and those who have already graduated.

5. *Begin to Build Plans for a Community Occupational Survey*

a. Discuss plans with community organizations and employers.

b. Set a target date for organizing a committee to begin planning the survey.

(Investigate the possibilities of utilizing the VIEW system. Contact the director, at the address already given, to explore ways of using this system.)

GETTING THE JOB DONE

The activities just outlined may seem overwhelming. After all, local information is only part of the information system, and the counselor has other responsibilities that will not wait. Obstacles may arise. School policy may require that he or she be available in the building at all times. Is it actually possible to collect enough local information to be useful?

Several suggestions may help the counselor resolve the time problem. First, career guidance and counseling are gaining more and more educational and community support. A priority higher than in the past will undoubtedly be given to local occupational and educational information. Its collection will be expected or even required. Second, support personnel can do much of the work (see Chapter 11.) Third, setting limited and practical immediate goals will relieve some of the pressure and reduce the frustration caused by competing demands. The goal will thus appear possible, and each accomplishment will represent a step toward it. A modified systems approach may be helpful in the planning.

The collection process, the persons involved, and the goal to be achieved may be thought of as a system. Each part, for example, the file of local employers, is a subsystem. A plan is made, with estimates of the time required for each part. The sequence of steps is based on the local priorities. For example, it was suggested earlier that information about local employers is most important and should be collected first. In a particular school, however, it may be more important to develop good relations with the employment service and begin referrals for testing and placement. As each subsystem is completed, it fits into the total local information system and contributes to the overall goal. The counselor thus proves himself or herself accountable for providing pupils with local information, makes use of local resources, and develops community support for the school guidance and counseling program.

The local occupational information service may also be conceptualized as a subsystem of the total information system. Without this local component, the system will not meet the needs of a large percentage of pupils.

SUMMARY

This chapter has emphasized the importance of local occupational, educational, and training information for career counseling and guidance. Major sources, such as employers, educational and training institutions, community agencies, and individuals, have been discussed, and procedures for including them in the information system have been suggested. A brief list of steps for conducting the community occupational survey and for following up on pupils has been given. Local occupational information has been characterized as a subsystem in the total information system.

PROJECTS AND EXPERIENTIAL ACTIVITIES

1. Visit an employer to discuss entry jobs and ways that a school-employer working relationship may be established.

2. Visit the state employment service to learn about its service, types of acceptable referrals, and the procedures the staff recommends for cooperative school–employment service working arrangements. If there is a CETA program available, include a visit to it to learn about local guidance, training, and placement services.

3. Identify examples of local occupational information in the media. Evaluate their informational value for high school and college students and adults.

4. Visit a school, college, or community agency guidance office and look over the supply of local occupational and educational information. Ask the counselor how it is collected and used.

5. If a computer guidance system is available, investigate the local occupational and educational information it provides. Evaluate the usefulness of the data and the effectiveness of the delivery system.

6. Using small groups from the class, ask each group to arrive at a list, in rank order, of the five most useful sources of information about the counselor-education program for someone considering making application for admission. At the conclusion, have the groups report results to the class. Were there any important types of information that were not available?

7. Make an inventory of resource persons on the counselor-education (or education) faculty. Find out how many nonguidance occupations each has had. Discuss the results in terms of what they imply for availability of resource persons on the faculty of a school or college or on the staff of an agency.

8. Use a role-playing situation to design a community occupational survey or a pupil follow-up study. If possible, include local persons who have some knowledge of the practical problems to be encountered: a school counselor who can discuss the availability of pupils' names and addresses and the adequacy of clerical help, or an employment service counselor who can describe the community's businesses and industries, typical entry jobs, and labor supply.

9. Prepare a follow-up form for occupational information and send copies to last year's counselor graduates in education. Evaluate the value of the responses for guidance.

10. Review recent issues of *Research in Education* for reports that describe local information programs and projects. Write to the ERIC centers listed in this chapter for lists of special reports about collecting and providing local information.

11. Inventory class members to determine what types of work they have done and determine for which of those jobs they could serve as resource persons. Then arrange one (or several) role-playing interview in which another class member who is considering one of the jobs interviews the resource person about it. At the conclusion of the interview(s) discuss the questions asked, the information provided, and whether or not bias was apparent in the worker's comments.

12. Arrange for each class member to spend up to a day shadowing someone on a job or in a training program with which they are not familiar. (The telephone directory is a good source of services and establishments.) Discuss the results in class in terms of effectiveness of this technique to learn about work and major positive and negative insights about the work or training.

ADDITIONAL REFERENCES

NOTE: See references for Chapter 5. Many apply to local information also.

Baer, Max F. *Occupational Information*. 3rd ed. Chicago: Science Research Associates, 1964. Chap. 14, "Developing Local Sources of Information," covers essentially the same local sources mentioned in this chapter. However, the author also describes a vocational development follow-up study, an interesting variation on the pupil follow-up.

Hansen, Lorraine Sundal. *Career Guidance Practices in School and Community*. Washington, D.C.: National Vocational Guidance Association, 1970. Examples of local information programs are given throughout this book. Skimming to locate relevant sections is recommended. Chap. 2, "Practices and Programs in the Schools," is a good starting point.

Norris, Willa, Franklin R. Zeran, Raymond N. Hatch, and James R. Engelkes. *The Information Service in Guidance*. 3rd ed. Chicago: Rand McNally, 1972. Local sources of information are given comprehensive treatment. Part 4, "Sources of Information—Local/Primary," is an excellent reference for this chapter.

7

Individual Counseling for Decision Making and Development

GOALS

1
To explain counselor roles and strategies in providing career-development assistance to individuals.

2
To describe the nature of the helping relationship in career counseling.

3
To describe the contribution of career-development theories to individual assistance.

4
To help the reader develop a personal style for helping individuals with career choices and plans.

To THIS POINT, we have focused on theories of career development and information. This chapter emphasizes individual counseling, and the next chapter emphasizes working with small groups. Chapter 9 discusses the total guidance program. These three chapters translate the theories and materials covered earlier into practice.

The role of the counselor is discussed first, followed by a review of the general principles of the helping relationship. Decision-making theory is then reviewed in conjunction with related guidance and counseling approaches. These three areas are synthesized into a counseling approach to facilitate career choice and implementation. The relationship of this approach to the information system is explained and illustrated.

THE COUNSELOR'S ROLE

The clearest, most concise, and most authoritative statement of the counselor's role has come from school counselors themselves. Its major features are summarized under the following headings: *who* the counselor is, *what* he or she does, *where* he or she works (ASCA, 1966).

The counselor in the school is a person who works as a member of the pupil personnel team to help pupils achieve growth, development, and self-fulfillment. He or she values each individual as unique and worthy. He or she perceives the school as a democratic institution dedicated to helping each individual achieve maximum development. He or she views society as providing almost limitless opportunities in complex, dynamic, and challenging environments. The school counselor is a professional with unique skills in the art and science of helping others in their quest for identity and fulfillment.

The critical importance of the career-counseling service is clearly set forth in the NVGA/AVA joint position paper and the ACES statement of counselor competencies. Most of the recommendations of the position paper apply to the type of assistance provided in face-to-face help, which could be group as well as individual. Specifically, it is recommended that each individual have the opportunity to understand the factors involved in choice, the rewards associated with each choice, the probabilities of success, the importance of attitudes and values in these choices, and the consequences. Each individual should know how to identify and analyze data essential to the choice process. Insuring that each person has opportunities requires availability of a substantial amount of individual assistance.

The unique career-development competencies needed by all counselors are succinctly stated in the ACES statement. The following competencies have specific implications for individual work and apply across the board, regardless of employment setting:

Career-assessment strategies and the skills necessary to assist individuals to use these data in the decision-making process

Individual and group-counseling practices and the skills necessary to assist individuals in career planning using both approaches

Career decision-making processes and the skills necessary to implement programs designed to facilitate career decision making for clients in educational and community agency settings

The unique career-development needs of special client groups (women, minorities, handicapped, disadvantaged, and adults) and the skills necessary to assist them in their development

The roles that life-style and leisure play in career development and the skills necessary to assist clients in selecting and preparing for occupations that coincide with various preferences

Synthesizing categories and the skills necessary to assist individuals to understand the interrelatedness of their career decisions and life roles[1]

The underlying theme of these competencies is helping individuals with decision making, individually or in groups, which is one of the most critical tasks of counselors. Decisions may be needed for immediate choices of work, or they may be made in a developmental context—to identify and try out special abilities. Effectiveness in decision making is one of the most, if not the most, critical factors in career development.

These values and competencies partially define the counselor's role. They indicate *who* the counselor is. What the counselor does is a second dimension.

Major Functions

Ten major functions make up the school counselor's work. Counseling—working face-to-face with individuals and small groups—is the major function. More than any other activity, it draws on the counselor's unique personal and professional helping capacities. Leadership in developing the guidance and counseling program is a second essential function. Career guidance, counseling, and development combine three specific services—appraisal, information, and placement—that contribute to pupils' personal, social, educational, and career development. Each function interacts with others to help the whole individual.

The counselor's five remaining functions are coordination of resources to provide needed help, parental assistance, consultation with staff and administration, research on pupil needs and effectiveness of services, and community-pupil relations. All these activities help pupils by making available a growth-facilitating relationship, appraisal, referral, environmental information, and appropriate learning experiences. They are facilitated by a supportive work setting.

The counselor's role is flexible and open-ended. He or she may emphasize certain aspects of particular local concern or may develop innovative, less time-consuming ways to provide traditional services. Current social and economic trends suggest that new approaches are needed, particularly for special groups.

[1]L. Sunny Hansen, "ACES Position Paper: Counselor Preparation for Career Development/Career Education," *Counselor Education and Supervision,* 17, No. 3 (1978), pp. 168–179. Copyright 1978 American Personnel and Guidance Association. Used by permission.

Recent developments in career education, use of computers, and ways of conceptualizing role dimensions add to the functions already given and clarify their application. Hoyt (1976, pp. 7–10) describes counselors' functions in career education from three perspectives; the composite picture gives considerable emphasis to leadership, coordination, consulting, and upgrading of career guidance service. The career-education function (see Chapter 10) gives a much clearer picture of what counselors can do to spread career-development assistance throughout an institution.

Table 5.1 (p. 162) identifies the career-education and guidance functions that are best handled by teacher/curriculum, computer, group counseling, individual counseling, and community. For individual counseling, primary responsibilities involve helping the individual see the relation between self and occupational-educational information and learn attitudes and skills needed for finding and holding a job. Responsibility shared with the four other services and facilities mentioned involves the following types of help: self-concept formulation and clarification; reality testing of occupational alternatives; implementation of choices; learning vocational skills; and economic awareness (Harris-Bowlsbey, 1975, p. 43).

Concepts of the dimensions and priorities in guidance and counseling further describe how the career counselor's functions may be planned and carried out. The cube model of Morrill, Oetting, and Hurst (1974) places counselor functioning on three dimensions corresponding to the sides of a cube, as shown in Figure 7.1.

Individual counseling is one method of intervention by direct services. It is the most costly in terms of time and money but is frequently the necessary strategy. Consultation and training, which are usually group approaches, spread the effects of career guidance much more widely and are often used in career education, for example, helping teachers learn how to present occupational information. Use of such media as computer guidance systems and slide-sound–group participation programs, is also growing rapidly.

The cube model, as well as others discussed here, incorporates the emphasis that MacKay (1975) recommends—that decisions are not isolated matchings of persons and educational programs or occupations but rather events in the lifelong developmental process. Decisions about particular jobs are part of the ongoing process of development; they may involve reality testing, role playing, and mastery of job-entry skills, developmental tasks, and job-coping skills.

Ivey's (1976) concept of the psychoeducator model gives major emphasis to the educational and developmental roles. Prevention is followed by remediation and rehabilitation. In some ways, the model is in line with the major thrust of career education (see Chapters 9 and 10).

These concepts of career-counselor functions show the variety of approaches available for work with many different subpopulations. One approach of particular importance involves contacting individuals in their own settings rather than waiting for them to come to the counselor's office. The target group can range from the individual to the institution (school, community). Primary groups include basic social units, such as the family, and associational groups, such as those made up of individuals brought together by choice or circumstances, such as classes or clubs. In this chapter, the main focus is on the individual; it is important to note, however, that each individual is a member of a number of groups.

Figure 7.1   The cube model of Morrill, Oetting, and Hurst

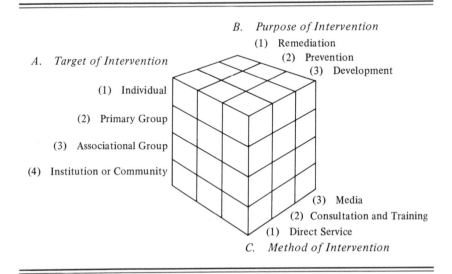

B.   *Purpose of Intervention*
(1) Remediation
(2) Prevention
(3) Development

A.   *Target of Intervention*

(1) Individual

(2) Primary Group

(3) Associational Group

(4) Institution or Community

(3) Media
(2) Consultation and Training
(1) Direct Service
C.   *Method of Intervention*

SOURCE: Weston H. Morrill, Eugene R. Oetting, and James C. Hurst, "Dimensions of Counselor Functioning," *Personnel and Guidance Journal,* 52, No. 6 (1974), 355. Copyright 1974 American Personnel and Guidance Association. Reprinted with permission.

The purpose of the help to the individual may be remediation, prevention, or developmental. Career decision making could be prevention but would typically be developmental—how to make optimum use of abilities and interests and avoid problems. The four types of counseling for career development suggested by Morrill and Forrest (1970) also show the multiple purposes of individual work. Type 1, usually short-term, helps the individual with a specific decision. Emphasis is on providing various types of self and occupational information and assistance with clarification of issues and problems. Type 2 focuses on the specific decision to be made and also on teaching decision-making skills for future use. Type 3 emphasizes the developmental process and views decisions as sequential activities in that process. Type 4 aims to help the individual in the developmental process by helping him or her to master tasks, utilize strengths, and build coping skills.

The setting has a substantial influence on the degree to which the counselor can implement his or her beliefs and carry out his or her functions. A reasonable pupil load is a major factor. Around 250 pupils per counselor is recommended by the ASCA statement referred to previously. Freedom from administrative, clerical, teaching, and disciplinary responsibilities is essential. Provisions should be made for research, study, and professional development. The freedom to hold school-hour conferences with pupils and to budget time as one sees fit is a necessary professional consideration. At times, the counselor might best fulfill his or her function by being absent from the school to confer with the staff of a community agency or meet the personnel director of a local industry. Freedom to try out new approaches is also characteristic of a facilitating and stimulating setting. Finally, adequate facilities, equipment, and budget are necessary. The counselor who lacks privacy or adequate files and records and is burdened with clerical tasks will find it next to impossible to use his or her expertise in helping others (ASCA, 1965, 1966, 1971).

Active Outreach

Many of the functions mentioned imply that the counselor must leave the office, go where the problems are, and seek out those who need help. Many of those who could profit from the counselor's assistance are reluctant to visit the office or ask for help (Calia, 1966; Grande, 1968). Furthermore, in order to effect changes that are beneficial to the school and the community, the counselor should have an impact on the institution; he or she should help the "system client" as well as the "student client" (U.S. Department of HEW, 1970). The counselor should also serve as a helper—a consultant—to other staff members (Lister, 1969). The counselor needs to invite teachers onto the guidance team ("Will the Real Guidance Counselor Please Stand Up?" 1971). Increased effort to understand and reach all groups—the disadvantaged, the discriminated against, the culturally different—is a top-priority need (Proctor, 1970; Aragon and Ulibarri, 1971; Atkin, 1972; Tiedt, 1972).

These emphases do not suggest a basic change in the counselor's role; it is, as Loughary (1971) says, still relevant and valid. But he, too, emphasizes the importance of the counselor's role as a social change agent—another way of saying that the counselor serves the system client. Sinick (1977) supports the concept and describes how the counselor can change society by his or her own impact on counselees, the environment, and employers, acting as a member of professional associations and as a citizen.

Outreach is part of the "new activist role" described by Rosen (1970). He advises the counselor to go out in the community, gather job information, become acquainted with employers and union leaders, and help pupils plan effective job strategies. The activist is not satisfied with helping pupils cope with the status quo. He or she uses knowledge of the community and counseling skills to motivate employers to develop more relevant and realistic requirements for employment. To use the outreach approach, the counselor has to first understand the situation. Thereafter, conditions that need to be changed become highly visible. Being a change agent is inseparably related to outreach.

Two related developments in counseling—accountability and differentiated staffing—have a direct bearing on the counselor's outreach role and potential. Support personnel free the counselor from some tasks and enable him or her to concentrate energies in needed areas. But support personnel can themselves offer guidance assistance to those who might otherwise be missed, such as minority groups, dropouts, and the unemployed.

The expectations of the public define one aspect of accountability. These expectations suggest outreach services (Gysbers, 1970; Richards, 1970). Counselors have become aware that the guidance consumer who pays the bills expects help will be provided when and where it is needed even if this requires the counselor to go more than halfway. If the *type* of assistance given is what is expected, one aspect of accountability is provided for. Demonstrating results is, of course, the major factor.

In the next section, principles of the helping relationship will be surveyed and trends will be described.

THE HELPING RELATIONSHIP

Discussions of counseling (Tyler, 1969, Chap. 3; Kell and Burow, 1970, Chap. 2) and research reports on the process (Carkhuff, 1969, Vols. 1 and 2) tend to recommend that the counseling relationship be characterized by the following conditions, variously named: acceptance, empathy, understanding or communication, trust, concern, respect, and openness (Tolbert, 1972a, pp. 134–135). These conditions make sense as important variables in a helping relationship and certainly seem desirable. The counselor should accept the other person, understand both intellectually and emotionally how the person feels, and demonstrate interest and concern. This and the other traits appear to be critical whether counseling a pupil, consulting with a teacher or principal, serving as a change agent, organizing a survey, or developing relationships with a community agency. But whether or not these conditions are absolutely essential for positive results has not been established. As Aubrey points out, the approach based on these conditions—particularly those characterized as the core facilitative conditions: empathy, respect, genuineness, and concreteness (Carkhuff, 1969, 1: 4)—is *therapeutic* and not necessarily suited to all the counselees with whom the school counselor works. The school counselor needs, according to Aubrey, "theoretical models congruent with educational purposes, and/or realistic designs which will enable guidance personnel to modify or change existing educational structures and practices" (1969, p. 277). Gladstein (1970) investigated the value of empathy in school counseling and found no evidence that it is essential. Core conditions appear to be assessed differently by counselees and judges, and the presence of these conditions does not insure satisfaction with counseling (Anthony and Lister, 1972).

Career counseling often requires considerable emphasis on information, decision making, and placement. There is enough evidence to support the position that facilitative conditions are helpful in the process, and their inclusion in the counseling climate is recommended, for they characterize a good learning and problem-solving environment. But at the same time the counselor may do a variety of other things that appear helpful. He or she may, for example, seek out a pupil who does not request help. He or she may provide information, suggest occupational information-getting interviews, or go with a pupil to visit a prospective employer. He or she may do these things without first building an ideal therapeutic relationship, for which sufficient time may not be available. He or she may provide a needed service to a counselee with whom empathy and openness are only partially developed. This is not to say that good human relationships are unnecessary. It simply says that the counseling session involves a number of factors and that a therapeutic relationship is not sufficient for decision making, nor does it completely overshadow all other aspects. Counselors for occupational decision making will combine as much of the therapeutic relationship with other counseling techniques as is practical in each situation.

In working with individuals and groups and serving as a consultant and social change agent in the school and community, counseling principles enable the counselor to put his or her role concept into action. Helping activities are based on a theory or set of beliefs about human beings and their development.

The value of adapting a specific theoretical position has been questioned. However, many theoretical positions have been formulated and are widely used (Stefflre, 1965; Patterson, 1966; Tolbert, 1972a). A particular counselor's approach is usually a blend of a theory or theories and a personal style (Shoben, 1962; Lister, 1964). It provides a road map for the counselor to help determine the goal and how to get there. It is a strategy for helping. Each counselor has some sort of theory, implicit or, ideally, explicit. He or she should be able to explain actions and expected results.

A review of these approaches or strategies is beyond the scope of this section. The important point is that the techniques and facilitative conditions taken up later are related to personal beliefs about the nature of human beings and the ways that growth and development take place.

Counseling the Disadvantaged

Questions have been raised about the suitability of the traditional verbal, self-explorative, feeling-oriented type of counseling with the culturally different, particularly blacks (Calia, 1966; Gross, 1969; Kincaid, 1969). Subcultural patterns of behavior, values, and attitudes toward community institutions underline the need for different approaches to the counseling relationship. Communication should involve modes other than verbal exchanges. Help should be action-oriented. The counselor shows understanding, interest, and concern, but he or she also does something to help the counselee (Calia, 1966; Gordon, 1967; Kincaid, 1969). He or she may assist the counselee in finding a job, go with him or her to resolve a difference with an administrator, or provide task-oriented group counseling.

The counselor needs to understand and respect cultural differences, and to show it (Vontress, 1967; Leacock, 1968). He or she needs to have faith in counselees, look for their strengths, and demonstrate respect (Washington, 1968). Help may focus on making immediate changes in the environment and planning specific remedial steps (Gordon, 1964). It should also involve long-range planning to build better relationships with pupils and to better understand them (Irvine, 1968). Counselor preferences may hinder acceptance of "different" counselees (Thompson, 1969). It may be difficult to feel honestly that the counselee is important and to make the effort needed to provide the critical help.

Adaptations in the counseling relationship are required for the disadvantaged. Faith, concern, understanding of their culture, and active involvement are the key characteristics. Counselors, under pressure to adhere to community and institutional demands, often find it difficult to build this kind of relationship. Professional preparation and personal lifestyle may also cause conflicts. Expanding the counselor's role to reach all groups, however, is another aspect of outreach counseling.

Counseling Women

The counselor functions already summarized amply cover the needs of *all* pupils. But customs, attitudes, and traditions may intrude in the counseling session and affect the helping relationship. One view is that it is virtually impossible for counselors to serve women unless they are or become, feminists (Gardner, 1971); otherwise, growth-facilitating help is not possible. Even the concepts of mental health for men and women differ, and counselors tend to stereotype women in a subservient, passive role. The "sexist" counselor is out of tune with the needs of women as a group. Such a counselor should instead make efforts to change attitudes and conditions that inhibit development of the potential of members of this special group. Only by intensive effort can the counselor hope to shed constricting attitudes.

Whether or not one agrees with this view, many would concur that there has been a tendency to neglect exploration of options for women (Ohlsen, 1968). Both counselees and counselors are influenced by learned roles and cultural pressures. Counseling that emphasizes exploration of values and educational and career opportunities is needed from an early age (Feingold, 1972). There are many reasons for a woman to have a career besides economic need, the frequently used subterfuge (Weary, 1972).

How do cultural influences, stereotypes, and limited educational and career opportunities make a difference in the counseling relationship? For one thing, females should be given more opportunity, and even challenged, to consider options and they should be given more information about opportunities—whether or not it is requested. Special sensitivity to counselee attitudes about what is normal and what is abnormal must be exhibited. For example, what counselor reactions might be evoked by a counselee who stated that her goal was to be an airline pilot rather than a hostess? How empathic would the male counselor be if an angry and frustrated counselee lashed out at "sexist" counselors and "male chauvinists"?

In Chapter 4, a number of factors that need to be considered in counseling women were discussed. More detailed information like that in the comprehensive review found in the 1975 *Handbook on Women Workers* (U.S. Department of Labor) is needed. Sections in this handbook on the education, training, and employment of women, laws affecting women's employment, and institutions and mechanisms to help improve women's status are of particular value.

Counseling Those at Mid-Life and Retirement

The review of characteristics of individuals in the mid-life through retirement periods in Chapter 4 indicates the areas of counseling concern. A great number of special programs are being developed (Harrison and Entine, 1976), but the emphasis is typically on group rather than individual work. Mid-life career programs may involve unanticipated problems caused by external events (Entine, 1977). In the postretirement period, career assistance may be provided to enable individuals to deal with the unique problems and needs of that stage, including supplementing income and finding appropriate leisure involvements. Sinick (1976) identifies major concerns with which the counselor may have to deal at both periods. For the mid-life period, motivations for career change should be explored, with special attention to indications of unrealistic expectations. Lack of self-confidence may be an important factor. A review of past achievements may be more useful than assessment with psychological measurement instruments. Assistance must frequently follow through with help for job finding and adjustment. In the retirement period, counselors should focus on role adjustments resulting from changes that have taken place, finding a satisfying use of time, and daily coping and maintenance matters. Although the typical problems and developmental tasks of the age periods may provide unique content, the process for developmental and decision-making counseling is quite similar to that discussed later; exploration of feeling, for example, is just as important for individuals at those stages as it is for those at high school and college levels.

Counselor attitudes about older persons, particularly those at the retirement age, are critical. I share with Sinick (1976) the belief that counselor age is not a barrier—young counselors can work effectively with those at mid-life or retirement. But counselor prejudices and biases can get in the way. If attitudes are negative, condescending, defensive, or apprehensive, the counselee will almost certainly be aware of it. In some cases, older persons bring up differences—for example, by commenting, "You really haven't had the experiences that I've had." This type of counselee attitude, although very threatening, should not put the counselor on the defensive.

In addition to one's own attitudes about working with older persons, it is important to be aware of counselees' feelings about counseling and guidance services, particularly if there is an attitude that implies that something is wrong with an individual, such as an emotional problem. The possibility of negative attitudes is less in career guidance than in psychotherapy, but it is still a factor, particularly with those who have had no prior contact with career counseling or who have had only negative experiences with it.

Counseling the Disabled

Most such assistance has been provided by rehabilitation counselors, but with the passage of PL 94-142 and the publication of guidelines for implementation (Humes, 1978), counselors at all educational levels will be more deeply involved with the disabled. Group procedures and environmental manipulations will frequently be used, but individual counseling will still be a major strategy. In addition to learning about the characteristics and limitations of those with various types of disabilities, the counselor must become aware of the limiting effects in occupational, training, and educational terms of each type of disability and how to interpret analyses made by other specialists. One major demand on the counselor may be reorganizing and accepting the disabled person as an individual with strengths and capabilities as well as limitations. Helping the individual face and successfully cope with disability is a major aspect of counseling. It is a critical problem for all ages—the active high school pupil who must spend years or perhaps a lifetime in a wheelchair as well as the middle-aged individual no longer able to work in a preferred occupation because of injury or illness. In addition to disabilities of recent onset, there are those the individual has always had, such as mental retardation and cerebral palsy. Each requires understanding and acceptance by the counselor, but certain types, such as mental retardation, call for special skills in communication and may tax the counselor's ability to be accepting and empathic and to believe in the potential of the individual.

The combination of other factors with a disability—such as advanced age and minority status—greatly complicates the counselor's task. In most help provided to members of special groups, more is usually needed than understanding and acceptance; the counselor must take active steps to help the individual—assist the person to get to a needed referral agency, change the environment, provide outreach services.

As far as the school counselor is concerned, the need for individual counseling with parents will certainly increase (Humes, 1978). Responsibilities will include counseling individual pupils representing a very wide range of disabilities, and these functions will likely be in addition to those for which the counselor is already responsible in the ongoing career-guidance program in the school.

Counseling Parents

One final factor involving relationships has to do with the school policy for conferring with parents. Does working closely with and holding conferences with parents have an impact on the counseling relationship? Rothney (1972, p. 90) takes the position that sharing information with parents, with discretion and adequate preparation of the parents, has a dual value. First, parents are taxpayers; they support or reject school programs in light of perceived benefits. Second, parents can provide valuable data about developmental patterns. Further, parent-counselor conferences often give rise to suggestions that are followed up at home, such as educational planning and choice of occupation (Jessell and Rothney, 1965).

Much can be said in favor of a policy of parent conferences in developmental counseling. Parents want information, appreciate help in planning with their children, and are generally enthusiastic. Perhaps some of the current criticisms of guidance and counseling would not be so severe if parents had been included in planning and sharing information.

The other side of the picture, however, suggests some hazards. If high school pupils are aware that counselors regularly hold parent conferences, it could have an adverse effect on their readiness to talk with counselors. If counselee approval were obtained for conferences, however, negative reactions would no doubt be lessened.

Rothney (1972, p. 90) suggests that the number of pupils affected negatively would be small. My experience tends to support this point of view.

Each counseling and guidance staff should determine its own position on this issue. I favor extensive use of parent conferences and close working relationships with parents. At the same time, the option of confidential conferences if pupils wish is recommended.

DECISION MAKING: A REVIEW

Decision making is perhaps the key element in career counseling and guidance. In Chapters 2 and 3, some aspects of decision making were discussed in conjunction with each vocational-development theory. Building on that material and using some concepts from decision theory, this section summarizes some of the critical factors in decision making and reviews applications to counseling and guidance. One of the decision-making models presented earlier will then be used in building an approach to career counseling.

The first concept is *alternatives.* The individual must have at least two options. No choice is possible otherwise. Second, there must be a need to make a decision. The decider needs a goal or *purpose.* He or she must choose among alternatives. All decision theories involve these two elements.

Sequential decision making is the third concept. Decisions are made continually. Each decision changes the information, or input, for subsequent decisions. Immediate decisions usually involve an awareness of potential effects on future ones. *Information,* or *input,* is the fourth element and consists of the material or data needed to carry forward the process. Information related to the purpose of the decision must be on hand to enable the decision maker to understand the options open.

The *utility* of a goal or outcome for the decision maker is one of the most useful concepts borrowed from decision theory. The utility of an outcome is its reward value for the individual. For example, the outcome of getting a job may be more desirable—have a higher utility—for a pupil than taking additional training.

The *probability* of each outcome is related to its utility. Two kinds of probabilities are involved. *Objective probability* is the more or less "factual" evidence of the likelihood of achieving an outcome. For example, nine out of ten persons with the counselee's ability succeed in auto mechanics. This type of probability, however, does not enter into decision making directly. Instead, it has an effect on the *subjective probability*—the individual's own estimate of the chances of success. His or her estimate, based on past experiences, self-concept, and level of aspiration, may be similar to or quite different from the objective probability.

Decision making is always, or practically always, done under conditions of *uncertainty;* there is an element of risk. But preference for risk may vary, that is, the utility of risk may vary with different individuals. Some prefer a considerable amount. Others may wish to avoid as much uncertainty as possible.

One final relevant concept is *maximizing gain.* The decision process is an effort to combine subjective probability with outcome utility to achieve maximum gain. For example, a male counselee is considering three alternatives: beginning as a helper in a machine shop; taking a program in machine shop in the vocational-technical center; or applying for an apprenticeship in the machinist trade. He is sure he can get the helper's job, reasonably sure he can be admitted to the vocational-technical program, but aware that he has a great deal of competition for the apprenticeship. His goal—the outcome of greatest utility for him—is to become a master craftsman. His subjective probability estimate of being admitted to the apprenticeship is much greater than the objective probability. He is confident that he will be admitted, although only one in thirty applicants will be accepted in this particular program. The high utility of the goal and the high subjective probability of being accepted combine to make this his choice.

Decision-theory concepts have been utilized in counseling, guidance, and vocational development; in addition to those covered in Chapter 3 some other innovative applications have been made. Some representative concepts are discussed next.

Decision Concepts in Counseling and Guidance

Kaldor and Zytowski (1969) use decision concepts in a theory of occupational choice that maximizes expected gain and includes the variable *indifference*, the person's attitude when the utility of two occupations is equal. Thoresen and Mehrens (1967) discuss lessening the discrepancy between subjective and objective probability estimates. The relationship appears to vary for different individuals and some will, for example, accept more risk than others. The less the discrepancy the more realistic the decision, in most cases. Thomas (1972) suggests that the majority of pupils seen by the counselor are faced with making and acting on decisions. To provide the sort of assistance needed, an approach is recommended in which the counselee first states the problem and lists the alternatives in writing. The counseling process then involves discussion and evaluation of alternatives, in keeping with decision concepts discussed previously. Morrill and Forrest (1970) suggest that vocational counseling be viewed in terms of dimensions related to career development. Four types are described, each representing a particular level of vocational development. Type 2, for example, focuses on both making a specific decision and learning decision-making skills for future use. Although decision-theory concepts play a major role in this type, they are also utilized in the other three, for example, providing information for an immediate decision, learning to view development as a series of decision points, and developing self-direction and the ability to change conditions rather than be controlled by them. Dilley (1968) outlines specific counselor behaviors that help the counselee in the decision-making process. Counselees are encouraged to take responsibility for themselves and to have faith in the future. The use of a decision-making strategy is facilitated both by explaining the strategy and promoting its use. Counselees are encouraged to expand the range of options and look at new possibilities. Finally, they are helped to interpret, synthesize, and apply information to the decision-making task and to arrive at their own decision. Dilley's lucid discussion provides the counselor with an excellent guide for decision-making help.

Jepsen's (1974, 1975) research on decision making has contributed to an understanding of the process. He defines decision-making behavior as *"the array of conscious attitudes, actions, and thoughts given in response to social expectations to assume a schooling or work position"* (1974, p. 285). Using concepts from decision theory, he investigated the process for high school juniors and found that pupils with similar backgrounds exhibit different vocational decision-making behaviors and that behaviors tended to group into four clusters: the range of activities considered, the frequency of planning activities, the level and specificity of long-range plans, and the selection of courses for the next year.

Frequency of planning activities showed only a moderate relation to such criteria as school-community activities, grade average, and amount of self-description. Additional research (1975) was carried out on the development of decision processes over the high school years. Results showed growth in information search strategy and elaborateness of rationale for occupational choice, that is, expanding the bases for choice. Both these processes contributed to the confidence felt about the occupational choice in the twelfth grade. Jepsen points out that more research is needed on developmental changes in decision-making behavior, but results so far strongly suggest that there is a maturing of some choice behaviors.

In other research (Jepsen, 1974), twelve occupational decision-making strategy types of high school pupils were identified. Strategy-Type 6, called active planners, consists of active, knowledgeable, self-aware planners, while Strategy-Type 3, called singular fatalists, consists of individuals who concentrate on a narrow range of occupations, do little searching for occupational information, and do not see the relationships of current activities to plans. Cooperative analysis of decision-making models did not show any one model to be superior (Jepsen and Dilley, 1974).

Vocational indecision has also been studied in an effort to identify factors that could be dealt with in counseling. The amount of risk the individual is willing to accept does not appear to be related to indecision (Davidshofer, 1976), but anxiety level does appear to inhibit educational and occupational choices (Hawkins, Bradley, and White, 1977). High school and college students who classify themselves as decided and undecided tend to differ in several ways: undecideds lack interpersonal competency, self-confidence, involvement, an identity, and effective decision-making skills (Holland and Holland, 1977). The pattern of traits, attitudes, and skills is related to the concept of anomie, which Holland and Holland define as the indecisive disposition. Only a small percentage of the undecided students may have this characteristic to such an extent that it acts as a barrier to choice; many undecided students do not need any special treatment and will make decisions when they must.

The process of decision making involves both intuition and cognitive processes, but the relative importance of each is a matter of controversy. Baumgardner (1976, 1977, 1977a) suggests that occupational choice is largely intuitive, particularly as one goes through college, and that the uncertainties of the world of work make logical planning and decision making ineffective. At the same time, it should be recognized that career-planning and decision-making theories involve subjective data, that the counselor's job is to help the counselee make the best possible use of both objective and subjective data, and that the realities of the world of work, such as an economic recession, must be considered (Herr, 1977; Osipow, 1977a). One major challenge of career-development counseling is to consider strengths, goals, and opportunities in a way that makes the best possible use of both intuitive and cognitive data in a systematic process. Both types of data are essential in career choice and development.

New concepts and theories about career-development and decision-making processes help to identify times at which choices must be made and strategies chosen for use in counseling. Crites's (1978) concept of the decision-making process provides a synthesis of theories and techniques that begins with general exploration, moves on to identification of the problem, and goes through an active phase of finding a solution to the presenting problem. A specific decision, however, may not be the goal; progress in development or improved general adjustment may be the most appropriate outcome. The diagnostic step is essential to the process; in it, the problem is identified, the reasons for it are uncovered, and the counselee's position in the career-development sequence is determined. Active collaboration of counselor and counselee occurs in the search for causes as well as at other stages. The counselor accepts and deals with the counselee's perceptions of reality, but the counselee assumes responsibility for what is done and selects action steps to take. Collaborative selection and interpretation of tests and the use of career information, including computers, may be part of the process.

The career-development concepts of Super, Kidd, and Watts (1977) are helpful in determining how to adapt counseling to a particular counselee. Lifestyle in their concepts means the number and types of roles taken and the width (amount of time) and depth (degree of involvement) of roles. For example, the occupational role tends to increase in width and intensity as the individual moves from childhood through adolescence and into early adulthood. Exploring these elements can lead to a better understanding of one's present situation and goals and the contribution of past experiences. Decision points occur before and at the time of taking up a new role or changing an old one; roles interact to varying degrees, so changes in one have some effect on others.

The time when decisions are approached is particularly significant for counseling: "The major types of career behaviors are observable in miniature in the decision-making process" (p. 13). Growth, exploration, and establishment take place at any age. The individual recognizes the need to make changes in roles, options and data about them are examined, and efforts are made to build a place in the new occupation. One of the major contributions of this concept of career life is the way it relates career decision making to the developmental process. This relationship is a critical element for counseling over the life span.

Decision-making concepts have wide application in individual and group counseling, guidance, and the total educational program in the school. Simulation techniques, such as career games, utilize decision concepts. Group techniques that combine learning and decision concepts have been shown to stimulate occupational information-seeking behavior (Krumboltz and Thoresen, 1964). The guidance and information systems discussed in Chapter 3 utilize decision concepts, and the career-education models described in Chapter 1 are designed to help pupils obtain and process needed information and arrive at suitable decisions. Project PLAN (Flanagan, 1969) involves short- and long-range decisions and feedback for evaluation. Learning how to manage one's own development, one of the major goals of PLAN, is essentially a process of learning how to make good decisions.

Decision-making skills are taught by the use of computer information systems, simulation, and individual counseling focusing on these skills. The computer programs already discussed use a decision-making process and in some cases teach it to the user. Evans and Cody (1969) were successful in teaching decision-making skills that transferred to other settings, using a counselinglike situation. Programmed materials have been shown to be effective in learning how to make decisions (Graff, Danish, and Austin, 1972). Elementary school pupils can learn decision-making skills with the help of a model for utilizing information about self and environment. Fear of making a poor or harmful decision is seen as the major obstacle to learning the skill (Smith, 1970).

A counseling procedure to facilitate decision making should be a synthesis of principles of the helping relationship plus decision-making concepts. The procedure suggested here combines these elements, the information system, and placement and follow-up. Until the suitability of plans has been evaluated and the counselee has either decided to continue with them or engage in further counseling, the process is not complete.

The development of new strategies, materials, technology, and concepts has important implications for decision-making counseling. For one thing, computer technology has greatly enhanced the counselor's effectiveness by practically taking over the provision of occupational information, analysis of the relationship of personal and environmental data, and teaching and evaluating of decision-making processes. Materials such as the career data books (Rossi, Bartlett, Campbell, Wise, and McLaughlin, 1975) provide interest and ability profiles for use in career exploration and evaluation goals. New multimedia and simulated materials can be used to increase the effectiveness of the counselor's work (Weinrach, 1978). Techniques such as the Self-Directed Search enable counselors to reach a large number of counselees economically (Krivatsy and Magoon, 1976). Whitehurst (1978) describes a ten- to fifteen-hour self-paced, individualized, career-guidance program for educational and career planning that includes several counselor-counselee conferences but is largely worked through by the counselee, aided by booklets and guidance-center resources. Users gave the program very positive evaluations. Each type of program or technique enables the counselor to make the most effective use possible of time spent face to face with the counselee.

The following decision-making strategy is adapted from Gelatt's Frame of Reference (Gelatt 1962; Gelatt, Varenhorst, and Carey, 1972). The acronym DECIDE is used for the process:

*D*ata,
*E*valuation, and
*C*ounseling
*I*n
*D*ecision-Making
*E*ffectiveness

This acronym does not indicate the exact steps or phases. It was devised by me and my students in a vocational-development class to provide a convenient label for the major elements in decision making. Data are collected and evaluated.

Counseling helps the individual assess the relation of data to his or her goal. The steps are as follows:

1. PURPOSE   The counselee needs to make a decision. He or she has at least two options.
2. INFORMATION   Information about the options is identified or obtained.
3. POSSIBILITIES   All possible courses of action are identified.
4. RESULTS POSSIBLE   Possible consequences of each alternative are examined.
5. RESULTS PROBABLE   The likelihood of each consequence is predicted.
6. VALUES   The personal desirability of each consequence is assessed.
7. DECISION   A choice is made. It may be
   a. Terminal
   b. Investigatory
8. FEEDBACK AND EVALUATION
   a. The counselee judges the suitability of his or her decision.
   b. The counselor evaluates the effectiveness of his or her help. Figure 7.2, adapted from Gelatt (1962), illustrates the process.

A Case in Point

This strategy may be illustrated by a brief example. A ninth-grade pupil is trying to decide whether to take the college preparatory or the vocational program. Data are needed for input. Program descriptions, test results, school marks, and occupational information are assembled. Additional information about preferences, hobbies, and parental attitudes is brought out in interviews. The two programs are the major options to be considered, though each will lead to more specific choices, such as auto mechanics or mechanical engineering. The pupil considers what is possible and what is probable and begins to favor the vocational-education route. The information about employment opportunities that has been assembled suggests that jobs will be available. Furthermore, the pupil sees this as the most rewarding role. Finally, having weighed the pros and cons of the two options, the pupil chooses the vocational program and plans to visit the vocational-technical center to obtain firsthand information about specific programs.

The counseling process has not been a rigid, lock-step experience. Values were given considerable weight. There was a shuttling back and forth, in which previous and future decision-making steps were brought in. For example, in the final selection-of-a-decision phase, new information was obtained. In the early stages of reviewing possibilities, values emerged as critical aspects of planning. The counselee engaged in a decision-making process that will be applicable to other situations involving choices.

Joe Prince, who was introduced in Chapter 1, is the counselee. Elliot Cohen, his counselor, completed graduate school two years ago with a master's degree. Joe has been referred by a teacher and his parents, but a few minutes after the beginning of

Figure 7.2   Gelatt's decision-making model used in the counseling approach

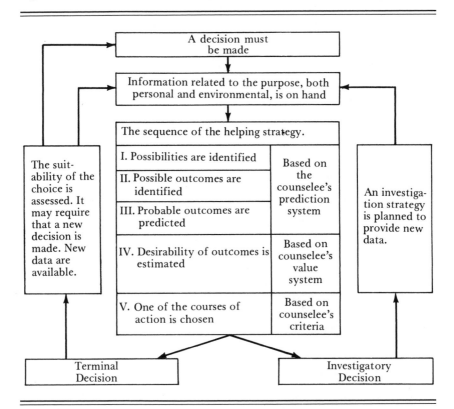

SOURCE: H. B. Gelatt, "Decision-Making: A Conceptual Frame of Reference for Counseling," *Journal of Counseling Psychology,* 9 (1962), adapted from p. 242. Copyright 1962 by the American Psychological Association. Reprinted by permission.

the first meeting he said he had to leave. Because Joe didn't show up for the next scheduled conference, the counselor took the initiative when he caught Joe in the hall a few days later. A discussion of the process used by the counselor follows, illustrated with transcripts of counselor and counselee interactions.

Seeing the Need for a Decision

Ideally, a counselee is aware of the need to decide and anxious to get started. If the counselee is not so motivated, the counselor may let the matter drop or may raise questions, make suggestions, confront or in other ways help the counselee see the need for a decision. The counselor infers the counselee's level of vocational development and uses this as a guide for the process. For example, if a counselee is at the early stages of exploration, the counselor would proceed differently than he or she would if the counselee is trying to decide between two carefully considered options. The process is carried out in a climate of interest, acceptance, and respect. The dimensions listed earlier are important in building trust, acceptance, and cooperation.

The counselor decides that he will try to motivate Joe to begin looking at options. In his judgment, Joe is vocationally immature in that he lacks self and environmental information, is unaware of the need for choice, and is reluctant to consider realistic choices.

COUNSELOR: I was sort of hoping we could talk further . . . you know, about where you're going. What happened?

COUNSELEE: Oh, I don't know. Didn't have much to say. I didn't want to take much of your time, I guess.

COUNSELOR: Joe, I'm interested. That's what my time's for . . . and you just have some things moving right on up to you. Like the end of school. You're going to have to do something.

The interview continues in the hall and later in the office. Elliot is mainly interested in showing that he wants to help, that he likes Joe, and that some choices will soon have to be made. Eventually, it turns out that the major decision revolves around college or some other alternative.

Obtaining Pertinent Information

Needed information may be personal, educational, or occupational. The pupil information service provides a record of the pupil's achievement, aptitudes, plans, and family data. Additional information is obtained in the interview, from tests and inventories, from teachers, and from parents; more may be available from the counselee's work or exploratory experiences. Environmental data about the school, for example, about school programs and organizations, may be known to the counselor. The information system provides data about educational, training, and occupational opportunities. Information may be related to the options being considered, or it may suggest additional ones.

Although a variety of data about the counselee are usually introduced during discussion of alternatives, test data require specific interpretive skill on the part of the counselor. Reliability should be adequate, and validity and norm groups should be relevant. For example, if test data on mechanical ability are used to estimate success at the vocational-technical center, the relationship of scores to success should be known, and norms should be based on students in the vocational-technical center.

If tests and inventories are to be administered to the counselee, it is suggested that the counselor

1. Discuss the purposes of testing and respond to the counselee's feelings about using them.
2. Select the instruments to be used with the counselee jointly and discuss them. The counselor describes the characteristics to be measured and suggests one or more specific instruments. The counselee makes the final selection.
3. Bring in results as needed, discuss them primarily in verbal terms, and relate them to such other data as school marks, hobbies, and plans.
4. Recognize and respond to counselee reactions. If the meaning of data is not accepted, it may be necessary to explore reasons for the resistance.
5. Help the counselee relate to various options.

Other nontest data, such as time distribution, autobiography, and rating scales may be used to help the counselee better understand the possible consequences of alternatives and to identify values.

The information system provides input as needed. Strategic reasons for its use in the total decision process are as follows:

1. *To Identify Possibilities*
Educational and training directories. Occupational file (or sources such as VIEW or computers). Books such as the *Occupational Outlook Handbook*. Local educational, training, and occupational resource persons and agencies.

2. *To Estimate Possible Outcomes*
The sources just listed, with special attention to requirements for admission to programs or qualifications for work.

3. *To Predict Probable Outcomes*
The sources just listed, particularly any technological aids that help in prediction and data that provide for an analysis of requirements, duties, and responsibilities. Local norms and expectancy tables, if available.

4. *To Estimate the Desirability of Outcomes*
Detailed information, such as files, books, films, and other sources that enable the counselee to project himself or herself into the role of worker or student. Interviews with resource persons and visits to job sites or training or educational institutions.

5. *To Arrive at a Choice*
Information on making application to schools or training institutions. Lists of employers. Services provided by school and community placement agencies.

The information system is arranged so that the pupil can easily move from survey and exploration to in-depth study of specific occupations or educational opportunities. Some materials are suitable for both uses, however. The *Occupational Outlook Handbook* is an excellent survey or browsing resource, and it also provides in-depth information on occupations and industries.

These general guides for use of the information system emphasize the close relationship of decision-making counseling to the system and the need for up-to-date, readily accessible data.

Identifying Possible Decisions

Many pupils, particularly the disadvantaged and girls, are not aware of all the options open to them. The counselor may suggest alternatives, such as a school program, a type of work, or a training opportunity. Considerable exploration may be done either by reading or by more active methods, such as visits and interviews.

The counselor maintains an accepting climate but may suggest additional possibilities for consideration. It should be clear, however, that he or she is not recommending a specific alternative, only presenting it for the counselee's consideration.

At this point, the counselee's prediction system assumes major importance. The counselor observes how he or she feels about possibilities. Does he or she predict too optimistically? Too pessimistically? Does he or she overlook critical data or give unrealistic weights to some in selecting or rejecting possibilities? What sort of decision strategy does he or she seem to be using? The counselor is in a position to learn how the counselee predicts and to help improve the validity of the process.

In Joe Prince's case, the counselor and counselee spend several brief sessions discussing possibilities. Outcomes and values quite naturally enter into the discussion, but the focus is on the options Joe *might* consider.

COUNSELOR: What do you think about college, anyway? I'm feeling that you are sort of drifting that way and you don't look forward to it.
COUNSELEE: I don't have the slightest idea I could pass. But there's too much of a hassle at home about it. I just keep quiet.
COUNSELOR: You'd take the path of least resistance? With those reservations? You don't expect to pass? It's not *your* choice?
COUNSELEE: What else can I do? I talked to you about stopping school and working on newspaper delivery full time. I don't have the nerve to even mention that at home!

Eventually, three options emerge that Joe feels should be considered:

1. Enroll in the community college transfer program after the completion of high school.
2. Change now to the distributive education program (DE) and work half-time as a newspaper distributor.
3. Complete high school in the general program and take the two-year terminal program in business at the vocational-technical center.

Identifying Possible Outcomes

As alternatives are identified, the consequences of each are forecast. This involves the counselee's prediction system to a greater degree than does the previous step. One of the counselor's major functions is to maintain an accepting and understanding climate that makes possible the expression of feeling as well as the thoughtful and careful examination and weighing of relevant data. A second major function is to bring in needed data and help the counselee understand their relationships to each other and to alternatives. Questions may be raised to help the counselee look ahead and predict consequences. Data may be organized to facilitate predictions. Expectancy tables are a good way to help the counselee understand probabilities of success.

Joe has considerable difficulty looking ahead and estimating the results of courses of action. Elliot pushes him to do so, however, by questioning, confronting, and responding to the feelings Joe expresses. The following dialogue is an example:

COUNSELOR: Well, how do you think it would go in the transfer program? You saw how your grades and tests compared with the transfer people . . .
COUNSELEE: Aw, I don't know. You can't tell. I might not . . . you just can't tell . . .
COUNSELOR: You're telling me there's no way to tell . . . just no way.
COUNSELEE: No way!
COUNSELOR: It doesn't matter what others have done . . .

Joe eventually becomes more specific about how well he thinks each of the options would work out. Information about parental attitude plays a large part in the evaluation. It is necessary for Joe to delve beneath his acquiescent manner and discuss his attitudes about his parents and the amount of control they exercise over him. After working through this difficult stage, Joe expresses the feeling that he has never been required to think and decide for himself. He states that he really feels good about doing something of his own for the first time.

Identifying Probable Outcomes

The difference between what is possible and what is probable is extremely important in deciding and in predicting consequences. Usually, possible and probable outcomes are considered at the same time. The counselee is estimating whether or not he *could* complete the auto mechanic course and get a job as he is weighing the probability that this *would* happen. It is, for example, a 99–1 or a 50–50 situation?

His prediction system or decision-making strategy is the basis for the way he looks at the future and the amount of uncertainty or risk he can accept. He may, for example, be willing to accept a substantial risk for considerable possible gain. Another counselee, however, may want to "play it safe" and consider only outcomes that are practically guaranteed. The counselee's strategy—to take chances, to bet on sure things, to avoid realities—could be discussed in the counseling session. The goal is to help him gain insight into how he makes decisions and to help him develop an effective decision-making approach for current and future choice situations.

Joe prefers a cautious approach to the future. He tends to underestimate his own potential and to avoid risk. In looking ahead, he feels that he can hold his own in the newspaper distribution job because he has done it successfully. Elliot tries some simulation exercises in which he describes a student and lists his options. He then asks Joe to choose one of the options for the pupil and predict what will happen as a result of the choice. The counselor does not try to change Joe's personality pattern of caution but does attempt to help him make subjective probabilities and objective probabilities more congruent. The following exchange takes place during one session:

COUNSELOR: You think you could make enough to live on, say, full time on the job.
COUNSELEE: My work's been OK. I could take over the whole south end of town. Two or three people do it now, and they're not dependable at all. People miss papers and are calling all the time.
COUNSELOR: You're confident that you could get it and do it.
COUNSELEE: Well, wouldn't you say so? Nobody's doing it right. They have a hard time keeping anybody on.
COUNSELOR: It seems almost a sure thing.
COUNSELEE: Yeah. It's better than this uncertainty about can you get in school? Can you pass? Can you get out and find a job? Maybe it'll never be much more than it is now, but that's good enough for me.

Further discussion brings out that this option is a dead-end job, that the pay is minimal, and that Joe's parents are strongly opposed to it. Joe begins to realize that the primary attraction of that course of action is lack of competition.

Evaluating the Outcomes

Values are considered throughout the process, but when possible options are identified, personal values become one of the most, if not the most, significant aspect. If the utility of an outcome is high, it can override other factors. Often, several options are almost equal in accessibility. The hierarchy of values is then the determining factor in choice.

Counseling can help the counselee make his or her values explicit. They will emerge in the discussion of options. The approach suggested by the question "Who do you want to be?" rather than "What do you want to do?" elicits value responses. Preparation of a list of life goals may help. Looking ahead through role-playing and trying to translate the self-concept into an occupational self-concept will help to crystallize what is really important, what is desirable, and what is of only incidental appeal.

It may become apparent that the counselee is acting on someone else's values or trying to please someone else. The facilitative climate makes it possible for these influences to be acknowledged and discussed. The counselor also may be reinforcing a course of action without realizing it. The following excerpt suggests that this was true in Joe's case.

COUNSELOR: You asked which I thought was best. You'd like some . . . uh, support . . .?
COUNSELEE: Well, I sort of think *you* think I ought to try the transfer program . . . you didn't exactly say it, but I just sort of feel it.
COUNSELOR: You think I'm pushing that . . .
COUNSELEE: Yeah. Sort of. You've been to college. Everybody here's been to college. You must think it's good. Besides, you sort of brighten up when I talk about it.

Choosing a Course of Action

Each counselee has personal criteria for choosing. The strategy to this point has been designed to help him or her become aware of the factors involved, look ahead, and anticipate consequences. It is *his* or *her* choice, and the counselee should accept the responsibility for it and for the consequences.

Some counselees find it difficult or impossible to make a choice. If the symptoms strongly suggest an emotional block, the counseling may be modified to become a more therapeutic relationship, or referral may be made for specialized help. The reason or reasons, however, can more often than not be handled in counseling for decision making. The counselee's level of general and vocational maturity may be so low that only time and additional experiences will increase his or her readiness. Conflicts with others, especially parents, may need to be explored. Parental goals often operate in subtle ways of which the counselee may not be aware. All possibilities may be equally unattractive or equally appealing. There may be a reluctance to give up the present uncommitted way of life and move in a definite direction.

Choices are not final, and they need not be more specific than the situation requires. Changes can usually be made. The counselee may decide to continue to investigate possibilities and use the new data in the decision-making process or may make a terminal decision. For both types of decision, feedback allows evaluation of its suitability. Both counselor and counselee can assess the appropriateness of the chosen option. Further counseling may be needed, either to adjust to the new situation or to consider other alternatives.

Each decision has an effect on the future. The process is cyclical. Data for new decisions are being accumulated as current ones are implemented. Feedback helps the individual evaluate both choice and strategy. A productive and satisfying strategy becomes a way of handling choices, just as a personally satisfying pattern of social interaction becomes part of one's personality. Decision points occur throughout life, and the same process can be used at any age.

Following Up the Decision

Assistance does not stop when the choice is made. Often the most critical step is the transition from decision to implementation. An occupation is selected and a job-procuring campaign is planned. After a couple of rebuffs, the counselee may become discouraged and stop trying. Another counselee may obtain a job but find the supervision objectionable and leave. The critical period for him or her is after work begins.

The school placement service and community agencies may be used as referral resources for the counselee. The information system contains names, telephone numbers, and addresses of local resource persons and agencies. The school placement service, of which the counselor may be a part, has information about specific job openings, training, and educational opportunities.

Decision making is thus implemented in two ways: the counselee is helped to carry out the decision and to perform satisfactorily in the new setting. Decision-making counseling is not completed until the suitability of the decision has been realistically determined.

This approach to helping is ideally suited for evaluation and for demonstrating accountability. Some questions that could be asked are as follows:

1. Was relevant information provided?
2. Were all possible alternatives considered?
3. Could the counselee foresee consequences?
4. How well did the counselee learn to make decisions?
5. Did the decision work out satisfactorily?

The last criterion is the critical one. If decisions are not satisfactory and plans do not work, all the help provided and all the material and equipment available will be evaluated by pupils and the community as wasted effort and expense.

SUMMARY

In this chapter, recent position papers of professional organizations, definitions of the counselor's role, the nature of the counseling relationship, and principles of decision making have been reviewed briefly as background for formulating a decision-making approach to helping. An active outreach role has been recommended, since many who are in need of counseling do not try to obtain help. A facilitative relationship is important, but the need to provide services may limit the time available to establish the optimal counseling climate.

Working with special groups, such as the disadvantaged, requires adaptations that do not depend entirely on verbal communication. Counseling those at mid-life and retirement age is an emerging concern, but it may pose some threat for both counselee and counselor. Expanded responsibility for career counseling with the disabled will result from recent legislation. Career counseling for women is a critical need, and efforts should be made to broaden their occupational horizons and help them deal with personal and social attitudes that limit their options. Parents play a significant role in the career planning of school-age youth and should be involved in the helping process in a way that is in keeping with ethical standards of confidentiality. Individual counseling, although time-consuming and relatively costly, has an important place in the total guidance program.

New concepts, materials, and technology not only help counselors improve the decision-making process but provide them with timesaving and growth-producing aids. Decision-making counseling makes use of both subjective and objective data and provides developmental help as well as assistance for specific and immediate occupational choices. Decision-making concepts can be synthesized with counseling procedures to provide a rationale for assisting counselees to make career plans. The model DECIDE incorporates major elements from Gelatt's paradigm into a comprehensive approach that begins with a recognition of the need to choose and ends with an evaluation of the suitability of the decision. The case of Joe Prince has been used to illustrate this approach. The information system provides needed input at strategic points in the process and is an essential supportive resource. The decision-making approach readily provides data for evaluation and accountability studies.

PROJECTS AND EXPERIENTIAL ACTIVITIES

1. Interview several persons and find out how they made decisions about jobs and/or education. Compare their strategies with the one described in this chapter.

2. Ask a counselor how he or she helps counselees deal with problems requiring decisions.

3. Prepare a simulation involving an individual who must choose among several alternatives. State the alternatives. Ask someone to select an alternative and explain the choice. Ask the individual to think aloud while making the decision.

4. Role-play different parts of the decision-making process, for example, helping the individual become aware that a decision is needed or identifying alternatives. Tape-record and play back.

5. Prepare a three- to five-minute example of some specific techniques of decision-making counseling, for example, interpreting a test score or helping a counselee use the *Occupational Outlook Handbook*. Tape-record or videotape the example. Prepare a manual of the type described by Ivey (1971) for microcounseling. Use it with others in your class or school.

6. Have class members form small groups and agree on the most difficult career problem they can imagine. Make up a brief description of someone who has this problem. Then decide on the first, second, and third steps the group would take in providing individual assistance. (Note: limit the problem to one for which you, as a counselor, would carry the helping process through to the conclusion.)

7. In small groups, discuss two major career decisions you have faced in the last several years and the problems encountered in making each one. Select one decision and decide which part of the decision-making counseling process would have been the most helpful in resolving the difficulty.

8. Use small groups to role-play a brief career-counseling episode of about five minutes. While the interview is in process, have other members of the group identify the decision-making steps used—for instance, identifying options or looking at possible outcomes. Which steps were more frequently used? Were they the most appropriate ones?

9. In small groups, list the five most critical factors that enter into decisions (for example, considering values, identifying possibilities, learning about options). Then eliminate four, one at a time, until one is left. What is the major reason for retaining the last one? Was it difficult to determine which factors should be eliminated?

10. Draw a line on a sheet of paper representing the life span and then divide it into ten-year segments. Indicate with a vertical mark major career decisions already made and those expected (for example, how many years do you plan to keep your first job before deciding to continue in it or move to another one?). Then for each of the decisions, put an "O" for objective and an "S" for subjective data to indicate which type had or is expected to have the most weight (in other words, is it primarily a cognitive or intuitive decision?). Compare results and determine which type of factor appears to be the most extensively used.

ADDITIONAL REFERENCES

Baer, Max F., and Edward C. Roeber. *Occupational Information.* 3rd ed. Chicago: Science Research Associates, 1964. Chap. 18, "Using Information in Counseling Interviews and Small Group Work," is a very helpful source of techniques for providing occupational information to counselees.

Crites, John O. "Career Counseling: A Comprehensive Approach." In *Career Counseling.* Eds. John M. Whiteley and Arthur Resnikoff. Monterey, Calif.: Brooks/Cole, 1978, pp. 74–99. This is an extremely lucid discussion of a model for individual career counseling. It will be helpful to read the full report in connection with the brief summary contained in this chapter. The synthesis of concepts from career-development theories is particularly noteworthy. Comments by Holland and Roe (pp. 128–138) will add to an understanding of issues involved.

Gelatt, H. B., Barbara Varenhorst, and Richard Carey. *Deciding* (student's book) and *Deciding: A Leader's Guide.* New York: College Entrance Examination Board, 1972. These two manuals provide an interesting and graphic portrayal of the decision-making approach used in this chapter. They are useful references for the counselor, as well as excellent materials for pupils to learn decision making.

Isaacson, Lee E. *Career Information in Counseling and Teaching.* 3rd ed. Boston: Allyn

& Bacon, 1977. Pp. 476–500 provide a helpful guide for using information in counseling.

Hoppock, Robert. *Occupational Information*. 4th ed. New York: McGraw-Hill, 1976. Three chapters are particularly helpful for decision-making counseling. Chap. 9, "Contributions of Client-Centered and Behavioral Counseling to Career Counseling," is useful as a synthesis of counseling and information-giving concepts. Chap. 10, "The Use of Occupational Information in Counseling—General Aspects," outlines an effective way to use the DOT and suggests approaches for particularly difficult occupational choice problems. Chap. 11, "The Use of Occupational Information in Counseling—Answering Questions," is very helpful in suggesting information that may be needed and emphasizing its significance for decision making and planning.

Krumboltz, John D., and Ronald D. Baker. "Behavioral Counseling for Vocational Decisions." In *Career Guidance for a New Age*. Ed. Henry Borow. Boston: Houghton Mifflin, 1973, pp. 235–283. A very helpful explanation with illustrative dialogue of decision-making counseling. Steps or phases are clearly shown.

Norris, Willa, Franklin R. Zeran, Raymond M. Hatch, and James R. Engelkes. *The Information Service in Guidance*. 3rd ed. Chicago: Rand McNally, 1972. Chap. 13, "The Use of Information in Counseling and Teaching," is a brief but helpful review of principles for providing information and facilitating decision making in counseling.

Rossi, Robert J., Wendy B. Bartlett, Emily A. Campbell, Lauress L. Wise, and Donald H. McLaughlin. *Using the Talent Profiles in Counseling: A Supplement to the Career Data Book*. Palo Alto, Calif.: American Institutes for Research, 1975. In the introduction (pp. 1–23), the use of the Talent Profiles in Counseling is discussed. The counseling strategies used in the three illustrative cases are very helpful in understanding a decision-making approach to career counseling.

Stiller, Alfred. "The Changing Role of Guidance Counselor in the Emerging School." In *Educating for Tomorrow*. Ed. Walter M. Lifton. New York: John Wiley & Sons, 1970. The author's description of the content and use of the information system is lucid and comprehensive. This is an excellent reading to help synthesize the information system and counseling.

Tolbert, E. L. *Introduction to Counseling*. 2nd ed. New York: McGraw-Hill, 1972. Chaps. 8 and 9, on using occupational information and test results in counseling, present the author's approach, with case illustrations. Chap. 6 is a discussion, with illustrations, of facilitative conditions in counseling.

Tyler, Leona E. *The Work of the Counselor*. 3rd ed. New York: Appleton-Century-Crofts, 1969. Chap. 9, "Facilitating Decisions," is recommended, particularly pp. 145–150 on blocks to decision making. Also relevant and helpful are Chap. 7, "Surveying Possibilities in the Self by Means of Tests," and Chap. 8, "Surveying Occupational Possibilities in Career Counseling."

———. "Counseling Girls and Women in the Year 2,000." In *Counseling Girls and Women Over the Life Span*. Eds. Edwin A. Whitfield and Alice Gustav. Washington, D.C.: National Vocational Guidance Association, 1972. The importance of career choice and decision making in counseling girls and women is convincingly presented.

8

Decision Making:

Group Counseling

GOALS

1
To explain the value of group counseling for career development.

2
To describe the group-counseling methods and techniques used to help promote career development.

3
To give information about a number of innovative approaches to group career counseling.

4
To help the student develop competency in planning, carrying out, and evaluating group career counseling.

ONE OF THE NEWEST HELPING STRATEGIES in the guidance profession is group counseling. Neither the concept nor the process appeared in guidance literature and counselor-preparation programs until relatively recently. Mahler (1971) says that group counseling has developed over the past thirty or forty years, but the term was practically unknown until the late 1950s (Anderson and Johnson, 1968). Prior to that time, it was felt that the term *counseling,* should be reserved for the one-to-one relationship (Bennett, 1963, p. viii; Anderson and Johnson, 1969). Early innovators used the term *multiple* rather than *group* (Driver, 1954), suggesting that the counselor was helping several persons simultaneously. Group interaction was, however, considered a helpful aspect of the process. In the past twenty years, the growth of group counseling has been phenomenal. School counseling and guidance services are a natural setting for it, and it is generally recognized as an approach that is needed in the educational institution (Cohn, 1967, p. 5).

It was pointed out in Chapter 7 that the National Vocational Guidance Association and the American Vocational Association emphasize assistance for career decisions in their joint position paper. Their recommendations apply to group as well as individual help. The same point is made in the ACES position paper: knowledge of and competencies in facilitating career development apply to group procedures as well as individual work. With the development of new techniques and materials, the incorporation of technology, the recognition of the benefits of multiple interactions in the helping process, and the need to spread helping services as widely as possible with the least possible cost, group career-counseling procedures have become one of the most widely used of all strategies. The trend shows every sign of continuing. This chapter discusses applications of the group processes and techniques to career development and decision making.

DEFINITIONS

The terms *group guidance* and *group counseling* are often used interchangeably. There are differences, however, primarily in the dimensions of content and process (Goldman, 1962). Group guidance deals mostly with phenomena in the environment, *outside* the group members themselves. For example, the group may discuss the programs at the vocational-technical center. The topic is selected by the leader or jointly by members and the leader, and the material is provided by an outside source. The leader may function as an information giver. Discussion, questions, and attitudinal reactions may be involved, but the emphasis is on learning about some aspect of the environment.

Group counseling, on the other hand, concentrates on the experiences and feelings of the participants. Topics are introduced by group members. The leader helps in the expression of feeling, clarifies reactions, and stimulates productive interaction among members.

Group guidance and counseling thus are usually conceptualized as different categories of helping rather than as different points on a continuum. Rinn (1961) found two distinct approaches to group work while investigating what educators wanted to know about groups. Some wished to learn more about effective *teaching-type* activities; others were more interested in *group dynamics*. Both his classification and Goldman's (1962) model portray basic differences. Burks and Pate (1970) classify group guidance, group counseling, sensitivity training, and group therapy on the basis of six factors, such as *setting, leader,* and *goals.* Group guidance is expected to result in factual learning, while group counseling encourages realistic planning, expectations, and effective use of resources.

These distinctions are widely accepted. Mahler's (1971) definition emphasizes these key points in group counseling:

1. Problems with developmental tasks are the members' main concerns.
2. Group interaction is the process for achieving goals.
3. The climate permits the lowering of defenses so that feelings can be revealed and explored.
4. Self-understanding and self-acceptance are the goals.

These characteristics serve as the basis for the approach to group counseling described in this chapter. Some modifications, to be explained later, are made for group *career* counseling.

Group guidance, as defined by Kirby (1971) and commented on by Hoppock (1971), emphasizes the following points:

1. It is a process of education in aspects of choice, growth, and development not covered in the school curriculum.
2. It involves educational, vocational, and social development.
3. Information giving is a major activity.
4. It is "incremental"—that is, concerned with gradual, marginal changes in accomplishing developmental tasks and helping with day-by-day decision making. But it is also concerned with the effects of these decisions and plans on later development and success.
5. It focuses on the here and now.
6. The leader needs special qualifications for this type of activity, although his or her competencies are not the same as those of the group-counseling leader.

There is, therefore, enough distinction between the two processes to discuss them separately. Group-counseling approaches are covered in this chapter. Those more clearly applicable to group guidance are discussed in Chapter 9 as an aspect of the total guidance program in school or agency. There is some overlap, but the unique contributions of each make separate treatment desirable.

The three dimensions of counselor function (Morrill, Oetting, and Hurst, 1974) discussed on pages 205–206 help to illustrate the place of group counseling in the total guidance program. In this case, the *target of intervention* is a small group—five to eight members drawn from primary or associational groups or from the institution or community. *Purpose* may be remediation, prevention, or development. In career-guidance programs, it would typically be development. The *method* is direct service, sometimes with media-assisted activities.

Primary and shared responsibilities in career guidance are illustrated in Figure

5.1 (page 162, Harris-Bowlsbey, 1975, p. 43). Group counseling has four areas of primary responsibility and three shared with other components. Areas of primary responsibility involve forming and clarifying self-concept, relating self- and occupational-educational information, teaching career planning and decision-making skills, and teaching job-seeking and job-holding skills and attitudes. Responsibility is shared with other guidance services for implementation of choice, teaching vocational skills, and helping with economic awareness and planning.

A GROUP-COUNSELING MODEL

Three assumptions are made about the essential elements of group counseling. First, career planning and decision making require input about occupations. Second, accurate data about the self, that is, about aptitudes, preferences, achievements, and values, are needed. Third, the procedure offers opportunities to explore personal meaning, identify and examine subjective aspects of the self, get feedback from others, and try on roles. With these basic assumptions as guides, the key points of group career counseling may be stated as follows:

1. GOAL   The goal is an acceptable and realistic occupational self-concept in keeping with the expected level of vocational development.
2. PROCESS   The process involves five types of activities:
    a. Exploring feelings, attitudes, and values in an accepting climate
    b. Interacting with others, emphasizing feedback on how others perceive personal occupational plans and goals
    c. Reviewing personal information and relating it to goals
    d. Obtaining and reviewing occupational, educational, and training information
    e. Practicing decision making
3. CONFIDENTIALITY   Participants reveal only as much as they choose to. They may, for example, withhold ability test scores just as they may withhold attitudes toward themselves or school. Furthermore, each member treats the group discussions as confidential.
4. MEMBERSHIP   Six to ten participants is the desirable size to promote interaction and feedback, permit some heterogeneity, and facilitate maximum participation of each member.
5. THE LEADER   The leader should be competent in both group counseling and career information. Major functions are
    a. Promoting a climate for interaction and personal exploration
    b. Insuring the input of needed information
    c. Assisting participants to learn decision-making strategies
6. SCHEDULING   A set number of meetings should not be specified. When members decide that group and individual goals have been reached, the sessions are terminated.

Before discussing this procedure further, a survey of group-counseling approaches will be presented because they are the basis for the group-counseling aspect of group career counseling. This review deals only with group counseling in schools, colleges, and agencies. Techniques like therapy and sensitivity training are beyond the scope of this chapter and are not directly applicable to those settings, although many techniques and procedures used in group counseling have been borrowed from them. (See the references at the end of this chapter.) In some settings, however, it would be difficult to discern differences between group counseling and sensitivity training, or even group therapy.

Components of the Model

There is a wide variety of approaches to group counseling. They all tend to embody certain shared characteristics and to have similar general goals, but the exact process used is not always clearly specified in research reports and programs (Zimpfer, 1968). In spite of this variability, it is reasonably accurate to describe the group-counseling procedure as follows:

1. THE LEADER   Qualifications are similar to those needed for individual counseling, with the addition of group skills. He or she conveys warmth, understanding, acceptance, and faith in each individual's ability to solve problems. The leader needs to be able to attend to a number of persons at one time, to understand the feelings being expressed, and to promote interaction among members (Kemp, 1970, p. 263). He or she has a clear concept of the nature and purpose of the group. The leader is aware, for example, of the differences between socioprocess behavior and psyche process behavior—that is, working through to a problem solution as contrasted with expressing and clarifying feelings (Kemp, 1970, p. 263).

2. THE SETTING.   The climate of group counseling is of critical importance. Kemp (1970, pp. 141–155) describes it as characterized by unconditional acceptance, feelings of adequacy, an open-minded view of authority, other-centered participation, trust, development of potential, and understanding. Each participant experiences a permissive, warm, supportive climate in which mutual care and concern are evident, and in which each person, including the leader, demonstrates mutual respect and endeavors to help each other member achieve growth and fulfillment.

3. THE PROCESS   The leader structures the situation by explaining the group purpose and the usual ways of proceeding. Structuring, however, may be specific or subtle; there may be a list of ground rules, or the structure may be implied by the leader's manner and the way he or she responds to participants' reactions. As the process continues, activities may range from completely unplanned spontaneous reactions to such specific exercises as asking members to introduce themselves or each other.

4. GROUP MEMBERS   The members of the group are usually somewhat homogeneous in regard to problems and plans. Diversity, however, may add to the value of the group experience. It is desirable for participants to take part voluntarily, be willing to interact with others, and be relatively well adjusted. The number of participants varies. It would seem difficult to carry out the kinds of interactions

discussed with more than six or eight, but some report groups as large as fifteen (Mahler, 1971).

Group Progress

Group progress tends to fall into stages: establishment, followed by transition, and finally acceptance of group norms and openness in bringing out personal feelings. Lifton (1966, pp. 108–109) describes movement on three levels—the content of topics discussed, feelings expressed regardless of content, and effects of the interpersonal relationships. Themes tend to be repeated, and increased self-understanding, understanding of others, and awareness of one's own feelings merge in the growth process. I have described movement in terms of initial feelings of confusion, some hostility, and resistance; then better understanding and acceptance of others; and finally group feeling—"We are a group," "We are concerned about each person here" (1972a, pp. 279–280). Kline's (Fullmer and Bernard, 1964, pp. 193–204) conceptualization of levels of maturity is one of the most helpful in describing the stages of group progress. Twelve stages in the individual progress from initial apprehension to creativity are suggested. The initial stages, after apprehension, are resistance, suspicion-apathy, skepticism, and ambivalence. At that point, progress becomes more positive. Confidence-trust, identity, and intimacy are the next three levels. The final three are self-acceptance or equilibrium, self-actualization, and creativity. Actually, few people reach the highest levels (Fullmer and Bernard, 1964, p. 205). The first ten levels probably best represent the stages of successful group counseling.

METHODS IN DETAIL

A pregroup meeting interview with each prospective member is helpful. The counselor explains the nature of the group and gives the counselee the opportunity to make his or her own decision about taking part.

Meetings of about one hour's duration are usually held once a week, with shorter meeting times for elementary school pupils. No set number of meetings is prescribed, but eight to twelve seems to be the usual practice. Often, the length of the group's existence is related to the length of the school term. Schedules change and groups disband.

Techniques frequently employed are reflection of feeling, clarification, and linking—relating one member's comments to those of another. Kemp (1970, pp. 191–203) lists group skills as listening, clarification, reflection, interpretation, linking, and summarization. It is not so much a matter of technique, however, as a basic attitude of concern, caring, and personal involvement. A group leader might confront, question, or give information in a way that is highly facilitative or might reflect in a threatening manner. Sometimes techniques like role playing are used. Exercises may be adapted from encounter-group procedures (Coulson, 1970).

Some typical applications and variations of this procedure are discussed next, to illustrate both usual and innovative implementations of group-counseling approaches. These include services to special groups as well as modifications of approaches. Those discussed are typical approach, discussion approach, group modeling, simulation, assertion training, fantasy in career exploration, peers as models, and parent participation. There are others, but these illustrate the approaches most often employed.

The Typical Approach

Group counseling is used on all educational levels and also for groups with special needs. Ohlsen (1968), in an extremely helpful article, describes applications to children. Careful selection of counselees by means of an initial interview is recommended. Problems are usually centered around lack of confidence or social skills. Major adaptations in the counselor's role needed for elementary school pupils are more active participation, more structure, and active techniques such as role playing. With primary school pupils, play materials may be helpful in facilitating communication. The basic approach is in keeping with that described previously.

An interesting application to counselor preparation is described by Rousseve (1965). Counselors-in-training met with high school pupils in an unstructured counseling group for an experience in self-development and group dynamics. The "leader" was less assertive than in the group-counseling approach described earlier, serving as more of a catalyst. Themes were identified at the first meeting and brought into subsequent sessions by the catalyst, one of the graduate students. The climate was informal and permissive, and the focus was on feelings. Results, in terms of personal attitudes and shared insights, represented typical goals of group counseling, in other words, the members felt that this kind of experience helped them to become more fully aware of themselves as persons and to gain better appreciation of personal adequacies.

The conventional group-counseling approach was used by Gilliland (1968) in a year-long program for black high school pupils. Emphasis was on providing conditions of positive regard, empathy, and congruence in order to facilitate exploration of feelings and progress toward self-fulfillment and enhancement of self-concept. Results indicated that group counseling had positive effects on both the achievement and the personal functioning of adolescents. Differences in responses of girls and boys to the group processes were noted. For example, boys took longer to enter into self-exploration and expression of feeling. Even so, group counseling worked well with both sexes.

Some other examples of application of the typical model further illustrate its potentialities. Creange (1971) reports on a ten-meeting program for underachieving ninth-graders. Groups of five members each were established to enable participants to explore feelings and attitudes. The purpose of the groups—to help them do something about underachievement—was explained to pupils. Counselors were free to use procedures they felt were appropriate; at times this involved giving directions and providing information. Results were all positive; the group-counseling approach, although used in a limited study, was judged to be an effective procedure.

Woodhull (1968) describes a group-counseling program that was effective with "noncollege-bound" high school pupils. Clough (1968) describes her experiences in group counseling with ninth-grade pupils. The report is an excellent guide for the counselor planning to use group-counseling procedures. Lerche (1968) describes a brief, seven-session group-counseling program with failing ninth-grade pupils. Although some positive results were obtained, it was concluded that a more lengthy period of help was needed. A study of the growth-producing effects of feedback, a widely used technique in group counseling, supported its value (Malouf, 1968). Pearson (1968, pp. 75–76) recommends the group-counseling approach for the culturally different. It gives the participants the opportunity and freedom to change without being forced to do so.

The usual format—the open, permissive, group-centered, feeling-oriented group—has applications to a variety of settings. Numerous positive results are reported but additional research, particularly involving theory-based hypotheses and replication, is needed.

The Discussion Approach

This type of group work could be described as cooperative problem solving through group discussion and analysis of a common problem. It is useful in building good interpersonal relations and is most effective with democratic, group-centered leadership. Kinnick (1968) found many similarities between group counseling and group discussion.

In fact, the differences between group counseling and group discussion are often obscured in practice. The discussion group addresses a topic of concern to the members, but feelings as well as intellectual responses and participant interaction are also involved. The focus, however, is usually on a problem or issue, and there is at least some effort to arrive at a consensus. The case conference (Hoppock, 1967, pp. 286–297) is an example. Those participating discuss a case, somewhat as is done in simulation, and offer suggestions. In the process, they interact with others, clarify feelings, and develop self-understanding. The group discussion leader reflects, clarifies, and synthesizes, very much as he or she does in group counseling, but focuses on the problem rather than on group interaction and exploration of feelings. Some pupils prefer a discussion group to a counseling group because they feel that it will remain at a more impersonal level. In the assumed safety of this type of group, they will participate in much the same style as do participants in group counseling.

Some writers tend to put more emphasis on problem solving as a major aspect of both processes than is done in the group-counseling model presented earlier in this chapter. Moore (1969) describes a group program for junior high school pupils, emphasizing changes in school organization, feelings about these changes, and reactions to individual development at this educational level. Developmentally oriented, the program was based on concerns pupils expressed. Two types of groups were used, emphasizing interpersonal relations skills and study skills. Results were generally positive. The group procedures were not described but appeared to involve discussion.

Group Modeling

Groups using models and verbal reinforcement have been successful in developing new behaviors. The model in one study (Krumboltz and Thoresen, 1964) was a tape-recorded interview of a pupil seeking information. The information-seeking responses were reinforced by the counselor in the tape recording and also by the group counselor after the tape recording was completed. Results demonstrated that models and reinforcement represent procedures that could be used successfully with groups. Films and other model presentations help counselees learn effective behavior and avoid problems (Krumboltz, 1966a; Hosford, 1969, p. 21). This approach provides a way to develop exploratory behavior and decision-making skills (Krumboltz and Hosford, 1967). In fact, microteaching and microcounseling (Ivey, 1971, p. 6) use elements of this procedure; a model is provided, and learner approximations of the model are reinforced.

A somewhat similar approach is suggested by Mayer, Rohen, and Whiteley (1969). Using social learning and cognitive dissonance theory, they suggest that models who provide dissonance-creating situations and with whom participants can identify promote constructive interaction and change. In an environment of minimal pressure and threat, the desired behavior is reinforced. Group members should differ; otherwise, all may take the same point of view. The suggested procedures have not been tested but appear to offer productive ways of utilizing modeling, reinforcement, and dissonance in group counseling.

Simulation

Two major types of simulation are work experiences and games. Neither is necessarily a group-counseling approach; guidance might be a more accurate classification. These types are taken up here, however, because they can be used in group counseling. Interaction among group members would increase the value of simulations. The game technique could actually serve as the basis of a group-counseling program.

The application of games to group counseling is best exemplified by Varenhorst's Life Career Game (1968). The group-counseling setting is considered necessary because the counselor can serve as a motivator and mobilizer of group efforts, help insure that group members work harmoniously, and assist in developing a group feeling. The simulation approach adds a new dimension to the usual type of group interaction. Participants can try out ideas and new ways of handling situations and dealing with others. Peers serve as models, and members learn from one another. Reinforcement is provided by the counselor and by other group members. Tryout of decisions is safe, because participants are not making irrevocable choices. As teams work together on planning the future for the case individual, they have an opportunity to share attitudes, learn cooperative working skills, and give and receive feedback.

The Life Career Game utilizes such prepared materials as cases, options available to the case individual, and expectancy tables based on census data. The group is divided into teams of four or five members each. The teams plan a number of years in the life of the case individual. Resource material describing available jobs and other choices is provided. Each team has a manual of rules and a description, school records, and family data on the case individual. Planning begins with the junior year or earlier, depending on the case. Each team's scores are computed for each year from decisions in four areas—home, leisure, work, and education. The better the decisions, the higher the scores. For example, points awarded in education increase with the grade average, a function of the number of hours studied as well as the ability level. (The element of chance is brought in through the use of a die.) Competitive scoring stimulates interest and motivates participants to make good decisions. General discussion occurs at the end of each round, during which teams give reasons for their choices. Alternatively, games may be played all the way through or continued in later sessions.

The potential benefits in a group-counseling setting are obvious. A task that involves participants' values, decision-making strategies, and group interactions can constitute an effective learning experience. Evaluations have tended to reveal positive results. Pupils have learned to move more quickly into a discussion of critical questions. Varenhorst (1968) reports multiple benefits, such as learning specific occupational and educational information, examining values, learning from other pupils, and sharing ideas. Pupils who had planned to drop out have stayed in school and shown improved ability in decision making.

Although simulation has content validity, more evaluative work needs to be done to assess its effects on current and future decisions. Research has not provided clear-cut support. Johnson and Euler (1972) did not find that ninth-grade pupils learned or retained more information than did those taught in occupational units. Further, participants did not perceive simulation as an interesting activity. To some extent, these results could be accounted for by the nature of the class (in a university school that frequently took part in innovative experiences) and the greater amount of information learned in the regular instructional groups. (The latter group learned more but forgot more rapidly.) Since the use of simulation was not part of an ongoing group-counseling procedure, its contribution to group counseling was not assessed.

Job simulation, the second type of experience (Krumboltz and Bergland, 1969), could be a group activity. It should work well when there is an opportunity for interaction after completing a particular simulation. I have found that a considerable amount of discussion ensues after each group member has tried out a job. A total of twenty job-simulation kits is currently available through Science Research Associates, 254 East Erie Street, Chicago, Illinois 60611. Professional, trade, clerical, and service occupations are represented. For example, there is an accountant kit, an electronics technician kit, and a secretary kit.

This type of simulation could be used in group guidance, as well as group counseling. The latter, however, allows for more extensive exploration of the attitudes and feelings evoked by the experience and for interaction among members about work skills, values, and goals.

Assertion Training

This technique includes procedures to help the individual respond naturally and effectively to others without being inhibited by undue anxiety. Typical methods involve role-playing of a situation in which the individual is either unable to present his or her own views or finds it very difficult to do so. One application has been in preparation for job interviews (McGovern, Tinsley, Liss-Levinson, Laventure, and Britton, 1975). Group members go through a series of meetings that first includes an explanation of the process of the employment interview to help them understand what usually takes place and to give some structure to an ambiguous situation. Then behavior rehearsal in small groups gives participants the opportunity to develop an assertive and personally satisfying communication style. The group experience is useful for individuals of various ages and degrees of experience, particularly women and minority group members.

Fantasy in Career Exploration

Quite often, this process involves preliminary preparation by use of relaxation techniques, which are followed by instructions to help participants go through a guided fantasy experience, as, for example, a workday in the future. Participants are asked to imagine very specific events of the day—the sort of place they live in, what they have for breakfast, and how they get to work. Other topics may involve mid-career change or retirement; there is no limit to possibilities, just so they fit the concerns of the group members. At the end of the experience, members discuss impressions, feelings, and insights. The results are viewed as information to be used in career planning.

Use of fantasy in group procedures, including applications in career guidance, has been increasing (Morgan and Skovholt, 1974; Skovholt and Hoenninger, 1977). Morgan and Skovholt enumerate a number of benefits from use of the technique, including a pleasurable experience, sharing of feelings, awareness of ignored or repressed feelings, and the bringing out of data useful for career guidance.

Peers as Models

Peers as models in group counseling can help with the educational achievement and occupational motivation of the disadvantaged (Vriend, 1969b). Furthermore, they have the potential to help with occupational, personal, and educational problems (Vriend, 1969a; Ettkin and Snyder, 1972). Peer counseling has been effective in helping high school "peer clients" and has contributed to the psychological education of pupils (Mosher and Sprinthall, 1971, pp. 19–36).

A qualified counselor is usually present to facilitate group development, but peers may work with subgroups of the total counseling group, counsel individuals, and serve as models for other participants. High-performing individuals are particularly helpful in work with the disadvantaged.

Parent Participation

The typical counseling approach described earlier has been used with groups of parents (Mallars, 1968). Usually, underachievement, physical or social handicaps, and other difficulties shared by their children serve as the basis for forming the group. One or two counselors may work with a small group of parents or with family units. Teachers and other specialists may be brought in (Fullmer, 1968).

No special adaptations of group-counseling methods are needed for work with parents. The accepting climate allows for expression of the negative feelings usually present when pupil problems have developed. Reflection of feelings, particularly positive ones, helps parents move toward constructive planning and away from looking for someone to blame (Mallars, 1968). Group work may help parents to plan steps they can take to assist their children (Heller and Gurney, 1968). There may, therefore, be times when the emphasis shifts from exploration and clarification of feelings to information giving and planning—for example, how to study or how to learn about occupations. Expected outcomes are increased understanding and acceptance of their children and some concrete ways of demonstrating interest and providing assistance.

CAREER-DEVELOPMENT THEORY AND GROUP STRATEGIES

Each of the group strategies described in the sections that follow is to some degree based on the career-development theories reviewed in Chapter 2. In many cases, the relation will be apparent, for example, at the high school and early college periods, exploration, reality testing, and tentative planning are emphasized. Moreover, various types of self- and occupational data are identified and reviewed. Extensive use is made of decision-making strategies.

Most group strategies in this chapter deal with career awareness, exploration, identity formation, and choice—all phases in the career-development process. Action steps, such as instituting a job search, which are also part of the process, are covered to some extent but are discussed more fully in Chapter 12 on placement.

Group-Counseling Programs

Many programs have been developed to provide group career-development experiences. Some of the best known are described here. In addition, several new programs that are similar to elements of career education covered in Chapter 10 are briefly reviewed.

The Sprague and Strong Plan

The most clear-cut example of a combination of group counseling and decision making is described by Sprague and Strong[1]. They call the approach Vocational Choice Group Counseling. Hewer's (1968) model was the starting point for development of the plan.

The general purpose of the group program was to help college students choose an occupation through group counseling with others facing the same problem. The cases of individual participants provided bases for discussion and suggestions. Group goals were to help each participant become an expert in vocational-choice problem solving, develop a comprehensive understanding of himself or herself, and organize and evaluate plans and goals through the process of group interaction. The group leader functioned primarily as a facilitator of group interaction, an expert on problem solving, and a resource person on measurement and occupational problems.

The program was announced in the student newspaper and on the bulletin board. Students were also referred by other counseling staff members. Each group included members of all college classes. A brief interview was held with each prospective member to explain the group procedure, discuss vocational choice problems, and screen out those with personality problems.

A total of nine weekly meetings of one hour each was scheduled. Participants took a battery of vocational-interest and personality inventories before the first meeting, so that results would be available by the second meeting.

The first meeting was devoted to introductions, an explanation of the purposes of the group, and a discussion of vocational problems and decision making. Each member described his or her career dilemma and reasons for joining the group. A copy of the *Occupational Outlook Handbook* and instructions for locating other information were given to each participant.

The second meeting was devoted to discussing the results of tests and inventories. Each participant received copies of the results for his or her personal file.

Sessions 3 through 9 were used for individual case presentations, discussion, and interaction. Progress reports were given at later sessions after case presentations. Worksheets on decision making and related subjects were handed out for study and background information. No pressure was put on participants to make decisions, but some progress toward defining goals was expected. Each member proceeded at his or her own pace to resolve problems and make plans.

Evaluation gave positive results. About three-fourths of those who participated in five groups polled responded to a follow-up questionnaire. Respondents stated that they enjoyed the group meetings, had achieved greater self-understanding, liked the case method, and considered it valuable. About half had either made a choice or were well on the way to doing so. The worksheets were rated as of questionable value. (Would group members rather interact than study?)

This program has been reviewed at length because, although designed for the

[1]Douglas G. Sprague and Donald J. Strong, "Vocational Choice Group Counseling," *Journal of College Student Personnel*, 11, No. 1 (1970), pp. 35–56. Copyright 1970 American Personnel and Guidance Association. Material adapted with permission.

college level, it has been the source of ideas used in the career group-counseling proposal presented later.

The Johnson Plan

Another innovative approach, intended to give first-year students a good start in the career decision-making process, was designed by Johnson (1972). A group training package for residence halls, it includes a series of group meetings that takes students through personal assessment, occupational exploration, tentative occupational choice, educational exploration related to the occupational choice, and tentative educational choice. After the meetings, students engage in tryout and exploratory experiences, using campus career-counseling resources as needed. The outline for the nine meetings, each about one hour in length, is as follows:

FIRST MEETING—INTRODUCTION   Explanation of the rationale of the program is followed by a "name game" activity to acquaint group members with one another.

SECOND MEETING—PERSONAL ASSESSMENT   (abilities and interests) A personal profile sheet that emphasizes interests is completed. A "guess who" group activity that uses the profile sheet is then conducted.

THIRD MEETING—PERSONAL ASSESSMENT   (values) An activity entitled The Millionaire is used to elicit occupational values and preferences.

FOURTH MEETING—PERSONAL ASSESSMENT   (occupational criteria) An occupational-preference sort is followed by discussion focusing on the criteria each individual would use in selecting an occupation.

FIFTH MEETING—OCCUPATIONAL EXPLORATION   The Name an Occupation (NANO) game, which involves naming occupations by groups and level of required education, is played.

SIXTH MEETING—OCCUPATIONAL CHOICE   The Salesman, an activity requiring each group member to make an occupational choice and "sell" it to the group, is played.

SEVENTH MEETING—EDUCATIONAL EXPLORATION   A game calling for educational majors to be listed under occupational groups is played.

EIGHTH MEETING—EDUCATIONAL CHOICE   The Salesman is played again, but this time each group member chooses an educational major and "sells" it to the group.

NINTH MEETING—IMPLEMENTATION   The last meeting is devoted to an activity requiring each group member to identify the next action to be taken in his or her decision making.

Formats for each session have been developed and tested. The following is one version of the approach used for meetings 6 and 8. The procedure was prepared by Diane Ducat, when she was a graduate student in counselor education at the University of Florida. Although it does not include the "salesman" activity, it illustrates the emphasis on feedback that is a major characteristic of the group meetings.

RATIONALE   This procedure is designed to elicit feedback from a small group on occupational choice. Time will be allotted each member to present his choice and receive feedback from group members. Emphasis will be placed on the reasons for choice and how the individual sees himself in a given career. The others will be asked if his choice coincides with their impressions and knowledge of the individual. The feedback is then used by the person to evaluate his tentative decision.

PROCEDURE   Read or paraphrase the following instructions to the group:

This hour is designed to provide information about how other group members see you in the occupation or occupational area you have tentatively chosen. You will be given *one minute* to describe the occupation and how you see yourself in it. Use the time to tell what occupation you have chosen and the reasons why you have selected this occupation or area. Be as specific as possible. For example, you might start off, "I have chosen the occupation of engineer because I like to build things and have always done well in math and science." Give as many reasons as possible within the one-minute time limit that support your plan.

The group will then be given *four minutes* to react. As a group member, try to imagine the person in the occupation he has presented. Again, be as specific as possible in giving evidence that confirms or contradicts his plan. Some examples of feedback might be:

I see you as happy as an interior designer because you are always rearranging your room in new and imaginative ways.

I can't picture you as a UN translator. You always cut language lab and you got a C in Spanish last quarter.

I don't think you will be happy as an English teacher, although I think you have the necessary skills. My uncle teaches English and he doesn't loaf after 3 P.M. He grades papers many nights. I don't think you have a good picture of the job.

After everyone has had an opportunity to get the reactions of others to his plan to enter an occupation or occupational area, there will be a brief discussion of the experience.

Now start the exercise by calling on one member to begin his one-minute presentation. When the time is up, start the feedback. Encourage all members of the group to give some, but do not waste time insisting. After the group has given four minutes of feedback, go on to the next person. Continue until each member has made a presentation and received reactions. As group leader, your job will be to watch the time (or appoint a timekeeper) so that everyone will get an equal opportunity. Since this procedure is set up for a 10-member group and a one-hour time period spend about 5 minutes on each person. It will take approximately 50 minutes to go around the group. If your group is larger, you may have to cut the presentation and feedback time. If the group is smaller, you can increase them proportionally. Allow approximately 10 minutes at the end for general discussion of the experience. Point out that the procedures do not evaluate the person as an individual. It only gives the others' perceptions of him in a particular career. If anyone has a plan that is strongly contradicted, you might ask him at the end of the meeting whether he would like to meet with one of the counselors. Encourage each member to weigh his feedback carefully. It is another source of information he can use in his occupational decision.

The Life Career-Development System

This group procedure is provided by specially trained and certified faciliators; training usually takes about three days and is available at a number of sites. The program is intended to help participants learn how to present the program to others and to increase their own facilitative skills. The system is adaptable for ninth-graders through adults and consists of a sixty-hour program based on the rationale that career development involves the total individual, including education, work, and leisure time[2].

The major strategy is to focus on participant learning and outcomes that are closely related to real-life situations and thus facilitate generalizing. A substantial experiential element is provided to enable participants to deal with actual career-development tasks. In each module, a pattern of orientation, experiencing, personalization, and behavioral follow-through is used.

Each module includes from six to nine fifty-minute sessions involving individual and group structured learning experiences. Scheduling may be concentrated or spread over a semester or a year. The modules cover the following areas:

1. EXPLORING SELF   Seven sessions are devoted to understanding interests, strengths and the like, and the relationship of self-understanding to career satisfaction.
2. DETERMINING VALUES   Six sessions are devoted to identifying values and examining their relationship to career planning.
3. SETTING GOALS   Six sessions are used for learning how to set goals and formulate satisfying ones, utilizing insights and understandings from previous meetings.
4. EXPANDING OPTIONS   This module uses six sessions to help participants become aware of new roles and opportunities, to expand options, and to explore ways to find meaning and satisfaction in work.
5. OVERCOMING BARRIERS   Six sessions are used for participants to learn how to identify and cope with barriers and obstacles to career development.
6. USING INFORMATION   Five regular sessions (fifty-minute) and one three-hour session are used to learn how to locate, evaluate, and use information in career planning.
7. WORKING EFFECTIVELY   Six sessions are devoted to helping participants learn

[2]Material in this section adapted by permission from Garry R. Walz and Libby Benjamin, "The Life Career Development System," in Garry R. Walz, Robert L. Smith, and Libby Benjamin (eds). *A Comprehensive View of Career Development*. Washington, D.C.: American Personnel and Guidance Association, 1974, pp. 71–79.

how to increase effectiveness in study and work and to become aware of the nature of effective job performance.

8. THINKING FUTURISTICALLY   Six sessions requiring six to eight fifty-minute periods are utilized to enable participants to look into the future, develop skill in forecasting, and formulate self-renewal strategies.

9. SELECTING MATES   Six sessions are devoted to various aspects of dating and marriage to help individuals understand stable and mutually satisfying relationships.

This program may serve as an organizing framework for a school or college career-guidance program. Agencies, too, could utilize it with individuals willing to make a relatively long-term commitment for participation.

The Life-Planning Workshop

This career program, adapted from materials designed for an industrial setting, provides a way of helping college students take an active role in life planning, develop self-understanding, and find their place in life (Johnson, 1977). It is helpful for preparing individuals to deal with a number of tasks, such as career planning and marriage decisions. The focus is on understanding one's present status and making projections into the future (Johnson, 1977). The process is shown in Figure 8.1.

The four basic areas of the workshop are shown in the circles. The numbered items are the major activities carried out in each area. For example, in the "life line" exercise, participants draw a line on a sheet of paper, with one end representing birth and the other death. An x is placed on the line to indicate the participant's current position. More than one line may be used to indicate the present stage in several life roles with different degrees of progress in each. The purpose of the exercise is to help participants think about what lies ahead and to evaluate progress. At the conclusion of the five- to six-hour meeting, participants leave with specific goals to accomplish.

The workshop may be conducted by counselors, counselors-in-training, or paraprofessionals who have had preparation for the task. An instructor's manual and other aids assist the facilitator. Groups usually contain four members, an appropriate number for the type of interaction, discussion, and modeling needed.

Evaluation data indicate that the workshop helps individuals. Moreover, three alternative methods of presentation—audio-visual, written, and leaderless—have also shown positive results. The developer describes the program as a viable alternative to in-office counseling.

DECIDING, Decisions and Outcomes, and How to Decide

Three programs developed by the College Entrance Examination Board provide well-developed and effective programs for several different populations. The

Figure 8.1   The life planning workshop experiential flow chart

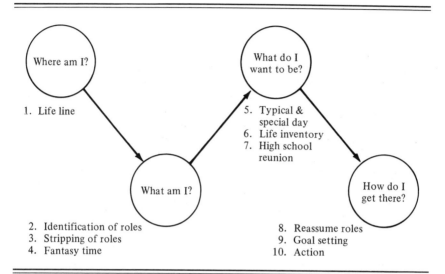

SOURCE: Robert B. Johnson, "Life Planning and Life Planning Workshops," *Personnel and Guidance Journal*, 55, No. 9, (1977), 547. Copyright 1977 American Personnel and Guidance Association. Used by permission.

programs, which may be obtained from the College Entrance Examination Board, are widely used and well accepted.

DECIDING (Carey, Gelatt, Miller, and Varenhorst, 1971) is designed for junior and senior high school pupils and features identification and analysis of values, finding and using relevant information, and developing action strategies. Program scheduling is flexible; it may be completed in from fifteen to forty-five hours and may be used in a brief, concentrated period or spread out over a full year. It may be a separate course or part of the existing curriculum.

Decisions and Outcomes (Carey, Gelatt, Miller, and Varenhorst, 1973), the second College Board decision-making program, is designed for teenagers, older students, and adults. The rationale is the same as for DECIDING; it assists individuals to learn and apply a rational decision-making process. Major sections cover values, information, and strategy, and there are numerous exercises for experiencing. It is suitable for a separate program or for inclusion in the regular curriculum. Other uses have been in college orientation, as part of the educational program, and for assisting mid-career men and women in career planning.

The third program is called How to Decide: A Guide for Women (Scholz, Prince, and Miller, 1976); it may be used by individuals alone or in groups. In groups, it is suitable for such helping procedures as career counseling, marriage counseling, group therapy, psychology courses, and business and industrial programs for women. Four major sections, in logical sequence, build decision-making skills. These sections seek answers to the following questions:

1. Where are you as a woman? Participants are helped to recognize that they have choices and can take control of their lives.
2. Who are you? The focus is on values and personal goals.
3. What do you need to know? This section shows that information enables individuals to make decisions about their lives. Barriers to choice and risk taking are covered, and participants are helped to recognize and deal with obstacles to decision making.
4. How do you take action? Discussions of examples of successful persons and analyses of personal barriers lead to an action plan based on learnings from the previous units.

The Vocational Exploration Group, or VEG

This structured group-counseling procedure published by Studies for Urban Man, Tempe, Arizona, focuses on job functions, job demands, and job satisfactions. Groups are limited to four to six individuals to provide time and opportunity for extensive participation in the two major methods of group interaction used—self-disclosure and peer feedback. Depending on the method of administration, the group process takes from two to four hours. Administration is completely outlined in a manual and needed materials—charts, books—are included in the kit. Counselors, teachers, and paraprofessionals usually serve as facilitators and are certified after going through a training program. Briefly, the program content is as follows:

Part 1
1. Members introduce each other. Each participant tells what he or she would do with a million dollars.
2. Participants categorize occupations by functions and needed training and identify those most and least liked.
3. Cool seat. Participants give feedback about suitable and unsuitable occupations for one another.
4. Participants choose suitable jobs and evaluate functions—data, people, things, aspects.
5. Participants expand alternatives presented in charts and illustrations.
6. Participants use books to learn about a number of occupations.

Part 2
1. Participants discuss job satisfiers
2. Participants discuss their interests and skills
3. Participants discuss preferred occupations and the preparation required

4. Participants evaluate preferred occupations
5. Participants evaluate preferred occupations in terms of satisfiers, interests, and abilities
6. Participants expand occupational alternatives
7. Participants decide on next steps

The program combines group counseling and decision-making techniques in a systematic process. Participants usually enjoy the activities and report that they learned a great deal. Positive results have been obtained with those seeking help from state employment services—for example, improvement in job-seeking behavior and job tenure and reduction in alienation and dogmatism. The VEG has been effective when used with high school pupils, including those with educational, economic, emotional, or physical handicaps (Neely and Kosier, 1977). Pupils tend to take the next step they have formulated (Cross, 1975). Comparisons of written responses versus group interaction have been made, but results need further study (Bergland and Lundquist, 1975).

Other Programs

Hewer (1968) describes the group-counseling program at the University of Minnesota. This program utilizes a case conference approach in which counselees describe their situations, plans, and difficulties and other group members suggest courses of action, predict success, estimate satisfaction, and otherwise serve as helpers. Group members are screened for potential to profit from this kind of counseling. Six to eight participants make up the group. Usually, seven or eight fifty-minute meetings are held. The counselor assists with reactions to suggestions and provides data. As would be expected, discussion and interaction range far beyond educational and vocational choice and planning. Parental attitudes, marriage, the university, and sex roles are other areas explored.

Group guidance for vocational choice and planning has typically used field trips, consultants, and films. However, active methods to obtain occupational information in conjunction with group counseling also have been used. Thompson (Thompson and Majunder, 1972) describes a program of "work exposure" for disadvantaged youth that involved intensive, on-site exposure of two weeks' duration each to five different health-related professions. Group as well as individual counseling was a part of the program, and guest speakers and other informational techniques were used. The program was judged effective in raising occupational and educational aspirations and improving self-concepts. Thompson concludes that the procedure is practical for large-scale use in the school program.

Going a step further, Hoffnung and Mills (1970) combined group counseling with work experience for disadvantaged youths in an apprenticeship program. The best results were obtained with twice-weekly meetings in which trainees' life situations were explored. The approach was client-centered, and the leader served mainly to clarify feelings, provide needed information, and reinforce openness and attempts at problem solving. Positive changes in attitude toward self, peers, and work resulted. Improved attitudes were demonstrated on the job as well as in the groups.

Many of the career-development programs designed for adults use a group approach, although not all could be classified as group counseling; the workshop and class formats are often used (Harrison and Entine, 1976). Group-counseling methods are particularly useful at the college level. The summary of programs at Illinois State University (Cochran and Rademacher, 1978) identifies six group-counseling services, primarily developmental and preventive. At all levels and in practically all settings, innovative programs are being tried out and evaluated.

Research Findings

Evidence on the effects of group career counseling are positive enough to demonstrate its value and suggest its potential. Eight-session group counseling with girls increased career awareness and factual knowledge of the occupational status of women (Woodcock and Herman, 1978). College programs for career development, utilizing group-counseling techniques, have helped students increase self-knowledge, engage in more planning activities, take more responsibility for decision making, and consider career areas related to interests (Mencke and Cochran, 1974; Babcock and Kaufman, 1976). The Mencke and Cochran study also revealed that career-development behaviors are more readily affected by intensive work than are career attitudes. This finding is particularly significant because of the part that behaviors play in career planning and decision making. A thirty-minute structured career-development program, Life Work Planning (Tichenor, 1977), which included a phase of value exploration and one of decision making, had positive effects on participants. Counseling activities were used to help individuals move from initial warm-up and group-forming activities through goal setting and decision making. Immediate and delayed evaluation showed that participants had improved significantly on two aspects of self-actualization—inner direction and self-regard.

Combining group counseling and computer guidance systems augments the effectiveness of each. The trend is to design computer systems around a career-development rationale with the computer doing those tasks that it can best handle. Group-counseling sessions are used to discuss and react to data obtained from the computer. Since use of the terminal is an individual activity, group counseling is particularly appropriate for giving individuals the opportunity to interact with one another in terms of what they have learned, to explore feelings about it, and to clarify goals. Table 5.1 (p. 162) shows that the computer shares responsibility with group counseling for a number of career-development tasks, such as self-concept clarification, relating self- and occupational information, and teaching decision-making skills. As computer-guidance systems become more widely used, additional programs for integration with both group counseling and group guidance will likely be developed; the combination has a great deal of potential.

Group counseling has been used successfully with disabled individuals to help them reach such career goals as learning job-interviewing skills, developing a more optimistic life perspective, and increasing vocational and personal maturity. Use by Roessler, Cook, and Lillard (1977) of two-hour group sessions over a five-week period with work-adjustment clients resulted in such gains. However, the authors suggest the need for additional research to determine whether these learnings contribute to employment and progress on the job. Grinnell and Lieberman (1977) used microcounseling with videotaped playback to increase the job-interviewing skills of mentally retarded young adults and produced substantial improvement in eye contact and body posture. The presence of a model and constant repetition of skills were shown to be the most effective procedures to insure mastery. These and other approaches should be particularly useful today in view of new demands for counselors to work with the disabled.

Other Applications

The number and variety of career group-counseling approaches are increasing so rapidly that it is difficult to describe all the developments. Often it is impossible to distinguish between group guidance and group counseling, because both approaches are combined in a single program. Moreover, group methods are increasingly used in placement (see Chapter 12) to build attitudes and skills that contribute to job finding and success.

Many new programs have been instituted at all levels; college is one example. Evans and Rector (1978) report on a credit course, Decision-Making for Career Development, that combines independent study, large group meetings, and small group-counseling sessions. Although the authors point out that evaluation results should be viewed with caution because of the possible influence of other variables, the evidence is that the course contributed to the career development of undergraduate students. Crane (1978) describes the effects of four two-hour group meetings to help students explore career concerns and learn decision-making processes. Techniques like the SDS fantasy exercises were used. Student evaluations were very positive. The Knefelkamp-Slepitza model was used by a college personnel team (Touchton, Wertheimer, Cornfeld, and Harrison, 1977) to develop a career-planning course for undergraduates. When compared with results of traditionally taught courses, students showed significant gains in the major course objective, cognitive complexity with respect to careers, and expressed greater satisfaction.

Similar progress is being made in schools, where many of these group programs are being conducted by guidance personnel as part of career education (see Chapter 10). The program to reduce stereotyping by eighth-grade girls and help them become aware of more occupational options is an example of many current projects (Cramer, Wise, and Colburn, 1977). On measures of both attitudes and cognitive learning (knowledge about women and careers) the pupils in the treatment groups made significant improvement over control pupils. The authors conclude that group career counseling is an effective strategy to use for this age group.

CAREER COUNSELING IN DETAIL

The studies and programs just described have been used in designing the group-counseling approach called group career counseling, whose rationale was outlined at the beginning of this chapter. The approach, with some brief illustrations, is described in the following section.

Decision-making and vocational-development concepts are also used in the process. The steps highlight phases, but each step does not represent a meeting. Structure is needed, although the amount suggested may seem extreme in light of widely used group methods. Acceptance, positive regard, and understanding characterize the climate; reflection of the real meaning of comments is a frequently used response. Participants should be interested in career planning, not more than one grade apart, and usually be juniors or seniors. Those in lower grade levels may participate, however.

Step 1. Recruit Participants

Let pupils know about the proposed group. Make a list of those interested. One counselor placed a notice on the guidance bulletin board and visited classrooms to make brief announcements. The responses were so numerous that all applicants could not be included.

Step 2. Interview Pupils

Inform pupils about the purposes and procedures of the group, screen those who are not suited to participation, review the purposes of taking part in the group, and explain that participation involves commitment, but that an individual can withdraw from the group if he or she wishes.

In the school that serves as an example, the counselor interviewed eighteen pupils to get two groups of six members each. Individual counseling was suggested for several students. Two appeared to be uncertain about their interest in attending regular meetings. It was announced that because of staff limitations only two groups could be started immediately and that additional groups would be scheduled later in the term.

Step 3. Select Group Members

Select between six and ten pupils to make up the group. Heterogeneity is recommended. The twelve pupils selected were juniors and seniors. There was a representative racial and sexual distribution. Four had firm college plans. Three were somewhat indefinite about college or post–high school preparation, and five planned to work after high school. Of these five, one was on the verge of dropping out. Group A, which will be used as the example, had the following membership:

Sally—definitely planning to attend college

Joe—a potential dropout

Mike—going to work after high school
Sandi—going to work after high school
Carl—undecided about post–high school preparation
Linda—undecided about post–high school preparation

Step 4. Start the Group

In the first meeting, have pupils introduce themselves or let each introduce another person that he or she does not know well. If the latter procedure is used, provide ten minutes for pairs to interview each other to obtain information for the introductions. Briefly discuss the process of vocational development, pointing out stages. The purpose of this session is to help break the ice and to orient participants to the process of career development.

The counselor suggested that members pair up and interview each other for a few minutes to prepare introductions. Although this began with a great deal of superficial joking and awkwardness, it turned out to be very effective. Members quickly moved to informal, friendly interaction, and several expressed surprise that they learned so many interesting things about the others, whom they had previously known only casually.

The counselor also explained that the group would meet an hour each week, at different times to avoid interrupting the same class each time, and that the number of meetings depended on group progress and preference.

Step 5. Orient to Decision Making

Introduce the process of decision making. Let members explain how they think decisions should be made. Explain simply the decision-making model described in Chapter 7 as the framework for later sessions. Two techniques that might stimulate pupil interest are:

1. Ask participants to interview someone prior to the session to find out how he or she decided on his or her current job.
2. Use a brief simulation, for example, describe a hypothetical pupil similar to those in the group and list several options from which he or she may select. Let participants select options for the pupil and explain their choices. The purpose of this phase is to help pupils learn how decisions are made and to understand the basis for the sequence of group activities.

The counselor used a simulation he had prepared to introduce decision making. A brief dittoed case of a pupil very similar to several of the group members was handed out. After it had been read, a second sheet listing four options for the pupil was distributed. Members were asked to select an option and explain their reasons. Then a third sheet, describing outcomes, was passed out. Discussion of the outcomes, the way the decisions were made, and the information that had been used and overlooked led to an in-depth analysis of the choice process.

Step 6. Determine Participant Purposes

Each member has a purpose for taking part in the group. It may, however, be vague and difficult to express. This phase resembles the unstructured type of group counseling, with its extensive use of reflection of feeling, clarification, and linking. The counselor could model these as well as self-disclosure and feedback techniques. Although participants may acknowledge intellectually that decision making requires a purpose, they must experience the need if genuine progress is to take place. It may be helpful to practice some responses, such as feedback, to encourage participants to react to each other in constructive ways.

The counselor began in an unstructured way, with the suggestion that members talk about what they would like to get out of group counseling. Sally, usually eager to talk about herself, began by saying that she was undecided about a college major. She didn't seem to be able to settle on anything for more than a week at a time. Joe found it more difficult to pinpoint his purpose. "I just don't seem to have much interest in anything. There must be something I'd like to do, but I can't find it." Carl was debating whether to enter vocational-technical training or college. He expressed concern about being able to find a job when he completed preparation. Mike said that he had to go to work after high school. He was expected to join his father in the family automobile agency, but had some reservations about this plan. Sandi explained that she was in the vocational office training program, but wanted to do more with her life than office work. Linda seemed to be completely undecided. "I'm confused. I don't even know where to start to say what I want to get out of this group! Just less confused?"

Interaction occurred spontaneously. Sally reacted to Joe by asserting that everybody has some interests and that he was keeping his from the group for some reason. Linda responded by defending Joe and insisting that it is possible to have no idea what one would like to do. Feedback developed naturally, with the counselor doing some modeling. For example, he said to Sandi, "When you say you want to do more than office work, it makes me feel that you've got some special kind of talent that you want to use. But you think that you *ought* to stay with secretarial work." In the process, some deeper reasons emerged. Linda later expressed her feelings in a slightly different way. "What I *really* wonder is what chances does a black girl have to do what she has the ability to do? That's in the picture. You can't understand that. Maybe Carl does." Carl replied that he knew it would make a difference, being black himself, but he believed that he could make it. "It even might help you. You know, 'tokenism.'"

By the end of the session, purposes had been clarified somewhat. An additional meeting using a more traditional approach could have been scheduled, but the counselor felt that further exploration of purposes and goals would naturally emerge in future meetings. Furthermore, he felt that it was preferable to adhere to the general plan to keep the group's attention focused on decision making.

Step 7. Provide Information to Counselees

The counselor provides each participant with a personal folder of information from his or her cumulative record, including a verbal description of test scores. Part of this phase is used to explain the meaning of test scores and other data, such as predictive validity of school marks.

If needed, additional tests and inventories, such as OVIS, Kuder C, DD, SCII, or DAT, could be administered at this time. Decisions about additional tests and inventories are made in the group, although different members might elect to take different tests—for example, some might want the GATB. Although for some tests and inventories there may be a delay in obtaining machine-scored results, this procedure is preferable to giving all participants the same battery at the beginning of the group work.

The objective of this phase is to develop self-understanding, both through use of test and other data and through interaction among members. The latter process has, of course, been taking place since the beginning of group counseling.

There was a great deal of interest in the information folder. The counselor had prepared for each member a summary sheet including course averages, test scores, and other data. Participants had rated themselves on the same factors on a form given out at the end of the previous session. College Board or ACT test results and norm booklets were included for Sally, Carl, and Linda, who had taken one of the tests. Some local expectancy table data were included for the community college and the vocational-technical center.

Participants decided that they wanted some additional tests to facilitate self-understanding. OVIS, SCII, and Kuder DD were described. Each participant decided to take one or more and to wait for the results before moving to the next phase. Several also wanted to take the GATB. Because a member of the guidance staff had been trained in administering it by the employment service and the school had purchased a set of materials, this presented no problems.

Inventory results, with the help of special fast scoring, were received in two weeks. The next session was used to give group interpretations of the inventories, answer questions, and explain how test and inventory data are related to other information. There was considerable interaction as results were reviewed. Members exclaimed such things as "What did you do on this?" and "Look at this! I don't know how that ever came out so high!" and "Do you think I'd make a good accountant?" They seemed to be testing the results with others or seeking confirmation for measured preferences. There was little discussion, however, of ability test scores. The counselor had made it clear that test and inventory results were each individual's personal information and that there would be no pressure to reveal any more information than one wished.

Step 8. Look at Options

Options are related to pupils' status and levels of vocational maturity. The options for seniors going to work after completing school are various jobs. A vocationally immature pupil's options might be different plans for exploration. Each member is asked to select three that he or she would like to consider.

The success of this phase depends to a large extent on how well interactions, including counselor suggestions, broaden the range of possibilities considered. It might be helpful to use employer interviews, resource persons, individual or group field trips, and information-system exploration with reports to the group to broaden horizons. The purpose of this phase, in addition to increasing the number of possibilities, is to break down unrealistic patterns of preferences and occupational stereotypes.

Each member was asked to come to the meeting with three options he or she might follow. Each was encouraged to suggest other possibilities to the individual who presented his or her choices. Although participants had attended a career fair the previous year and several career days during the past two years, they exhibited a decided lack of information about occupations, college programs, and technical training. Because the group seemed to feel this lack acutely, the counselor assumed that they were highly enough motivated to obtain information themselves and report on it the next session. Each member took a special assignment—programs at the community college, occupations in health-related fields (a visit to a local hospital), or major occupations in the community (a visit to the employment service). The purpose was to expand the number of possibilities that might be considered rather than to collect in-depth information about particular occupations. Since interests were quite heterogeneous, the counselor did not think it feasible to use a particular set of films (such as the WERC series), take all members on the same field trip, or invite consultants.

The main problems with the reports turned out to be completing them in the allotted time. Sally went on and on about health-related careers, insisted on distributing a collection of pamphlets, and wanted the group to invite the hospital staff member with whom she had talked to a meeting. Joe was impressed with the "fantastic number of things you can take at the community college. Anything you ever heard of is there!" Some participants' plans were changed, but the main value was the additional possibilities of which they became aware.

Step 9. Consider Possibilities and Probabilities

Now that pupils have several possible courses of action in mind, the focus moves to trying out educational and occupational roles in the group. Each member makes a brief presentation of his or her preferred option, describing how he or she sees himself or herself in the role. Each other member gives two or three minutes' feedback on how well he or she thinks the role fits, based on what he or she knows about the person and about the occupational or educational program. The counselor helps keep the feedback on a constructive level and corrects misinformation about occupations or educational programs. (Feedback is often unrealistically positive, however. The problem is to help participants give sincere reactions when some are not complimentary.)

Predictions of success, values, and other aspects of decision making are brought out in this process. The group must observe time limits so that each participant will have a chance. At the conclusion, unstructured discussion is helpful. Discussion may be quite brief or may continue for several sessions. Each participant should keep in mind that "feedback" is how others perceive him or her, regardless of whether or not he or she agrees with it. It may be decided to try other options on the group or to bring in resource persons to help clarify questions that have arisen.

Each individual compares what he or she has decided with his or her original purpose. Presumably, the group would continue until each member reaches a decision related to his or her purpose. Decisions can be for further exploration or for definite courses of action. The decision is the individual's although, if the group wishes, there could be feedback on the perceived strengths and limitations of the individual for that choice.

The preferred-option presentations and feedback continued over several sessions. The interaction seemed more like unstructured group counseling than had any previous session, even though the counselor carefully limited the amount of time for presentation and feedback. Each member became a "counselor," reflecting, questioning, supporting, challenging, and giving information.

Pressure was not exerted on the participants to make final choices, but most of them expressed a first and a second preference. Mike decided to talk with his parents about the possibility of journalism. He wanted to take at least a year or so of college and try to get a part-time job on the local newspaper. A second choice was to become an airline pilot, and he was going to visit a school that offered basic training. Joining his father's automobile agency was a poor third. Mike felt that he knew what he wanted and could at least get his point of view across to his parents. Joe's plans were for further exploration. "I'm going to visit a lot of places and talk to a lot of people. And get some work if I can. I don't think I'll do much studying. Maybe I will. But I plan to see what's going on out in the world. After all, I got next year in school and maybe got the service, too. So I have time." Sally stayed undecided, and the group devoted a final session to her, following through on the plan that the group would continue until each member had made a reasonably satisfactory decision. It was finally agreed, however, that she would probably have to go to college, try various programs, and make up her mind later. After all, the only major decision she had to make as a high school junior was whether or not to attend college. Later she would need to decide on the type of college and make application. She felt that this would not be a major problem, since she preferred the state university.

Step 10. Implement

Each individual plans and describes how he or she will carry out his or her decision. Resource persons may be helpful for job-hunting strategies, college applications, and practicing employment interviews. For junior high pupils, reports could be made on the programs to be taken. For those planning more exploration, a strategy could be described. This is an often-neglected phase, but one that is extremely important. Support and counseling are often needed at this point as much or more than at any other time.

Implementation involves the tryout and evaluation of decision and plans. The group is not a terminal one-shot phenomenon. It meets again, perhaps after a long interval, to report on progress. The success of exploratory plans and post–high school educational applications could be reported. The testing of occupational decisions would come later. The school placement service could help arrange for follow-up of those employed locally.

The last two activities, follow-up while in school and post–high school meetings, present some massive difficulties. With heavy case loads and an array of other responsibilities, counselors often feel that the best procedure is to complete one group and begin the next. But it is more important to follow through with fewer pupils than to give brief and unevaluated help to a much larger number. In the procedure described, evaluation is built in. The process is self-correcting.

Plans for implementation and feedback took up the last session. It was agreed that the group should meet again in the spring to follow up on its progress. Members were quite positive in their opinion that a meeting, or at least some kind of contact, should be planned for the year following high school. The group also evaluated the counseling sessions very positively, saying that they knew themselves much better than they had expected and had rather clear ideas about what they could accomplish in the future.

SUMMARY

Group-counseling methods and decision-making concepts can be combined in a model for group-career counseling. Much of the work that has ben done on this group process has involved college students, using group members' problems as content. A group career-counseling model derived from existing programs, group-counseling principles, career-development theory and decision-making concepts has been described and illustrated in this chapter. The major features of this procedure are a facilitative climate to stimulate interaction and exploration of feelings, testing of tentative educational and occupational roles, and utilization of various sorts of information as input to facilitate decision making. Considerable use was made of career-development concepts to help pupils understand their present situation and the decision situations that will be encountered in the future.

PROJECTS AND EXPERIENTIAL ACTIVITIES

1. Visit a school guidance office to determine the use made of group counseling. If possible, observe or sit in on a group session.

2. Practice a group procedure with high school or college student volunteers. Set a limited goal, such as discussion of career plans. Let the group know that you are doing it for practice. Record and play back the session for personal evaluation. Did your responses help members discuss and clarify goals?

3. Use some of the following materials to learn about techniques that could be incorporated into group career counseling. *Carl Rogers Conducts an Encounter Group,* available from the American Personnel and Guidance Association, 1607 New Hampshire Avenue, N.W., Washington, D.C. 20009. Other tapes, films, and videotapes are listed by Helen L. Stevens, J. Joseph Doerr, and Roger Chatten in "Audiovisual Materials for Group Workers," *Personnel and Guidance Journal,* 49, No. 8 (1971), 657–658.

4. Practice a group technique with colleagues. For example, practice linking members' relations.

5. Participate in some type of group experience. It is usually not difficult to join a discussion, encounter, or counseling group in the community or on the campus. Observe the dynamics of the group, the techniques the leader uses, and the types of interaction that develop.

6. Form small groups and try out one or more of the group exercises designed to help with career planning and decision making. Discuss the results in terms of perceived values for future work setting and personal help to you. Some suggested group exercises:
   a. the life line
   b. a fantasy experience
   c. role stripping (one procedure is to write four or five important roles you play on separate pieces of paper, rank them in importance, discard them one by one, and discuss your feelings about each deletion. (Other techniques that could be tried out are given in the chapter and in additional references.)

7. Develop your own brief group-counseling procedure, using career-development theory, group-counseling techniques, and decision-making/developmental exercises. Identify the setting and clientele for which the procedure is suitable— elementary school, middle school, high school, college, a program for re-entry men and women. If possible, try it out and ask participants to evaluate results.

ADDITIONAL REFERENCES

Boy, Angelo V., and Gerald J. Pine. *The Counselor in the Schools: A Reconceptualization.* Boston: Houghton Mifflin, 1968. Chap. 10, "His Awareness of Group Counseling," is particularly helpful in clarifying terms and concepts, describing the group-counseling procedure, and illustrating the process. The description of the important linking function, for example, is lucid and interesting.

Cohn, Benjamin, ed. *Guidelines for Future Research on Group Counseling in the Public School Setting.* Washington, D.C.: American Personnel and Guidance Association, 1967. Pp. 4–12 are a general introduction to purposes, issues, and problems related to group counseling in the school. The monograph deals primarily with research and evaluation. Later sections are valuable resource materials for planning evaluation studies.

Coulson, William. "Inside the Basic Encounter Group." *The Counseling Psychologist*, 2, No. 2 (1970), 1–27. For an understandable, relatively brief discussion of the encounter group, with illustrative material, this is highly recommended. The responses by authorities that follow help the reader to understand different points of view toward this approach to group work.

Dye, H. Allen. *Fundamental Group Procedures for School Counselors*. Boston: Houghton Mifflin, 1968. This discussion of group procedures for the school counselor is particularly useful as a handy reference when initiating and conducting group counseling.

Fullmer, Daniel W., and Harold W. Bernard. *The School Counselor-Consultant*. Boston: Houghton Mifflin, 1972. The place of group work and group counseling in the schools is clearly explained on pp. 170–183. The authors develop the concept of the counselor-consultant as a planner and provider of group services, a significant trend in school guidance.

Gazda, George M., ed. *Theories and Methods of Group Counseling in the Schools*. Springfield, Ill.: Charles C Thomas, 1969. Several chapters are excellent readings on group counseling. Mahler's article is a good starting point, particularly for an explanation of stages in group development. Blakeman and Day's description of activity group counseling and Varenhorst's chapter on behavioral group counseling are highly recommended.

Gazda, George M. "Group Procedures." *Counseling Today and Tomorrow*, 1, No. 2 (1972), 8–22 (and audiotape). Gazda's discussion is part of APGA's cassette series on major trends in guidance and counseling. It gives an excellent overview of group procedures and guidelines for conducting developmental group counseling.

Golembiewski, Robert T., and Arthur Blumberg, eds. *Sensitivity Training and the Laboratory Approach*. Itasca, Ill.: F. E. Peacock, 1970. This is a helpful reference for those who wish to learn more about sensitivity groups and techniques that might be adapted to group career counseling. For example, feedback is discussed on pp. 60–64 and 69–73.

Hoppock, Robert. *Occupational Information*. 4th ed. New York: McGraw-Hill, 1976. A number of the techniques Hoppock describes can be adapted for use in group counseling. For example, the case conference, discussed on pp. 209–215, has been used extensively in the group-counseling programs described in this chapter.

Kemp, C. Gratton. *Foundations of Group Counseling*. New York: McGraw-Hill, 1970. This is an excellent reference on group counseling. A reading of the book will help one understand the process, the dynamics, and the leader's role. The scales given on pp. 301–308 are useful for evaluating group work.

Lifton, Walter M. *Working with Groups*. 2nd ed. New York: John Wiley & Sons, 1966. Chap. 4, "A Group in Action," is an excellent illustration of group interaction with commentary.

Mowrer, O. Hobart. "Integrity Groups: Principles and Procedures." *The Counseling Psychologist,* 3, No. 2 (1972), 7–33. Integrity groups represent an interesting approach to therapeutic group work. The article also includes a summary of the development of the small-group movement and a discussion of the current issues.

Tolbert, E. L. *Introduction to Counseling.* 2nd ed. New York: McGraw-Hill, 1972. Group counseling is discussed and illustrated on pp. 16–17, 126–129, 172–174, 279–282, and 296–299.

9

Career-Guidance Programs

GOALS

1

To explain how career guidance contributes to pupil personnel services in educational institutions.

2

To describe career-guidance program planning.

3

To describe staffing patterns for career guidance.

4

To discuss group-guidance procedures that may be used in the program.

5

To explain how the counselor can promote guidance programs in the school and the community.

6

To make the reader aware of the many settings in several countries in which career-guidance programs operate.

THE COUNSELOR PLAYS THE KEY ROLE in initiating, building, and coordinating career-guidance services. New guidance models are certain to include the counselor on the educational team that works toward the major career-development goals he or she has promoted more or less alone in the past.

The counselor's key role is emphasized in statements from professional organizations. The NVGA/AVA position paper makes clear the counselor's coordination, leadership, supervisory, and consulting responsibilities. It points out that "effective implementation of career guidance in an educational setting necessitates that guidance leadership identify not only what has to be accomplished, but also what has the capabilities for coordinating and delivering specific program elements" (NVGA/AVA, 1973, p. 6). The counselor competencies specifically related to these responsibilities are clearly identified in the position paper of the Association for Counselor Education and Supervision.

1. Consultation strategies and the skills necessary to assist others (teachers, parents, and peers) to deliver indirect career-guidance services
2. Program development and curricular-infusion strategies and the skills necessary to design and implement career awareness, self-development, career exploration, and job-placement programs within educational and community-agency settings
3. Organizational development and change processes and the skills necessary to facilitate change in educators' attitudes toward career education.[1]

These competencies, which stress work with the total staff, apply to this chapter and the next and emphasize or state unequivocally that the career counselor has a central role in building and directing the school or agency program.

This chapter covers services offered for pupils, program models, and staffing. Group approaches are discussed next, and interaction with other staff members is the last topic. The counselor can and should enlist the support of all school personnel in helping pupils with decision making, planning, and career development. All pupil personnel services should cooperate in accomplishing these objectives, as well as in meeting other pupil needs. The broad focus is on health, home, social, and economic, as well as career, problems. The total pupil personnel program may seem at times to merge with instruction, but differences exist, and they should be understood for effective operation of these specialized services.

This chapter is essential background for understanding career education or any other plan for schoolwide guidance. The next chapter describes in detail and gives examples of many of the principles introduced here. Emphasis in Chapter 10 is on *career education* as one approach to promoting career development in educational institutions.

[1]L. Sunny Hansen, "ACES Position Paper: Counselor Preparation for Career Development/Career Education," *Counselor Education and Supervision,* 17, No. 3 (1978), pp. 177–178. Copyright 1978 American Personnel and Guidance Association. Used by permission.

PUPIL PERSONNEL SERVICES

"Pupil personnel services" is an umbrella label for a number of pupil-oriented functions, which usually include the following:

1. PSYCHOLOGICAL SERVICES   Diagnostic, remedial, and therapeutic services provided by a school psychologist.
2. SOCIAL-WORK SERVICES   Home-school relations, problems related to child welfare, home-school legal matters, and assistance for home problems that interfere with school progress and general adjustment. The social-work orientation is currently more pronounced than when this function was handled by the "visiting teacher."
3. HEALTH SERVICES   Primary emphasis on physical health and services provided by medical doctors, nurses, and other health-related professionals. Emotional health services may be provided by psychiatrists as well as school psychologists.
4. SPEECH AND HEARING THERAPY SERVICES   Diagnosis and remediation of speech and hearing difficulties. Individual or group-treatment methods may be used. Consultation with parents is frequent.
5. ATTENDANCE SERVICES   Monitoring and assurance of regular attendance or appropriate educational experiences for those unable to participate in regular classes. In addition, data on the pupil population are maintained.
6. PUPIL APPRAISAL SERVICE   Collection of data about pupils, primarily by means of standardized tests and measurements.
7. REMEDIAL INSTRUCTIONAL SERVICES   Identification and remediation of learning difficulties. The trend is to include these in a program of child-study services involving psychologists, special education personnel, and specialists.
8. GUIDANCE SERVICES   Help with self-understanding, planning, decision making, and utilizing of potential.

A comment should be made about the term *guidance*. Objections have been raised to it and its demise has been predicted, but it appears to be durable, relevant, and understandable. I prefer it because, in spite of its shifting meanings over the years, it still describes the kinds of services that are performed. The changes in meaning will be discussed later, but the term seems able to incorporate them.

The following guidance services are, in essence, the same ones given in the discussion of the role of the counselor in Chapter 7:

1. Counseling—individual and group
2. Group guidance and orientation
3. Testing and assessment
4. Occupational, educational, and social-personal information
5. Consultation with teachers, parents, and pupils
6. In-service education
7. Placement
8. Research and evaluation

These services are either carried out or supervised by the counselor. Some areas overlap other pupil personnel workers, and it is obvious that these other specialists can make a substantial contribution to the goals of the guidance service.

At the community college level, the overall service may be called student personnel services, student affairs, or a similar title. The major services include counseling, career placement, housing, health, and student activities. Organizational patterns vary a great deal, and the trend is toward emphasis on student development and involvement of students in the guidance process—for example, by peer counseling.

Agencies usually have nothing similar to the pupil personnel or student personnel organization. Career-development responsibilities of counselors depend on the purpose of the organization and on staff competencies and assignments. In some agencies, it is up to the individual to decide whether or not to use techniques like group career counseling and to accumulate information on occupations and educational opportunities for use with counselees. In others, such as the employment service, career-guidance procedures are relatively standardized, and informational materials are provided.

PROGRAM PLANNING

In Schools

The difficulty of focusing on pupil needs and the search for better ways to deliver services have resulted in new program designs. Peters's (1970, p. 31) pupil behavioral system establishes a staff to cover various areas and levels of help. The National Conference on Pupil Personnel Services (Leibman, Goldman, and Battle, 1971) calls for a major reorganization of the educational structure, including the addition of a learning-development consultant. This worker would be an expert coordinator-facilitator. A less radical revision is suggested by International Research Commission on Pupil Personnel Services, or IRCOPPS (Stoughton, McKenna, and Cook, 1969, pp. 34–35), which recommends a positive, preventive role, a focus on service rather than the professional role, increased help to parents and teachers, and increased cooperative work with the community. More recent models emphasize consulting as a major program element, a school-community organization, and the synthesis of career guidance with instructional programs.

Setting up a career-development program draws on career-development theories and program-development techniques. The first suggest what should be done, when, and why. For example, they emphasize exploration during the high school years. Program-development techniques, such as the systems approach (Ryan, 1974; Jones, Helliwell, and Ganschow, 1975), provide strategies for determining needs, establishing goals and objectives, deciding on functions, making staff assignments, and evaluating results. The last step provides data on how well the program has achieved its objectives and indicates the degree of success in meeting accountability requirements. Demonstrating effectiveness (see Chapter 13) is particularly critical because of increasingly tight restrictions on budgets and termination of programs that are not shown to be meeting needs successfully.

The use of needs-survey data can be of immense value in program planning, particularly when they are derived for a range of ages. The National Assessment of Career and Educational Development included ages nine, thirteen, seventeen, and adults in a nationwide survey that covered five critical areas (Miller, 1978, pp. 2–3): preparation for career decisions, career and occupational capabilities, skills needed in the world of work, work habits, and work attitudes. Results are reported in a series of manuals (Aubrey, 1978; Miller, 1978; Mitchell, 1978; Westbrook, 1978). The manuals are designed to facilitate local planning; suggested steps help the user incorporate results in programs that are being set up (Miller, 1978, pp. 7–8). First, the user selects objectives related to his or her own program priorities. Next, the program planner reviews each specific question (exercise) to rate its relevance for local objectives. Although regional results are given, local administration of exercises is possible if the user feels these types of data are needed. Results of the nationwide survey can then be reviewed in the data-analysis section of the reports. With these results and the suggestions about appropriate career-development activities provided in the reports, the user has a wealth of material for program planning. Results of the four age-level surveys are too extensive to summarize, but a sample from the survey of seventeen-year-olds will show the potential value for program building.

Under the subobjective of "relate own personal characteristics to occupational requirements," result 18 is as follows: "More males than females are able to name an activity in which they were interested that might be useful for a job. High Metro [High ability pupils] and Post-HS exceed the national average on this item" (Mitchell, 1978, p. 16). Implications and suggestions for practice are given; a part of one statement is as follows (the responses to several other questions served as a basis for the statement of implications of this subgoal):

> Probably one of the most significant results of this item [subgoal] is that only 2.2% of the respondents saw school or academic areas as activities that might be useful for a job. . . . The implications of this are so obvious—and so embarrassing—that they will not be repeated here. A first step might be for each staff member who works with Seventeens to define, in terms of student competencies, the knowledges, skills, attitudes, interests, and values she/he is trying to help the students achieve (Mitchell, 1978, pp. 16–17).

Tables give breakdowns of responses by sex, region, race, parental education, and size and type of community. Overall, there was a very low response to exercises that asked to show how the preferred activity—hobby, sport, game, or other activity—related to occupational exploration or choice (Mitchell, 1978, pp. 48–49).

There is a definite need for guidance programs in new educational programs like alternative schools and community education, but less theorizing and planning has been done in these settings than in public schools and postsecondary institutions (Tolbert, 1978, pp. 270–275). These innovative educational programs are excellent settings for career-development. For example, community education brings together the school and community resources to meet identified needs of individuals of all ages, generates a sense of community, and gives members a sense of control over their lives. Careers, broadly defined, could be expected to be a major aspect of the needs of most community members. The same is true for alternative schools, which include a variety of institutions designed to meet the needs of specific groups of pupils—open schools, schools without walls, and learning centers. A major purpose of many alternative schools is to help pupils with career development. Programs are heavily experiential and exploratory and include activities to enhance career development; in fact, some of the programs discussed in Chapter 10 are actually alternative education. On the whole, however, an organized career-development program does not appear to be included in alternative schools. At the same time, in many cases these institutions obviously do an excellent job of career guidance (Jennings and Nathan, 1977).

In Industry

Relatively few career-development programs have been established in business and industrial settings, but a few examples indicate innovative practices and hint at the possibility of a much greater involvement. One example involves a career-development program aimed at helping employees do occupational planning. Designed for high-level scientific specialists, it included individual crisis counseling, preparation of a small group of managers in career-counseling skills, and short-term group career counseling (Hopson, 1973). Career-development assistance was particularly relevant; after an initial period of work, employees had to make choices about future positions, and turnover was a problem. Results were quite positive, and the basic elements of the program were adapted by the establishment.

Much of what could be called "career guidance" in business and industry involves assistance in various forms for taking education or training programs offered by either the establishment or by local schools and colleges (Lusterman, 1977). In some instances, outside consultants are called in to provide special group-development activities, such as communications training (Emener and Rye, 1975). As Kunze (1973) indicates, the cost of any kind of program has to be considered in terms of financial benefits to the establishment; what is best in terms of the individual's long-range career development may not be a high priority for the particular business or industry. New legislation on affirmative action, employment of the disadvantaged, and manpower programs may increase the need for career-development services, but if counseling and guidance functions are instituted, they are often provided by supervisors and other employees already part of the establishment.

Few counselors seem to consider the industrial setting a place where they can use their skills. One negative aspect may be the lack of models. It is difficult to find someone who portrays the career-development counselor working in business and industry to discuss the role with counselor-education students.

Closer cooperation between business and industry and the schools is recommended by Wirtz (1975, pp. 170–175). It could lead to programs that assist the employee in his or her career development, perhaps as a joint school-community-employer enterprise. Increasing public concern about mid-career changes and the pre- and postretirement years also may help stimulate interest and action. At the present time, however, a number of factors, such as economic conditions, labor supply, and lack of awareness of the potential contribution of career-development services, are major obstacles to instituting career-development programs in business settings.

In Other Countries

Career-guidance programs in other countries, particularly England and Western Europe, have developed outside the school system and tend to have a placement rather than a developmental rationale. A great deal of emphasis is put on the transition from school to work, and agencies in the community provide services (Reubens, 1977, pp. 237–239). Considerable attention is given to the job market, while in the United States there is less concern about this aspect and more emphasis on career development prior to the actual transition. Both these conditions are changing, however, at least to some degree.

There are some notable examples of career-development programs in other countries and an increase in the development types of services provided through the school years (Tolbert, 1976). Even though cultures differ and political, economic, and educational systems impose constraints on what may be done, the career problems faced by individuals are very similar, and much can be gained from exchange of ideas. For example, Ginzberg (1977, p. iii) points out that one lesson to be learned from a study of guidance programs in other countries is that the transition from school to work calls for a closer relation between schools and community placement agencies; neither can do an adequate job alone. In the United States there is increasing interest in problems in the transition process; placement, for example, has become a major service in many school systems. A growing amount of research is available on the process, including research on re-entry for those who have been out of the labor force as well as on initial entry for young people.

Several references are devoted to career guidance in other countries, and several organizations provide for exchange of information. A special issue of the *Vocational Guidance Quarterly* (Tolbert, 1976) contains descriptions of career guidance in six Western European countries, Canada, and Japan. Reubens's (1977) study provides descriptions and analyses, focusing mainly on school-to-work transition services, of career-guidance services in Western Europe, Canada, Australia, Japan, and the United States. Drapala's (1977) *Guidance in Other Countries* covers a number of guidance programs, but not specifically career services. Both the Canadian *School Guidance Worker* (Guidance Centre, Faculty of Education, University of Toronto, 100 Yonge Street, Toronto, Ontario, Canada, M4W 2K8) and the *British Journal of Guidance and Counselling* (Careers Research and Advisory Centre, Bateman Street, Cambridge, England) frequently publish articles on career guidance and development. *L'Orientation scolaire et professionnelle* (I.N.O.P., 41 rue Gay-Lussac, Paris 5e, France) reports studies and program descriptions in France (in French), many of which deal with career problems and issues.

Three organizations facilitate participation and exchange of information in international aspects of career guidance. The International Relations Committee of the American Personnel and Guidance Association collects and publishes in a newsletter information about practices in other countries, meetings, convention programs, travel opportunities, and accounts of counselors' work. Information about membership can be obtained by writing to the APGA International Relations Committee, American Personnel and Guidance Association, 1607 New Hampshire Avenue, N.W., Washington, D.C. 20009. The International Association for Educational and Vocational Guidance (IAEVG) holds biennial meetings and publishes a bulletin and a report of international meetings. Information about membership can be obtained from Dr. William Bingham, U.S. National Correspondent, IAEVG, 70 Frost Avenue, East Brunswick, New Jersey 08816. The International Round Table for the Advancement of Counselling (IRTAC) also holds biennial meetings, which are attended by counselors from many different countries. Information can be obtained from Dr. Derek Hope, Secretary, IRTAC, Brunel University, Uxbridge, Middlesex UB8 3PH, United Kingdom.

STAFFING

Guidance usually predated pupil personnel services in the school; "guidance counselors" were, more often than not, teachers who divided their time between instruction and miscellaneous counseling and guidance duties. There was a close working relation among these guidance counselors, pupils, teachers, and administrators. Often, pupil personnel services were provided at the county level; they were introduced into the school later (Humes, 1971). Counselors tended to be identified with the school and pupil personnel workers with the district. Assigning the counselor to the pupil personnel team is viewed by some as likely to increase the distance between counselors on the one hand, and pupils, teachers, administrators, and parents on the other. The organizational "team" plan, then, has certain advantages and some built-in limitations (Tolbert, 1972a, pp. 40–42). Increased professional status, expanded resources, and potential effectiveness must be weighed against the possible diminishment of the close working relationship with pupils and staff and the counselor's position of eminence in the school. The problem has not been resolved, but the hope is that it will not impede provision of needed services to pupils, parents, and staff.

Differentiated Staffing

Differentiated staffing has been mentioned several times as a trend of considerable importance for counselors. It has tremendous significance for the provision of guidance services. Stiller (1967, p. 260) describes two levels, one of which is personal growth-producing contacts and the other support, information-giving, and orientation. Within the guidance service, therefore, there should be two levels of workers with appropriate responsibilities. Additional levels might be involved—for example, pupil helpers. Lobitz (1970) used pupils as tutors and Mosher and Sprinthall (1971) involved them in peer counseling.

The differentiated staffing approach to organizing guidance services appears to be gaining more and more acceptance and to meet definite needs. Support personnel (discussed in Chapter 11) are earning a solid position on the guidance team. The consultant, representing a level different from that of the regular staff counselor, has been used in some situations. Along these lines, one state association (FPGA, 1971) has suggested three levels of counseling personnel: support personnel, professional counselors, and supervising counselors. The last level is equipped by training and experience to perform a leadership function in improving services, opening up channels of communication within the school and between the school and the community, and evaluating the effectiveness of services. Each level should be accountable to the one above it, with the supervising counselor responsible to the institution head. This is in line with the American School Counselor Association Statement of Policy (ASCA, 1965, p. 97), which recognizes the need for different levels of professional preparation and certification. Levels have also been recognized by the Washington State Certification Program (Brammer and Springer, 1971). Hoppock's "occupational information consultant" (Hoppock and Novick, 1971), however, does not represent a level as much as a specialty differentiation. The specialty type of differentiated staffing utilizes a horizontal arrangement in which role differences are significant.

Differentiated staffing offers the opportunity for effective teachers to remain in the classroom; advancement is not limited to administrative and supervisory positions. It provides the individual who wants more responsibility and remuneration the chance to obtain them. At the same time, it does not reduce the importance and contribution of other staff members. It is closely related to the concept of accountability, focusing on the best way to meet pupil needs and specifying responsibility. There are other advantages and some disadvantages, too, but these suggest that the concept may be a durable one.

Career guidance and counseling, probably more than any other aspect of guidance, can be improved and strengthened by differentiated staffing. A start has already been made, judging from the use of support personnel and the definite signs of an emerging consultant level. The former is in some cases a support person specifically responsible for career guidance and placement. Further, there is a critical need at the levels of planning, leadership, and coordination for those who can initiate and develop career education in the schools, build school-community relations, plan and supervise placement and follow-up, and communicate to others the degree to which the guidance service is discharging its responsibilities for accountability.

Other Possibilities

A second possible direction for school guidance services has two related emphases: providing services where they are needed and using deliberate changes in the environment to help pupils. Zerface and Cox (1971) suggest a radical reorganization. They would move the counselor from the school to a community Human

Development Center to avoid some of the conflicts and identification problems caused by school-based work. Less startling is Caldwell's (1970) *contextual counseling,* in which the counselor moves out of the office and endeavors to have an impact in the classroom and on the curriculum. The thrust is to find ways to carry counseling, as the author puts it, "where the action is." Behavioral counseling plays a major role in this approach, as well as in the recommendations of Matheny (1971), who suggests that counselors utilize *environmental* engineering in the school and community to help pupils solve problems, learn problem-solving skills, cope successfully with new situations, and assess their potential.

NEW MODES OF STAFF PREPARATION

The preparation of counselors and guidance workers may have some impact on the nature of guidance services. Berdie (1972) proposes a new type of preparation and a new role, the *applied behavioral scientist.* A guidance worker (Berdie uses the term *counselor* but the concept goes beyond a strict definition of the counselor) would have a thorough grounding in the research and theory of the behavioral sciences, in place of the present preparation. The guidance worker would apply this expertise to all kinds of problems at the school level. The counselor would be what the title implies, a scientist who uses theory and research findings to facilitate pupils' day-to-day learning and development. Application of the concept would usher in sweeping changes; guidance would certainly have a different look!

Less revolutionary, at least at first glance, is a new approach to counselor certification. Brammer and Springer (1971) describe the Washington State Certification Plan, which emphasizes behaviorally stated standards related to validated methods of helping pupils. Each counselor, with the assistance of a consultant, goes through a sequence of steps to meet certification requirements. The new elements are the behaviorally stated objectives, the consultant to help the counselor prepare for and remedy weak areas brought out by the certification process, and the examining panel. These procedures are ways to insure that counselors can do what is expected of them.

The recommendations by Wirtz (1975, pp. 170–172) have tremendous implications for staff preparation for career counseling. The proposed education-work councils would bring the educational institutions, unions, and community members together to build realistic, effective work-experience and career-guidance programs. In addition, all high school pupils would receive at least five hours of career guidance a year from both professionally trained counselors in the school and community advisers with relevant types of work experience. There would also be an opportunity for at least five hundred hours of work experience for high school youth, provided by cooperative efforts of the school, the employer, and the community at large. This experience would be designed to help individuals learn about the world of work and its personal meaning for them and to become involved in an experiential learning activity. It is clear from these recommendations that major program changes are called for, but expanding the career-guidance program, bringing together the school and community, and adding realism to exploratory and planning experiences are needed improvements if career guidance is to be a vital factor in the lives of young people.

Regardless of the specific approach used in setting up career-guidance programs, the most significant factor is the counselor's competencies in career guidance and counseling. The position paper of the Association for Counselor Education and Supervision points out the need for the counselor to work with others as a team member, to become involved in the business-labor-industrial setting, as well as the home and the community, and to work through curricular change and consulting. These factors, with the specific career-development competencies recommended for counselors in all settings (used throughout this book), are the bases for the most significant trends in career-development programs today.

GROUP GUIDANCE APPROACHES

Guidance activities for groups are among the oldest types of assistance. Orientation, guidance units and courses, career days, college days, field trips, films, displays, and bulletin boards are approaches that have been widely used. If these and some of the newer developments are carefully planned and integrated into the guidance program, they can provide essential developmental help in an economical way.

Group guidance is not used alone; it is allied with other guidance and counseling activities so as to create maximum benefits for them. For example, Doverspike (1971) describes the Guidance and Counseling, or GUICO, approach, which combines the best features of guidance and counseling. Structure and assignments are used, as well as group interaction, feedback, and exploration of feelings. In many cases, group-guidance procedures are used separately from group counseling.

Orientation as Group Guidance

In any transition from one setting to another, orientation is needed to ease the shock and pave the way for effective movement into the new situation. Programs have been offered for pupils first entering school and for those moving from one school level to another—for example, from junior high to senior high school and from school to college or work. College orientation programs have been the most highly developed, probably because college entrance is a discontinuity in the developmental sequence.

To facilitate decision making and career development, orientation must provide a thorough understanding of the educational opportunities of the new setting. Ideally, this process begins before movement to the new environment and before choices are made and includes input from all who will be involved. For example, as pupils near the end of junior high school, the counselor could visit their school to explain the high school programs and distribute take-home material. Parents could participate in these meetings and in visits and tours of the high school. Pupils at the receiving school can help plan and carry out orientation. Follow-up in small group and individual conferences could enable newcomers to further clarify plans before making choices.

One-shot orientation, terminated when classes begin, loses much of its potential value. The trend is for activities to continue through the first month or so, or even the first term. Large group meetings, that is, of twenty to thirty people, are frequently used for discussion of problems, policies, and opportunities. They provide a setting in which pupils can raise questions, express views, and perceive the personal relevance of the information that is disseminated. In fact, an orientation focus may permeate many other guidance activities that occur all year long; it may continue in the classroom, with teachers orienting pupils to the purposes of courses, effective study methods, and occupations to which courses lead.

Guidance Courses or Units for Career Planning

Group-guidance courses and units cover the full range of pupil problems and needs, but discussion here is limited to those aimed at career guidance. The purpose of these procedures is to help pupils learn about careers and about themselves and make choices and plans appropriate to their level of career maturity. Although the concepts of vocational maturity and vocational development serve as guidelines for all types of career counseling and guidance activities, nowhere is their applicability more obvious than in setting the level, content, and goals of the course or unit. Much of the difficulty experienced with courses in the past seems to be traceable to inappropriate activities and teachers who lacked an understanding of developmental levels.

Three significant trends may infuse life into courses and units. Career-development theory provides guidelines for appropriate content and procedures at different school levels. Techniques and materials, such as job simulations, life career games, and decision-making programs like DECIDE, add interest and realism to group meetings. A third factor, mentioned earlier, is the emphasis on career education. No doubt the kinds of activities included in this new educational concept will swallow up career courses and units in a total school career-development program. In the process, however, we may expect to see a greatly expanded use of the course-unit format.

The teaching of courses and units and their grade placement are important matters in insuring success and effectiveness. Hoppock (1967, pp. 199–200) suggests that they be taught by the counselor. It is a demanding job, and one that must be done well if the program is to be a success. Units in regular courses require an understanding of the world of work and knowledge about sources of needed information; a well-developed information system can be of tremendous value to teachers of both units and courses. Scheduling the program at points at which the information is needed—just before major choice points—is recommended.

Planning the content and approach is a joint leader-pupil process. It is essential that the content be important to the participants. The variety of techniques described by Hoppock—for example, pupils following up graduates and dropouts (1976, pp. 164–175)—and by Norris, Zeran, Hatch, and Engelkes (1972, pp

415–443), as well as simulation and other methods, can be incorporated in the sequence. Surveys of currently enrolled pupils, community surveys, and inventories of needs and interests of group participants can be used as planning guides.

Research has tended to support the value of this approach (Sinick, Gorman, and Hoppock, 1971; Hoppock, 1976, pp. 283–287; Norris, Zeran, Hatch, and Engelkes, 1972, pp. 452–453). As new procedures are developed, for example, computer information systems, decision-making aids, and experiential activities, even more substantial gains are predicted.

Career Days and College Days

Career days and college days have had a long history of usage in the high school. Career days have typically featured a school assembly to discuss the importance of career planning, followed by a series of meetings in which individuals in various occupations discuss their work. College days follow a similar format, but college representatives meet with groups of interested pupils after a general orientation meeting.

For both procedures, planning should be carefully done to insure that the occupations or institutions represented are related to interests. Preparatory and follow-up activities are needed so pupils can select the most appropriate sessions and can incorporate what is learned into what they already know about their interests, abilities, and plans.

These two procedures fill a definite need in the information service. Face-to-face contact with representatives of occupations, training, and educational institutions is a unique and often stimulating experience for pupils. Interest, in turn, may be generated in other aspects of the information system, such as the occupational file. Such variations as scheduling occupational representatives' visits over a period of time give pupils the opportunity to learn about a greater range of possibilities. Combining schools can provide more coverage—that is, a wider variety of occupations and educational institutions may be included. Career fairs, with exhibits and occupational representatives, promote school-community-industry-business cooperation and are usually evaluated enthusiastically by participants.

RELATIONSHIPS WITH THE SCHOOL STAFF

The job of facilitating vocational development and decision making cannot be done by counselors alone. A total school effort is needed. Certain aspects can best be carried out by other members of the pupil personnel team: teachers, vocational-education coordinators, administrators, and supervisors. Many staff members are usually actively involved in some phase of career guidance and are ready and willing to do more. In some schools, one of the most significant services the counselor can perform is to organize existing efforts. In the process, gaps in services become apparent and needs may be identified.

One of the most critical aspects of the counselor's job is building cooperative working relationships with the school staff. Without cooperation, communication, and a two-way flow of information and assistance the guidance service may become isolated and relatively ineffective. Isolation is a particularly serious hazard for career guidance and counseling. Of first importance to prevent this from happening is administrative support and understanding. Teacher cooperation, active participation in promoting career development, and assistance with evaluation and improvement of services are also needed. Cooperative relationships with vocational teachers are particularly important. The selection, information-getting, guidance, placement, and follow-up functions performed routinely by these staff members have considerable potential value for the career guidance and development service.

The Counselor as Change Agent

A great deal has been said in earlier chapters about the counselor as a change agent in the school and community. Why the emphasis? Isn't practically everything the counselor does in working with the administration, teachers, pupils, parents, and the community playing the change-agent role? Baker and Cramer (1972) would say no. They take the position that a change agent deliberately attempts to change conditions in the institution or community that are harmful to those he or she is trying to help. They suggest that research shows that counselor actions may be located on a continuum from *status quo* through *counseling model* to *change-agent model*. In my judgment, however, consultation, in-service education, and other counselor actions represent change-agent activities. The degree to which they are used to help change such conditions as attitudes, school organization, and community customs indicates the extent to which the counselor implements the change-agent role.

This position differs from that of Baker and Cramer. Furthermore, it somewhat contradicts their view that counselors, in their present position of minimal power and status, may be best advised to assume the counseling role of helper to the individual in handling present needs and problems (Baker and Cramer, 1972). This image of the counselor is in keeping with the role that Baker and Hansen (1972) found to be preferred in a survey of counselors: the change-oriented counselor who is *interested* in change but prefers to help the counselee become a self-directed change agent. The survey revealed that few would be strong *status quo* advocates or strong change agents.

Recognizing that the counselor's capacity to be a true change agent is limited, Cook (1971, pp. 478–489) suggests roles such as feedback agent and strategies such as using pupils as guidance aides. These seem to be positive and effective ways of working, even though the counselor may feel that he or she should be more assertive or even be a distinct irritant to the school and community (Stewart and Warnath, 1965, p. 45). The counselor needs to exert his or her influence through the institution, not so much because of the danger that he or she will be unpopular or lose his or her job but because if anyone in the school has the know-how and skill to initiate change, it is the counselor. There is always a reservoir of talent and energy for positive change, which can be used to help to identify, stimulate, and develop.

New tools and techniques are available for the counselor to use in influencing staff members. One of the most effective techniques—consultation—is discussed in the next section. There are others, such as communication skills and guidance techniques, that may be demonstrated in the classroom and/or taught to teachers, and new materials, such as slide-sound presentations. In addition, more is known about the change process, and the counselor can utilize this knowledge to his or her advantage. For example, Dustin (1974) lists five principles concerning the change process, ranging from sources of pressure for change (from outside), the direction of change (from the top down), the locus of change (systems change from within), the extent of initial change (superficial), and the results of failure for change to take effect (overreaction resulting in sweeping changes). Blocher (1977) describes how change can be effected in the school environment by counselor-teacher partnership in which the counselor helps the teacher identify and face challenge, supports new behaviors and attitudes, and assists with evaluation. In this process, the counselor models an open, involved, risk-taking behavior that leads to a changed environment. The process is basically a consulting relationship. Huse (1978) describes how the principles of organizational development (OD) can be used to improve the institution's ability to manage its own operation and cope with outside pressures and demands.

Moving beyond the school, new developments in change strategies may be used to lessen or eliminate destructive conditions in the community. Lewis and Lewis (1977) identify four major functions in which counselors may be involved as community change agents. First is the identification of need; counselors are in an excellent position to gather firsthand information about unhealthy conditions and also to describe actions to generate a healthy, positive climate. A knowledge of resources is second, and coordination of resources is a function for which the counselor is well prepared. Third, the counselor has skills that may be taught to others; and fourth, he or she can serve as an advocate for those who need support.

An additional benefit of becoming involved in a wide variety of challenging and varied activities, working closely with a wide range of individuals, and seeing needed changes take place is protection against counselor burnout. One source of this condition is the shocking difference between what the student in counselor education expects and what the work is really like (Warnath and Shelton, 1976). Being involved with others in highly significant endeavours should counteract some of the feelings of being on a treadmill, of isolation, and of infrequent reward identified as leading to burnout.

It is not an either-or matter—the counselor can be a change agent to a degree that balances his or her own professional goals with the possibilities that exist in the school and community. Change tends to be cumulative. Unless there is a severe setback, improvements accomplished this year add to the sum total of those made last year.

Cooperating with the Staff

The statement that the counselor should have teaching experience so that he or she will be "accepted" by the school staff has been made many times. Acceptance, confidence, trust, and professional respect grow out of the counselor's performance rather than his or her teaching credentials. Admittedly, similar backgrounds make it initially possible to speak the same language, but subsequent actions make the difference.

The major factors in building cooperative relationships are, in my opinion, two-way understanding and service. Getting across the counselor's role is one of the most critical factors. Written material may help. Presentations or even demonstrations at staff meetings may be effective. Videotaping, with audience participation, may facilitate development of feelings of rapport and involvement. Materials such as *Teachers and Counselors Work Together* (American Personnel and Guidance Association, 1965), *The Teacher Looks at Guidance* (Schwartz, Johnson, and Nicol, 1961), *Parents and the Counselor* (Berdie, Grams, and Vance, 1960), and *Meet Your Secondary School Counselor* (American School Counselor Association, 1971) can be very useful reading material. But the most relevant will probably be handouts prepared by the counselor in conjunction with what he or she has said or demonstrated.

A face-to-face meeting with each teacher (or perhaps with small groups) is suggested as the most productive approach, though time-consuming. For vocational teachers, this should include a tour of the facilities, if possible while pupils are at work. In this type of conference, the counselor emphasizes the help he or she can provide, his or her consulting and referral functions, and the resource materials he or she has on hand. Publications such as *The Teacher's Role in Career Development* (Tennyson, Soldahl, and Mueller, 1965), *Career Decisions* (National Vocational Guidance Association, 1969), and *The Parent's Role in Career Development* (Knapp and Bedford, 1967) are useful for staff members. An explanation of the information system should also convey the potential benefits of working closely with guidance services.

It is helpful in dealing with vocational teachers to compare plans for collecting local occupational and educational information, placement, and follow-up. Vocational teachers do a great deal of work in these areas, and mutually satisfactory working plans will improve the total school guidance program as well as enhance rapport.

Consultation has been frequently mentioned as one of the guidance staff's services. Only in recent years has this aspect of service assumed its rightful status. It is, in my opinion, equal in potential to any other new trend. With differentiated staffing and the demonstrated ability of support personnel to provide direct assistance of various kinds, consultation becomes increasingly important. Some tentative evidence shows that administrators regard the role positively (Tolbert, 1972b). Authorities in the field have given more and more attention to the role (Roeber, Walz, and Smith, 1969, pp. 133–154; Perrone, Ryan, and Zeran, 1970, pp. 133–145; Lundquist and Chamley, 1971; Munson, 1971, pp. 152–171; Pancrazio, 1971; Fullmer and Bernard, 1972, pp. 268–279). A specialized consultant, the "occupational information consultant," is described by Hoppock and Novick (1971). Consultation role concepts vary somewhat, but there seems to be general agreement that the consultant has a high level of professional competence and can work effectively to help the third person, provide needed information, and assist the consultee to clarify his or her own thinking.

The consultation process is not very different from in-service education, though it is more personalized. In fact, in-service education is a way of enhancing rapport with the school staff, if it is seen as helping them do a better job, provide assistance to pupils, and develop more effective classroom procedures. Quite often, teachers ask for help if they feel the counselor has something to offer. The case group in-service process described by Foreman, Poppen, and Frost (1967) illustrates the combination of in-service education with consultation. In the C-groups (case groups), discussion of pupil cases followed an initial orientation to developmental principles and case-study methods. Specialists, such as reading teachers, were available as needed. The school counselor and an outside consultant-counselor served as the consultants. Groups dealt with special cases, professional problems, and feelings and moved in the direction of sensitivity training groups (T-groups). Reactions of participants were positive. This in-service approach was well received. Dinkmeyer and Arciniega (1972) describe the rationale and procedure for the C-group and show how it enables the counselor to carry out the consulting and change agent roles to best effect.

Providing help to the teacher in the classroom is another way consultation and in-service education can be fused. Two examples, both involving behavior modification, vividly illustrate this approach. Stetter (1971) and Foley and Willson (1971) describe procedures in which the counselor enlists the teacher's collaboration in planning and carrying out a behavior reward program for pupils who are poor achievers, behavior problems, or both. Stetter reports positive gains in both citizenship and science achievement for eleven pupils. Procedures like these are of tremendous help in building good counselor-staff relationships.

Consultation has assumed so much visibility and acceptance in the last few years that two special issues of the *Personnel and Guidance Journal* have been devoted to it (Vol. 56, Nos. 6 and 7, 1978). Much of the emphasis is on mental health consultation, but many models could be used in building career-guidance programs. Moreover, roles and applications vary with particular consultants and purposes of assistance. Five basic types of interventions are identified (Blake and Mouton, 1978). First is *acceptance,* in which the counselor helps the consultee clarify conflicting attitudes and gain a more accurate perception of the problem situation. Second, a *catalytic* intervention helps the consultee collect and reassess data to arrive at a solution. *Confrontation,* the third type, challenges the consultee to deal with distortions and values that get in the way of solutions. In the fourth type, *prescription,* the solution is provided, either by telling the consultee what to do or doing it for him or her. Finally, *theory and principles* intervention involves giving and helping the consultee internalize tested ways of dealing with the problem. The authors point out that some consultants use one type of intervention while others employ a combination. Whatever is done should be related to the consultee's needs.

A number of strategies for change are explained and illustrated, and programs are described in these journal issues. One that deals specifically with career development is Born Free, a large-scale career-development program aimed at broadening the range of career opportunities of individuals from elementary school to college by reducing sex-role stereotyping (Hansen and Kelerleber, 1978). The project involves a consultation model, a career-development model, and a change-process model. Data and training packets were prepared to use with indirect intervention with educators. The consultation model is defined as eclectic, with emphasis on development, process, and collaboration. The collaborative consultation approach helped the consultee discover, define, take responsibility for the problem, and develop and carry out plans for change—in this case, for the problem of sex-role stereotyping. Two levels of consultation were involved: first, the central office project staff consulted with the field staffs in particular institutions; second, the field staff worked directly with counselors, faculty, and others in the school or college. Change-process principles employed included involving local staff at the start of the program, identifying interested members in the specific institutions, encouraging institution self-study and needs analysis, and giving local staff members skills to assist them to influence others.

The consulting- change-agent process was adapted to the needs and attitudes of each institution. For example, in one elementary school, teachers used a questionnaire to determine pupils' opinions about possible and desired occupations. The restricted options pupils listed for both types convinced teachers of a definite need for a career-development program to expand both expectations and aspirations.

The project is an excellent example of using consultation to build career-development programs in educational institutions. The complete article should be read, as this brief account does not do justice to the careful planning and skilled application of techniques.

Relations with the Administration

The success of the guidance service depends on administrative support all the way up to the superintendent (Malcolm and Hays, 1969). School-board support and state-level backing for guidance services through standards, allocation of funds, and announced priorities are essential. But the school principal is, in the final analysis, the key person in the support of guidance and counseling services. He or she influences the school's climate for guidance and counseling services. He or she facilitates or impedes utilization of services and cooperative working relationships. The principal's attitude toward the counselor enhances or diminishes the role. If he or she perceives the counselor as a professional, requiring autonomy and flexibility in planning his or her work and providing a vital school service, his or her perceptions will have a schoolwide effect.

An excellent statement of both principals' and counselors' responsibilities is contained in *Principals and Counselors Work Together* (ASCA, NASSP, AASA, 1968). Fifteen questions directed at principals examine their awareness of their responsibility to provide a growth-producing climate, the contributions the counselor can make to curriculum planning and modification, and the importance of a reasonable counselor-pupil ratio. Twelve questions focus on the principal's expectations of counselors. Questions relate to communication of role and services and awareness of the expectations of others. The items contained in this brief pamphlet serve as an excellent guide for preparation of a joint statement on roles and responsibilities by counselor and principal.

Guidance workers often wait for the principal to tell them what to do. It is the former's responsibility, instead, to have clear ideas of their role and services and to present these to the principal, using the approach, "This is how I feel I can make my greatest contribution." Together they work out a mutually satisfying statement of responsibilities. Although it may be time-consuming and focus excessively on details, a *written* statement developed at the outset should insure better working relationships and a higher level of support for guidance services than otherwise. If a statement cannot be agreed on, it is better to know at the start than six months or a year later. The counselor can then decide whether or not to accept the working conditions.

Working in Differentiated Staffing Patterns

This relatively new concept in school staffing has two implications for the guidance service. Counselors need to develop effective procedures to work with the different levels of teaching personnel in the schools. Guidance services can use differentiated staff arrangements for more effective service.

Many schools have instituted elements of differentiated staffing, such as team teaching and teacher aides. These partial uses do not constitute comprehensive reorganization of staff to increase efficiency through defining roles and assigning different responsibilities (Olivero, 1970). They do, however, represent methods of utilizing staff for improved educational results. It is important for the counselor to develop ways to work with these partial measures as well as with a total program of differentiated staffing.

Predicting the future development of the differentiated staffing plan is difficult but many counselors probably will encounter some version of it in their work. It touches on several critical areas in education, and thus is likely to be in existence in one form or another for many years to come.

The staffing levels, which may involve three or four classifications, have implications for the ˙work of the guidance department. For example, suppose that there are master teachers, senior teachers, staff teachers, and associate teachers, representing different levels of experience and expertise. How will lines of communication between the guidance and teaching staffs be established? Will the counselor typically work with the staff teacher, who may be carrying most of the teaching load, or should he or she deal with the senior teacher, who may be an expert on method and content? Presumably, provisions are made for supervision and in-service education in the differentiated staff arrangement. Difficulties may arise if guidance workers are not aware of, or do not work in a way compatible with, the staff organization.

In my opinion, differentiated staffing offers new and promising ways to develop effective working relationships and to build career development into the curriculum. Combining the counselor's career-development competencies with the master teacher's teaching skills should result in some excellent course-based experience to help pupils in career development. Working out procedures by which the guidance staff can serve as consultants to the beginning associate teachers should provide fertile ground for building guidance-teaching cooperation in the early stages of professional development.

SUMMARY

The career-development counselor works as a member of the pupil personnel team and needs to be familiar with the roles of other members. Since he or she is primarily a member of the guidance staff, however, his or her first responsibility is to work closely with other services in this specific area. Team membership has advantages and disadvantages, but if the focus is on helping pupils, conflicts and overlaps may be avoided. Differential staffing allows great extension of the effectiveness of career-guidance services, and it appears to be an important trend for the future. Outreach approaches, another significant development, are being explored through a variety of models. New roles for the counselor are being formulated, and it is difficult to predict what the school counselor of 1990 will be like.

A great variety of group guidance approaches, such as orientation, can facilitate career development. Counselors' major impact on career development and guidance, however, will be through the curriculum. Many new programs are being developed, which are discussed in the next chapter. In both school and community, the counselor has the opportunity to serve as a consultant and a change agent to build conditions that will contribute to career development.

PROJECTS AND EXPERIENTIAL ACTIVITIES

1. Visit a high school and obtain a description of the pupil personnel program. It would be helpful to interview the pupil personnel staff at the county or city level to learn about the services they provide the school.

2. Inventory the career-development activities carried on at a school.

3. Use a theory (or theories) of career development as a basis to prepare a brief module or exercise that contributes to career development. Try it out in class.

4. In small groups, plan the outline of an orientation program for the counselor-education program. Decide on who would do what, when and for how long. When plans are completed, present them to the class. Discuss the plans in terms of needs felt by the class members when they entered the program.

5. Practice in small groups the role of a career-development consultant. Select a setting (elementary school, middle/junior high school, secondary school, community college, college, community agency) and agree on a career-development need or problem experienced by the institution. Next, agree on how you would go about serving as a consultant to deal with the problem. (Prior reading in the two special issues of the *Personnel and Guidance Journal* will be helpful.) Present problems and consultation plans to the class.

6. Identify a career-development problem in the community. (A call to a local guidance director, the Chamber of Commerce, or the employment service should give some good indications of problems.) In class, divide into small groups and pretend you are change-agent consultants responsible for planning and carrying out ways to ameliorate the negative condition. After plans are made, report them to the class. Discuss similarities and differences in plans.

7. Shadow a counselor or guidance director in a setting of your choice for a day. Discuss results in small groups, organized by similarity of agencies or institutions visited. Identify the major features of the program that promote efficiency and those that reduce effectiveness. Report your conclusions to the class and discuss their importance for students' career planning.

ADDITIONAL REFERENCES

Aubrey, Roger F. *Career Development Needs of Thirteen Year Olds.* Washington, D.C.: American Personnel and Guidance Association, 1978. Results and implications of the 1973–1974 National Assessment of Educational Progress Career and Occupational Development Needs Survey of thirteen-year-olds.

Bingham, William C. *The Counselor and Youth Employment.* Boston: Houghton Mifflin, 1973. A brief but valuable reference on career guidance. Chap. 4, on facilitating career development in the schools, gives an excellent overview of services, personnel, and facilities.

Carlson, Jon, Howard Splete, and Roy Kern, eds. *The Consulting Process.* Washington, D.C.: American Personnel and Guidance Association, 1975. Reprints from American Personnel and Guidance Association journals covering all phases of consulting. Although only a few are specifically on career guidance, the other principles and procedures discussed are applicable to it. This volume of well-selected articles is a convenient reference to check for special needs.

Cook, David R. "Guidance and Institutional Change." In *Guidance for Education in Revolution.* Ed. David R. Cook. Boston: Allyn & Bacon, 1971, pp. 453–491. The nature of the educational system is examined and suggestions for ways to function as a change agent are discussed. This book is an excellent reference for anyone planning to move into the change-agent's role.

Cunha, Joseph E., Darryl Laramore, Bruce L. Lowery, Anita M. Mitchell, Thomas W. Smith, and Dale C. Woolley, eds. *Career Development: A California Model for Career Guidance Curriculum K–Adult.* Fullerton, Calif.: California Personnel and Guidance Association, 1972. This helpful guide to planning career development covers specification of goals, implementation of the program, and evaluation. Examples of objectives are particularly helpful.

Hansen, Lorraine Sundal. *Career Guidance Practice in School and Community.* Washington, D.C.: National Vocational Guidance Association, 1970. The programs and courses discussed in Chap. 2 illustrate career development in action. The counselor's role in curriculum building is clearly illustrated in a number of examples.

Hoppock, Robert. *Occupational Information.* 4th ed. New York: McGraw-Hill, 1976. An excellent source of information about group guidance and career courses and units. Chaps. 12 through 19 describe specific techniques and procedures for use in a number of settings.

Miller, Juliet V. *Career Development Needs of Nine Year Olds.* Washington, D.C.: American Personnel and Guidance Association, 1978. Results and implications of the 1973–1974 National Assessment of Educational Progress Career and Occupational Development Needs Survey.

Mitchell, Anita M. *Career Development Needs of Seventeen Year Olds.* Washington, D.C.: American Personnel and Guidance Association, 1978. Results of the 1973–1974 National Assessment of Educational Progress (Career and Occupational Development Needs Survey). The section on career and occupational development is summarized and implications for practice are given. This book is an excellent resource for gaining an overview of the career development of this age group and for improving career-development programs.

Mitchell, Anita M., and James A. Saum, eds. *A Master Plan for Pupil Services.* Fullerton, Calif.: California Personnel and Guidance Association, 1972. This useful guide to building pupil personnel services incorporates an up-to-date emphasis on accountability.

Personnel and Guidance Journal 56, Nos. 6 and 7 (1978). These two issues, both featuring consultation, are one of the most useful and interesting sources of information on this important new counseling strategy. No. 6 covers models and procedures, plus programs in schools and colleges and mental health programs. No. 7 contains eight articles on specific uses of consulting techniques and two on the preparation of consultants. (The brief summary in this chapter of Hansen and Kelerleber's article on Born Free is based on a report in this issue.)

Peters, Herman. *Interpreting Guidance Programs to the Public.* Boston: Houghton Mifflin, 1968. This entire book is a valuable source for background material on building good relationships with the community.

Pietrofesa, John J., George Leonard, and Roy F. Giroux, eds. *Career Education and the Counselor.* Washington D.C.: American Personnel and Guidance Association, 1975. A book of reprints that contains a number of excellent articles on career-guidance activities and programs that cover the life span. Although the articles have appeared in American Personnel and Guidance Association journals, this volume brings them together in a convenient, valuable reference book.

Roeber, Edward. *Interpreting Guidance Programs to School Personnel.* Boston: Houghton Mifflin, 1968. This is an excellent reference to accompany Peters's book. Practical procedures for building good working relationships with other staff members are described and illustrated.

Ryan, T. Antoinette. *Guidance Services.* Danville, Ill. Interstate Printers and Publishers, 1978. An extremely useful and readable reference with numerous examples that use the systems approach in guidance services. Chaps. 7 through 11 emphasize career aspects and are particularly relevant, but all the chapters provide important background material.

Tolbert, E. L. *An Introduction to Guidance,* Boston: Little, Brown, 1978. Chap. 6, "The Framework for Guidance: Programs, Roles, and Services," gives the author's perceptions of the major types of guidance-program models currently in use.

Westbrook, Bert W. *Career Development Needs of Adults.* Washington, D.C.: American Personnel and Guidance Association, 1978. Results and implications of the 1973–1974 National Assessment of Educational Progress Career and Occupational Development Needs Survey of adults aged twenty-six to thirty-five.

Wirtz, Willard. *The Boundless Resource*. Washington, D.C.: The New Republic Book Company, 1975. Chap. 4, "New Means," describes how career guidance can be a community project and shows how the community education-work council could expand the effectiveness of the school career-guidance effort. The author recommends what amounts to a new and different kind of career-guidance program and is quite specific about what should be done to implement it. The whole book is recommended reading.

·10

Career Education

GOALS

1
To explain the origin, rationale, and present status of the concept of career education.

2
To describe the counselor's role in career education.

3
To describe innovative applications in a variety of settings.

4
To help the reader form conclusions about the effectiveness of career education.

5
To describe how career-education programs are instituted and managed.

6
To give an overview of the resources for career education.

7
To help the reader form a personal position about participation in this type of program.

CAREER EDUCATION IS BETTER VIEWED as a concept than as a program; it is a way to reform the entire educational system, including adult education. Although a specific definition (Hoyt, n.d.) has not been given, specific elements have tended to emerge and become part of the concept. The statement of a local implementor given by Preli covers many of these elements: "Career education is an effort aimed at refocusing American education and the actions of the broader community in ways that will help the individual acquire and utilize the knowledge, skills, and attitudes necessary for each to make work a meaningful, productive, satisfying part of his or her way of living" (1978, p. 1). This explanation combines ideas that have been developed since the introduction of career education. It is not final, nor would it be likely to receive very wide approval. Career education, as an educational concept, is evolving and is interpreted differently by those who theorize and implement. But this explanation includes major elements that portray the present status.

Although this explanation includes the key elements, additional clarification is needed. The concept of work covers humanistic values, not just the job one does for income; it includes unpaid work and leisure activities—whatever the individual does to "become *someone* through doing *something*" (Hoyt, 1976, p. 33). "Refocusing" means that there should be basic reforms in educational institutions rather than addition of new techniques, procedures, and programs. The relationship between the educational institution and the community should be collaborative, because neither can do the job alone. To be successful, career education requires the active involvement of school, community, employer, and family. Full use must be made of community resources. Preparation for work is viewed as *one* of the goals of education, not the only one. Bringing career education into the curriculum is more a matter of *threading* rather than infusing; the latter process could be viewed as adding to an already full curriculum, while the former can result in giving new meaning to what is taught (Hoyt, 1977, pp. 4–5A).

BACKGROUND OF THE CONCEPT

As Harris-Bowlsbey (1975, pp. 6–8) points out, many elements of the concept of career education have been in evidence for some time. Theories of career development and decision making, awareness of needs of special groups, use of information resources and assessment techniques, including those for vocational development, the central role of career in one's life, and the need for career guidance are well established. But the overall concept of reorganization of the educational system around career, broadly defined, was introduced in 1971 by Sidney Marland, then commissioner of education (Marland, 1972; Herr, 1974, pp. 48–49b). Dr. Marland used the term *career education* for the first time, but efforts by the U.S. Office of Education to promote the concept began much earlier, and the roots of the concept reach back into the research and theorizing on career development.

Marland suggested four models for career education: school-based, experience-based, community-based, and residential-based. The Ohio Center for Vocational and

Technical Education was given a contract by the Office of Education to develop the school-based model. The rationale and objectives were established, and a number of exemplary programs were set up. Other contractors were used to establish and try out the three remaining models. The Office of Education did not give a specific definition of career education or method of implementation, so the meaning of the concept could be developed at the state and local levels. Even so, early publications provided indications of major factors involved (U.S. Department of Health, Education, and Welfare, 1971). For example, one fundamental idea was that all lifelong education experiences and facilities should be organized to help the individual both appreciate the importance and dignity of work and be successful in the world of work. Further, recognizing the developmental nature of career planning, the elementary school emphasis should be primarily on career awareness; in the middle grades and early high school, it should be on career exploration; and in later high school years, it should be on preparation for work or further education. In addition, a process of entry into and exit from educational or training programs should continue throughout life as needed. The idea of career clusters—organizing related occupations into groups as an aid to exploration and choice—was also included.

Commissioner Marland provided money for model programs from discretionary funds allocated to him, and model developmental efforts were instituted in every state. There was immediate, enthusiastic reception for the concept across the country. In 1974, career education was mandated by Congress (PL 93-380), and federal law established the Office of Career Education and provided funds for furthering the concept. The Office of Education published an official policy paper on it. Since then, progress has been substantial. Although there have been less than three hundred federally funded projects, over five thousand of the seventeen thousand school districts in the United States have provided some kind of program, even though few are providing what could be called a comprehensive program (Hoyt, 1976, pp. 10, 38).

Indications are that the concept has established a firm base and will grow in the years ahead. It reflects the public's felt needs as well as or better than any educational movement since those around the turn of the century. It is in tune with the times—demands for accountability, a decreasing job market, an increasingly complex technological society, insistent criticisms of education, and increased concern about the need for lifelong guidance and education. Wirtz (1975, pp. 47, 70, 170–184) characterizes it as a vital concept and recommends programs that mesh well with it. Recent legislation has shown strong congressional support; for example, PL 95-207 emphasizes the central place of career education in all types of educational agencies and institutions.

Much of the task of stimulating the spread of career education has been carried out by Kenneth Hoyt, director of the Office of Career Education, U.S. Office of Education. Several years ago, the National Institute of Education (NIE) took over responsibility for a number of programs, but reorganization of the NIE has reduced the priority of career education. Funds provided by PL 95-207, however, still provide substantial support.

PURPOSES AND GOALS

One of the earliest statements about career education lists these goals:

1. To prepare individuals to leave and return to the educational system at times of choice throughout life
2. To help increase the relevance of school by focusing on pupils' career choices
3. To increase knowledge of the world of work
4. To help individuals develop positive attitudes toward work
5. To prepare individuals for the next step, whether it be work, training, or education
6. To eliminate the distinction between "vocational" and "academic" courses (U.S. Department of Health, Education, and Welfare, 1971, pp. 2–3)

The "Learner Outcomes" and "Educational Changes" sections of the career-education policy paper of the Office of Education (Hoyt, 1975, pp. 10–14) summarize career-education goals as follows. The individual leaving the educational program, at whatever level exit occurs, should have the following:

1. Needed academic skills for a changing society
2. Good work habits
3. The ability to choose, and positive work values on which to base choices
4. Skills to get and hold a job
5. A comprehensive understanding of self, work opportunities, and facilities for further education or training
6. The ability to negotiate the next step—work, education, or training—successfully
7. A personally suitable combination of work and lifestyle values

The changes needed in educational programs are

1. More and better vocational-education offerings at secondary levels
2. More variety in school courses and less emphasis on separate tracks
3. Evaluation in terms of performance
4. Credit for out-of-school learning
5. Increased use of noncertified resource persons from the business-labor-industry community
6. A flexible open entry-exit system
7. An increase in adult and recurrent educational programs
8. A year-round public school with multiple points for entry and exit
9. Revision of teacher education to incorporate career education
10. Substantial increases in all aspects of career guidance
11. Increased opportunities for teachers to use their preferred strategies and materials to increase pupil achievement

12. Increased use of educational technology

13. Increased involvement of pupils, parents, teachers, and members of the business-industry-labor community in policy making

14. Greater involvement of educational institutions in community services, such as community education and human services programs

All these statements emphasize the importance of helping promote career development as a lifelong process and as a reflection of life development (Harris-Bowlsbey, 1975, p. iii). The comprehensive nature of these goals is also emphasized in PL 95-207, which states that career education is appropriate for all individuals, has an essential role in the school, has the potential for improving both the quality and holding power of education and helping pupils relate career aspirations to the work world, and is important for both educational institutions and community career-oriented agencies.

Another way to look at goals involves the elements and pupil outcomes of the school-based model (Herr, 1974, p. 50B):

ELEMENT	OUTCOME
Career Awareness	Career Identity
Self-Awareness	Self-Identity
Appreciations, Attitudes	Self–Social Fulfillment
Decision-Making Skills	Career Decisions
Economic Awareness	Economic Understanding
Skill Awareness and Beginning Competence	Employment Skills
Employability Skills	Career Placement
Educational Awareness	Educational Identity

These goals provide the framework for establishing objectives for each element at each grade level and indicate that career education encompasses major aspects of human development. The programs described later in this chapter give purposes and goals in somewhat different ways, but the eight elements and outcomes just listed appear in one form or another in practically all of them. In fact, Marland (1974, p. 100) characterizes these elements and outcomes as an operational definition of career education.

Well over half the states have adopted policy statements about career education and have established the position of coordinator. As mentioned previously, about a third of the school districts in the United States have at least made a start on a program. Several hundred federally funded projects are in operation (Hoyt, 1976, p. 10). Much of the federal financing has come from vocational-education funds, while other offices and agencies, such as the NIE, have contributed lesser amounts. Many publications about career education have been prepared by the NIE, the Office of Education, the Ohio State Center for Vocational and Technical Education (now including the ERIC Clearinghouse in Career Education), the Center for Occupational Education (North Carolina State University at Raleigh), and state and local school systems. Many of the summaries of career-education programs given in this section are based on materials from these sources.

The development of programs and the spread of the philosophy of career education has been affected by the Youth Employment and Demonstration Projects Act of 1977 (YEDPA). This legislation is aimed at problems of youth employment, unemployment, and underemployment, particularly for the economically disadvantaged. It requires that the Department of Labor prime sponsors in communities (under CETA) work closely with local school systems and that a specific amount of CETA funds go to school programs. It will now be possible to use CETA funds for career education for in-school youth. Productive strategies involve a kindergarten through grade twelve career-education program, emphasis on dropout prevention, alternative schools, such as the experienced-based types discussed later, and effective career-guidance services (Mangum, 1978, pp. 46–47). Some preliminary steps have been taken to set up programs, but it is too early to discern major trends and implementation strategies.

The career-education programs described next are representative; many other excellent ones could just as well have been included. Any discussion of career-education programs would be incomplete without including the four original models mentioned previously. These models, particularly the first two, have done much to stimulate nationwide interest in career education.

THE FOUR BASIC MODELS

In 1971, the Office of Education funded four basic models or approaches to career education intended to reach "all segments of the population at those points in their lives and in the contexts which promise the most impact" (Herr, 1974, p. 49B). These models were the school-based comprehensive career-education model (CCEM) for elementary, middle, and high schools; the employer-based career education model (EBCE), later changed to the experience-based career-education model; the home-based model; and the residential-based model. Programs based on these models have been in operation for several years, and evaluations have been completed or are in process.

The School-Based Comprehensive Career-Education Model

Six sites were selected for development and field testing of the school-based model: Mesa, Arizona; Los Angeles, California; Jefferson County, Colorado; Atlanta, Georgia; Pontiac, Michigan; and Hackensack, New Jersey. The Center for Vocational and Technical Education, Ohio State University, was designated as the prime sponsor, coordinator, and director for developing the model, materials, and units for use in schools throughout the nation. In developing the model, general goals were translated into the elements and outcomes mentioned previously (p. 289).

Brief descriptions of two of these programs are included to show diversities and similarities. Although the same framework served as a basis for all CCEMs, each site was responsible for developing the model according to its own needs and preferences. Thus, each has unique and innovative features.

The Mesa Program

This program has demonstrated a unique approach from the start. It defines the term *career* as "individualized planning for comprehensive life goals"[1]. The manual further states that "Mesa's career guidance programs and counseling personnel must be able to provide individual planning assistance to help students set 'life' or 'career' goals in such areas as: (1) occupations, (2) education, (3) personal and social behavior, (4) learning how to learn, (5) social responsibility (i.e., citizenship development), and (6) leisure time activity" (p. 1).

The manual gives a lucid description of the seven steps taken toward these goals, explains how they were carried out, and describes how the results of each step were used. The steps, beginning with identification of target groups affected and terminating with designation of evaluative procedures for counselor performance and pupil behaviors, show careful design of program development. Emphasis was on career education and accountability, with a total community approach, and counselors played a key role from the start.

Application of this strategy included collection of needs data from representative samples in small groups who used card sorts in four areas of needs: interpersonal, intrapersonal, academic learning, and educational-vocational. Guidance-program resources were assessed next. Counselors kept records to show how time was spent and the purposes of services. Results showed current priorities, which were compared with priorities derived from needs data. The final resources inventory showed what was being done, who was doing it, the effectiveness of activities, and available facilities.

Next, needs and current practices were compared. When unmet needs were identified, goals were formulated to take care of them. For example, the resources inventory showed that only about 5 percent of the counselors' time was devoted to helping pupils get along with others, but this need had priority for pupils. The result was the decision that at least 20 percent of the counselors' time would be designated for dealing with such needs.

After that came structuring the guidance program, selecting target groups, materials, and procedures, and disseminating information to pupils, parents, and teachers. The dissemination aspect was designed both to inform and to elicit input from others.

Next, goals were formulated, and from these, objectives were developed. By this time, data were available to build the actual program. Counselors met in group sessions to plan ways to reach goals. Available materials and procedures were reviewed and, if suitable, adopted. The general strategy for reaching goals by the

---

[1]Mesa Public Schools. *Accountability for Counselors*. Mesa, Ariz.: Board of Education. Mesa Public Schools. *Toward Accountability*. Mesa, Ariz.: Board of Education.

mastery of the specific objectives derived from each was to use counseling-learning units keyed to the specific objectives. Flow charts were developed for each goal showing level of learning (comprehension, application, and analysis), thus facilitating the most productive ordering of objectives. These steps provided the bases for constructing units.

A tentative career-education matrix, prepared with input from state career-education project directors and containing the eight career-education elements mentioned earlier and four developmental grade levels (primary, intermediate, junior high, and high school), served as the program framework. After reviews by school and lay persons, the final matrix was prepared. It contained eight elements and outcomes, arranged by the four educational levels. Thirty-three element themes and 217 goal statements were included. For example, an element theme for *career awareness* in the high school is that "the student will understand the variety of occupations found in the world of work." One goal statement for this theme is that "the student will know the detailed characteristics of his chosen field." From the goal statements, objectives were derived to serve as the bases for the construction of classroom units by teachers and counselors in a team relationship. (A large number of instructional materials and staff-training modules are available to other schools.)

Recent developments emphasize three major aspects: development of centers designated the "place"—or "preparing for life activities center"—development of learning charts for K–12 that thread career guidance into the total curriculum, and the Career Integration Implementation Program, (or CIIP), designed to prepare adults to assist young people in career development. The projects established to implement these recent developments include a training component to help teachers thread career education into classroom activities and a community resource service that helps schools use community resources through tours, pupil observations, and other methods. A planning component works with all aspects of the program, particularly refinement of experiences at each grade level, concepts used in the program, and evaluation of results. The guidance and placement component assists counselors in upgrading school services and also facilitates the transition of pupils to work, education, or training. Career-development curriculum materials are collected or prepared and made available by the staff of the curriculum component. Finally, the evaluation component provides help in all types of functions that assess program effectiveness.

The "place," (preparing for life activities center) program being tried out in a number of schools (and later to be adopted by all secondary schools) is a full-service career resource center that includes current educational, occupational, and recreational opportunity information, a self-study laboratory, a motivational laboratory, a teacher resources area, and a placement area. The center is directed by a career-development counselor who is a full-time paraprofessional. Pupil assistants, peer counselors, community volunteers, and counselor-education interns are also used as staff. Building the center involved establishing goals, inventorying needs, deciding on evaluation methods, and formulating strategies for initiating and improving guidance programs. Staff-training materials have been developed in module form.

Learning charts are being developed for each grade; career education is not listed as a separate category because it is threaded into other areas. For example, at the fifth-grade level in social studies, one pupil skill is "describes the ways of living with various occupations." At the sixth-grade level, in language communications skills, the pupil "tells how language skills are used in various occupations." Much of career education falls in the area of citizenship and personal development. For example, at the third-grade level, a task to be accomplished is matching "various jobs with developing interests and abilities" (Mesa School System, 1977). In this way, the purposes of career education are threaded throughout the curriculum, and effective use is made of special facilities like career centers.

CIIP will orient, train, and involve all adults who assist young people's career development: counselors, teachers, nonteaching staff, parents, employers, and community leaders. All the career-education components of the total program, such as career centers, curriculum materials, and staff-development procedures, will be used to provide a comprehensive program. A task force will plan for ways to prepare all groups for effective involvement and will develop strategies for such goals as threading career education into the curriculum and using the community as a learning laboratory. Process, product, and impact evaluation are also part of the plan. In addition, the project includes financial incentives for staff members to develop and implement career-education activities. This program is expected to bring all elements together into a comprehensive career-education model at the secondary level.

The Center for Career Development provides a number of ongoing career-development services and helps maintain linkage between the world of education and the world of work through a school-community advisory council that holds regular meetings with the center staff.

The Los Angeles Project

This project was developed in Belmont High School, three junior high schools, and six elementary schools. Its overall purpose was to establish a system that would give each pupil who leaves high school entry-level skills for work as well as those necessary for gaining admission to post-secondary education (Sampieri, 1972). A two-year planning period, starting in 1972, was used to develop and review career-education curricula, carry out needs assessment, and plan a districtwide program (Sampieri, 1975). Initial work shows the use of the major career-education concepts of the Office of Education and the National Institute of Education (Sampieri, 1972).

Four major phases made up the kindergarten through grade twelve career-education sequence. In Phase I (kindergarten through grade six), the focus was on career awareness. In Phase II (grades seven and eight), career exploration was emphasized. Phase III (grades nine and ten) was concerned with career orientation, and Phase IV (grades eleven and twelve) provided for acquisition of specific career competencies.

Career awareness, the emphasis of the first level, involved awareness of self, the personal and social significance of work, and the broad range of career opportunities.

In grades seven and eight, pupils evaluated interests, abilities, and values and identified needs in relation to life careers for more intensive exploration in the next phase. The career orientation phase involved a more detailed study of occupations and the initiation of skill development in career areas. In Phase IV, intensive preparation for carrying out post–high school plans was provided. Intensified guidance and counseling helped with planning and placement.

The project staff consisted of thirty-three persons, including thirty teachers, an administrator, a secondary-school counselor, and a "career-advisor"—a new guidance role designed to help pupils take advantage of available occupational training programs (Winder, 1972). The project's curriculum supervisor served as group leader, and consultants assisted with the work. Parents were involved in every step of the process and were given the information needed to support their children. (The organization chart also shows a "career guidance supervisor" and "paraprofessional aides," but their functions are not described.)

This major curriculum-development task was to some extent structured by the guidelines established by the prime sponsor, the Center for Vocational and Technical Education at Ohio State University. These guidelines consist of a matrix, one of whose dimensions is the eight elements of career education selected by the center; the other dimension is the thirteen grade levels (kindergarten through grade twelve). Units related to goals were located, screened, and revised if necessary. The Los Angeles CCEM developed about thirty-five units.

The total curriculum-building process thus involved identification of the major elements described, cooperative goal identification by representatives of all specialties and levels, a synthesizing and organizing function performed by the contracting center, preparation and testing of units, in-service education, delivery, use, and revision.

The shift in guidance emphasis apparent in this new plan was of considerable significance to both teachers and counselors. Guidance became an integral part of the curriculum and the teacher's responsibility. Units emphasized such guidance concepts as self-understanding and self-acceptance. Guidance and counseling personnel functioned in a consultative and referral role for those needing special assistance and provided information for pupil decision making.

A thorough, well-designed evaluation program was part of the initial project. Before the new system was installed, the status of such program components as the dropout rate was assessed. Prior to this, the attitudes of parents, pupils, and staff toward career education were surveyed. (All groups gave very positive responses.) Field testing was done to validate units before their use in the program, and pre- and posttests assessed pupil progress. Process evaluation conducted by the local project staff, the center staff, and the Institute for Vocational Development was systematically carried out. Finally, an accountability evaluation of the major goals of the project was made. Each of these assessments and evaluations is essential, but the last one is critical.

In three years of developmental work, fourteen implementation options were developed. Each option was based on a common rationale, which is initiating a career-education program to meet a particular need. Starting out on a five-year implementation program with relatively small models to test effectiveness before they went into operation, five projects were selected by area administrators. In addition, the career-education staff made a systematic, determined effort to develop relationships with the business community and sell the program to them.

The first project set up under this program, the Los Angeles County Alliance for Career Education, brings together representatives from education, business, and industry to build career education in the county. Some programs are conducted by the alliance and some are carried out by other agencies or offices, such as industry-education councils. A close working relationship is maintained between the Office of Career Education and the Alliance for Career Education.

The second project, Career Expo '75, was a ten-day exhibition of career materials by over five hundred firms and agencies. Each detail was systematically planned, from enlisting the help of community organizations to preparing for the visits.

The third project, The Personnel Exchange Program, was originally designed to enable daylong exchanges between those in education and business. In practice, most of the visiting has been done by educators. At the time of the report, over ninety teachers and counselors had been placed. Informal evaluations indicate that the program is well received and considered very helpful.

Competency-Based Career Education is the fourth major project to be implemented. Its purpose is to insure that every pupil is able to demonstrate an entry-level job skill before he or she leaves school. The skills may be acquired in any way, for example, through the regional occupational programs or the community colleges. The project takes considerable coordination and building of cooperative relations in both the school and the workplace. Progress at the time of the report was enough to justify plans to make the program part of the school curriculum the following year.

The fifth project, Secondary School Options, is designed to test a new secondary-school model that could readily incorporate career-education principles and techniques. Although various options have been considered, the general plan is to organize a "school within a school" that has an open-classroom structure, allows pupils to work on projects both in and outside the school, and involves evaluation by measuring success in mastering competencies rather than grades.

The focus is on helping each individual assume responsibility for his or her actions and take an active role in shaping his or her future. The process is to test and refine carefully developed procedures in small-scale studies while simultaneously building support in the school and community, particularly in business and industry.

The Experienced-Based Career-Education Model

This model was originally called the employer-based career education model but objections arose to the implications that business and industry would be conducting public education. To reflect the community involvement in learning, the name was later changed to "experience-based." After a series of feasibility studies, four regional settings were selected to develop operational programs as alternatives for high school pupils who for one reason or another cannot profit from the regular high school.

The sites, each in different social and economic settings and each supported by a coordinating laboratory, are as follows:

1. Appalachian Educational Laboratory, Charleston, West Virginia. The program is coordinated by the Appalachia Educational Laboratory. It involves the state government offices and industrial resources of Charleston, West Virginia.
2. Far West High School, Oakland Public High School District, Oakland, California. This program is coordinated by the Far West Laboratory. It is in an urban setting with ethnic mix of blacks, Chicanos, Asians, and whites.
3. Community Experience for Career Education (CE)2, Tigard, Northwest Regional Education Laboratory, Portland, Oregon. The setting is a Portland suburb with a mixture of rural and metropolitan traditions.
4. The Academy, Olney High School, Philadelphia, Pennsylvania. Coordinated by Research for Better Schools. The setting for this model is the central city (Hagans, 1976, p. 6).

Additionally, a number of pilot sites to evaluate the EBCE model are receiving technical assistance from the coordinating laboratories. Other schools have asked for and received assistance in implementing part of the model. In all, eighty different educational agencies in forty-six states plus the District of Columbia are operating or planning to operate EBCE programs (*Roll Call of Sites*, 1976, p. 2)

Definitions of EBCE vary somewhat, but the following statement from *A Comparison of Four Experienced-Based Career-Education Programs* gives the basic elements:

> Experienced-based Career Education is a new approach to secondary education . . . to help bridge the gap between the classroom and the community. . . . It combines learning activities outside and within the school into a balanced, comprehensive, individualized program for high school students. The community is analyzed for its potential as a learning resource. Student experiences in the community are then carefully planned, supervised, and evaluated.
>
> Students learn subject matter normally studied in the classroom, but they learn through the practical application of academic disciplines in the workaday world. They explore important new dimensions about themselves and potential careers, and they learn how to make informed career decisions (*Education and Work Program*, 1976, unnumbered).

EBCE differs from traditional work/education programs in several ways. It provides unpaid work experience, career exploration in various locations, experiential learning in academic subjects, and significant pupil role in developing a personalized educational plan. It places greater emphasis on career development than alternative schools do. It prepares for college, work, and further training. It is for a wide variety of pupils: those who want to compare academic learning with the real world; those who want to explore careers firsthand; the college-bound pupil who wishes to verify a career choice; the job-bound pupil who wants to pursue a career interest, learn basic skills, and get ready for employment. Future plans for EBCE call for ways to implement programs, probably through state educational agencies, with technical assistance from the four model programs.

A brief review of some major features of one of the programs illustrates its innovative features and utilization of guidance and counseling (Education and Work Program, 1977, pp. 2–3, 12–13, 34–35). In the Appalachian program, five basic areas form the basis for a concept-centered, community-integrated curriculum. Individual programs based on learning objectives are set up for each pupil; two aides—program guides and student guides—are used. A career-planning and decision-making skills course is required. Pupils spend 70 to 80 percent of their time at community sites to complete their personalized academic and career programs.

Self-assessment instruments are used in program planning. In the process, the pupil analyzes work and work settings and compares preferences with opportunities in a cycle of assessment, placement, information collection, and reassessment. Guidance and counseling are woven into all pupil learning. In addition, small group-counseling and guidance sessions are used. Local high school counselors assist with counseling, inservice education, and consultation.

As of 1976, 100 pupils in grades eleven and twelve were enrolled in the program, which had already graduated 165. Approximately 145 local businesses and agencies were participating.

The EBCE is staffed by a director of operations, learning coordinators, counselor-coordinators, and support personnel. Each learning coordinator is a teacher-facilitator and coordinates and manages the programs of about twenty pupils. The counselor-coordinators perform special counseling and guidance functions and back up the first-line guidance of the learning coordinators. The support staff consists of personnel for clerical and transportation services. A community advisory council obtains input about the program, gives feedback to the staff, and assists in enlisting experience sites (Appalachia Educational Laboratory, 1976, pp. 11-1, 11-7, Hyre and Henderson, 1976).

The cooperation of experience sites is obtained early, followed by site analysis; referral procedures are then established. Resource persons are oriented to the program's purposes and methods. A manual has been prepared for site analysis and for other activities in this phase of program building.

The new pupil first goes through a week of orientation to learn how the system works and to begin program planning. The *Student Program Guide* is used by learning coordinator and pupil to plan career experiences and the academic program. After completing the career-planning section, the pupil consults the *List of Experience Site Placement Opportunities* and the *Experience Site Learning Guide* to select experience sites. Initial choices are requested according to a standard procedure. Courses are selected using the academic program part of the *Student Program Guide*.

Pupil projects then are planned, and pupils go into the community to spend three to thirteen weeks at various work sites. One day a week is spent with the learning coordinator, who also visits pupils at work sites. An activity sheet is used for guiding and recording learning experiences. A cross-reference catalogue identifies resources and activities to assist in project planning and data collection to compile project reports. Evaluation is done at the completion of a planned activity, with an ongoing quality check on the pupils' work. A system has been developed to convert work completed into Carnegie units.

A manual called the *Student Career Guide* is used to enhance career development. The guide is designed to enable pupils to explore occupations and relate them to personal abilities and interests. Credits can be earned in career education as well as academic areas.

The total program has been field-tested and is ready for use in other school systems. This program and the decision-making materials that have been developed (which are discussed later in this chapter) are considered particularly useful for CETA projects and educational activities. Technical assistance for program building is available from the laboratory.

Extensive field-testing evaluations have provided evidence of the effectiveness and acceptability of the EBCE program. Students, graduates, parents, and community resource agencies uniformly rate EBCE highly effective. Practically all the community work-site participants say they would recommend the program to others (Buckman, 1976; Education and Work Program, 1976, pp. 22–24A). Pupil attitudes toward school, oral communication skills, and perceived effects on success in further education and work are all very positive. A final and critical evaluation measures public confidence and support for the program; the four school districts associated with the pilot projects have substantially taken over the management and financial support of the programs. EBCE is currently being implemented with local funds by other districts that took part in evaluation studies.

The Home-Based Career-Education Model

This model was developed and tested in Providence, Rhode Island. It was designed for adult populations, including the homebound—young adults who have not made career choices, retired individuals, and housewives without outside employment. Its initial objectives were

1. to develop educational delivery systems in the home and community.
2. to provide new career-education programs for adults.
3. to establish a guidance and career-placement system to assist individuals in occupational and related life roles.
4. to develop more competent workers for the world of work.
5. to enhance the quality of the home as a learning center (Herr, 1974, p. 51B).

A continuous community-needs assessment was carried out to provide data for establishing priorities; evaluation was done through information from follow-ups. Results of studies have shown that users made and carried out plans and that they were almost 100 percent positive in their evaluations (Education and Work Group, 1977–1978, pp. 134–135; Tolbert, 1978, p. 266). In spite of the favorable evaluation and extensive use of the service, the model received a low priority rating from the National Institute of Education because it had not been demonstrated that the home-based unemployed or underemployed needed this type of help. Even so, after the federal funding ended, the state continued to operate the service.

The model is innovative, with outreach the major strategy. Radio, television, and other media were used to reach prospective counselees. Typically, paraprofessionals carried out counseling by telephone to help clients assess their present situations, capabilities, and limitations; to give information; to help with decision making; and to assist in carrying out plans. An information component contained data about occupations, trends, and job openings. Local information, tailored to client needs, was developed by an information unit. An evaluation component provided feedback about program effectiveness.

The Residential-Based Career-Education Model

This model was set up in 1971 for a developmental period of five years at a cost of $20 million. A vacant Strategic Air Command base at Glasgow, Montana, was used as the tryout site.

The rural/residential model was designed to help the unemployed, problem-ridden rural family become self-sufficient by housing the total family unit at the residential training site for a comprehensive career-education program. The goal was to prepare the family to function effectively and become economically independent in everyday society. Families were recruited from a six-state area: Idaho, Montana, Nebraska, North Dakota, South Dakota, and Wyoming.

Six criteria were used to screen applicants for the program:

1. The unit must constitute a family.
2. The family must have an income less than one and one-half times the local poverty level.
3. The family must live in a rural place.
4. The head of the family must be able to work.
5. The head of the family must be between the ages of eighteeen and forty-nine years.
6. The head of the family must have sufficient education to benefit from participation in a career-education program similar to Mountain-Plains [completion of at least sixth grade] (Bale, Park, and Meekin, 1976, p. i).

It is estimated that 2.3 million families nationwide—about 11 million individuals—would be eligible on the basis of these criteria.

The program, designed to be seven months in length, provided a comprehensive and integrated array of services according to client need, including basic education; specific job-skill training; placement home management, health care, and parenting training; and personal, family, and career counseling (Bale, Park, and Meekin, 1976 p. i). In addition, the model provided a laboratory for testing strategies that involve family units in education (Career Education Task Force, 1973, pp. 105–106).

The field-testing site has accommodated two hundred families at a time. Although it is very expensive, the program could be cost-effective if it successfully rehabilitates families. Cost-effective data, however, are not available (Education and Work Group, 1977–1978, p. 160). But other evaluative data are promising. Three families applied for each one accepted. About 75 percent completed the program, and about 80 percent of those were on the job within a week. Employers reported being satisfied with workers. Families also showed strong gains in acceptance of self and others, personal judgment ability, and ability to focus on the task at hand. Average cost was about $14,000 per family, but it is estimated that it would take less than ten years for families to pay back the government's investment (Education and Work Group, 1977–1978, pp. 170–173).

A great deal has been learned about career education from field-testing of these four models, and new programs are being developed, particularly for the school-based and experience-based models. Pupils, teachers, and parents enthusiastically support career education, but active administrative backing and direct assistance and materials for teachers are essential. Implementation requires relatively long-term support, including adequate funding (Education and Work Group, 1977–1978, pp. 212–213, 223–224).

RANGE OF PROGRAMS

Because of the number and great variety of approaches to career education, it is not possible to list or discuss them all. In the next sections, however, brief descriptions of some programs are given, illustrating applications in various settings.

Elementary and Middle School

Programs for the CCEM school-based model cover the kindergarten-grade twelve range although models that have been developed emphasize the early and middle grades. Hoyt, Pinson, Laramore, and Mangum (1973) describe planning and program implementation at the elementary level, and Evans, Hoyt, and Mangum (1973) cover the middle-junior high school grades.

Many special high school programs assume that developmental work was done at earlier levels, since implementation of career education typically calls for kindergarten through grade twelve, or even kindergarten through grade fourteen organization and infusion. The Orange County Consortium Career Education Project is an example of this type of implementation. Based in Orange County, California, the project included four elementary schools, two junior high schools, two high schools, and a community college (discussed in the next section). Funding was provided by the state and various parts of the Vocational Education Act. The director's objective was to thread career education so thoroughly into the curriculum that it would achieve a permanent status and would not be visible as a separate program. Major features of the program are a teacher-developed curriculum, a guidance program, career centers, and a coordinated work experience/regional occupational program (Hewett, 1975, pp. 1–19).

Curriculum development began with a needs assessment, which revealed, among other things, that teachers spent little time on career education, but they were willing to do more. Pupils' reports indicated that they had very little information about careers.

Consultants defined goals and objectives. Teachers began to develop curriculum materials for some of the Office of Education's occupational clusters. A matrix showing career-education concepts was constructed vertically by year, kindergarten through grade fourteen, and horizontally by each grade and subject area. For the years kindergarten–six, seven–nine, and ten–fourteen, four levels of awareness and five developmental stages were identified as a guide for curriculum construction.

Materials were developed for the total program, and in-service education was given teachers to help them use materials to infuse career education.

In order to provide the most effective assistance possible and maintain program momentum, facilitators were designated for each school. Their roles varied with the school, but typical services included helping teachers select career-oriented curriculum materials, setting up career resource rooms, helping teachers field-test units, and assisting them in trying out new units.

Major emphasis was on the elementary-school curriculum, because the assumption was that pupils in early grades are more flexible organizationally and because pupils who had a good start would demand changes in later school years. A wide variety of innovative practices to combine basic skills and career awareness were instituted, such as career corners in classroom, elective courses on career areas, audio-visual materials, woodworking experiences in the shop (including the kindergarten level), and puppet shows.

Units and other curriculum activities at the junior high school level were developed from the career-education matrix; facilitators were particularly important in helping teachers use materials and techniques. Career labs, minicourses, and visiting speakers were among the popular approaches used. One example is a ten-day unit on science for seventh-graders that the facilitator and teacher set up in ten stations around the school to give pupils a variety of career-related learning experiences.

Guidance personnel, working with facilitators, developed new strategies to help pupils identify interests, explore careers, and plan for the future. Since regularly assigned counselors were not available in the elementary schools, teachers at this level, assisted by counselors for other age groups and district consultants, developed guidance units—for example, a second-grade program on awareness of the changing work roles of men and women. At the junior high level, guidance emphasis was on helping pupils identify goals and begin preparing to achieve them. The career-development curriculum helped pupils become aware of options, and counseling and group guidance helped them become aware of and relate personal attributes to educational areas and career clusters. Counseling priority surveys were used to identify areas for occupational exploration, and structured group activities were employed in some ninth-grade classes to help with high school course selection.

Guidance is not as separate and distinct from the career-education program as it may appear from the preceding discussion. Both curriculum and guidance focus on the career development of pupils.

Community College

In some programs, the range of the career-education program is from kindergarten through grade fourteen and the community college is included in the overall plan. In other situations, the community college has developed its own program, which may be coordinated with local high schools but is separate from them. Since this type of institution usually devotes a large part of its program to both occupational preparation and transfer programs, career education is an obvious necessity. In many cases, a great deal is already being done about career education, although often more through separate services—a course or a computer guidance program—than through a program based on the career-education models already discussed. Few comprehensive programs are reported (Hewett, n.d., pp. 3–12), and extensive model-building programs like the CCEM are not in operation.

Although Hoyt (1977b) points out that the community college movement and career education have a great deal in common, he finds very little comprehensive career education in this setting, although there are many bits and pieces. It is clear that career education at this level is different from the high school model partly because of the diversity of students and the increasing emphasis on adult and continuing education. Moreover, there are variations between institutions because of location, size, and student body.

Building career education into the community/junior college involves establishing close relationships with similar activities in the high school and adopting a broad definition of work. Increased use of community resources, expanded faculty involvement in guidance services rather than leaving those services to student personnel workers, and efforts based on a concept of career development as a lifelong process are also needed (Hoyt, 1977b).

The Orange County Consortium Career Education Project is one example of a community college career program as part of a kindergarten through grade fourteen system (Hewett, 1975, p. 12). The project has developed a curriculum for regular and continuing education classes and for local community education. Teams of teachers have been active in developing units and over thirty have been prepared. Many continuing-education courses are open entry and exit, and students can move at their own pace. The guidance and counseling component features a career-planning center to give individuals personal help in career planning and decision making. Services include individual and group counseling, classes in such areas as job-getting skills, and occupation/educational information. VIEW, computerized local job banks, and catalogues of educational institutions are among the available resources. In all, the center has information available on more than twenty thousand occupational and training opportunities.

Vocational-Technical Centers

The status of comprehensive career education in vocational-technical centers is in many ways similar to that in the community college—there are many parts and separate services but few comprehensive models. This type of institution, which focuses on community needs, utilizes local resources, and adapts to continuing and adult education, quite naturally includes important aspects of career education. But unless there is a deliberate effort to introduce the career-education concept, these separate elements do not amount to a comprehensive career-education program. Even so, the many innovative career-development techniques being used at this level facilitate integration of the concept into the total program.

College Level

At the higher-education level there are an enormous number of services and offices that provide career guidance (Swails, 1977), but comprehensive career education is not yet very much in evidence. It would seem that colleges of education should be among the leaders in incorporating career education into programs, but little is being done even there (Leonard and Splete, 1978). Hoyt (1976c) did not find any college or university that could be identified as an "exemplary career education institution." Although there is considerable debate about applicability (Krupka and Vener, 1978; Nash and Saurman, 1978; Stoler and Stoler, 1978), Hoyt states that there is no question that college students need career-development assistance and expect colleges to prepare them for a career. If the college or university does not have this as one of its important goals, students and the public should be informed (Hoyt, 1975). The point is well made that career education is an important concept for the college or university.

Although there is a lack of use of the term *career education*—and even at times a hostile attitude toward it—there is a real concern among higher-education staff and students—and also among employers—about the "poor preparation for work which college students seem to receive" (Rosen and Olson, 1977, p. 54). Some positive steps have been taken, but critical problems remain, such as integrating experiential and abstract learning and establishing education credentials that reflect students' performance ability in both education and work. The synthesis of career education and the liberal arts is meeting considerable resistance, but its advantages are recognized (Craig, 1978).

A statewide proposal to promote career education at the college and university level is given in the report of the Chancellor's Advisory Committee in California (Ferrin and Arbeiter, 1975, pp. 22–24). This report makes a number of recommendations to the state university system that emphasize the importance of career education. Among other things, it encourages institutions to work closely with local industry-education groups and continuously evaluate their career-guidance programs. The report clearly supports career education as an important function of contemporary higher education.

Community Programs and Agencies

Many of the programs already described serve adults of all ages through counseling and guidance, training, education, and placement. The community-based career-education model is one example. CETA is the largest program of all; funded on a national level, but with local control, it has tremendous potential for providing career-development experiences to qualified individuals. In addition, legislation permits use of CETA funds to support career education in secondary schools. Programs are also offered by community colleges and vocational-technical centers, local institutions that include adults among their clientele.

A large and growing number of programs, not part of other institutions or organizations, provide career education to adults. Advocates of Women in San Francisco is an example. Begun in 1971, it includes three major programs and three special services (Hewett, n.d., pp. 1–19). The major programs are as follows:

1. Recruitment and career counseling to help women enter apprenticeship training. Contacts are made with employers and unions to assist in placement.
2. Recruitment, career counseling, and workshops to help women moving into management jobs. Job development is also done to help with placement.
3. Job and training program listings for the area and short-term group career counseling to assist with planning and decision making.

The three special services involve consulting with employers on affirmative action and equal employment guidelines, training programs for both employers and employees on implementing affirmative action policies, and workshops and conferences for women interested in starting their own businesses. Advocates for Women helps women identify interests and abilities and plan training and skill development that will lead to chosen careers. It also endeavors to reduce occupational stereotypes among both clients and employers.

With the trend toward expanding career opportunities for women, minority groups, and the disadvantaged, and increasing concern about the career needs (broadly defined) of mid-life and older persons, it seems safe to predict an increase in such programs. Moreover, recognition of the close relationship between personal-social problems and career maladjustment should lead other community agencies to give serious consideration to making at least some effort in the career-education direction. Increases in services seem inevitable in spite of taxpayers' revolts and similar moves to reduce government expenditures.

EVALUATION OF PROGRAMS

In keeping with the importance of accountability, career education is being evaluated in terms of both process and results. Most of the programs described have been evaluated, and the results are being used for program modification and improvement. The nature and definition of career education is developing as a result of these continuing evaluations.

Large-Scale Evaluations

Leifer and Lesser (1976) analyzed research on the development of career awareness in young children and available materials to foster this process, primarily to identify needs and to recommend research priorities. They recommend that efforts be devoted to expanding occupational options, reducing the effects of stereotypes, and combining the resources of the home, school, and media to develop career awareness in young children. Bhaerman (1977), after reviewing studies of the effects of career education on basic academic achievement, concludes that it does not hurt achievement in the basic subject areas and usually appears to have a positive effect. Achievement is a critical area, for competence in the basic skills is a major goal of career education and is particularly important in the current "back to basics" climate.

A synthesis of the evaluations of forty-five federally funded kindergarten through grade twelve career-education programs (Bonnet, 1977) reveals a number of significant features related to the nature and effectiveness of programs. Programs were quite different, and infusion or threading took many different forms. It was not possible to conclude which strategies or techniques are best. In regard to specific accomplishments based on learner objectives, evaluation results are as follows:

1. EFFECTS ON BASIC ACADEMIC SKILLS   Overall, the effects were neither positive nor negative, but in some instances there were significant gains in reading both from a statistical and an educational standpoint. In addition, many teachers stated that they felt that career education helped development of basic skills.

2. VALUES THAT FOSTER A DESIRE TO WORK   There was good evidence of success in this area.

3. CAREER DECISION-MAKING SKILLS   Although somewhat sparse, available evidence supported the conclusion that career education strengthened these skills.

4. JOB-SPECIFIC OCCUPATIONAL AND INTERPERSONAL SKILLS   The first were not evaluated, but for the second the evidence was inconclusive but encouraging.

5. SELF-UNDERSTANDING AND UNDERSTANDING OF EDUCATIONAL AND OCCUPATIONAL OPPORTUNIITIES   Objective data on self-understanding were lacking, but career awareness was achieved in most cases, and this aspect of career education was considered to be effectively done.

6. CONSISTENCY OF CAREER PLANS AND DECISIONS   It was too early to judge the impact of career education on this goal.

In other areas, such as finding meaning in work and productive use of leisure, few evaluation results are available, but those reviewed are encouraging. There are gaps, however, in evaluation data, and conclusions about the achievement of other goals cannot be reached.

The report of the National Advisory Council on Career Education (1976), based on data from program reviews, state career-education coordinators, and reports on specific treatments, concludes that career education improves career awareness, shows some indications of facilitating positive changes in self-concept and work habits, and helps build decision-making skills. K–12 pupils respond positively to career education, and attitudes tend to improve with increased participation. The report also found that efforts designed to improve career decision-making skills need a theoretical base for optimum success. Enderlein's (1976) review of career-education evaluation studies reveals positive effects on academic growth, decision-making ability, and knowledge of the world of work. Although much of the research was at the elementary school level with a focus on career awareness, the review does note that pupils at both elementary and secondary levels who had participated in career education were better able to make decisions that required analysis of abilities, needs, interests, occupational roles, and the relation of self to career plans than those who had not participated.

The reports by Datta (1977) and High (1977) provide further evidence of the effects of career education. Datta reviewed findings from four Office of Education demonstration projects and found a number of positive indications. Academic achievement in reading and math was higher for pupils, including those from low-income families, who had participated in career education. Evidence also showed definite growth in career awareness at the elementary school level. When those in grades three through twelve who had high exposure to career education were compared with those with limited exposure, the high-exposure pupils had greater understanding of the skills and abilities required for careers. High draws on extensive evidence to show that career education contributes to development of basic skills, builds positive work values, helps pupils develop decision-making and job-getting skills, facilitates development of abilities needed for success on the job, helps pupils develop self-understanding and acquire a knowledge of occupational opportunities, and helps them become aware of means for changing choices and learn how to evaluate the flexibility of alternatives. As High says, "Career education is still a long way from aviation's supersonic jet transports that regularly and reliably, day after day, carry passengers some 3,800 miles across the Atlantic Ocean from Washington to Paris in 3 hours and 50 minutes. But we do have increasing evidence that career education can 'get off the ground' in relation to the goals which it purports to address" (p. 7).

Process evaluations of the CCEMs (Education and Work Group, 1977, pp. 212–213, 223) show that career education is well received by parents, pupils, and teachers and that strong administrative support and teacher involvement are needed to build effective programs. It was also found that the development of career education is a slow process and requires the best possible use of local talent. Process evaluation is essential for effective program building, even though it does not indicate changes in pupils.

Smaller Summaries

Studies of specific programs, such as those by Omvig, Tulloch, and Thomas (1975) and Omvig and Thomas (1977), demonstrate that career education has a positive effect on the career maturity and career competencies of sixth- and eighth-grade pupils, that academic achievement is not adversely affected, and that girls are consistently higher than boys in career maturity.

There is an ongoing effort to upgrade the quality of evaluation studies of career education to test the effectiveness of various approaches and identify strategies and techniques that can be used in other settings. Tallmadge (1977) describes procedures for collecting convincing evidence about program effectiveness, enumerates criteria for program evaluation, and gives examples of convincing and unconvincing evaluation reports. He points out that school administrators are reluctant to initiate changes unless there is evidence that substantial benefits will be forthcoming. An extensive, well-designed search for transportable career-education activities (Hamilton and Mitchell, 1978) found relatively few that clearly demonstrated results that could be accounted for by the career-education activity itself and that could be recommended for dissemination to other schools and school systems. These efforts to upgrade evaluations are extremely important, because convincing evidence will be needed to maintain and expand career-education programs in the face of the "back to basics" movement.

BUILDING CAREER-EDUCATION PROGRAMS

The counselor can view program building in two ways. The first involves the overall strategy by school and community for initiating and managing career education in the institution. The second, more relevant for guidance personnel, deals with staffing. Practices vary, and no one best approach can be recommended for either general program building or counselor participation in initiating or carrying out services.

Strategy

Although there is no single approach that can be called the "best" approach, there seems to be a consensus that a series of steps based on a systems approach is a productive way to organize programs (Mannback and Stillwell, 1974; Ryan, 1974). The steps used in many of the programs already described include, first, identification of decision makers, decision points, and individuals in school and community who should participate in reviews of actions and give input for revision and further development (Jacobson and Mitchell, 1977).[2] Next, a model is selected, either by adopting or modifying available ones or by building a new procedure. After adoption or construction, the model is presented to key persons for approval. Following this step, a "task, talent, time analysis" (Jacobson and Mitchell, 1977, p. 196) is prepared to outline the steps in the program-building process.

Program goals are formulated next, based on the model, the particular school or school system, and the conditions and problems of the society. Following the needs assessment (which follows initial goal formulation), these goals are refined to give direction to the program. The needs assessment covers both desired outcome and current program evaluation. Significant groups, such as pupils and parents, select from a prepared list the outcomes they consider important. The current practices

[2]Adaptation of material from Thomas J. Jacobson and Anita M. Mitchell, "How to Develop a District Master Plan for Career Guidance and Counseling," Vocational Guidance Quarterly, Vol. 25, No. 3, 1977, pp. 195–202. Copyright 1977 American Personnel and Guidance Association. Used by permission.

assessment is then carried out, again using the list of possible outcomes developed from the model, to determine what is already being done.

Objectives are formulated next. There should be an adequate number to provide evidence of success in reaching each goal but not so many that the program is bogged down in detail. The plan used by Jacobson and Mitchell involves four functional levels:

1. AWARENESS   Knowledge
2. INTERNALIZATION IN TERMS OF SELF   Students relate knowledge to their own life plans
3. ACTION   Students utilize the knowledge and understanding in their own career planning
4. EVALUATION   Students evaluate the effects of their action and decide whether to persist in the same direction, change directions, or leave that learning as completed or abandoned (1977, p. 198)

Next, personnel, facility, and equipment resources are assessed. Investigation of such factors as teachers' attitudes about the program and administrators' level of support and enthusiasm is also included. Then strategies are selected. The inventory of current practices is a source of potentially useful strategies, but new ones may have to be devised. Those used should involve the greatest efficiency for the least possible expenditure of time and resources.

Competency analysis, staff development, and staffing strategies are three related steps that follow. Needed competencies are listed, staff abilities are surveyed, and necessary staff development is planned. Finally, staff assignments are made.

Criterion measures must be specified for data collection before and after the program to provide the basis for judging what has been accomplished. In this way, accountability can be evaluated (Krumboltz, 1974). The major question to be asked is, "Does it work?" In light of results, changes may need to be made in the program. Further evaluation is then carried out.

Budget preparation is another essential step; it reflects the cost of the programs, including new personnel and facilities that must be added.

This type of approach has both advantages and disadvantages, as Jacobson and Mitchell (1977) point out. It takes time and commitment, and it increases the number of decision makers, thus adding to complexity as participants raise numerous objections. Reactions, however, tend to become positive as work progresses.

Staffing

The successful development of career education in the school (or in any setting) is largely dependent on the effectiveness of the person with major responsibility for the task. Thus, the administrative organization is extremely important, particularly because success also depends on the cooperation and support of so many different groups—teachers, school administrators, counselors, parents, and business and industrial representatives. Five different administrative plans have been identified by Hausmann and Green (1977):

1. The school superintendent retains authority for planning and implementation.
2. There is a full-time districtwide coordinator.
3. A part-time coordinator serves the district. (This coordinator is similar to the full-time coordinator, except that he or she has other duties, such as teaching.)
4. A school resource person is used. This is a district position held by someone with other teaching, guidance, or staff responsibilities. The emphasis is on resource assistance rather than on coordinating, developing, or implementing.
5. A career-education facilitator serves two or more districts with both instruction and information. The facilitator may have a staff and be located in a regional center.

Another pattern, which appears to have good potential, involves use of a lay person to work with teachers and others to thread career education into the curriculum. Individuals retired from business or the military are examples. This arrangement is sometimes used when funds are not available for employing a coordinator.

Specific groups in the school prefer different arrangements of personnel. Guidance personnel, for example, favor the full-time coordinator. Secondary teachers appear to prefer the resource person, but the choice may reflect a lack of enthusiasm for career education—they would prefer to send pupils to someone rather than take on the responsibility for career education. The full- or part-time coordinator, however, was the most acceptable overall.

Infusion or threading of career education is basically the responsibility of teachers, with encouragement and support provided by the administrator. Career-education outcomes should be threaded into teachers' instructional objectives (Hoyt, 1977a). A team effort by all involved in the instructional delivery system is needed for this to be accomplished (Preli, 1978, pp. 25–26). Teachers must be willing to change, understand the concept of career education, recognize the need for it, and be aware of their role in promoting it (Preli, 1978, pp. 25–26). The teacher's role is critical; if anything of consequence is to come from the career-education movement, it must become a part of the ongoing teaching-learning process (Hoyt, 1976, pp. 34–35). If this is not done, career education may become a separate program with little effect. On the other hand, the danger of diffusion to the vanishing point must be faced. Thus, career education must be understood, accepted, and implemented by teachers.

PROGRAM RESOURCES

There is a wide array of resources for building career education in educational institutions. The community is, of course, the major one; it contains individuals, agencies, programs, businesses, industries, and an almost limitless number of resources to make career education a viable concept. The school can provide experiences, resource persons and activities over and above what is usually expected. For instance, many teachers have worked in noneducational occupations and can serve as information sources. A typical needs survey might not tap all the potential in the institution unless a special effort is made to do so. Community colleges, vocational-technical centers, colleges, universities, and apprenticeship programs are also community educational resources.

Local businesses and industries provide the world-of-work laboratory essential for career education. However, cooperative planning to make productive use of opportunities, for instance, community education-work councils, is needed. Not only does this collaboration add to the effectiveness of career education, it brings school and community closer together and engenders mutual understanding and respect. These effects have been demonstrated over and over again in programs described earlier.

National Organizations

Long before the term *career education* gained widespread recognition, its principles were practiced by many national organizations that have programs in communities (Hoyt, 1977c). These community programs serve as resources for career education and they also provide clues about ways to build effective school programs. In addition, using existing resources re-emphasizes a central tenet of career education not to build yet another structure on top of those already in existence but rather to use effectively those already available. For example, through their Explorer program, the Boy Scouts help young men and women learn about occupations as they relate to lifestyles and bring them in contact with community business and industrial volunteer leaders. The Girl Scouts are also active in career development, including programs to reduce the effects of sex stereotyping and activities to promote career exploration. Both groups are currently planning ways to facilitate career awareness in younger age groups.

Other organizations supporting career education include Junior Achievement, the National Association of Manufacturers, the National Association for Industry-Education Cooperation, and the Chamber of Commerce. Special business programs, such as those at the American Telephone and Telegraph Company, General Motors, and General Electric, have done much to improve the quality of career education in the schools.

Government agencies (Government Resources, 1977), local, state, and national, offer a wide variety of resources ranging from free and inexpensive printed matter to resource persons and consultants to financial support for programs. The government employment service and CETA are also valuable resources for job finding, work experience, and printed information (see Chapter 5). Many of the guides for initiating and improving career education cited in this chapter were prepared by government agencies.

Kits, Program Guides, and Other Materials

A great many planning guides, in-service education programs, infusion materials, and books have been produced for use in career education. The number is so large that grants were awarded for preparation of a two-volume guide, *How to Select and Evaluate Instructional Material* (Program Plan, 1977–1978, 1977 p. 141). In this guide over seven hundred commercial and non-commercial products—textbooks, teachers' guides, workbooks, films, slides, and tapes for all age groups—are analyzed.

The Center for Vocational Education, Ohio State University, has developed a large variety of materials for all ages and all aspects of career education, including program frameworks, staff-development guides, and community involvement aids. The following items are representative:

1. The Career Planning Support System, or CPSS. An integrated set of handbooks, guides, survey questionnaires, and filmstrip/audio-tape presentations for schools to use in building, managing, and evaluating a needs-based career-guidance program in the high school.
2. A rural school career-guidance, counseling, placement, and follow-through system. A series of publications to help rural schools build a complete career-guidance program. Part of the project is the preparation of a cadre of state leadership personnel to help counselors use the program. Staff development guides are included.
3. The National Career Guidance Communication Network for Rural and Small Schools. Developed by a consortium of the Center for Vocational Education, Columbus, Ohio; ERIC Clearinghouse for Rural Education and Small Schools, New Mexico State University; and the Far West Laboratory.

REACTIONS TO THE CONCEPT

Any new educational concept, particularly one that has wide visibility, generates strong opposition as well as support. Controversy, however, is a stimulating and growth-producing activity, and in most instances the debates on career education have resulted in sharpening and improving both principles and practices.

Major Criticisms

The major issues involve three points: the difference between career education and vocational education, the meaning of the term *work,* and the relation of career education to postsecondary education (Hoyt, 1976, pp. 22–29).

Some critics feel that career education is the same as vocational education (Grubb and Lazerson, 1975). In my experience, some college officials and lay persons share this view, which is based on a superficial understanding of the purposes of career education. It is difficult to understand, however, how this issue could be raised by anyone who has in-depth knowledge of the philosophy of career education. Hoyt (1976, pp. 22–23) enumerates the essential differences: Career education is for all individuals at all educational levels; it permeates all teaching and learning activities, and it includes vocational education for those who choose the option of specific vocational preparation. In addition, it is built on a base of career-development theory and research and is a lifelong process.

Questions have also been raised about the importance and value of work in the individual's life today (Grubb and Lazerson, 1975; Baumgardner, 1977). It has been suggested that career education could, unless there is a shift in focus toward more humanistic values, emphasize an industrial ethic that has caused many current problems (Agne and Nash, 1973; Peterson and Park, 1975). Hoyt (1975b, pp. 24–25) responds by pointing out that the definition of work includes both paid and unpaid activities and that the emphasis is on finding purpose and a sense of mastery in whatever is done. Career education does not force, shape, or brainwash individuals to fit into niches in an industrial society but instead increases their control over their lives.

A number of educators, parents, and pupils (quite frequently guidance paraprofessionals) have implicitly or explicitly indicated that career education is for the high school pupil going directly to work, not for the college-bound. The same attitude is expressed by some writers (Grubb and Lazerson, 1975). Labor unions and minority group leaders have expressed fears that chances for higher education will be reduced through emphasis on getting ready to go to work (Kearney and Clayton, 1973; Sessions, 1975; Carroll and Edwards, 1978; Kemble, 1978). Some minority group members feel that career education is a program to assure business and industry of a pool of cheap labor. Career education, however, is for all pupils regardless of the expected level of educational attainment. Moreover, it aims to help the individual make the best choices for further education or training. If, for example, a pupil makes a reasoned choice of vocational-technical education or apprenticeship over college attendance, the decision may be best for him or her *even though* there seems to be a widespread attitude that college is always the most desirable option. Career education could just as well help a job-oriented pupil choose college. Its purpose is to lead to better choices not to lower-level ones. It is, therefore, just as important for the academically talented and gifted as it is for any other pupil.

One rather persistent criticism arises from perceptions of what career education professes to do but cannot accomplish. Hoyt (1976, p. 27) lists five statements that have been named as goals or results of career education but that actually are not based on stated policy:

1. Every high school graduate should have a marketable skill.
2. Unemployment will decrease.
3. Pupils are prepared for entry-level rather than professional jobs.

4. Pupils' aspirations for attending college will be reduced.

5. Pupils' expectations and aspirations will be lowered.

Hoyt points out that none of these statements is a valid goal or result. First, career-education policy advocates that each pupil leaving *formal education* have marketable job skills; this goal is quite different from saying that every pupil leaving *high school* should have these skills. Next, although career education is credited with having the goal of reducing unemployment (Grubb and Lazerson, 1975; Kroll, 1976), this is actually not the case. Although even in the depression years of the 1930s there were unfilled jobs because no applicants had the needed skills, unemployment depends on too many factors to expect an educational program to make a significant difference. What, for example, could career education or any educational program do to counteract the effects of an oil embargo?

Comments already made apply to criticisms about lowered expectations and reduced likelihood of college attendance. If evaluation of career-education programs was made in terms of the number who attend college, results could be quite misleading and would not give any indication of the programs' effectiveness. It bears repeating that career education is for career planning and decision making at all levels of education and work.

Other Criticisms

Hoyt (1976, p. 28) enumerates and responds to a series of criticisms that center around critics' assertions that career education cannot accomplish what should be reasonable goals. Although substantial evidence of success in achieving all these goals is not yet available, career education *is* designed to have an impact in those areas the critics single out. For example, critics state that career education cannot reduce the likelihood of preparing pupils for dead-end jobs, nor can it get them ready for a progression of jobs. But two major goals of career education are adaptability and preparing pupils to get and hold jobs. The same is true for the criticism that career education does not develop avenues of upward mobility; such major focuses of career education as job-coping skills and lifelong learning pave the way for occupational progress.

Other concerns expressed by labor organizations (Davis, 1978) involve expectations that an effective program can be built without substantial expenditures, that some aspects of education may be turned over to employers, and that child-labor and minimum-wage laws may be relaxed. Part of the concern results from lack of participation by labor in the early planning for career education. This condition has to some extent been remedied, and unions are aware of the potential of career education (Hutton, 1978). There is recognition, too, that it has much to offer women and minorities, provided there is an awareness of the difficult problems that must be solved for effective implementation, for career education is not a panacea (Carroll and Edwards, 1978).

Two additional criticisms involve solving social problems and increasing satisfaction with school and work. Certainly career education cannot solve all social problems, but it should have an impact on a number, for example, sex stereotyping and racial bias. In addition, it has been shown over and over that work satisfaction and physical and mental health are related (O'Toole, 1973, Chap. 3). Career education, then, should help reduce physical and mental-health problems. Finally, one thrust of career education is toward increasing satisfaction with school and work. Satisfaction is not the only criterion to use to measure the effectiveness of career education, but it is among the major ones. As Hoyt (1976, pp. 28–29) says, career education makes a deliberate attempt to reduce pupil and worker alienation, increase self-understanding and identification of work values, and find personally meaningful ways to use potential; career-development theory and research support the position that career education will be effective in reaching these goals.

THE COUNSELOR'S ROLE

Counselors have a central role in career education. This fact has been made abundantly clear in the NVGA/AVA and ACES position papers, in the writing of authorities on the subject (Hoyt, Evans, Mackin, and Mangum, 1972, pp. 127–129; Marland, 1974, pp. 189–214), in the work of practitioners (Hoyt, 1976a), and in reports of the Office of Education (Hoyt, 1975, pp. 9–10; Preli, 1978). Figure 7.1 (p. 206) indicates some of the specific career-education functions the counselor carries out, primarily in terms of individual and group counseling. A continuing study is being made to further clarify the counselor's role and preparation (*APGA Wins Contract for Career Education Study,* 1978, pp. 1, 11).

One of the most lucid statements of the counselor's role was prepared by the American Personnel and Guidance Association; it is organized in terms of counselor leadership and participatory functions for career-education programs at *any* educational level.

Leadership Functions
1. Provide leadership in the identification and programming implementation of individual career-development tasks
2. Provide leadership in the identification, classification, and use of self-, educational, and occupational information
3. Provide leadership in the assimilation and application of career decision-making methods and materials
4. Provide leadership in eliminating the influence of both racism and sexism as cultural restrictions of opportunities available to minority persons, females, and others who may be affected
5. Provide leadership in expanding the variety and appropriateness of assessment devices and procedures required for sound personal, educational, and occupational decision making

6. Provide leadership in emphasizing the importance of carrying out the functions of career counseling.

Participatory Functions

7. Serve as a liaison between the educational and community-resource groups
8. Conduct career-guidance needs-assessment surveys
9. Organize and operate part-time and full-time educational, occupational, and job-placement programs
10. Conduct follow-up, follow-through, and job-adjustment activities
11. Participate in curriculum revision
12. Participate in efforts to involve the home and family in career education
13. Participate in efforts to monitor and assess operations and communicate the results of these activities to other practitioners and clientele, as appropriate[3]

The counselor's critical functions are enthusiastic endorsement and collaborative work with teachers, parents, employers, and community members to promote career education (Hoyt, 1975b). Work with teachers is particularly important. To be fully implemented, career education must be infused or threaded into the teaching-learning process and the teacher is the key person to do the day-to-day work (Preli, 1978, p. 5). Counselors experienced in career education speak of an "orchestrator" role—that is, helping teachers infuse career education is best accomplished through the power of persuasion rather than through the power of the counselor's position (Hoyt, 1976, p. 11A).

Counselors have a vital role to play in career education, one that makes use of counseling, consulting, and programming skills in a collaborative working relationship with the many others involved in the process. It is particularly important today that counselors be knowledgeable about the role as well as the content and methods of career education if they are to participate fully in this promising approach to providing career guidance for all pupils.

SUMMARY

Career education offers an excellent way to implement career-development theory and techniques throughout the school, college, or agency, and it has aroused nationwide enthusiasm and support. The philosophy of career education sees preparation for work to be one goal of education but not the only one. Moreover, *work* is broadly defined and covers much more than the paid, full-time occupation. Recent legislation attests to the timeliness and public acceptance of this philosophy.

Career education involves both educational institutions and the community and

[3]L. Sunny Hansen, "ACES Position Paper: Counselor Preparation for Career Development/Career Education," *Counselor Education and Supervision,* Vol. 17, No. 3, 1978, pp. 168–179. Copyright 1978 American Personnel and Guidance Association. Used by permission.

uses threading into the curriculum as the central strategy. Counselors have a significant role in career education and should prepare for effective participation by mastering appropriate skills and knowledge. A number of career-education programs have been described in this chapter, including the four CCEM models. Although most of the developmental work has been done in K–12 institutions, innovative and promising practices are visible in many other settings. Guidelines for implementation have been reviewed, and the systems approach appears to be the most efficient. A key strategy in career education is to utilize community resources; a large number are readily available. Some type of school-community committee is needed to facilitate collaborative action. There is a large and rapidly growing quantity of materials that can be used for initiating, administrating, and improving career education.

PROJECTS AND EXPERIENTIAL ACTIVITIES

1. Select one of the following on-site observations:
   a. Visit a school and ask the counselor or administrator how he or she defines career education and if any implementation has taken place. If so, talk to several teachers about their attitudes about the concept and what they are doing to implement it.
   b. Locate a school (or other institution) that is considered to have a model program and visit it to learn about policies and activities. If possible, observe a class or other example of career-education threading.
2. Consider your career interests and select a community college, college, or other post–high school institution, visit it, and talk to those in charge of the student personnel services and the placement service. Ask how they define career education and if the concept is being implemented in any way in the institution. If possible, observe an activity that is identified as career education.
3. Visit a community agency, special project, or other type of community service of interest to you as a possible work setting and ask what is being done to help clients in career development. Ask counselors how they feel about the importance of the ACES list of skills and knowledge that all counselors should have. (Note: This experience is appropriate for any agency—the employment service, a CETA office, a mental-health center, programs for drug users, halfway houses for penal inmates.)
4. Check to see if your department has a supply of career-education materials on hand. If so, preview samples and evaluate their effectiveness.
5. If career-education units, modules, and the like are available, try them out in class or in small groups. The staff-development ones are particularly appropriate, because they are designed for counselors, teachers, and administrators. Modules and units for pupils, however, will be helpful in experiencing career education from the target group's point of view.

6. Form small groups and role-play a school staff meeting consisting of a counselor, teacher(s), and an administrator. The counselor's task is to explain why he or she has a vital role to play in career education. At the conclusion, have class members rate the effectiveness of the presentation.

7. Form small groups and prepare a brief module for threading career education into the counselor-education program. The first step would be to identify a theme that should be included. Then agree on goals, objectives, activities, materials, and methods of evaluation. Try out the completed module in the class.

ADDITIONAL REFERENCES

Career Education and the Curriculum. Guidance Monograph Series No. IX. Boston: Houghton Mifflin, 1975. This series, introduced by a volume on career counseling and guidance, contains nine monographs on applications to specific subject areas. It is an invaluable set of references for the counselor, teacher, or administrator.

Evans, Rupert N., Kenneth B. Hoyt, and Garth L. Mangum. *Career Education in the Middle/Junior High Schools.* Salt Lake City, Utah: Olympus Publishing Company, 1973. Designed for teachers, counselors, and administrators who work with middle-school pupils, this book explains how exploration, the major career-development task of this educational level, may be implemented in the classroom.

Hewett, Kathryn D. *Eleven Career Education Programs.* Cambridge, Mass.: Abt Publications, 1975. Interesting, vivid, and comprehensive descriptions of career-education programs in schools, colleges, and special community services. Some program summaries in this chapter are based on descriptions given in the book. One of the best compilations of practices available.

Hoyt, Kenneth B. *A Primer for Career Education.* Washington, D.C.: U.S. Department of Health, Education, and Welfare, n.d. A review of career education that covers everything the beginner needs to know. An excellent introductory reading. Highly recommended.

————. *Career Education: What It Is and How to Do It.* Salt Lake City, Utah: Olympus Publishing Company, 1972. One of the most popular references on career education, this book takes the reader from basic concepts through all the steps and levels in implementation. Highly recommended.

————. *An Introduction to Career Education.* Washington, D.C.: U.S. Government Printing Office, 1975. The first comprehensive conceptual statement on career education from the Office of Education, this book covers definition, concepts, assumptions, implementation, priorities, and learner outcomes and has served as the basis for program planning and evaluation.

————. *Career Education Needs of Special Populations.* Washington, D.C.: Department of Health, Education, and Welfare, 1976 (ED 132-428). An analysis of career-development needs of low-income, minority, gifted and talented, and handicapped people. A particularly valuable reference for insuring that career education reaches those important but often-neglected segments of the population.

————. *Community Resources for Career Education*. Washington, D.C.: Department of Health, Education, and Welfare, 1976 (ED 130-118). A very helpful description of resources that can contribute to career education. Principles and guidelines for school-community collaboration are discussed. Eleven national programs that have local organizations are described. The work of community career-education action councils is explained. Valuable reading for learning about what's out there to help build career education.

————. *Refining the Career Education Concept*. Washington, D.C.: U.S. Government Printing Office, 1976. A series of essays that gives counselors, teachers, and administrators a comprehensive view of what has been done, the problems and issues that need to be confronted, the fallacies of some criticisms, and next steps.

————. *The School Counselor and Career Education*. Washington, D.C.: U.S. Government Printing Office, 1976. The counselor's role is described, and the experiences of twelve counselors who implemented a number of innovative practices are recounted. An invaluable manual for counselors who want to "break into" career education.

————. *Career Education Implications for Counselors*. Washington, D.C.: U.S. Government Printing Office, 1977. This monograph supplements *The School Counselor and Career Education* (1976) and emphasizes the key role the counselor plays in implementing the concept. Suggestions are also made for preparation of counselors and career-planning assistance at the post–high school level.

————. *Refining the Career Education Concept, Part II*. Washington, D.C.: U.S. Government Printing Office, 1977. Articles in this monograph are more recent than those in *Refining the Career Education Concept* (1976). Among other topics, the manpower field and the community college setting are dealt with.

Hoyt, Kenneth B., Nancy M. Pinson, Darryl Laramore, and Garth L. Mangum. *Career Education and the Elementary School Teacher*. Salt Lake City, Utah: Olympus Publishing Company, 1973. A how-to-do-it book, beginning with basic principles, that covers grades K–6. Considerable emphasis is given to the part that home and community can play in career education. An invaluable reference for the student or teacher wanting to learn about and become involved in career education.

Hoyt, Kenneth B., and Jean Hebeler, eds. *Career Education for Gifted and Talented Students*. Salt Lake City, Utah: Olympus Publishing Company, 1974. A book based on presentations at a conference of national leaders highly qualified to deal with the career-education needs of the gifted and talented. Background concepts, exemplary programs, and implications for curriculum development are covered. The book makes an impressive case for the importance of career education for this group.

Hoyt, Kenneth, Rupert Evans, Garth Mangum, Ella Bowen, and Donald Gale. *Career Education in the High School*. Salt Lake City, Utah: Olympus Publishing Company, 1977. An important reference for those who are learning about secondary-level career education or who are involved in implementing it. Such major aspects as decision making, values clarification, and use of community resources are covered. Numerous illustrations of innovative practices and programs are included.

Marland, Sidney P. *Career Education.* New York: McGraw-Hill, 1977. A clear and comprehensive statement of the development and meaning of career education by the originator of the concept. A very important reference for the educator who wants to acquire an understanding of this dynamic and timely approach to education. The counselor's role is discussed on pp. 189–214.

Preli, Barbara Stock. *Career Education: Teaching/Learning Process.* Washington, D.C.: U.S. Government Printing Office, 1978. Particularly valuable for what it has to say about the teacher's role in career education, this monograph will be helpful in preparing counselors to work with teachers in threading career education into the curriculum.

Super, Donald E. *Career Education and the Meaning of Work.* Washington, D.C.: Department of Health, Education, and Welfare, 1976 (ED 128 593). A review of life stages, developmental tasks, career patterns, and their relation to career education. Includes a discussion of the meaning and importance of work for individuals at various occupational levels and those who are members of subgroups.

Valley, John R. *Career Education of Adults.* Washington, D.C.: U.S. Government Printing Office, 1977. An examination, with descriptions of practices, of career-development needs of adults, and recommendations for provisions of services. At this important level, career education is viewed as much more complex than for preadults.

Wirtz, Willard. *The Boundless Resource.* Washington, D.C.: The New Republic Book Company, 1975. One of the best available references on the community education-work councils, and excellent strategy to bring community resources into the career-education program. The recommendations on pp. 169–185 give strong support to the career-education concept.

11

Working with

Support Personnel

GOALS

1

To describe the helping roles that support personnel can
occupy in career guidance.

2

To promote an understanding of how counselors supervise the
work of support personnel.

3

To make the reader aware of the career-guidance functions that
support personnel can carry out.

4

To explain how support personnel are selected and prepared for
career-guidance functions.

5

To list programs in which support personnel are used.

THE USE OF SUPPORT PERSONNEL is a new approach to increasing the effectiveness of guidance workers and counselors. Support personnel have emerged in response to needs derived from the demands of special groups, the specialization of guidance tasks, the pressures of outreach in guidance, and public demands for accountability. It is somewhat surprising that this role is relatively new to the guidance profession, since it has a long history in other fields, particularly in the helping professions. It may be a sign of increasing professionalization and professional security, particularly in light of the timely demise of the slogan "Special guidance workers are not needed because every teacher is a counselor" (Hill, 1968, pp. 5–6). It is no longer a matter of whether or not to utilize support personnel but of *how* to use them (Samler, 1968b). Many schools are grappling with the problem of utilization of support personnel, and many others will soon follow. Part of the motivation is no doubt economic, but expanding the scope and increasing the efficiency of services are also major factors.

The NVGA/AVA and ACES position papers do not describe in detail the place of career-guidance support personnel, but their role is implied in a number of policy statements. The NVGA/AVA position paper identifies roles for parents, peers, and community volunteers (pp. 7–8). The cooperation of these persons can enhance the counselor's efforts, help bring school and community closer together, and provide the opportunity to teach others specific guidance techniques to use in helping relationships. The ACES position paper emphasizes the importance of collaborative relationships to thread career education into the curriculum, including work with many who are classified as support persons. In addition, the importance of preparing others to use counseling and guidance skills is emphasized (p. 177). Moreover, as discussed in Chapter 10, the use of support personnel in career education, regardless of setting, is widespread.

Wirtz (1975, pp. 40, 66, 68–69, 172) believes that support personnel should complement the counselor's work in helping pupils gain a realistic understanding of the world of work and assisting in managing information resources. The programs and strategies for bridging the gap described by Ferrin and Arbeiter (1975, Chap. 3) use support personnel in a number of ways, although their participation is not described in detail.

In addition, employment is provided for those who work in this capacity as they help to increase the efficiency and effectiveness of services; while assisting others, they may participate in therapeutic work experiences for themselves (Gatewood and Teare, 1976). Despite the potential for a substantial contribution to career guidance and counseling, however, the use of support personnel has not come up to expectations, due in part to shortcomings in job development and defining jobs in terms of the institutions' or agencies' goals (Gatewood and Teare, 1976).

The support-personnel role has not developed without controversy. Some of the earlier efforts were severely criticized (Odgers, 1964), just as stoutly defended (Gordon, 1965), and mediated (Hill, 1965). Conflicts arose over the preparation of guidance personnel for the Counselor Advisor University Summer Education, or CAUSE, program, sponsored by the Department of Labor, which utilized a relatively brief period of training, with the implied possibility of advancement through on-the-job experience. The issues have been more or less settled, at least for this type of program (APGA, 1965; Zimpfer, Frederickson, Salim, and Sanford, 1971, p. 3), but similar problems will doubtless arise from time to time as educators, counselors, and administrators hammer out the details of support personnel's preparation and employment. For example, the counseling profession has recently criticized the counseling offered in CETA programs, questioning its adequacy and the qualifications of its counselors. Recommendations have been made for greater use of the services of professional counselors in upgrading the quality of assistance (see p. 152).

The obvious need for support personnel in guidance counseling has led to preparation of a well-developed report by the American Personnel and Guidance Association on roles and training for support personnel (APGA, 1967) and establishment of a Committee on Support Personnel for Guidance in the School. This committee applied the principles of the APGA statement to school counseling. The resulting monograph, *Support Personnel in School Guidance Programs* (Zimpfer et al., 1971), along with the APGA guidelines, is the most useful reference on the subject for school counselors. These references are referred to frequently in this chapter.

SUPPORT PERSONNEL ROLES

A number of terms are used to characterize this role, among them *nonprofessional, subprofessional, paraprofessional, aide* (Zimpfer et al., 1971, p. 3), *occupational specialist* (Florida State Department of Education, 1971), *outreach liaison person,* and *community job adviser* (FPGA, 1971). Levels within the role have been suggested distinguishing simple tasks involving minimal contact with pupils from those requiring judgment and extensive interpersonal relations (Zimpfer et al., 1971, p. 3). *Support personnel* appears to be the name most widely used, most readily understood, and most accepted, and it will be used here to indicate all types.

The role is defined by guidelines, rather than a specific job description, in both the APGA statement and the resulting monograph. Its major identifying features, which could serve as a basis for a specific job description, are as follows: Support personnel

1. serve in a hierarchic relationship with the counselor and under his or her direct supervision.
2. carry out specific duties that contribute to the counseling function but do not involve counseling. Their responsibilities involve a limited aspect of the program while the counselor has overall responsibilities for supervision and planning.
3. are on a level below the counselor in the differentiated staffing pattern and are on a different level from clerical and secretarial personnel. The latter distinction is based on (a) the guidance orientation of their preparation, and (b) the guidance nature of their responsibilities.

4. carry out activities that involve the implementation of theory and research. A theoretical background is not essential for their work.

5. provide both indirect and direct help to pupils, parents, teachers, and others.

6. have different career patterns from counselors. The lines of advancement for support personnel do not routinely lead to professional counselor status; the individual must meet the orthodox requirements in order to become a counselor.[1]

The APGA statement and the resulting monograph represent the most lucid, up-to-date, and practical role statement available. The following discussion is based on those two publications.

Direct types of helping functions of support personnel are as follows:

Individual Interviewing Function
1. Secure information from an interviewee by means of a semi-structured or structured interview schedule. The information elicited would tend to be factual and limited in nature.

2. Give information prepared in advance and approved by the counselor for its appropriateness for the interviewee. Such information would usually be factual rather than interpretative.

3. Explain in practical lay terms the purposes and procedures involved in the services to the counselee.

4. Engage the counselee in informal, casual discussion as a means of putting him or her at ease and establishing an openness to counseling. Such a dyadic activity may be especially important when performed by an interviewer who is making initial contact with potential counselees who are hostile toward, or apprehensive of, counseling.

5. Provide informal follow-up support to a former counselee.

Small-Group Interviewing or Discussion Function
1. In structured groups with a largely preplanned program, guide discussion as a discussion leader.

2. Describe staff and material available to the group, an an information resource person, or tell the group how and where to acquire needed resources.

3. Act as recorder in a variety of small-group discussion or counseling situations, under the supervision of the counselor.

4. Observe verbal and nonverbal interaction in groups, following predetermined cues and procedures for making observations.

5. Participate in informal, superficial social conversation in a small group of counselees to help put them at ease and to establish the beginning of helping relationships that may be provided by forthcoming counseling.

[1] Adapted from David Zimpfer, Ronald Fredrickson, Mitchell Salim, and Alpheus Sanford, *Support Personnel in School Guidance Programs* (Washington, D.C.: American Personnel and Guidance Association, 1971), p. 4. Copyright 1971 by the American Personnel and Guidance Association. Adapted with permission.

6. Informally provide information and support to former counselees.

7. Perform outreach activities.[2]

These helping functions are characterized by either direct counselor supervision or the performance of a structured activity. They relate to many of the career-guidance and counseling responsibilities and functions discussed earlier and greatly expand the helping potential of the guidance service. The functions just listed are the most sensitive ones, because the support person deals face-to-face with the individuals to whom guidance assistance is provided.

Indirect activities make up the greater portion of the work. They are as follows:

Information-Gathering and Processing Function

1. Administer, score, and profile routine standardized tests and other appraisal instruments (nonclinical type).

2. Obtain and maintain routine information on the scope and character of the world of work with current reference to employment trends, in accordance with instructions established by the counselor.

3. Contact various sources for needed records and related information relevant to counseling.

4. Search for new sources of information about counselees and/or the environment, under direction of the counselor.

5. Prepare educational, occupational, and personal-social information for verbal and graphic presentation or transmittal to others for use in accordance with instructions established by the counselor.

6. Under the counselor's supervision, search for new sources to which the counselee may be referred.

7. Secure specific special information about former counselees on request and under the supervision of the counselor.

8. Operate technical communications media involving printed and electronic processes of a visual-auditory nature for the counselee's benefit.

Referral Function

1. Initiate general contacts with specific referral agencies.

2. Initiate contact for specific individuals with given referral agencies.

3. Aid individuals in making proper contact with referral agencies.

Placement and Routine Follow-up Function

1. Through appropriate channels, establish and maintain working relationships with organized placement agencies in the community.

[2]Adapted from APGA Sub-Committee on Support Personnel, "Support Personnel for the Counselor: Their Technical and Non-Technical Roles and Preparation," *Personnel and Guidance Journal,* 45, (1967), 860–861. Copyright 1967 by the American Personnel and Guidance Association. Adapted with permission.

2. Develop specific placement opportunities (under the supervision of the counselor) for the individual cases not handled through cooperation with other placement agencies.

3. Maintain continuous surveys of placement conditions and trends as requested by the counselor.

4. Search for new placement resources that may be useful to counselees.

5. Secure follow-up information of a routine nature according to a general follow-up plan.

Program Planning and Management Function
1. Perform routine collecting and analytical statistical operations as a research assistant.

2. Procure and prepare supplies of materials of various sorts for the counselor.

3. Prepare standardized reports of contacts with counselees, potential counselees, and referral, placement, and follow-up agencies and persons.

4. Maintain appropriate personnel and information records for the counselor.

5. Supervise and coordinate the activities of clerical or other skilled personnel under the general supervision of the counselor.[3]

These functions are heavily bound up with career guidance and consume a considerable amount of the counselor's time. With support personnel assistance, much could be done that previously could not even have been attempted. For example, extensive use could be made of local information; surveys, follow-ups, and identification of community resources would be possible and practical.

In planning the work of the support personnel, the three-level design of Zimpfer, Frederickson, Salim, and Sanford (1971, p. 38) is extremely helpful. Using the scale categories of *people, data, knowledge,* and *autonomy,* they arrange activities according to their level of complexity and extent of contacts with others. For example, Level I in the people category involves data *about* pupils. Posting test results in the cumulative record is an illustrative task. Level II could involve preparing or collecting materials to be used by others with counselees. For example, the support person might contact the administrative office, or the office of a school previously attended, to collect needed pupil records. At Level III, the support person could engage in face-to-face contact with those from whom appraisal data are collected. For example, he or she might use a series of questions to obtain factual and specific information from a pupil, parent, or teacher.

Using the ten areas of professional responsibility of the school counselor—for example, counseling, pupil appraisal, and placement—Zimpfer, Frederickson, Salim, and Sanford (1971, pp. 56–62) have suggested duties for support personnel at each of the three levels. This breakdown should be familiar to every counselor planning to work with, or currently working with, support personnel.

---

[3]"Support Personnel for the Counselor," pp. 860–861.

SUPPORT PERSONNEL FUNCTIONS

The direct and indirect functions listed earlier suggest specific types of activities the support personnel can undertake to help with career counseling and guidance. The monograph *Support Personnel in School Guidance Programs* (Zimpfer et al., 1971, pp. 56–62) provides the most complete list available and indicates the relative frequency of tasks. The greatest number involve educational and occupational planning, with counseling second, and pupil appraisal third. As the level increases, that is, as support personnel become more competent, the number of suggested counseling and educational and occupational information tasks increases, but the number of pupil-appraisal tasks decreases (Zimpfer et al., 1971, p. 40).

Counselor reactions also suggest services that would provide assistance. A random sample 5 percent of the members of the American School Counselor Association showed enthusiastic support for this role, with the strongest preference for functions that provide indirect help to the counselee, such as obtaining information. The least preferred single item was planning specific referrals (Zimpfer et al., p. 30). Clearly, counselor reactions suggest that they might keep support personnel from engaging in face-to-face counseling-like activities. But the range of responses is revealing. Almost half the respondents considered the lowest ranked task of all a suitable activity for support personnel! It might be expected that close cooperative working relationships, plus clear-cut delineation of roles, would lead to increased opportunity for face-to-face work with pupils, parents, teachers, and employers. This has certainly been the case in most situations I have observed in the occupational specialist program.

Handling Information

In the discussion of the information system, the assistance of support personnel was mentioned. This service is essential for career guidance and it consumes an inordinate amount of the counselor's time if undertaken even minimally. This assistance is not busywork to keep the support person out of the way and occupied. Collecting, organizing, and disseminating career information, as well as being a vital service, immeasurably broadens the knowledge of the assistant. Although the support person has typically had work experience outside the schools, he or she has often been engaged in a narrow range of occupations. Ordering and classifying printed material, setting up an occupational file, and reviewing film strips and slides tend to give a support person a broad understanding of the world of work. The support person soon becomes the expert on where to find what. He or she will be called on by pupils, teachers, and counselors for all sorts of information. If systems like VIEW or computers are available, a support person can provide the needed orientation and instructions for pupils, relieving the counselor of this responsibility.

Collection of local information is an opportunity par excellence for the support person to assist the counselor and extend the scope of the guidance service. Contacts with referral resources can be made, working relations established, and referral guidelines agreed on. In fact, support personnel can be quite helpful with both referral and follow-up. For example, the support person may actually accompany the counselee to the employment service if this appears desirable. Contacts with employers, collection of information about training and educational opportunities, and job development for difficult-to-place students are additional tasks the support person can undertake that augment the local aspect of the guidance service.

If the support person becomes the expert on information, there may be both positive and negative concomitants. On the positive side are the feelings of importance and satisfaction that accrue from this status. I have observed this phenomenon over and over again. On the negative side, however, the counselor may feel increasingly left out, particularly if others go first to the support person for current and comprehensive information. The negative aspects need not arise, however. If information-getting activities are jointly planned and if the information is recorded, for example, on a form or card for use by all guidance personnel, it will not be the sole province of one individual. All play a part in planning the system, and all know what is available. Recording the data may seem an onerous task to some support personnel (and to some counselors) but it is strongly recommended. It will help the counselor and support personnel be collaborators, rather than competitors, in learning about opportunities in the community, and in getting the greatest possible benefit from the data.

Both policy and practice suggest that dissemination is an appropriate function for the support person. It offers a tremendous range of ways for support personnel to assist the counselor. Activities range from preparing materials for teachers and counselors to leading a group guidance discussion. Some individuals have expressed considerable apprehension about acceptance by pupils and teachers in group sessions because of lack of formal education and teaching credentials. As a rule, these feelings are quickly dispelled once the sessions begins. Acceptance and enthusiasm are usually quite apparent. Even so, not all support personnel like all activities equally well. Several with whom I am acquainted enjoy taking an active part in an assembly or other large group program. Others much prefer to work directly with individuals and small groups. Still others obtain their greatest satisfaction from going out into the community to help dropouts and follow up those placed in jobs or training situations. It is certainly desirable to consider the support person's competences and preferences when planning functions. Further, support and encouragement to try new activities may be helpful. I have been repeatedly struck by the potential of support personnel, once they get their bearings in the new job and begin to feel they are accomplishing something worthwhile. They can do an astonishing variety of highly demanding tasks with skill and enthusiasm.

Helping with Local Surveys

Closely akin to information collecting is participation in local occupational and educational surveys. It was suggested in discussion of the information system that the counselor defer involvement in a community survey until other activities of higher priority are completed. But if the services of support personnel are available, surveys can be made much sooner.

Planning a survey is a good way for the counselor and support persons to develop good working relationships. Much of the planning and implementation could be supervised by the support personnel. For example, they could follow up nonrespondents to mailed questionnaires or reschedule interviews for those who were missed in a personal-contact survey. Tabulating results, preparing visual aids, and assembling the report could also be supervised by support personnel, but they should not be saddled with clerical work. Their guidance orientation and preparation makes them more valuable in other functions. Furthermore, it is important to maintain a distinction between clerical workers and support personnel for the latter's morale. Support personnel suitable for a guidance role tend to dislike detailed clerical work and to feel that they are relegated to a decidely inferior role when they are required to do it. (The morale of the clerical staff is important, too, but this is the type of work for which they were employed.)

A specialized type of survey might serve as a start. One school district used support personnel to interview employers about entry jobs. Not all local businesses and industries were covered, but enough of a start was made to broaden the interviewers' perspectives and to collect very useful guidance information. In another situation, local training opportunities were surveyed. Those taking part managed to spend considerable time talking with students and learned much more about the programs than was contained in catalogues and brochures.

One of the most persistent (and justified) complaints of counselors is that they do not have the time to survey local occupational and training opportunities, including the follow-up of students who have gone into work or training in the community. The use of support personnel will help make it possible to carry out these essential guidance functions.

Helping with Placement

An increasingly critical attitude toward education and guidance has given these two functions prominence. Whether we like it or not, guidance services are expected to provide placement and to do at least some evaluation of the actual suitability of job or training plans. In my opinion, these are the two most valuable services support personnel can provide. A school may have an excellent career-education program and high quality of guidance and counseling services, do an excellent job helping pupils select and gain admission to colleges, and assist a sizable number to enter suitable vocational-training programs, but if graduates cannot find suitable jobs the program's success is endangered. One frequently voiced question about career education is whether or not jobs will actually be available when pupils have completed the work. This question is often directed at the guidance service.

The guidance department and support personnel cannot ordinarily manufacture jobs. (As a matter of fact, they *can,* to some extent. Programs like JOBS and NYC provide *new* jobs. Guidance personnel might help initiate such a program locally.) But they can locate existing opportunities, become active in job development, and help pupils obtain placement. This is a time-consuming and demanding function. Job openings change rapidly. Continued contact must be maintained with employers. Good school-employer relations depend on referral of qualified applicants. Thus, the placement worker must not only have good contacts with employers but also be able to interpret job requirements in terms of pupil qualifications.

The placement function also involves interpretation of job requirements in terms of school programs. Often, the problem is not a dearth of jobs but a lack of qualified workers. In some cases, changes in, or additions to, the school program will enable pupils to qualify for local jobs they could not otherwise obtain. Additional work at the vocational-technical center or the community college may be needed. A well-organized placement service can inform pupils of the needed qualifications and help them plan to reach the required level of proficiency.

Maintaining up-to-date placement information and conducting follow-ups could be major responsibilities of the support personnel. These functions should be combined, because placement visits to an establishment provide the opportunity to check on the progress of earlier placements. Although some placements will result from decision making in counseling, many will be made without such help. Support personnel, therefore, should be able to meet with pupils to find out the sorts of jobs or training they want and their qualifications and should be competent to follow through with the actual placement. That is, they should be able to operate on their own, within the framework of established policy and procedures.

Helping with Community Relations

All activities that put the guidance staff in contact with the community have an impact on community relations. Those that bring parents and other community persons to the school are extremely important, but those that carry some aspect of the school program to the community may be the most significant. It is in the latter type of activity that support persons can make their greatest contribution. First, much of what they do will take them into the community, increase the visibility of the guidance service, and promote the belief that the school is interested in, and concerned about, the community. Second, in many if not most cases, support persons will have a rapport with community members that many educators do not. Their backgrounds and experiences may be similar. It does not seem essential that they be indigenous to the community, unless they are working in a particularly alienated subculture, but they must be able to communicate with individuals from a wide range of occupations and socioeconomic levels.

Specific activities the support person may undertake to enhance community relations primarily involve helping community residents and involving the community in the helping process. There are others, of course, such as appearing before groups to describe the guidance program, preparing displays and news releases, and assisting with television programs. More impact, however, results from what guidance personnel, including the support personnel, *do* than from what they *say* they do.

It is important that the support person understand the school and the guidance program and realize that every task he or she carries out is, in effect, a form of public relations. Thus, attitudes about work as well as status in the program are important.

One support person who felt isolated and insignificant at his school was heard to comment several times, "I don't know what's going on up there (in the school). They're always going around in circles and nobody tells me anything!" It is not difficult to imagine the image these comments evoked in community members.

In sum, outreach activities are the most effective way for support personnel to help the counselor build good community relations. Planning is needed to establish priorities and to insure counselor–support personnel cooperation.

CHOOSING AND TRAINING

Preparation has a bearing on selection. Support personnel may be selected to perform specific duties, work at different levels, or utilize skills or attributes they already have. In some situations, job duties are grouped by level of difficulty, and support personnel are employed to handle the simpler ones. In others, client need is the basis for jobs; the result is usually more varied and interesting occupations for support personnel (Gatewood and Teare, 1976).

For general selection purposes, criteria include the potential ability to perform specific duties; the capacity to work with counselors, counselees, and others in the specific job setting; and liking for this type of activity (APGA, 1967). Academic ability and achievement should not be general admission criteria.

Training programs vary considerably. Zimpfer, Frederickson, Salim, and Sanford (1971, pp. 13–16) report examples of brief preservice and in-service preparation, summer college work preceding in-service education, and two-year college programs. There is a definite lack of consistency in patterns of preparation.

In-Service Training

The preservice phase, when it exists, is often relatively brief, and the in-service portion is longer and more critical (APGA, 1967). The latter should be carefully planned to include practice, laboratory work, and a final field experience under counselor supervision (APGA, 1967). The training program described by Carlson, Cavins, and Dinkmeyer (1969) developed for the Deerfield School District Project illustrates these points. The "guidance assistants" in this project were at a more advanced academic level than is usually expected of support personnel (the bachelor's degree and teacher certification), but their on-the-job preparation followed a pattern applicable to other groups. The yearlong program began in the fall with orientation to the school district, referral agencies, specific schools, and pupil personnel teams. The assistants were then given classroom instruction, in part by members of the pupil personnel teams. Three graduate-level courses were also included in the program, for enrichment and to motivate the assistants to continue their education. A particularly interesting feature of the in-service part of the program was the use of simulation and feedback to develop skill in specific tasks prior to engaging in them.

The in-service preparation of the paraprofessionals in the Detroit Career Guidance Project (Schlossberg, Woodruff, and Leonard, 1971, p. 16) primarily involved participation on a team composed of a professional guidance consultant, a support person, and student clerical assistants. Roles such as the "bridge" role were formulated, and assignments were given for in-service education (Schlossberg et al., 1971, pp. 31–32; Leonard and Vriend, 1975). This preparation program allowed for immediate involvement utilizing the support person's previous knowledge of the inner-city neighborhood and its residents, with less emphasis on previous academic qualifications and achievement. Both this and the Deerfield project illustrate the importance of selecting support personnel for the specific tasks to be accomplished.

Preparation programs for the "occupational specialist" (Legislature of the State of Florida, 1970; Florida State Department of Education, 1971) have generally involved a week or so of preschool orientation covering such topics as school organization, community resources, role definition, and human relations. Preservice preparation, however, is not required by state guidelines. The major emphasis is on in-service training, in programs developed by local school districts and involving cooperation with local colleges, other education units, industries, and businesses. Districts may develop cooperative plans. This program will be discussed further later in this chapter.

The most helpful guidelines for the preparation of support personnel are contained in the monograph by Zimpfer, Frederickson, Salim, and Sanford (1971, pp. 40–43). They emphasize a training rationale flexible enough to take into account trainees' different backgrounds; permitting preparation at levels I, II, or III; focusing on specific tasks; and utilizing nontraditional teaching approaches, such as simulation, laboratory practice, and self-evaluation. The participation of counselors—those with whom support persons will work—is essential. Both pre- and in-service training are needed. Considerable attention should be given to making support persons feel important and accepted and to helping them perceive their work as significant for the school.

Three major training phases are suggested. Human relations skills, clerical and audio-visual skills, and guidance skills—the first being most basic—are fundamental. Much of the training in the other skills should be tailored to the specific situation. For example, in a particular school it may be necessary to learn to assist with life career games, contact employers about job openings, or help pupils learn how to conduct themselves during a job interview. The authors state that their model is designed for a short summer training period followed by a year of in-service work. An individual starting at Level I could conceivably reach Level III by the third year.

The listing of activities by levels and counselor functions and the proficiency check list given in Zimpfer et al. (1971, pp. 56–64) are invaluable guides for the counselor who is developing a training program. They should be carefully reviewed, along with local needs, in setting up such a program.

Counselor Supervision

It is generally agreed that the bulk of preparation should be done on the job. Some state guidance supervisors feel that training should utilize a joint team approach involving counselor educators, state department of education personnel, and counselors (Zimpfer et al., 1971, p. 27). But Jones and Cox (1970) found that counselors, counselor educators, and guidance directors would prefer to assign the major training role to the school counselor. Exceptions were in-group and individual counseling, but these were considered appropriate for support personnel by only a small percentage of respondents. Consultants provide an outsider's view, which can be quite valuable in resolving conflicts, clarifying roles, and detecting program strengths and weaknesses. The major responsibility for supervision, follow-up, and climate setting, however, will still be the counselor's. The most critical phase of the preparation, the practical experience, or practicum, is directly under the counselor's supervision. It is reasonable to assume that the counselor's day-to-day supervision is the most significant aspect of training.

Building rapport and providing a climate in which the support person feels important, worthy, and accepted are prerequisites to in-service education. In one program that I observed, much of the preservice discussion centered on acceptance by the school staff, particularly by the counselor. Though some counselors, principals, and superintendents did take part in the training program, the apprehension of the new support personnel, many of whom had had no academic work beyond high school, was not reduced. Their feelings were not entirely without basis, however, Many counselors had heard on the grapevine that they might be replaced by support personnel. Their feelings were somewhat like those described elsewhere (Grosser, 1969; Zimpfer et al., 1971, pp. 16–18): threat, defensiveness, and anxiety, particularly when support personnel dealt directly with pupils and others.

Just as has been reported for other programs (Zimpfer et al., 1971, pp. 17–21), however, close working relationships, the opportunity to discuss feelings and attitudes, and the pressure to search for answers to common problems tended to dispel these initial negative feelings. The early preparation of a role statement or job description, worked out jointly by counselors and support personnel, is one way to help build cooperative working relationships. Another is to set up a mutually satisfactory system of keeping the counselor informed about the support person's activities. A third is to insure that hierarchical lines are followed in supervision and assignment of duties—for example, that the principal does not bypass the counselor to deal directly with the support personnel.

An approach that is particularly relevant to teaching interviewing and human relations skills should be mentioned. *Microcounseling* has been shown to be effective for developing three basic human relations skills: "attending behavior," "expression of feeling," and "reflection of feeling" (Haase and DiMattia, 1970). Because proficiency tends to decrease over time (Haase, DiMattia, and Guttman, 1972), methods of continuous reinforcement need to be investigated. There is evidence that lay counselors (support personnel) can develop facilitative skills (Carkhuff, 1968) and can help others and achieve personal growth in the process (Carkhuff and Griffin, 1970). The procedures used involved scales developed to rate facilitative conditions, immediate feedback, and focus on specific human relations skills. Although these skills are generally regarded as important to the work of support personnel, additional areas of knowledge and competence are needed for help with career development and guidance.

PROGRAMS USING SUPPORT PERSONNEL

The most comprehensive reviews of programs involving support personnel are by Grosser (1968, 1969) and Zimpfer, Frederickson, Salim, and Sanford (1971, pp. 12–16). The former deals primarily with community agencies; although it is recommended reading, it is not as directly relevant to this chapter as the latter. Only a few school programs are covered. The authors of the APGA monograph report that a recent nationwide study identified fewer than 150 support personnel for survey purposes (Zimpfer et al., 1971, p. 12). More recently, support persons have been used in increasing numbers in information services (Chapter 5), career education (Chapter 10), and placement (Chapter 12). The following are examples, some current and some older, of effective programs.

Detroit, Michigan

Support personnel play a significant role in the Detroit Development Guidance Project (Hansen, 1970, pp. 23–27; Schlossberg, Woodruff, and Leonard, 1971). The program was designed to help inner-city Detroit pupils raise and broaden their career and training goals, to develop a model for educational-career guidance for inner-city pupils in grades 1–12, to involve school personnel in cooperative planning and development, and to evaluate the model through systematic study of pupil plans and attitudes (Monacel, Fort, and Sloan, n.d., p. 7).

Two types of support personnel are used: student aides and adult community aides. A training workbook on roles based on project staff experiences has been prepared. The staff recommends that the training of support personnel involve counselors and that it be continuous, on-the-job, and utilize action-type experiences (Schlossberg et al., 1971, p. 3). The role of support personnel (they use the term *paraprofessionals*) is succinctly described. Called *career community aides,* their main function is to work with parents and the community. Providing liaison between the school career-guidance program and the community, a function for which they are uniquely well equipped, is their major responsibility. Each school's team is made up of a professional guidance consultant; a support person who is a qualified, deserving pupil from the senior high school serving in a half-time liaison and clerical capacity; and a second support person, an unemployed community adult who serves as liaison with pupils, parents, and community agencies (Schlossberg et al., 1971, p. 16). Some of the activities of these aides emphasize the "bridge" role; they organize parent groups, accompany pupils on field trips, assist with occupational surveys, and perform clerical work.

The roles of support personnel are as follows:

1. THE BRIDGE ROLE   Serving as the link between the community and the school
2. THE PROGRAMMER ROLE   Developing programs based on what parents and the community need to know
3. THE GUIDANCE ROLE   Helping through listening, reflecting, suggesting, and referral to the counselor or a helping agent

4. THE CLERICAL ROLE   Helping the counselor to keep files in order, preparing
bulletin boards, and similar activities (Schlossberg et al., 1971, pp. 30–41)

Evaluations have revealed positive results for the experimental schools compared
with control schools. Pupils exhibit a significant rise in level of aspiration, show
more growth in occupational knowledge and planning, re-examine their values
more, show a more acceptable attitude toward counselors, demonstrate gains in
achievement, and reveal a greater need for professional assistance. They perceive
information as more readily available and also state that they have been helped to
learn about employment opportunities (Schlossberg et al., 1971, pp. 26–27;
Leonard and Vriend, 1975). Although the support personnel were not specifically
evaluated, it seems reasonable to infer that they were a major factor in the positive
results.

Programs for Occupational Specialists and Human Services Aides

Two programs I have observed prepare occupational specialists (Legislature of the
State of Florida, 1970; Florida State Department of Education, 1917) and human
services associates (Lynch and Wehn, 1972). To some extent, these two programs
represent the extremes in support personnel concepts. The first was established by
the Florida legislature out of concern about the dearth of counselors, "academic bias"
on the part of those serving in the schools as well as in counselor-preparation
programs, and lack of attention to the job and to training-bound students. There
was a feeling, too, that many counselors lacked work experience in other than
educational settings.

One factor in starting the program that caused considerable concern and
resentment on the part of counselors was the policy statement that occupational
specialists could be used to replace up to 50 percent of the guidance workers in a
district. This limit was later removed. Much effort had to be devoted to ameliorating
the negative effects of this policy and to dealing with the hostilities engendered.

The suggested duties of the occupational specialist focus on career guidance, job
placement, and follow-up of those entering work or training. Each district is
required to establish a training program, which is then approved by the Florida State
Department of Education. The guidelines are quite permissive; no overall model
program has yet been prepared, although several demonstration training programs
have been funded by the state. New training modules covering basic competencies
have, however, been distributed by the state office to all counties (Rand, 1979).
Some counties have joined together to provide pre- and in-service education. Some
teaching modules have been prepared by the Department of Education—for
example, on the use of the *Occupational Outlook Handbook*.

In 1976 there were approximately six hundred occupational specialists in the
state, with personnel in practically every county. Process and product evaluations
indicate that the program has reached a sizable number of pupils and has been of
substantial assistance to them.

A recent survey ("Occupational Specialists Identify Training Needs," 1978) revealed that occupational specialists feel they need more training in relation to pupils, particularly the socially deprived, emotionally disturbed, and handicapped. In-service programs have been instituted to meet these needs.

A program that uses occupational specialists, Comprehensive Humanistic Oriented Implementation of Career Education, or CHOICE, was established in Pasco County, Florida, to combat the high dropout rate (Panther, 1975). Occupational specialists staff the career-education element; other components are guidance (staffed by counselors), reading, and media (staffed by specialists in these areas). Counselors emphasize consultation with occupational specialists and teachers about guidance procedures and individual and group counseling for pupils. Although the support personnel had some preparation for the career-guidance functions they carried out and were supervised by counselors, the latter should have been more directly involved in career-education activities. To put full responsibility for this element on support personnel implies that career guidance and career education are not as complex or significant as other aspects of the helping process. Although available evidence suggests that the support personnel do an effective job with the career-guidance function, current policy makes it clear that the counselor has significant participation and leadership roles to play.

The other program prepares mental-health support personnel to serve in community agencies, schools, colleges, hospitals, and other institutions and service agencies. The program is conducted by Santa Fe Community College, Gainesville, Florida, and has been in operation since 1973. Trainees go through an intensive program of group work, including laboratory experiences with feedback, and also take academic courses in psychology and related subjects. The focus is on developing sensitivity to others and becoming a facilitator for individual and group growth. Career guidance as such is not part of the preparation. A considerable amount of research is built in to evaluate the effectiveness of the instructional program and to identify and validate promotion and graduation criteria.

Students engage in practicums early in the program; those who have progressed sufficiently may do so in community agencies and schools. Toward the end of the program, the practicum and intern emphases are increased. Students work full-time in agencies but continue to attend regular weekly supervision meetings conducted by staff members. Self-selection is emphasized. The attrition rate is fairly high, largely as a result of trainees' decisions that the role is not one they want to fill.

Other Programs

Hopke (1976) describes several programs using support personnel in innovative ways. In one, the New York State Bureau of Guidance investigated using counselor assistants in secondary schools. The program goals were to prepare support personnel to take over the less demanding tasks from the counselor, to identify those who could profit from the training, to provide tasks suitable for support personnel to carry out, and to define the role of counselor assistant as contrasted with those of counselor and clerk. The study showed that the supervising counselors' role was to develop suitable activities to help solve problems that arose and to encourage the assistants to participate in professional meetings.

In another program, efforts were directed at improving guidance services in San Francisco high schools using volunteers. The major purpose of the volunteers was to provide an informal drop-in college and career information service and a place to discuss problems. Results indicated that this use of volunteer support personnel is feasible, that staff and students utilize them, and that flexibility is necessary for successful operation. Hopke concludes that support personnel are here to stay and their number will grow substantially.

Career-guidance programs for adults—women, minorities, and mid-career changers—use support personnel for a substantial part of their service. Much of this type of help is by peers who do not have formal counselor preparation but who have backgrounds similar to those of counselees. Some specific training for the task is provided; empathy, understanding, ability to relate to other adults, and knowledge of career development are considered the needed competencies (Harrison and Entine, 1976).

The use of school and college students as support personnel is a new development in helping services. The major focus is on personal and social competence, and less attention is given to career development (Tolbert, 1978, pp. 239–251). Some programs, however, have emphasized educational development. Brown (1965) describes a student-led first year college group-counseling program that resulted in improved marks. Student counselors were carefully selected and prepared to handle a structured program. Lobitz (1970) describes a high school group-counseling program in which seniors enrolled in independent study programs tutored failing pupils. The percentage of those receiving passing grades was much greater for the experimental (coached) group than for the control group. Though the number of pupils involved was small, the project illustrates an innovative way to provide learning experiences for both advanced pupils and those experiencing academic difficulties.

A variety of other programs use pupils, graduate students, and parents as support personnel. Jacobson (1972) rates both parents and pupils as very helpful in operating career-development centers in San Diego. Volunteer parents and pupils provide information and refer users to available facilities. Several different types of staffing patterns have been used in these centers, with the number running a center ranging from one support person to fourteen individuals, including counselors and various categories of support personnel, such as student assistants and community volunteers (Hopke, 1976). The use of support personnel is considered essential for effective staffing of the career centers, and full-time assignment is more desirable than part-time utilization. For one thing, pupils make greater use of full-time than part-time staff support personnel. In addition, many of the essential activities, such as updating information files and organizing programs, require continuity on the job. It was also concluded that counselor supervision is essential; support personnel alone cannot be expected to manage all career-center activities.

Graduate students have provided career counseling services on a "circuit rider" basis to small rural schools in New Mexico with very positive results (Cross, 1970). A number of programs have also used pupils as helpers. The psychological education program described by Mosher and Sprinthall (1971) used pupils to counsel peers. At the college level in connection with a personality course, student-led groups were rated as good learning experiences; the student leaders were judged very effective and were well accepted by faculty members conducting the same kinds of groups (Wrenn and Mencke, 1972). Mitchell, Rubin, Bozarth, and Wyrick (1971) point out the increasing use of students to counsel other students and describe a short-term training program that helped dormitory counselors improve their ability to provide empathic understanding.

SUMMARY

In recent years, support personnel have emerged on the guidance scene. Controversy has surrounded their preparation and role, but guidelines have been formulated to provide for their effective use in guidance and counseling settings. Career-guidance functions such as handling information and helping with local surveys, placement, and community relations have been discussed in this chapter. Training models involving levels of preparation have been described, and the importance of close supervision by the counselor has been discussed. Finally, several programs involving support personnel in career guidance have been described.

PROJECTS AND EXPERIENTIAL ACTIVITIES

1. Interview a counselor about his or her definition of the term *support personnel* and his or her feelings about utilizing them. You might have the opportunity to interview a counselor who is working with a support person. If so, also interview the support person about his or her role definition and satisfactions and dissatisfactions with the work.

2. Visit a program that prepares support personnel (of any type, such as teacher aides or medical services aides), perhaps in a community college. Observe the program and inquire about the focus of the training.

3. List the functions carried out by a guidance or counseling service, such as a high school guidance service, a college counseling and placement center, or a rehabilitation agency. List the functions that could be undertaken by a support person who has had a brief period of specific training.

4. Role-play the following situation in small groups: Half of the group members are counselors on the staff of the educational institution or community agency. The other half are new support personnel in their first orientation meeting with counselors. First, all group members select the setting and describe it briefly. Then play the roles for a short period of time. Next, counselors assume that you are now in a supervision session with the support persons. Select a problem, topic, or issue with which to deal (for example, a problem that counselors have noted, a

difficulty experienced by support personnel, a question about policy raised by support personnel). Play roles in this situation for a few minutes. At the conclusion, "counselors" and "support personnel" should discuss the positive and negative aspects of both sessions. How could the sessions be made more productive?

5. Invite a group of support personnel from schools, colleges, or community agencies to meet with the class. Ask them to present a panel discussion on the topic "I wish counselors would. . . ." Follow the presentations with questions and discussion. At the conclusion, ask for summaries of what was learned.

6. Form small, role-playing groups, half of which are counselors and half of which are support persons, and discuss the following two issues:

a. No advancement is possible for support personnel.

b. Support personnel feel that they are just as proficient as counselors in working with individuals and small groups. Thus, they need no specified amount of supervision.

Be prepared to present your views to the other groups. After positions have been discussed in the small groups, present them to the whole class. When the presentations are finished, share the feelings you have experienced in formulating a position and listening to those of other groups.

ADDITIONAL REFERENCES

Delworth, Ursula, ed. "The Paraprofessionals are Coming!" *Personnel and Guidance Journal,* 53, No. 4 (1974), 250. This is a special issue of the *Personnel and Guidance Journal* that deals with support personnel. Three articles discuss the movement, six describe programs, three deal with training, three cover new roles and opinions of support personnel, and a final one is on needed improvements. Few of these articles, deal specifically with career development, but the principles, guidelines, and practices discussed in other articles are applicable to the subject of career development.

Feild, Hubert S., and Robert Gatewood. "The Paraprofessionals and the Organization." *Personnel and Guidance Journal,* 55, No. 4 (1976), 181–185. This article deals with the problem of the career development of paraprofessionals themselves and offers a number of suggestions for their more effective participation in the work of the school or agency. Very useful for anyone working with support personnel.

Grosser, Charles. "The Role of the Nonprofessional in the Manpower Development Programs." In *Counseling the Disadvantaged Youth.* Eds. William E. Amos and Jean Dresden Grambs. Englewood Cliffs, N.J.: Prentice-Hall, 1968, pp. 291–320. This is an excellent summary of the use of support personnel in community programs, many of which emphasize career guidance. Selection, training, and problems in work relationships are covered.

————. "Using the Nonprofessional." In *Breakthrough for Disadvantaged Youth.*

U.S. Department of Labor, Washington, D.C.: U.S. Government Printing Office, 1969, pp. 213–232. This reference contains substantially the same information as "The Role of the Nonprofessional in the Manpower Development Programs" (1968).

Hansen, Lorraine Sundal. *Career Guidance Practices in School and Community.* Washington, D.C.: National Vocational Guidance Association, 1970, Chaps. 2 and 3. A number of career-guidance programs are described, including many in which support personnel are used. Although the role of support personnel in each is covered only briefly, ways in which they may participate in career-development and guidance programs are suggested. It is also possible to identify functions and services that could be handled by support personnel if they were used.

Tolbert, E. L. *An Introduction to Guidance.* Boston: Little, Brown, 1978. Chap. 12, "Support Personnel and Expanded Service," provides an overview of the use of support personnel, including a summary of research studies on their effectiveness. Some attention is given to their use in career guidance.

Zimpfer, David, Ronald Frederickson, Mitchell Salim, and Alpheus Sanford. *Support Personnel in School Guidance Programs.* Washington, D.C.: American Personnel and Guidance Association, 1971. This excellent publication is a must for every counselor who is working with support personnel or expects to do so. It is appropriate as assigned reading in counselor-education programs.

12

Placement Counseling

GOALS

1
To discuss the differing views of placement by educational
institutions.

2
To discuss the various types of placement.

3
To explain how placement and decision-making counseling
are related.

4
To describe how a placement service may be established
and maintained.

5
To make the student aware of various ways in which placement
services are provided.

ONLY A FEW YEARS AGO, in the first edition of this book, placement was described as the most controversial topic covered in the discussion of career guidance and career development. The situation has changed radically. Where placement already was a major factor, expansion has taken place. Additional emphasis has been provided in the community through CETA programs. Many colleges and universities are upgrading placement services by providing a developmental emphasis, by offering training in job-getting skills, and by increased use of technology, as in computer matching of student and employer.

The greatest change has taken place at the school level. There has been an upsurge in school placement services; some states have instituted mandatory placement services (*Guidelines for Placement Services and Follow-Up Studies,* 1973; Ferrin and Arbeiter, 1975, pp. 38–40; Harris, 1977). Almost half the nation's school districts now have some kind of placement service, over 90 percent provide referral to job openings, almost the same percentage teach job-search techniques, and more than half make an effort to identify jobs for pupils (Wiggins, 1978). Over half the districts with placement programs reported that they were initiated in the past five years ("Washington Briefs," 1977, p. 785). Increasingly, placement is recognized as an aspect of career education (Fuller, 1972; Moore, 1972; Buckingham and Lee, 1973; Ferrin and Arbeiter, 1975, pp. 1–4). A critical feature of this new model for education will be the success of graduates in finding suitable employment.

Wirtz (1975, pp. 58–59, 65) highlights the need for placement services in his advocacy of community education-work councils; full use should be made of both school and community resources to "ferry people . . . across the gap between education and employment" (p. 65). Moreover, he recommends that laws, practices, and customs that restrict the employment of individuals be carefully studied to determine changes that may be needed (pp. 175–176).

Professional position papers emphasize the crucial role placement plays in bridging the gap between school and work or further education or training. The NVGA/AVA position paper recommends only that the guidance team coordinate a school job-placement program. The ACES position paper, however, points out that, regardless of setting, counselors should have knowledge about "job-placement services and the skills necessary to assist clients to seek, acquire, and maintain employment"[1] (p. 177). Counselors should be able to design and implement job-placement programs in educational and community agency settings, help counselees use community placement resources, conduct follow-up programs to evaluate the suitability of placements, and assist with needed job adjustment (Hansen, 1978).

There are clear indications that placement, particularly that which is aimed at helping young people make the transition from education to work, has tremendous support from a wide range of persons and institutions. In addition, the need of older groups for services are becoming widely recognized. Placement today is much more than a service for helping with initial entry into the world of work.

---

[1] L. Sunny Hansen "ACES Position Paper: Counselor Preparation for Career Development/Career Education" *Counselor Education and Supervision,* Vol. 17, No. 3, 1978, pp. 168–179. Copyright 1978 American Personnel and Guidance Association. Used by permission.

IS PLACEMENT THE SCHOOL'S BUSINESS?

Most school-leavers need placement assistance, but counselors often seem unaware of the magnitude of this problem. The majority of pupils, both graduates and dropouts, move directly into the world of work. The percentages vary strikingly from school to school, but overall more go to work, or look for work, than enter any kind of post–high school training or education. As the world of work becomes more complex, involves more specialization, and is increasingly subject to unpredictable changes, the task of finding a job becomes more demanding.

Many counselors have not personally experienced this difficulty to an appreciable degree. Early in the 1970s, the demand for counseling and guidance personnel exceeded the supply; quite often, the employer took the initiative in seeking out prospects. Furthermore, extensive and well-developed placement services were available through colleges and professional organizations. The sophistication of graduate students equipped them to make contacts, plan strategies, and find job openings. Only recently, with the levelling off of job opportunities, have some counselors experienced what is commonplace in many other fields of working—the need to search for a job opening, compete for it with a number of other qualified applicants, and cope with rejection after rejection. As one counselor said, "I'm supposed to be able to help other people get jobs and I don't know how to find one for myself!"

Critics of the schools have stated that education is the only "industry" that is not interested in its product. This is an exaggeration, but there is enough truth in the accusation for it to hurt. Although substantial interest is frequently demonstrated in the success of the "product" in college, there are other "products" who merit concern. The criticism is deserved unless the school helps all pupils successfully take the next step.

Vocational-development theory supports the occupational-placement concept. The level of vocational development of high school pupils is characterized by exploration, choice of directions, and tryout experiences. Typically, pupils are not ready to move efficiently into the labor market, that is, to locate potential jobs, identify those that best utilize their talents, apply, and adjust to the job or continue the search. A pupil may have learned a great deal about the decision-making process, about himself or herself, and about the world of work, and may have made good career plans, but he or she is not necessarily able to implement those plans. The disadvantaged usually experience even greater-than-average job-finding difficulty. They have had less opportunity in home, family, and neighborhood to develop the essential understandings and skills.

Increasingly, high schools provide placement services. Colleges and universities maintain extensive placement services. Provision is made for campus interviews by prospective employers. Credential files are maintained for students' and employers' convenience. Community colleges, vocational-technical schools, and private vocational schools also provide placement services. Wiggins (1978) reflects a growing concern about the importance of high-quality school placement services and points out that this service requires the best efforts of the professional counselor.

Differing Viewpoints

Opinions about the school's role in providing placement vary. Official statements about the role of the school counselor (ASCA, 1965, p. 102) assert that placement, including job placement, is a counselor responsibility. Hansen (1968) questions the advisability of involvement. Odgers (1968) points out that placement is a responsibility of the school guidance program, whether or not it is shared with the employment service or other agencies, so that it may be kept within the guidance framework. He remarks on the massive commitment of staff and resources the school would of necessity make if it seriously undertook this function. Thompson (1964, pp. 494–495) speculates that other agencies will tend to assume the job-placement function and that schools will take less responsibility for it. Andrews (1957, p. 10) gives ten reasons why the school should provide placement services, emphasizing the guidance aspect of the process.

Job placement by the school has many advocates. Hoppock (1976, pp. 87–88) recommends seeing counselees through placement, partly to insure that they have done an adequate job of reality testing and partly to evaluate the effectiveness of help. Norris, Zeran, Hatch, and Engelkes (1972, pp. 350–354) support vocational placement, including utilization of community resources when they are available. Herr and Cramer (1972, pp. 214–216) consider placement the end product of the school's efforts to help with career development. Placement is viewed as a transition process, as well as an event for which the pupil is helped to prepare himself or herself psychologically and practically. Isaacson (1977, p. 320) points out that the question of providing or not providing job placement is academic, since schools are already doing it. Sinick (1970, Chap. 6) includes both placement and postplacement as aspects of school guidance work, the latter for checking on the effectiveness of services. The school's uniquely favorable position for providing effective placement is seen by Riccio and Quaranta (1968, p. 54) as a major reason for including this service in the school guidance program. Summarizing research on guidance for job- and technical school–bound pupils, Miller (1969, p. 3) concludes that job placement should be provided. The most conclusive argument, however, is the fact that a large number of school districts are setting up placement services, and there are some statewide mandatory programs.

A complete summary of opposing points of view has not been attempted. It is apparent, nevertheless, that a number of knowledgeable professionals support the inclusion of this service. There seems to be agreement that the school should utilize existing community agencies, such as the employment service, to the fullest extent possible. A stated or implied point of view is that the school is the agency best qualified to insure a guidance emphasis in placement. In career education, placement appears to be an essential phase (Fuller, 1972; Miller, 1972). In fact, the pattern of moving in and out of the educational process throughout life that is part of the career-education rationale suggests that a two-way placement process will be needed. As means become available, attitudes may become more positive. When computers are used and the burden of clerical work is lessened, local job placement appears to be more favorably viewed. Perhaps it is less the principle that is opposed than the work involved.

Counselor's Attitudes

In past years, placement did not rank very high on the school counselors' list of priorities. The service has not been indexed in the *Personnel and Guidance Journal* since June 1970, although reports could have been included under "Vocational Development and Adjustment." Ashcraft's (1966) survey of counselors in a five-state area revealed that slightly over half helped pupils find part-time jobs. Full-time job placement was not mentioned in the report. Roemmich (1967) surveyed NDEA trainees to determine specific behaviors performed and rankings of the importance of the various functions. The results are difficult to relate to job placement because of the specific nature of the items, but it may be inferred that job placement was one of the lowest-ranking items in terms of both *work performed* and *importance*. (Some activities that ranked higher on both scales may have involved job placement, but "telephone employers to solicit employment for students" is the only one that specified a job-placement activity.) Interestingly enough, "assist students in making application for college" ranked relatively high on both scales. The findings agree with those of Carmical and Calvin (1970) and Maser (1971). The Counselor Function Inventory was used in both surveys, and limited samples were involved. In both, placement, whether for part-time or full-time work, was near the bottom of the scale. Herr's (1969) survey of guidance supervisors, using questions based on the ASCA Counselor Role Statement, found substantial support for a general placement function. However, job placement was not distinguished from school and college placement, and it is thus not possible to attribute the strong endorsement to job placement alone. Crary's (1966) survey suggests that counselor educators see little need for emphasis on this service. There is some evidence, however, that pupils tend to think of the counselor as the person to see for help with job placement (Kennedy and Frederickson, 1969). In general, it appears that counselors neither feel job placement to be their responsibility nor devote an appreciable amount of time and effort to it.

This attitude toward job placement may be related to the way guidance services developed in this country. As Thompson (1964, pp. 494–495) points out, educational and vocational guidance first appeared in American schools as help with choice and planning and later moved out into the community to provide job placement. In England, by contrast, guidance *began* as a placement function and was then extended backward to encompass school training. The same circumstances surrounded the development of guidance in other European countries, where it typically started outside the school, was more practically oriented, and involved parents to a very substantial degree (Cote, 1971).

Several factors appear to be related to and probably largely responsible for the emergence of placement as an important function for counselors in schools as well as those in a variety of other settings. Accountability is one. The changing economic picture is another. The rapid spread of the career-education concept is the third. Increased concern about the needs of the deprived, the neglected, the disadvantaged, and other subpopulations is a fourth. There is no doubt that the rising average age of the population has stimulated development of helping services for mid-life and older persons. Sophisticated technology has to some extent generated increased interest in the whole career-guidance area, including placement; now the counselor is relieved of amassing information and spending lengthy periods of time providing it to individuals and groups. Regardless of the reasons, placement appears to be gaining increased status among counselors in all settings.

The need for counseling expertise is particularly important now. Although many of the time-consuming placement-related tasks may be handled by support personnel, placement demands the skills of the professional counselor. For example, a high quality of placement is critical in the movement of previously barred workers (women, blacks, the handicapped) into new positions. Job development may be needed for many if help is to be effective. Providing information may appear on the surface to be a simple task, but it often evokes strong emotional reactions in recipients. The prospect of confronting prospective employers may challenge the counselee to decide who he or she is and what his or her values are. These situations demand the most competent counseling. Another element, which I have experienced repeatedly in working with high school and college students, needs to be recognized: There seems to be a real discontinuity in the helping process when, after a decision has been made and the counselee is ready to implement it, no provisions are made for further help. Some counselees seem to feel that the counselor has walked out on the "hard part" of the helping process.

The British System

A closer look at the development and status of the British system offers some contrasts that may help us view our own in a new perspective and foresee trends in career guidance and counseling. In Britain, placement is an important function. The youth employment officer (Heginbotham, 1951, Chap. 12; Rae, 1965–1966) works in the schools under the general administration of the Ministry of Labor and the local education authority to provide career information, individual advice, and placement. Heginbotham (1951, Chaps. 13–15) gives a detailed account of the services to pupils, which are not considered complete until a suitable job has been found. These services are quite extensive and include career weeks, exploratory work experiences, special career orientation for women, career advisers' meetings with parents, and special help in career centers for those having difficulty in holding a job. Two aspects of the work are particularly significant. There is intensive follow-up of placements, and assistance is provided to those experiencing adjustment problems related to the new job. In order to deal with recent high levels of unemployment among young people after completion of high school, such innovative procedures as job-preparation units have been set up to help maintain skills and the incentive to work (Heginbotham, 1978).

The youth employment officer has no counterpart in American schools. Likewise, there is no position like that of the American school counselor in the British school (Mitchell, 1969). The British situation is changing to some extent with the emerging interest in career development, however. Recent programs of research and counselor preparation emphasize the school's role in promoting career development and self-understanding (Department of Psychology, 1971; Hopson and Hough,

1971). Much of the new material being prepared is aimed at the teacher, but "school counselor" courses are being offered. The Youth Employment Service (Department of Employment, 1971) is reorganizing, but it is not yet clear whether the changes will result in a position more like that of our school counselor. There is a trend toward installing a "career teacher" in the schools to provide educational guidance and assistance for general development and preparation for social life after school, rather than strictly occupational choice and placement (Herr and Watts, 1978). The "career adviser" takes over when the individual is ready to go to work and helps with job placement and adjustment. The future might see a merging of career-development activities in the school and the occupational guidance and placement functions of the Youth Employment Service. The converse might take place in our schools, and more of the placement function might be assumed by school counselors, particularly when there is increased emphasis on outreach services.

CANDIDATES FOR PLACEMENT

In Chapters 1 and 2, brief descriptions were given of high school pupils who need placement as well as other guidance services. Sam Baker, nineteen years old, a high school dropout, is a good example. When financial responsibilities begin to close in on him during his senior year in high school, he needs help in locating a type of assistance that will provide some family support along with the opportunity to complete high school and enter college. Someone could refer him to the appropriate community agency. Several sources of help could be checked. But Sam does not know where to begin. The employment service could be a starting point for information about programs for persons in his situation. He does not know that several community-service clubs have scholarship funds for cases like his, and one local industry has a work-study program that would enable him to take the college program of his choice. He fails to obtain the financial assistance he needs because of his lack of knowledge about the possibilities and because the school guidance service is not aware of community resources.

Jack Buell presents another kind of placement problem. His understanding of work and training are very limited. His attitudes and behaviors do not help in either job applications or admission to training. He is in need of job placement, and it is particularly important that he be well prepared for interviews in order to make a good impression. Further, he badly needs some leads for jobs for which he could qualify and that would give him the opportunity to test occupational interests.

Henry Fuller, a nineteen year old dropout, is in a similar situation. He took an unskilled job and was one of the first to be discharged during a general layoff. A good placement service might have helped him take a critical look at the dead-end job he accepted. Later, he could have turned to a placement service rather than drifting and complaining.

Ralph Hart is an example of a pupil who needs college placement help in order to consider the pros and cons of community college versus four-year college and to prepare to move to the next educational level. He has a number of concerns about the freedom and demands of college life, some realistic and some not; he is not ready to cope with the transition. His parents should be brought into the placement process, as their understanding and support are likely a major factor in Ralph's decisions and his success in carrying them out.

These are only a few illustrations of individuals who need placement assistance. Dropouts are overrepresented deliberately to emphasize the needs of this large category, which probably receives less help than any other. In the typical school, those going from graduation to work are usually the largest single group, and the one for whom the greatest job placement effort should be expended.

The mid-life changers like Bill Powell, the pre- and postretirement people like Orville Harmon and George Fuller, the re-entry individuals like Mabel Hillman, and the handicapped like Harry Sparks also usually lack helping resources and merit a fair share of attention. No doubt you can recall many individuals who needed but did not receive placement help. Likewise, you can probably recall some who, as a result of a happy series of circumstances, obtained topnotch placement help from school staff, friends, agencies, or parents. This happens, but far too infrequently and often to those who need it least.

TYPES OF PLACEMENT

In College

This placement activity is probably the best known and most widely accepted. Few negative reactions would be evoked by the statement that the school guidance service provides college placement. The bulk of the school's educational-vocational guidance efforts are traditionally devoted to this function. Many schools are "judged" by the criterion of their graduates' rate of admission to "name" colleges and universities.

The intention here is not to denigrate college placement. If anything, its importance should be enhanced. More care and attention should be devoted to providing pupils with relevant data and helping them determine the meaning of college for their career development and test choices by realistic rather than glamour- or prestige-oriented criteria. But college-placement efforts should be balanced with those devoted to other goals. Even though improvements are needed, college placement has been the most thoroughly researched and practiced in educational institutions. Both high schools and colleges devote personnel and resources to the process. College representatives visit high schools for face-to-face contacts with prospective applicants. College catalogues, yearbooks, brochures, and newspapers are provided free. Tours, visits, and even weekends on campus are offered. Materials prepared by the institution or by commercial publishers describe programs, costs, and environments (both physical and psychological) and provide test norm data. Directories list and describe institutions. Computerized college-placement services help with difficult placements.

High schools provide information services and college days, while resource persons (such as alumni clubs) provide data and assistance. College admission tests are administered by school personnel. School records are designed to contain the data needed for college applications. Application forms (transcripts of grades, test results, ratings, and recommendations by school staff members) are prepared in the school office. There is an abundance of literature on the organization and management of placement services for the college-bound, for example, Herr and Cramer (1968) and Barr (1970). Some publications have been prepared in response to widespread concern about the lack of attention to educational guidance in counselor preparation. Two noteworthy ones are *Preparing School Counselors in Educational Guidance* (1967) and *Pre-Service and In-Service Preparation of School Counselors for Educational Guidance* (Cramer, 1970). The bulk of these two publications deals with college placement. There is considerable research on criteria for success in college, college characteristics, and the impact of the college on the student (Herr; 1967; Astin and Panos, 1969). This wealth of data presents the counselor with a tremendous job of keeping up to date.

From the pupils' side of the process, planning should begin early. Successive educational choices, even at the junior high school level, help in the formulation of educational goals. Test data, as well as experiences in taking tests, facilitates educational planning. Super (1967) points out the potential value of relating concept of self and college characteristics in the context of an exploratory vocational-development stage.

The college-placement function should include parents, who, as Barre points out (1970, pp. 12–13), are the most significant factor in college choice but know least about requirements, programs, and institutional characteristics. The placement process involves parents, primarily to orient them to college requirements but also to give them the background for helping their children follow through with plans. A "mock admissions session" is an effective way to deal with many of their questions. Parents are often particularly concerned about test scores and the effects they will have on college admissions. Group work to explain the meaning of these data seems to be particularly appreciated. The wealth of well-prepared interpretive material distributed by test services is not always clearly understood. In some cases, it varies from parents' expectations, and plan modifications are needed.

College guidance and placement for the disadvantaged should be a special concern. Barre (1970, p. 14) emphasizes the need to avoid a middle-class bias. College opportunities for the disadvantaged are increasing, but new efforts must be made by both counselor and school to help pupils reach the attitudinal and intellectual status for successful college admission and performance (Gordon, 1967; Barre, 1970, pp. 14–18).

College placement must not be left to the senior year; preparation should begin much earlier. The long-term process, such as learning about abilities, is clearly guidance. However, specialized assistance is needed during the last year or so, when choices are made and applications prepared. Help is needed to locate a suitable institution, make application, and cope with the school-to-college transition. Sources of financial aid should be identified. All the previous preparation may be wasted if these culminating placement services are not available.

Herr, Dillenbeck, and Swisher (1970, pp. 19–20) identify the three goals of guidance for the college-bound as an understanding of personal values, goals, and abilities; synthesis of personal understanding with information of available options in the decision-making process; and both intellectual and emotional preparation for college. In addition to suggestions for the preparation of effective counselors for the college-bound, Warner, Tibby, and Putnam (1970) provide a list of valuable resource material.

The college-placement process requires that the counselor have at his or her disposal materials such as directories, college catalogues, and other information, including confidential data, that he or she has collected. Barre (1970, pp. 5–6) points out the value of survey and follow-up data to better understand the qualities needed for success and thus provide help for the guidance of future applicants. If a number of pupils attend the same institution, the counselor can compare his or her personal and detailed knowledge of the individuals with their reactions to the demands and climate of the institution. It thus becomes a matter of José, or Brian, or Susan, each with his or her unique patterns of strengths and weaknesses, finding the state university challenging, impossible, permissive, or restricting. This cumulative information is invaluable to the counselor in helping current pupils understand the prospective college environment and make their own choices.

In Vocational Programs

Placement services should be available for vocational programs in the school, post–high school training such as vocational-technical schools, private vocational schools, and apprenticeships. Placement for training appears to be accepted and is often referred to as a guidance activity. The emphasis is on acquainting the pupil with training opportunities and helping him or her to decide on the program he or she wishes to enter. The problem, however, is quite different for job placement. If preferences, abilities, and goals point toward a particular preparation program, the pupil may usually enter it, since openings are usually available. Apprenticeship training more nearly resembles job placement, since the number of openings is limited and there is usually competition for those available.

Training placement usually needs upgrading. Many pupil decisions seem to be hit or miss and based on limited information. Opportunities should be well publicized. Pupils should be helped to assess their preferences and potentials, decide on the direction they wish to take, and choose the specific training course that is most suitable. They should then talk with the vocational teacher in the high school or the counselor or admissions officer in the community college or vocational-technical center, whichever is appropriate. Substantial improvement in services has been made in recent years through the use of computer programs such as those discussed in Chapter 5 and with the help of community programs such as CETA. The types of programs are for individuals who have specific talents and interests; they are not catchalls for those who lack interest and aptitude for academic work.

In Jobs

Job placement goes beyond decision making and planning to identifying a specific job opening to which the individual may apply, helping him or her get ready to apply, and following up on results and assisting with adjustments to the new situation. For example, a new counselee may state, "I want to work in electronics. TV repair. Any kind of work that is electronics." He may have taken the work-study cooperative program in school and worked part-time in a television sales and repair shop in conjunction with his high school program. He may have some knowledge about a number of job openings, and his coordinator may know about several others. Placement should not be too difficult in this case. The coordinator might utilize the guidance department for additional pupil information and might draw on the information system for additional details about trends and new developments appearing in the electronics field.

A more typical, and more demanding, situation is that of a pupil who is not in a work-study program. A senior girl is ready for graduation with no clear-cut occupational goals. She has "thought about" college, business school, and the community college and decides with counseling help that she would prefer to enter some type of health-related work. She begins to make the rounds to see what is available, checking hospitals, dental offices, clinics, and community agencies. She may take the first job offered, regardless of its suitability. She will probably not know the questions she should ask when interviewed or ways to communicate the contribution she can make to the organization. If she fails to obtain a job after several interviews, she may become discouraged and take any job she can find.

The job-placement service should be of considerable help in these and similar types of situations. First, it could give the pupil several suggestions about where to go and who to see. Second, the counselor has extensive pupil information readily available. He or she either knows the pupil personally or can obtain information from records and from those who are acquainted with the pupil. The counselor knows the requirements of specific jobs and the nature of the work settings and can introduce the applicant to the prospective employer. Furthermore, the counselor can provide psychological support. Few high school-age individuals have had much experience in applying for jobs. What may appear to a counselor to be a routine interview is often a very novel and threatening experience for a young person.

Job placement involves three major types of activities. First is the job listing and referral service, which contains openings that are either called in or located through the placement worker's routine contacts. Second is a process for locating openings that suit specific applicants. Third is the procedure for referring applicants to prospective employers. The total placement process may appear rather simple and straightforward at first glance—the counselor simply gives the counselee a list of jobs, and the counselee makes applications.

The process, however, is complex and demanding. Ferman (1969, pp. 184–188), discussing services for the disadvantaged, specifies six activities basic to the total placement service. These include identifying job openings and other job-placement services, matching the individual and the job, preparing the individual for the interviews and tests to be encountered, providing on-the-job supportive help, and completing follow-up. The employer's knowledge of the types of training applicants have completed is a factor in satisfactory placement.

Job development is the second aspect of placement. As Ferman points out (1969, pp. 190–191), the first stage in building a placement service is primarily a matter of locating job openings and finding applicants to fill them. As the service is improved and expanded, however, the *job developer* endeavors to persuade employers to tailor jobs to applicants. This process is used extensively in placement projects for special groups (Ferman, 1969, pp. 195–202). Cheney (Cheney and Kish, 1970) describes a veterans' hospital placement program that effectively uses job development. The "development" emphasis, which involves extensive use of employment service lists, calls to employers, and leads from individuals, is credited with making a substantial contribution to the success of the placement programs. Although job development has often been used for difficult placements (Gleason, 1968), it is an approach the school needs. For one thing, it may counteract the negative attitudes some pupil personnel workers express about the prescriptive, directive, "slot-filling" nature of placement.

A third aspect of job placement is the utilization of community agencies and services. The most helpful are the employment service and the rehabilitation service. They not only provide placement but also serve as sources of information about other training and placement programs. Especially because new facilities, services, and procedures are regularly being added, a personal visit is the most effective way to learn about current programs. For example, the Job Bank program (U.S. Department of Labor, 1970a, pp. 199–205; 1971b) of the employment service, a long-range project, is beginning to make nationwide, up-to-date job information available. During 1972, statewide job banks were partially operational in every state. CETA is another major resource.

PLACEMENT AS DECISION-MAKING COUNSELING

The counseling approach described in Chapter 7 included implementation of the decision—taking a course, joining a club, changing a program, entering a training program, or getting a job—as a phase of the process. If the decision is about a job, the counseling process monitors obtaining the job and evaluating its suitability. The degree of assistance in implementation varies. For example, the counselee may find the job on his or her own, obtain the help of a community agency or some other resource, or be placed by the school guidance service. Placement is part of the counseling process, but it may be done in different ways.

Conceptualizing placement as part of counseling offers several distinct advantages. The counselor is in a better position than anyone else to help the counselee prepare for placement and look at opportunities in terms of values, goals, abilities, and limitations. The quality of the decision can be assessed only *after* implementation. Decision making can be learned by carrying it through to reality testing, and only then can the counselor evaluate the effectiveness of his or her efforts to teach decision-making skills.

One of the best ways to prepare to cope with future changes is to learn to deal with current ones. Thus, the "evaluated placement" appears to be an invaluable part of the guidance process for the pupil. It not only helps the job seeker resolve his or her immediate problem but is also a learning experience in developing skills to deal with future ones.

THE PLACEMENT SERVICE

Because placement is considered an aspect of the guidance service, a separate placement staff and facilities are not suggested. Maximum use is made of all available personnel and resources, and responsibilities are allocated to those who can carry them out. Realistically, it may not be possible to do all that is needed. Priorities will very likely have to be established.

Organizing

No single plan or model is used in schools, and there does not appear to be a general procedure that can be recommended. Three general organizational patterns are suggested by Andrews (1957, pp. 12–16), Norris, Zeran, Hatch, and Engelkes (1972, pp. 352–354), and Isaacson (1977, pp. 320–322). The first, the *decentralized* plan, provides service at the school level. A similar procedure is in effect now, on a partial basis, in vocational and work-study programs. Teachers and coordinators undertake a great deal of placement, with some placement provided by the guidance office. The second approach, the *centralized* plan, provides one placement office for the school, or for several schools, specifically devoted to placement services. Other variations use combinations of these two organizational patterns. There may be a central school office for placement, but recommendations and other data are obtained from teachers. Staff members may continue to maintain placement contacts and actually carry out placement functions. A *cooperative* plan, utilizing both school and public placement services, is sometimes identified as a distinct type (Isaacson, 1977, p. 321), but it is assumed here that each approach already mentioned would work cooperatively with community resources. Although a combination of centralized and decentralized plans would usually be desirable, the best plan for a particular school will depend on its needs and characteristics (Norris, Zeran, Hatch, and Engelkes, 1972, p. 353). Furthermore, the availability of support personnel and technological aids has an effect on service design and operation.

Steps in initiating and building a school placement service give a sequence to major tasks. A rationale and purpose should be formulated, priorities established, and a publicity campaign developed. Then those involved need to plan the procedures to be used. For example, how will the placement service coordinate its work with that of the vocational teachers? How will cooperative relationships with the employment service be initiated? Will part-time as well as full-time work be covered? How will contacts be made with employers? What efforts will be made toward job development? Wide publicity, in both school and community, will be helpful in gaining support and cooperation. Many employers will recognize placement as a service to them as well as to pupils and will provide enthusiastic support.

Staffing

As mentioned, placement does not require a separate staff. Although there are advantages to a full-time placement staff, the dangers of narrow focus, hierarchical prestige, and lack of feedback for the whole staff make having one a less than desirable arrangement. Making the placement service an additional duty of an already overloaded staff whose orientation is toward other emphases would be disastrous, however, as would assigning these duties to staff members who have no experiential background and preparation for the work. Therefore, as I see it, the major staffing problem is to assign a specific portion of the guidance service's time to placement. If new staff has to be added, increasing the regular counseling and support personnel is recommended. Some work experience in business and industry is desirable, particularly for support personnel. Andrews (1957, p. 18) suggests a "placement specialist" and outlines qualifications. The Newton, Massachusetts, school system, described later in this chapter, uses a job-placement coordinator to head the total placement program (Circle, 1968, p. 55).

The placement service staff should consist of counselors, support personnel, and clerical workers. The auxiliary staff should consist of all teachers in the school, including vocational teachers (who might, however, prefer to carry out their own placement activities independently). Job placement is a total school enterprise. Community resources, particularly the employment service, also represent auxiliary staffs, in the sense that they extend the school placement function. The same is true of admissions officers at community colleges and vocational-technical centers, apprenticeship representatives, and the like.

No proposed ratio of staff to pupils is suggested, since there has not been enough experimentation or tryout to establish guidelines. Additional staff will usually be needed, however. Furthermore, the percentage of pupils going to work, the number in vocational courses that provide some placement help, and the cooperation of employers all have a bearing on the amount of time and effort job placement will require. Also, placement in colleges and training programs should not be neglected, so staffing cannot be based on shifting personnel responsibilities.

Community advisory committees and education-work councils can help in policy making and publicity and perhaps do some of the work. In my experience, employers, community agency representatives, and service organizations have been more than willing to contribute ideas and energy.

Setting Up an Office

Building the job- and training-placement service requires little additional space and facilities, other than several files. If the office has VIEW equipment, for example, local training information is recorded on the cards. The major records needed are pupil registration cards, job-order records, and pupils' qualification records (Andrews, 1957, pp. 24–35; Circle, 1968, pp. 62–66). If employers visit the school to talk with counselors or interview pupils, the office should be easily accessible from the building entrance. Adequate telephone service is a critical need; if the school lines are busy much of the day, calls about job openings may be missed.

Identifying Job Openings

In conjunction with publicity, community contacts, and other preliminary activities, the job-order file is begun. Job surveys may be conducted, along the lines suggested in Chapter 6. Pupils can participate very effectively in collecting information. Andrews (1957, pp. 21–27) lists the data needed from employers, such as the minimum age for applicants and general and specific qualifications required. A system for recording and classifying notifications of openings needs to be established. One such system, used in the Newton school system, is described on pages 358–361. This particular system has been carefully designed and evaluated and provides an excellent starting point for a school designing its own plan. Buckingham and Lee (1973, pp. 12–14) give a helpful discussion of ways to gain employers' cooperation.

PLACEMENT IN PRACTICE

Identifying those in need of placement may be done by publicizing the service through notices and announcements to pupils and teachers, by distributing registration cards, and by referrals. Surveys may help identify those who should be contacted.

The Procedure

The first step in job placement could be an interview to determine job preferences, previous work experience, specific competencies, and occupational goals. Even though the school cumulative record is available, time will be saved by using a special informational form (or card) in this interview. The school may want to design its own form, including a system that will facilitate quick identification of applicants according to their preferences and qualifications—with, for example, tabs, punched holes, or color coding. Designing the form with the cooperation of local employers may be best.

A referral form for the applicant to present to the employer also will be needed in job-placement work. This second form can include a space for the prospective employer to note the decision about the applicant, and the form can be returned to the counselor. Employer feedback is helpful in preparing later applicants for interviews. Samples of form letters and announcements that may be used are given in Circle (1968, pp. 54–67).

During the interview, the counselor can go over appropriate openings in the job-order file. Pros and cons of these openings may be discussed. Counseling may help in clarifying goals, deciding on next steps, and planning for job interviews. If a suitable job (or jobs) is available, the applicant is given the referral form to present to the employer. After interview(s), the applicant reports results to the placement office.

The applicant might be referred to the employment service, rather than to an employer, if needed help indicated that this would be the most productive next step. Guidelines previously developed with the employment service would help the counselor in making such a judgment and in deciding on the procedure to be followed.

If no suitable openings were available, the counselor might follow one of several courses of action. First, he or she might call or have a support person call employers to learn if an opening were available or expected in the near future. Second, the counselor might decide that the pupil is a case for job development, supervised either by himself or herself or by support personnel. If the placement is for a later date, perhaps the end of the school year, the applicant may be told to check back from time to time as new jobs are called in. His or her application should automatically be checked against new job orders, probably by the clerk-secretary or support person, and the pupil should be contacted when a suitable opening materializes.

Follow-up of placements, or what Sinick (1970, p. 64) calls "postplacement services," is an essential phase. These services overlap the actual placement and serve to insure that it is successful. As Sinick (1970, pp. 65–67), points out, follow-up helps others besides the pupil who has been placed; the guidance staff, the school, and the employers all receive benefits. For some individuals, postplacement may be the time when counseling is most needed.

The follow-up may be done by telephone, mail, or visit. The latter is the most effective and the most time-consuming. Support personnel should be able to handle this task very well, referring appropriate problems to the counselor. Sinick (1970, pp. 64–68) gives a helpful explanation of this phase of placement, suggesting systematic follow-ups beginning thirty days after the counselee begins the new job and arranged so as not to interfere with work hours. It may be necessary to contact or visit the counselee after work or to set up late hours in the placement service.

An accurate record of the results of placements, including the time devoted to them, is extremely valuable for at least two reasons. It permits evaluation of the service and provides the kind of "hard data" needed to convince school boards, voters, and legislators of the effects guidance can have.

Placement for Dropouts

It must be decided whether or not the school placement service will provide assistance to dropouts. Helping those who are leaving school is suggested as a first priority. Working with high school–age dropouts in the community would be second, if the service is capable of doing so. Ideally, dropouts would be contacted at the time they leave school. For those missed, a check of the school and district attendance record may be helpful. Unemployed graduates in the community should already be registered with the employment service. If plans are developed to help out-of-school youth, it is advisable to cooperate with the welfare office and the employment service to identify those for whom the school placement service would be appropriate. It seems highly unlikely, however, that a school placement service would have the staff and facilities to help others in addition to its current pupils. In fact, it would seem inadvisable to attempt it; there are other agencies and programs established specifically for this purpose. It may be beneficial however, to work out arrangements with other placement programs in the community so that referrals may be easily made when unemployed or underemployed adults request help.

Building Job-Search and Job-Getting Skills

Along with the trend to increase school placement services has come recognition that individuals need specific competencies not only to locate places of potential employment but also to make effective presentations, both verbal and written, to prospective employers. The Virginia plan (Harris, 1977) identifies a number of competencies pupils should develop, including those for making job-search plans, writing effective letters of application and résumés, and participating effectively in job interviews. Franchak (1976) emphasizes the need for such skills to be developed though the school placement service. Florida law and guidelines (Guidelines for Placement Services and Follow-up Studies, 1973) do not state that job-finding and job-getting skills are required, but a program called the Employability Skills Series has been developed with state support to help pupils acquire these competencies. Group procedures like those discussed in Chapter 8 usually aim to develop these skills along with others, such as self-understanding.

There is evidence that placement services that include preparation in job-getting and job-holding skills contribute to the individual's effectiveness in the application process (McGovern, Tinsley, Liss-Levinson, Laventure and Britton, 1975; Clowers and Fraser, 1977). One placement program that involved a schoolwide approach, a career-placement specialist, and collaborative working relationships with the public employment service also emphasized job-getting skills along with other features. These skills—résumé preparation, interviewing effectiveness, occupational information, career planning, and decision making—were regarded as one of the service's most significant contributions. The unemployment rate of graduates from schools with the total service was much lower than that for a similar institution without it. Wiggins (1978) also emphasizes the need for skill development and points out that if placement services are to be effective, they must be part of the total counseling program; just providing "facts" to young people will not do the job.

Working with Community Services

The work of the school placement service can be immeasurably enhanced by cooperative working arrangements with community agencies. The employment service is one major placement agency; the local rehabilitation office is another. Community education-work councils can mobilize community resources to facilitate the transition from education to jobs. The programs described in Chapter 10 illustrate a variety of cooperative working relationships with community resources.

One of the most effective ways to build community relations is to help pupils obtain jobs or enter training programs. If the placement is suitable—if the new worker likes the job and has the characteristics the employer seeks—both will have positive attitudes toward the school and the guidance service. If dropouts and graduates without plans or work are followed up and helped, another gain has been scored for the guidance program. The cumulative effect of many such individual services can contribute significantly to good community relations. While they may not convince community members to approve school bond issues, they will at least not have a negative effect.

Involving others in the community in the helping process is perhaps the most effective way of improving community relations. Some of the staunchest supporters of guidance services I have encountered are those who have served as resource persons for career interviews, discussed an occupation at a career day, or served as hosts for industrial or business field trips. Asking a community person to serve as a *participant* appears to have a very salutary effect. Interest is aroused, questions asked, and understanding developed. Many of the programs Hansen describes (1970, Chaps. 2 and 3) have involved the community heavily in the guidance process and illustrate this approach to improving school-community relations.

The school or school district placement service may find itself competing with the youth service of the employment service unless close cooperation is maintained. This is particularly true of the employment agencies' new services, which are designed to provide summer employment and placement for high school graduates and dropouts. There is evidence that mutual understanding between the schools and the employment services could be improved (Rossmann and Prebonich, 1968). Building and maintaining good working relationships with the employment service can be handled successfully by a placement specialist (Franchak, 1976).

Two factors involving ethical and legal issues need to be considered in managing placement services. One is the handling of pupils' records, the information contained in them, and other information brought out in counseling. The other involves laws regulating employment, such as those relating to minimum age and prohibition of discrimination. Counselors should know and be guided by ethical standards in handling information about pupils (Tolbert, 1978, pp. 289–290). This reminder should in no way inhibit the use of needed information in placement, but it is well to be aware of the guidelines to be observed. Laws concerning employment are changing, and counselors must keep up with what is current at the national and state levels. Examples are minimum age laws; antidiscrimination statues for women, minorities, and older persons; and eligibility requirements for programs like CETA and the Job Corps. Although the counselor is not responsible for enforcing or interpreting laws, he or she may need to discuss their applications with pupils, parents, or others (Norris, Zeran, Hatch, and Engelkes, 1972, p. 357). Brief summaries in Norris, Zeran, Hatch, and Engelkes (1972, pp. 357–364) and Isaacson (1977, pp. 323–326) will be helpful, but more recent information is needed. State departments of education, local employment services, the Department of Labor, and members of Congress are sources of information about the most recent regulations.

PLACEMENT PROGRAMS AND SERVICES

In the past few years, the increase in placement work has resulted in publication of information about a great variety of programs and services. Descriptions of typical endeavors are given here to show organizational patterns, staffing procedures, and techniques.

Newton, Massachusetts

Circle (1968, Section 3) describes the planning and operation of this school system's job-placement service and presents valuable guidelines derived from it. The program was developed to provide career-development experiences for pupils, help build positive attitudes toward the world of work, and introduce the essential aspect of vocational decision making into the school guidance program. Originally, the placement service's organizational structure was a combined plan utilizing a central office and decentralized placement activities in each school. The Career Guidance Resource Center at Newton North High School continued the program independently after the combined plan was discontinued.

   The organization of the placement service illustrates effective planning and execution. A summary of the steps involved in the program's implementation follows.

1. Material on job placement and job program descriptions was reviewed.
2. Three surveys were conducted:
   a. A follow-up of graduates, which revealed that they had received little assistance from job-placement agencies.
   b. A survey of pupils then attending high school, which showed that most intended to work or were already working part-time.
   c. A survey of those applying for working permits, which indicated very little anticipated use of any placement services.
3. School job-placement activities were studied. A few relatively isolated placement efforts were found.
4. A community advisory committee was established by the following procedures:[2]
   a. Presidents of major service clubs were contacted by telephone and the placement program was explained. They were asked to request club members to
      (1) list job openings with the school placement service
      (2) volunteer for membership on an advisory committee.
   b. An eighteen-member advisory committee was established. Half the members were from service clubs, the chairman was from the Chamber of Commerce, and the remaining members were selected to represent all facets of community life.

[2]This description was brought up to date by Mrs. Myra Trachtenberg, Newton North High School.

5. The advisory committee did the following:
   a. Provided a good public image.
   b. Provided an imposing list of names for a letterhead.
   c. Handled publicity.
   d. Provided advice on the most effective ways to approach employers. The committee agreed that an employer would react positively when contacted for job orders if
      (1) he or she personally knew someone in the group that made the request.
      (2) the request had the endorsement of respected persons in the community.
      (3) the request for job openings was made to the employer in person at his or her place of business.
      (4) the advantages to him or her were pointed out.
6. A steering committee was appointed. This was a working committee composed of school personnel interested in the job-placement program; it included a representative from the employment service. The committee approved the operating plans formulated by the director and agreed that the service would be called Jobs for Youth.
7. A list of employers was compiled. The working papers of pupils for the past two years, the Chamber of Commerce's list of businesses, the city directory, and the Yellow Pages provided the basic list.
8. Letters were mailed to approximately 1,500 employers to solicit job openings and stimulate interest and cooperation prior to the initiation of personal contacts.
9. Pupils were recruited and trained to make personal contacts with employers to locate jobs. The procedure was as follows:
   a. Two pupil "leaders" were responsible for contacting employers in each of the twelve "villages" in Newton.
   b. Meetings were held with the pupil leaders to prepare them for contacting employers.
   c. Leaders contacted a limited number of employers (ten) in their villages to try out the procedure and to provide data for comparing the personal contact approach with the mailed request. (The former was far more effective.)
   d. Pupil leaders recruited two additional pupils for each ten employers in their villages. Training sessions were held and work schedules established. Practically all of the leaders and over half of the team members completed their tasks.

The personal job survey provided so much information that present contacts are handled by telephone. The experience revealed, however, that some screening of employers should be done to eliminate those with very low potential for employment of high school pupils. The frustrations of team members who were repeatedly turned down partially accounted for the failure to complete interview assignments.

The Career Guidance Resource Center at Newton North High School functions as the central office and disseminates information. Job orders may be called in, provided by pupils, gleaned from newspapers, or gotten in other ways, but in each case, complete information is obtained. Direct verbal contact with the employer is the only satisfactory method. The information required is quite detailed; fourteen items, such as "the person to whom to apply," "job title and description," and "starting date," are covered.

When complete job information is obtained, it is disseminated to students via a prominently posted Jobs for Youth bulletin board and a card file of all current job listings. The job-listing and job-seeking procedure is as follows:

1. Each opening is given a job-order number for identification.
2. A job-order form, giving complete information, is made up. One copy is kept in the card file students use. A second copy is held in reserve in case the original is accidentally removed.
3. A job description label showing all the information except the firm's name, address, and telephone number, and the name of the person to whom to apply is prepared for the bulletin board.
4. A pupil learns about jobs from the bulletin board and contacts the career center on those of interest. The pupil is given the name of the establishment that has the job opening. A card of introduction and suggestions about employment interviews are provided if the pupil wishes to apply.
5. The interested pupil calls the employer for an appointment. A job interview is set up.
6. After the interview, the employer is contacted to see if the job is still open and if additional positions are available.
7. If the job is closed, it is deleted from the card file.
8. A call to the employer after a week or so is made to learn whether the job has been filled and to update the job listings.
9. The Career Guidance Resource Center maintains the following files:
   a. Job-order forms, classified as "open" or "closed."
   b. An alphabetical file of all employers, with notations about openings and positions filled.
   c. A card file based on the six-digit DOT classification system for access to different information.

Each employer who has hired a pupil is listed and briefly described on a card in the appropriate occupational classification.

The school's part in the placement process consists primarily of notifying pupils of openings and providing introduction cards. The schools do not screen applicants, although the qualifications employers are seeking are pointed out to potential applicants. The school sees itself as performing a service to students rather than to employers. A rather lengthy pupil registration card was mandatory in the early stages of the service but is no longer required.

Some job development was done the second year of the program. Specific needs included jobs for pupils in special education, half-day jobs for those in work-study programs, and jobs for pupils referred by counselors and psychologists. Efforts were also made to locate exploratory-experience jobs for those going on to college.

Potential employers identified for the lists already prepared were contacted, and placement needs were explained. Special mailings were used to tap new sources. These efforts were generally successful, except for junior high school pupils and those wanting exploratory experiences related to professional occupations. More intensive job development is planned in these two areas.

Sarasota County, Florida

An increasing number of educational institutions are taking the position that placement should be a cooperative process involving pupils, school, and community. Sarasota County, Florida, is an example (Preston, 1977). The 25 to 30 percent of the pupils in each graduating class who typically need placement assistance are identified by a pregraduate data survey in March to locate those who would like placement assistance. Pupils who request it are contacted by a school-based counselor or occupational specialist. An interview is held, and the student's records are reviewed to facilitate planning. At the same time, a district-level coordinator identifies job openings and carries out job development, making full use of community resources. Extensive program publicity through local organizations and media stimulates the cooperation of local employers; for example, all eighteen hundred members of the Chamber of Commerce are contacted. For each job identified, a school-based placement worker obtains information. A district office coordination plan limits the number of calls to each employer to obtain detailed job information.

When the job information is on hand, students are again interviewed and referred to openings for which they are qualified. Applicants are also given assistance in preparing for the interview and developing job-holding skills. Interview results are reported by both applicant and employer, and additional job interviews may be scheduled if needed. Six months after graduation, a follow-up needs assessment is conducted to check job progress and to identify those who require additional assistance. Those still out of work are interviewed by the central office placement person, and personal assistance is provided where needed.

The extensive use of community agencies and resources has increased program effectiveness and held down costs. CETA has provided support in a number of ways, including assigning a research and placement specialist to the central office and making on-the-job training available. Evaluations indicate that the program is cost effective, is highly regarded by both applicants and employers, and has held down the unemployment rate for recent high school graduates.

Services Using Computers

Computers are now being used in placement services, as described in Chapter 5. For example, Project PLACE, a computer-based occupational and educational placement service in a number of Dayton, Ohio, high schools, utilizes the Time Share GIS network for information on careers, colleges, and financial aid. A job-placement service matches pupils to jobs in the Dayton area (Chamberlain, Kaser, and Rhoads, 1975). Both pupils and employers enter information into the computer system; terminals in schools give pupils data about jobs for which they qualify. In addition, job-placement specialists meet with employers to do job development and promote their use of Project PLACE. Educational placement is facilitated by the GIS system, which is used for detailed information on institutions and opportunities for financial aid and is updated yearly.

GRAD II, a system developed by the College Placement Council, Inc. and adapted for use at the University of Florida Career Resources Center, uses a computer to match students with prospective employers. Covering all academic majors in the university, the computer matches on the basis of degree level, major, career field or fields (as many as three), geographic preference, and type of employer. The program does not identify specific jobs, it provides a list of employers that meet students' needs. It serves as a screening device for students to use in selecting recruiters to interview on campus or to contact in other ways. The list is also made available to employers. GRAD II does not provide placement, but it does help make the total job-search process more efficient.

Another service is the Computer Assisted Placement Service for Pupils, or CAPS, located in Florida (van Camp, 1978). Designed for use in secondary schools, community colleges, and area vocational-technical centers, the service makes data about students available to over twelve thousand employers. Schools or other institutions register with CAPS and give information about programs, enrollments, and other data. In turn, employers provide information about hiring interests. The third component is student registration, which includes information about occupational preferences and training. Processing of these data provides the content for regularly published CAP-O-GRAMS for employers, listing information about students. Other data, such as employment status reports and program enrollments, are also available to participating institutions. Initial reactions from employers have been very favorable. The CAPS program is a service of the recently established Center for Career Development (Woolley, 1978), which also has added a VIEW deck to the state VIEW system for apprenticeable occupations.

SUMMARY

In past years, placement has been described as one of the major guidance services, but only recently have high schools taken steps to institute programs that are on a par with those in higher education. Position statements by professional counseling organizations favor placement services, and public opinion supports their installation. Placement services in England offer assistance in evaluating our own programs, and they have been described in this chapter. In addition, several cases of individuals who need placement have been described. Types of placement have been discussed, including college, vocational programs, and work. Strategies for organizing and staffing placement services and several programs have also been described, including those that emphasize building job-getting skills and those that use computers.

PROJECTS AND EXPERIENTIAL ACTIVITIES

1. Visit the employment service to learn about its programs and placement procedures. Visit other placement services in the community, including private placement services, to learn about their procedures, types of clients, and services.

2. Interview a counselor about his or her attitudes toward job placement and college placement.

3. Compare the attitudes toward job placement of staff members in a college placement office with those of a high school guidance director.

4. Interview a high school vocational teacher to find out what kind of job placement he or she does and what he or she thinks of a school job-placement service.

5. Role-play a step in planning a placement service. Invite school and employment-service counselors to be present if the step you choose involves cooperative school-community relations. Include employers if the role playing involves industry-school cooperation. Structure a specific problem, such as maintaining contact with local industry or working out procedures for dealing with dropouts.

6. Review the want ad section in a local newspaper. What kinds of jobs are most frequently listed? Of how much help would this resource be to high school dropouts and graduates?

7. Form small groups and go through the experience of interviewing for a counseling or guidance position. Have each group describe the employment setting briefly (school, college, community agency). Formulate questions that an interviewer probably would ask, then select one person to role-play the interviewer and one to play the applicant. Role-play the interview for several minutes, then have all group members critique the session. Rotate roles so each group member acts as both interviewer and interviewee. Note particularly in the critique how well the interviewee communicated strengths and competencies and his or her ability to make a positive contribution to the agency or organization.

8. In class, decide on the most important feature a placement service for counselor-education students should have. Then, in small groups, formulate procedures for implementing this procedure. Share these procedures with the total group. Discuss the major strategies proposed. Note particularly the emphasis (or lack of it) on personal responsibility and skill building for job applicants.

ADDITIONAL REFERENCES

Andrews, Margaret E. *Providing School Placement Services*. Chicago: Science Research Associates, 1957. This brief publication, only forty-three pages long, is an excellent introduction to school placement services. All the essential elements are covered in concise, readable form.

Barre, Mary E. *College Information and Guidance.* Boston: Houghton Mifflin, 1970. Although this chapter has devoted little attention to college placement, it is a necessary part of the school placement service. Barre's monograph covers the process well and discusses the college "climate," which is often omitted in discussions of college choice.

Bolles, Richard N. *What Color is your Parachute?* Berkeley, Calif.: Ten Speed Press, 1977. A guide for job hunting and job changing that draws a very positive reaction from counselor-education students. One of the most useful of the many publications on this topic.

Buckingham, Lillian, and Arthur M. Lee. *Placement and Follow-up in Career Education.* Raleigh, N. C.: North Carolina State University at Raleigh, 1973. A brief, useful manual for establishing a school placement and follow-up service, this book is particularly helpful in showing the necessity for the involvement of school, community, and home.

Capehart, Bertis E. *Placement Services.* Ann Arbor, Mich.: Prakken Publications, 1977. This manual, which contains a complete guide for setting up a placement service, was developed with support from the Office of Education as a curriculum project. Job placement is viewed as a series of coordinated services, including school-community interaction, staff training, and curriculum development to enable young people to secure and progress in suitable jobs. A wealth of useful forms is included.

Circle, D. F. "The Career Information Service: A Guide to Its Development and Use." Newton, Mass.: Newton Public Schools, 1968 (ED 021 300). Section 3, "Job Placement Service," is the source of the brief description of the Newton job-placement service in this chapter. The original is extremely helpful for planning a placement service. This is a highly recommended reference.

College Entrance Examination Board. *Preparing School Counselors in Educational Guidance.* New York: College Entrance Examination Board, 1967. This book is a collection of papers presented at the 1966 College Board Invitational Conference on the preparation of school counselors in educational guidance. Some of the individual reports have been referred to in this chapter; other valuable ones have not. The entire volume is particularly useful for those working with the college-bound.

Cramer, Stanley H., ed. *Pre-Service and In-Service Preparation of School Counselors for Educational Guidance.* Washington, D.C.: American Personnel and Guidance Association, 1970. This book was prepared in response to the concern of ACES about the quality of college-placement counseling. The papers, several of which were used as references for this chapter, are useful for both counselors and counselor educators. Some attention is given to post–high school education other than college. The annotated bibliography of college directories and other materials on college placement is a valuable resource.

Ferman, Louis A. "Job Placement, Creation, and Development." In *Breakthrough for Disadvantaged Youth.* U.S. Department of Labor, Washington, D.C.: U.S. Government Printing Office, 1969, pp. 181–212. Although this report is oriented toward placement for the disadvantaged, it is a useful reference for the school counselor. The discussion of placement, job creation, and job development are particularly valuable. Federal programs that have dealt extensively with job placement are reviewed and their strengths and weaknesses summarized.

Ferrin, Richard I., and Solomon Arbeiter. *Bridging the Gap: Education-to-Work Linkages,* and *Supplemental Report, Bridging the Gap: A Selection of Education-to-Work Linkages.* Princeton, N. J.: College Entrance Examination Board, 1975. Although "linkages" cover much more than job placement, the analyses of means, barriers, and possible strategies, and the program descriptions in the supplemental report are valuable reading for gaining a comprehensive understanding of how the movement from education to work may be facilitated.

Ginzberg, Eli. *The Manpower Connection.* Cambridge, Mass.: Harvard University Press, 1975. Almost any part of this book is excellent background reading for deepening one's understanding of problems and issues in job placement. Chaps. 16 and 17 are particularly valuable for gaining an understanding of the impact of manpower and public employment programs.

Gleason, Clyde W. "Employment Opportunities for Disadvantaged Youth." In *Counseling the Disadvantaged Youth.* Eds. William E. Amos and Jean Dresden Grambs. Englewood Cliffs, N.J.: Prentice-Hall, 1968, pp. 206–235. The emphasis in this reference is on description of special placement programs for the disadvantaged. It is helpful background reading, but up-to-date information on such programs is also needed.

Hoppock, Robert. *Occupational Information,* 4th ed. New York: McGraw-Hill, 1976. Hoppock is one of the few authorities in the guidance profession who over the years has consistently emphasized the importance of career guidance, including placement. Here, the emphasis is on preparation for placement rather than on the actual job-getting process.

Isaacson, Lee E. *Career Information in Counseling and Teaching.* 3rd ed. Boston: Allyn & Bacon, 1977. Chap. 9 is a very useful reference on work-experience programs. apprenticeship, and CETA. Educational and occupational placement, including legal aspects, are discussed in Chap. 10.

Norris, Willa, Franklin R. Zeran, Raymond N. Hatch and James R. Engelkes. *The Information Service in Guidance,* 3rd ed. Chicago: Rand McNally, 1972. Placement, including the school's responsibilities for it and its legal aspects, are covered on pp. 348–366. A brief but helpful review.

Shippen, Samuel J., and Raymond A. Wasil. *Placement and Follow-up.* Lexington, Mass.: Xerox Individualized Publishing Program, 1977. A very useful manual by a number of experts on school placement and follow-up services, emphasizing a developmental approach. The comprehensive coverage includes the areas of information, exploration, counseling, placement, follow-up, and legislation.

Sinick, Daniel. *Occupational Information and Guidance.* Boston: Houghton Mifflin, 1970. This entire monograph is recommended reading in connection with this chapter; Part 2, "Job Placement," particularly Chap. 6, is one of the most useful references available on the nature and operation of the school placement service.

U.S. Department of Labor. *1975 Handbook on Women Workers.* Washington, D.C.: U.S. Department of Labor, 1975. A comprehensive reference on women workers.

Pp. 209–240 are particularly useful for those returning to school or in need of job assistance. Part 2 is an excellent review of laws and legislation affecting women workers.

Wirtz, Willard. *The Boundless Resource.* Washington, D.C.: New Republic Book Company, 1975. A major theme throughout this book is the importance of school-community-employer cooperation in placement. The proposals on pp. 170–185 give a succinct overview of the major new strategies suggested.

13

Evaluation for Accountability

GOALS

1
To discuss the meaning and importance of accountability
for counselors.

2
To explain the relationship between evaluation and
accountability.

3
To describe the various purposes of evaluation.

4
To help the reader learn how to evaluate his or her own work
as well as school- or agencywide programs.

THE QUESTIONS RAISED IN CHAPTER I about the value of guidance need to be reconsidered. How can career guidance and counseling be evaluated? How can goals be established that are meaningful for the profession, those served, and the public—which provides, as Rothney (1972, pp. 65–66) puts it, the "sanctions" for the service?

Each occupation has its own accountability. Those served are becoming more articulate about its responsibilities and how they are judged. Consumers are taking a closer look at what they are getting and expressing approval or disapproval more openly. Education is no exception. Pupils, parents, and taxpayers in general are exercising more initiative in stating what should be accomplished and how results should be assessed. This attitude may well be the way of the future, not just a passing educational fad.

The ACES position paper on counselor competencies adds support to the position that evaluation is a major aspect of the counselor's responsibilities. Moreover, attention to accountability and evaluation is essential if counseling is to move ahead with the times (Oetting and Hawkes, 1974).

ACCOUNTABILITY IN GUIDANCE AND COUNSELING

The current emphasis on accountability occasionally implies that education has accomplished very little or even that schools have "failed." Countering this extreme and overdramatized position is beyond the scope of this book. But in the long view, the growth and development of education in this country is nothing short of phenomenal. The system, including its guidance component, has no counterpart in any other time or place. The contemporary movement to remedy imperfections is a tribute to both the viability of the system and the quality of personnel involved. The concept of accountability provides a fresh approach to solving problems and improving the educational process.

The term *accountability,* as Barro (1970) observes, is too new to have a standard definition. Its basic meaning is that schools and the educational personnel who operate them—teachers, counselors, administrators—are responsible for outcomes. Few would disagree with this point of view. Major questions and issues arise, however, when implementation is considered. "Responsibility" is not new to the schools. Goals of education have been set, and the school's success in achieving them has been assessed. But the term *accountability* seems to ring a bell. Its popularity may be due more to novelty than to serviceability (Barro, 1970). Novelty or not, it appears to be the major new concept in education and other helping services today, and one that will be with us for years to come. Efforts to develop a comprehensive definition are only beginning.

Views of Accountability

The degree of enthusiasm for accountability evinced by guidance and counseling personnel varies considerably. Carey and Garris (1971) express the fear that emphasis on the popular definition of accountability at this stage of professional maturity will lead to a mechanistic orientation that will be disastrous to the humanistic approach. They suggest that accountability for *school counseling* should focus on role development, improved certification standards, and upgrading of the quality of help. But one may ask whether or not the publics served by the counselor will be willing to wait for such steps to be taken; instead, a strategy of simultaneous role development and identification of outcome indices is recommended (Humes, 1972). Humes (1972) further points out, in response to assertions that guidance results cannot be assessed objectively, that other noncognitive areas in education can be evaluated in terms of behavioral outcomes.

The need for the profession to move toward establishing behavioral objectives and making explicit the methods of assessing them appears to be pressing. The conditions that have led to this situation are identified by Barro (1970) as federally stimulated emphasis on evaluation, the trend toward cost evaluation in education, the priority on effective help for the disadvantaged, and an increased consumer voice in education. Guidance and pupil personnel workers need hard data to counteract efforts to cut staffs ("A Question of Survival," 1972). Walz (1971) describes the situation as a major crisis in continued public support for counseling and guidance services. But counselor reactions to this crisis are mixed (Walz, 1972). Some assert that accountability is contrary to the goals of counseling. Others conclude that they are already employing it. A third reaction is to develop a limited definition of accountability and insist that only that approach be used. The issues and controversy still exist, and resolution of the problem does not appear to be at hand.

Part of the problem seems to be guidance workers' interpretations of the concept. Walz (1972) gives a lucid explanation of the meaning of accountability for pupil personnel workers, pointing out that it involves a statement of the service's goals, preferably in behavioral terms; a specified way to measure the degree to which these outcomes are achieved; and communication of these goals and the service's degree of success in teaching them to the public. Accountability prescribes specific responsibilities and identifies the person or organization to whom the individual performing the service is responsible. This is one of the difficult problems: counselors may be accountable to the guidance director or the principal, but pupils, parents, and community members may regard counselors as accountable to them. They may insist that the service provide the the sort of help they consider relevant, regardless of school and pupil personnel policies. In fact, parents may refuse to support a school service that functions counter to their expectations. To date, policy statements to help eliminate this confusion are lacking. Certainly, the community has a role to play in establishing goals. At least one guide to community involvement in setting and ranking goals emphasizes this approach (Lang and Rose, 1972). At the same time, there seems to be some apprehension among counselors and guidance workers about inappropriate goals established by lay persons.

The reactions of guidance workers may be a necessary phase in the process of developing workable approaches to accountability. Walz (1972) suggests that this is the case and identifies four positive approaches. One, the self-study and hard-look-at-goals approach may be more effective than hasty adoption of a list of behavioral outcomes and performance standards. Two, it may be more productive to utilize new resources and find new ways to provide services than to further systematize, that is, reshuffle and relabel, existing procedures. Three, it may be productive to involve individuals at all levels in setting goals and reviewing progress. Four, a large-scale study and adoption of accountability procedures that offer professional groups the opportunity to enhance communication with all agencies and persons involved increase interest and cooperation.

It appears, therefore, that the question is no longer whether or not to adopt accountability, but what kind (Lieberman, 1970; Hartnett, 1971, pp. 1–2). The problems for guidance and counseling are in many ways more difficult than the extremely complex ones facing classroom teachers. Evaluation is itself difficult enough (Ginzberg, 1971, pp. 218–219). But accountability, while basically identical to evaluation, has several additional features that further complicate operation of a service program. First, it emphasizes efficient use of resources to achieve goals. Second, it should be possible for outside observers to assess results (Hartnett, 1971, pp. 5–6). Accountability, therefore, does not replace evaluation but adds important dimensions to it.

What is true for educational institutions is equally important for agencies and community services. There is a trend to make systematic reviews of their productivity and to base funding on results. In short, regardless of setting, the demand for counselors to be accountable is insistent and growing.

Counselor's Goals and Objectives

Setting goals is perhaps the most critical aspect of the process of evaluation and accountability. Ginzberg (1971, p. 253) puts his finger on the critical point when he states that society's expectations of guidance workers and guidance workers' goals are not necessarily the same. Though evaluation may never be as precise and effective as is desirable, the goals evaluated may not be those the public regards as the most relevant. Improving the quality of evaluation does not in itself resolve the problem of accountability.

Goals may be derived to some extent from the opinions and expectations of the publics served—pupils, teachers, parents, and community persons. Sources of goals also include the current guidance program, the needs of pupils in the school and school system, and outside sources, such as the objectives of other guidance programs (Sullivan and O'Hare, 1971, p. 13). Information from teachers, parents, and others is an aspect of pupil needs.

In stating goals and objectives, counselors, more than any other educators, face an acute dilemma. They must strike a balance between the excessively precise and trivial and the broadly ambiguous (Hartnett, 1971, p. 14). An analogy to engineering, in which the system is designed to turn out the highest-quality product with maximum efficiency, is helpful to a point. But education is a process of human interactions, not the processing of raw materials (Dyer, 1970). On the one hand, the position may be taken that the larger goals of counseling and guidance are too subtle, personal, and idiosyncratic to be expressed in precise terms. On the other hand, one may argue that guidance and counseling do, in fact, make a difference in the lives of pupils and that the difference should be observable and measurable. My opinion is closer to the latter position. There are effects that probably cannot be measured and that constitute the "large questions" (Hartnett, 1971, p. 14)—for example, does guidance provide an essential school service? But such questions can be broken down into specific elements for evaluation. The more elusive aspects of growth, development, and identity formation may present "hard problems. [But] they are problems that must be tackled" (Dyer, 1970, p. 211).

The goal of counseling and guidance should be changes in behavior that the counselee wishes to make that are not in extreme conflict with the values of society and that result in differences discernible to others (Krumboltz, 1966b, pp. 4–5). Utilizing these criteria will lead to establishment of behavioral objectives, identification of specific objectives for each counselee, and a valid assessment of results (Krumboltz 1966b, pp. 8–10). This approach leads to an evaluation strategy that involves a series of logical steps (O'Hare and Lasser, 1971, pp. 45–54). First, desired outcomes are stated precisely, in terms of observable behaviors. Next, criteria are established to assess the status of these outcomes before, during, and following the guidance process. Third, the guidance service components, for example, processes and situations, are identified. Cost effectiveness is considered, and comparisons made between the results of programs. Not all these steps must be taken simultaneously. A school may be *making progress* toward evaluation by clearly stating program outcomes.

The total framework just outlined represents a comprehensive evaluation. The procedure is clearly outlined by O'Hare and Lasser (1971, Chap. 4); Chapter 5 in the same reference illustrates the use of several different types of outcomes in evaluation. This book is an extremely valuable reference for a guidance staff planning program evaluations.

Vocational-development theory provides the guidelines for specifying long-range, immediate, and intermediate objectives for the career-development and guidance program. Herr and Cramer (1972, Chap. 5) review significant career-development concepts and describe and illustrate approaches to writing objectives. The California Personnel and Guidance Association monograph (Sullivan and O'Hare, 1971, Chap. 2) explains the approach of a task force of California educators in which process objectives were identified by the use of data from current programs, surveys of needs, and external sources. Four levels of responsibility were established:

1. Policy—board of education and legislature
2. Program—administrative staff
3. Operational—pupil personnel staff
4. Behavioral—pupils and pupil personnel staff (pupils also have responsibilities and are accountable)

Pupil personnel staffs are primarily concerned with the operational and behaviroal levels (carrying out the program, assessing results, and making needed modifications), but the policy and program levels have an impact on what is done at these levels.

Setting up the goals and building the guidance and career-development program are based on three dimensions, as shown in Figure 13.1. The "domains" represent

Figure 13.1   Three-dimensional model for pupil personnel objectives

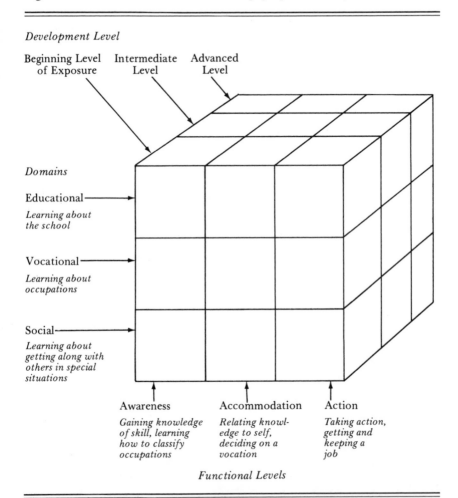

SOURCE: Howard J. Sullivan and Robert W. O'Hare, *Accountability in Pupil Personnel Services: A Process Guide for the Development of Objectives* (Fullerton, Calif.: California Personnel and Guidance Association, 1971), p. 12. Reproduced with permission.

the areas of the objectives. The "functional levels," as suggested by the examples, range from learning about the environment and the self through relating self-knowledge and environmental knowledge in making decisions to engaging in purposeful and consistent behavior. "Development levels" are the stages at which an objective is used. The level sequencing is quite flexible and dependent on the particular behavior in question. For example, behaviors could be dispersed through the twelve grades or accomplished during the last year in high school. Development levels, as well as domains and functional levels, are based on vocational-development theory.

This format is a very practical one for the guidance and pupil personnel staff to use in preparing objectives and is not as demanding as it might first appear. Every cell in the figure need not be filled—in other words, every activity does not have to be provided in every grade (Sullivan and O'Hare, 1971, p. 13).

GUIDELINES FOR EVALUATION

Recent years have witnessed a marked increase in interest in and use of evaluation procedures. Many of the programs described in Chapter 10 have had both internal and external evaluations. More attention is being paid to providing data about results to those responsible for decisions about programs; for example, Wergin, Munson, Garrison, and Braskamp (1976) describe an evaluation program that was deliberately political in its intent to have an impact on influential persons.

The California Plan

The California Personnel and Guidance Association monograph (Sullivan and O'Hare, 1971, pp. 30–32, 106) also provides excellent guidelines for carrying the process from the initial formulation of objectives to final assessment. The Situation, Population, Outcome, Process, or SPOP, format for writing objectives explained in this publication is particularly helpful. For each objective, each of these four elements is specified (Sullivan and O'Hare, 1971, p. 106). An example is as follows:

Santa Ana Unified School District
Sample Objective
Saddleback High School
Goals of Counseling and Guidance
EDUCATIONAL
1.0 DISTRICT GOAL   To assist each student in his efforts to develop and utilize his potential in making a place for himself in the school, in the community and in the larger society of the state and nation.
1.2 PROGRAM OBJECTIVE   For the student to become aware of his academic abilities, limitations and educational interests.
OPERATIONAL OBJECTIVE
Situation: Given Saddleback High School, a four-year high school located in a business and industrial community with a student population coming primarily from middle- and lower-class families, 26% of which are of minority ethnic origin.
Population: All students.

Treatment: After small group discussions or individual conferences in which the counselor interprets test scores, with each student having a copy of his own test scores.

Outcome: Upon request by the counselor, 80% of all students will be able to report accurately their own academic strengths and weaknesses and their academic aptitude as indicated by test scores.

The district goal is the general objective. The program objective is only one of many, but it illustrates the format. The situation indicates the locale in which results will be assessed. In the example, the school and community are identified and their significant features described. The population specifies who will be assessed. The outcome indicates the behavior that is supposed to result, and to what degree. In the example, 80 percent of the students should be able to report the findings of tests about their traits.

In the evaluation process, a criterion-referenced test was used. Norm-referenced measurements can also be employed, but the former are more useful in determining whether or not pupils have reached an acceptable level on the criteria. Furthermore, evaluation may be *formative* or *summative*. In the first type, the program is evaluated while it is still being developed; in the second, evaluation is carried out after the program has been established. Formative evaluation and criterion-referenced measurements are, as Sullivan and O'Hare point out, particularly useful in improving the type of program discussed here.

The National Assessment Program

This project, for which planning began in 1964, provides extensive help in setting up evaluation activities (Womer, 1970; McQueen, 1971). Subject areas, academic skills, and citizenship are covered; the category of "career and occupational development" is of special relevance here. The career-development objectives do not represent the outcomes of any single subject but cut across learnings in general education, guidance, and counseling. Specific vocational skills are not included. The following career-development dimensions were assessed: self-evaluation, career-planning, attitudes toward work, employment-seeking skills, work habits, and skills useful in many occupations (National Assessment of Educational Progress,

Achievement was measured at four age levels—nine, thirteen, seventeen, and young adults between twenty-six and thirty-five—during 1972 and 1973. Over thirty thousand pupils at each of the first three stages and about twenty thousand young adults were tested each year. Career and occupational development were measured again in 1978 and 1979, on a six-year cycle.

The National Assessment has led to four reports on career-development needs for ages nine, thirteen, seventeen, and adults aged twenty-six to thirty-five (see pp. 266–267 and the Additional References for Chapter 9). The reports discuss implications and suggest activities to promote career development. Since it is possible to use the exercises for local needs surveys, national, regional, and community comparisons and evaluations can be made. Although the surveys are cross-sectional, they give a vivid picture of some important facets of career development for almost three decades of life.

Planning, Programming, Budgeting System

Accountability may be instituted in a school or school system by utilizing the Planning, Programming, Budgeting System, or PPBS (Humes, 1972). This approach, although similar in many ways to the systems approach (Hosford and Ryan, 1970), makes possible the comparison of program costs and achievements. In an application to guidance, a program analysis of a junior high school program was made. Goals stating the general purposes of the program were formulated. For example, one goal was helping pupils attain maximum personal and educational development. The objectives drawn from the goals are quite specific, measurable, and scheduled for accomplishment within a designated time limit. For example, one objective was personal and educational growth for 90 percent of the pupils. Success in reaching this goal was assessed by a counselor-completed rating sheet for the period from grades seven through nine. Constraints, a third factor in PPBS, are limitations or obstacles that may hinder attainment of goals and objectives. In the example, one constraint was an obsolete role definition for the counselor.

Additional steps in PPBS include program description, evaluation, desirable program changes according to priority, methods of making program changes, and financial plans. Humes points out weaknesses in the approach and suggests ways that it could be improved.

More emphasis on PPBS may be expected in schools and colleges as allocation of funds becomes more critical. Regardless of the counseling and guidance worker's degree of enthusiasm for this and the systems approach, he or she would do well to learn about them.

An Office of Education Procedure

A particularly highly developed evaluation system is the one used to select exemplary career-education projects to submit to the Joint Dissemination Review Panel of the U.S. Office of Education to make available well-evaluated models to school systems. This evaluation program is noteworthy as an illustration of a carefully executed assessment of specific career-guidance activities to identify procedures for practioners. The American Institutes for Research carried out evaluations in three stages (Hamilton and Mitchell, 1978). Of the 257 career-education activities analyzed, only ten were selected to submit to the Joint Dissemination Review Panel. Of these ten, six were initially approved for dissemination and a seventh was accepted after the needed evaluation information was provided. Seven reports on activities have been released (see Additional References).

The project staff also developed comprehensive criteria for evaluation (Hamilton and Mitchell, 1978, pp. 9–12) and a handbook *(Ways to Evaluate Different Types of Career Education Activities: A Handbook of Evaluation Models)* for local evaluations that includes clear, practical procedures for six evaluation models (Mitchell, 1978).

The major groups of factors used and several representative items illustrate their comprehensiveness. (The complete criteria will be of considerable help to those planning evaluation.) The major criteria are the effectiveness of the activity, its importance, and its replicability, generalizability, and practicability (Hamilton and Mitchell, 1978, p. 6). Under the subcategory of "evaluation," some representative items are as follows:

FOCUS   Evaluation data are available on those activity objectives that are relevant to improvement of career education skills.

AVAILABILITY   Information required for validation of activity success can be obtained. Available information is adequate to validate activity success.

EVALUATION SAMPLE   Critical descriptive and statistical data related to characterizing the activity group are provided. In instances where the evaluation group was only a portion of the activity group, procedures for selecting the group are specified.

EDUCATIONAL SIGNIFICANCE   Educational significance is demonstrated if the performance of the activity group is greater with respect to activity objectives than would be expected for appropriate reference groups, e.g., using typical instructional materials and procedures with a group comparable to activity participants (Hamilton and Mitchell, 1978, pp. 10–11).

Evaluation Models

Even more valuable to the practitioner are the six evaluation models and examples of applications in the handbook. Although the term *career education* is used, with some adaptations, the procedures would be useful for all sorts of settings because the problems identified as typical for career education are often present in other programs. These evaluation problems are that guidance activities are started without consideration of underlying assumptions or premises, that there is no comprehensive understanding of major conditions or factors that affect the program, that there is no identification of alternative strategies, that programs may be shaped by local conditions so generalizations are not possible, and that data needed for evaluation are not clearly identified (Mitchell, 1978, p. 1).

The models provide for assessment of specific components of the career-education program, but they can be combined for a more comprehensive evaluation. Those that identify the major components of a comprehensive career-education program are as follows:

1. Evaluation of supplementary activities, such as field trips
2. Evaluation of career-education facilities, such as housing
3. Evaluation of indirect interventions, such as those activities designed to insure that students are exposed to accurate and comprehensive occupational information

4. Evaluation of staff development, such as programs to improve the use of facilitative techniques

5. Evaluation of product development, such as career-development exercises for group use

6. Evaluation of curriculum implementation, such as threading career-education concepts into the curriculum

These models clearly show that a career-education program has several major components and that evaluation must be designed to get at the unique features of these components. Examples of applications help the reader apply the models to his or her own situation. The manual also contains an annotated list of resource materials covering all types of evaluation, assessment instruments, and research reports.

OBJECTIVES AND EVALUATIVE RESEARCH

Research methods and procedures are significant only to the extent that they contribute in some way to the improvement of guidance and provide ways to assess success in reaching goals. The critical questions are: "What are we trying to do?" "What is the situation now?" "How well does the procedure work?" After these questions are clearly stated, research and evaluation designs and techniques are used to help answer them. The degree of success in reaching goals indicates the extent to which the requirements of accountability have been met.

In recent years substantial progress has been made in developing research and evaluation procedures and techniques that will help the guidance and counseling staff answer the questions just raised. A review of examples, general research methods, and specific techniques is beyond the scope of this chapter. Excellent summaries have been published by Brayfield and Crites (1964), Thoresen (1969), Tyler (1969, Chap. 14), and Goldman (1978).

The counselor may play one or more of several research roles. He or she may be a *consumer, producer, stimulator, teacher of the problem-solving method,* or *program evaluator* (Tolbert, 1967, p. 2; Tolbert, 1972b, pp. 363–364). Of these roles, the *producer* in an action research–oriented approach will be most extensively used (Cramer, Herr, Morris, and Frantz, 1970, p. 1). This is an extremely important role, particularly for evaluation and accountability. More than a decade ago, Moore (1967) stated that, while public faith and confidence has for a time supported the guidance service, eventually more concrete evidence would be required. He emphasized the contribution that local research and evaluation can make in providing this evidence. I strongly endorse these statements about the value of local research and believe that support personnel and computers should enable the counselor to improve both the scope and sophistication of local evaluative studies.

Research Types

Five types of research are particularly well adapted to answering the kinds of questions the counselor faces: descriptive, follow-up, environmental assessment, program evaluation, and single-case designs (Cramer, et al., 1970, pp. 2–6; Frey, 1978). Each of these types can be built into the ongoing program and can provide data for evaluation, program improvement, and accountability.

Descriptive research is the most basic, would ordinarily be done first, and provides information needed by all school personnel. Usually, a great variety of extremely significant data is scattered throughout records, reports, and other sources. Pulled together and organized, these data can give a valuable description of the pupil population. Additional information, such as occupational goals, may be obtained directly from pupils. A starting point might be an inventory of knowledge and attitudes about the guidance and counseling program—for example, how well it is known and what type of help it is expected to provide. For career guidance, data about occupational and educational plans, usually contained in the cumulative records, would be helpful in program planning. Description may also involve comparisons of, for example, achievement and potential (Cramer et al., 1970, Chaps. 2–5). These authors describe techniques for organizing descriptive data, including the preparation of local norms, expectancy tables, and correlations. The latter two are particularly useful for introducing the "comparison" element to description. Cramer, Herr, Morris, and Frantz (1970, Chap. 10) and Buchheimer and Weiner (1967) also describe procedures for studying student attitudes, and Cramer (1967) explains how the opinion survey may be designed and carried out. These references are excellent guides to conducting descriptive studies.

The second type suggested by Cramer, Herr, Morris, and Frantz is the *follow-up study*. This technique was discussed earlier in connection with the information system and the guidance and counseling process. In my opinion, it is more a phase of guidance than a type of research, but its use in research and evaluation is important. As a phase of *guidance,* follow-up would not include every pupil—although theoretically it should. In *evaluation,* every pupil would be contacted. The follow-up can provide the most meaningful data about the effectiveness of the guidance and educational program and is thus closely related to accountability.

The follow-up must be carefully planned, executed, and interpreted to be useful. Misuses and misinterpretations result from inadequate sampling, misinterpretation of cause-effect relationships, and overgeneralization. Poor returns, particularly if they represent a biased group, may give a very distorted picture. It is particularly important to determine whether the respondents are similar to the group about whom generalizations are made. Two particularly useful references for planning, conducting, and interpreting follow-up research are by Cramer, Herr, Morris, and Frantz (1970, Chap. 8) and Hansen and Herr (1967, pp. 100–114).

Environmental assessment is the third type of research in which counselors are likely to be involved. The concept of institutional "press" is a relatively new one (Cramer et al., 1970, pp. 4–5, Chap. 6) and has significant implications for guidance. Environmental data are essential for the change-agent role, because they describe the pressures, demands, and influences of the institution. Cramer, Herr, Morris, and Frantz explain how press may be assessed and how the counselor may use the results of this type of research.

The fourth type, *program evaluation,* is one with which the counseling and guidance staff will inevitably be involved. Accrediting associations must carry out evaluations from time to time. Evaluation may involve staff, facilities, process, or products. Evaluative criteria and related procedures judge program effectiveness on the basis of input, that is, personnel available, services provided, equipment on hand, and use of time. Accountability puts more emphasis on outcomes. In the former type, it is assumed that if personnel, equipment, and facilities are adequate, guidance will be effective.

The fifth type of research, the *single-case design,* has been widely recognized as a productive approach to counseling and guidance research (Anton, 1978; Frey, 1978). It is adaptable for the day-to-day work of counselors and can be carried out in the school, agency, or community setting. Frey (1978) identifies three patterns of single-case analysis; psychohistory, to understand the lives of historical figures; case study, to understand the lives of contemporary counselees; and intensive designs, to analyze the effects of some kind of treatment. All these approaches involve collection and analysis of all sorts of data about the case, including repeated measurements over time to detect changes. The general approach can be used to study several cases at a time instead of only one; practicing counselors may find some versions of both the single and multiple case useful in relating theory to practice and validating their own work (Thoresen, 1978).

Additional Strategies

A number of suggestions have been made to improve the quality, utility, and relevance of research in counseling and guidance; these suggestions are applicable regardless of the counselor's work setting, and they provide effective ways to demonstrate accountability. Goldman (1976, 1977, 1978) recommends the single-case design to improve the relevance and utility of guidance research. He also suggests more emphasis on field studies, an increase in systematic observations, an increase in the use of interviews instead of questionnaires, and more emphasis on practice-oriented studies. In order to deal with problems arising from the ethics involved in research on human subjects and experimenter effects, Goldman suggests that the researcher make a contractual agreement with participants and explain as much as possible about what is going to happen in the procedure, to build an open, collaborative relationship in the research process. Other recommendations (Sprinthall, 1975) emphasize the importance of focusing on significant questions, conducting studies in the work or educational setting, and providing flexibility in design so needed changes can be made as the study progresses.

Moving beyond research planning and execution, new strategies have been formulated to derive the most possible value from completed studies. Meta-analysis (Glass, 1976; Smith and Glass, 1977; Mehrens, 1978) uses existing studies rather than new data, combining results of large numbers of separate, often very specific research projects to check the stability of findings. For Glass, meta-analysis means "the statistical analysis of a large number of analysis results from individual studies for the purpose of integrating the findings" (1976, p. 3). The procedure promises to show which information may be used with confidence and which is transitory and accidental.

Opinions differ about the areas that should have research priority to improve guidance and counseling practice. Mehrens (1978) takes issue with Goldman's analysis of the shortcomings and recommends more rigor, stating that rigor does not necessarily interfere with relevance. In the final analysis, we need all types of research in career guidance and career education. Improving the quality of evaluation depends on improving the quality of the research on which it is based.

Although evaluation involves use of research concepts and techniques, the two differ in a number of important ways, even though some of the research models already mentioned are more like evaluation than research—for example, field studies. But evaluation is aimed at providing information needed by those making decisions about career guidance and career education and is based on program goals and objectives. Further, evaluation is flexible so it can accommodate changes along the way, a procedure that would disrupt the typical research project (Oetting and Hawkes, 1974; Burck and Peterson, 1975). The term used by Oetting and Hawkes, *evaluative research,* appeals to me as one that best describes the process.

Models for evaluation demonstrate a remarkable degree of innovation and utility and cover much more than "what happened?" Results are crucial to accountability, but program planners, counselors, administrators, and the public need to know more than only what happened. Even though the major accountability focus is on the impact the program has on users—product evaluation—synthesis of evaluation and research is needed in the evaluation process.

Some evaluation strategies that focus on elements besides goals and objectives use innovative procedures to expand on one or more of the types of research given to facilitate program improvement. Brown (1978) identifies three of these as *goal-free, responsive,* and *transactional;* each emphasizes individuals, processes, and values and can be applied to the ongoing guidance or personnel programs. In the goal-free approach, the evaluator deliberately does not learn about program goals but instead searches for program effects intended and not intended, particularly any side effects. In the responsive approach, emphasis is on what is actually done, as contrasted with the written program description; informal reports are given to the administrator at frequent intervals. Thus, careful observation of what acutally happens and how those involved feel about their functions is used extensively. In the transactional approach, emphasis is on conflicts that arise as the program is carried out—the attitudes of those who favor it and those who are antagonistic to it. A greater administrator involvement than usual is required, but success results from program improvements that save the administrator time in the long run.

None of these strategies should be the sole evaluation used; more typical goal-oriented studies should also be carried out. The suggestions that follow for practical applications primarily emphasize product evaluation, that is, effects on the individuals served. (Books cited in the Additional References for this chapter give detailed information about implementing other types.) For accountability, this is the most significant type of evaluation. Moreoever, it requires that goals be clearly formulated and stated in terms that make sense to the many publics involved—teachers, administrators, parents, legislators.

THE FOLLOW-UP IN EVALUATION

The primary purpose of evaluation is to estimate the effectiveness of help and to identify needed improvements. Input evidence, such as number and qualification of counselors, and process variables, such as evidence of counselee growth, are important. Outcome data are the most significant, the most difficult to obtain, and the most ambiguous insofar as cause and effect are concerned. Evidence obtained from evaluation procedures may be used in several ways. But there is no substitute for information about what happens to pupils after they leave school. If priorities for evaluation must be established, the follow-up study should be given top rank.

The most significant criterion for career guidance and counseling—for the whole career-development program, in fact—is what happens to the individual when he or she goes to work. Whether work is entered after high school, vocational training, or college, the suitability of the job is the ultimate criterion. "Suitability," however, is subject to many interpretations. Furthermore, it is difficult to identify outcomes that may be specifically attributed to the guidance services.

Follow-up for evaluation is no different from follow-up to collect data for the information service. Contact is made by mail, telephone, or visit after the worker has had time to estimate the suitability of the job. A reasonable interval is one to three months. Because follow-up contacts may be made by various persons, coordination is needed to prevent duplication. For example, the vocational teacher may be following up pupils, the counselor may be following up those with whom he or she has worked, and contacts may be made to collect data for the information service. A central file of names, addresses, and follow-up results is a necessity.

It is difficult to specify the total span of time to be covered by the follow-up. If several contacts are made during the first five or six months on the job, rather reliable estimates of suitability should be obtained, and they may suffice for evaluation. But long-range career pattern information is also important. What happens after one or two years? Is progress evident? Were good decisions made? Is there evidence that the career-development and guidance program had a lasting effect? The final decision about the extent of the follow-up should be based on its specific purposes and criteria, but relatively long-term data add greatly to the value of program evaluation.

Relating criteria to career development and guidance is difficult, but effective behaviors can be inferred to be at least partially the result of the school program. For example, if teaching decision-making skills was part of the school program and former pupils indicate that these skills have helped them to develop good plans, at least some credit can be taken by the school. Behavioral objectives will facilitate linking school emphases to later activities. For example, if one criterion is the *behavioral objective* of having three interviews for jobs related to training, performance of this activity can be credited with some confidence to the career-development and guidance program. If the goal is for 80 percent of former pupils to carry out this procedure, and 80 percent of them do so, the goal has been reached. Whether or not the same percentage would have done the same thing if there were no career development in the school cannot be judged. Experimentation is needed to give evidence of the comparative effectiveness of programs and techniques.

Personnel and facilities should be provided for the follow-up. Not only is it possible to evaluate program effectiveness, but additional assistance may be given to those who are experiencing difficulties. This extra step not only helps the individual but also enables the guidance service to raise its "batting average." If, for example, ten former pupils are well satisfied and successful and ten are not, helping eight of the latter will raise the success rate from 50 percent to 90 percent. Although this illustration may seem extreme, a *little more assistance* is often all that is needed, and without providing it the guidance service has stopped just short of doing a complete job. It may be too much to expect that counselors undertake this kind of follow-up, but schools can hardly afford to omit this phase of the guidance serivce, for both humanistic and practical reasons. It has multiple potential values, which Sinick (1970, pp. 65–66) emphasizes in describing how "postplacement services" contribute to counselees, guidance services, schools, and employers.

For Education and Training

Although the education or training follow-up is an intermediate step to job follow-up, it is an essential part of the evaluation program. Systematic procedures are needed for checking on those who selected a vocational-education program in the high school. Plans can be worked out with the vocational-education teacher, who usually maintains a record of each pupil's progress. For example, the boy who enters diversified occupations to become an auto mechanic is admitted on the basis of some criteria. Often, however, these criteria are neither known nor utilized by guidance personnel. Sometimes personal biases enter into the admission process, and follow-up will enable both teacher and guidance worker to determine the really critical criteria.

Evaluation of the success of those entering post–high school training or education is even more important. This training represents a very specific choice and commitment, and its suitability should be a major concern of the high school guidance service. Follow-up may be facilitated by the training institution; many routinely send progress reports to high schools. Information from the former pupil, however, is essential in the evaluation process.

Training and educational follow-up are linked directly to the goals of the guidance service. Areas that cover the information the guidance service needs to assess its own help and that of the total program include the following:

1. How well the respondent likes the program (tasks, colleagues, and teachers).
2. How well it meets expectations.
3. The effectiveness of the help received in selecting the program. (For example, was the information received adequate?)
4. Estimates of progress.
5. The degree to which the program will enable the student to reach his or her career goals.

6. Problems or difficulties encountered and suggestions for high school pupils considering the program.

Other areas could be covered, but these cover the information the guidance service needs to assess both its own help and that of the total career-development program.

The follow-up data should also indicate that additional needed assistance will be provided. In most cases this could be given by guidance personnel at the training or educational institution. The high school's main function could be to suggest to the respondent that he or she contact a counselor. If the current institution takes the initiative, this suggestion could be communicated to a counselor. Ethical practices, particularly those related to confidentiality, must be observed, but this would not usually prevent positive action by the school counselor. In one example, a student in a specialized post–high school training program needed help for home-related and personal problems. As is often the case, the troubled student was reluctant to approach the guidance office. Without breaking any confidences, the school counselor mentioned this to the vocational school counselor and suggested that the student be contacted in a way that would appear to be a routine interview with new students. The contact was made and provided the opportunity for the student to discuss problems that were making it difficult for him to do satisfactory work.

Several methods of contacting former pupils may be used. The interview held either at the individual's home or at the work or training site is the most informative and mutually helpful, though the most time-consuming. Support personnel could help carry out this type of follow-up. Former pupils may be invited to return to the school for follow-up interviews, but this is not likely to result in very many contacts. The school guidance service will have to take the initiative to obtain comprehensive results, and the mailed questionnaires may be the only practical method. Lack of responses may present a serious difficulty. I have followed up a number of groups and have typically received around 50 to 60 percent returns from mailed questionnaires even after repeated appeals. Telephone calls and personal notes to nonrespondents resulted in no more than a 10 or 15 percent increase.

Circle (1968, Section 4) gives an excellent review of research on the follow-up and describes the plan developed for the Newton, Massachusetts, schools. The report provides an excellent guide for planning a follow-up study in connection with placement services.

For Improving the Curriculum

The success of pupils in work, training, or education may be largely due to the curriculum. Multiple influences, including the home, community, and personal attributes, play a part, and no curriculum can account for all the successes or failures in career choice and adjustment. There are, however, curriculum factors that can contribute to the career development of pupils.

The follow-up provides information about former pupils' occupations, and these data suggest the types of programs the school should emphasize. But other factors must be given consideration. If the labor market is tight, the jobs entered may be the only ones available. Lack of relevant preparation, however, may prevent pupils from getting jobs that are available. For example, there may be a need for welders, but such training is not provided. The follow-up, if used alone, would not reveal this situation, since few former pupils would be in this type of work. Further, new businesses or industries may be opening and providing jobs that have previously been unavailable. Follow-up data should be compared with information about current and predicted opportunities in the community.

A breakdown of the *directions* that pupils take—college, industry, business, technical training—will give excellent guidelines for establishing curriculum priorities. The unemployed group needs special attention for estimating necessary preparation in vocational skills as well as needed career-development emphases. Resources can then be utilized in ways that are the most effective for the greatest number. Programs that lead nowhere should be dropped in order to strengthen those that are more relevant.

The follow-up provides data about the adequacy of existing programs. For example, if those in office jobs tend to agree that their levels of skills are inadequate or that some important skills were not covered in classes, changes can be made to remedy deficiencies. Employers' evaluations are particularly useful. For example, in one evaluation employers stated that many new shopworkers did not seem to be aware of the need for promptness and were unable to work under supervision. To remedy this situation, shop instructors organized classes into industry-type groups, with foremen and a system of time cards for checking in and out. Other on-the-job practices were adopted so that the school situation provided a realistic orientation to the world of work.

The procedure for identifying significant data in follow-ups and translating them into priorities for curriculum development should be established with care. Participation of guidance personnel on the curriculum committee is one way to bring critical information before the group that can make essential changes and modifications.

Follow-up data inevitably have implications for the career-education and development program. Results indicate the levels of vocational maturity that were achieved. For example, it should be possible to determine how much awareness there is of the factors that need to be considered in career choice and planning, the effectiveness of decision making, and the implementation of occupation values.

For Improving the Career-Guidance Program

The career-guidance program includes follow-up as part of the total process. Follow-up of counseling and placement, however, will not necessarily reach all pupils and may not cover the time span desired. The all-pupil systematic follow-up can be designed to reveal the effectiveness of next steps for both graduates and dropouts and to indicate the positive impact of career guidance service. The following are areas that could be covered when former pupils are contacted.

1. KNOWLEDGE OF THE GUIDANCE PROGRAM   If pupils do not know about the guidance program, or if they have a misconception of what it is supposed to do, a better job of communicating with them is obviously needed.

2. UTILIZATION OF THE SERVICES   If a pupil needed some sort of assistance and for one reason or another did not obtain it, the availability of services should be assessed. For example, is more of an outreach approach needed? Should teachers be encouraged to make more extensive use of referrals? Are counselors and other guidance staff members actually available, or are they busy most of the time in committee work and administrative duties?

3. EFFECTIVENESS OF ASSISTANCE   Some of the help provided, for example, career days, career films, or occupational files, may not be recognized by former pupils as part of the guidance service. If evaluation of specific items is to be accomplished, each item will have to be identified in the follow-up. Even so, the impact of particular features is one of the most difficult types of information to extract from returns. If the individual accomplished his or her goals, it may not be possible to determine the part played by the career-guidance service or any one aspect of it. If he or she did not, it may also be impossible to determine whether or not it was the fault of the guidance service. Framing appropriate questions, however, may help make it possible to identify effective or ineffective elements. For example, was career information lacking or obsolete? Was counseling helpful in decision making? Did placement help the pupil locate a suitable job, school, or college?

4. PERCENTAGE OF PUPILS HELPED   Follow-up data will begin to reveal trends as more and more are collected. If a substantial percentage of pupils have found a technique or service helpful, its value is substantiated. Trends may similarly reveal weaknesses. For example, suppose that dropouts tend to express the feeling that they were overlooked and ignored until the exit interview. The procedure for identifying and contacting potential dropouts needs to be improved. Early identification may in turn highlight the need for better in-school placement, an expanded work-study program, group counseling, or improved referral and placement services.

Follow-up information is most significant for evaluation and improvement of the school career-guidance and counseling service. But it is often, however, the missing ingredient. When follow-up information is obtained, it is often a one-time effort whose results are filed after little analysis. Its importance, however, is analogous to that of similar data in a variety of other fields. In test construction, the ultimate evidence of validity is how well the test predicts future performance. In business and industry, the ultimate criterion is how well the product or service satisfies those who use it. In career counseling and guidance, regardless of setting, the success of the "product" in achieving life goals is the ultimate criterion.

For Public Relations

The school's responsibility for college placement has long been recognized by both educators and lay persons. The inference may easily be made, therefore, that the school is primarily a college-preparatory institution. The follow-up of those who go to work or enter vocational training after high school should have an effect on community attitudes toward the school. Contact with employers and workers publicizes the fact that guidance goals are relevant to all pupils.

In addition to the public relations effect of the follow-up itself, it is advantageous to tell the community through the newspapers, radio, television, and by talks to community groups what is being done, why, and how it is working. Too often, schools and colleges cannot state where their "products" are, what they are doing, and the degree of success they are experiencing—and do not appear particularly concerned about the questions. Follow-up thus provides the content for an effective public relations program.

SUMMARY

The career-guidance and counseling service and the career-education program, utilizing a variety of sources, establish goals and objectives for which they are accountable. Results of services—suitable work, education, or training—are so important to school and community that carefully designed evaluation is critical to estimate effectiveness and make needed improvements. Research, particularly some newer approaches, makes available powerful techniques and strategies for improvement of evaluation. Research and evaluation, however, are different in several essential ways—for example, evaluation provides data needed by decision makers and is goal oriented.

A variety of evaluation strategies are available to the practitioner for assessing each major phase of a program. Although input, context, and process evaluation are important, follow-up data are considered the most significant for evaluating and improving the service. A variety of significant information may be obtained by the follow-up. This information should be used to evaluate and improve both the school program and the career-guidance and counseling service.

PROJECTS AND EXPERIENTIAL ACTIVITIES

1. Interview a fellow student or colleague as if you were conducting a follow-up interview for evaluating guidance services. Prepare an interview guide for this purpose, paying particular attention to ways to identify the specific services that were helpful.

2. Select a specific aspect of the career-guidance program (for example, the career day, occupational file, or in-school program placement) and design an evaluation study.

3. Design a follow-up questionnaire to be used with pupils going directly to work after school.

4. State in behavioral terms the objectives of some aspects of the career-guidance service. Prepare a follow-up form to assess these objectives.

5. In small groups, select a counseling setting. Then assume that you are to appear before the budget-making group to justify funds for your counseling service. What will you be accountable for and how will you show that you have achieved the desired results? Each group should report to the class. Discuss the significance of program goals for the service and the community.

6. In small groups, assume that you have the task of evaluating graduates of the counselor-education program. Establish one goal and one objective and describe how you would estimate success in achieving the objective. Identify the type of evaluation used. Report results to the class. Is the objective significant? Can progress toward it be assessed?

7. In small groups, role-play the following situation: One group member is applying for a job and has been asked by the interviewing committee to talk about the evidence of results of career guidance and counseling and/or career education. Ask one group member to role-play the applicant while the others serve as the group interview committee. After a five- or six-minute interview, discuss results. Did the applicant present useful evaluation data from his or her own experiences and from evaluative research? Rotate applicants and repeat the process several times, following up each interview session with a discussion.

ADDITIONAL REFERENCES

American Institutes for Research. *Evaluated, Exemplary Activities in Career Education (K-12),* Palo Alto, Calif.: American Institutes for Research, 1978. Seven reports contain descriptions of exemplary career-education activities approved for dissemination. Each of these reports includes a description of the evaluation process that could serve as a model for other educational institutions. The seven reports are as follows:

Baker, Octave V., and Virginia Lish. *Project CERES* (Career Education Responsive to Every Student), Ceres United School District, Ceres, California.

Baker, Octave V., and Norman Steinaker. *Project MATCH* (Matching Attitudes and Talents to Career Horizons), Ontario-Montclair School District, Ontario, California.

Hamilton, Jack A., and Jeanne Leffler. *Project CAP* (Career Awareness Program), Boston Mountains Educational Cooperative, Greenland, Arkansas.

Hamilton, Jack A., and John D. Ross. *Project EQUALITY,* Highline Public Schools, Seattle, Washington.

Kaplan, Carol B., and Lee Downey. *Project CDCC* (Career Development Centered Curriculum), Coloma Community School District, Coloma, Michigan.

McBain, Susan L., and Joyce McKay. *Developmental Career Guidance Project,* Pima County, Arizona.

McBain, Susan L., and Nicholas J. Topougis. *Career Development Program,* Akron Public Schools, Akron, Ohio.

Bingham, William C. "Assessing Career Guidance Outcomes." In *A Comprehensive View of Career Development*. Eds. Garry R. Walz, Robert L. Smith, and Libby Benjamin. Washington, D.C.: American Personnel and Guidance Association, 1974, pp. 80–93. A useful, brief overview of evaluation and accountability that covers issues, obstacles, and application of results.

College Entrance Examination Board. *Research Guidelines for High School Counselors*. New York: College Entrance Examination Board, 1967. This is an excellent, easy-to-understand guide for all types of research. Illustrations and procedures are specifically related to the work of the secondary-school counselor.

Cramer, Stanley H., Edwin L. Herr, Charles H. Morris, and Thomas T. Frantz. *Research and the School Counselor*. Boston: Houghton Mifflin, 1970. This is one of the most useful references available for the counselor when planning and carrying out research and evaluative studies. Emphasis is, appropriately, on what the counselor can do in his or her school to improve guidance and counseling services. Data processing is introduced, and there is a concise summary of several major research programs.

Frey, David. "Science and the Single Case in Counseling Research." *Personnel and Guidance Journal*, 56, No. 5 (1978), 263–268. This is the lead article by the guest editor of the special-feature section on the single case in counseling research. It and three other articles on this type of research constitute a valuable resource for counselors who are learning about these practical, on-the-job research strategies.

Goldman, Leo, ed. *Research Methods for Counselors: Practical Approaches in Field Settings*. New York: John Wiley, 1978. A very useful reference for planning and conducting studies in the local work setting. The aim of the book is to bring research and evaluation to the practitioner; the sixteen authors accomplish this task in an impressive manner.

Herr, Edwin L., and Stanley H. Cramer. *Vocational Guidance and Career Development in the Schools: Toward a Systems Approach*. Boston: Houghton Mifflin, 1972. Chap. 5 relates career-development theory to the objectives of the career-development program, describes approaches to writing objectives, and gives examples. This is a particularly good reference for this chapter.

Krumboltz, John D. *Stating the Goals of Counseling*. Fullerton, Calif.: Personnel and Guidance Association, 1966. An extremely helpful statement on how to cast counseling goals in terms that can facilitate assessment and program improvement.

Mitchell, A. M., ed. *Ways to Evaluate Different Types of Career-Education Activities: A Handbook of Evaluation Models*. Palo Alto, Calif.: American Institutes for Research, 1978. An extremely useful easy-to-understand guide for conducting evaluations. Purposes of evaluation are discussed and six models are given in how-to-do-it fashion with cartoons that illuminate as well as amuse. The annotated list of references is an invaluable source of information for planning and carrying out evaluations.

National Assessment of Educational Progress. *Objectives for Career and Occupational Development*. Denver: National Assessment of Educational Progress, 1971. This is a valuable statement of career-development objectives for ages nine, thirteen, seventeen, and adults. It is a useful guide for planning the career-development program in the schools. The procedure used for formulating the objectives is described, and the assessment schedule is given. The objectives for the second assessment are given in *Career and Occupational Development Objectives: Second Assessment* (1977) Objectives are listed in two categories: knowledge, abilities, and attitudes for (1) career decisions, and (2) career success.

O'Hare, Robert W., and Barbara Lasser. *Evaluating Pupil Personnel Programs.* Fullerton, Calif.: California Personnel and Guidance Association, 1971. This book is a must for school counseling and guidance personnel, both for an overview of trends and for planning program evaluation. Strategies are concisely and lucidly stated, and examples are given.

Sinick, David. *Occupational Information and Guidance.* Boston: Houghton Mifflin, 1970. The postplacement service discussed on pp. 65–72 is a good illustration of the evaluation follow-up recommended in this chapter.

Sullivan, Howard J., and Robert W. O'Hare, eds. *Accountability in Pupil Personnel Services: A Process Guide for the Development of Objectives.* Fullerton, Calif.: California Personnel and Guidance Association, 1971. This monograph, which was prepared under the auspices of the Bureau of Pupil Personnel Services, California State Department of Education, is a valuable resource for the guidance staff. It has been referred to extensively in this chapter, and a careful and complete study of it is highly recommended.

Tolbert, E. L. *Research for Teachers and Counselors.* Minneapolis: Burgess, 1967. Chap. 8 illustrates how the counselor, as a consumer of research, can analyze and apply the work of others. On-the-job action-type research is discussed and illustrated on pp. 57–62.

———. *An Introduction to Guidance.* Boston: Little, Brown, 1978. Chap. 13 summarizes points of view on research and accountability, discusses various types of programs, and suggests ways to implement the results of evaluation to improve services.

Upton, A., B. Lowery, and B. Varenhorst. *A Planning Model for Developing a Career Guidance Curriculum.* Fullerton, Calif.: California Personnel and Guidance Association, 1978. The program planning model developed by the Bureau of Pupil Personnel Services of the California State Department of Education is described here, and the book also includes a very useful chapter on the evaluation process.

ACES Position Paper:

Counselor Preparation for

Career Development*/Career Education†

RECOMMENDATIONS

Recognizing the inadequacies felt by many counselors in meeting the career-guidance needs of children, youth, and adults in our society, ACES makes the following seven recommendations to counselor educators and supervisors as a beginning step toward improving preservice and in-service training in career development, career guidance, and career education:

1. Counselor preparation should train counselors for major leadership functions in the provision of career guidance for children, youth, and adults.

2. Counselor preparation should emphasize that career education, broadly defined with major emphasis on self- and value development, provides the most feasible framework within which to deliver comprehensive career guidance to all persons.

3. Counselor preparation should draw on career-development theory and research to provide a solid conceptual framework, organizing center, and central focus for career education and career guidance.

4. Counselor preparation should train counselors for collaborative relationships with other educators, the community, and parents to infuse career education into the curriculum.

---

*The definitions of career and career development used are the same as those used in the NVGA-AVA position paper on career development, career being defined as a time-extended working out of a purposeful life pattern. Career development is seen as a series of positions or roles—of which occupation is only one—occupied by a person in a lifetime.

†*Counselor Education and Supervision*, Vol. 17, No. 3, March 1978, pp. 168–179. Reprinted by permission. Copyright 1978 American Personnel and Guidance Association.

5. Counselor preparation should provide counselors with skills in the development of guidance-based career-education programs, including the identification of developmental tasks, objectives, and strategies for program implementation and evaluation appropriate to the specific population served.

6. Counselor preparation should provide counselors with skills in organizational development and the change process in order that they may more effectively implement career education and career guidance in schools and agencies.

7. Counselor educators should initiate and encourage research on career development, career guidance, and career education to provide documentation for program outcomes.

The following sections of this paper provide the background and rationale for these recommendations, along with further delineation of the counselor competencies needed to develop more effective career-guidance and career-education programs.

BACKGROUND

In July 1974, the president of ACES appointed the Commission on Counselor Preparation for Career Development/Career Education. The commission, composed of persons representing each geographical region of ACES, was charged with a variety of tasks revolving around the career-development component in the preparation and supervision of counselors. This position paper was developed by the commission in an effort to explore and make recommendations regarding the roles and responsibilities of counselor educators and supervisors in the preparation and upgrading of counselors in career development and career education.

RATIONALE FOR CHANGE IN COUNSELOR
PREPARATION AND SUPERVISION

Counseling, as well as other socially oriented professions, must be responsive to social change if it is to remain a viable service to contemporary individuals and institutions. Through the years the profession has demonstrated its responsiveness by continuing modification and expansion of services to meet the ever-changing needs of a variety of clients. Although the formal counseling profession was formed under a vocational-guidance rubric in the early 1900s, it has evolved through a number of cycles and changes in emphases, for the most part in response to social demands. For example, few people would question the superb response of the profession to one of its greatest challenges: the National Defense Education Act of 1958.

Today, again because of the needs of various publics, a still-greater challenge to the profession is occurring. That challenge, which is being heralded by persons within as well as outside the profession, is the challenge of career-development. The need to make career development one of the highest priorities of the profession can be attributed to a number of current social factors converging to stimulate interest in the career-development needs of individuals of all ages. The position paper on career development by the NVGA-AVA Commission on Career Guidance and Vocational Education (1973) reflects several of these factors.

1. The growing complexity of the occupational and organizational structure of society makes it difficult for a person to assimilate and organize the data necessary to formulate a career.
2. Increasingly rapid technological change demands human adaptability and responsiveness.
3. National concern is increasing over the need to develop all human talent, including the talents of women and minorities.
4. People are conducting an ardent search for values that will give meaning to life.
5. People need specialized training to obtain entry-level jobs.
6. Students who have difficulty relating their education to the rest of their lives express disenchantment.

Nationwide studies of both secondary and postsecondary students have reaffirmed that individuals of all ages and stages of life desire more help in career planning and career decision making than they have been receiving. Because of this need, it is becoming increasingly evident that much greater attention must be given to career development if both individuals and society are to realize their fullest potential. In response to these social forces, a number of individuals and groups have actively advocated a greater career-development thrust in the counseling profession.

THE CALL FOR CHANGE: A DECADE OF CONCERN

For more than a decade, individuals and divisions of APGA have been actively involved in the promotion and development of career-guidance programs. Since 1965, a large number of national, regional, and state conferences have been held to identify career-development needs of various client groups and to develop effective methods of career guidance. In addition, numerous publications and position statements have been formulated to promote career-development programs for all persons.

CONFERENCES

In 1966, NVGA sponsored a conference entitled Implementing Career Development Theory and Research Through the Curriculum. The conference brought together a variety of professional personnel to engage in dialogue and identify methods for moving from theory to practice in career development. During the late 1960s, Ohio State University's Center for Research and Leadership Development in Vocational and Technical Education organized and conducted several conferences to explore the vocational aspects of guidance. These landmark seminars considered career guidance from the cradle to the grave and involved persons from a wide spectrum of professions, including psychology, sociology, guidance, general education, vocational education, government, labor, and the business and industrial community. The National Seminar on Vocational Guidance (1966), jointly sponsored by APGA and AVA, was one of the first conscious attempts to continue the dialogue among all those involved in the vocational guidance of youth.

Several conferences focused on counselor education and supervision. An AVA–APGA–sponsored national seminar on vocational guidance (1967) was largely devoted to counselor preparation for career guidance. In 1966, the College Entrance Examination Board supported a conference to examine critical issues in the preparation of counselors to meet the career-guidance needs of students planning for a wide variety of kinds of postsecondary education. In December 1965, the U.S. Office of Education supported a major conference entitled the Vocational Aspects of Counselor Education. Participants in this conference proposed changes in counselor preparation that are as relevant today as they were then. These changes include greater attention to career-development theory and practice, business-labor-education cooperation, curriculum development, field experiences, and placement services.

PUBLICATIONS

APGA, and particularly NVGA, sponsored the publication of several professional references designed to promote effective career-guidance practices for all individuals. Representative examples include *Teachers' Role in Career Development* (1963), *Man in a World* (1964), *Career Guidance Practices in School and Community* (1970), *Career Guidance for a New Age* (1973), and *Vocational Guidance and Human Development* (1974). In addition, every major division journal of APGA has included one or more articles regarding career development, career education, and career guidance. Illustrative of APGA's high priority for career development is the May 1975 special issue of *Personnel and Guidance Journal,* which was entitled Career Development: Guidance and Education.

NVGA-AVA POSITION PAPER

If the 1960s could be depicted as the recreation of concern for career development, then the 1970s might well be described as a period of position statements attempting to clarify the roles and responsibilities of counselors, teachers, administrators, and others in the delivery of career guidance. NVGA and AVA jointly wrote and adopted a position paper in 1973 that has considerable significance for the counseling profession. The position paper was an attempt to bring together, in a single statement, the basic elements of career development and to examine its potential for all education from kindergarten to adulthood. NVGA's position is that a career-guidance program should assist the individual to assimilate and integrate knowledge, experiences, and appreciations related to

1. Self-understanding, which includes persons' perceptions of their own characteristics and their relationships to others and to the environment;
2. Understanding of the working society and those factors that affect its constancy and change, including worker attitudes, life-styles, and mobility;
3. Awareness of the part that leisure plays in a person's life;
4. Understanding of the multiple factors to be considered in career planning; and
5. Understanding of the information and skills necessary to achieve self-fulfillment in work and leisure.

The position paper continued by outlining 18 career-guidance experiences in which each individual should have an opportunity to participate. In addition, NVGA and AVA placed the career-guidance leadership and coordination responsibilities directly on professional guidance personnel. Roles of counselors, teachers, administrators, peers, and the community in well-functioning career-guidance programs were also described.

APGA POSITION PAPER

Career-guidance personnel have strongly supported increased counselor and teacher involvement in career education. An APGA position paper entitled Career Guidance: Role and Functions of Counseling and Guidance Personnel Practitioners in Career Education was adopted by the APGA Senate in March 1975. APGA endorsed the following 13 counselor roles as desirable in career-education programs at any educational level. The counselor should

Leadership Functions

1. Provide leadership in the identification and programmatic implementation of individual career-development tasks;
2. Provide leadership in the identification, classification, and use of self-, educational, and occupational information;
3. Provide leadership in the assimilation and application of career decision-making methods and materials;
4. Provide leadership in eliminating the influence of both racism and sexism as

cultural restrictors of opportunities available to minority persons, females, and others who may be affected;

5. Provide leadership in expanding the variety and appropriateness of assessment devices and procedures required for sound personal, educational, and occupational decision making; and

6. Provide leadership in emphasizing the importance of carrying out the functions of career counseling.

Participatory Functions

7. Serve as liaison between the educational- and community-resource groups;

8. Conduct career-guidance needs-assessment surveys;

9. Organize and operate part-time and full-time educational, occupational, and job-placement programs;

10. Conduct follow-up, follow-through, and job-adjustment activities;

11. Participate in curriculum revision;

12. Participate in efforts to involve the home and family in career education; and

13. Participate in efforts to monitor and assess operations and communicate the results of those activities to other practitioners and clientele, as appropriate.

APGA's position is that the implications of these roles for counselor functioning and preparation are great. Those of most significance follow.

1. A change toward further emphasizing the counselor as a member of the career-education team and away from emphasis on the counselor as an isolated professional;

2. A change toward greater counselor involvement in the business-labor-industrial community as well as in the home environment;

3. A change toward emphasizing career education in life-style terms and away from the narrow view of occupational guidance often emphasized in the past;

4. A change toward emphasizing the counselor as a major influencer of curriculum change and away from a view of the counselor as one who helps students adjust to the curriculum;

5. A change toward helping others use some of the expertise and understandings developed by the personnel and guidance movement (The direction is away from attempting to make such data the exclusive province of the counselor);

6. A change toward using the concept of work as a means of helping students acquire self-understanding and personal meaningfulness; and

7. A change toward counselor activity and involvement in the broader environment.

APGA recognizes that to effect these kinds of changes massive in-service education efforts must take place as well as significant changes in the professional preparation programs for preservice counselors. The roles proposed in this position paper and the resulting changes in functioning are consistent with those implied by the NVGA-AVA position paper on career development, as well as statements by key guidance leaders during the last decade.

CAREER-DEVELOPMENT NEEDS OF SPECIAL GROUPS

One of the most fundamental developments of this decade has been the increasing amount of attention directed toward the special career-development needs of groups that have not traditionally been priority recipients of career guidance. Increasingly, women, ethnic-minority groups, the disadvantaged and handicapped, and persons in midlife are demanding high-quality career counseling. As equalization of opportunity continues to become a reality, career-guidance programs must be developed for all persons, with special attention focused on needs that may be characteristic of males and females of a particular race, age, or socioeconomic status.

FEDERAL LEGISLATION

In an effort to secure the necessary funding to implement the changes recommended by these position statements, individuals, and special-interest groups, APGA committed itself to legislative efforts aimed at obtaining these resources. APGA's efforts are organized in two basic legislative areas. Of highest priority is lobbying for the passage of federal legislation specifically designed to improve career-guidance and counseling programs and personnel. Such a career-guidance-and-counseling act would provide funding support for program development as well as for professional personnel development. The second major area involves influencing legislation that is not totally devoted to career guidance but that has a career-guidance component. APGA seeks to assure that professional guidance personnel play a major role in decision making regarding programs in the guidance component and that trained guidance personnel either provide the direct or supervise the indirect services called for in the career-guidance component of the legislation.

SUMMARY

Any major proposed change in counselor preparation and supervision requires a strong rationale that this section has attempted to provide. Major forces both within and outside the counseling profession are calling for significant reform in the focus and functioning of counselors at every level. Change is called for by professional publications, by conferences, by position statements, by special-interest groups, as well as by APGA itself.

Given such widespread support by professional organizations and individuals, how can practicing and preservice counselors be prepared to provide extensive career guidance? ACES's mandate for providing leadership is clear, for it has the major responsibility in this endeavor. Through its regional and state divisions and through efforts of individual counselor educators and supervisors, ACES must create and implement necessary programs even if sufficient federal support is not available.

POSITION OF ACES

ACES concurs with the observations and recommendations regarding desirable changes in counselor role and function incorporated in the APGA's position paper, Career Guidance: Role and Functions of Counseling and Guidance Personnel Practitioners in Career Education, and the NVGA-AVA position paper on career development. ACES's position is that all students and adults must be provided with career-guidance opportunities to ensure that they

1. Understand that career development is a lifelong process based on an interwoven and sequential series of educational, occupational, leisure, and family choices;
2. Examine their own interests, values, aptitudes, and aspirations in an effort to increase self-awareness and self-understanding;
3. Develop a personally satisfying set of work values that leads them to believe that work, in some form, can be desirable to them;
4. Recognize that paid and unpaid work have dignity;
5. Understand the role of leisure in career development;
6. Understand the process of reasoned decision making and the ownership of those decisions in terms of their consequences;
7. Recognize that educational and occupational decisions are interrelated with family, work, and leisure;
8. Gather the kinds of data necessary to make well-informed career decisions;
9. Become aware of and explore a variety of occupational alternatives;
10. Explore possible rewards, satisfactions, life-styles, and negative aspects associated with various occupational options;
11. Consider the probability of success and failure for various occupations;
12. Understand the important role of interpersonal and basic employability skills in occupational success;
13. Identify and use a variety of resources in the school and community to maximize career-development potential;
14. Know and understand the entrance, transition, and decision points in education and the problems of adjustment that might occur in relation to these points;
15. Obtain chosen vocational skills and use available placement services to gain satisfactory entrance into employment in relation to occupational aspirations and beginning competencies; and

16. Know and understand the value of continuing education to update or acquire additional occupational skills or leisure pursuits.

ROLE OF THE COUNSELING PROFESSION

ACES believes that counselors must take a major leadership position in the provision of the kinds of career-guidance programs implied in the preceding list. ACES also recognizes that although counselors play a major leadership function in the provision of career-guidance programs they are by no means the only persons responsible for the delivery of programs to children, youth, and adults. Parents, teachers, peers, administrators, and members of the community must all assume active roles if effective career-guidance programs are to reach all students and adults. Thus, in addition to the provision of direct career-guidance services, counselors must also take responsibility for the facilitation of various kinds of indirect services.

ACES's position is that career education, broadly defined with major emphasis on self- and value development, provides the most feasible framework within which to deliver comprehensive career-guidance programs to all persons. Career education is a unifying concept around which counselors and other professional personnel can conveniently rally. The counselor should take an active leadership role in the development and implementation of guidance-based career-education programs. This career-development emphasis should occur not only in the public schools (K–12) but also in institutions of postsecondary education and community agencies.

NECESSARY COUNSELOR COMPETENCIES IN CAREER GUIDANCE

In order to assume and maintain leadership positions in the delivery of career guidance to all individuals, ACES believes that counselors must have a set of at least 15 common areas of competence that should be acquired during preservice or in-service training. Counselors, regardless of their employment setting, should have knowledge and competencies in the following areas:

1. Career- and human-development theory and research and the skills necessary to translate this knowledge into developmental career-guidance and career-education programs;

2. Career-information resources and the necessary skills to assist teachers, administrators, community-agency personnel, paraprofessionals, and peers to integrate this kind of information into the teaching-counseling process;

3. Career-assessment strategies and the skills necessary to assist individuals to use these data in the decision-making process;

4. Individual- and group-counseling practices and the skills necessary to assist individuals in career planning using both approaches;

5. Career decision-making processes and the skills necessary to implement programs designed to facilitate career decision making for clients in educational and community-agency settings;

6. Job-placement services and the skills necessary to assist clients to seek, acquire, and maintain employment;

7. The unique career-development needs of special client groups (women, minorities, handicapped, disadvantaged, and adults) and the skills necessary to assist them in their development;

8. Sexism and racism and the necessary skills to reduce institutional discrimination in order to broaden the career opportunities available for all persons;

9. The roles that life-style and leisure play in career development and the skills necessary to assist clients in selecting and preparing for occupations that coincide with various preferences;

10. Consultation strategies and the skills necessary to assist others (teachers, parents, and peers) to deliver indirect career-guidance services;

11. Synthesizing strategies and the skills necessary to assist individuals to understand the interrelatedness of their career decisions and life roles;

12. Program development and curricular-infusion strategies and the skills necessary to design and implement career awareness, self-development, career exploration, and job-placement programs within educational and community-agency settings;

13. Organizational development and change processes and the skills necessary to facilitate change in educators' attitudes toward career education;

14. Program-evaluation techniques and the skills necessary to acquire evidence of the effectiveness of career-guidance and career-education programming; and

15. Educational trends and state and federal legislation that may influence the development and implementation of career-guidance programs.

ROLE OF COUNSELOR EDUCATORS AND SUPERVISORS

Elaborating on the seven initial recommendations, ACES believes that counselor educators have a responsibility to help preservice counselors become effective facilitators of change as well as provide consultative in-service training in schools and agencies. Counselor educators should also provide staff development for other counselor educators, educational administrators, and teacher educators to help bring about a collaborative effort in career education. Counselor educators should also be prepared to offer consultation to related local, state, and national professional associations. In addition, counselor preparation should take leadership in identifying a more complete set of career-development competencies, behaviorally stated and measurable, that counselors need to function effectively in career guidance and career education.

ROLE OF ACES

As the professional association representing counselor educators and supervisors, ACES must take the leadership role to assure that practicing counselors as well as preservice counselors acquire the necessary competencies in career guidance and career education. Accepting this mandate for leadership, ACES will

1. Continue to support APGA's efforts for passage of federal legislation designed to meet human needs through the further development of career-guidance programs and career-guidance personnel;
2. Strongly support the career-development movement in public schools, institutions of postsecondary education, and community agencies;
3. Propose changes in counselor-preparation and state certification standards to include expanded competencies in career guidance and career education;
4. Develop and implement national, regional, and state seminars to assist counselor educators and supervisors in acquiring the necessary skills to train others in the career guidance competencies cited;
5. Recommend that at least one special issue of *Counselor Education and Supervision* be devoted to career development in counselor education and supervision;
6. Support the development of a series of training materials based on how-to aspects of career development in counselor education and supervision (Suggested topics might include career development through career education, career development through group counseling, career development through individual counseling, and career development of special groups. A complementary series of color videotapes might also be developed and distributed through APGA publications);
7. Strongly urge individual ACES members to examine all aspects of their counselor-education and supervision programs—theory, practicum, assessment, and internship—to modify them as appropriate, and to find new ways to infuse career development into various elements of the training program; and
8. Seek the support and cooperation of related organizations such as ASCA, NVGA, and AVA to assist in the training and retraining of counselor educators and counselor supervisors for career development.

COMMISSION MEMBERS
Betty Bosdell, Northern Illinois University (DeKalb)
Owen Caskey, Texas Tech University (Lubbock)
F. J. Eicke, University of Mississippi

L. Sunny Hansen, chairperson, University of Minnesota (Minneapolis)

Joan Hartzke, Lewis and Clark College (Portland, Ore.)

Thomas H. Hohenshil, Virginia Polytechnic Institute and State University (Blacksburg)

Philip Perrone, University of Wisconsin-Madison

Nancy Pinson, Maryland State Department of Education (Baltimore)

Charles Ryan, University of Maine at Orono

Nancy Schlossberg, University of Maryland (College Park)

Robert Williams, Andrews University (Berrien Springs, Mich.)

Appendix **B**

Career Development
and Career Guidance*

A National Vocational Guidance Association
and American Vocational Association
Joint Position Paper

INTRODUCTION

Much has been written in recent years about the concept of career development and its applications in various settings. These writings are scattered in a variety of books, professional journals, conference proceedings and unpublished papers, and reflect a diversity of opinion. Because of this, the American Vocational Association and the National Vocational Guidance Association felt the need to bring together in a position statement the basic elements of career development and examine its potential for all of education, from kindergarten through adulthood.

To accomplish this, the associations established a joint commission in 1971 to prepare a position paper on career development. Commission members included W. Wesley Tennyson, chairman, William Bingham, Harry Drier, Charles Foster, Kenneth Hoyt, Doris Jefferies, David H. Pritchard, Robert A. Williams, Norman C. Gysbers (unofficial), Allan J. Miller (unofficial). Harold Reed (unofficial) and Donald Severson (unofficial). The group's recommended paper was reviewed and modified by the AVA Guidance Division's Policy and Planning Committee and the NVGA Board of Directors.

The resulting paper is a partial response to the need for a coherent policy in that it describes the concept of career development in general terms, but discussion of its application is limited specifically to the school setting. In discussing the application

*National Vocational Guidance Newsletter, 1973, vol. 13, no. 1, pp 5–8. Reprinted by permission.

of career development to the school, however, it is important to understand that details, such as the nature of the delivery systems needed to implement this concept, are not covered in this paper. Such discussion is needed but is not within the scope of this paper.

The paper was officially adopted by the Board of Directors of the National Vocational Guidance Association in May, 1973. The Board of Directors of the American Vocational Association officially adopted it as an American Vocational Association Guidance position paper on career development in July, 1973.

A position paper such as this is the result of the work of many people and thus may not represent the opinion of any one individual or group: It was written to stimulate thought and discussion. Among the many uses this document has are the following:

It can serve as a rationale for state and federal legislation on career guidance, counseling and placement.

It also can serve as an aid in developing new programs or improving and extending existing programs at the state and local level.

It can be used by federal, state and local educational personnel in pre- and in-service education.

PART I

THE PROCESS OF CAREER DEVELOPMENT

In order to be whole persons, men and women naturally must engage in activities they consider to be significant. The need to make judgments about using time and assuming roles recurs throughout life. A person formulates a career by continuously evaluating both what he wants to do with his life and the actions that will enable him to achieve his personal goals. Career development occurs as educational and vocational pursuits interact with other life pursuits. It continues throughout life.

CAREER DEVELOPMENT AS PART OF HUMAN DEVELOPMENT

As with other normal aspects of human development, career development is not totally dependent upon external forces or programs. Rather, it reflects a personal growth pattern that, in some respects, differs for each individual. However, certain common patterns of growth, coupled with individual variations, allow generalization about normal development patterns and career sequences.

Certain basic principles regarding human development apply whether one speaks about physical, emotional, intellectual, social, or career development. At least seven developmental dimensions are important in the design and implementation of programs for career development. These are as follows:

1. Development occurs during the lifetime of an individual. It can be described in maturational terms denoting progression through life stages and the mastery of developmental tasks at each stage. Although research evidence is lacking, it seems unlikely that intervention can substantially shorten this maturational process.

2. Individual development is influenced by both heredity and environment. Psychological, sociological, educational, political, economic, and physical factors affect development. Appropriate intervention strategies which focus upon these factors can influence the quality of individual development.

3. Development is a continuous process. Individual development can best be facilitated by intervention strategies that begin in the early years and continue throughout the life of the person. Programs which focus only at certain points or at certain stages in the individual's life will have limited effectiveness.

4. Although development is continuous, certain aspects are dominant at various periods in the life span. Programs designed to facilitate career development should account for the dominant aspects at given stages.

5. Individual development involves a progressive differentiation and integration of the person's self and his perceived world. Intervention strategies need to be designed to assist individuals during normal maturational stages of career development rather than to provide remedial assistance to individuals whose development has been damaged or retarded.

6. While common developmental stages can be observed and described during childhood and adult life, individual differences in progressing through these stages can be expected. Intervention programs should provide for these differences, making no assumption that something is "wrong" with those who progress at atypical rates.

7. Excessive deprivation with respect to any single aspect of human development can retard optimal development in other areas. Optimal human development programs are comprehensive in nature, not limited to any single facet. It is recognized that those who suffer from deprivation may require special and intensive assistance. Where deprivation is long term, short term intervention is not likely to be sufficient.

Building upon such principles as the foregoing offers the only assurance that a program of career guidance will have a constructive and educative influence in shaping human potential and providing the means for its expression.

WORK VALUES AS PART OF HUMAN VALUES

Just as career development is a part of human development, the values a person formulates with regard to work and to himself as a worker are a part of his larger value system. Human values, including work values, begin to develop early in life.

These values are influenced by society and by the attitudes and values held by family, associates, and peers. The educational institution, as an instrument of society, plays a decidedly important part in value formation and clarification particularly in the clarification of previously formed values that may not be fully understood. Through the clarification and formulation of values, an individual finds meaning, direction, and purpose in life and participates as a responsible citizen. The values a person formulates about workers and their work is a topic which needs the attention of those who set goals and priorities for education.

The United States was founded when the classical work ethic was universally held. That ethic embraced a number of work values, including the following:

1. All honest work possesses worth and dignity.
2. A man is known best through his achievements and what he contributes to society.
3. A task well done is its own reward.
4. A worker should do his very best at all times and not quit a job until it is finished.
5. Hard work is the best and the surest route to occupational success.
6. The pride an individual can find in himself is derived, in large part, from the pride he finds through achievement in his work.
7. A man deserves nothing that he has not earned through his work.

These values and beliefs have played a fundamental part in national progress. In recent years, the emergence of some new values and a change in the relative importance of others is markedly altering the nature of jobs and organizations, and for many persons, their career development. These changes lead to a recognition that the United States is experiencing the evolution of a new epoch: the post-individual era. In this present period of transition, it is difficult to speak with assurance about values and value positions. Several observations, however, seem to have validity.

First, for many workers, the classical work ethic no longer constitutes a viable set of work values. Although this ethic was eminently appropriate in the agrarian period when work was viewed as an essential prerequisite to individual survival, its base has been somewhat eroded. Today, technology increasingly provides for material needs and banishes somewhat the fear of scarcity.

Second, technological advances in industrial productivity, stimulated by both automation and cybernation, have created working conditions that have further eroded the bases for the traditional work ethic. This is particularly true for individuals engaged in assembly line jobs where tasks and responsibilities are narrowly defined and the worker is viewed and treated as an operating unit. While most employers would be pleased if the classical version of the work ethic were still regarded as meaningful by all employees, it is a fact that management decisions and assembly line techniques have affected worker motivation.

Third, the continuing substitution of mechanical and electrical energy for human energy in performing work will lead eventually to a somewhat greater emphasis on new career calling for adaptability, self-expression, and interdependence. With machines increasingly absorbing tasks and activities that are programmable, future industrial workers will function in situations where programming is not feasible and where a high degree of variability exists. For those who will pursue production-oriented careers, this change in job function may lead to a revitalization of the traditional work ethic, though in modified form.

Fourth, as the nation moves into this post-industrial period, the provision of services will become increasingly important. An expansion of occupational opportunities in services is a natural consequence of automation and cybernation. The formulation of work values deeply rooted in a desire to help fellow humans may well motivate the career development of many individuals. Work viewed as service may assume a set of values that diverges considerably from those which underlie work conceived as a means to society's maintenance. Such services may still be offered for profit.

Many of the values which characterize the classical version of the work ethic remain alive and viable in the post-industrial period. Achievement, self-control, independence and delay of gratification are values that continue to hold great importance for many individuals, directing their vocational behavior and molding their career development. For others however, and particularly for some young people, values of self-expression, interdependence, service, and search for meaning in work are playing a more prominent role in the way they structure their work lives. In facilitating career development, educators should not attempt to impose any particular set of work values on all. Yet education must provide each student with the opportunity to develop a comprehensive set of personal values upon which he can rely when making career plans and decisions. Today more than ever before, there is every reason to allow students to explore their own basic natures and to formulate career plans in keeping with their own values. Perhaps the single most important characteristic of the post-industrial era will be the tolerance it accords to the individual's human values.

THE MEANING OF CAREER

One may view "career" from several perspectives. In general, the term is defined differently depending on whether the viewer seeks to relate it to institutions, organizations and occupations, or whether he intends to relate it to persons. At one extreme is the equation of career and occupation, including the advances a person makes in his occupation. At the other extreme is the view that career denotes a general life pattern which includes virtually all activities. Some writers would delimit the latter interpretation by suggesting the major life domains which engage the individual in multiple roles—e.g., worker, family member, community participant and leisure-time participant.

Between these two extremes, some sociologists and psychologists have used the term "career" to refer to the sequence of occupations, jobs, and positions held during the course of life. This definition may be applied in considering developmental movement through societal structures, but it conveys no sense of an active person interacting with his environment.

The position taken in this paper is that the term "career" means a time-extended working out of a purposeful life pattern through *work* undertaken by the individual. Career can easily be differentiated from the term "career development," which refers to the total constellation of psychological, sociological, educational, physical, economic, and chance factors that combine to shape the career of any given individual.

The meaning of the word "career" then, is directly dependent upon the meaning attached to the word "work." Work, as conceived for this paper, may be defined as an expenditure of effort designed to effect some change, however slight, in some province of civilization. It is not simply an arbitrary or gratuitous action, but something which, from some viewpoint within society, *ought* to be done. The concept carries the intention that human effort will lead to an improvement of the individuals' own condition or that of some element of society.

Viewed in this way, work is not directly attached to paid employment. It may also include efforts of an educational or a vocational nature. Thus, education for work, as well as certain elements of leisure undertaken to benefit society or which contribute to a sense of individual purpose and achievement, are included in this definition.

While these definitions provide a framework for the educator who will facilitate career development, it must be emphasized that a person's career does not unfold independently of other areas of his development. Ultimately the educator, whatever his title, must concern himself with the total development of a person, and this implies a consideration of how work and career mesh with other life pursuits in a reasoned style of living.

FREEDOM TO CHOOSE

A basic value, rooted deeply in moral heritage, political philosophy, and the traditions of society, is the concept of individual freedom and responsibility. The strength of this nation in the past has rested in part upon the natural differences in individual talents and the freedom of each individual to develop and express his talents in a unique way. The theory underlying career development is consonant with this fundamental democratic value. Preservation of the individual's integrity disavows any type of prescriptive guidance which commits the individual to particular directions. Individuals, however, must be made aware of the values society places on different talents and the relative demand for different kinds of talents.

PART II
CAREER GUIDANCE AS AN INTERVENTION PROCESS

THE NEED FOR CAREER GUIDANCE

Today there are many social factors which converge to stimulate an interest in the career development needs of persons of all ages. Some of these are as follows:

1. Growing complexity in the occupational and organizational structure of society which makes it difficult for a person to assimilate and organize the data necessary to formulate a career.
2. Ever more rapid technological change demanding human adaptability and responsiveness.
3. Increasing national concern with the need to develop all human talent, including the talents of women and minorities.
4. An ardent search for values which will give meaning to life.
5. The need for specialized training to obtain entry jobs.
6. The apparent disenchantment expressed by students who have difficulty relating their education to their lives.

Each of these factors impinges on the individual in ways that make achieving self-fulfillment more difficult.

In the past, some managerial personnel in business and industry have held a "non-careerism" attitude which viewed the typical job as an isolated event in a person's life. Whether this attitude is tenable in the postindustrial period is seriously questioned today. The evolving view is that a job should be considered a stage in an integrated, life-long career—a step on a career lattice which involves both horizontal and vertical dimensions. On the horizontal level it involves patterns of choice at one point in time, such as: "Should I combine employment with study? Or should I engage in volunteer work along with my employment?" Vertically, it involves choices along a time line, such as: "How do my options or behavior at this point relate to options or behavior in the near, intermediate or distant future?" As new questions are raised about the opportunities work provides for learning and self-development, the need for expanded programs of career guidance becomes apparent.

THE NATURE OF CAREER GUIDANCE

The nature of guidance for career development cannot be viewed as a static, tradition-based set of related services that assist individuals in making single occupational choices. The content of any career guidance program must be developed from initial assessment of the present and future career development needs of the individual; it must also account for impinging environmental factors that could affect the development and fulfillment of career expectations. Career guidance content can be organized in many ways to facilitate the individual's development. Whatever its form, the program should encourage the individual to assume responsibility for his own career development.

A career guidance program assists the individual to assimilate and integrate knowledge, experience and appreciations related to the following career development elements:

1. Self-understanding, which includes a person's relationship to his own characteristics and perceptions, and his relationship to others and the environment.

2. Understanding of the work society and those factors that affect its constant change, including worker attitudes and discipline.
3. Awareness of the part leisure time may play in a person's life.
4. Understanding of the necessity for and the multitude of factors to be considered in career planning.
5. Understanding of the information and skills necessary to achieve self-fulfillment in work and leisure.

An illumination of these content areas may include career guidance experiences to insure that each individual:

Gathers the kinds of data necessary to make rational career decisions.

Understands the necessary considerations for making choices and accepts responsibility for the decisions made.

Explores the possible rewards and satisfactions associated with each career choice considered.

Develops through work the attitude that he is a contributor to life and the community.

Determines success and failure probabilities in any occupational area considered.

Explores the possible work conditions associated with occupational options.

Shows an understanding of the varied attitudes toward work and workers held by himself and by others.

Recognizes how workers can bring dignity to their work.

Considers the possible and even predictable value changes in society which could affect a person's life.

Understands the important role of interpersonal and basic employment skills in occupational success.

Classifies the different values and attitudes individuals may hold and the possible effects these may have on decisions and choices.

Understands that career development is lifelong, based upon a sequential series of educational and occupational choices.

Determines the possible personal risk, cost, and other related consequences of each career decision and is willing to assume responsibility for each consequence.

Systematically analyzes school and nonschool experiences as he plans and makes career-related decisions.

Explores the worker characteristics and work skills necessary to achieve success in occupational areas under consideration.

Identifies and uses a wide variety of resources in the school and community to maximize career development potential.

Knows and understands the entrance, transition and decision points in education and the problems of adjustment that might occur in relation to these points.

Obtains necessary employability skills and uses available placement services to gain satisfactory entry into employment in line with occupational aspirations and beginning competencies.

RESPONSIBILITIES FOR FACILITATING CAREER GUIDANCE

Effective implementation of career guidance in an educational setting necessitates that guidance leadership identify not only what has to be accomplished, but who has the capabilities for coordinating and delivering specific program elements. This is of particular importance if the education establishment is to reduce the past confusion and mis-interpretation of who holds responsibilities for career guidance and when it should be accomplished. To some, career guidance means merely a body of content in which volunteers participate at will: others see its functions as solely those of the professionally prepared school counselor. Obviously, neither of these viewpoints is correct. A clear identification of those persons who have primary, secondary, and shared roles and responsibilities in meeting student career development needs is urgently required.

To assure program quality, consistency and sequence, some one person must be assigned responsibility for overall coordination of the career guidance program. The competencies needed by that person include the following:

1. A thorough understanding of career development theory and research.
2. Group process, human relations and consultative skills.
3. A knowledge of curriculum and how curriculum is developed.
4. An understanding of the relationship between values, goals, choices and information in decision-making.
5. A knowledge of the history of work and its changing meanings.
6. An understanding of the changing nature of manpower, womanpower and economic outlooks.
7. Familiarity with various strategies and resources for facilitating career development, including the utilization of the school, the community and the home.

It is the position of this paper that the guidance specialist possesses many of these qualifications and is in a position to coordinate the career guidance program. Other educational personnel having these qualifications also are in a position to coordinate the program.

The advent of career education has focused the interest of school people upon the career development needs of young people and has provided an opportunity for all educational personnel to extend their involvement. Career guidance, to be functional in meeting the career development needs of today's population, must be planned only after accounting for the needs of those to be served and the impinging environmental conditions that exist. This means, then, that the combined skills of the guidance team, vocational educators, academic teachers, administrators, parents, peers and others in the individual's environment need to be identified and appropriate learning experiences provided to make full use of the contributions they can provide. For descriptive purposes these role definitions will be discussed under the headings guidance specialists, vocational educator, academic teacher, principal, peers, and employers and other community members.

GUIDANCE SPECIALISTS

The guidance team has appropriate understandings and competencies to serve as facilitator and change agent in (1) assisting in school curriculum development and instructional methods, (2) assisting the individual in his career development, and (3) communicating with parents and others. The guidance team is composed of a number of specialists including, but not limited to, education personnel with the following titles: Elementary Career Development Specialist, Elementary Counselors, Junior Career Exploratory Teacher, Orientation and Group Guidance Specialist, Occupational and Educational Information Specialist, Job Placement Specialist, Post-Secondary Student Personnel Workers, Guidance Counselor, Cooperative Work Experience Coordinator, Vocational Appraisal Specialist.

The responsibilities of the guidance team can be classified as follows:

A. *Program Leadership and Coordination*
1. Coordinate the career guidance program.
2. Provide staff with the understandings necessary to assist each student to obtain a full, competency-based learning experience.
3. Coordinate the acquisition and use of appropriate occupational, educational and labor market information.
4. Help staff understand the process of human growth and development and assess needs of specific individuals.
5. Help staff plan for sequential student learning experiences in career development.
6. Coordinate the development and use of a comprehensive, cumulative pupil data system that can be readily used by all students.
7. Identify and coordinate the use of school and community resources needed to facilitate career guidance.
8. Coordinate the evaluation of students' learning experiences and use the resulting data in counseling with students, in consulting with the instructional staff and parents, and in modifying the curriculum.
9. Coordinate a job placement program for the school and provide for job adjustment counseling.
10. Provide individual and group counseling and guidance so that students will be stimulated to continually and systematically interrelate and expand their experiences, knowledges, understandings, skills, and appreciation as they grow and develop throughout life.

B. *Student Direction*
1. Help each student to realize that each person has a unique set of characteristics and that, to plan realistically, each must appraise himself fairly.
2. Enable each student to make use of available assessment tools and techniques in examining his personal characteristics.

3. Assist students in identifying realistic role models.
4. Assist students in developing the employability skills necessary for entry into employment where opportunities exist.

VOCATIONAL EDUCATORS

Vocational educators carry many of the same responsibilities as guidance specialists in facilitating the career development of students who are enrolled in vocational education courses. Their unique contributions to a comprehensive career education program may include the following:

1. Provide realistic educational and occupational information to students and staff based on knowledge of occupational fields and continuous contact with workers and work settings.
2. Identify and recruit resource persons in the employment community to assist in the school program.
3. Provide exploratory experiences in vocational classrooms, labs, and shops for students not enrolled in occupational preparation programs and assist those teachers who wish to incorporate "hands on" types of activities in their courses.
4. Identify basic and academic skills and knowledge needed to succeed in the occupations of their field and communicate this information to academic teachers and guidance specialists.
5. Assist academic teachers and guidance specialists in designing appropriate occupational exploration experiences.
6. Provide students with information about vocational offerings and guidance specialists with information about the kinds of careers for which students are prepared.
7. Assist students enrolled in vocational programs to analyze and interpret their learning experiences for better understanding of self in relation to occupations and the world of work.
8. Plan and provide vocational instruction which prepares students to enter, adjust, progress and change jobs in an occupational field.
9. Assist students in identifying a wide range of occupations for which their vocational instruction is applicable.
10. Encourage employers to assist in expanding student awareness of career opportunities.
11. Arrange observation activities or part-time employment for students and school staff to help them learn more about occupations and work settings.
12. Participate in the planning and implementation of a comprehensive career education program.

ACADEMIC TEACHERS

The academic teacher also has a vital set of responsibilities in career guidance which require the ability to accomplish the following:

1. Provide for easy transition of students from home to school, from one school environment to another, and from school to further education or employment.
2. Provide students with curriculum and related learning experiences to insure the development of basic concepts of work and the importance of those who perform work.
3. Provide group guidance experiences, with appropriate aid from guidance specialists and vocational educators, to regularly demonstrate the relationship between learning and job requirements.
4. Help parents understand and encourage the career development process as it relates to their children.
5. Provide opportunities within the curriculum for students to have decision-making experiences related to educational and vocational planning.
6. Assist students in synthesizing accumulated career development experiences to prepare them for educational transitions.
7. Provide career exploratory experiences to help students gain an understanding of worker characteristics and work requirements.
8. Provide experiences to help students increase their understanding of their own capabilities, interests and possible limitations.
9. Provide for career preparation experiences that will enable the individual to acquire skills necessary to enter and remain in the world of work at a level appropriate to his capabilities and expectations.
10. Provide, as an extension of the in-school learning experience, opportunities for the individual to experience work first-hand in a nonthreatening environment.

PRINCIPALS

The principal carries ultimate responsibility in his building for the guidance program. More specifically, his responsibilities are as follows:

1. Provide active encouragement and support of the program.
2. Espouse the idea of career guidance as a responsibility of each staff member.
3. Commit himself to experimentation and flexibility in program and curriculum.
4. Arrange for in-service education of staff in career guidance and human relations.
5. Organize and encourage the development of a career guidance committee composed of staff members, students, parents, and community leaders.

6. Provide necessary personnel, space, facilities and materials.

7. Encourage constant evaluation and improvement of the program.

COMMUNITY MEMBERS

Although school staff members are extremely important in assisting youths in their career development, there are other persons who also provide valuable assistance. They include parents peers and other community members.

1. Parents

Without question parents can and should be the most influential role models and counselors to their children. Having some measure of direct control over the environment in which their children have been reared, they have the unique opportunity to expose them to experiences appropriate for self-fulfillment. As their children enter public education, parents share, but do not give up, the responsibility for their development. Parents who take full advantage of the information given them by school staff members concerning the interest, aptitudes, failures and achievements of their children, can use this background of information to provide the following career guidance and counseling:

a. Assistance in analyzing their children's interests, capabilities and limitations.

b. Explanations of the traits required, and working conditions and life styles of workers in work areas with which they are most familiar.

c. Discussion of work values developed as a result of past experiences and of the consequences they have experienced.

d. Discussions of the economic condition of the family as it applies to the children's education and training needs and assistance in planning a course of action.

e. Help in using the knowledge, experience, and services of relatives, friends, fellow workers and other resources in exploring the world of work and in planning and preparing for their children's role in the work society.

f. Provision of a model and counseling to their children during critical developmental periods of their lives in an attempt to have children establish and maintain positive attitudes towards themselves and others.

g. Exemplification of the attitude that *all* persons have dignity and worth no matter what their position in the world of work.

h. Provision of situations that allow children to experience decision-making and to accept responsibility for the consequences of their decisions.

i. Maintenance of open communication between school and home so that the experiences of both settings can be used in meeting student needs.

j. Provision of opportunities for children to work and accept responsibility of the home and community.

2. Peers

As youths establish and experience interpersonal relationships with their peers, they need to understand how to analyze and use these experiences in their career development. A person's friends and associates have an intense effect upon his values, attitude formation and career expectations. Opportunities should be provided to allow young persons to share their ideas with each other.

The guidance team is in a particular strategic position to capitalize upon the influence that young persons may have upon each other. Research is beginning to demonstrate that peer influence can be harnessed and directed to contribute to the favorable development of youth. The strategy involves teaching selected youngsters certain skills of counseling and human relations and then using these young persons in a para-professional capacity. The use of this or similar strategies will enable youth and young adults to accurately perceive the challenges and responsibilities of being an active member of the school's guidance team.

3. Employers and Other Community Members

As contemporary schools open their doors to allow for expanded community involvement, it is appropriate to discuss the possible roles members of the community may play. Employers, employees, clergy, retired workers, community agency personnel and others should be viewed as potential guidance team members. Educators and parents must be ready and willing to team up with other community members, especially when they find a child needs specialized information or assistance related to career development. Employers should provide work stations and observation experiences and be available as career speakers for school programs. Industry and business should demand a significant role in the education of youth, rather than the token role they've had in the past. Since employers can provide actual work settings, staff who understand the traits of workers, and skill competencies needed for entry jobs and job retention, it would be tragic if education failed to utilize this resource.

Career guidance specialists, working in cooperation with vocational educators, can do much to encourage full use of all community resources available for the career development of young people.

Bibliography

"A Question of Survival." *Guidepost,* 14, No. 7 (1972), 1–2.

Adams, Arthur J., and Thomas H. Stone "Satisfaction of Need for Achievement in Work and Leisure Time Activities." *Journal of Vocational Behavior,* 11, No. 2 (1977), 174–181.

Agne, Russell M., and Robert J. Nash, "School Counselors: The Conscience of Career Education." *School Counselor,* 21, No. 2 (1973), 90–101.

American College Testing Program. *Career Planning Program: Counselor's Manual, 1971-72.* Iowa City, Ia: American College Testing Program, 1972.

———. *Assessment of Career Development Handbook.* Boston: Houghton Mifflin Company, 1974.

American Personnel and Guidance Association. "Statement on CAUSE." *Personnel and Guidance Journal,* 44, No. 1 (1965), 107–108.

———. *Teachers and Counselors Work Together.* Washington, D.C.: American Personnel and Guidance Association, 1965.

———. "Support Personnel for the Counselor: Their Technical and Non-Technical Roles and Preparation." *Personnel and Guidance Journal,* 45, No. 8 (1967), 857–861.

American Psychological Association Task Force on Employment Testing of Minority Groups. "Job Testing and the Disadvantaged." *American Psychologist,* 24, No. 7 (1969), 637–650.

American School Counselor Association. "Statement of Policy for Secondary School Counselors," and "Guidelines for Implementation of the ASCA Statement of Policy for Secondary School Counselors." In *Counseling, A Growing Profession.* Ed. John W. Loughary. Washington, D.C.: American Personnel and Guidance Association, 1965, 94–106.

———. *The Role of the Secondary School Counselor.* Washington, D.C.: American Personnel and Guidance Association, 1966.

American School Counselor Association, National Association of Secondary School Principals, and the American Association of School Administrators. *Principals and Counselors Work Together.* Washington, D.C.: American Personnel and Guidance Association, 1968.

———. *Meet Your Secondary School Counselor.* Washington, D.C.: American Personnel and Guidance Association, 1971.

Amos, William E., and Jean Dresden Grambs. eds. *Counseling the Disadvantaged Youth.* Englewood Cliffs, N.J.: Prentice-Hall, 1968.

Anderson, Alan R., and Donald L. Johnson. "Using Group Procedures to Improve Human Relations in the School Social System." *The School Counselor,* 15, No. 5 (1968), 334–342.

Andrews, Margaret E. *Providing School Placement Services.* Chicago: Science Research Associates, 1957.

Anthony, John, and James Lister. "Secondary School Counseling: A Preliminary Investigation." *The School Counselor,* 19, No. 5 (1972), 378–382.

Anton, Jane L. "Intensive Experimental Designs: A Model for the Counselor/Researcher." *Personnel and Guidance Journal,* 56, No. 5 (1978), 273–278.

"APGA Wins Contract for Career Education Study." *Guidepost,* 21, No. 6 (1978) 1, 11.

Appalachia Educational Laboratory. *Administrative Manual for EBCE.* Charleston, W. VA., 1976.

Aragon, John A., and Sabine R. Ulibarri. "Learn, Amigo, Learn," *Personnel and Guidance Journal,* 50, No. 2 (1971), 87–89.

Ashbrook, James B. "Comment." *Journal of Counseling Psychology* 14, No. 5 (1967), 403–406.

Ashcraft, Rock. "A Five State Survey of Counselor Duties, Problems and Responsibilities." *The School Counselor,* 13, No. 4 (1966), 230–232.

Astin, Alexander W., and Robert J. Panos. *The Educational and Vocational Development of College Students.* Washington, D.C.: American Council on Education, 1969.

Atkin, Jerry. "Counseling in an Age of Crisis." *Personnel and Guidance Journal,* 50, No. 9 (1972), 719–724.

Aubrey, Roger F. *Career Development Needs of Thirteen Years Olds.* Washington, D.C.: American Personnel and Guidance Association, 1978.

Babcock, Robert J., and Marylin Ann Kaufman. "Effectiveness of a Career Course." *Vocational Guidance Quarterly,* 24, No. 3 (1976), 261–266.

Baer, Max F., and Edward C. Roeber. *Occupational Information.* 3rd ed. Chicago: Science Research Associates, 1964.

Baker, Stanley B., and Stanley H. Cramer. "Counselor or Change Agent: Support for the Profession." *Personnel and Guidance Journal,* 50, No. 8 (1972), 661–666.

Baker, Stanley B., and James C. Hansen. "School Counselor Attitudes on a Status Quo-Change Agent Measurement Scale." *The School Counselor,* 19, No. 4 (1972), 243–248.

Bale, Richard, Donna R. Park, and Robert W. McMeekin, Jr. *Family-Centered Residential Career Education and the Rural Poor: A National Needs Assessment* (summary). Washington, D.C.: National Institute of Education, 1976.

Barnett, Rosalind. "Personality Correlates of Vocational Planning." *Genetic Psychology Monographs,* 83 (1971), 309–356.

Barre, Mary E. *College Information and Guidance.* Boston: Houghton Mifflin Company, 1970.

Barrett, Thomas C., and Howard E. A. Tinsley. "Measuring Vocational Self-Concept Crystallization." *Journal of Vocational Behavior,* 11, No. 3 (1977), 305–313.

Barro, Stephen M. "An Approach to Developing Accountability Measures for the Public Schools." *Phi Delta Kappan,* 52, No. 4 (1970), 196–205.

Barry, William A., and Edward S. Bordin. "Personality Development and the Vocational Choice of the Ministry." *Journal of Counseling Psychology,* 14, No. 5 (1967) 395–403.

Bauernfeind, Robert H. *Building a School Testing Program*. Boston: Houghton Mifflin Company, 1968.

Baumgardner, Steve R., "The Impact of College Experience on Conventional Career Logic." *Journal of Counseling Psychology*, 23, No. 1 (1976), 40–45.

————. "Vocational Planning: The Great Swindle." *Personnel and Guidance Journal*, 56, No. 1 (1977), 17–22.

————. "Reactions to Reactions." *Personnel and Guidance Journal*, 56, No. 1 (1977a), 28.

Baxter, Neale. "JOB-FLO: How to Learn if There's a Job in Dallas when You're Jobless in Des Moines." *Occupational Outlook Quarterly*, 20, No. 2 (1976), 2–7.

Beall, L., and Edward S. Bordin. "The Development and Personality of Engineers." *Personnel and Guidance Journal*, 43, No. 1 (1965), 23–32.

Belitsky, A. Harvey. "Private Vocational Schools: An Underutilized Training Resource." *Vocational Guidance Quarterly*, 19, No. 2 (1970), 127–130.

Benedict, David Speare. "A Generalist Counselor in Industry." *Personnel and Guidance Journal*, 51, No. 10 (1973), 717–722.

Bennett, G. K., H. G. Seashore, and A. G. Wesman. *The Differential Aptitude Tests*. New York: Psychological Corporation (n. d.).

Bennett, Margaret E. *Guidance and Counseling in Groups*. 2nd ed. New York: McGraw-Hill, 1963.

Berdie, Ralph F., Armin Grams, and Forrest Vance. *Parents and the Counselor*. Washington, D.C.: National Vocational Guidance Association, 1960.

————. "Comment." *Journal of Counseling Psychology*, 11, No. 1 (1964), 12.

Bergland, Bruce W., and Gerald W. Lundquist. "The Vocational Exploration Group and Minority Youth: An Experimental Outcome Study." *Journal of Vocational Behavior*, 7, No. 3 (1975), 289–296.

Bernstein, Jean. "The Elementary School: Training Ground for Sex Role Stereotypes." *Personnel and Guidance Journal*, 51, No. 2 (1972), 97–104.

Betz, Ellen L. "Vocational Behavior and Career Development, 1976: A Review." *Journal of Vocational Behavior*, 11, No. 2 (1977), 129–152.

Betz, Robert L., Kenneth B. Engle, George G. Mallinson. "Perceptions of Non-College-Bound, Vocationally Oriented High School Graduates." *Personnel and Guidance Journal*, 47, No. 10 (1969), 988–994.

Bhaerman, Robert D. *Career Education and Basic Academic Achievement*. Washington, D.C.: U.S. Government Printing Office, 1977.

Bingham, William C., and Elaine W. House. "Counselors' Attitudes Toward Women and Work." *Vocational Guidance Quarterly*, 22, No. 1 (1973), 16–23.

Blake, Robert R., and Jane Srygley Mouton. "Toward a General Theory of Consultation." *Personnel and Guidance Journal*, 56, No. 6 (1978), 328–330.

Blau, Peter H., Herbert S. Parmes, John W. Gustad, Richard Jessor, and Richard C. Wilcox. "Occupational Choice: A Conceptual Framework." *Industrial and Labor Relations*, 9, No. 4 (1956), 531–543.

Blocher, Donald H. "The Counselor's Impact on Learning Environments." *Personnel and Guidance Journal*, 55, No. 6 (1977), 352–355.

Bohn, Martin J. "Field Trial and Evaluation of a System." In *Computer-Assisted*

Counseling. Ed. Donald E. Super. New York: Teachers College Press, 1970, 83–99.

Bonnet, Deborah G. *What Does Career Education Do for Kids?* Crawfordsville, Ind.: New Education Directions, 1977 (ED 143-831).

Bordin, Edward S., Barbara Nachman, and Stanley J. Segal. "An Articulated Framework for Vocational Development." *Journal of Counseling Psychology,* 10, No. 2 (1963), 107–117.

Borow, Henry. "Career Development: A Future for Counseling." In *Counseling and Guidance in the Twentieth Century.* Eds. William H. Van Hoose and John J. Pietrofesa. Boston: Houghton Mifflin Company, 1970, 30–46.

Bosdell, Berry, and Robert L. Frank. "Evaluating Counseling Effectiveness." In *Research Guidelines for High School Counselors.* Association for Counselor Education and Supervision. New York: College Entrance Examination Board, 1967, 71–87.

Bowlsbey, JoAnn H., Jack R. Rayman, and Doris L. Bryson. *Discover: Field Trial Report.* Westminster, Md.: Discover Foundation, 1976.

Bradley, Richard W. "Person-Referenced Test Interpretation: A Learning Process." *Measurement and Evaluation in Guidance,* 10, No. 4 (1978), 201–210.

Bradley, Richard W., and Margaret S. Thacker. "Developing Local Sources of Career Information." *Vocational Guidance Quarterly,* 26, No. 3 (1978), 268–272.

Brakel, Eugene. "Parents: The Neglected Party in Pre-College Counseling." *The School Counselor,* 16, No. 3 (1969), 216–217.

Brammer, Lawrence M. "Informal Helping Systems in Selected Subcultures." *Personnel and Guidance Journal,* 56, No. 8 (1978), 476–479.

Brammer, Lawrence M., and Springer, Harry C. "A Radical Change in Counselor Education and Certification." *Personnel and Guidance Journal,* 49, No. 10 (1971), 803–808.

Brandhorst, Ted. "ERIC: Reminders of How it Can Help You." *Phi Delta Kappan,* 58, No. 8 (1977), 627–630.

Brayfield, Arthur H., and John O. Crites. "Research on Vocational Guidance: Status and Prospect." In *Man in a World at Work.* Ed. Henry Borow. Boston: Houghton Mifflin Company, 1964, 310–340.

Brazziel, William F. "Beyond the Sound and the Fury." *Measurement and Evaluation in Guidance,* 3, No. 1 (1970), 7–9.

Brenton, Myron. "Education of the Handicapped: Historic and Current Facts." In *Mainstreaming.* Ed. Marjorie Watson. Washington, D.C.: National Education Association, 1977, 7–14.

Brown, Fred. "Test Review." *Measurement and Evaluation in Guidance,* 5, No. 1 (1972), 315–319.

Brown, Robert D. "Implications of New Evaluation Strategies for Accountability in Student Affairs." *Journal of College Student Personnel,* 19, No. 2 (1978), 123–126.

Brown, William F. "Student-to-Student Counseling for Academic Adjustment." *Personnel and Guidance Journal,* 43, No. 8 (1965), 811–817.

Brunkan, Richard J., and John O. Crites. "An Inventory to Measure the Parental Attitude Variables in Roe's Theory of Vocational Choice." *Journal of Counseling Psychology,* 11, No. 1 (1964), 3–11.

Buchheimer, Arnold and Max Weiner. "Studying Student Attitudes." In *Research Guidelines for High School Counselors.* Association for Counselor Education and Supervision: New York: College Entrance Examination Board, 1967, 1–15.

Buckingham, Lillian, and Arthur M. Lee. *Placement and Follow-Up in Career Education.* Raleigh, N.C.: North Carolina State University at Raleigh, 1973.

Buckman, Ronald B. "The Impact of EBCE—An Evaluator's Viewpoint." *Illinois Career Educational Journal,* 33, No. 3 (1976), 32–36.

Burck, Harman D., and Gary W. Peterson. "Needed: More Evaluation, Not Research," *Personnel and Guidance Journal,* 53, No. 8 (1975), 563–569.

Bureau of Labor Statistics. *Industry and Occupational Outlook for the Southeast, 1974-1985.* Atlanta: Southeastern Regional Office, U.S. Department of Labor, 1978.

Burks, Herbert M., Jr., and Robert H. Pate, Jr. "Group Procedures Terminology: Babel Revisited." *The School Counselor,* 18, No. 1 (1970), 53–60.

Byrne, Richard Hill. Review of *Vocational Education and Guidance: A System for the Seventies,* by James A. Rhodes. In *Personnel and Guidance Journal,* 49, No. 10 (1971), 875–876.

Calderone, JoAnne, and David H. Hampson. "EBCE: The Future." *Illinois Career Education Journal,* 33, No. 3 (1976), 42–43.

Caldwell, Edson. "Counseling in Context." *Personnel and Guidance Journal,* 49, No. 4 (1970), 271–278.

Calia, Vincent F. "The Culturally Deprived Client: A Reformulation of the Counselor's Role." *Journal of Counseling Psychology,* 13, No. 1 (1966), 100–108.

California Pilot Career Guidance Center. *Newsletter,* 1, No. 1 (1974), 2–3.

Cameron, Howard K. "Cultural Myopia." *Measurement and Evaluation in Guidance,* 3, No. 1 (1970), 10–17.

Capehart, Bertis E. "Education Cooperation Activities and Services of American Iron and Steel Institute." *Vocational Guidance Quarterly,* 15, No. 4 (1967), 305–306.

Career Education Task Force. *Forward Plan for Career Education Research and Development.* Washington, D.C.: National Institute of Education, 1973.

Carey, Albert R., and Donald L. Garris. "Accountability for School Counselors." *The School Counselor,* 18, No. 5 (1971), 321–326.

Carey, Max. "Five Million Opportunities." *Occupational Outlook Quarterly,* 15, No. 1 (1971), 2–11.

Carey, Richard, H. B. Gelatt, Gordon P. Miller, and Barbara B. Varenhorst. *Deciding.* New York: College Entrance Examination Board, 1971.

———. *Decisions and Outcomes.* New York: College Entrance Examination Board, 1973.

Carkhuff, Robert R. "Differential Functioning of Lay and Professional Helpers." *Journal of Counseling Psychology,* 15, No. 2 (1968), 117–126.

Carkhuff, Robert R., and Andrew H. Griffin. "The Selection and Training of Human Relations Specialists." *Journal of Counseling Psychology,* 17, No. 5 (1970), 443–450.

Carlson, Jon, David D. Cavins, and Don Dinkmeyer. "Guidance for All Through Support Personnel." *The School Counselor,* 16, No. 5 (1969), 360–366.

Carmical, LaVerne, and Leland Calvin, Jr. "Functions Selected by School Counselors." *The School Counselor,* 17, No. 4 (1970), 280–285.

Carr, H. C., and M. A. Young. "Industry–Education Cooperation." *Vocational Guidance Quarterly,* 15, No. 4 (1967), 302–304.

Carroll, Terresa, and Kenneth R. Edwards. "Women and Minorities as Beneficiaries of Career Education." *Journal of Career Education,* 4, No. 4 (1978), 27–34.

Chamberlain, William, Joyce Kaser, and Kenneth Rhoads. "An Innovative Approach to Placement in Dayton Schools." *Phi Delta Kappan,* 56, No. 9 (1975), 615.

Cheney, Truman, and George B. Kish. "Job Development in a Veterans Administration Hospital." *Vocational Guidance Quarterly,* 19, No. 1 (1970), 61–65.

Chick, Joyce M. *Innovations in the Use of Career Information.* Boston: Houghton Mifflin Company, 1970.

Ching, J. Frederic. "A Unique Program in Industry–Education Cooperation." *Vocational Guidance Quarterly,* 15, No. 3 (1967), 225–228.

Christensen, Edward W. "When Counseling Puerto Ricans. . . ." *Personnel and Guidance Journal,* 55, No. 7 (1977), 412–415.

Circle, D. F. "The Career Information Service: A Guide to Its Development and Use." Newton, Mass. Public Schools, 1968 (ED 021 300).

Clark, Kenneth E. *The Vocational Interests of Non-professional Men.* Minneapolis: University of Minnesota Press, 1961.

Clark, Kenneth E., and David P. Campbell. *Manual: Minnesota Vocational Interest Inventory.* New York: Psychological Corporation, 1965.

Clark, Matt, and Mariana Gosnell. "Treating the Old and Sick." *Newsweek,* February 28, 1977, 64–65.

Clark, Victoria M. "A Local Occupational Survey." *Vocational Guidance Quarterly,* 10, No. 2 (1962), 115–117.

Clarke, Robert, H. B. Gelatt, and Louis Levine. "A Decision-Making Paradigm of Local Guidance Research." *Personnel and Guidance Journal,* 44, No. 1 (1965), 40–51.

Clough, Deborah. "A First Approach to Group Counseling." *The School Counselor,* 15, No. 5 (1968), 377–381.

Clowers, Michael R., and Robert T. Fraser. "Employment Interview Literature: A Perspective for the Counselor." *Vocational Guidance Quarterly,* 26, No. 1 (1977), 13–26.

Cochran, Donald J., and Betty Green Rademacher. "University Career Development Programming." *Journal of College Student Personnel,* 19, No. 3 (1978), 275–281.

Cohn, Benjamin, ed. *Guidelines for Future Research on Group Counseling in the Public School Setting.* Washington, D.C.: American Personnel and Guidance Association, 1967.

Cole, Robert W., and Rita Dunn. "A New Lease on Life for Education of the Handicapped." *Phi Delta Kappan,* 59, No. 1 (1977), 3–10.

Cook, David R. "Guidance and Institutional Change." In *Guidance for Education in Revolution.* Ed. David R. Cook. Boston: Allyn & Bacon, 1971.

Cook, Desmond L. *Program Evaluation and Review Technique.* Washington, D.C.: U.S. Government Printing Office, 1966.

Cote, Theodore J. "Vocational Guidance European Style." In *Contemporary Concepts in Vocational Education.* Ed. Gordon F. Law. Washington, D.C.: American Vocational Association, 1971.

Coulson, William. "Inside a Basic Encounter Group." *The Counseling Psychologist,* 2, No. 2 (1970), 1–27.

Cox, Jennings G., and Richard W. Thoreson. "Client–Counselor Matching: A Test of the Holland Model." *Journal of Counseling Psychology,* 24, No. 2 (1977), 158–161.

Craig, Robert Paul. "A Need for Moderation: Career Education and the Liberal Arts." *Journal of Career Education,* 4, No. 4 (1978), 49–55.

Cramer, Stanley H. "The Opinion Survey as a Research Technique." In *Research Guidelines for High School Counselors.* Association for Counselor Education and Supervision. New York: College Entrance Examination Board, 1967, 88–89.

———. *Pre-Service and In-Service Preparation of School Counselors for Educational Guidance.* Washington, D.C.: American Personnel and Guidance Association, 1970.

Cramer, Stanley H., Edwin L. Herr, Charles N. Morris, and Thomas T. Frantz. *Research and the School Counselor.* Boston: Houghton Mifflin Company, 1970.

Cramer, Stanley H., Pamela Sharrett Wise, and David E. Colburn. "An Evaluation of a Treatment to Expand Perceptions of Junior High School Girls." *School Counselor,* 25, No. 2 (1977), 124–129.

Crane, Jeffrey K. "A Structured Group for Career Exploration." *Journal of College Student Personnel,* 19, No. 2 (1978), 182.

Crary, Robert Wall. "Specialized Counseling–A New Trend?" *Personnel and Guidance Journal,* 44, No. 10 (1966), 1056–1061.

Crawford, Paul. "Counselor Responsibility in Investigating Private Vocational Schools." *Vocational Guidance Quarterly,* 17, No. 3 (1969), 173–177.

Creange, Norman G. "Group Counseling for Underachieving Ninth Graders." *The School Counselor,* 18, No. 4 (1971), 279–285.

Crites, John O. "A Model for the Measurement of Vocational Maturity." *Journal of Counseling Psychology,* 8, No. 3 (1961), 255–259.

———. "Measurement of Vocational Maturity in Adolescence." In *Vocational Behavior Readings in Theory and Research,* Ed. Donald G. Zytowski. New York: Holt, Rinehart and Winston, 1968, 149–162.

———. *Vocational Psychology.* New York: McGraw-Hill, 1969.

———. *The Maturity of Vocational Attitudes in Adolescence.* Washington, D.C.: American Personnel and Guidance Association, 1971.

———. "The Career Maturity Inventory." In *Measuring Vocational Maturity for Counseling and Evaluation.* Ed. Donald E. Super. Washington, D.C.: National Vocational Guidance Association, 1974, 25–39.

———. "A Comprehensive Model of Career Development in Early Adulthood." *Journal of Vocational Behavior,* 9, No. 1 (1976), 105–118.

———. "Career Counseling: A Comprehensive Approach." In *Career Counseling.*

Eds. John M. Whiteley and Arthur Resnikoff. Monterey, California: Brooks/Cole Publishing, 1978a, 74–99.

――――. "Career Counseling: A Review of Major Approaches." In *Career Counseling*. Eds. John M. Whiteley and Arthur Resnikoff. Monterey, California: Brooks/Cole Publishing, 1978b, 18–56.

――――. *Theory and Research Handbook,* CMI. 2nd ed. Del Monte Park, Monterey Park, Calif.: CTB/McGraw-Hill, 1978c.

Cross, Ellen Gail. "The Effects of a Vocational Exploration Group Program with Middle and High School Students." University of Florida, dissertation, 1975.

Cross, William C. "A Career Guidance Program for Small Rural Schools." *Vocational Guidance Quarterly,* 19, No. 2 (1970), 146–150.

Cunha, Joseph E., Darryl Laramore, Bruce L. Lowery, Anita M. Mitchell, Thomas W. Smith, and Dale C. Woolley, eds. *Career Development: A California Model for Career Guidance Curriculum K-Adult.* Fullerton, Calif.: California Personnel and Guidance Association, 1972.

Cunningham, Claude H., Herbert L. Alston, Eugene B. Doughtie, and James A. Wakefield, Jr. "Use of Holland's Vocational Theory with Potential High School Dropouts." *Journal of Vocational Behavior,* 10, No. 1 (1977), 35–38.

Cutts, Catherine C. "The Self-Directed Search." *Measurement and Evaluation in Guidance,* 10, No. 2 (1977), 117–120.

Datta, Lois-Ellin et al. *Career Education–What Proof Do we Have That it Works?* Washington, D.C.: U.S. Office of Education, 1977 (ED 151 516).

Daughtrey, William E., Jr. "Vocational Evaluation: Some Fundamental Propositions." *Vocational Evaluation and Work Adjustment Bulletin,* 5, No. 1 (1972), 12–17.

Davidshofer, Charles O. "Risk Taking and Vocational Choice: A Reevaluation." *Journal of Counseling Psychology,* 23, No. 2 (1976), 151–154.

Davis, Donald A., Nellie Hagan, and Judith Strouf. "Occupational Choice of Twelve-Year-Olds." *Personnel and Guidance Journal,* 40, No. 7 (1962), 628–629.

Davis, Walter G. "Introduction to the Special Issue on Labor's View on Career Education." *Journal of Career Education,* 4, No. 4 (1978), 2–5.

Dawis, René V., and Lloyd H. Lofquist. "Personality Style and the Process of Work Adjustment." *Journal of Counseling Psychology,* 23, No. 1 (1976), 55–59.

D'Costa, Ayers G., David W. Winefordner, John G. Odgers, and Paul B. Koons, Jr. *Ohio Vocational Interest Survey: Manual for Interpretation.* New York: Harcourt, Brace, Jovanovich, 1970.

Demain, Cathy, and George S. DuBato. "CC-LSD:Career Conferences-Let Students Do It." *Vocational Guidance Quarterly,* 19, No. 2 (1970), 141–144.

Department of Employment. *People and Jobs–A Modern Employment Service.* London: Department of Employment, The Employment Service, 1971.

Department of Psychology, The University of Leeds. *Vocational Guidance Research Unit Newsletter,* 1, No. 1 (1971).

Diamond, Esther E. "Minimizing Sex Bias in Testing." *Measurement and Evaluation in Guidance,* 9, No. 1 (1976), 28–34.

――――. "Issues of Sex Bias and Sex Fairness in Career Interest Measurement:

Background and Current Status." In *Sex-Fair Interest Measurement: Research Implications.* Eds. Carol Kehr Tittle and Donald G. Zytowski. Washington, D.C.: National Institute of Education, 1978, 3–9.

Dilley, Josiah S. "Decision-Making Ability and Vocational Maturity." *Personnel and Guidance Journal.* 44, No. 4 (1965), 423–427.

———. "Counselor Actions That Facilitate Decision Making." *The School Counselor,* 15, No. 4 (1968), 247–252.

Dinkmeyer, Don, and Mike Arciniega. "Affecting the Learning Climate Through 'C' Groups with Teachers." *The School Counselor,* 19, No. 4 (1972), 249–253.

DISCOVER Foundation. *A Computer-Based Career Development and Counselor Support System—The College/Adult System.* Westminster, Md.: DISCOVER Foundation, 1977a.

Dolliver, Robert H., and Robert N. Hansen. "Second Review." *Measurement and Evaluation in Guidance,* 10, No. 2 (1977), 120–123.

Doverspike, James E. "GUICO: A Synthesized Group Approach." *Personnel and Guidance Journal,* 50, No. 3 (1971), 182–187.

Drapela, Victor J., ed. *Guidance in Other Countries.* Tampa: University of South Florida, 1977.

Driver, Helen Irene. *Multiple Counseling: A Small Group Discussion Method for Personal Growth.* Madison, Wis.: Monona Publications, 1954.

Dudley, Gordon A., and David V. Tiedeman. *Career Development: Exploration and Commitment.* Muncie, Ind.: Accelerated Development, Inc., 1977.

Dunn, James A. "Career Education and Guidance in the PLAN System of Individualized Education." In *Career Education and the Technology of Career Development.* Palo Alto, Calif.: American Institutes for Research, 1971, 81–116.

Dustin, Richard, "Training for Institutional Change." *Personnel and Guidance Journal,* 52, No. 6 (1974), 422–427.

Dyer, Henry S. "Toward Objective Criteria of Professional Accountability in the Schools of New York City." *Phi Delta Kappan,* 52, No. 4 (1970), 206–211.

Education and Work. *The Community is the Teacher.* Washington, D.C.: National Institute of Education, 1976a.

Education and Work Group. *Program Plan for Fiscal Years 1977/1978.* Washington, D.C.: National Institute of Education, 1977.

Education and Work Program. *A Comparison of Four Experienced-Based Career Education Programs.* Washington, D.C.: National Institute of Education, 1976.

Edwards, Keith J., and Douglas R. Whitney. "Structural Analysis of Holland's Personality Types Using Factor and Configural Analysis." *Journal of Counseling Psychology,* 19, No. 2 (1972), 136–145.

Egan, Christine. "You're a What? *Occupational Outlook Quarterly,* 21, No. 1 (1977), 30–31.

———. "Apprenticeship Now." *Occupational Outlook Quarterly,* 22, No. 2 (1978), 2–19.

Elder, Lawrence A. "An Inservice Community Occupational Survey." *Vocational Guidance Quarterly,* 17, No. 3 (1969), 185–188.

Elton, Charles P., and Harriet A. Rose. "Male Occupational Constancy and Change:

Its Prediction According to Holland's Theory," Part 2. *Journal of Counseling Psychology,* 17, No. 6 (1970), 1–19.

Emener, William G., and Donald R Rye. "Counselor Education Applied to Industry. *Counselor Education and Supervision,* 15, No. 1 (1975), 72–76.

Enderlein, Thomas. *A Review of Career Education Evaluation Studies.* Washington, D.C.: U.S. Office of Education, 1976 (ED 141-584).

Entine, Alan D. "Mid-life Counseling: Prognosis and Potential." *Personnel and Guidance Journal,* 55, No. 3 (1976), 112–114.

———. "Counseling for Mid-Life and Beyond." *Vocational Guidance Quarterly,* 25, No. 4 (1977), 332–336.

Esposito, Ronald P. "The Relationship Between the Motive to Avoid Success and Vocational Choice." *Journal of Vocational Behavior,* 10, No. 3 (1977), 347–357.

ETS. "SIGI Evaluation Data," Princeton, N.J.: Educational Testing Service, n. d. (mimeographed).

Ettkin, Larry, and Lester Snyder. "A Model for Peer Group Counseling Based on Role-Playing." *The School Counselor,* 19, No. 3 (1972), 215–218.

Evans, John R., and John J. Cody. "Transfer of Decision-Making Skills Learned in a Counseling-Like Setting to Similar and Dissimilar Situations." *Journal of Counseling Psychology,* 16, No. 5 (1969), 427–432.

Evans, John R., and Alice P. Rector. "Evaluation of a College Course in Career Decision Making." *Journal of College Student Personnel,* 19, No. 2 (1978), 163–168.

Evans, Rupert N., Kenneth B. Hoyt, and Garth L. Mangum. *Career Education in the Middle/Junior High School.* Salt Lake City, Utah: Olympus Publishing, 1973.

Farmer, Helen. "INQUIRY Project: Computer-Assisted Counseling Centers for Adults." *Counseling Psychologist,* 6, No. 1 (1976), 50–54.

Farmer, Helen S., and Thomas E. Backer. *Women at Work: A Counselor's Sourcebook.* Los Angeles: Interaction Research Institute, 1975.

Feinberg, Lawrence B. "The Job Game." In Weinrach, Stephen G., "Re:Views," *Personnel and Guidance Journal,* 56, No. 1 (1977), 60.

Feingold, S. Norman. "Counseling Women in the New Morality." In *Counseling Girls and Women over the Life Span.* Eds. Edwin A. Whitfield and Alice Gustav. Washington, D.C.: National Vocational Guidance Association, 1972, 47–64.

Ferman, Louis A. "Job Placement, Creation and Development." In *Breakthrough for Disadvantaged Youth.* Washington, D.C.: U.S. Government Printing Office, 1969, 181–212.

Ferrin, Richard I., and Solomon Arbeiter. *Bridging the Gap: A Study of Education-to-Work Linkages.* New York: College Entrance Examination Board, 1975.

Flanagan, John C. "The Implication of Project Talent and Related Research for Guidance." *Measurement and Evaluation in Guidance* 2 (1969), 116–123.

———. "The Psychologist's Role in Youth's Quest for Fulfillment." Div. 15, presidential address, American Psychological Association Convention, 1970.

———. "Some Pertinent Findings of Project Talent." *Vocational Guidance Quarterly,* 22, No. 2 (1973a), 92–95.

————. "The First 15 Years of Project Talent: Implications for Career Guidance." *Vocational Guidance Quarterly,* 22, No. 1 (1973b), 8–14.

————. "Planning Career Goals Based on Data from Project Talent." *Vocational Guidance Quarterly,* 25, No. 3 (1977), 270–273.

————. "A Research Approach to Improving our Quality of Life." *American Psychologist,* 33, No. 2 (1978), 138–147.

Flanagan, John C., John T. Dailey, Mation F. Shaycoft, William A. Gorham, David B. Orr, and Isadore Goldberg. *Design for a Study of American Youth.* Boston: Houghton Mifflin Company, 1962.

Flanagan, John C., F. B. Davis, John T. Dailey, Mation F. Shaycoft, David B. Orr, Isadore Goldberg, and C. A. Neyman, Jr. *The American High School Student.* Pittsburgh: Project Talent, 1964.

Flanagan, John C., David V. Tiedeman, Mary B. Willis, and Donald H. McLaughlin. *The Career Data Book: Results from Project Talent's Five-Year Follow-Up Study.* Palo Alto, Calif.: American Institutes for Research, 1973.

Florida Personnel and Guidance Association. "Differentiated Staffing for Counseling and Guidance Services in Florida Educational Institutions and Allied Agencies." March 1971 (mimeographed).

Florida State Department of Education. "New Legislation Relative to the Requirement to Provide Occupational Specialists in the Districts." Tallahassee: 1971 (mimeographed).

Foley, Wayne E., and John W. Willson. "Contracted Behavioral Counseling: A Model for Classroom Intervention." *The School Counselor,* 19, No. 2 (1971), 126–129.

Foreman, Milton E., William A. Poppen, and Jack M. Frost. "Case Groups: An In-Service Education Technique." *Personnel and Guidance Journal,* 46, No. 4 (1967), 388–392.

Forrest, David J., and Albert S. Thompson. "The Career Development Inventory." In *Measuring Vocational Maturity for Counseling and Evaluation.* Ed. Donald E. Super. Washington, D.C.: National Vocational Guidance Association, 1974, 53–66.

Fozard, James L., and Samuel J. Popkin. "Optimizing Adult Development." *American Psychologist,* 33, No. 11 (1978), 975–989.

Franchak, Stephen J. "School-Based Job Placement: Does It Work?" *Florida Vocational Journal,* 2, No. 4 (1976), 28–32.

Frey, David H. "Science and the Single Case in Counseling Research." *Personnel and Guidance Journal,* 56, No. 5 (1978), 263–268.

Friend, Byron L. "Apprenticeships in the '70's." *Vocational Guidance Quarterly,* 20, No. 4 (1972), 291–293.

Fuller, Robert W. "Eight Steps for Developing a Career Education Program." *Thrust for Educational Leadership,* 1, No. 5 (1972), 21–23.

Fullmer, Daniel W. "An Evolving Model for Group Work in the Elementary School:Counselor-Teacher-Parent Teams." *Elementary School Guidance and Counseling,* 3, No. 1 (1968), 57–64.

Fullmer, Daniel W., and Harold W. Bernard. *Counseling: Content and Process.* Chicago: Science Research Associates, 1964.

————. *The School Counselor Consultant*. Boston: Houghton Mifflin Company, 1972.

Galinsky, M. David. "Personality Development and Vocational Choice of Clinical Psychologists and Physicists." *Journal of Counseling Psychology,* 9, No. 4 (1962), 299–305.

Galinsky, M. David, and Irene Fast. "Vocational Choice as a Focus on the Identity Search." *Journal of Counseling Psychology* 13, No. 1 (1966), 89–92.

Gardner, Joann. "Sexist Counseling Must Stop." *Personnel and Guidance Journal,* 49, No. 9 (1971), 705–714.

Gatewood, Robert D., and Robert J. Teare. "Paraprofessional Utilization: Motives and Job-Assignment Techniques." *Vocational Guidance Quarterly,* 25, No. 2 (1976), 138–144.

Gay, Evan G., David J. Weiss, Darwin D. Hendel, Rene V. Dawis, and Lloyd H. Lofquist. *Manual for the Minnesota Importance Questionnaire.* Minneapolis: University of Minnesota, 1971.

Gelatt, H. B. "Decision-Making: A Conceptual Frame of Reference for Counseling." *Journal of Counseling Psychology,* 9, No. 3 (1962), 240–245.

————. "Information and Decision Theories Applied to College Choice and Planning." In *Preparing School Counselors in Educational Guidance.* Princeton, N.J.: College Entrance Examination Board, 1967, 101–114.

Gelatt, H. B., and R. B. Clarke. "Role of Subjective Probabilities in the Decision Process." *Journal of Counseling Psychology,* 14, No. 4 (1967), 332–341.

Gelatt, H. B., Barbara Varenhorst, and Richard Carey. *Deciding.* New York: College Entrance Examination Board, 1972.

Gilliland, Burl E. "Small Group Counseling with Negro Adolescents in a Public High School." *Journal of Counseling Psychology,* 15, No. 2 (1968), 147–152.

Ginzberg, Eli. "Toward a Theory of Occupational Choice." *Personnel and Guidance Journal,* 30, No. 8 (1952), 491–494.

————. "Autobiography," "The Development of a Developmental Theory of Occupational Choice," and "Selected Writings." In *Guidance in the Twentieth Century.* Eds. William H. Van Hoose and John Pietrofesa. Boston: Houghton Mifflin Company, 1970, 58–67.

————. *Career Guidance.* New York: McGraw-Hill, 1971.

————. "On Career Guidance." *Counseling: Today and Tomorrow,* 1, No. 1 (1972a), 7–17.

————. "Toward a Theory of Occupational Choice: A Restatement." *Vocational Guidance Quarterly,* 20, No. 3 (1972b), 169–176.

————. *The Manpower Connection—Education and Work.* Cambridge, Mass.: Harvard University Press, 1975.

————. "Preface." In *Bridges to Work,* Ed. Beatrice G. Reubens. New York: Conservation of Human Resources, Columbia University, 1977, i–iv.

Ginzberg, Eli, Sol W. Ginzberg, Sidney Axelrod, and John Herma. *Occupational Choice: An Approach to a General Theory.* New York: Columbia University Press, 1951.

Gladstein, Gerald A. "Is Empathy Important in Counseling?" *Personnel and Guidance Journal,* 48, No. 10 (1970), 823–827.

Glass, Gene V. "Primary, Secondary, and Meta-Analysis of Research." *Educational Researcher,* 5 (1976), 3–8.

Gleason, Clyde W. "Employment Opportunities for Disadvantaged Youth," In *Counseling the Disadvantaged Youth.* Eds. William E. Amos and Jean Dresden Grambs. Englewood Cliffs, N.J.: Prentice-Hall, 1968, 206–235.

Goldman, Leo. "Group Guidance:Content and Process." *Personnel and Guidance Journal,* 40, No. 6 (1962), 518–522.

———. "Tests and Counseling: The Marriage that Failed." *Measurement and Evaluation in Guidance,* 4, No. 4 (1972), 213–220.

———. "A Revolution in Counseling Research." *Journal of Counseling Psychology,* 23, No. 6 (1976), 543–552.

———. "Toward More Meaningful Research." *Personnel and Guidance Journal,* 55, No. 6 (1977), 363–368.

Goldman, Leo (ed). *Research Methods for Counselors: Practical Approaches in Field Settings.* New York: John Wiley, 1978.

Gordon, Edmund W. "Social Status Differences:Counseling and Guidance for Disadvantaged Youth." In *Guidance and the School Dropout.* Eds. Daniel Schreiber and Bernard A. Kaplan. Washington, D.C.: National Education Association, 1964, 193–208.

———. "The Socially Disadvantaged Student: Implications for the Preparation of Guidance Specialists." In *Preparing School Counselors in Educational Guidance.* Princeton, N.J.: College Entrance Examination Board, 1967, 67–88.

Gordon, Jesse E. "The Concern for Cause." *Counselor Education and Supervision,* 4, No. 3 (1965), 131–141.

———. "Counseling the Disadvantaged Boy." In *Counseling the Disadvantaged Youth.* Eds. William E. Amos and Jean Dresden Grambs. Englewood Cliffs, N.J.: Prentice-Hall, 1968, 119–168.

Gould, Roger, "Adult Life Stages: Growth Toward Self-Tolerance." *Psychology Today,* 8, No. 9 (1975), 74–78.

"Government Resources for Career Education." *Occupational Outlook Quarterly,* 21, No. 2 (1977), 22–27.

Graff, Robert W., Steven Danish, and Brian Austin. "Reactions to Three Kinds of Vocational-Educational Counseling." *Journal of Counseling Psychology,* 19, No. 3 (1972), 224–228.

Grande, Peter P. "Attitudes of Counselors and Disadvantaged Students Toward School Guidance." *Personnel and Guidance Journal,* 46, No. 9 (1968), 889–892.

Greco, Maria Elena, and Roderick J. McDavis. "Cuban-American College Students: Needs, Cultural Attitudes, and Vocational Development Program Suggestions." *Journal of College Student Personnel,* 19, No. 3 (1978), 254–258.

Green, Lawrence B., and Harry J. Parker. "Parental Influence upon Adolescents' Occupational Choice: A Test of an Aspect of Roe's Theory." *Journal of Counseling Psychology,* 12, No. 4 (1965), 379–383.

Greenhaus, Jeffrey H., and William E. Simon. "Self-Esteem, Career Salience, and the Choice of an Ideal Occupation." *Journal of Vocational Behavior,* 8, No. 1 (1976), 51–58.

————. "Career Salience, Work Values, and Vocational Indecision." *Journal of Vocational Behavior*, 10, No. 1 (1977), 104–110.

Gribbons, Warren D. "Evaluation of an Eighth Grade Group Guidance Program." *Personnel and Guidance Journal*, 38, No. 9 (1960), 740–745.

Gribbons, Warren D., and Paul R. Lohnes. "Relationships Among Measures of Readiness for Vocational Planning." *Journal of Counseling Psychology*, 11, No. 1 (1964a), 13–19.

————. "Validation of Vocational Planning Interview Scales." *Journal of Counseling Psychology*, 11, No. 1 (1964b), 20–25.

————. *Emerging Careers*. New York: Teachers College Press, 1968.

————. "Eighth Grade Vocational Maturity in Relation to Nine-Year Career Patterns." *Journal of Counseling Psychology*, 16, No. 6 (1969), 557–562.

Grigg, Austin E. "Childhood Experience with Parental Attitude: A Test of Roe's Hypothesis." *Journal of Counseling Psychology*, 6, No. 2 (1959), 153–156.

Grinnell, Richard M., Jr., and Alice Lieberman, "Teaching the Mentally Retarded Job Interviewing Skills." *Journal of Counseling Psychology*, 24, No. 4 (1977), 332–337.

Gross, Edward. "Counselors Under Fire: Youth Opportunity Centers." *Personnel and Guidance Journal*, 47, No. 5 (1969), 404–409.

Grosser, Charles. "The Role of the Nonprofessional in the Manpower Development Program." In *Counseling the Disadvantaged Youth*. Eds. William E. Amos and Jean Dresden Grambs. Englewood Cliffs, N.J.: Prentice-Hall, 1968, 291–320.

————. "Using the Nonprofessional." In *Breakthrough for Disadvantaged Youth*. U.S. Department of Labor. Washington, D.C.: U.S. Government Printing Office, 1969, 213–232.

Grubb, W. Morton, and Marvin Lazerson. "Rally 'round the Workplace: Continuities and Fallacies in Career Education." *Harvard Educational Review*, 45, No. 4 (1975), 451–474.

Guidelines for Placement Services and Follow-Up Studies. Tallahassee: State of Florida Department of Education, 1973.

Guidepost. "APGA/DOL Discuss Plans for Improved Standards." 20, No. 14 (1978), 1–5.

————. "Survey Yields Interesting View of Counselors' Needs." 19, No. 15 (1977), 12.

Gutsch, Kenneth U., and Richard H. Logan, III. "Newspapers as a Means of Disseminating Occupational Information." *Vocational Guidance Quarterly*, 15, No. 3 (1967), 186–190.

Gysbers, Norman C. "Wanted: Active-Involved Counselors." APGA Convention, New Orleans, 1970 (mimeographed).

Haase, Richard F., and Dominic J. DiMattia. "The Application of the Micro-Counseling Paradigm to the Training of Support Personnel in Counseling." *Counselor Education and Supervision*, 10, No. 1 (1970), 16–22.

Haase, Richard F., Dominic J. DiMattia, and Mary A. Julius Guttman. "Training of Support Personnel in Three Human Relations Skills: A Systematic One-Year Follow-Up." *Counselor Education and Supervision*, 11, No. 3 (1972), 194–199.

Hagans, Rex W. "What is Experienced-Based Career Education." *Illinois Career Education Journal*, 33, No. 3 (1976), 6–10.

Hagen, Douglas. "Careers and Family Atmosphere: A Test of Roe's Theory." *Journal of Counseling Psychology*, 7, No. 4 (1960), 251–256.

Hamilton, Jack A., and Anita M. Mitchell. *Identification of Evaluated, Exemplary Activities in Career Education (K-12)*. Palo Alto, Calif.: American Institutes for Research, 1978.

Hansen, James C., and Edwin L. Herr. "The Follow-Up Study." In *Research Guidelines for High School Counselors*. Association for Counselor Education and Supervision. New York: College Entrance Examination Board, 1967, 100–114.

Hansen, Jo-Ida C. "Coding SCII Items According to Holland's Vocational Theory." *Measurement and Evaluation in Guidance*, 10, No. 2 (1977), 75–83.

Hansen, Lorraine S. "Editorial: The Placement Function." *The School Counselor*, 15, No. 3 (1968), 166.

———. *Career Guidance Practices in School and Community*. Washington, D.C.: National Vocational Guidance Association, 1970.

Hansen, L. Sunny. "ACES Position Paper: Counselor Preparation for Career Development/Career Education." *Counselor Education and Supervision*, 17, No. 3 (1978), 168–179.

Hansen, L. Sunny, and Dennis L. Keierleber. "BORN FREE: A Collaborative Consultation Model for Career Development and Sex-Role Stereotyping." *Personnel and Guidance Journal*, 56, No. 7 (1978), 395–399.

Hanson, Gary R., and Nancy S. Cole. "The Career Planning Program—More Than a Test Battery." *Measurement and Evaluation in Guidance*, 5, No. 3 (1972), 415–419.

Harren, Vincent A. "The Vocational Decision-Making Process Among College Males." *Journal of Counseling Psychology*, 13, No. 3 (1966), 271–277.

Harris, Thomas L. "Employment Counseling and Placement Services for Secondary School Students." *Vocational Guidance Quarterly*, 26, No. 2 (1977), 166–168.

Harris-Bowlsbey, JoAnn. *Structure and Technology for Facilitating Human Development Through Career Education*. DeKalb, Ill.: ERIC Clearinghouse in Career Education, 1975.

Harrison, Laurie R., and Alan D. Entine. "Existing Programs and Emerging Strategies." *Counseling Psychologist*, 6, No. 1 (1976), 45–49.

Hartnett, Rodney T. *Accountability in Higher Education*. Princeton, N.J.: College Entrance Examination Board, 1971.

Hausmann, Evalyn L., and Gary Green. "An Examination and Analysis of Career Education Administrative Arrangements at the Local Level." *Journal of Career Education*, 4, No. 2 (1977), 24–34.

Havighurst, Robert J. "Youth in Exploration and Man Emergent." In *Man in a World at Work*. Ed. Henry Borow. Boston: Houghton Mifflin Company, 1964, 215–236.

———. *Developmental Tasks and Education*. 3rd ed. New York: David McKay Company, 1972.

Hawkins, John G., Richard W. Bradley, and Gordon W. White. "Anxiety and the

Process of Deciding About a Major and a Vocation." *Journal of Counseling Psychology*, 24, No. 5 (1977), 398–403.

Heddesheimer, Janet. "Multiple Motivations for Mid-Career Changes." *Personnel and Guidance Journal*, 55, No. 3 (1976), 109–111.

Heginbotham, H. *The Youth Employment Service*. London: Methuen and Company, Ltd., 1951.

———. "Meeting the Challenge." City of Birmingham Education Department, 1978 (mimeographed).

Heller, Blanche, and David Gurney. "Involving Parents in Group Counseling with Junior High Underachievers." *The School Counselor*, 15, No. 5 (1968), 394–397.

Henjum, Raymond J., and John W. M. Rothney. "Parental Action on Counselor's Suggestions." *Vocational Guidance Quarterly*, 18, No. 1 (1969), 54–58.

Herr, Edwin L. "Student Personality and College Climate. In *Preparing School Counselors in Educational Guidance*. New York: College Entrance Examination Board, 1967, 23–40.

———. "The Perceptions of State Supervisors of Guidance of Appropriateness of Counselor Function, the Function of Counselors, and Counselor Preparation." *Counselor Education and Supervision*, 8, No. 4 (1969), 241–257.

———. (ed) *Vocational Guidance and Human Development*. Boston: Houghton Mifflin Company, 1974.

———. "Manpower Policies, Vocational Guidance, and Career Development." In *Vocational Guidance and Human Development*. Ed. Edwin L. Herr. Boston: Houghton Mifflin Company, 1974b, 32–62.

———. "Vocational Planning: An Alternate View." *Personnel and Guidance Journal*, 56, No. 1 (1977), 25–27.

Herr, Edwin L. and Stanley H. Cramer. *Guidance of the College-Bound*. New York: Appleton-Century-Crofts, 1968.

———. *Vocational Guidance and Career Development in the Schools: Toward a Systems Approach*. Boston: Houghton Mifflin Company, 1972.

Herr, Edwin L., Douglas D. Dillenbeck, and John D. Swisher. "Content and Preparation Strategies Relative to Pre-College Guidance and Counseling." In *Pre-Service and In-Service Preparation of School Counselors for Educational Guidance*. Ed. Stanley H. Cramer. Washington, D.C.: American Personnel and Guidance Association, 1970, 13–42.

Herr, Edwin L., and A. G. Watts. "British and American Models of Career Education: An Overview." *Vocational Guidance Quarterly*, 27, No. 2 (1978), 101–113.

Herrick, Neal Q. "Government Approaches to the Humanization of Work." *Vocational Guidance Quarterly*, 24, No. 2 (1975), 169–171.

Hershenson, David B., and Robert Roth. "A Decisional Process Model of Vocational Development." *Journal of Counseling Psychology*, 13, No. 3 (1966), 368–370.

Hershenson, David B., and William R. Langbauer. "Sequencing of Intrapsychic Stages of Vocational Development." *Journal of Counseling Psychology*, 20, No. 6 (1973), 519–521.

Hershenson, David B., and Gerard J. Lavery. "Sequencing of Vocational Development Stages: Further Studies." *Journal of Vocational Behavior,* 12, No. 1 (1978). 102–108.

Hewer, Vivian H. "Group Counseling." *Vocational Guidance Quarterly,* 16, No. 4 (1968), 250–257.

Hewett, Kathryn D. *Career Education Catalogue.* Cambridge, Mass.: ABT Publications, n.d.

High, Sidney C., Jr. "Can Career Education Get Off the Ground?" *Occupational Outlook Quarterly,* 21, No. 2 (1977), 4–7.

Hill, George E. "The Cause 'Debate'—Comments on the Odgers-Gordon Article." *Counselor Education and Supervision,* 4, No. 3 (1965), 142–146.

———. *Staffing Guidance Programs.* Boston: Houghton Mifflin Company, 1968.

Hoffman, Paul R. "Some Comments on Vocational Evaluation as Activity Counseling." *Vocational Evaluation and Work Adjustment Bulletin,* 5, No. 1 (1972), 22–25.

Holland, John L. "Some Explorations with Occupational Titles." *Journal of Counseling Psychology,* 8, No. 1 (1961), 82–87.

———. *The Vocational Preference Inventory,* 6th rev. ed. Palo Alto, Calif.: Consulting Psychologist Press, Inc. 1965.

———. *The Psychology of Vocational Choice.* Waltham, Mass.: Blaisdell, 1966.

———. *Making Vocational Choices.* Englewood Cliffs, N.J.: Prentice-Hall, 1973.

———. *Manual for the Vocational Preference Inventory.* Palo Alto, Calif.: Consulting Psychologists Press, Inc., 1975.

———. "Career Counseling: Then, Now, and What's Next?" In *Career Counseling.* Eds. John M. Whiteley and Arthur Resnikoff. Monterey, Calif.: Brooks/Cole Publishing, 1978a, 57–62.

———. "A New Synthesis for an Old Method and A New Analysis of Some Old Phenomena." In *Career Counseling.* Eds. John M. Whiteley and Arthur Resnikoff. Monterey, Calif.: Brooks/Cole Publishing, 1978b, 128–135.

Holland, John L., and Gary D. Gottfredson. "Using a Typology of Persons and Environments to Explain Careers: Some Extensions and Clarifications." In *Career Counseling.* Eds. John M. Whiteley and Arthur Resnikoff. Monterey, Calif.: Brooks/Cole Publishing, 1978, 146–170.

Holland, John L., and Joan E. Holland. "Vocational Indecision: More Evidence and Speculation." *Journal of Counseling Psychology,* 24, No. 5 (1977), 404–414.

Holland, John L., Gary D. Gottfredson, and Joan E. Holland. "The New Edition of the Self-Directed Search." 1977 (mimeographed).

Hollander, John W. "Development of a Realistic Vocational Choice." *Journal of Counseling Psychology,* 14, No. 4 (1967), 314–318.

Hollingshead, August B. *Elmtown's Youth.* New York: John Wiley, 1949.

Hooper, Pat. "CETA Program Grants and the School Counselor." *ASCA Newsletter,* 15, No. 4 (1978), 6.

Hopke, William E. "Vocational Paraprofessional or Support Personnel as a Part of the Guidance Team." *Vocational Guidance Quarterly,* 25, No. 2 (1976), 130–137.

Hoppock, Robert. *Occupational Information.* 3rd ed. New York: McGraw-Hill, 1967.

————. "Occupations and Guidance." In *Counseling and Guidance in the Twentieth Century*. Eds. William H. Van Hoose and John Pietrofesa. Boston: Houghton Mifflin Company, 1970, 90–97.

————. "Comment." *Personnel and Guidance Journal*, 49, No. 8 (1971), 598–599.

————. *Occupational Information*. 4th ed. New York: McGraw-Hill, 1976.

Hoppock, Robert, and Bernard Novick. "The Occupational Information Consultant: A New Profession?" *Personnel and Guidance Journal*, 49, No. 7 (1971), 555–558.

Hopson, Barrie, "Career Development in Industry: The Diary of an Experiment." *British Journal of Guidance and Counseling*, 1, No. 1 (1973), 51–61.

Hopson, Barrie and John Haynes. *Career Guidance*. London: Heinemann, 1972.

Hopson, Barrie, and Patricia Hough. "Careers Teaching Program." Department of Psychology, The University of Leeds, 1971 (mimeographed).

Hosford, Ray E. "Behavioral Counseling—A Contemporary Overview." *The Counseling Psychologist*, 1, No. 4 (1969), 1–32.

Hosford, Ray E., and T. Antoinette Ryan. "Systems Design in the Development of Counseling and Guidance Programs." *Personnel and Guidance Journal*, 49, No. 3 (1970), 221–230.

Howell, Frank M., Wolfgang Frese, and Carlton R. Sollie. "Ginzberg's Theory of Occupational Choice: A Reanalysis of Increasing Realism." *Journal of Vocational Behavior*, 11, No. 3 (1977), pp. 332–346.

Hoyt, Kenneth B. "The Role of Career Counseling and Placement in the College and University." Paper prepared for presentation at the College Placement Council Meeting, Washington, D.C.: May, 1975c.

————. *Refining the Career Education Concept*. Washington, D.C.: U.S. Government Printing Office, 1976.

————. *The School Counselor*. Washington, D.C.: U.S. Government Printing Office, 1976a.

————. *Application of the Concept of Career Education to Higher Education: An Idealistic Model*. Washington, D.C.: U.S. Government Printing Office, 1976c.

————. "Basic Issues in Implementation of Career Education." Talk prepared for the National Conference for State Coordinators of Career Education, San Francisco, Calif., 1977.

————. "Career Education in the Community College: An Evolving Concept." Paper presented at the AACJC National Convention, Denver, 1977a.

————. "Career Education: Challenges for Counselors." *Vocational Guidance Quarterly*, 23, No. 4 (1975b), 303–310.

————. "Community Resources for Career Education." *Occupational Outlook Quarterly*, 21, No. 2 (1977c), 10–21.

————. *An Introduction to Career Education*. Washington, D.C.: U.S. Government Printing Office, 1975.

Hoyt, Kenneth B., and Jean R. Hebeler, eds. *Career Education for Gifted and Talented Students*. Salt Lake City, Utah: Olympus Publishing Co., 1974.

Hoyt, Kenneth B., Rupert N. Evans, Edward Mackin, and Garth L. Mangum. *Career Education*. Salt Lake City Utah: Olympus Publishing Co., 1972.

Hoyt, Kenneth, Rupert Evans, Garth Mangum, Ella Bowen, and Donald Gale. *Career Education in the High School.* Salt Lake City, Utah: Olympus Publishing Co., 1977.

Hoyt, Kenneth B., Nancy M. Pinson, Darryl Laramore, and Garth L. Mangum. *Career Education and the Elementary School Teacher.* Salt Lake City, Utah: Olympus Publishing Co., 1973.

Huffnung, Robert J., and Robert B. Mills. "Situational Group Counseling with Disadvantaged Youth." *Personnel and Guidance Journal,* 48, No. 6 (1970), 458–464.

Humes, Charles W., II. "Are Counselors Part of Pupil Personnel Services?" *The School Counselor,* 18, No. 5 (1971), 316–319.

———. "Program Budgeting in Guidance." *The School Counselor,* 19, No. 5 (1972), 313–318.

———. "School Counselors and PL 94-142." *School Counselor,* 25, No. 3 (1978), 192–195.

Hummel, Thomas J., James W. Lichtenberg, and Warren F. Shaffer. CLIENT I: A Computer Program which Stimulates Client Behavior in an Initial Interview." *Journal of Counseling Psychology,* 22, No. 2 (1975), 164–169.

Huse, Edgar F. "Organization Development." *Personnel and Guidance Journal,* 56, No. 7 (1978), 403–406.

Hutchinson, Thomas, and Anne Roe. "Studies of Occupational History. Part II. Attractiveness of Developmental Groups of the Roe System." *Journal of Counseling Psychology,* 15, No. 2 (1968), 107–110.

Hutton, Carroll M. "Career Education Strategies: A UAW View." *Journal of Career Education,* 4, No. 4 (1978), 13–17.

Hyre, C. Steven, and Harold L. Henderson. "An Alternative Curriculum." American Educational Research Association, San Francisco, April 22, 1976.

Illich, Ivan. *Deschooling Society.* New York: Harper and Row, 1970.

Irvine, David J. "Needed for Disadvantaged Youth: An Expanded Concept of Counseling." *The School Counselor,* 15, No. 3 (1968), 176–179.

Isaacson, Lee E. *Career Information in Counseling and Teaching.* 3rd ed. Boston: Allyn & Bacon, 1977.

Ivey, Allen E. *Microcounseling.* Springfield, Ill.: Charles C Thomas, 1971.

———. "Counseling Psychology, the Psychoeducator Model and the Future." *Counseling Psychologist,* 6, No. 3 (1976), 72–75.

Jacobson, Thomas J. "Career Guidance Centers." *Personnel and Guidance Journal.* 50, No. 7 (1972), 599–604.

———. *A Study of Career Centers in the State of California.* Le Mesa, Calif.: Grossmont Union High School District, 1975.

Jacobson, Thomas J., and Anita M. Mitchell. "How to Develop a District Master Plan for Career Guidance and Counseling." *Vocational Guidance Quarterly,* 25, No. 3 (1977), 195–202.

Jennings, Wayne, and Joe Nathan. "Startling/Disturbing Research on School Program Effectiveness." *Phi Delta Kappan,* 58, No. 7 (1977), 568–572.

Jepsen, David A. "Occupational Decision Development over the High School Years." *Journal of Vocational Behavior,* 7, No. 2 (1975), 225–237.

————. "Vocational Decision-Making Strategy-Types: An Exploratory Study." *Vocational Guidance Quarterly*, 23, No. 1 (1974), 17–23.

Jepsen, David A., and Josiah S. Dilley. "Vocational Decision-Making Models: A Review and Comparative Analysis." *Review of Educational Research*, 44, No. 3 (1974), 331–349.

Jessell, John C., and John W. M. Rothney. "The Effectiveness of Parent-Counselor Conferences." *Personnel and Guidance Journal*, 44, No. 2 (1965), 142–145.

Johnson, Edward, and Bonnie Briggs. "At Our Fingertips." *Vocational Guidance Quarterly*, 20, No. 4 (1972), 303–304.

Johnson, Larry, and Ralph H. Johnson. "High School Preparation, Occupation, and Job Satisfaction." *Vocational Guidance Quarterly*, 20, No. 4 (1972), 287–290.

Johnson, Richard H. "ACADEM, Decision-Making Program for University of Florida Freshmen." Department of Counselor Education, University of Florida, 1972 (mimeographed).

Johnson, Richard H. and Delores E. Euler. "Effect of the Life Career Games on Learning and Retention of Educational-Occupational Information." *The School Counselor*, 19, No. 3 (1972), 155–159.

Johnson, Robert B. "Life Planning and Life Planning Workshops." *Personnel and Guidance Journal*, 55, No. 9 (1977), 546–549.

Jones, G. Brian, Carolyn B. Helliwell, and Laurie H. Ganschow. "A Planning Model for Career Guidance." *Vocational Guidance Quarterly*, 23, No. 3 (1975), 220–225.

Jones, Lawrence K., and Wray K. Cox. "Support Personnel: Attitudes Toward Functions and Training Responsibility." *Counselor Education and Supervision*, 10, No. 1 (1970), 51–55.

Jordaan, Jean Pierre. "Career Development: Theory, Research, Practice." *Pupil Personnel Services Journal*, 6, No. 1 (1977), 41–59.

Jordaan, Jean Pierre and Martha B. Heyde. *Vocational Maturity During the High School Years*. New York: Teachers College Press, 1979.

Kaldor, Donald R., and Donald G. Zytowski. "A Maximizing Model of Occupational Decision-Making." *Personnel and Guidance Journal*, 47, No. 8 (1969), 781–788.

Kanzaki, George A. "Fifty Years (1925-1975) of Stability in the Social Status of Occupations." *Vocational Guidance Quarterly*, 25, No. 2 (1976), 101–105.

Kaplan, Herbert H. "A Case for Better Training in Pre-College Guidance: Counselors Speak Out." In *Pre-Service and In-Service Preparation of School Counselors for Educational Guidance*. Ed. Stanley H. Cramer. Washington, D.C.: American Personnel and Guidance Association, 1970, 5–12.

Katz, Martin R. *You: Today and Tomorrow*. Princeton, N.J.: Educational Testing Service, 1958.

————. *Decisions and Values*. New York: College Entrance Examination Board, 1963.

————. "A Model of Guidance for Career Decision-Making." *Vocational Guidance Quarterly*, 15, No. 1 (1966), 2–10.

Kearney, Annette G., and Robert L. Clayton. "Career Education and Blacks: Trick or Treat?" *School Counselor*, 21, No. 2 (1973), 102–108.

Kell, Bill L., and Josephine Morse Burow. *Developmental Counseling and Therapy*. Boston: Houghton Mifflin Company, 1970.

Kemble, Eugenia. "Possibilities and Shortcomings in Career Education." *Journal of Career Education*, 4, No. 4 (1978), 6–12.

Kemp, C. Gratton. *Foundations of Group Counseling*. New York: McGraw-Hill, 1970.

Kennedy, John J., and Ronald H. Frederickson. "Student Assessment of Counselor Assistance in Selected Problem Areas." *Counselor Education and Supervision*, 8, No. 3 (1969), 206–212.

Kincaid, Marylou. "Identity and Therapy in the Black Community." *Personnel and Guidance Journal*, 47, No. 9 (1969), 884–890.

Kinnick, Bernard C. "Group Discussion and Group Counseling Applied to Student Problem Solving." *The School Counselor*, 15, No. 5 (1968), 350–356.

Kirby, Jonell H. "Group Guidance." *Personnel and Guidance Journal*, 49, No. 8 (1971), 593–598.

Knapp, Dale L. and James H. Bedford. *The Parent's Role in Career Development*. Washington, D.C.: American Personnel and Guidance Association, 1967.

Knapp, Robert R., Lila Knapp, and Peter M. Buttafuoco. "Interest Changes and the Classification of Occupations." *Measurement and Evaluation in Guidance*, 11, No. 1 (1978), 14–19.

Knefelkamp, L. Lee, and Ron Slepitza. "A Cognitive-Developmental Model of Career Development—An Adaptation of the Perry Scheme." In *Career Counseling*. Eds. John M. Whiteley and Arthur Resnikoff. Monterey, Calif.: Brooks/Cole Publishing, 1978, 232–245.

Kramer, Bruce J. "Follow-Up?—Forget it!" *The School Counselor*, 17, No. 3 (1970), 228–232.

Krippner, Stanley. "Junior High School Students' Vocational Preferences and Their Parents' Occupational Levels." *Personnel and Guidance Journal*, 41, No. 7 (1963), 590–595.

Krivatsy, Susana E., and Thomas M. Magoon. "Differential Effects of Three Vocational Counseling Treatments." *Journal of Counseling Psychology*, 23, No. 2 (1976), 112–118.

Kroll, Arthur M. "Career Education's Impact on Employability and Unemployment: Expectations and Realities." *Vocational Guidance Quarterly*, 24, No. 3 (1976), 209–218.

Kroll, Arthur Maynard, Lillian Brandon Dinklage, Jennifer Lee, Eileen Dorothy Morley, and Eugene Heber Wilson. *Career Development*. New York: John Wiley, 1970.

Krumboltz, John D. "Promoting Adaptive Behavior." In *Revolution in Counseling*. Ed. John D. Krumboltz. Boston: Houghton Mifflin Company, 1966a, 3–26.

———. "A Social Learning Theory of CDM." In *A Social Learning Theory of Career Decision-Making*. Eds. Anita A. Mitchell, G. Brian Jones, and John D. Krumboltz. Palo Alto, Calif.: American Institutes for Research, 1975, 13–39.

———. "A Social Learning Theory of Career Decision Making." In *Social Learning and Career Decision-Making*. Eds. Anita M. Mitchell, G. Brian Jones, and John D. Krumboltz. Cranston, R.I.: Carroll Press, 1979, 19–49.

Krumboltz, John D. and Bruce Bergland. "Experiencing Work Almost Like It Is." *Educational Technology*, 9, No. 3 (1969), 47–49.

Krumboltz, John D., and Raymond E. Hosford. "Behavioral Counseling in the Elementary School." *Elementary School Guidance and Counseling*, 1, No. 1 (1967), 27–40.

Krumboltz, John D., and Carl E. Thoresen. "The Effect of Behavioral Counseling in Group and Individual Settings on Information-Seeking Behaviors." *Journal of Counseling Psychology*, 11, No. 4 (1964), 324–333.

Krupka, Lawrence R., and Arthur M. Vener. "Career Education and the University: A Faculty Perspective." *Personnel and Guidance Journal*, 57, No. 2 (1978), 112–114.

Kuder, G. Frederic. *Occupational Interest Survey General Manual*. Chicago: Science Research Associates, 1970.

Kunze, Karl R. "Industry Resources Available to Counselors." *Vocational Guidance Quarterly*, 16, No. 2 (1967), 137–142.

———. "Business and Industry Look Out for Their Own." *Personnel and Guidance Journal*, 52, No. 3 (1973), 145–149.

Kurland, Norman D. "A National Strategy for Lifelong Learning." *Phi Delta Kappan*, 59, No. 6 (1978), 385–389.

Kuvlesky, William P., and Rumaldo Z. Juarez. "Mexican American Youth and the American Dream." In *Career Behavior of Special Groups*. Eds. J. Steven Picou and Robert E. Campbell. Columbus, Ohio: Charles E. Merrill Publishing Co., 1975, 241–296.

Lang, Carroll A., and Keith Rose. *Educational Goals and Objectives: A Model Program for Community and Professional Involvement*. Bloomington, Ind.: *Phi Delta Kappa*, 1972.

Laramore, Darryl. "Counselors Make Occupational Information Packages." *Vocational Guidance Quarterly*, 19, No. 3 (1971), 220–224.

Laramore, Darryl, and Jack M. Thompson. "Counselors Learn About the World of Work." *Vocational Guidance Quarterly*, 19, No. 2 (1970), 140–141.

Leacock, Eleanor. "The Concept of Culture and Its Significance for School Counselors." *Personnel and Guidance Journal*, 46, No. 9 (1968), 844–851.

Legislature of the State of Florida. House Bill No. 3893, chapter 70-317. Tallahassee, 1970.

Leibman, O. Bernard, Leo Goldman, and Haron J. Battle. "Report of the National Conference of Pupil Personnel Services." 1971 (dittoed).

Leifer, Aimee Dorr, and Gerald S. Lesser. *The Development of Career Awareness in Young Children*. Washington, D.C.: National Institute of Education, 1976.

Leonard, George E. "Career Guidance in the Elementary School." *Elementary School Guidance and Counseling*, 6, No. 3 (1972), 283–286.

Leonard, George E., and Howard H. Splete. "Career Education in Colleges of Education: A Neglected Responsibility," *Journal of Career Education*, 4, No. 4 (1978), 42–48.

Leonard, George E., and Thelma J. Vriend. "Update: The Developmental Career Guidance Project." *Personnel and Guidance Journal*, 53, No. 9 (1975) 668–671.

Lerche, Mary E. "Seven Sessions with Failing Students." *The School Counselor*, 15, No. 5 (1968), 382–385.

Levinson, Daniel J. "The Mid-Life Transition: A Period in Adult Psychological Development." *Psychiatry*, 40, No. 2 (1977), 99–112.

Lewis, Michael D., and Judith A. Lewis. "The Counselor's Impact on Community Environments." *Personnel and Guidance Journal*, 55, No. 6 (1977), 356–358.

Lieberman, Myron. "An Overview of Accountability." *Phi Delta Kappan*, 52, No. 4 (1970), 194–195.

Lifton, Walter M. *Working with Groups*. New York: John Wiley, 1966.

Lister, James L. "The Counselor's Personal Theory." *Counselor Education and Supervision*, 3, No. 4 (1964), 207–213.

———. "The Consultant to Counselors: A New Professional Role." *The School Counselor*, 16, No. 5 (1969), 349–354.

Lobitz, W. Charles. "Maximizing the High School Counselor's Effectiveness: The Use of Senior Tutors." *The School Counselor*, 18, No. 2 (1970), 127–129.

LoCascio, Ralph. "The Vocational Maturity of Diverse Groups: Theory and Measurement." In *Measuring Vocational Maturity for Counseling and Evaluation*. Ed. Donald E. Super. Washington, D.C.: National Vocational Guidance Association, 1974, 123–133.

LoCascio, Ralph, Jeanne Nesselroth, and Mark Thomas. "The Career Development Inventory: Use and Findings with Inner City Drop-Outs." *Journal of Vocational Behavior*, 8, No 3 (1976), 285–292.

Lofquist, Lloyd H., and Rene V. Dawis. *Applications of the Theory of Work Adjustment to Rehabilitation Counseling*. Minneapolis: University of Minnesota, 1972.

Loughary, John W. "To Grow or Not to Grow." *The School Counselor*, 18, No. 5 (1971), 327–334.

Lowenthal, Marjorie Fiske, Majda Thurnher, David Chiriboga, and Associates. *Four Stages of Life*. San Francisco: Josey-Bass Publishers, 1976.

Lundquist, Gerald W., and John C. Chamley. "Counselor-Consultant: A Move Toward Effectiveness." *The School Counselor*, 18, No. 5 (1971), 362–366.

Lunneborg, Patricia W., and Clifford E. Lunneborg. "Roe's Classification of Occupations in Predicting Academic Achievement." *Journal of Counseling Psychology*, 15, No. 1 (1968), 8–16.

Lusterman, Seymour. *Education in Industry*. New York: The Conference Board, Inc. 1977.

Lynch, Stanley, and Marcia Wehr. "The Human Service Associate: An Emergency Para-Professional Model." *Program Summaries and Abstracts, 1972 Convention*. Washington, D.C.: American Personnel and Guidance Association, 1972, 29.

MacKay, William R. "The Decision Fallacy: Is It If or When?" *Vocational Guidance Quarterly*, 23, No. 3 (1975), 227–231.

Mager, Robert F. *Preparing Instructional Objectives*. Palo Alto, Calif.: Fearon, 1962.

Mahler, Clarence A. "Group Counseling." *Personnel and Guidance Journal*. 49, No. 8 (1971), 601–608.

Malcolm, David D. and Donald G. Hays. *Expectations and Commitments*. Washington, D.C.: American Personnel and Guidance Association 1969.

Mallars, Patricia B. "Thinking About Group Counseling for Parents?" *The School Counselor*, 15, No. 5 (1968), 374–376.

Malouf, Phelon J. "Direct Feedback: Helpful or Disruptive in Group Counseling?" *The School Counselor*, 15, No. 5 (1968), 390–393.

Mangum, Garth L. *Career Education and the Comprehensive Employment and Training Act*. Washington, D.C.: U.S. Government Printing Office, 1978.

Mannbach, Alfred J., and William E. Stilwell. "Installing Career Education: A System Approach." *Vocational Guidance Quarterly*, 22, No. 3 (1974), 180–188.

Maola, Joseph and Gary Kane. "Comparison of Computer-Based Versus Counselor-Based Occupational Information Systems with Disadvantaged Vocational Students." *Journal of Counseling Psychology*, 23, No. 2 (1976), 163–165.

Marland, Sidney P., Jr. "Career Education Now." *Vocational Guidance Quarterly*, 20, No. 3 (1972), 188–192.

———. *Career Education*. New York: McGraw-Hill, 1974.

Martin, Ann M. *The Theory and Practice of Communicating Educational and Vocational Information*. Boston: Houghton Mifflin Company, 1970.

Maser, Arthur L. "Counselor Function in Secondary Schools." *The School Counselor*, 18, No. 5 (1971), 367–382.

Mastie, Marjorie M. "Differential Aptitude Tests, Form S and T, with Career Planning Program." *Measurement and Evaluation in Guidance*, 9, No. 2 (1976), 87–95.

Matheny, Kenneth. "Counselors as Environmental Engineers." *Personnel and Guidance Journal*, 49, No. 6 (1971), 439–444.

Mathis, Harold I. "The Disadvantaged and the Aptitude Barrier." *Personnel and Guidance Journal*, 47, No. 5 (1969), 467–472.

Mayer, G. Roy, Terrence M. Rohen, and Dan Whitley. "Group Counseling with Children: A Cognitive-Behavioral Approach." *Journal of Counseling Psychology*, 16, No. 2 (1969), 142–149.

McDaniels, Carl. "Leisure and Career Development in Mid-Life: A Rationale." *Vocational Guidance Quarterly*, 25, No. 4 (1977), 344–350.

McGovern, Thomas V., Diane J. Tinsley, Nechama Liss-Levinson, Rene O. Laventure, and Ginny Britton. "Assertion Training for Job Interviews." *Counseling Psychologist*, 5, No. 4 (1975), 65–68.

McKinlay, Bruce. *Developing a Career Information System*. Eugene, Ore.: Oregon Career Information System, 1974.

McLaughlin, Donald H., and David V. Tiedeman. "Eleven-Year Career Stability and Change as Reflected in Project Talent Data Through the Flanagan, Holland, and Roe Occupational Classification Systems." *Journal of Vocational Behavior*, 5, No. 2 (1974), 177–196.

McQueen, Mildred. "Accountability (Part Three-The National Assessment)." Research Report. Chicago: Science Research Associates, 1971.

Mehrens, William A. "Rigor and Reality in Counseling Research." *Measurement and Evaluation in Guidance*, 11, No. 1 (1978), 8–13.

Meir, Eichmann I. "Empirical Test of Roe's Structure of Occupations and an Alternative Structure." *Journal of Counseling Psychology*, 17, No. 1 (1970), 41–48.

Mencke, Reed A., and Donald J. Cochran. "Impact of a Counseling Outreach Workshop on Vocational Development." *Journal of Counseling Psychology,* 21, No. 3 (1974), 185–190.

Mesa Public Schools. *Accountability for Counselors.* Mesa, Ariz.: Board of Education, n.d.

————. *Toward Accountability.* Mesa, Ariz.: Board of Education, n. d.

Mesa School System. *Mesa Public Schools, K-6 Learning Chart.* Mesa, Ariz.: Board of Education, 1977.

Military-Civilian Occupational Source Book. Fort Sheridan, Ill.: United States Military Enlistment Processing Command, 1978.

Miller, A. J. "The Emerging School-Based Comprehensive Education Model." Columbus, Ohio: National Conference on Career Education, 1972.

Miller, C. Dean, and Gene Oetting. "Barriers to Employment and the Disadvantaged." *Personnel and Guidance Journal,* 56, No. 2 (1977), 89–93.

Miller, Delbert G. and William H. Form. *Industrial Sociology.* New York: Harper and Brothers, 1951.

Miller Juliet V. *Intensive High School Occupational Guidance Approaches for Initial Work and Technical School Placement.* Ann Arbor, Mich.: ERIC Clearinghouse on Counseling and Personnel Services, 1969.

————. *Career Development Needs of Nine Year Olds.* Washington, D.C.: American Personnel and Guidance Association, 1978.

Mitchell, A. M., ed. *Ways to Evaluate Different Types of Career Education Activities: A Handbook of Evaluation Models.* Palo Alto, Calif.: American Institutes for Research, 1978.

Mitchell, Anita M. *Career Development Needs of Seventeen Year Olds.* Washington, D.C.: American Personnel and Guidance Association, 1978b.

Mitchell, Anita M., G. Brian Jones, and John D. Krumboltz, eds. *A Social Learning Theory of Career Decision Making.* Palo Alto, Calif.: American Institutes for Research, 1975.

Mitchell, Kevin M., Stanford E. Rubin, Jerold D. Bozarth, and Thomas J. Wyrick. "Effects of Short-Term Training on Residence Hall Assistants." *Counselor Education and Supervision,* 10, No. 4 (1971), 310–318.

Mitchell, Marianne H. "A Comparison of Pupil Personnel Services in Britain and the United States." *The School Counselor,* 16, No. 4 (1969), 255–259.

Monacel, Louis D., Herschel W. Fort, and Felix R. Sloan. *Development Career Guidance in Action.* Detroit, Mich.: Wayne State University and Detroit Public Schools, n.d.

Mondale, Walter F. "The Lifetime Learning ACT: Proposed Legislation," *Counseling Psychologist,* 6, No. 1 (1976), 67–68.

Moore, Gilbert D. "Introduction." In *Research Guidelines for High School Counselors.* Association for Counselor Education and Supervision. New York: College Entrance Examination Board, 1967, vii–xii.

Moore, Lorraine. "A Developmental Approach to Group Counseling with Seventh Graders." *The School Counselor,* 16, No. 4 (1969), 272–276.

Moore, William. "Administrative Needs and Problems in the Installation of Career

Education Programs." Columbus, Ohio: National Conference on Career Education, 1972.

Morgan, James I., and Thomas M. Skovholt. "Using Inner Experience: Fantasy and Daydreams in Career Counseling." *Journal of Counseling Psychology*, 24, No. 5 (1977), 391–397.

Morrill, Weston, H., and David J. Forrest. "Dimensions of Counseling for Career Development." *Personnel and Guidance Journal*, 49, No. 4 (1970), 299–305.

Morrill, Weston H., Eugene R. Oetting, and James C. Hurst. "Dimensions of Counselor Functioning." *Personnel and Guidance Journal*, 52, No. 6 (1974), 354–359.

Morrison, Edward J. "Trends in vocational-Technical Education and Curriculum." *Vocational Guidance Quarterly*, 18, No. 4 (1970), 243–248.

Moser, Helen P., William Dubin, and Irving M. Shelsky. "A Proposed Modification of the Roe Occupational Classification." *Journal of Counseling Psychology*, 3, No. 1 (1956), 27–31.

Mosher, Ralph L., and Norman A. Sprinthall. "Psychological Education: A Means to Promote Personal Development During Adolescence." *Counseling Psychologist*, 2, No. 4 (1971), 3–84.

Munger, Daniel I. "The Occupational Information Speaker's Bureau." *Vocational Guidance Quarterly*, 15, No. 4 (1967), 265–266.

Munley, Patrick H. "Erik Erikson's Theory of Psychological Development and Vocational Behavior." *Journal of Counseling Psychology*, 22, No. 4 (1975), 314–319.

———. "Erikson's Theory of Psychological Development and Career Development." *Journal of Vocational Behavior*, 10, No. 3 (1977), 261–269.

Munson, Harold L. *Foundations of Developmental Guidance*, Boston: Allyn & Bacon, 1971.

Musselman, Dayton L. "Career Exposition: Big Time Version of an Old Guidance Technique." *Vocational Guidance Quarterly*, 18, No. 1 (1969), 49–53.

Myers, Isabel Briggs. *Introduction to Type.* Swarthmore, Pa.: 1970.

Myers, Roger A. "IBM ECES: A Preliminary Report on the First Year of Field Trials in Genesee County, Michigan." In *Career Education and the Technology of Career Development*. American Institutes for Research. Palo Alto, Calif.: American Institutes for Research, 1972, 159–160.

Myers, Roger A., Richard H. Lindeman, Albert S. Thompson, and Theodora A. Patrick. "Effects of Educational and Career Exploration and Career Exploration System on Vocational Maturity." *Journal of Vocational Behavior*, 6, No. 2 (1975), 245–254.

Nachmann, Barbara. "Childhood Experience and Vocational Choice in Law, Dentistry, and Social Work." *Journal of Counseling Psychology*, 7, No. 4 (1960), 243–250.

Nafziger, Dean H., John L. Holland, Samuel T. Helms, and James M. McPartland. "Applying an Occupational Classification to the Work Histories of Young Women." *Journal of Vocational Behavior*, 5, No. 3 (1974), 331–345.

Nash, Robert J., and Kenneth P. Saurman. "Learning to Earn is not Learning to

Live: Student Development Educators as Meaning Makers" and "Nash-Saurman Reaction to the Stolers." *Personnel and Guidance Journal,* 57, No. 2 (1978), 84–89, 94–95.

National Advisory Council on Career Education. *The Efficacy of Career Education* Washington, D.C.: National Advisory Council on Career Education, 1976 (ED 130–092).

National Assessment of Educational Progress. *Objectives for Career and Occupational Development.* Denver: National Assessment of Educational Progress, 1971.

———. "17-Year Old 'Dropouts' Lag in Skills Needed to Get, Keep Job." *NAEP Newsletter,* 11, No. 2 (1978), 1, 3–4.

———. "Guidelines for the Preparation and Evaluation of Nonprint Career Media." *Vocational Guidance Quarterly,* 26, No. 2 (1977), 99–107.

National Vocational Guidance Association. *Career Decisions.* Washington, D.C.: American Personnel and Guidance Association, 1969.

———. *Guidelines for the Preparation and Evaluation of Career Information Media.* Washington, D.C.: National Vocational Guidance Association, 1971.

———. *Bibliography of Current Information.* Washington, D.C.: American Personnel and Guidance Association, 1978.

National Vocational Guidance Association and American Vocational Association. "Career Development and Career Guidance," *NVGA Newsletter,* 13, No. 1 (1973), 5–8.

Neely, Margery A., and Mary W. Kosier. "Physically Impaired Students and the Vocational Exploration Group." *Vocational Guidance Quarterly,* 26, No. 1 (1977), 37–44.

Neff, Walter S. "Psychoanalytic Conceptions of the Meaning of Work." *Psychiatry,* 28, No. 4 (1965), 324–333.

———. "Problems of Work Evaluation." *Personnel and Guidance Journal,* 44, No. 7 (1966), 682–688.

Noeth, Richard J., and Dale J. Prediger. "Career Development over the High School Years." *Vocational Guidance Quarterly,* 26, No. 3 (1978), 244–254.

Norris, Lila, and Donald J. Cochran. "The SIGI Prediction System: Predicting College Grades with and without Tests." *Measurement and Evaluation in Guidance,* 10, No. 3 (1977), 134–140.

Norris, Willa, Franklin R. Zeran, Raymond N. Hatch, and James R. Engelkes. *The Information Service in Guidance.* 3rd ed. Chicago: Rand McNally, 1972.

Norton, Joseph L. "Current Status of the Measurement of Vocational Maturity." *Vocational Guidance Quarterly,* 18, No. 3 (1970), 165–170.

"Occupational Specialists Identify Training Needs," *Florida Vocational Journal,* 3, No. 6 (1978), 32.

Odgers, John G. "Cause for Concern." *Counselor Education and Supervision,* 4, No. 1 (1964), 17–20.

———. "Placement: A Counselor's Job." *The School Counselor,* 15, No. 5 (1968), 398–400.

Oetting, Eugene R., and James F. Hawkes. "Training Professionals for Evaluative Research." *Personnel and Guidance Journal,* 52, No. 6 (1974), 434–438.

Oetting, Gene, and Dean C. Miller. "Work and the Disadvantaged: The Work

Adjustment Hierarchy." *Personnel and Guidance Journal,* 56, No. 1 (1977), 29–35.

O'Hara, Robert P., and David V. Tiedeman. "Vocational Self-Concept in Adolescence." *Journal of Counseling Psychology,* 6, No. 4 (1959), 292–301.

O'Hare, Robert W., and Barbara Lasser. *Evaluating Pupil Personnel Programs.* Fullerton, Calif.: California Personnel and Guidance Association, 1971.

Ohlsen, Merle M. "Counseling Children in Groups." *The School Counselor,* 15, No. 5 (1968), 343–349.

Olivero, James L. "The Meaning and Application of Differentiated Staffing in Teaching." *Phi Delta Kappan,* 52, No. 1 (1970), 36–40.

Omvig, Clayton P., and Edward G. Thomas. "Relationship between Career Education, Sex, and Career Maturity of Sixth and Eighth Grade Pupils." *Journal of Vocational Behavior,* 11, No. 3 (1977), 322–331.

Omvig, Clayton P., Rodney W. Tulloch, and Edward G. Thomas. "The Effects of Career Education on Career Maturity." *Journal of Vocational Behavior,* 7, No. 2 (1975), 265–273.

O'Neil, James M. "Holland's Theoretical Signs of Consistency and Differentiation and their Relationship to Academic Potential and Achievement." *Journal of Vocational Behavior,* 11, No. 2 (1977), 166–173.

O'Neil, James M., and Thomas M. Magoon. "The Predictive Power of Holland's Investigative Personality Type and Consistency Levels Using the Self-Directed Search." *Journal of Vocational Behavior,* 10, No. 1 (1977), 39–46.

Oregon Career Information System. Eugene, Oregon: University of Oregon n. d.

Osipow, Samuel H. "Consistency of Occupational Choices and Roe's Classification of Occupations." *Vocational Guidance Quarterly,* 14, No. 4 (1966), 285–286.

————. "The Relevance of Theories of Career Development to Special Groups: Problems, Needed Data, and Implications." In *Career Behavior of Special Groups.* Eds. J. Steven Picou and Robert E. Campbell. Columbus, Ohio: Charles E. Merrill, 1975, 9–22.

————. "Vocational Behavior and Career Development, 1975: A Review." *Journal of Vocational Behavior,* 9, No. 2 (1976), 129–145.

————. "The Great Expose Swindle: A Reader's Reaction." *Personnel and Guidance Journal,* 56, No. 1 (1977a), 23–24.

O'Toole, James. *Work in America.* Cambridge, Mass.: MIT Press, 1973.

P.L. 95-207, Career Education Incentive Act, Dec. 13, 1977.

Pallone, Nathaniel J., Robert B. Hurley, and Fred S. Rickard. "Emphases in Job Satisfaction Research: 1968–1969." *Journal of Vocational Behavior,* 1, No. 1 (1971), 11–28.

Pallone, Nathaniel J., Fred S. Rickard, and Robert B. Hurley. "Job Satisfaction Research of 1966–67." *Personnel and Guidance Journal,* 48, No. 6 (1970), 469–478.

Pancrazio, James J. "The School Counselor as a Human Relations Consultant." *The School Counselor,* 19, No. 2 (1971), 81–87.

Panther, Edward E. "Career Education's Missing Link: Support Personnel." *Vocational Guidance Quarterly,* 24, No. 1 (1975), 73–76.

Parsons, George E., and James V. Wigtil. "Occupational Mobility as Measured by

Holland's Theory of Career Selection." *Journal* of *Vocational Behavior,* 5, No. 3 (1974), 321–330.

Patterson, C. H. *Theories of Counseling and Psychotherapy.* New York: Harper and Row, 1966.

Patterson, Lewis E. "Career Information: Experience is the Best Teacher." *Vocational Guidance Quarterly,* 25, No. 2 (1976), 112–118.

Pearson, Richard. "Working with the Disadvantaged Through Groups." In *Counseling the Disadvantaged Youth.* Ed. William E. Amos and Jean Dresden Grambs. Englewood Cliffs, N.J.: Prentice-Hall, 1968, 54–79.

Peatling, John H. "Careers and a Sense of Justice in Mid-Life." *Vocational Guidance Quarterly,* 25, No. 4 (1977), 303–308.

Peatling, John H., and David V. Tiedeman. *Career Development: Designing Self.* Muncie, Ind.: Accelerated Development, Inc., 1977.

Perrone, Philip A. "Teaching Vocational Aspects of Development in Eighth Grade." *Vocational Guidance Quarterly,* 22, No. 3 (1972), 204–209.

Perrone, Philip A., Antoinette Ryan, and Franklin R. Zeran. *Guidance and the Emerging Adolescent.* Scranton, Pa.: International Textbook Company, 1970.

Peters, Herman J. *The Guidance Process.* Itasca, Ill.: Peacock, 1970.

Peterson, James A., and Dick Park. "Values in Career Education: Some Pitfalls." Phi Delta Kappan, 61, No. 9 (1975), 621–623.

Pietrofesa, John J., and Howard Splete. *Career Development: Theory and Research.* New York: Grune and Stratton, 1975.

Pipho, Chris. "Minimum Competency Testing in 1978: A Look at State Standards." *Phi Delta Kappan,* 59, No. 9 (1978), 585–587.

Prediger, Dale J. *Converting Test Data to Counseling Information.* Iowa City, Ia.: American College Testing Program, 1971a.

———. "Data Information Conversion in Test Interpretation." *Journal of Counseling Psychology,* 18, No. 4 (1971b), 306–313.

———. "Tests and Developmental Career Guidance: The Untried Relationship." *Measurement and Evaluation in Guidance,* 5, No. 3 (1972), 426–429.

———. "A World of Work Map for Career Exploration." *Vocational Guidance Quarterly,* 24, No. 3 (1976), 198–208.

Prediger, Dale J., John D. Roth, and Richard J. Noeth. *Nationwide Study of Student Career Development: Summary of Results.* Iowa City, Ia: American College Testing Program, 1973.

Preli, Barbara Stock. *Career Education: Teaching/Learning Process.* Washington, D.C.: U.S. Government Printing Office, 1978.

Preparing School Counselors in Educational Guidance. New York: College Entrance Examination Board, 1967.

Preston, Jim. "Community Resources and Job Placement." *Florida Vocational Journal,* 3, No. 3 (1977), 19–23.

Proctor, Samuel A. "Reversing the Spiral Toward Futility." *Personnel and Guidance Journal,* 48, No. 9 (1970), 707–712.

Project Talent, Bulletin No. 7. "New Studies by Project Talent." July, 1972, p. 7.

Pucinski, Roman C., and Sharlene Pearlman Hirach, eds. *The Courage to Change.* Englewood Cliffs, N.J.: Prentice-Hall, 1971.

Putnam, Barbara A., and James C. Hansen. "Relationship of Self-Concept and Feminine Role Concept to Vocational Maturity in Young Women." *Journal of Counseling Psychology,* 18, No. 5 (1972), 436–440.

Rae, W. Leslie: "The Work of a British Youth Employment Officer." *Vocational Guidance Quarterly,* 14, No. 2 (1965–66), 103–107.

Rand, Herb. "Occupational Specialists' Training Competencies." *Florida Vocational Journal,* 4, No. 7 (1979), 34.

Rayman, Jack R., and JoAnn Harris-Bowlsbey. DISCOVER: A Model for a Systematic Career Guidance Program." *Vocational Guidance Quarterly,* 26, No. 1 (1977), 3–11.

Rayman, Jack R., Doris L. Bryson, and JoAnne B. Day. "Toward A Systematic Computerized Career Development Program for College Students." *Journal of College Student Personnel,* 19, No. 3 (1978), 202–207.

Reardon, Robert C., and Dorothy Domkowski. "Building Instruction into a Career Information Center." *Vocational Guidance Quarterly,* 25, No. 3 (1977), 274–278.

Reed, Harold J., Joseph Seiler, and Saul Leshner. "Research in Counseling the Disadvantaged." APGA Convention, Las Vegas, 1969.

Renzulli, Joseph S. "What Makes Giftedness?" *Phi Delta Kappan,* 60, No. 3 (1978), 180–184, 261.

Reubens, Beatrice G. *Bridges to Work.* New York: Conservation of Human Resources, Columbia University, 1977.

Rhodes, James A. *Vocational Education and Guidance: A System for the Seventies.* Columbus, Ohio: Charles E. Merrill, 1970.

Riccio, Anthony C., and Joseph J. Quaranta. *Establishing Guidance Programs in Secondary Schools.* Boston: Houghton Mifflin Company, 1968.

Richards, Kenneth W. "Who are the Consumers of Guidance and What Do They Want?" APGA Convention, 1970 (mimeographed).

Richardson, Mary Sue. "Vocational Maturity in Counseling Girls and Young Women." In *Measuring Vocational Maturity for Counseling and Evaluation.* Ed. Donald E. Super. Washington, D.C.: National Vocational Guidance Association, 1974, 135–143.

Rinn, John L. "Group Guidance: Two Processes." *Personnel and Guidance Journal,* 39, No. 7 (1961), 591–594.

Roberts, Nick J. "Establishing a Need for a Vocational Guidance Program at the Elementary and Middle School Level." *Elementary School Guidance and Counseling,* 6, No. 4 (1972), 252–257.

Roe, Anne. *The Psychology of Occupations.* New York: John Wiley, 1956.

———. "Early Determinants of Vocational Choice." *Journal of Counseling Psychology,* 4, No. 3 (1957), 212–217.

———. "Comment," *Journal of Counseling Psychology,* 10, No. 2 (1963), 117.

———. "Perspectives on Vocational Development." In *Perspectives on Vocational Development.* Eds. John M. Whiteley and Arthur Resnikoff. Washington, D.C.: American Personnel and Guidance Association, 1972, 62–68.

Roe, Anne, W. D. Hubbard, Thomas Hutchinson, and Thomas Bateman. "Studies of Occupational History, Part I: Job Changes and the Classification of Occupations." *Journal of Counseling Psychology,* 3, No. 4 (1966), 387–393.

Roe, Anne and Dennis Klos. "Classification of Occupations." In *Perspectives on Vocational Development*. Eds. John M. Whiteley and Arthur Resnikoff. Washington, D.C.: American Personnel and Guidance Association, 1972, 199–221.

Roe, Anne, and Marvin Siegelman. *The Origin of Interests*. Washington, D.C.: American Personnel and Guidance Association, 1964.

Roeber, Edward C., Garry R. Walz, and Glenn E. Smith. *A Strategy for Guidance*. New York: Macmillan, 1969.

Roemmich, Herman. "Counselor Functions in Terms of Behavioral Tasks." *The School Counselor*, 14, No. 5 (1967), 312–317.

Roessler, Richard, Daniel Cook, and Delbert Lillard. "Effects of Systematic Group Counseling on Work Adjustment Clients." *Journal of Counseling Psychology*, 24, No. 4 (1977), 313–317.

Roll Call of Sites. *Update*, 1, No. 1 (1976), 2–8.

Rosen, David, and Layton Olson. "Postsecondary Education and Work Programs Based on Outcomes for Students." *Journal of Career Education*, 4, No. 1 (1977), 53–63.

Rosen, Howard. "Guidance Counselor–A New Activist Role," *Occupational Outlook Quarterly*, 14, No. 3 (1970), 20–22.

Rosen, Stuart D., David J. Weiss, Darwin D. Hendel, René V. Dawis, and Lloyd H. Lofquist. *Occupational Reinforcer Patterns*. Minneapolis: University of Minnesota, 1972.

Rossi, Robert J., Wendy B. Bartlett, Emily A. Campbell, Lauress L. Wise, and Donald H. McLaughlin. *Using the Talent Profiles in Counseling: A Supplement to the Career Data Book*. Palo Alto, Calif.: American Institutes for Research, 1975.

Rossman, Jack E., and Elaine M. Prebonich. "School Counselor-Employment Service Relations: The Minnesota Report." *Vocational Guidance Quarterly*, 16, No. 4 (1968), 258–263.

Rothney, John W. M. *Adaptive Counseling in Schools*. Englewood Cliffs, N.J.: Prentice-Hall, 1972.

Rousseve, Ronald J. "A Counselor Education Pilot Project in 'Guided' Group Interaction." *Personnel and Guidance Journal*, 44, No. 1 (1965), 52–57.

Ruiz, Rene A., and Amado M. Padilla. "Counseling Latinos." *Personnel and Guidance Journal*, 55, No. 7 (1977), 401–408.

Ryan, T. Antoinette. "A Systems Approach to Career Education." *Vocational Guidance Quarterly*, 22, No. 3 (1974), 172–179.

Salomone, Paul R., and Robert B. Salaney. "The Applicability of Holland's Theory to Non-Professional Workers." *Journal of Vocational Behavior*, 13, No. 1 (1978), 63–74.

Samler, Joseph. "Vocational Counseling: A Pattern and a Projection." *Vocational Guidance Quarterly*, 17, No. 1 (1968), 2–11.

———. *Vocational Counselor and Social Action*. Washington, D.C.: National Vocational Guidance Association, 1970.

Sampieri, Robert A. "Comprehensive Career Education Model." *Thrust for Education Leadership*, 1, No. 5 (1972), 10–14.

———. "Los Angeles Comprehensive Career Education Program." In *Eleven Career*

Education Programs. Ed. Kathryn D. Hewett. Cambridge, Mass.: ABT Publications, 1975, 1–20.

Sandler, Bernice. "Title IX: Antisexism's Big Legal Stick." *American Education,* 13, No. 4 (1977), 6–9.

Schlossberg, Nancy K., James Woodruff, and George E. Leonard. "A Workbook and Manual for Paraprofessionals in Guidance." Detroit: Developmental Career Guidance Project, 1971 (mimeographed).

Scholz, Nelle Tumin, Judith Sosebee Prince, and Gordon Porter Miller. *How to Decide.* Princeton, N.J.: College Entrance Examination Board, 1975.

Schutz, Richard A., and Donald H. Blocher, "Self-Satisfaction and Level of Occupational Choice." *Personnel and Guidance Journal,* 39, No. 7 (1961), 595–598.

Schwartz, G. R., Elizabeth Johnson, and Jason Nicol. *The Teacher Looks at Guidance.* Washington, D.C.: National Vocational Guidance Association, 1961.

Sears, Robert R. "Sources of Life Satisfactions of the Terman Gifted Men." *American Psychologist,* 32, No. 2 (1977), 119–128.

Segal, Stanley J. "A Psychoanalytic Analysis of Personality Factors in Vocational Choice." *Journal of Counseling Psychology,* 8, No. 3 (1961), 202–210.

Seiler, Joseph. "Preparing the Disadvantaged for Tests." *Vocational Guidance Quarterly,* 19, No. 3 (1971), 201–205.

Sessions, John A. "Misdirecting Career Education: A Union View." *Vocational Guidance Quarterly,* 23, No. 4 (1975), 311–316.

Sharf, Richard S. "Evaluation of a Computer-Based Narrative Interpretation of a Test Battery." *Measurement and Evaluation in Guidance,* 11, No. 1 (1978), 50–53.

Sheppard, Harold L. "The Emerging Pattern of Second Careers." *Vocational Guidance Quarterly,* 20, No. 2 (1971), 89–95.

———. *Research and Development Strategy on Employment-Related Problems of Older Workers.* Washington, D.C.: American Institutes for Research, 1978.

Shoben, Edward Joseph, Jr. "The Counselor's Theory as Personal Trait." *Personnel and Guidance Journal,* 40, No. 7 (1962), 617–621.

Simon, J. "An Existential View of Vocational Development." *Personnel and Guidance Journal,* 44, No. 6 (1966), 604–610.

Sinick, Daniel. *Occupational Information and Guidance.* Boston: Houghton Mifflin Company, 1970.

———. "Counseling Older Persons: Career Change and Retirement." *Vocational Guidance Quarterly,* 25, No. 1 (1976), 18–25.

———. "Can Vocational Counselors Change Society?" *Vocational Guidance Quarterly,* 25, No. 3 (1977), 245–251.

Sinick, Daniel, William E. Gorman, and Robert Hoppock. "Research on the Teaching of Occupations: 1965–1970." *Vocational Guidance Quarterly,* 20, No. 2 (1971), 129–137.

Skovholt, Thomas M., and Ronald W. Hoenninger. "Guided Fantasy in Career Counseling." *Personnel and Guidance Journal,* 52, No. 10 (1974), 693–696.

Slakter, Malcolm J., and Stanley H. Cramer. "Risk Taking and Vocational or Curriculum Choice." *Vocational Guidance Quarterly,* 18, No. 2 (1969), 127–132.

Smaby, Marlowe H., and George C. Holton. "Using Career Resource People Effectively." *School Counselor,* 23, No. 2 (1975), 116–120.

Small, Leonard. "A Theory of Vocational Choice." *Vocational Guidance Quarterly.* No. 1 (1952), 29–31.

———. "Personality Determinants of Vocational Choice." *Psychological Monographs,* 67, No. 1 (1953).

Smith, Edward D. "Vocational Aspects of Elementary School Guidance Programs: Objectives and Activities." *Vocational Guidance Quarterly,* 18, No. 4 (1970), 273–279.

Smith, Mary Lee, and Gene V. Glass. "Meta-Analysis of Psychotherapy Outcome Studies." *American Psychologist,* 32, No. 9 (1977), 752–760.

Sorenson, Garth. "Ohio Vocational Interest Survey." *Measurement and Evaluation in Guidance,* 7, No. 2 (1974), 140–143.

Spencer, Barbara G., Gerald O. Windham, and John H. Peterson, Jr. "Occupational Orientation of an American Indian Group." In *Career Behavior of Special Groups.* Eds. J. Steven Picou and Robert E. Campbell. Columbus, Ohio: Charles E. Merrill, 1975, 199–223.

Sprague, Douglas G., and Donald J. Strong. "Vocational Choice Group Counseling." *Journal of College Student Personnel,* 11, No. 1 (1970), 35–45.

Sprinthall, Norman A. "Fantasy and Reality in Research: How to Move Beyond the Unproductive Paradox." *Counselor Education and Supervision,* 14, No. 4 (1975), 310–322.

Stahmann, Robert F. "Test Review." *Journal of Counseling Psychology,* 19, No. 1 (1972), 85–86.

Standley, Nancy V. "Kierkegaard and Man's Vocation." *Vocational Guidance Quarterly,* 20, No. 2 (1971) 119–122.

Stefflre, Buford, ed. *Theories of Counseling.* New York: McGraw-Hill, 1965.

Stephens, W. Richard. *Social Reforms and the Origins of Vocational Guidance.* Washington, D.C.: American Personnel and Guidance Association, 1970.

Stetter, Dick. "Into the Classroom with Behavior Modification." *The School Counselor,* 19, No. 2 (1971), 110–114.

Stevenson, Gloria. "Apprenticeship." *Occupational Outlook Quarterly,* 15, No. 1 (1971), 17–19.

Stewart, Lawrence H., and Charles F. Warnath. *The Counselor and Society.* Boston: Houghton Mifflin Company, 1965.

Stiller, Alfred, "Casting the Future." In *School Counseling.* Ed. Alfred Stiller. Washington, D.C.: American Personnel and Guidance Association, 1967.

Stoler, Mark A., and Jennie Versteeg Stoler. "Hidden Agendas and the Learning Earning Controversy: A Reply to Robert J. Nash and Kenneth P. Saurman." *Personnel and Guidance Journal,* 57, No. 2 (1978), 91–93.

Stoughton, Robert W., James W. McKenna, and Richard P. Cook. *Pupil Personnel Services.* Connecticut State Department of Education, National Association of Pupil Personnel Administrators, 1969.

Stripling, Robert O. "Can Counselors Cope with the Dynamics of College Choice?" In *Preparing School Counselors in Educational Choice.* New York: College Entrance Examination Board, 1967, 16–22.

Subcommittee on Career Guidance of the Committee on Specialized Personnel. *Career Guidance.* Washington, D.C.: U.S. Department of Labor, 1967.

Subweeks, Leslie L. "School Counselors Spend Summer Vacations in the Employment Service." *Vocational Guidance Quarterly,* 20, No. 4 (1972), 299–302.

Sue, Derald W. "Asian-Americans: Social-psychological Forces Affecting their Life Styles." In *Career Behavior of Special Groups.* Eds. J. Steven Picou and Robert W. Campbell. Columbus, Ohio: Charles E. Merrill, 1975, 97–121.

———. "Generalizations, Yes–Stereotypes, No!" *Personnel and Guidance Journal,* 56, No. 1 (1977), 5.

Sullivan, Howard J., and Robert W. O'Hare. *Accountability in Pupil Personnel Services: A Process Guide for the Development of Objectives.* Fullerton, Cal.: California Personnel and Guidance Association, 1971.

Super, Donald E. "The Critical Ninth Grade: Vocational Choice or Vocational Exploration." *Personnel and Guidance Journal,* 39, No. 2 (1960), 106–109.

———. "A Developmental Approach to Vocational Guidance: Recent Theory and Results." *Vocational Guidance Quarterly,* 13, No. 1 (1964), 1–10.

———. *The Psychology of Careers.* New York: Harper & Brothers. 1957.

———. "Retrospect, Circumspect, and Prospect." In *Measuring Vocational Maturity for Counseling and Evaluation.* Ed. Donald E. Super. Washington, D.C.: National Vocational Guidance Association, 1974a, pp. 161–169.

———. "A Theory of Vocational Development." *American Psychologist,* 8, No. 4, 1953, 185–190.

———. "Vocational Development Theory: Persons, Positions, and Processes." *Counseling Psychologist,* 1, No. 1, 1969b, 2–9.

———. "Vocational Maturity in Mid-Career," *Vocational Guidance Quarterly,* 25, No. 4, 1977, 294–302.

———. "Vocational Maturity Theory: Toward Implementing a Psychology of Career Education and Guidance." In *Measuring Vocational Maturity for Counseling and Evaluation.* Ed. Donald E. Super. Washington, D.C.: National Vocational Guidance Association, 1974, pp. 9–24.

———. *Work Values Inventory.* Boston: Houghton Mifflin, 1970b.

Super, Donald E., and Martin J. Bohn. *Occupational Psychology.* Belmont, Cal.: Wadsworth, 1970.

Super, Donald E., John O. Crites, Raymond C. Hummel, Helen Moser, Phoebe L. Overstreet, and Charles F. Warnath. *Vocational Development: A Framework for Research.* New York: Teachers College 1957.

Super, Donald E., and David J. Forrest. *Career Development Inventory, Form I, Preliminary Manual.* New York: Teachers College, 1972 (mimeographed).

Super, Donald E., Jennifer Kidd, and A. G. Watts. "A Life-Span and Life-Space Approach to and Descriptive Framework of Career Development." Cambridge, England: National Institute of Careers Education and Counselling, 1977, (mimeographed).

Super, Donald E., Ruth S. Kowalski, and Elizabeth H. Gotkin. *Floundering and Trial after High School.* New York: Teachers College, 1967 (mimeographed).

Super, Donald E., and Phoebe L. Overstreet. *The Vocational Maturity of Ninth Grade Boys.* New York: Teachers College, 1960.

Super, Donald E., Reuben Starishevsky, Norman Matlin, and Jean Pierre Jordaan. *Career Development: Self-Concept Theory.* Princeton, N.J.: College Entrance Examination Board, 1963.

Super, Donald E., Rubin S. Zelkowitz, and Albert S. Thompson. "Career Development Inventory, Adult Form I." New York: Teachers College, 1975 (mimeographed).

Swails, Richard G. "Career Education in Action in the Multiversity: The Management of a Career Development and Placement Center." *Journal of Career Education,* 4, No. 2 (1977), 35–44.

Switzer, David K., Austin E. Grigg, Jerome S. Miller, and Robert K. Young. "Early Experiences and Occupational Choice: A Test of Roe's Hypothesis." *Journal of Counseling Psychology,* 9, No. 1 (1962), 45–48.

Takai, Ricky, and John L. Holland. "The Relative Influence of the Vocational Card Sort, the Self-Directed Search, and the Vocational Exploration and Insight Kit on High School Girls." Baltimore: John Hopkins University (n. d.).

Tallmadge, G. Kasten. *The Joint Dissemination Review Panel IDEABOOK.* Washington, D.C.: National Institute of Education, 1977 (ED 148 329).

Tennyson, W. Wesley, Thomas A. Soldahl, and Charlotte Mueller. *The Teacher's Role in Career Development.* Washington, D.C.: American Personnel and Guidance Association, 1965.

Thomas, G. Patience. "Feasible Alternatives Counseling." *The School Counselor,* 19, No. 4 (1972), 237–242.

Thomas, L. Eugene. "Mid-Career Change: Self-Selected or Externally Mandated?" *Vocational Guidance Quarterly,* 25, No. 4 (1977), 320–328.

Thomas, L. Eugene, Richard L. Mela, Paula I. Robbins, and David W. Harvey. "Corporate Dropouts: A Preliminary Typology." *Vocational Guidance Quarterly,* 24, No. 3 (1976), 220–228.

Thomas, Mark J. "Realism and Socioeconomic Status (SES) of Occupational Plans of Low SES Black and White Male Adolescents." *Journal of Counseling Psychology,* 23, No. 1 (1976), 46–49.

Thompson, Albert S. "School Settings for Vocational Guidance." In *Man in a World at Work.* Ed. Henry Borow. Boston: Houghton Mifflin Company, 1964, 487–509.

Thompson, Charles L. "The Secondary School Counselor's Ideal Client." *Journal of Counseling Psychology,* 16, No. 1 (1969), 69–74.

Thompson, Donald L., and Ranjit K. Majunder. "Work Exposure: A New Concept in Vocational Guidance for Disadvantaged Youth." *Research Reports, 1972 Convention.* Washington, D.C.: American Personnel and Guidance Association, 1972, 86–87.

Thoresen, Carl. "Relevance and Research in Counseling." *Review of Educational Research,* 39, No. 2 (1969), 263–281.

————, ed. "Guidance and Counseling." *Review of Educational Research,* 39, No. 2 (1969).

————. "Making Better Science Intensively." *Personnel and Guidance Journal,* 56, No. 5 (1978), 279–282.

Thoresen, Carl E., and Craig K. Ewart. "Behavioral Self-Control and Career

Warner, Richard, Edward Tibby, and Barbara Putnam. "Educational Information and Guidance: A Selected Annotated Bibliography." In *Pre-Service and In-Service Preparation of School Counselors for Educational Guidance.* Ed. Stanley H. Cramer. Washington, D.C.: American Personnel and Guidance Association, 1970, 52–68.

Washington, Bennetta B. "Counseling the Disadvantaged Girl." In *Counseling the Disadvantaged Youth.* Eds. William E. Amos and Jean D. Grambs. Englewood Cliffs, N.J.: Prentice-Hall, 1968, 169–189.

"Washington Briefs," *Phi Delta Kappan,* 58, No. 10 (1977), 785.

Weary, Bettina. "A Job Choice of One's Own." In *Counseling Girls and Women Over the Life Span.* Ed. Edwin A. Whitefield. Washington, D.C.: National Vocational Guidance Association, 1972, 65–73.

Weinrach, Steve. "Guidelines for the Systematic Selection, Evaluation, and Use of Simulated Guidance Materials." *Personnel and Guidance Journal,* 56, No. 5 (1978), 288–292.

Wergin, Jon F., Paul J. Munson, Clifford Garrison, and Larry Braskamp. "Evaluating Career Education Programs Politically: A Case Study." *Vocational Guidance Quarterly,* 25, No. 1 (1976), 26–34.

Wesman, Alexander G. "Testing and Counseling: Fact and Fancy." *Measurement and Evaluation in Guidance,* 5, No. 3 (1972), 397–402.

Westbrook, Bert W. "The Relationship Between Vocational Maturity and Appropriateness of Vocational Choices of Ninth-Grade Pupils." *Measurement and Evaluation in Guidance,* 9, No. 2 (1976), 75–80.

————. *Career Development Needs of Adults.* Washington, D.C.: American Personnel and Guidance Association, 1978.

Westbrook, Bert W., and Marjorie M. Mastie. "The Cognitive Vocational Maturity Test." In *Measuring Vocational Maturity for Counseling and Evaluation.* Ed. Donald E. Super. Washington, D.C.: Vocational Guidance Association, 1974, 41–50.

Wheeler, Melissa. "A Master Plan for Students with Special Needs." *Florida Vocational Journal,* 3, No. 7 (1978), 11–14.

Whitehurst, Melvin. "An Individualized Career Exploration Program." *Journal of College Student Personnel,* 19, No. 2 (1978), 186–187.

Whiteley, John M. "Career Counseling: An Overview." In *Career Counseling.* Eds. John M. Whiteley and Arthur Resnikoff. Monterey, Calif.: Brooks/Cole Publishing, 1978, 1–17.

Whitfield, Edwin A., Jerome J. Miller, and Lawrence Johnson. "The California Regional Career Guidance Center." San Diego: Department of Education, 1978.

Wiggins, James D. "More Placement Services—No More Placements." *School Counselor,* 26, No. 1 (1978), 46–49.

"Will the Real Guidance Counselor Please Stand Up?" *Guidance Newsletter.* Chicago: Science Research Associates, September-October 1971.

Williamson, E. G. *Counseling Adolescents.* New York: McGraw-Hill, 1950.

Wilson, Sandra Reitz, and Lauress L. Wise, *The American Citizen: 11 Years After High School.* Palo Alto, Calif.: American Institutes for Research, 1975.

Winder, George. "Realizing Career Objectives Through Regional Occupational Centers and Programs." *Thrust for Education Leadership,* 1, No. 5 (1972), 42–47.

Winters, R. Arthur, and James C. Hansen. "Toward an Understanding of Work-Leisure Relationships." *Vocational Guidance Quarterly*, 24, No. 3 (1976), 238–243.

Wirtz, Willard. *The Boundless Resource*. Washington, D.C.: New Republic Book Company, 1975.

Wise, Robert, Ivan Charner, and Mary Lou Randour. "A Conceptual Framework for Career Awareness in Career Decision Making." In *Career Counseling*. Eds. John M. Whiteley and Arthur Resnikoff. Monterey, Calif.: Brooks/Cole Publishing, 1978, 216–231.

Witwer, Gloria, and Lawrence H. Stewart. "Personality Correlates of Preference for Risk Among Occupation-Oriented Junior College Students." *Vocational Guidance Quarterly*, 20, No. 4 (1972), 259–265.

Wolfson, Karen P. "Career Development Patterns for College Women." *Journal of Counseling Psychology*, 23, No. 2 (1976), 119–125.

Womer, Frank B. "The National Assessment of Educational Progress: Concept and Organization." *Caps Capsule*, 3, No. 2 (1970), 1–7.

Woodcock, Penny Robinson, and Al Herman. "Fostering Career Awareness in Tenth-Grade Girls," *School Counselor*, 25, No. 4 (1978), 256–259, 262–263.

Woodhull, Walter, Jr. "Group Counseling with High School's 'Second Best.' " *The School Counselor*, 15, No. 5 (1968), 363–366.

Woolley, Bill. "The Center for Career Development Services: An Overview." *Florida Vocational Journal*, 4, No. 1 (1978), 22–24.

"Words and Figures." *Manpower*, 4, No. 2 (1972), 20.

Wrenn, Robert L., and Reed Mencke. "Students Who Counsel Students." *Personnel and Guidance Journal*, 50, No. 8 (1972), 687–689.

Yen, Flora B., and Charles C. Healy. "The Effects of Work Experience on Two Scales of Career Development." *Measurement and Evaluation in Guidance*, 10, No. 3 (1977), 175–177.

Youngman, Geraldine, and Margaret Sadongei. "Counseling the American Indian Child." *Elementary School Guidance and Counseling*, 8, No. 4 (1974), 273–277.

Zaccaria, Joseph S. *Theories of Occupational Choice and Vocational Development*, Boston: Houghton Mifflin Company, 1970.

Zerface, James P., and Walter H. Cox. "School Counselors, Leave Home." *Personnel and Guidance Journal*, 49, No. 5 (1971), 371–375.

Zener, Thelma Baldwin, and Leslie Schnuelle. "An Evaluation of the Self Directed Search: A Guide to Educational and Vocational Planning." Baltimore: Johns Hopkins University, 1972 (mimeographed).

Ziller, Robert C. "Vocational Choice and Utility for Risk." *Journal of Counseling Psychology*, 4, No. 1 (1957), 61–64.

Zimpfer, David G. "Some Conceptual and Research Problems in Group Counseling." *The School Counselor*, 15, No. 5 (1968), 326–333.

Zimpfer, David, Ronald Frederickson, Mitchell Salim, and Alpheus Sanford. *Support Personnel in School Guidance Programs*. Washington, D.C.: American Personnel and Guidance Association, 1971.

Zytowski, Donald G. "Toward a Theory of Career Development for Women." *Personnel and Guidance Journal*, 47, No. 7 (1969), 660–664.

Authors Cited

Adams, Arthur J., 115
Agne, Russell M., 312
Alston, Herbert L., 72
Anderson, Alan R., 231
Andrews, Margaret E., 343, 352, 353, 354
Anthony, John, 208
Anton, Jane L., 379
Aragon, John A., 207
Abreiter, Solomon, 303, 321, 341
Arciniega, Mike, 278
Ashbrook, James B., 74
Ashcraft, Rock, 344
Astin, Alexander W., 348
Atkin, Jerry, 207
Aubrey, Roger F., 125, 126, 266
Austin, Brian, 217

Babcock, Robert J., 250
Backer, Thomas E., 120, 121, 124, 133
Baer, Max F., 191, 194
Baker, Stanley B., 275
Bale, Richard, 299
Barnett, Rosalind, 113
Barre, Mary E., 348, 349
Barrett, Thomas C., 45
Barro, Stephen M., 368, 369
Barry, William A., 74
Bartlett, Wendy B., 40, 217
Bateman, Thomas, 63
Battle, Haron J., 265
Bauernfeind, Robert H., 107
Baumgardner, Steve R., 6, 33, 215, 312
Beall, L., 74
Bedford, James H., 277
Belitsky, A. Harvey, 150
Bennett, G. K., 103
Bennett, Margaret E., 231
Berdie, Ralph F., 63, 271, 277
Bergland, Bruce, 239, 249
Bernard, Harold W., 235, 277
Bernstein, Jean, 113
Betz, Ellen L., 34, 71, 74, 109, 110, 124, 133
Betz, Robert L., 113
Bhaerman, Robert D., 305
Bingham, William C., 123, 269

Blake, Robert R., 278
Blau, Peter H., 75
Blocher, Donald H., 70, 276
Bohn, Martin J., 44, 115, 167
Bonnet, Deborah G., 305
Bordin, Edward S., 73, 74
Bowlsbey, Joann, 173
Bozarth, Jerold, 337
Bradley, Richard W., 104, 196, 215
Brammer, Lawrence M., 127, 270, 271
Brandhorst, Ted, 189
Braskamp, Larry, 373
Brayfield, Arthur H., 79, 377
Brazziel, William F., 106
Brenton, Myron, 136
Briggs, Bonnie, 197
Britton, Ginny, 240, 356
Brobst, Harry K., 192
Brown, Fred, 72
Brown, Robert D., 380
Brunkan, Richard J., 63, 66
Bryson, Doris, L., 170, 173
Buchheimer, Arnold, 378
Buckingham, Lillian, 341, 354
Buckman, Ronald B., 298
Burck, Harman D., 380
Buros, Oscar Krisen, 106
Burow, Josephine, 208
Buttafuoco, Peter M., 63
Byrne, Richard, 6

Caldwell, Edson, 271
Calia, Vincent F., 207, 209
Calvin, Leland, Jr., 344
Cameron, Howard K., 106
Campbell, David P., 108
Campbell, Emily A., 40, 217
Capehart, Bertis E., 186
Carey, Albert R., 368
Carey, Richard, 85, 217, 247
Carkhuff, Robert R., 208, 332
Carlson, Jon, 330
Carmical, La Verne, 344
Carr, H. C., 186
Carroll, Terresa, 312, 313
Cavins, David A., 330

Subject Index

We would like to know your reactions to this second edition of COUNSELING FOR CAREER DEVELOPMENT. Your evaluation of the book will help us to respond to both the interest and needs of the readers of future editions. Please fill out the questionnaire and return it to: **College Marketing, Houghton Mifflin Company, One Beacon Street, Boston, MA 02107**

1. Do you feel that the style of the book is clear?   YES _____

    NO _____

    Readable?   YES _____

    NO _____

    Please comment. _____

    _____

    _____

    _____

2. Are terms and concepts defined adequately when they are first introduced? _____

    _____

    _____

3. Did the illustrations make discussions in the book easier to understand? _____

    _____

4. Which chapter did you find most interesting? _____

    _____

5. Which chapter was the least interesting? _____

    _____

6. Which features of the book did you particularly like or dislike?

    Why? _____

    _____

    _____

    _____

7. Do you plan to keep this book in your professional library? _____

8. What helped you most in understanding the material covered? (Check only those appropriate to this book.)

Goals at the beginning of chapters _____

Definitions of terms _____

Descriptions of programs _____

Examples of practices, for example, the counseling case _____

Chapter summaries _____

Experiential activities at chapter ends _____

Other (please specify) _____